BIGGER BETTER. bargains®

2002 EDITION

Other Localize Shopping Books by Sue Goldstein

The Underground Shopper/Atlanta

The Underground Shopper/Boston

The Underground Shopper/Chicago

The Underground Shopper Dallas/Ft. Worth

The Underground Shopper/Detroit

The Underground Shopper/Houston

The Underground Shopper/Minneapolis/St. Paul

The Underground Shopper/New York

The Underground Shopper Phoenix

The Underground Shopper/San Antonio & Austin

The Underground Shopper/Southeast Florida

The Underground Shopper/Tulsa

National Books by Sue Goldstein

The Factory Outlet Guide   Viking/Penguin

Great Buys for Kids   Viking/Penguin

Great Buys for People Over 50   Viking/Penguin

Great Buys on Mail Order   Viking/Penguin

The Underground Shopper's Guide to Fitness & Health   Ballantine/Faucett

The Underground Shopper's Guide to Mail Order Discount Shopper:
1,2,3 Editions (Andrews & McNeel)

The Underground Shopper's Guide to Off-Price Shopping   Warner Books

The Home Shopper   McGraw Hill

Secrets from The Underground Shopper   Taylor Publishing

Coming Soon: Local

Bigger Better Bargains/Orlando

Bigger Better Bargains/Phoenix

Bigger Better Bargains/North Carolina

Bigger Better Bargains/Houston

Bigger Better Bargains/Sacramento

To Die For in Dallas/Fort Worth

Coming Soon: National

BiggerBetterBargains Online
By Sue Goldstein

Two Old Broads Who Love to Shop
By Sue Goldstein and Tammy Faye Bakker Messner

*Living the Good Life in Dallas/Fort Worth
at Half the Price!™*

BIGGER BETTER
bargains ®

2002 EDITION

SUE GOLDSTEIN
Founder of the Underground Shopper™

Published by: Shopping Business, Inc.
PMB 428
1070 W. Round Grove Road, Suite 300
Lewisville, TX 75067
469/293-SHOP; 866/273-SHOP

Printed in Canada

10 9 8 7 6 5 4 3 2 1

ISBN 0-9711598-0-7

Special thanks for Art Direction, Cover Design, Layout and

Desktop Publishing, Schlegel Marketing Communications

Database Administration and Editing, Ken Kraft & Steve Walker

Art Illustrations, Advertisement Layout and Design, Lee Evans

Web Design, PhotoSynthesis, Inc., Joshua Goldstein

Photography, Mark Butler

Printed by Printcrafters Inc.

To Bob who helped me make it through the nights; to Josh who jumped in when I most needed him and came through with a terrific web design; and to Irena, who married Josh, I finally have a daughter!

And to merchants, readers, listeners and viewers of the former Underground Shopper series of books, radio show, web site and TV segments...thank you from the bottom of my heart for being so loyal and so loving. I finally agree with you. Regardless of what name I go by, I'm still the Diva—just with a new dress on.

Table of Contents

Introduction

Categories/Chapters

Table of Contents

Indices

Disclaimer

In the center of the book, you can't help but notice there's a special color advertising section. Make no mistake, these are paid ads. But for as long as I've been writing and publishing local guidebooks, I have tried to always be fair in my appraisals of the shopping scene and hand-pick those merchants and services that I whole-heartedly endorse for my advertising base.

I would not accept monies from stores that I find disreputable, despicable, disgusting, degrading or undeserving. Period. I shop them and write them as I see them. So do the shoppers who are hired as researchers.

We try to ensure a perfect write-up. We verify everything at the last minute. When we shop a store or service, we look at the following:

- Quality of the merchandise
- Selection
- Service
- Amenities
- Convenience
- Price
- Something out of the ordinary that makes them special

There's nothing scientific about the process. We could calculate to the minutest details...but we don't. You probably don't either.

No doubt, our ratings are somewhat "subjective" though we try to be "objective." Let's face it, even the greatest store, with the greatest prices and the greatest selection can have an "off" day and be merchandise-lacking and service-kaput! Tough. If that's the day we shopped them, so be it.

If Bigger Better Bargains is not the best book on bargain shopping in the Metroplex, let me have it..right between the eyes.

Log on to our website at www.biggerbetterbargains and send me an email at Diva@biggerbetterbargains. Let me know where I've failed or click on the icon: askthediva and tell me I've fallen off the deep end instead of the deep discounts.

Of course, I welcome you to my call-in radio show every Saturday from 2-4 on Talk Radio KLIF 570 A.M. Call me, talk to me, so I can show you the way to bigger better bargains! You may even win some Diva Dollars from merchants in town who want to introduce you to a new (radio) wave of saving without ever sacrificing quality.

And lastly, join me every Friday on Channel 5 during the 10 AM news broadcast with Michael Scott and Brenda-Teele Jackson. My segment, "Shopping with Sue" is also rebroadcast on Sunday mornings.

Too, you can always write me snail mail at PMB 428, 1079 W. Round Grove Road, Suite 300, Lewisville, TX 75067; or as a last resort, call me at 469/293-SHOP (7467).

Acknowledgements

The opening lines to The Tale of Two Cities if I remember my high school English Lit class was something like…"It was the best of times and the worse of times."

Rather than belabor the worst of times, let me move on to now which is definitely bigger, definitely better, and most certainly a bargain, this book!

Bigger Better Bargains Guide to Shopping in the Dallas/Ft. Worth area has always been my life, my love.

The thought that I would never be able to talk to you about "bargains" (as some thought it a "dirty" word) was just one of the reasons I left my 30 years of being The Underground Shopper behind.

It was an era that I am most proud, but since I'm fairly well-known, I guess you might say I'm aboveground now. Most folks in this area know who I am. I'm not going anywhere. I'm still here to introduce you to the new places in town that have surfaced when my back was turned and to teach you the ways of living the good life-at half the price ™. Remember, you don't have to be cheap to love a bargain…you just have to be smart!™

This year, we'll publish another local book, To Die For plus a national edition of Bigger Better Bargains/Online.

In the works, too, is another national book co-authored with Tammy Faye Bakker Messner entitled, Two Old Broads Who Love to Shop. Yes, *that* Tammy Faye. It's going to be a very good year.

This was a tough year. I hope to make those who believed in me proud.

In my personal life, my husband, Bob Blair, has not only been the rock behind my avalanche, but the lone flower amongst the weeds. He proved not only his unwavering love and devotion, but also his showed his true colors and led us all on the path towards civility.

It's hard to turn the other cheek. But he helped me move on and proved to me, without a doubt, that behind every good woman, they may even be a better man.

As the President of my new company, part of his duties include being my soul mate on the radio. It has really worked. Better than even I had hoped. He takes my abuse that is meant in jest (though there is a twinge of reality) and he's always ready to take on a new day and a new challenge with a smile and determination. To have that kind of outlook is truly remarkable. I love him; but most importantly, I envy his sense of self and admire his pureness, without a mean bone in his body.

I hope I learn from him. With his strength to lean on, I know I can't lose. It's never too late to begin anew and I am so lucky to have him to share the trip.

Then my son Josh, who rose to the occasion, took the bull by the horn, and created www.biggerbetterbargains.com. I thought his passion was only for photography. He is good; no, he's great. Moreover, he sacrificed many years of a carefree childhood with much of the carefree missing. Being a single parent was hard at times; being a single parent's child was even harder.

Though he is self-taught in many ways, you can't teach him to be passionate. About everything. From politics to ecology issues, honesty to his art, his contributions to the website is obvious. Just click on our online store (Click and Shop) and you can see he's been busy. He's now back to doing his own thing but he established the foundation and I'm mighty proud of his efforts.

You're right. I am a typical Jewish mother boasting about her very talented son. So, if you are looking for museum-quality photographs, go to www.joshuagoldstein.net and see for yourself. Of course, if you bought a few, that would be nice. (Just don't tell him I told you so.)

My life besides my family was fairly isolated this year but I managed to fill up any idle hours with lawyers, several of them. They not only performed admirably, but became friends as well. Heading the team right up to the summary judgment, Frank Wright, Esq. of Winstead, Sechrist and Minnick was first to the team; Joel Reese of the same firm joined us as it heated up. The two of them are different kinds of lawyers. They're actually honest. Expensive, yes, but try to see the other side's prospective, too, and refused to play the "dirty little games" some lawyers stoop to.

I liked that about them. They really raised the bar to the 'nth degree.

I may not be the greatest proponent of the legal profession, but I can assure you, these were not your run of the mill. Another lawyer on the team included Ross Garssen and legal secretary Linda Ladner. If they didn't cost so much, I just might call them daily. I know, though, I can always call them my friends.

Mark McPherson, Esq. www.McTexLaw.com is another fine corporate lawyer. He knows that an uphill battle takes time but he has walked the walk with me all the way. I have no hesitancy in recommending him either.

Now, here comes the "Ex's." The inspiration was contagious when swarms of former employees came a-callin'. "What can we do?" they asked. Not one, two, but at least fifty have not only asked to come to work, but volunteered their services. It's hard to employ them all, even for free, but I would have if I had more room, more computers and a whole lot more than one book, one radio show, one TV segment, and one website...or so I thought!

It was time, though, for many of them to move on. I would have liked to hold on a little longer, but I always knew they were behind me all the way and not behind my back whispering. Those who ultimately joined me were very special in so many ways. There are no words that I can say to adequately express my gratitude, my appreciation, and my thanks for an effort that went well beyond the call of duty-even those who started at the very beginning and moved on somewhere along the way.

Some like Jeannie Bellomy, Ian Leech, Chris Sopher, Eric Sham, Sharon Sham, Patricia Saunders, Faythe Hunter, Mara Davis, Melva Thorpe, Jason Landry, Alan Abtahi and Rhonda Reddick, for example, have carved out new careers and new employment, but for a brief time, they were the transition team that helped me to the next level of wholeness.

I thought selling my business after almost 30 years was a smart move. Boy, was I wrong! In hindsight, I have learned a very important lesson. It's never the paper you sign that's the deciding factor as to whether you've just consummated a potentially successful business deal. It's the people. Need I say more?

When we finally got down to my new and improved business, it was a wonderful blending of talent and support from you-thousands of you who sent me an email or wrote me a personal note. The resounding, "You go, girl" and "We love you, Diva," were enough to make a grown girl cry-but it was just the push I needed to get over the hump of feeling sorry for myself.

Getting down to business began seriously with Laurie Lawrence who was first to jump into the hopper and became my Chief Researcher. A young mother of two, former Ft. Worth resident who had moved to Orlando several years ago, who was hired originally as the Orlando shopper. She was good. She was fast. Then when the company who hired her closed, she was first to reach out and say, "Can I help you?" she cried.

I put her to work. She was in charge of this year's Dallas/Ft. Worth research. Little did she realize what she was getting into? In spite of her experience shopping the Orlando market, Dallas/Ft. Worth was twice the size as Orlando and I expected it to be shopped in half the time. She jumped in, cell phone in hand, and tackled it morning, noon and night, without one complaint until the very end when she got the flu and couldn't work for a few hours. How many employees do you know that would do it for FREE, no less?

This woman worked diligently for six months full time for not one penny. She loved to shop. She loved the project. And she loved me. To repay her is still up in the air. But what's so remarkable, she'd do it again. I promised her one weekend at a spa and to go shopping. The perfect reward for a job well done. Besides, what a perfect recompense to a shopper whose feet are killing her. Then, for the rest of my appreciation, well that is still up in the air. Later, she says, let's worry about this later.

Danielle Downey-Wilett jumped in to help out with baby in tow. As a brand new mother, she was able to juggle bottles and bargain write-ups with much dexterity. A double thank you.

Ken Kraft was next to jump on the bandwagon. He developed a fabulous database that organized all my shopping secrets-by city, by brand, by category, by sizes, well, the answers come so fast, it doesn't even matter if I have a "senior moment" and can't remember off the top of my head. No wonder I can tell you "where to go!" with one click of the mouse. (Here, you thought it was all in my memory bank!)

You won't believe how many times I wailed, Ken, I can't save the ratings! How do I find this or that? My questions were numerous, his patience was indomitable. He also is our desktop publisher, putting tags in where labels needed to be in bold, or organizing the table of contents. In fact, whatever the assignment, he is always willing and able. With his own physical limitations, he's just the best. I know I couldn't be without him.

His wife Vickie also was kept busy from her wheelchair developing the online book entries, which means thousands of web sites that she was able to shop from home, for free. A great project, a great couple that I shall never be able to repay (You're going to hear this line a lot!) but I can say thank you from the bottom of my heart. With all that they deal with on an everyday basis, I never heard one peep of heartache. They are truly amazing.

Now how many employers do you know that has organized a staff of this caliber with this kind of dedication who were all willing to work for free (rather than work for free in their previous job and not agree to it!)

Nevertheless, others also came to the rescue but had families to support. Steve Walker was one who is head of some radio station's engineering duties but remains my devoted editor and publishing liaison to the distribution community. His name should be familiar. He's worked with me for more than a dozen years. The only difference is today he's a proud daddy to Jeremy and he and his wife Sherry are expecting a little girl in the fall. He was there from day one and working together has always been effortless, so why not?

He was also instrumental in helping us with our online store in between moving to a new house, maintaining a full-time job and other demands on his time. He always comes through. What price do you put on such loyalty, much less his skills?

Then there's Mike Simeone, the seasoned voice behind many of our radio commercials as well as our technical guru. He not only hooked us up with phones and computers, gathers the props for TV, screens the callers on the radio show and soon will be seen on TV, but has been a big booster to me emotionally (and vice versa.) With all this acclaim, he still responds to my many "Mikey, I need you" cries of woe, he still comes running. You know how it is when you can't pull up a program or you can't find a write-up? He's so adept plus he calls me "Sunshine." How can I not smile? Together, as we say, we shall overcome.

Starting out, Chris Sopher was our radio conduit, from plugging in our monitors to running the database on the air. He and his finance Veronica are planning their upcoming February wedding and are committed to doing it all for less. They've both been there when I needed help. If you want anything fixed and it has wires, Chris is who to plug into.

During the summer, Fayth Hunter and her son Justin came to work bringing bagels and doing the "books." Then, they took a dip in the pool. Nice job if you can get it. A big thank you.

Cover and Art Direction for the book was under the watchful and creative eye of the tiger, Lance Schlegel, most recently seen on Channel 8 when he and Amanda tied the knot. Butterflies were released instead of rice as their wedding's final gesture. I thought it a fitting gift to begin their lives together in a new form, flying free. Then, after their honeymoon, I started nagging him about the layout. Fortunately, he's a pro (214/824-2425) who can tend to any graphic design project. Thank him for the beautiful cover, layout and other design elements and hire him. He's started his own Design Studio and can really do wonderful things with on a Mac.

Then there's Lee Evans, a real pro with years and years of experience designing web sites and advertising campaigns. Since he had designed many of the logos for my segments on Channel 11 and worked at Channel 8, too, I knew he was a formidable designer. I just didn't realize what a gentleman he was. Thank him for all the ads right up to the very last minute-and I mean minute If you need a web designer or ad maker, who can make deadlines without ruffling his feathers, give Lee at call at 940/243-3281 or email him at 3lee@gte.net. And thanks to his wife Denise, who worked side by side while she was off for the summer. (She's a teacher during the year.)

Then behind the scenes, there's Lou Richardson, who can work the Excel spreadsheets, handle the bookkeeping duties and manage the checkbook, all with a single bound. Invoices go out, payroll taxes get paid (don't you worry there) and the checkbook balances—all because of her.

Additionally, I'd like to give a nod of extra special thanks to Christy Cheek, Channel 5 producer who gave me my "Shopping with Sue" time slot, Sabrina Smith, a woman of like-minds who helped me along the way, Manship Smith for delivering some terrific new clients and his wife, Jane, who while battling breast cancer herself, never failed to stop by to see how I was doing, these are all friends who are irreplaceable.

And to one friend who stood by me during the early legal skirmishes and never flinched, my dear friend, Wayne Robinson. You only need one friend like him who was with me day in and day out as I teetered between up and over, over and out. Some days I wanted to give up; other days, I wanted to give in. He wouldn't let me do either and helped me weather the storm. I told Bob, when I die, he can marry Wayne. (Wayne's wife Barbara is also on my dear friend's list.)

If you need a fabulous commercial real estate broker, he's the barracuda with a deft hand. Give him a call at Henry S. Miller, 972/386-1427.

Then, the list gets longer. I couldn't have been any luckier than to have so many friends and business associates. Just a few: Jeannie Bellomy and Ian Leech for their backbone; Jeff Rupley, GM/United Group Printing for being such a wonderful printing partner; Nick Mayrath, a fabulous CPA who's not only honest but can add; Lon Bason and Jeff Hillary, the honchos at KLIF for the opportunity to have a radio presence, Rob Hassen, KLIF Sales Manager and Melissa Meyers, Account Executive, who believes we are a viable money-maker; Tommy Snodgrass, a long-time client, along with Dixie Hargrove from Dixie's Fashion Accessories and Billy Oyster of Dallas Gold & Silver who were the first to sign on the dotted line, thanks for the vote of confidence.

I probably forgot some really important people, but please forgive me. Here's a blanket thank you for helping me making it through this tumultuous year.

This edition certainly marks my tenacity for the past 30 years. It also marks the year when I lost a dear friend and colleague, Sandi Trybom. She was a truly special and loving woman when all those around her were not. I miss her a lot but especially those times when she's not accompanying me to a speech.

Those were the good old days when she was introduced to "kugel" and 15,000-square-foot homes, some of the richest ladies in Dallas and some of the cheapest. To and from each occasion, we always had our eyes open for the garage sales. We always made a detour and never came home empty-handed.

Sandi, this book's for you.

Ratings, Codes and Designations

100 Best

 In the center section of the book, you'll find color ads to some of our 100 Best Winners who were chosen by shoppers on our web site and my team of professional shoppers. For those not participating in our 100 Best Marketing Program, you will see the logo alongside their writeups. When you see the 100 Best logo on their doors or advertising programs, you know we think they're the best of the best. Higher than a 5-star and judged by those who shop them. Trust them. They're in a class all by themselves.

Star Ratings: Merchants of Goods & Products

Please see the Disclaimer on page **ix** for the criteia of these ratings.

★★★★★	Top Dog
★★★★	Not quite, but Close
★★★	Definitely Worth a Trip
★★	Not Bad
★	Don't Bother
No ★	Unless it's a typo, beware!

Diamond Ratings: Service-Based Merchants

Not every merchant can be judged on price alone. A merchant who provides a service that is superior to others in the same business is given the highest rating (5 diamonds); sometimes, they charge a little less but give you a lot more. You know what I mean. Those special touches when they go the extra mile…when a moving company will work into the wee hours of the night to be sure you get all your stuff into your new house or the printer who will make a second press check to make sure that the color pages are just right.

Therefore, the diamonds are graduated from:

◆◆◆◆◆	Spectacular and Well Beyond the Call of Duty
◆◆◆◆	No complaints, whatsoever
◆◆◆	Got what I paid for
◆◆	Adequate
◆	Wouldn't recommend them to my mother-in-law
No ◆	Botched the job, beware!

To Die For

 Ever walked into a store and said, "This is to die for?" Sorry, but it may be a sexist-only phrase, but somehow women understand it implicitly. You'll see just the tip of the "To Die For" stores—our top 10 in Dallas/Fort Worth. Next year, you'll see an entire book full.

So, we decided to give you a taste. Look for the heart symbol with the cupid's arrow puncturing through. It's 10 we knew you'd want to hear about-and it is a start to something big. There are lots of fabulous finds where money is not the ONLY object of consideration. When you walk into a To Die For store, you want to shout, "Wow!" It's drop-dead gorgeous, who cares what it costs, I want it regardless of the price! Get it?

Online Bargains

 There are also websites associated with bricks and mortar stores. Some just give static information on their locations and their history—think of it like an online brochure.

Then, they are those that have bricks and mortar stores who also want you to take advantage of shopping online, too. Then, if you need to return it, they'd like for you to return it to the closest physical location. Another service; another tool to get you into their shops.

It's also a way to reach into your pockets for additional discounts. Some tout their promotions; others, provide a downloadable coupon. Either way, it's a good deal.

But in the Top 10 Online stores highlighted with the computer screen and a circle 10, the only way

Online Shopping

When you shop any of our Top 10, you can trust we know these merchants well. At the time of publication, all met our criteria for inclusion include being a secured site, relationships with professional organizations, such as the Better Business Bureau, a toll-free number for easy communication, an easy return policy, a variety of delivery options and of course, quality merchandise at sensational prices.

to save is through their online store. These are e-commerce sites exclusively. That means they can make it without a store front. And for you, it's the only way to buy.

For example, www.overstocks.com is a fabulous place to whet your appetite. Name brand and designer items covering a wide range of merchandise, superb customer service, a top-notch management team, plenty of solid financing and a history of a least one year of personally shopping them.

It's also another carrot we've thrown in to the Dallas/Fort Worth book to show you that we take bargain shopping to its greatest heights. The world is now our marketplace and we'll go to the ends of the earth just to save some money. Your money. Watch for our national Bigger Better Bargains/Online next year, too, 'cause we're not going to leave a stone unturned.

You deserve to know what's under every rock and we're going to share our finds. Once you've shopped those who made it to the Top 10 Online represent the quality, integrity and power of the web. We wanted you to have a piece of the pie. Enjoy.

So whether it's across town, across the country, the continent, the world, welcome to the wonderful world of bargains.

National Merchant

 Map of the USA indicates the store is either a chain and available coast-to-coast, has the capacity of accepting mail orders nationwide, has a catalog, and of course, the Internet provides that capacity without having to draw you a map. Once you get the hang of it, you'll love it.

Other Codes

Some codes you may run across in the headers or writeups include:

MO	Mail Order
PQ	Price Quote
PS	Periodic Sale
NV	Not Shopped; just a rumor

How we do a few other things.

Credit Cards

All merchants listed take credit cards. If they only take cash, we'll indicate in their heading with a $ sign. However, instead of wasting space, we've eliminated the credit cards they accept because they all accept credit cards these days. If they don't, we tell you.

Addresses

To conserve space, we only list three store addresses. If there are more than three stores, to find the one nearest you, go to www.switchboard.com, www.whitepages or www.yellowpages; or check directory assistance.

Toll-free Numbers

We just used the area codes of 800, 888, 877, 866 without the one before it. We assumed you knew to dial it.

Prices Listed

Prices that are listed in the write-ups are strictly illustrative of the prices and the savings. As you well know, they change. Don't expect to see that item with that price tag on when you shop.

Blanket Apology

Up front, I admit we might have goofed. Inadvertently, there is an error. In spite of proof-reading 'til we're blue in the face, we may still have egg on our face. But at least it's Eggs Benedict. (See online www.wolfermans.com).

To conserve space, it was necessary to draw the line on the number of listings. I had wanted to share more online sites and To Die For stores but was given the stop sign when I turned in 200 more listings than the book could hold.

Sorry about that. I also eliminated this year all periodic sales. Listen to the radio show, visit our website often and we'll be including those in a special place online to ensure you don't miss a trick.

Foreword

Since 1972, I've been writing these kinds of books. This year marks the first year...of the rest of my life with bigger better bargains. However, you still know I founded The Underground Shopper but as of right now, I will not be using that name. Maybe one day, I'll go back to it, but not now.

There are some rules of thumb (and feet) when it comes to shopping for bargains.

1. Don't shop when you're hungry-especially in a grocery store. When your stomach is growling, "Feed me," you'll make terrible choices. Same with other shopping categories. Funerals, for example. Don't shop for one when you're grieving. You'll generally wind up buying something that's way too expensive; or something you could do without. We argued about where to put Discount Caskets and decided to wait until we go back to using the name "underground."

2. Don't shop in stiletto heels.

3. Leave your credit cards at home. If you don't have the cash, it's just too easy to put it on a credit card. Save them for a rainy day or in an emergency. You'll be glad you did.

4. Make a list of things you need. Browse for comparison-purposes only; then buy when you can really afford it.

5. Shop alone. You don't need a group experience to convince you that you really need that fuchsia chair.

6. Be conservative. Just because something's cheap, don't think you need to buy it just because...What if you get it home and you have nothing to wear with it? Then, you'll run to the corner and spend even more for a blouse to go with it. You know you'll regret it in the morning.

7. Plan a shopping route that is efficient. Combine bargain stops and make your time and gas go a long way.

8. Don't buy something because some movie star wore it to the Academy Awards or everybody's got one and you should, too.

9. Read ads so you'll be familiar with what things costs. At least when a store is claiming it's on sale or marked down, you'll be armed with some information that could prove invaluable.

10. Lastly, if it's too good to be true…read the book. If it's a great buy, it's more than likely within these pages. If not, let us know.

Enjoy your finds.

Sue Goldstein

Appendix (or is it my stomach)?

On August 24, 2001, I will undergo a gastric bypass performed by Dr. David Provost at Southwestern Medical Center/Zales/Lipshy Medical Hospital.

It's basically the same procedure that Carnie Wilson had that helped her lose all that weight.

I am hoping that I will also do so. Who but you have not noticed. I have always struggled with my weight all of my life. Up and down I go, where it would stop, I didn't know.

But as most of us who reach that weight that made me freak out, enough already. I could hardly walk the flea markets without an aching back and pains in my legs and knees. My greatest love, shopping, was becoming unbearable. Online is great but I also want it all. And nothing beats scrounging around-that is, if I could walk, and bend, and grab before someone else beat me to it. I knew it was now or never.

Watch Deborah Ferguson and the Channel 5 News Team take you from start to, well, my goal weight, at long last. Chin(s) up!

What started as just a dream, has now turned to reality and I'm counting the days before Dr. Provost and I meet again, under the (operating) lights. Unless he sews a pizza into my new little stomach, things are finally going to change…for the better and the Diva will finally be able to do Dallas without buckling under from her weight.

Stay tuned for my belly buster. I probably won't be joining you in any celebrations if champagne or diet Cokes are being served. There will be a few "no-no's" but life sure will get better without them. I want to feel better. I want to meet the challenge at long last. And I want to last until my ratings equal my pounds lost each week. So, I'll need your help.

Nothing has worked for many of us who suffer from morbid obesity. It's a disease, as Dr. Provost, says. I won't feel ashamed or feel guilty any more. I couldn't fight this disease with any of the options out there. Though I had lost on every program I tried, it all came back and more.

So this is it...a permanent weight loss regime and though I am scared, I am really excited, too. Imagine, this year I've been blessed with a new name, a new husband, a new daughter-in-law, and now a new dress, by next year, size 6?

I also met a superb group of folks who are either "weighting" for their surgery date or have already gone to the other side. I've met literally hundreds who have lost hundreds, no thousands of pounds, and are doing great. What a difference touching your toes makes. It's all those little things *plus* the big things, like living to celebrate your next birthday, that makes it all worthwhile.

I never knew there were so many of us who behind all the layers of fat are just like everybody else, wanting to live life to the fullest but couldn't. Now, we can live the good life-at half price, and still get filled up.

I love you all and thanks for your prayers.

Special thanks to Georgeanne, Julie and Washell...we'll all in this together. Do or die–t, let's drink our two ounces and cheer to our new life!

Log on to my website for my weighty tome plus my monthly pic and pound report.

If you are one of us and need to lose 100 pounds, I pray you also get the chance that Humana is giving me. At least, from all the success stories in my group, not one of them has any regrets. If nothing else, let's talk. When all is said and done, I will be able to lead you in the right direction if you need it, a doctor that I can recommend, and how my life has just begun.

Like everything else, I know you're behind me all the way. I hope, though, my behind goes all away in the process.

Antiques & Auctions

★★★★★ Accent Antiques   972/226-9830
616 Hwy. 80   Mon-Sat 9-5:30; Sun 11:30-5:30
Sunnyvale, TX 75182

Oui, Oui, monsieurs and madames. Pardon my French, but welcome to Accent Antiques, a 14,000-square-foot showplace specializing in French and Italian antiques. Save yourself a trip to the Eiffel Tower and keep yourself grounded by the hand-picked French antiques of owner Ron Robinson. Don't expect tourist class prices, though. These are jet-setting, Concorde prices all the way. His jewels reign supreme in his worldly warehouse, hardly regal, but you don't want to pay for the overhead, anyway. The selection is stellar, from French to country French, Continental, Majolica, lots of bombe secretaries and chests, Louis XV and XVI armoires, rush chairs, gilt armchairs and treasures, all pricey but discounted dramatically. Since most of his clientele are dealers, you might as well shop where the dealers shop. Pocket their commission and have a bite next door at the Eastfork Restaurant.

★★★★ Antique Co. Mall   972/548-2929
213 E. Virginia St.   Mon-Sat 10-5:30; Sun 11-5
McKinney, TX 75069

Frankly, my dear, foo dogs make the best house pets. No mess. No fuss. No barking. To buy them, you'd be barking up the right tree shopping at the largest antique mall in McKinney. This 22,000-square-foot emporium is home to more than 200 dealers with the same critical eye toward finding those buried treasures. Look and see furniture galore plus glassware, toys, rhinestone tiaras to roll-top desks, pottery to pipes, autographed memorabilia to antique coins, jewelry and old-time photographs. For the country touch, add a weathervane, a rusty porch chair, a washed fence post, various cows, screen doors, faded quilts, granny's lace, old crockery and cast iron skillets. Hang out at their smaller Lewisville location at 201 S. Mill Street in Lewisville, 972/219-1335.

★★★★★ Antiqueland
1300 Custer Rd.
Plano, TX 75075

972/509-7878
Mon-Wed 10-6; Thu-Sat 10-8; Sun 11-6
www.antiquelandusa.com

AntiqueLand is a Plano landmark with over 85,000 square feet of opulent shopping. Housed in this former Wal-Mart store, shop at over 350 vendors, grab a bite at their Palm Court Restaurant and enjoy the four antique malls under one umbrella (The others are Unlimited Ltd., Dallas; Forestwood, Dallas; Antique Colony in Fort Worth and Antique Mall at Rufe Snow in North Richland Hills). About half of the mall is split with 80 percent antiques and 20 percent reproductions. The other half houses antiques and designer furnishings representing American, French, English and Primitive furniture and collectibles. There are also design-related spaces, a TV lounge for couch potatoes and a meeting /classroom for seminars. Their newest location is now open at Denton Factory Stores.

★★★★★ Antiques & Moore
3708 W. Pioneer Pkwy.
Arlington, TX 76013

817/543-1060
Mon-Sat 10-6; Sun Noon-6

Sometimes more is not better. In this case, this Moore is. One of the originators of the antique mall craze, expect Sue Moore to be leading the pack (rats) with the myriad of merchants who are part of Antiques & Moore. Her ability to hand-pick a unique blend of over 175 individual dealers and put together a showcase gallery of collectibles all within this 50,000-square-foot emporium is testimony to her antique acumen. One particular favorite is the western boutique featuring **DOUBLE D RANCH** wear for the lady desiring a contemporary southwest wardrobe, including **DIAN MALOUF** jewelry. Other favorites include glass, china, crystal, Dresden dolls, birdhouses by **SHARMON HOLMQUIST**, lamps made from teapots—there is Moore than enough to feast your eyes on. Plan in advance and you can savor a feast, if not a nibble in the Tea Room open 7 days a week.

★★ Atrium Antique Mall, The
3404 Belt Line Rd.
Farmers Branch, TX 75234

972/243-2406
Mon-Sat 9-7; Sun 11-7
www.atriumantiques.com

Step right up, ladies and gentlemen, tell ya what I'm gonna do! Every month, Parker Antiques (Architecturals and Fine Reproductions) open their doors to a $2 million auction. Other times, you can shop their 140,000-square-foot antique mall that you've probably passed a hundred times driving down Belt Line. Both reproductions and old objects d'art are displayed. Central checkout will tell you if the owner of the item is willing to deal. If there's room to negotiate, most often you'll be dealing with one of Eddie Parker's relatives. They seem to own most of the booth spaces. Nevertheless, you'll love the stuff. Unfortunately their prices aren't anything to smile over. Frankly, my dear, I think they're over-rated!

★ Bargain House
1839 N. Galloway
Mesquite, TX 75149

972/288-9151
Mon-Fri 10-5; Sat 11-5

Marie McBride is a legend in her own time. For more than 20 years, collecting and selling someone else's castoffs has made her the maven of Mesquite. Her 7,000-square-foot shop is brimming with antique and flea market booths. If you're in the mood for love (seats) and other furniture finds, you should have no trouble furnishing your entire house with bargains from here. Consider outfitting the following rooms: dining room, living room, master bedroom, kids' rooms, guest room, dinette, entryway, library...they've got it all. Then check out all the little chotshkas (those are knick-knacks in Yiddish). They also are blooming with flowers, both silk and dry, to bring the outdoors in with little maintenance. The other part of McBride's is where you'll find lots of housewares to spruce up your home. China, glassware, vases, figurines—and it figures that birds of a feather will be singing cheap-cheap after pecking around these cheap price tags.

★★ Cabbage Patch Antiques   972/272-8928

901 S. Jupiter Rd.   Wed-Sat 10-6
Garland, TX 75042

If you didn't fall off a cabbage truck, you'll marvel at the mirth of merchandise here. Leave your troubles at the doorstep and smile when you enter this patch of good cheer. Some authentic antiques (over 100 years old) and some reproductions are in mixed company but would still feel comfortable in anybody's home. Blooming beautiful floral arrangements, candles, potpourri and home decor items complete this idyllic scene. Join their buying club for $30 and receive discounts on all purchases. Layaway and interest-free financing add additional incentives for buying here. On Jupiter Rd. near the Forest Lane intersection.

★★★★★ Choices on Park Hill   817/927-1854

2978 Park Hill   Tue-Fri 10-6; Sat 10-5
University at Park Hill
Fort Worth, TX 76109

A little here, a little there, you find a little bit of everything, everywhere. Choices on Park Hill gives you the option of spending from less than a buck to the investment of a lifetime on pieces averaging multi-thousand dollars. But how can you go wrong when there are three stories of home furnishings, accessories and jewelry to choose from? This consignment shop offers some of the most elite pieces to be found in all of Tarrant County and beyond. One dealer even travels the world in search of fine antique jewelry and another shows works of art from Fort Worth's own **HENRIETTA MILAN**. We gasped at one that was appraised for $4,000 but selling at less than half with a price tag of $1,800. Find it all—from **LALIQUE** crystal to Scandinavian wood carvings; Persian rugs to vintage clothing from the '30s and '40s; to Flow Blue and Majolica collections; custom and fine jewelry, vintage stained glass and so much more. Nothing quite like it in the Metroplex. Turn someone else's treasure into your treasure. Then climb to the pinnacle, the third floor. Patty Stroud keeps slipcovers and window treatments, faux paintings and tromp l'oeil. Then it will be obvious why Choices on Park Hill is not for the faint-hearted. If you're waffling about where to shop, turn over by TCU and the entrance to the zoo where you'll find Choices, and lots of them.

★★ Clements Antiques of Texas   972/564-1520

206 E. Hwy. 80, Bldg. A   Mon-Sat 9-5
Forney, TX 75126

If you're a die-hard fan of antique shopping, you already know about the strip. Clements is one of the originals—the formidable founding father of antique shopping in the Metroplex. Just 25 miles east of downtown Dallas, you can't miss them, first shop on the left, with statuary welcoming you in. More than 60,000 square feet of antiquity, some in need of repair, others in perfect shape, some museum-quality, others just treasures in your own mind. Auctions and estate sales are legendary and usually the prices open within reason. Very cordial to novices and well-stocked for the demanding antique shopper. You can trust a legend.

★★ Cobwebs Antiques Mall   972/423-8697
1400 Ave. J   Mon-Sat 10-5; Sun 1-5
Plano, TX 75074

Weaving a web of possibilities, this mall can entangle you even if you weren't looking for anything in particular. There's something for everyone, from estate jewelry to vintage clothing, Primitive to Victorian furniture, Depression glass to Early Americana. And just when you think you've exhausted the inventory, a grand ole tearoom appears just in the nick of time. Open Mon-Sat 11-2:30, shoppers appreciate a time-out, too. Take a step back in time in historic old Plano, right off 15th Street and remember the good ole days when shopping was affordable and an antique mall was walkable (without having to participate in a marathon.)

★★★★ Divine Designs   972/248-7149
18101-B Preston Rd., Suite 201   Mon-Sat 10-6
Dallas, TX 75252

From the divine to the sublime, this is where they intersect. At the corner (NW) of Preston and Frankfort, this almost Plano outpost is anything but plain, though some things are just plain old. Antiques are co-mingled with high-end looking accessories, furniture with custom silk floral arrangements, artwork, crystal, lamps, candles, tabletop accessories and custom-made iron furniture with an accompanying custom-made pad to cushion the blow. Not a store to be ignored, their contribution to the genre of "bargain boutiques" is noted and well-positioned to be a favorite on your "to shop" list.

★★★★ Dusty Attic, The   972/613-5093
3330 N. Galloway, #225   Mon-Sat 10-6; Thu 10-8; Sun 1-5
Mesquite, TX 75150   antiquescollectibles.homepage.com

Going up to the attic doesn't mean bring the **KLEENEX**.® You won't sneeze when visiting here because there's not an ounce of dust in spite of their name. Just down the street from Town East Mall, this attic is the combined efforts of almost 500 vendors jammed-packed into this 30,000-square-foot plethora of possibilities. From crafts and Southwest items in one half to antiques in the other, you'll see it all—but never together. On the crafts side, you'll see clothes, ceramics, yard art, birdhouses and such; on the antiques side, you'll see everything from **FENTON** glass, art deco furniture to Victorian hats, primitive accents to **PRECIOUS MOMENTS**. Nice synergism. Nice shopping at this dusty attic.

Englishman's Interiors   972/386-5996
14655 Midway Rd.   Tue-Sat 10-5:30
Dallas, TX 75001   www.englishmans.com

At the northwest corner of Midway and Proton, Englishman's Interiors (formerly Antiques) has raised the bar several notches. What a showplace. Opened in June, 1999, it's just north of the Crown Plaza Hotel Suites, and is 30,000 square feet of English tea and crumpets. It's one of the most breathtaking showrooms in the city, sure to make a trip to London a close second to shopping at a British marketplace for antiques. Their forte is antique reproductions. As seen on the *Ainsley Harriot Show*, no one could identify the real **STAFFORDSHIRE** Foo Dogs from the repro dogs. But don't think they closed their original 15,000 square feet of Englishman's Antiques down the street and north of Belt Line. No siree, cherie. Cheerio!

★★ Estate Warehouse   214/760-2424
905 Slocum   Tue-Sat 10-6
Dallas, TX 75207

Shop the estate sales all in one place at the Estate Warehouse. Near the Design District, behind the Greyhound Bus Station, finding this place is like Columbus falling off the face of the earth. Once you've discovered it, it's not like charting an unknown territory. With enough estate stuff in their warehouse to make a day of it, expect to wear your grubbies. Some of the crannies have not been unearthed in months—maybe years. Nevertheless, it's a fun day of down-to-earth shopping at pretty decent prices. Antiques, rugs, books, records, china and crystal, lamps, furniture, from chic to cheap.

★★★★ Forestwood Antique Mall   972/661-0001
5333 Forest Lane   Mon-Sat 10-7; Sun Noon-6
Dallas, TX 75244   www.antiquelandusa.com

This Austin, Texas-based company took off in 1998 acquiring antique malls all over the country. Today, they own 20 malls, have $40 million in sales and are already, the largest antique mall owner in the U.S. So there. Now you have it. Forestwood is one of them, which means you have access to buying and selling online as well. Sherri King's the manager here so everything's running smoothly with the 200-300 dealers. Half is serious antiques, expensive French armoires, English antiques, china, pottery and collector books, for example; the other side is less pricey with French beds, armoires, bookcases, costume and Victorian jewelry and more. Dine in the Garden Tea Room, Mon-Sat from 11-3, and enjoy!

★★★★★ Gallery Batavia   214/288-4523
4908 W Lovers Lane   Mon-Sat 10-6; Sun Noon-6
Dallas, TX 75205

Congratulations! This Gallery has moved uptown and is now housed inside Park Cities Antiques. These women first opened their business in a storage facility in Lewisville. Though shoppers eventually found their way to their "appointment only" way of life, they finally decided to go public. We applaud their decision. Just who are they and what do they sell? Well, for years, these women lived in Indonesia and want to share their love for the Indonesian furniture with their Metroplex brethren. Indeed, you, too, will love their imported antique finds. Both old and authentic pieces plus reproductions should give you a taste of both old and new (that looks like old.) Choose accessories such as bronzes, hand-woven textiles, batiks, accent tables, cabinets, chairs, benches, all with that Far Eastern flavor. But it's the prices that will set your heart a-flutter. A turn-of-the-century cabinet with inset glass sold for $698, and an antique, solid teak bench sold for $659. Travel to Highland Park and welcome this Gallery to your list of bargain haunts for the haute couture of furniture. Nothing ordinary about this Eastern delight. Pieces are extraordinary. And at last, available, seven days a week.

Gathering, The   214/741-4888
1515 Turtle Creek Blvd.   Mon-Sat 10-6
Dallas, TX 75207

Giving additional clout to the expression, "It's To Die For," this Design District outpost gathers about 30 dealers of antiques, art and accessories and opens their doors to the public. Each dealer is a specialist—one in original impressionists to traditional paintings, another in Oriental area rugs, others with furniture and 18th and 19th century European antiques, another in chandeliers and clocks—get the picture? Add glassware, silver, antique lighting, tapestries, bronzes and more and just when you think you've had your fill, step into the cafe. (Mon-Fri 11-3.)

★★★★★ Harris Antiques & Classic Design   817/246-8400
7600 Scott St.   Mon-Sat 8:30-5:30
Fort Worth, TX 76108

Fort Worth and antiques are synonymous with the Harris family. Separated by real and unreal (antiques or reproductions), this wholesaler offers the real McCoy and the look-alikes. Since retail stores buy from them, what's good for the goose is good for the gander, right? The selection is staggering: hundreds of chairs, armoires, tables, headboards, hand-carved desks, china cabinets, leaded-glass lamps and even **CHIPPENDALE** items within their 445,000-square-foot showroom and warehouse. Miles and miles before you sleep, you better get going.

★★★ Jayroe's Premier Antiques   972/960-8516
5333 Forest Lane   Mon-Sat 10-7; Sun Noon-6
Dallas, TX 75244

Located at Forestwood Antique Mall, between Inwood and the Tollway, Jay Jayroe's the name, have odd-size bed, will travel. Not just an antique dealer, but he offers the service of converting that odd-size antique bed into a double, queen or sometimes a king. If you buy the bed from him, the conversion costs $100, or $150 if you bring in another bed. The conversion, by the way, won't detract from the value of the antique or do any damage to the bed. Plus, it's completely reversible. Just think—what if you were a basketball player and seven feet tall? That's not reversible. But it's nice to have a bed fit the frame, right? There's more—like restored French-import antiques, (armoires in particular,) mirrors, clocks and tables, too.

★★★★★ Linda's Treasures & Antiques   214/824-7915
1929 Greenville   Mon-Sat 11-7; Sun 1-6
Dallas, TX 75206   www.lindastreasures.com

This Perdue's not into chickens. Instead, Linda Perdue sells used furniture "cheep, cheep!" Named as the best used furniture store for years by *The Dallas Observer*, you won't be disappointed. The possibilities are endless. Heads up to lower Greenville for English or art deco armoires, vanities, chests, tables, buffets, dining room tables, chairs and beds. Into collectibles? Pick up a unique gift, a piece of collectible pottery, china, and jewelry, both old and new. Then bump into original artwork, paintings, pottery, carousel horses and then hop aboard an assortment of anything and everything for the bar. Drink up.

Little Red's Antiques   972/564-2200
10274 W. Hwy. 80   Mon-Tue, Thu-Sat 9-5; Sun 1-5; Closed Wed
PO Box 128
Forney, TX 75126

What do you get when you open your doors to 40,000 square feet of European antiques and reproductions? Little Red's, that's what. Richard Whaley is behind Little Red's (dad was the original Red) and has located his treasure-trove in the groves of Forney's Antique Row. Whatever your pleasure, whether antique or a reproduction, they've got it. Even if you don't have a cast-iron stomach for wandering down the many miles of aisles, if you're looking for cast-iron, it's one of their specialties. Looking for something to flank your entryway? This is where I bought my two stately Great Dane guard dogs...ceramic, of course. From majestic armoires to Majorca pottery, patio sets to old-fashioned street signs, urns to yard ornaments, sideboards to pianos, it's their outdoor lamps for $250 (wired and ready to glow) that light my fire. One of the highlights in the Forney strip.

★★★★ Love Field Antique Mall   214/357-6500
6500 Cedar Springs   Mon-Sat 10-7; Sun 12-7
Cedar Springs at Mockingbird   www.lovefieldantiquemall.com
Dallas, TX 75235

Since 1989, Love Field Antique Mall has been home to over 250 antique shops, a showcase gallery, lots of unique gifts, and seventy cars ready for a new "minnie" driver. If you can find Love Field, you can find this 70,000-square-foot mall. If you're looking to store your antique car, they have climate-controlled spaces with security to protect your classic. And for your next meeting, luncheon, shower or get-together, why not indulge your guests with a home cooked feast in their private dining room? Groups up to 20 can be accommodated. If just shopping and working up an appetite, Cafe Avion (214/351-9989) will sate your hunger pains. Open Mon-Sat 11-2:30.

★★★★★ Miller's Antiques & Pine Furniture Warehouse   214/741-9020
1225 N. Industrial   Mon-Sat 10-5; Sun Noon-5
Dallas, TX 75207

Oh Danny, boy have you hit paydirt, or what! This is how the West was won. If you're looking for pine furniture for that **RALPH LAUREN** look, look no further than the wagon wheels out front. Wholesale pricing on one of the largest selections of secretaries (the four-legged kind), parlor seats, **DUNCAN PHYFE** and **CHIPPENDALE** armoires, chests, beds, dining room suites, the whole shebang. Mix and match in mahogany, oak, pine and walnut from accent pieces to an entire house full of deco. Prices are exceptional in this 10,000-square-foot outpost. Take I-35 to the Market Center exit and head west to Industrial.

★★★★ Montgomery Street Antique Mall   817/735-9685
2601 Montgomery at I-30   Mon-Sat 10-6; Sun Noon-6
Fort Worth, TX 76107   www.300-antiques-4sale.com

You might feel Bewitched if you try to visit the website of Montgomery Street Antique Mall. The site is not updated and not much information is available. Instead, wiggle your nose, start the car or put on your jogging shoes because the only way you're going to take advantage of these deals is to stop in and see for yourself. Here's where you'll find over 270 dealers, all wheelin' and dealin' under one roof. And it's probably the biggest antique mall you're going to find in Fort Worth so it's well worth the trip. Besides all the antique deals and steals on everything from furniture to glass and pottery, advertising to books, porcelains, housewares, toys, sporting goods, metals and jewelry, you'll also find an area filled with reproductions. Even **BEANIE BABIES** and **DEPARTMENT 56** are popping up on these shelves. Amenities include strollers and wheelchairs. Then be sure to savor a few moments and relish over your purchases in The Secret Garden Tea Room. But since the early bird catches the worm, the tearoom closes at 4 PM.

◆◆◆◆ Norma Baker Antiques   817/335-1152
3311 W. 7th St.   Mon-Sat 10-5
Fort Worth, TX 76107

Dress to impress—your table that is. If your flatware is looking a little flat and your crystal just doesn't have that ping, head to Norma Baker, the lady with "glass." Shine up any meal with new flatware, or just find all those missing or damaged pieces. Consider The Shining by adding pieces or a complete collection of cut glass. Top it off with some eye-catching antiques such as a dining room suite where you can invite the entire neigborhood in for tea. Finally, you could accrue an entire tea set by filling in all those missing pieces. And if you still can't find those missing pieces, Norma Baker will find them for you for a small finder's fee. Take advantage of FREE wedding gift-wrap and bridal registry when it comes time to bestow that gift upon the happy couple. Prices, though, are not their priority. Service is. *Call toll-free: 800/742-1107*

★★★★★ Old Home Supply   817/927-8004
1801 College Ave.   Mon-Fri 8:30-5; Sat 9-5; Sun 1-5
Fort Worth, TX 76110

Oh, give me a home, where architectural salvage and relics do roam, and I'll point you to Old Home Supply, one of the seven wonders of the world. Housed in the historic Fairmont District in downtown Fort Worth (including the Tasty Bakery Building), you are shopping from the good old days to be used in all the good days ahead. Occupying four corners, these four buildings will open the doors to making not only a dramatic entrance, but furnishing your home with all the accompanying artifacts that give your house that personal touch. Pining for pedestal sinks and coveting claw-foot tubs? Then stay flush and pick out the plumbs from one of the buildings that houses the plumbing extracts. Choose from literally hundreds of them. Sink your limbs into the sink or into the tub, either way you have a luxurious cleansing experience. Then it's off to building number two for the lights. Most are even rewired and ready to turn on the town. Another building is for green thumbs who don't want to spend a finger more than necessary to accessorize their garden, patio, porch or entry way. Find objects from the past that make perfect accessories for today. Most everything they carry is restored to mint condition, you can save even more if you want to put that shine on yourself. Stained and bevel glass, antique cabinetry and hardware, glass doorknobs, solid wood doors (hard to find those these days), ornamental crown moldings—grab a truck load and have yourself a field day. When it comes time to shop for architectural salvage, be it salvage or antique, the relics are all here in practically a block-long shopper's Mecca. Why travel to Greece? Grease your engines and rev up those motors. Retro is "in" and Old Home Supply is where it's at!

★★★ On Consignment   214/827-3600
2927 N. Henderson   Mon-Sat 10-5:30
Dallas, TX 75206

Hoochie-coochie, what a great place to find a perfect bar, apartment sized. For $75, what a find! A small price to pay for a little addition to your home's decor. Say "thanks for the memorabilia" at this Henderson haunt. One of the first antique consignment concepts in town, what comes in, goes out fast. Shop often for home furnishings and decorative accents, a nice mix of traditional and antique home furnishings. From chandeliers to armoires, iron beds to desks, tables to sofas, in spite of its Henderson location, they all may be "too good to be threw!"

★★★★ Park Cities Antiques   214/350-5983
4908 W. Lovers Lane   Mon-Sat 10-6; Sun Noon-6
Dallas, TX 75209   www.parkcitiesantiques.com

P ark Avenue can't hold a candle to Park Cities Antiques. If those on the Avenue put their noses up, it just might be why Caryl Smarr and David Lee, the owners, love to play Genie with their prices. Located on a street made famous for lovers of fine antiques, you can find them in all their glory as you wander in and out among the displays. See 18th century English and French furniture, collectibles, estate jewelry and even fine linens ready to relocate to another empty nester. Fill up your home with memories from someone else's past. You'll be surprised how fulfilling it can be just surrounding yourself with a touch of history. As you meander through 90 specialty shops offering African, English,

French, Oriental and Primitives to garden antiques, majolica, silver and more, you'll know why this repository for The Wrecking Bar's architectural remains is where aspiring Park Cityites should shop for a piece of p-jazz. Three blocks west of Inwood, near the Shelton School, this stand-alone building is strictly the real McCoy for the hoi-polloi.

★★★ Pease-Cobb   817/763-5108
3923 Camp Bowie Blvd.   Daily 10-5:30
Fort Worth, TX 76107

The dig is on. Excavate all the rest but dust off some great deals at this site located between Virginia and Belle Place. Nestled into every corner are great finds, finding their way from their home to yours. Light the way with table lamps and lighting fixtures while you take home estate furniture, rugs, bric-a-brac and more, lovingly displayed in vignette settings to give an overall appeal. (Besides, where else can you get such hands-on decorating ideas?) All priced to sell. And if you're looking to sell, take advantage of Pease-Cobb's 60/40 split on consignment items. Dig around, turn around, pick up those items in your cellar, perch yourself in the attic and empty out those old trunks. You might be surprised how you can consign them and get a pretty penny. Got too much to haul in? Simply arrange an estate sale at your very own estate. They will arrange, with pleasure.

★★★★★ Philbeck's Antiques & Reproductions   972/564-9842
119 E. Hwy. 80   Mon-Fri 9-5; Sat 9-5:30
Forney, TX 75126

If you're looking for the real McCoy, you'll find it here. And if you're the Hatfields just wanting everyone to think it's the real McCoy, you'll find that here, too. Randy and Gayle Philbeck will custom make pine reproductions that look every bit out of the pages of **RALPH LAUREN** to your specifications. So fire away and move along through the many rooms while you take a little of this and a little of that. Your eyes will be able to look up, over and through old stained glass, iron and horned chandeliers. If you get lost, just make your way to the back where you can take cover in the warehouse among armoires, buffets, desks, dressers, candlesticks and chests. Now the Hatfields and McCoys may not be very cultured but even they would be impressed with the selection of direct imports from Germany, England, Czech Republic and Indonesia. So call a truce and head over to Philbeck's Antiques and Reproductions for a unique experience in the heart of the Antique Capital of Forney, Texas.

◆◆◆◆◆ Smith Antiques   817/265-7048
3650 Garner Blvd.   Mon-Fri 7:30-4
Arlington, TX 76013

Breathe new life into that old furniture. Though Smith Antiques may no longer sell antiques, they have created a niche for themselves as antique restorers. And not to rub you the wrong way, their work is top notch. Like a cosmetic surgeon, they're medical geniuses at removing nicks and filling crannies until your antiques gain a more youthful appearance. Don't you wish a face-lift was this easy? Well, at least it can be for your treasured antiques and with pick up and delivery service available for a charge, you'll be sure each piece receives the private room TLC it deserves. And speaking of service, most work is completed within two to three weeks. If it was your face, you'd still be black and blue.

★★★★ **Texas Antique Connection, The**   **817/429-0922**
7429 E. Lancaster   Mon-Fri 9-5; Sat 9-Noon
Fort Worth, TX 76112

Partake in the pleasure of hunting for buried treasure. Those French ships might just have missed the New Orleans port and come ashore at The Texas Antique Collection. With Belgian and French antiques along with hand-carved mahogany reproductions from Indonesia, your ship should set sail with the rudder in gear. Drop anchor and spend some time looking over the wide selection of authentic and reproductions "shore" to fit any decor or budget. Then when you think you couldn't possibly make it through another hour afloat, you'll want to moor—next door. Classic Designs (www.classicdesign.com) offers a bounty of furniture, accessories, bronzes, pottery, autographs, books and more. Bury the gold in the back yard and take along some chump change because when they advertise their inventory sale, it's time to proceed full steam ahead. Make those land lovers appreciate a good deal when you sea one. You'll enjoy a day of strolling along Lancaster where there's a multitude of little antique stores and galleries. Look back in time and remember those days gone by.

★★★★★ **Unlimited Ltd. Antique Mall**   **972/490-4085**
15201 Midway Rd. (North of Beltline)   Mon-Sun 10-6
Addison, TX 75244   www.antiqueland.com

The sky's the limit at this antique mall. Over 150 vendors are joined at the hip—displaying everything from antique and classic furniture to artwork, collectibles and more. You may feel like walking to the moon and back again in this 40,000-square-foot showroom, but you'll be walking on clouds after seeing some of their price tags. A bright surprise is how well some antiques are preserved in over 135 showcases. And don't let a bout with hunger rain on your parade. Pull up a tuffet in The Garden Tea Room open Tue-Sun 11:30-3:30, especially if you have a hankerin' for a blooming treat of sandwiches and desserts. Then head back to seventh heaven for all those goodies that best be sat on rather than eaten.

★★★★★ **Wholesale Antique**   **972/564-4433**
Hwy. 80 and Country Rds. (Exit 212-217)   Tue-Sat 11-6; Sat 11-6; Sun 12-5
Forney, TX 75126

Older can definitely result in a bigger, better bargain. This 10,000-square-foot den of antiquity is located at Hwy. 80 and Country Roads (Exit 212-217) in Forney, a favorite strip of antique wheeler dealers. You, too, can wheel and deal where the dealer's deal. Shop wholesale and save the needless markups. (Hey, that has a nice ring to it!) Save money on good-looking solid mahogany, walnut or oak dining room and bedroom suites and assorted pieces to complete the 1900-1940 look. Fifteen minutes east of LBJ, they also have booths at Unlimited on Midway, Forestwood Antique Mall, Forest and Inwood and at The Colony.

Apparel: Children's

★★ Carter's For Kids
972/724-6770
3000 Grapevine Mills Pkwy.
Mon-Sat 10-9:30; Sun 11-8
Grapevine, TX 76051
www.carters.com

Since 1865, Carter's has been considered one of the oldest and largest manufacturers of infants' and children's apparel in the U.S. Lucky for those shopping Grapevine Mills, Fort Worth Outlet Square or Gainseville Factory Stores because there's a Carter's Outlet in all those locations. There, you'll see the popular and patented drop seat pj's that made Carter's For Kids as well known as liver pills. Whether it's baby's sleepwear or play clothes, expect about 20-30 percent off and more during sales and end-of-the-season closeouts. Sizes newborn to size 7 in boys; newborn to size 6X in girls. The store's equally divided between boys and girls so we can't file any discrimination charges. But I wouldn't recommend charging anything on Saturdays as it's a madhouse with wailing babies and wall-to-wall mothers. Try shopping weekdays for peace of mind. *Call toll-free: 800/253-3079*

★★★ Chelsea's Tea Room & Boutique
817/276-8100
2421-C Westpark Row
Mon-Fri 10-6; Sat 10-5:30; Sun Noon-5
Pantego, TX 76013

Coffee, tea, and tea parties. What a terrific combo. Ta! Ta! Chelsea's Tea Room and Boutique caters to little girls and boys in a very elegant atmosphere. Experience true southern hospitality, charm and grace when shopping for baby and children's clothing. Find the perfect outfit for any special occasion, whether it be a portrait or you're just a stickler for perfection. Boy's sizes 0-7 and girl's sizes 0-14 will have wardrobes that include **CHICKEN NOODLE**, **COTTON COLLECTION**, **NANETTE**, **WEEBOK**, **ZOODLES** and more. Even preemie sizes and maternity samples round out (pardon the expression) their inventory. And sampling prices at 15-20 percent off retail makes that tea a little easier to swallow. Then, there's always just the tearoom...a perfect place for that tea party or any other child-like soiree.

★★★★★ **Children's Orchard**   **972/612-7177**
3000 Custer, Suite 106   Mon-Fri 10-7; Sat 10-6; Sun Noon-5
SE Corner Parker and Custer   www.childrensorchard.com
Plano, TX 75023

Talk about taking a bite out of the red apple! This resale chain is building a forest nationwide. Their modus operandi—franchising. Go to their website for details. Only top brands are invited in with the potential of saving customers up to 70 percent. Look, see and shop gently-used and new kids' clothing, toys, furniture, equipment, books and accessories! But the best part? They buy your castoffs up front. That means, no waiting for months to collect that check when your consignment clothes sell. Visit also in Grapevine, 200 West NW Highway and Lewisville, 291 E. Round Grove Rd. Another plus, this chain supports the Family Builders Adoption Network, helping to find supportive adoptive families for hard to place children. *Call toll-free: 800/999-KIDS*

★★★★ **Children's Store, The**   **972/442-2708**
101 S. Ballard   Tue-Fri 10-5:30; Sat 10-5
Wylie, TX 75098

Now that you know where Buffalo Gap is, it's time to find Wylie—that eastern bastion of Plano that houses some great little refuges from high prices. Save 20-50 percent on lotsa-lotsa children's lines: **CASH-CASH, COTTONTAILS, HEARTSTRINGS, KNITWAYS, LITTLE ME, MAGGICE BREEN, MONDAY'S CHILD, NAUTICA, NICHOLE RUTH OF CAROLINA, TICKLE ME**, well, forget tickling, just belly-laugh all the way home. Girls' clothing and some boys, too, up to size 14, as well as some preteen and ladies' sizes. Some mother and daughter dresses were perfect for that Easter Parade or Christmas photo. Also, dressmaking fabric, buttons, lace, braid trim, ribbons of all sizes and colors, and all sewing supplies to do your own thing. Call for directions.

★★★★ **Chocolate Soup**   **214/363-6981**
1214 Preston Royal Plaza   Mon, Thu-Fri 10-8; Tue-Wed, Sat 10-6; Sun 1-5
Dallas, TX 75230

Oh how sweet it is when your savings are big. Unwrap some new duds for the youngen's with the variety of Chocolate Soup labeled apparel that comes directly from their factory in Kansas City. These designer look-a-likes will fatten up any wardrobe in girl's sizes 0-12 and boys to size 7, but shopping at the end of the season will sweeten the deal. Slurp, slurp! Splurge by adding some crackers like **BUSTER BROWN, CARRIAGE BOUTIQUE, HEARTSTRINGS, LE TOP, NAUTICA, S.F. BLUES**, and more—all at savings that average 25 percent off retail. It's time you shake that bonbon down to the southeast corner of Preston and Royal for more Chocolate Soup...before it melts in your hands!

★★★★★ **Consolidated Clothiers**   **214/678-0060**
2246 Vantage   Mon-Fri 9-5
Dallas, TX 75207

Mary may have a little lamb but Consolidated Clothiers has the discounts on fine children's clothing. Bah-bah-gains can be found on these racks with manufacturers' closeouts with famous names like **HOUSE OF HATTAN, KATHERINE REBECCA, LAVENDER, MONDAY'S CHILD, SAN FRANCISCO BLUE, TOO TOE PICCOLO, VIVA LA FETE** and more. Inventory rushes in faster than the tide, so don't wait for a blue moon to hit the bargains. And at Consolidated Clothiers, it's not against the rules to outfit the entire family. Frankly, you never know what lies behind closed doors. Knock three times and whisper low. These folks offer plenty of advantages to shop the Vantage Street Warehouse District. Located just west of Wycliff Ave, you can buy your pizza at CiCi's Pizza, buy your children's clothes at this CC. You'll C !

★★★★★ Just Kidstuff   972/240-5500
4125 Broadway, Suite 120   Mon-Sat 10-6
Garland, TX 75041

Just Kidstuff is a parent's just reward for all the sacrifices they make. Just keeping kids clothed is a priority (you can't send them to school naked) so trading in last year's barely worn for this year's latest can be a Godsend. This resale shop satisfies that well-known wail, "I've got nothing to wear!" Clothing and accessories arrive daily by the trunk-fuls. Just stop in and save up to 70 percent off retail and see why children's resale is a hot commodity every season. From the day they are born, teach them the value of comparative shopping and they'll come up a winner every time by shopping the resale route. From infants to size 7 for Juniors and size 20 for boys, it's just kidstuff, but what the heck. You can indulge them with a whole new wardrobe at these prices on Broadway!

★★★★★ Kidswap   214/890-7927
6728 Snider Plaza   Mon-Fri 10-6; Sat 10-5
Dallas, TX 75205

It's child's play when shopping for deals is this easy. Mother May I please have a place to shop where they have my size and I won't have to worry if I outgrow them too quick. Hide and seek out designer and name brands for boys and girls sized infants through juniors. Rock a Bye baby in due time with maternity wear. Tag—you're it. Tags in this gang include **BABY GUESS?**, **BUSTER BROWN**, **CARTERS**, **DIOR**, **DKNY**, **GAP**, **GYMBOREE**, **LEVI'S**, **LIMITED TOO**, **NIKE**, **POLO** and **TOMMY HILFIGER**. The stork has even added a new little addition to Kidswap with the arrival of overruns and brand new clothes from **FLAP-DOODLE**. We teach our children that rewards come with sacrifices. Although prices on chi-chi clothes reflect a low-brow approach to country club living, swap their clothes, not your kids, and make out like a bandit.

Mudpuppy   817/731-2581
5714 Locke   Mon-Sat 10-6
Locke at Camp Bowie
Fort Worth, TX 76107-5020

Saving money is never a dirty word, unless you're shopping at Mudpuppy. No need to clean out the bank account when shopping for clean children's clothing. Just dig in your heels and start reeling through the racks for children's clothing sized 0-16 for girls and 0-20 for boys. Even maternity styles and infants' accessories can be found lining the shelves. Just because they've been worn before doesn't mean they should have to stain your budget. Jana Minter keeps her store spic-n-span so labels like Neiman's feel right at home keeping company with **CARTERS**, **GAP**, **GYMBOREE**, **LEVI'S**, **OSHKOSH B'GOSH**, and **POLO**. Who cares if they're not even wet behind the ears? And to add to the mix, Jana's got doggies in the window now as she has adopted waifs from the Humane Societies and helps place these orphans in loving homes. As a matter of fact, single-handedly, she has helped place more than 30 puppies and doggies in homes since January 2001. Now, that deserves a standing ovation!

★★★★★ Once Upon a Child   972/618-5800
7200 Independence Pkwy.   Mon-Fri 10-7; Sat 10-6; Sun Noon-5
Plano, TX 75025   www.ouac.com

Once Upon A Child, there stood a great children's resale shop. With racks and racks of great names like **BUSTER BROWN** who was playing nicely with **CARTER'S** while **CHRISTIAN DIOR** was filling the **GAP** that was left by the hole dug by **GYMBOREE** who was dressed in **LEVI'S** while bouncing on his **POLO** stick. Okay, so we took some liberties while we were shopping. But remember, we were, once upon a time, children, too. Shelves were brimming with toys and infant accessories from **CENTURY**, **EVEN-FLO**, **FISHER PRICE**, **GERRY**, **GRACO**, **KOLOCRAFT**, **IN STEP** and **SAFETY FIRST**. Everyone was very happy to be saving so much money. Then one day, a big change took place and all the world decided to shop the resale way. But at Once Upon a Child, there's no wait for your money. "Kid's stuff with previous experience" is welcomed and paid for up front—except for the 20 percent new discounted inventory. This franchised chain is building momentum and growing by leaps and bounds. In the Metroplex alone, you can shop at 5904 S. Cooper St. #3, Arlington, TX 76017, 817/466-8380; 2661 Midway Rd, Carrollton, TX 75006, 972/250-6603; 2311 Cross Timbers Rd #317, Flower Mound, TX 75028, 972/874-0779; 3046 Lavon Drive #144, Garland, TX 75040, 972/495-4662; 2030 Glade Road, #206, Grapevine, TX 76051, 817/481-6210; 3557 N. Belt Line Rd., Irving, TX 75062, 972/252-4688 and the location above. Other locations throughout Texas should tell you this is one big whopper!

Small Fry   940/387-9915
330 Sunset   Mon-Sat 10-6
Denton, TX 76201

Do not, I repeat, do not associate this Small Fry with Small Fry World. They are like night and day. One's full price. The other, you can save as much as 50 percent on all the famous brands you've come to enjoy from department and specialty stores. Which one do I recommend? Duh-h-h! How do they do it? Well, for one, they operate out of two adorable cottages in Denton where the cost of doing business is less. Secondly, they buy market samples, promotional goods and whatever deals they can muster that are current and sought-after in babies' layettes, clothing for girls from preemies to 16, boys' clothing from preemies to 7 and gifts for both. Order up an entire wardrobe for your children, grandchildren, or anybody's children and don't look back, Dress your small fries and hold the ketchup. **ALLISON ROSE, AMY BYER, BABY TOGS, BISCOTTI, CALVIN KLEIN, CHICKEN NOODLE, CITY KIDS, CLAIRE LYNN, COTTON COLLECTION, DORISSA, FELTMAN, GOOD LAD, KC PARKER, KNITWAVES, LE TOP, LITTLE ME, MICHAEL SIMON, MONDAY'S CHILD, MULBERRIBUSH, SCHWAB, SIMI, TICKLE ME, TODDLE TYKE, ZOODLES** and **ZYNO** are some of the brands to be had. Shipping is available nationwide. If you prefer to shop via phone, just tell them what you're looking for, what size, how much and the gift it on its way. From birthdays to holidays, you don't want to forget how adorable they can look with the perfect outfit. And if you're watching those pennies from heaven, the force will be with you here. Of course, nothing will stop those diehards who want to see first hand, touch every hanger, and hold up every jumper and jumpsuit. Go for it, but you won't go broke. That's what makes them the the award-winner in the Children's Category. They won't lead you astray. Head north to Denton on I-35, exit Hwy. 377 (which turns into Carroll), Exit 465B. Turn right on Sunset, and you'll see those adorable children's cottages where the designer clothes are hanging out at 30-50 percent off, everyday. Mail orders welcomed nationwide. ***Call toll-free: 888/442-9002***

★★★★ Spankie's Rethreads   972/227-8822
169 Historic Town Square   Tue-Sat 10-6
Lancaster, TX 75146

Spankie's is the perfect place to dress up those little rascals. This historic old building makes classic fashions come alive. Suit up boys and girls in sizes 0-16. Darling attire can be acquired from **BUSTER BROWN**, **CARTER'S**, **BABY GUESS?**, **GAP KIDS**, **GYMBOREE**, **HUSH PUPPY**, **LEVI'S**, **MONKEY WEAR**, **NAUTICA**, **OSHKOSH B'GOSH**, **POLO**, **REEBOK**, **TOMMY HILFIGER**, and just like their Christmas list, it goes on and on. Colored tags allow for even greater savings with yellow and orange tags offering an additional 50 percent off. But keep your eyes peeled for pink and purple ones 'cause those are the ones that offer a whopping 75 percent off their already low, low price. Be sure, if need be, to consider the maternity outfits and baby extras such as accessories and toys. Gotta have, gotta have!

★★★★★ Sprouts Children's Boutique   817/788-8020
1101 Cheek Sparger   Tue-Thu 10-6; Fri 10-4; Sat 11-3
Tara Village Shopping Center
Colleyville, TX 76034

If your children are growing faster than your bank account, then count on Sprouts Children's Boutique for savings on the best in designer kids' clothes. Here's the place to dress up those darling little ones in sizes 0-14 for both boys and girls. Make any special occasion an affair to remember with elegant dresses, ruffles and lace and little boys' shortalls and knee-high socks. Don't forget the penny loafers and patent leathers to complete the look. Even first communion dresses, dancewear, costumes, baby items and maternity are available at Sprouts. Look closely and find new market samples and closeouts scattered throughout the inventory mix. But their claim to fame is the special occasion outfits for both moms-to-be and kids to play dressup, for real and surreal. Costumes are tough to find in the resale world, so this is a plus but here's a twist. New leotards for dance class and their accompanying counterparts, new tap and ballet shoes. At least you can find them.

★★★★★ Yesterdaze Kids   817/284-5437
7269 Glenview Drive   Tue-Fri 11-5; Sat Noon-4
North Richland Hills, TX 76180

Never on Sundays or Mondays, but every other daze, this is where your children's wardrobes can be complete. This children's resale clothes shopping machine is like wishful thinking come true. What a welcome relief for the cause of parental rights. Write your own ticket. Bring in clothes that they've outgrown though practically new; or buy someone else's outgrowns and practically new and build an entirely new wardrobe. Follow the store's light brick path just minutes from North Hills Mall. Sizes newborn to 18 for both boys and girls are hanging around just waiting for a new home. Designer duds, toys, gifts, books, baby accessories and more can be bought or sold. Coincidentally, the owner's name is Sandy Parrent and she's the Store Mother. Though this darling little house is home to one of the best resale shops in the Big Metroplex, you can huff and puff and try to blow the house down, but its 1,300 square feet are firmly rooted into the bargain scene. Forget it. Your budget will remain intact all through the shopping process.

Apparel: Family

★★★★ American T-Shirt   **972/289-8262**
1228 Scyene Rd., #209   Mon-Fri 9-5; Sat 10-3
Mesquite, TX 75149   www.american-t-shirts.com

As American as apple pie, American T-Shirt is in the business of helping businesses grow. With everything available—from aprons, athletic apparel, bags and totes, blankets, denim wear, fleece and golf shirts, headwear, loungewear and outerwear, emblazon your name on these items and strut your stuff. Add to that shorts, sweaters, towels, turtlenecks and, of course, T-shirts and you should finally get the message. All from names you know including **ANVIL**, **FRUIT OF THE LOOM**, **GILDAN**, **HANES**, **JERZEES**, **LEE**, **OUTER BANKS**, **RAWLINS** and **VAN HEUSEN**. Order by the piece, the dozen or by the case. This wholesale distributor has no minimum orders, but the more you buy, the more you'll save. They will even custom embroider most products. Call for a free brochure, their $5 catalog, or shop online. *Call toll-free: 800/782-0214*

bluefly.com   **877/BLUEFLY (258-3359)**
    www.bluefly.com

Bluefly don't bother me, unless you've got the savings of Bluefly.com. The buzz on saving up to 75 percent off is here, clear as the morning sunshine. Shoo away the imposters and go straight for big names like **CALVIN KLEIN**, **DONNA KARAN**, **FENDI**, **G-SHOCK**, **HUGO BOSS**, **LEVI'S**, **LONDON FOG**, **NIKE**, **PRADA**, **PUMA**, **RALPH LAUREN**, **ZENGA** and others. Be sure to land on this site often with over 500 designers available at any given time. There's no telling what you might find for men, women, children and even your home. Turn that frown upside down with Bluefly deals like **GUCCI** silk ties that retail for $125 for $64. It's a cakewalk to spend only $16 on kid's plush sweaters or a cashmere scarf by **TSE** that might retail for $245 but here it was $125. Don't stick to the same old variety with **ONLY HEARTS** sheer bralettes for $19. Around the house enjoy **BELLINO** fine linens and **JONATHAN ADLER** pottery. Don't swat at unwanted items when you have a full 90 days to return them. Raise an antenna since the buzzword is Bluefly.com for swarms of values. Forget the "Off" and get on with the program.

★★★ Dickies Factory Outlet   817/877-0387
521 W. Vickery   Mon-Sat 9:30-5:30
Fort Worth, TX 76104   www.dickies.com

Here's a name you should know since Dickies' has been providing quality work clothes for men and women since 1922. Uniforms can really put a dent in the wallet. That is why shopping at the outlet is not only smart, it's downright thrifty. And what's really nifty is their complete satisfaction guarantee. If for any reason you're not happy with your purchase, either now or later, just return it for a new item or complete refund. Now that's customer care. Workpants will run around $17 and khakis $18 for both men and women. Coveralls will fit the bill at $21 and pocket tees are $7. Children's school uniforms can be a real pain year after year. But this outfit can be a real boon to your budget if a uniform is required.

★★★★★ Haggar Clothing Co. Warehouse   214/956-4431
6113 Lemmon Ave.   Mon-Sat 10-6
Dallas, TX 75209   www.haggar.com

The Haggar Clothing Co. Warehouse store makes a believer in savings as big as Texas. This Texas-bred manufacturer is a staple in Texans' wardrobes. Their clothes are as easy to put on as they are to wear. And everything somehow coordinates, from modern dress-up to golf, khaki wear to business casual. If there's a Friday in your work week lineup, expect the lines to be long here. It's the perfect place for your entire classic casual wardrobe. Plus you will save up to 50 percent. The selection, too, is supersized with slacks, sport coats, suits, shirts, shorts, jackets, jeans and ties. Every figure type can be type-cast. Women's clothing, an afterthought, but comparable.

★★★★ Harold's Outlet Store   254/582-0133
104 NE I-35   Mon-Sat 10-8; Sun 11-6
Hillsboro, TX 76645   www.harolds.com

Creme de la creme! Only the best in women's and men's wear can be found hanging on the racks of Harold's Outlet Store. But lighten up. These price tags arrive at a fraction of their original costs. Love those bargains? Love is in the air each February (or there about) when Harold's offers their multi-million dollar inventory via a warehouse sale. It's the best Valentine's Day present you can give yourself. Somehow, when they alter the price tag, the hordes of bargain shoppers descend upon the convention center. But everyday bargain shoppers can benefit by heading to Hillsboro.

Jeans Warehouse   972/247-2800
11171 Harry Hines   Mon-Sun 9-7
Dallas, TX 75229

Denim, jeans, dungarees, if it's in your genes, shop for them and don't pay retail. Be a rebel and save on these denim magnates: **BOSS**, **CALVIN KLEIN**, **COSMO**, **GUESS?**, **JNCO**, **LEVI'S**, **POLO**, **SOUTHPOLE**, **TOMMY HILFIGER**, **WRANGLER** and more. We struck out, though, and didn't get "**LUCKY**." Make a radical change and resist the habit of traveling to the mall for your family's jeans. Find pants, shorts, jackets, tops, capri's—all in denim and all in sizes to fit any man, woman, teen or child. Rise up, Metroplex, and save 25 percent or more on your favorite styles at this congregation of genetic aberrations.

★★★★★ **T-Shirt Outlet**   **972/241-7030**
14015 N. Stemmons   Mon-Sat 10-8
Farmers Branch, TX 75234

Prices on shirts start at $3 each for S-M-L-XL and $4 each for 2XL-4XL but for the whole team, that's a different story. Win the game on high prices and shop at this bold yet beautiful bargain T-shirt factory. For silk-screening T-Shirts, expect to pay a $35 set up charge per color to be imprinted. Then it'll cost $1 per side of printing on a white shirt and $1.50 per side of printing on colored shirts. The minimum order for printed T-shirts is three dozen but smaller orders for just T-shirts can be had at a price slightly higher. They can be either be 100 percent cotton or 50-50 (cotton/polyester combination). Why not get with the program and get your team's name up there front and center, (or back and center, either side will generate results.) The T-shirts are so inexpensive, and these folks have all the equipment to churn out the quantities fast, in time for the first batter to go to bat. The children's T-shirts cost five for $10 (that's $2 a shirt) and thats the lowest we've found in the Metroplex. Too, adults can get the same quantity at the same price. No kidding. But oversized T's (2XL and 3XL) are a tad higher, three for $10. Still the lowest in town. Looks like this is where we'll be getting our "cheapest link" shirts. Stay tuned.

★★★★ **Tommy Hilfiger Outlet**   **972/874-0172**
3000 Grapevine Mills Pkwy.   Mon-Sat 10-9:30, Sun 11-8
Grapevine Mills Mall   www.tommy.com
Grapevine, TX 76051

If Tommy is a friend of yours, you might want to stop by his store and check out deals on clothing for men, women and children. There's no mistaking the savings with prices clearly marked an average of 40 percent off. Sport the look complete with logo T-shirts starting at just $15. Cozy up to one of the many clearance racks to save an extra 50 percent off their already low outlet prices. It's like having a friend in the business when savings like that can add up to a whopping 80 percent. So who cares if they're last year's style? Sure looks like this year's, huh? Classic styling that never knows from one season to the next. Wholesome, all-American, clean-cut, this is a **TOMMY HILFIGER** kind of guy and gal.

4

Apparel: Men's

★★★ Apparel World
4949 Beeman Ave.
Dallas, TX 75223

214/887-8999
Mon-Fri 8:30-4:30

Jump into this apparel shop for the real deal on jumpsuits at wholesale prices. That's right. This really is the manufacturer's outlet (look for "Lorch" on the front of the building; once inside, you'll see the sign for Apparel World) offering a large selection of jumpsuits suited to fit men sized 38-short to 60-long. Leap for joy with factory-direct pricing on knits and long sleeved shirts sizes S-2XL. You're bound to find something with this expansive inventory that includes everything from socks to sweaters. Just don't you sweat it. Finding this location is easy once you find the Lorch Building. Make a beeline and you'll be fine. *Call toll-free: 800/397-3086*

★★★★ Barry Mfg. Co.
4141 Independence Drive
Dallas, TX 75237

972/298-3366
Mon-Thu 9-7; Fri 9-8; Sat 9-7; Sun Noon-5
www.bettermenswear.com

How does same day alterations on suits sound, like just another line at a singles' bar...or the truth, and nothing but? Well, if we're lying we're dying 'cause men can size up this situation with same day alterations whether a small, a tall or a guy who's big and tall up to size 60. Let the fat robin sing about savings on single-and double-breasted suits, rayon/linen blends, polyester and wool, all priced up to 50 percent off comparable retail, from $99-$169. Shoes by **GEORGIO BRUTINI** and **STACY ADAMS**, some were walking out the door for as low as $39.99. Check directory for multiple locations.

★★★★★ Big and Tall Fashions for Less
951 W I-20, Suite 105
Arlington, TX 76017

817/468-5900
Mon-Fri 10-8; Sat 10-7; Sun Noon-5

Don't be chained down to just one store. Big and Tall Fashions for Less has eight locations throughout the Metroplex. Shop often for big deals on big sizes counting all the way up to 66 in jeans and 70 in suits. Make room for improvements with other garments sized to 6X and XLT-5XLT. Big taste and lots of style for Texans in **ADOLFO**, **ARROW**, **DUCK HEAD**, **HAGGAR**, **HARMONY**, **IZOD**, **LEVI'S** (545s up to size 60), **PALM BEACH**, **RALPH LAUREN** and **WRANGLER** for prices less than you might find elsewhere.

Some of these sizes, you just won't find elsewhere, either. So make it easy and take advantage of one-stop shopping at this location between Matlock and Cooper. Even men that are big can be beautiful. They just look silly with their hairy legs showing from too short pants or their shirt sleeves resting at their elbow. At last, here's one store that can deliver the real-l-l-y big bargains. Check directory for multiple locations and make some big or tall guy one happy fella!

★★★ Casual Male Big & Tall   817/468-8224
3200 S. Cooper, #101   Mon-Sat 10-7; Sun Noon-5
Arlington, TX 76015   www.thinkbig.com

This chain has really made a comeback. Since 1973, this company has been catering to big and tall men who wear sizes 1X-6X and waist sizes 36-66. They now are a big chain, with over 400 stores, a new apparel catalog, and an e-commerce site. They carry active and sportswear, blazers and sports jackets, outerwear and accessories plus boots, dress and athletic shoes. Brother stores are Repp Big and Tall and B & T Factory Stores. But for now, let's just concentrate on Casual Male. Sensible prices will put your senses on alert. See the savings on **HARBOR BAY** (comparable to **DOCKERS**), which is always a favorite. Feel the comfort of kicking back in a pair of **LEVI'S** or **WRANGLER**'s. Dress like the little guys in big boy's clothes. Prices are also lower than retail and even lower still during special promotions. Check directory for multiple locations in the Metroplex. ➤

★★★★★ Corporate Traditions   214/638-5050
1140 Empire Central   Mon-Fri 9-5; Sat 9-2
Dallas, TX 75247   www.corptrad.com

Keep abreast of the latest trends while holding strong to basic traditions and in the end, your wardrobe will be befitting the chairman of the board. Meet for lunch at The Palm, write the contract when the espresso is served and tip the waiter well. Welcome to Corporate Traditions. Whether you've already arrived or are still making waves to the top, rise above the rubble and shop smart. It's a tradition in this household to be pampered with the finest in customer service while shopping for the finest men's clothing at the lowest possible price. So while taking advantage of what might feel like an employee discount price, create a relationship with Anita Green and staff. Her 4,000-square-foot showroom contains the wardrobe for a king. Only the finest European and American designers are even talked about or considered. Don't even think about entering if you're a "schlump!" And if you don't know what the word means, you better ask before daring to step foot inside. Coordinate your entire wardrobe from top to bottom, suits to shoes, shirts to belts, ties to socks, slacks to shorts, it's a one-stop source for the designing man out to make a mark in the world. To test your designer vocabulary, here are a few to impress you with: **ASHWORTH**, **AUSTIN REED**, **AXIS** (Bob's favorite golf shirt), **BALLIN**, **BARRY BRICKEN**, **COOGI**, **CUTTER & BUCK**, **DESCENTE**, **HAUPT**, **JACK VICTOR**, **JHANE BARNES**, **LORD WEST** formal wear, **ST. CROIX**, **TALLIA** and **TERZOD**. Now for the more fiscally-endowed, what about an **IKE BEHAR** custom shirt? And what is your favorite shoe? **ALLEN EDMONDS**, **COLE-HAAN** and **TIMBERLAND**? They've got them, you get them. The price is right! *Call toll-free: 800/438-7848*

★★★★ David's Big and Tall Shop   817/731-3691
6730 Camp Bowie   Mon-Sat 9:30-7
Fort Worth, TX 76116   www.hardtofit.com

Like a fine wine, after almost 30 years in the business, David's Big and Tall has only improved with age. Keeping up with the (Too Tall) Jones's has just gotten easier—owing to the discounts that run big and tall here. They've been doing it for so long, it's gotten into their blood. Streaming sales make the savings an even flow. And the bigger the better with sizes running 48-70 in coats and jackets. No senior moments here because if you can't remember what you came in for, Michele the store manager is more than willing to help find it. Pull up in **CREEKWOOD** and drop anchor in **DOCKERS** while fishing through the **SALMON RIVER** for just the right fit in sizes 36-70. **IZOD** will look great on the golf course, while the discounted prices on everything else are heavenly. Are you listening, God? Members of the clergy get an additional 10 percent off. Hallelujah, brother. Just don't get too carried away and expect their website to be a website soon. The name's registered, but so far, there's nothing there.

★★★★ Far East Outlet   214/637-6828
1336 Inwood Rd.   Mon-Sat 10-5:30
Inwood Trade Center
Dallas, TX 75247

The Far East does not have to be far out of your way. Take time to explore new fashions in a not-so-new outlet. For almost 30 years, this store has been discounting men's and boy's clothing (sorry, they no longer offer women's) an average of 30-50 percent off retail. Dress up the little tykes in savings on boys' suits sizes 4-20, including slim and regular that retail for $99 for only $39. Fancy that! It's one of the few resources that cater to the Kiddos hoping to capture them while they're young and groom a customer for life. Then when they're all grown up, Far East Outlet be able to sell them men's all wool suits in sizes 36-60 (reg/long) and 36-44 (short) for $165 ($360 elsewhere). Polish it off with dress shirts for $16, silk shirts for $12 and ties for $9. If the Far East is foreign, then expect these names to be also. But from what country, I don't know. Sounds Italian to me but even so, they don't ring a bell: **CLASSICO UOMO**, **EUROPA COLLECTION**, **GINA CAPPELIO** and **LINEA CLASSICA**. If you don't care about familiarity, you'll get your money's worth sans designer label. Sayonara, baby!

★★★★★ Gent-ly Owned Men's Consignery   972/733-1115
17610 Midway, #108   Mon-Fri 11-7; Sat 11-5
Dallas, TX 75287   www.gentlyowned.com

Only a true gentlemen would be caught dead inside Gent-ly Owned Men's Consignery. So what, if you can't remember their name. Just think: Gent-ly Owned. Log onto their website. It's quite a looker. And you can be, too, in what they call, "Liquid Wardrobes." Fluid, eternal, tasteful, elegant, and think of it like the days when men were men and sales personnel treated you as such. Think of the men in your life. And think great names at fabulous prices. Though small in square footage, they make up for it in quality and service. Okay, the prices are great, too, but when was the last time you were REALLY waited on in a men's shop? I mean REALLY waited on. Todd Shevlin is at your service the minute you enter his store. Upscale with names like **ARMANI**, **CANALI**, **COLE-HAAN**, **COOGI**, **HUGO BOSS**, **NICOLE MILLER**, **PERRY ELLIS**, **POLO**, **TOMMY HILFIGER**, **VERSACE** and **ZEGNA**. Impressed yet? Business and casual wear including market samples are all wholesale priced. Who cares if some CEO jet-setter wears it once and then consigns it here? Given graciously, I'm sure, so that they can spread their good will by giving to the needy. Maybe even the greedy. We're not all Mark Cubans and Ross Perots, now are we? The best in American and European designer labels await you. Don't just be a customer, either. Learn how to be a consigner and profit from your outgrown clothes. Maybe you've developed that midlife spread? Maybe you've just entered your midlife crisis? Either way, make some room in your closet to consign what you're not wearing and buy something you will. Out with the old, in with the new...new to you, anyway. And laugh all the way to the executive washroom.

★★★★★ Gentry Men's Resale   817/428-4196
8218 Grapevine Hwy.   Mon-Fri 10-6; Sat 10-5
North Richland Hills, TX 76180

As a member of the club, this Gentry is dedicated to providing Tarrant County with an exclusive "Men's Only" resale shop. Yes ladies, you're welcome to shop but don't expect to place any new threads on your empty hangers. They may discriminate, but in this case, they are unanimous in saving you tons of money. Only the finest men's clothing struts its stuff these doors, checking in at fabulous prices. Rub elbows with **ALEXANDER JULIAN, AUSTIN REED, BROOKS BROTHERS, HART SCHAFFNER & MARX, HICKEY FREEMAN, NEIMAN MARCUS, PERRY ELLIS, POLO** by **RALPH LAUREN** and **TOMMY HILFIGER**. They may be exclusive but not to Club Gentry. They even welcome clothes from **THE GAP, IZOD** or **LEVI'S** just because men like 'em and wear 'em. Sizes are allowed from boys 12 to men's 54 XL. Special appearances are made by sample makers and special buys on leather wallets, watches, ties and gifts. Get with the program. Nobody pays retail these days and everyone knows just because someone previously owned it, doesn't mean it's not new to you. If you're going to spend money to be a member of the club, make it one with a hot tub.

International Suit & Shoe Warehouse   972/780-2599
4030 W. Camp Wisdom Rd.   Mon-Fri 10-8; Sat 10-7
Dallas, TX 75237

It's a good thing they call this land of ours a melting pot because International Suit and Shoe Warehouse is having a meltdown and citizens of the Metroplex will be the benefactors. This huge liquidation center is big on private label suits and sportswear discounted up to 70 percent. Don't be a drip by thinking that it has to have a designer label to make it quality. Many of those fancy-shmancy designer suits are made for the designers with one label, and also for International Suit without. It could even be the exact same suit. The only difference, the price. Now we're talking my language. Shoes, too, but they have the names still on like **GIORGIO BRUTINI** and **STACY ADAMS**. Heard of them, haven't you? And when you're buying everything from polyester to virgin wool suits for just $89-$329, you better understand what's in the mix. Pour yourself into sizes 36 to 60-inch shirts—a "neck" of a deal in sizes 14-22, 32-37 sleeve. Don't leave empty handed since some alterations can be performed on the spot—just $4 hems and $5 cuffs. International Suit and Shoe Warehouse is owned by Big and Tall Menswear for Less and has an additional location in North Dallas at 635 Preston Rd., corner of LBJ, 972/239-1984. Dy-no-mite!

★★ Jos. A. Bank Clothiers   972/248-4330
1713 Preston Rd. Suite C   Mon-Fri 10-8; Sat 10-6; Sun Noon-5
Plano, TX 75093

Farewell to you fair maidens. Jos. A. Bank is now for men only. And whether you're a banker or tanker, they can get you covered. Direct from their own factory, executives have known for years where to file and sharpen their corporate appearance. By looking down the button-downs and up to the pinstripes, men have sized up their wardrobes and concluded they could bank on Jos. A. Bank. Clothes in sizes 37S-50XL with additional sizing available through their catalog. Their prices are steep. Even during sales, you might shell out $375-$575. Not bad if you make pretty hefty deposits in your bank but if you're driven to succeed, pull up to this bank and see what your statement reads at the end of the month. Your bottom line will reflect good taste but big savings, probably not. Jos A. Bank's is legendary for their "Business Express" program, though, which consists of a 100 percent wool suit coat (two- or three-button, or double-breasted) with a coordinating pant, pleated or plain, for $375. Step up the corporate ladder in mix'n match separates that match your style. Alterations are available for an additional charge and ready in seven days. Close the deal at this Jos. A Bank's located across from Borders at Preston and Park, or look for them at 4025 Northwest Highway, Dallas, 214/691-9199, and in Lewisville at Vista Ridge Mall, 972/315-2577. Stay ahead of the competition by requesting their catalog.

K & G Men's Center   **972/438-6100**
3417 E. John Carpenter Frwy.   Fri 10-9; Sat 10-7; Sun Noon-6
Irving, TX 75062   www.kgmens.com

This chain is on the move and in the groove concurrently. With 55 men's stores, two ladies' stores and six combo stores, expect that some changes will be in store for their Metroplex locations soon, and maybe even online sales. But for the moment, call the 800 number for the store nearest you. Five area locations are open Fridays, Saturdays, Sundays, holidays and every day of the week from the day after Thanksgiving until New Years. Now that we've got the particulars, let's shop. Expect to save 30-70 percent throughout their warehouses in sizes 36 Short to 54 Extra Long (almost every man has his limits). Wool suits for just $99 (compared to $300) is their claim to fame. Two-button, three-button, four-button and double-breasted styles cover the gamut. Silk ties are always $7.99. Oxford dress shirts were only $19.99 and their tie collection (values to $30-plus) will get you all choked up for just $7.99. Make a stable statement with famous footwear ranging from $49.99-$64.99, compared to $72-$100. And since they don't advertise their brands, we will. **ADOLFO**, **CHAPS** by **RALPH LAUREN**, **CHRISTIAN DIOR**, **PIERRE CARDIN**, **PURITAN** and more are dressing up these racks. This location's 1/2 mile east of Texas Stadium at the Grauwyler exit; others can be found at 4400 Little Rd., in Arlington, 817/561-5100 and on N. Central Expressway at Arapaho in Richardson, 972/234-8688. *Call toll-free: 800-4KGMENS*

Men's Wearhouse, The   **214/369-1841**
8239 Preston Rd.   Mon-Fri 10-9; Sat 9:30-6; Sun Noon-6
Dallas, TX 75225   www.menswearhouse.com

By George, I think they've bought it. If it's not one chain, then it's another. Good old George is buying them up like we buy a case of Diet Coke. If there's a good price one day, we buy a couple of cases. So does George. Only he buys chains of men's stores and puts them under his tutelage. Men's Wearhouse is a well-run, well-stocked, power-buying men's chain with labels like **BOTANY 500**, **CHAPS** by **RALPH LAUREN**, **EVAN PICONE**, **GIVENCHY** and **PIERRE CARDIN**. They deliver the deals, period. Men, save 30-40 percent any way you cut it. They are a force to contend with...no matter how you grimace with "I guarantee it!" By George, it works. My only complaint, he put the first write-up anybody ever did about his store on his wall in Houston, Texas in 1973 when I wrote the *Underground Shopper* for Houston. And today, after all those TV touts about his store, only his partner will take my calls. George, I guarantee the next time I call, "You will talk to me!" because I'm going to say I'm a producer for The Tonight Show. Next year, I'll report on your response. *Call toll-free: 800/776-SUIT*

★★★ Repp Big & Tall   **817/784-8091**
4100 S. Cooper St.   Mon-Sat 10-9; Sun Noon-5
Arlington, TX 76015   www.reppltd.com

Here's a store that will suit you just fine, no matter what your suit size. Looking to size up that large loving man measuring 6'4" or taller or sporting a waistline of 36-58? Then look no further than Repp Big & Tall. If he's really a BMOC, be sure to give him a wardrobe befitting his stature in sizes to 8X or waists to size 70-72. The stores in the Dallas area are all their "Premier Stores" with brands such as: **NAUTI-**

CA, **POLO**, **RALPH LAUREN**, **TOMMY HILFIGER**, and their own Repp label in all the classic fashions and colors for men. Nothing discount about it but if you're a guy with an eye for fashion, you buy what you like. So be it. Designer shirts were standing tall around the store for $50 to $69.50. Been searching for more brands? Then find them represented in the Repp Big & Tall catalog including **CUTTER & BUCK**, **ENRO**, **GANT**, **HEARTLAND**, **IZOD**, **LEVI'S**, **NEW BALANCE**, **PALM BEACH**, Ralph Lauren, **SEBAGO**, **WORLD TRAVELLER**, and it doesn't take long to see that the list is huge. Just like the sizes and selection. Enro dress shirts were $34.50, **WORLD CLASS TRAVELER** cotton trousers were $52.50, Levi's 545 jeans were $49.50 and cotton pocket T-shirts were $14.50. Alterations are very reasonable, should you need a few minor adjustments. Their no-hassle return policy makes shopping easy. The other Metroplex locations are: 1025 N. Central Expressway, Plano, 972/423-4215; and 1725 N. Town East Blvd., Mesquite, 972/270-4476. 🦅

★★★★ S & K Famous Brand Menswear   972/874-1927

Grapevine Mills Mall
3000 Grapevine Mills Pkwy.
Grapevine, TX 76051

Mon-Sat 10-9:30; Sun 11-8:30
www.skmenswear.com

Your man will look like he stepped off the cover of GQ with the current designer fashions available at S&K. And you'll even feel rich enough to rub elbows with those in Fortune magazine knowing you saved 20-50 percent and more off everything in the store. If you're a fan of the Men's Warehouse, then you'll soon be cheering for S & K Famous Brand Menswear, too. Though in direct competition, one headquartered in Richmond, VA and the other in the Bay Area of San Francisco, they are quite similar in their offerings. Here you can join their Elite Rewards program that offers a point system for every dollar you spend annually. In exchange, you receive valuable discounts like a $100 savings voucher, gift certificates for up to $200, pre-sale notifications and their fit for life guarantee. If you should gain or lose weight you won't have to wait to fit back into those clothes. Just bring them into any S&K and they will alter them for FREE...for life. Lots of sportswear and over a thousand suits in stock from names like **BILL BLASS**, **BRASSBRO**, **CLAIBORNE**, **DANIEL HESTER**, **EVAN-PICONE**, **FENZIA**, **JOHNNY BENCH**, **JONES NEW YORK**, **NINO CERRITO**, **OLEG CASSINI**, **PIERRE CARDIN** et al. Looking to save even more? Apply for their S&K credit card and receive 90 days same as cash and 10 percent off your purchases. The savings just keep coming but the service stands strong. Measuring and catering to your every need. Making you a true VIP or S & K. Other locations in the area include Fort Worth Outlet Square Mall, 817/335-6305; Prime Outlets, Hillsboro, 254/582-0082 and Tanger Factory Outlet Center, I-20 in Terrell, 972/524-6034. *Call toll-free: 800/285-7848* 🦅

5

Apparel: Resale

★★★★★ ACO Upscale Resale Shop   972/727-4751
801 E. Main St.   Mon-Wed, Fri 10-6; Thu 10-8; Sat 10-5
Allen, TX 75002

ACO stands for the Allen Community Outreach, a **UNITED WAY AFFILIATE**. What lies behind their front door #1 are some of the best deals on top brands in the Metroplex. Besides, when you shop here, the proceeds benefit the programs of Allen's Community Outreach. How's that for doing double duty just by shopping once? By virtue of its proximity to Plano-Allen-McKinney, that far northern hub that is growing faster than your can drive on the George Bush Tollway, expect to sing their praises on designer clothing with names like **ANNE KLEIN**, **CACHE**, **CAROLE LITTLE**, **GAP**, **HILFIGER**, **IZOD**, **LITTLE TIMES**, **LIZ CLAIBORNE**, **OSHKOSH B'GOSH**, **PERRY ELLIS**, **POLO** and **TALBOTS**. Of course, most are gently worn, but hardly noticeable. Expect the price tags to reflect its use. Fashions (men's, ladies', infants' and childrenswear) hang out like clothes on a line, but these are definitely not washed up. Instead, they are pressed and cleaned and selling cheap. Okay, so I said the word. How else would you describe a men's suit for $18? Things for the baby, from strollers to car seats, playpens to porta-potties, keep your budget flush. Add toys, collectibles, housewares, small appliances, bridal wear and more to the mix, stir up an ounce of charity and load up the bags. Finally, being a "Bag Lady" has an entirely new meaning. When they have their famous bag sale, you load up as much as you can into a bag for only $15 total. Run, don't walk. If not, you'll come home empty-handed. Merchandise moves fast. Donations, of course, are also welcomed and always needed. So clean out those closets, the garage and the attic and donate to a worthy cause. Tax receipts are provided.

★★★★ Almost New   972/231-6333
2141 E. Arapaho Rd., #140   Tue-Sat 11-7
Richardson, TX 75081

Almost, virtually, nearly, practically, basically, just about new are the only words to describe these clothes as they make their way through the door. Only the freshest, hippest, trendiest (okay, there were a few traditionals who snuck in, I'll admit) find their way onto these racks. But if these ladies' sportswear and career fashions can make the cut, you can, too, in sizes 2-26. In due time, the racks are sporting maternity wear for those expecting the unexpected. Or if the little one has already sprouted, childrenswear from infants to size 14 can be found for both boys and girls. And should those little skirt huggers require additional care, bedding, toys and small infant furniture is also available.

★★★★ Backroom Raggs   972/227-4600
129 Historic Town Square   Tue-Sat 10-6
Lancaster, TX 75146

If you're interested in one of the 8 million stories in the big city, consider the one entitled, "From Raggs to Riches." Instead of Tuesdays with Morrie, try Thursdays at the Backroom. That's when they put the pedal to the medal and win all the awards. Garments fly off the racks, in names from department store stock to designer duds, no rugs, just rags with an additional one-third off their already low prices. Mix 'em up and spit 'em out, from consigned goods to right-of-the-line new accessories including the sought-after **BRIGHTON** belts, watches, bracelets and such. Shine on wardrobes from all the better lines from **DANA BUCHMAN** to **NEIMAN MARCUS** and many more. Lend an ear toward **LIZ CLAIBORNE** or **CAROLE LITTLE** from $10-$100 and fill in the gaps with great looking accessories. Inventory moves in and out fast so make hay while the sun shines Tuesday-Saturday. A total wardrobe can be had, so go girl! From the boardroom to the ballroom, the classroom to the dining room, strike a deal for your closet. Full size range available; sizes 2-28 are well represented.

★★★★★ Champagne Taste   972/233-9999
5211 Forest Lane, Suite 115   Tues-Sat 11-6
Dallas, TX 75244

Marcia Stone leaves no stone unturned when merchandising her consignment shop. If you have champange taste, regardless of whether it's **MOET** or any other sparkling imbibing allure, you can always enjoy her bubbly spirit and bargain-based attitude. Just don't overdo it unless, of course, you come with a designated driver. It can be intoxicating. The clothing mix is maximum: Designer and couturier castoffs, from business attire to ballgowns, casual to cocktail, plus everything else that it takes to make an entire fashion statement: jewelry, shoes, bags, hats, fragrances, furs...and some antiques and collectibles. A full size range, from sizes 4-44. Located at the northeast corner of Forest and Inwood, you can bag a bargain, or two, or three. Okay, so I bought a pair of wool pants, a strand of amber beads, a real **COACH** bag (at 30 percent off), a **PRADA** wallet, an **ARMANI** suit and a **BCBG** top—all for under $250. Now, put that in your pocket and sock-it-to-them!

★★★ Chapter Two   972/594-7722
1111 W. Airport Frwy., Suite 123   Mon-Wed, Fri 10-6; Thu 10-7; Sat 10-5
Irving, TX 75062

Sometimes you just don't get it at first. But by the time you're on Chapter Two, it all makes sense. Just because these fashions weren't housed in your closet first doesn't mean they're not perfectly acceptable now. Ah, it's crystal clear. Let somebody else do the breaking in, and then you break out in your new wardrobe that everybody thinks is new. Fool Mother Nature once in a while. It's fun. Evening wear, career wear, sports wear, casual wear, something to wear to the club, it's all part of closet reorganization. Whatever needs to be worn can be done without wearing a hole in your pocket. Consider, instead, buying a new wallet. Well, almost new, and at half the price. When you're pulling out that credit card, do you think anybody will scream, "Shame, shame on you?" Examine it all...as you never know what lies beyond Door #1. Accessories, shoes and jewelry proceed to add a finished look. Finished looking? Not yet! Skim through racks of **CAROLE LITTLE**, **ESCADA**, **EMANUEL**, **LIZ CLAIBORNE** and bring out the Texan in you with big deals on **BMW** and **DOUBLE RANCHWEAR**. Read between the lines, or tags, and find sizes 4-18 with an occasional plus size. Cash in on greater deals in the "back room" where everything is marked half price. Bring in your consignments, but be sure they are cleaned, in season, on hangers and be sure you bring a minimum of five items. This store is indeed a page turner. I wonder how it ends?

★★★★ Chic to Chic Designer Resale   972/713-7733
7529 Campbell Rd., #303   Mon-Sat 10-6
Dallas, TX 75248

From one chic to another, Chic to Chic is the place to go for women's designer resale. Step out in style. Kick up your heels. Make it a night on the town. And no one has to know it's not the outfit's first time around the block. Designer rethreads from sizes 0-16 may be well worn, or should we say, "Worn well"! No one will ever know it's not new, except you. Let's make it our little secret, just Chic to Chic. Take advantage of great discounts on eveningwear and dress it up with great shoes (sizes 5-10) and accessories. Putting it all together makes it a whole new look. So now who's wearing old duds? Returns not allowed. Be sure before you plunk down the cash. And remember, this is just between us, Chic to Chic.

Clothes Circuit, The   214/696-8634
6105 Sherry Lane   Mon-Fri 10-7; Thu 10-8; Sat 10-6; Sun Noon-6
Dallas, TX 75225   www.clothescircuit.com

Best Have a glass of sherry and decide there's nothing's quite as luxurious as wearing the castoffs of the rich and famous. Ask Tammy Faye, who used to be one of them. The first time she donned a **ST. JOHNS KNITS** from a resale shop, she was hooked. So, do as the rich-and-famous do—the ones who want to keep up appearances, that is. This is one "Decidedly Upscale Resale" and one of the best in Dallas. Just review some of these movers and shakers: **ARMANI**, **BCBG**, **CALVIN KLEIN**, **DKNY**, **DONNA KARAN**, **ESCADA**, **RALPH LAUREN**...and of course, **ST. JOHNS KNITS**—all priced to thrill while allowing you to dress to kill. Automatic price-downs make it imperative to shop often. Sizes, unfortunately, are limited to unheard of 2 to 14, but the upper limit is ever-growing and maternitywear units are making their appearance regularly now. Their accessories department is world renowned. Where else could you find the accoutrements to carry off the social circuit? Wait 'til you see the bags by **BOTTEGA**, **FENDI**, **GUCCI**, **JUDITH LEIBER** and **PRADA**; belts by **BRIGHTON**, **COACH**, DKNY and Judith Leiber. No "Red Apple" sales here, but their Yellow Banana Sale is legendary. They reduce their already 30-40 percent off items an additional 20 percent. Then twice a year, in late January and late July, they have their Back Room Sale, where prices are slashed to a pittance while last season's goods on the floor are marked another 50 percent off (prices as low as $5.) They also mark down items an additional 10 percent off during their Random Tuesdays sales, which are unannounced and decided....at random. So, meet you Tuesday Morning, eh?

★★★★★ Clothes Haven   817/861-2373
3100-C W. Arkansas Lane   Mon-Fri 10-6; Sat 10-5
Arlington, TX 76016

Sneak away to this Clothes Haven and no one will ever know you didn't buy it new. And who cares if they do? It's your money that's being saved, not theirs. And when you're saving on suits, sportswear, dresses and more, what more do you want? How about men's fashions for fractions of their original cost? Or ooh and aah over the special children's room carrying a variety of infant sizes to pre-teen for both boys and girls. Then bring on the whole family because they can all have their pick—shoes, belts, accessories and more. Savings are substantial, selection equally so, and service plentiful. But this secret didn't stay sacred for long. All of those living and working in North Arlington are already on to them.

★★★★ Dot's Closet   214/826-4099
5812 Live Oak St.   Mon-Fri 10-6; Sat 10-5
Dallas, TX 75214

Read between the dotted lines because shopping at Dot's Closet helps raise money for terminally ill patients. It's more like a bargain basement without the basement. The variety gives the amateur vertigo. Whirling around the racks and stacks include clothing, furniture, housewares, small appliances, collectibles, yard ornaments, jewelry, purses, belts, shoes and more. We're talking trash to treasures here. Clean out your closets and help support Dot's bottom line as well as yours. At Dot's, you've got to buy something. Lending a helping hand is a good way to start. Bring in your unwanted items for tax relief and it just might give some relief to a family in need.

★★★★★ Double Exposure   817/737-8038
6205 Sunset   Mon-Sat 10-5
Fort Worth, TX 76116

Do a double take here. Double your pleasure. Double your savings. Double the fun. But don't let double vision interfere with your seeing straight. The discounts are obvious and stare you down. Twice the selection of men's and women's clothing but don't overlook other great finds. Cozy furnishings for the house are the beginning to making your house a home. Mix in an eclectic collection of artwork, vases, books, candy dishes, mirrors and lamps. Unearth a treasure chest of jewelry, then go looking for the right shoes, purse, hat to coordinate with the new outfit. Now hear this. The selection of earrings is all ears. This place is doubly good when the savings double, triple, quadruple, get the picture? Just shutter to think of letting this camera get overexposed because once it's gone, it's gone. Better grab it before it disappears. Double Exposure is located just behind the Ridglea Presbyterian Church where helping friends and family of Fort Worth's Junior League make their way. Make their day by lending a hand; make your day by lending a hand. A good deed deserves another. You deserve that (tax) break today!

★★★★ Encore Resale Boutique   817/292-4927
5358 Wedgmont Circle N.   Mon-Sat 10-5
Fort Worth, TX 76133

Tony would be proud to award this shop in the savings category for best discounts in a featured resale shop. Encore offers reduced rates on gently-worn men's and women's fashions in a variety of sizes to fit even the most discriminating tastes. "Annie Get Your Gun" because the family's coming in from "Oklahoma" and we need to save on the "Rent." Let the "Cats" out of the bag and tell Joseph he can get "An Amazing Technicolor Dream Coat" here for less than he might pay elsewhere. "Miss Saigon" wouldn't miss a good deal and neither should you. Encore Resale Boutique offers a "Chorus Line" for consignments with a 50/50 split. It's a "Midsummer Nights Dream" come true.

★★★★★ Encore, Encore   972/317-3772
1301 W. F.M. 407, Suite 104   Tue-Wed, Fri-Sat 10:30-5; Thu 10:30-7
Lewisville, TX 75077

The audiences roar "Encore, Encore," for some things are better given a second look. Command big performances on the first Tuesday of each month, rightfully labeled "Hot Tuesday" where most of the store's inventory is reduced 50 percent and the remaining coats, evening wear, better leather and sterling silver is dropped 30 percent. Rise to your feet as **ANN TAYLOR**, **ARGENTI**, **CALVIN KLEIN**, **ESCADA**, **ESPRIT**, **GOTEX**, **LIZ CLAIBORNE** and **TOMMY HILFIGER** take center stage. Ticket prices originally started at $80-$110 but when it's an Encore performance, prices were SRO at just $5 and up. Pick any seat in the house from slacks and jeans to skirts, dresses, silk shorts and more for career, casual or evening wear. The orchestra plays on jewelry, accessories, designer handbags priced $20-$60 and even a few teen things, too. There's a new show every day and for those stars that make recurring appearances, mark-downs occur every five weeks with color tag discounts up to 50 percent. Street performances are available three times a year during their sidewalk sales in February, July and October. Take advantage of their command performances and shop early. With only two dressing rooms to act in, making room for a change is not a pretty picture. Write your own version with consignments accepted by appointment only. Lewisville Readers voted Encore, Encore Denton's best resale shop four years in a row. Located on F.M. 407, 1/2 mile west of I-35 E. Consignments accepted by appointment only.

★★★★ Fashions For Fractions Boutique   214/630-5611
5554 Harry Hines Blvd.   Mon-Sat 10-5:30
Dallas, TX 75235

Love 'em or leave 'em, either way, you can be a winner. Turn those fashions loose and let them hang out here where they will be grabbed up to serve another purpose. From your closet to God's ears, there is much to be salvaged at this Salvation Army thrift store. Taking on a new outlook in life, here's where you can get some of the best designer labels at such low prices, it is almost sacreligious. Without skirting the issue, this is where you'll find racks and racks of **CALVIN KLEIN**, **CHAUS**, **GLORIA VANDERBILT**, **GUESS?**, **JONES NEW YORK**, **LIZ CLAIBORNE**, **POLO** and **SCOTT MCCLINTOCK**. Break the mold with prices just fractions of their original retail. Spend your shopping time wisely by dividing yourself evenly between departments. Calculate the savings on clothing, sporting goods, housewares, exercise equipment, small appliances, wall decor and more. Bring your donations with you and if they can't fit through the door, such as a car, boat or motorcycle, just push three on their voice messaging system for complete details. Be sure to look for stores in Farmers Branch, Irving, Grand Prairie and two in Oak Cliff.

★★★★★ Fifth Avenue Rags   972/248-7337
17610 Midway Rd., Suite 132   Mon-Fri 11-6; Sat 11-5
Dallas, TX 75287

The best resale attraction in Dallas for almost two decades is still Fifth Avenue Rags. Suit up in great career wear from **CASABLANCA**, **DKNY**, **EPISODE**, **JONES NEW YORK**, **LIZ CLAIBORNE**, **MODA**, **RAMPAGE**, **SAVILLE** and **ST. JOHNS KNITS**. Paint the town red with a splash of eveningwear or cruise on by keeping afloat in the assorted deals in casual wear. Find it all from head to toe in sizes 2-20. After all, it's our ability to accessorize that separates us from the animals (well, some of us). Get the job done with jewelry, belts, bags, shoes, hats and more. Consignments are welcome at a ten-item minimum and all garments must be clean and on hangers.

Gavrel Furs   817/335-3877
2735 W. 7th St.   Mon-Sat 10-5
Fort Worth, TX 76107

Furiously we hit Fort Worth to see what's been hopping down the bunny trail. Lo and behold, Gravel Furs has hit pay dirt. What started as the storage and restyling of furs, both contemporary and vintage, has turned into a place to find gorgeous restyled furs plus fur and cloth coats that didn't sell at specialty stores. Or at least didn't sell out. So what you might see are racks and racks of cashmere or angora coats that retailed up to $1,500 for under $500. Now put that in your bonnet, or hat, or muff, and top off a winter's chill. Or, for lighter moments, wrap up in a boa. You can't go wrong with one from here. Across from the old Montgomery Ward's on 7th Street, a perfect wrap to an event down the street at the Will Rogers Coliseum.

★★★★★ Genesis II

5417 W. Lovers Lane
Dallas, TX 75209

214/351-6394
Mon-Fri 10-5:30; Sat 10-5

In the beginning, God created the heavens; and then later brought forth Genesis II. Proceeds from this charitable collection of fashion dynasties make for wonderful fodder at society luncheons. Wow, what a wonderful caché of designers—some new with the price tags still intact; others worn once, without a wrinkle in sight. A never-been-worn Neiman's embroidered jacket was a staggering $10 (retail $100), a **RALPH LAUREN** silk summer dress at $125 was a measly $10, and a **CAROLE LITTLE** red skirt for $50 was marked to only $8. The couturier line-up's star-studded: **CHANEL, GIANFRANCO FERRE, ISSEY MIYAKE, MOSHINO, ST. JOHNS KNITS** and others. More than 750 women have benefited through the services offered through Genesis Women's.

Genesis Thrift Store

2918 Oak Lawn
Dallas, TX 75219

214/520-6644
Mon-Fri 10-5; Sat 10-4:30

No doubt about it. These "Bargains of Eden" will have you coming and going. At the corner of Oak Lawn and Cedar Springs, this is the first of two upscale thrift stores that benefit the Genesis shelter. So whether you're bringing in a donation, or buying and donating those funds to the cause, you'll feel like a winner either way. Within their large 7,000-square-foot expanse, every item is organized and displayed in an appealing fashion, by size and by category. Clothing for men, women and children have relocated from some of the finest closets in town. Too, there's also a plethora of other items like toys, furniture, household goods whose proceeds all benefit the Genesis Shelter, a full-service care facility. Within this 14-room facility, they can accommodate women and their children into a six to eight-week rehabilitation program that includes help in finding housing, jobs and providing 24-hour counseling (especially in the area of self-esteem). Alcove, a Jewish Women's Council, offers this child-care assistance facility FREE giving women a real second chance at re-establishing a healthier lifestyle (one without the batterer). All women are screened prior to entering the program for drugs (they're the only shelter that does so). There are times when you cannot get help, but there is never a time when you cannot give it. Visit their second location for upscale resale at 5417 Lovers Lane. They, too, support the Genesis shelter and accept just about anything you might have that's not currently being put to good use. Everything's cleaned and polished making the need to rummage a thing of the past. Viva La Rumba instead!

★★★★★ Hope Chest Resale Shop

4209 McKinney Ave., Suite 200
Dallas, TX 75205

214/520-1087
Tue-Sat 10-5

You gotta have Hope. And when you're supporting the Hope Cottage folks, who can resist? Seasonal samples are donated along with decorative gift items that are sure to bring down the house. This one-stop haven for maternity, baby and children's resale items, men's and women's clothing, toys and household items not only generates money for mothers-to-be who are considering adoption, or families waiting to adopt, it sure comes in handy when the baby or child is ready to call John and Jane Doe, Mom and Dad. Worthy cause, agreed. But don't forget that you like a bargain now and then, too.

★★★★ Labels Designer Resale Boutique   972/713-8600

18101 Preston Rd., Suite A105   Mon-Fri 10-7; Sat 10-6; Sun Noon-5
Dallas, TX 75252

Pamper yourself with the service, service, and more service here. Yes, it's one of the finest resale boutiques in town. Yes, you'll be able to rub elbows with **ANNE KLEIN**, **ANN TAYLOR**, **CHANEL**, **DONNA KARAN**, **ESCADA**, **FENDI**, **GUCCI**, **JILL SANDERS**, **PRADA** and **ST.JOHNS KNITS**. Just don't get too comfortable. Unless you're dressed the part, you'll feel out-of-your-element. But don't you know the richest women in town are usually the least adorned. They don't need the outward trappings to ensure their net worth. Nevertheless, this place is definitely for the upper crust. Only the best will survive, as a shopper or as a consignee. Put your carefully cared for outfits up for consignment. You'll take in 50 percent of the selling price and if you have more than your fill, pick up is free. Size range is typical of resale, size 2-14 mostly. They work with The Family Place, a charity for abused women and your consigned items go a long way in helping to make a fresh start for someone in need. Find Labels Designer Resale Boutique on the northwest corner of Frankford and Preston, next to the Mediterraneo Restaurant.

★★★★ Larger Than Life—Rubenesque Resale   214/342-8550

10233 E. Northwest Hwy., Suite 435   Tues-Sat 10-6; Thu 10-8
Northlake Shopping Center
Dallas, TX 75238

Large and in charge. That ought to be the motto of this store. Bursting with stylish fashions for the big and beautiful women our there who want to look sleek and chic on the cheap. Shopping for plus sizes has always been slim pickin's, pardon the expression, in other resale shops, but not here. This shop comes fully equipped with wardrobes for the amply endowed. Both new and barely, starting at size 14 and up...whatever comes through the door. Snatch up good-looking garb at 1/3 to 1/2 off the original retail value. Get it all—from moving up the corporate ladder to eveningwear that will have you movin' and groovin' into the wee hours of those nights out on the town. Separates from great names like **BALI**, **BON WORTH**, **CHADWICK'S**, **ELIZABETH**, **JUST MY SIZE** and **LANE BRYANT** will size up a nice wardrobe at great savings. As I've said before, it's Larger Than Life 'cause bigger bargains are better. (Now say that three times!) Corner of Easton and Ferndale.

★★★★★ My Secret Closet   972/267-1144

17194 Preston   Mon-Thur 10-7; Fri-Sat 10-6; Sun 1-5
Dallas, TX 75252

The cat's out of the bag. Did you know some women will fill their closets with expensive clothes that are hardly, if ever, worn? Well, now you do. And when they need more room, they unload here. Welcome to My Secret Closet—that's only a secret for so long. There comes a time when you just can't keep it "in" any longer, blabbermouth. Here's the place to nab that nearly new garb from the rich (still) or the once rich. Maybe even the famous. When friends ask, there's no need to disclose where you bought the clothes. Keep it a secret, if you must. Merchandise is divided into three distinct groups for casual, career and couture occasions. Feel like a million bucks with service to match. I do know ladies who lunch and buy very expensive clothes and only wear them once or twice. That silk blouse, wool jacket or pair of fine shoes can look brand new for years—but here, it's a slam dunk deal. It's no secret that a ballgown goes to just one ball, or that the only way we can afford **CHANEL** is if we're owner No. 5. So, the secret's out. This neat, petite boutique with perky blonde personnel takes in consignments of the highest caliber and resells them for the lowest prices. New **VERSACE** jeans were originally $98, marked down 30 percent and then another 15 on top of that. Suits were going for about $95; blazers, $45; blouses, $10. Pick up everything you loved at **BANANA REPUBLIC**, **GAP** and **HAROLD'S** last year, here for a lot less. We found new fashions from **LUCIA LUKKEN** like broomstick skirts, velvet patchwork jackets and chenille sweaters selling a little above wholesale. Belts and handbags said **KATE SPADE** and **D & G**, but the tag stated "faux" so we said phooey. A never-worn market sample linen dress with ethnic embroidery was $24 so we grabbed it and forever held our peace. Can you keep a secret? We saw it in a famous catalog for $85 plus shipping. Seeing is believing, and I'm a believer now. Amen!

★★★ My Sister's Closet 214/826-6977
6434 E. Mockingbird Lane., Suite 105
Dallas, TX 75214

Tue-Sat 10-5

If you loved rummaging through your sister's closet in high school, think of how much more fun it will be now—28 years later. This store has held its own while others around them have gone in and out. Keep it in the family as we say, and cash in with a 50/50 split on your old (and not so old) clothes in sizes 4-20. No need to borrow at these prices. Consignments accepted and kept for two to three months. Bring in or take home **CAROLE LITTLE**, **CHANEL**, **LESLIE LUCKS** and **LIZ CLAIBORNE**—or is it Liz, for short. Open a diary of good deeds with jewelry, shoes, belts, bags, scarves, hats and just about anything that can accessorize that outfit and now you're dressed to the nines for maybe a five. Take a peek into this sister's closet but remember to look for colored tags that indicate special sale prices. If you're still talking to your sister, you might want to invite her to join you on your next shopping spree to this Sister's Closet. Remember, you used to share everything!

★★★★ My Sister's Room 903/597-8500
216 W. 9th
Tyler, TX 75701

Mon 10-4; Tue-Fri 10-5; Sat 10-4

Sisters rejoice. Make room for new attire and retire some of the old. My Sister's Room is open for business. Ladies, welcome in a whole new look from casual wear to After 5 in sizes ranging from Petite to Plus and fit for everyone in between. Girlfriends include **CAROLE LITTLE**, **DONNA KARAN**, **ELLEN TRACY**, **LANE BYRANT** and even **LIZ CLAIBORNE**—all have made a visit to My Sister's Room. Consignment are accepted but must first be cleaned, pressed and on hangers. Current styles and in-season clothing only with a consignment split of 50/50. Now open on Mondays. Anything less would be splitting heirs.

★★★ North's Plus Size Fashions 817/737-2174
5405 Birchman Ave.
Fort Worth, TX 76107

Tue-Fri 10-6; Sat 10-5

Tired of shopping on the one small rack in the back of the store at the typical consignment or resale shops? Worry worts, relax. Grow weary no more. Muster up your strength and head south to North's Plus Size Fashions. Sorry skinny minis, unless you're a size 16 and above, there's not much here for you except accessories. But for those who represent the woman of girth, the big and beautiful masses, there's a world of value. Rack after rack, you won't have to wrack your brain looking for an outfit that has some oomph. Fashionable wear for work and play run the full gamut. Try on tops and blazers, suits and slacks, dresses and skirts. Even sweaters for the winter and cover-ups for the summer are available for zaftig females. Heat things up with a large selection of active wear but should you need a little number for a night on the town, the numbers are pathetically few. Big girls don't cry except when they can't find a prom dress when they need it most. Other than that, North's Plus Size Fashions has everything a full-figured woman would want at a price they can afford.

★★★★ ReThreads   972/233-9323

411 Preston Valley Shopping Ctr   Mon-Wed, Fri 10-6:30; Thu 10-8; Sat 10-6; Sun 12-6
Dallas, TX 75205

This is the place for tired wardrobes, clothes with lots of tread still left and many miles to go. ReVitalize, ReJuvenate, ReTaliate against high prices. Trade in, trade up, trade your old way of thinking into a more contemporary mindset about wearing someone else's wardrobe. It's in. It's smart. Who cares? Whether you're buying or selling, this is one significant option to consider on the road to consignment men's and women's apparel, shoes and accessories. All here waiting to ReTire to your closets. Buy them by the closets full; sell them by the closets full. Both ways, you'll come out a winner.

★★★★★ Revente-Upscale Resale   214/823-2800

5400 E. Mockingbird Lane, Suite 113   Mon-Thu 11-7; Fri-Sat 10-6
Mockingbird Central Plaza
Dallas, TX 75206

Accepting consignments six days a week, it's almost impossible not to find something new that hasn't been abused. Across from the old Dr Pepper site and now part of the resurgence of Uptown, you will find one of the best-laid plans for women's wardrobes. Peek into the closets of Highland Park and see **BCBG**, **BETSY JOHNSON**, **CHANEL**, **DANA BUCHANAN**, **DONNA KARAN**, **ELLEN TRACY**, **EMANUEL**, **ESCADA**, **JIL SANDER**, **ST. JOHNS KNITS** and more. But don't shut your wallet until you've seen the **COACH**, **KATE SPADE** (the real ones) and **PRADA** handbags in perfectly pristine condition. Sizes 2-18 are waiting for their relocation papers. Consignors split 50/50 and there's a 60-day sale period, or else it's bye-bye. Also find accessories such as jewelry, shoes, scarves, hats, the whole shebang. Near Jason's Deli, why don't you order a roast beef sandwich with mustard and shopping spree combo on your next lunch hour?

★★★★★ Ritzy Raggs Ladies Resale   817/377-1199

6714 Camp Bowie   Tue-Sat 10-5
Town West Center
Fort Worth, TX 76116

Puttin on the Ritz, even if it was someone else's has never been easier, or more cost-effective. Consider this shop among Tarrant County's more prestigious addresses. After all, members of the TCU theatre guild can only be seen in a dress once per opening. And with six performances a year, that's a lot of new threads. Glitzy beaded ones, that is. Take advantage of these designer labels and prices designed for those who are price conscientious. Make an appearance in **ADOLPHO**, **AFTER FIVE**, **ALBERT NIPPON**, **ANNE KLEIN**, **ARMANI**, **BIZ**, **CHANEL**, **CRISSA**, **DIANE FREIS**, **ESCADA**, **HARI**, **KASPER**, **RALPH LAUREN**, **ST. JOHN'S KNITS**, **TERIJON** and **UNGARO**. But there's more than meets the eye since even the rich and famous get down and dirty (but not in theses clothes, of course.) Choose from dresses, sportswear, shoes, belts, purses, active wear, suits, casual ensembles and separates. Equally impressive is the selection of coats and wraps available in season. Become a seasoned shopper and shop for some Ritzy Raggs. Consignments are also accepted when pressed, cleaned and presented on hangers. Find them hanging out in the West Town Shopping Center.

★★★★ Robin Hood Designer Resale   214/360-9666
6609 Hillcrest Rd.   Mon-Fri 10-6; Sat 10-5
Dallas, TX 75205

Now you can't accuse them of stealing from the rich but rather consigning from the rich. But when it comes to giving to the poor, they're guilty as charged. Fair maidens can don designer suits, pants, jeans, T-shirts, dresses, blouses, blazers and the list goes on. Countrymen (and women) will sing praises to Robin Hood and his merry band of labels including **ANN TAYLOR**, **BANANA REPUBLIC**, **GAP/GAP EXPRESS**, **J. CREW**, **RALPH LAUREN**, **ST. JOHN'S KNITS** and **XOXO**. Hugs and kisses to the Mustangs. This shop is located directly across the street and for all those skinny, short-skirted coeds running around campus, there's plenty to choose from in sizes 2-8. Anything larger, and this Mustang runs out of gas.

★★★★ S & P Trading Co.   214/369-8977
6104 Luther Lane   Mon-Sat 10-6
Preston Center
Dallas, TX 75225

S & P is like the A & P, only for women hungry for designer clothing, resale and samples. If you're a size 2 (and in need of drink supplements) to size 16, here is a place for all things beautiful. Apparel and accessories will keep you coming and going to any event, from casual to corporate, cruise to the country club...at a fraction of what they cost new. This expanded closet houses more clothes in 1,200 square feet than any other store in Preston Center. That's a fact worth noting. Don't, therefore, bring in a truckload of clothing expecting them to take it all in. Consignments are accepted for 60 days with a 50/50 split,unless your item sells for more than $100, then you get 60 percent. You might remember that S & P could stand for being S-tylish and P-riced right. After all, if you want to "trade up," this is the way to go.

★★★★★ Second Glance   817/581-1909
6304 Rufe Snow Drive   Mon-Sat 9-5
Fort Worth, TX 76148

Look once, look twice, oh what the heck, look again because every time you find yourself looking, chances are, you'll find something to buy. And buying here is a two-fold experience, both positive. The diligent efforts of this shop help keep the programs supporting abused women running so be sure and give them a second chance...oops, glance. Go ahead. Make their day. Run around town doing your good deeds and secure good deals in the process. Wearing second-hand clothes is like giving a first-hand opportunity for a woman who has suffered from abuse. She and her children can buy what they need; proceeds of the shop benefit the entire program. You'll find plenty of resale clothing for all including new clothing for men, women and children. You can also find picture-perfect home furnishings, accessories, household items, bedding, appliances, collectibles and even a few antiques. Got a little extra time on Saturday? Then visit the corner of Watauga and Rufe Snow where there's an enormous rummage sale that catapults itself into a colossal savings event. Be sure to visit their other locations at 2400 W. Pioneer Pkwy. in Arlington, 817/277-8658, and 1629 Northwest Hwy., Grapevine, 817/416-2953. Remember that shopping for charity is more than just finding a bargain, it's giving something in return. These volunteers give of themselves daily to provide a safe haven for battered and abused women along with their children. How can you help? Well, don't come empty-handed. Donations and volunteers are always welcomed.

★★★ St. Michael's Exchange   214/521-3862
#5 Highland Park Village   Mon-Sat 9:30-5
Highland Village, TX 75205

Mom's and Dad's listen up. There's a way to keep those rug rats dressed and not have to take a second mortgage on the house (and in Highland Park, that is a significant savings, wouldn't you say?) Did you hear that? Discounts on previously broken-in (but still in great shape) children's clothing help the St. Michael's Episcopal Church while still being empathetic towards each family's budget. There's plenty for them to wear to church from suits to frilly dresses, but when you get home, you're not alone when you break out those jeans and sun dresses. Kids go through clothes so quickly that making a stop here can become an event. Clean out the kids' closets and drawers, bag it up and drop it off for a tax credit donation. Then pick out some new (at least to them) clothes and re-fill those empty drawers at home. Not only will you be getting a bargain, but you'll be teaching your children the value of charity. After all, charity does begin at home.

★★★ Tinka's   972/716-9944
142 Spring Creek Shopping Village   Mon-Sat 10-6
NW Corner Coit & Belt Line
Dallas, TX 75248

Were not sure where the name came from but the values speak for themselves. Tinka's consignment boutique offers an elegant shopping atmosphere for women of all ages in search of clothing for any occasion with lots of designer labels, After-5 and prom dresses, suits, skirts, blouses, pants and much more. Find new and used inventory, sizes 2-22 and all marked well below retail. Tinka's offers a laundry list of designer labels cleaned, pressed and ready to be dressed out and up with accessories including jewelry, shoes, handbags, hats, belts, scarves, sunglasses, did we leave anything out? Tinka, dinka, party, too.

★★★★★ Western Wear Exchange   817/738-4048
2809 Alta Mere   Mon-Sat 10-6
Fort Worth, TX 76116

Promenade your partner to and fro-m this resale shop for all good things you'll need to wear to a western event. You can't show up in chiffon and lace, you know, or you'll be skinned and tarred. This resale and consignment shop is the only one catering to westernwear. Gently-worn, please, not worn out. Pick through your collection and get rid of those you're not wearing. Somebody else will and save some money in the process. Jeans, shirts, boots, belts, buckles, vest and hats for the entire family start the ball rolling. Thank you, ma'am, you don't have to pay exorbitant prices on your everyday western wear or for that once-in-a-while, let's make like a Texan part, and do it up big. Big hair, fancy skin boots and a pair of leather jeans should do it!

6

Apparel: Vintage & Costume

★★★★ Ahab Bowen
2614 Boll St.
Dallas, TX 75204

214/720-1874
Mon-Sat Noon-6; Sun 1-5

Get in the groove at Ahab Bowen. Yeah baby, a little mojo goes a long way. Guys 'n Dolls can cover up in just about any vintage or classic style from the '40s, '50s and '60s all the way to the taste as diverse and distinctive as the '70s. Hey, just put it all together for your own eclectic ensemble. Even a little funk with some '78s can be found casually lining the shelves. The repertoire is tagged generally about $40 or less. Frankly, my dear, I don't give a—well, actually, we do care enough to buy the very best. But, we do believe that paying more and getting less is for the birds. And these cats make sure you do just the opposite. Ahab's isn't just blowing smoke screens around the fashion scene. He's breaking the molds and creating it. Break out at your next semi-formal occasion by donning a new Age of Aquarius, period. Authenticate the evening with hats, handbags, costume jewelry, scarves, ties, boots and zoots. Let's do the time warp again!

★★★★★ Hale's Costume
2902 Race
Fort Worth, TX 76111

817/838-7126
Tue-Fri 10-6; Sat 10-4; Mon By Appt.

Lions and Tigers and Bears, oh my, is this the greatest place for costumes or what? Even if you need a little gore or want a selection that is galore, you will find it here. This black and yellow addition to Fort Worth, off Hwy. 121 and Sylvania Avenue, is a stop worth making, especially if you're in the market for a non-traditional bridal ensemble. Owner/creator Beverly Hale and her daughter have the magic touch when finding the garment that responds to a particular theme —medieval, western or surreal. No matter what is in store for the party, look the part with everything from custom-made costumes to old favorites including Dracula, Grim Reaper, Cinderella, Dorothy and her entourage, Peter Pan and pirates. Throw your own Wild West party and get suited up here. Costumes for saloon girls, cowboys, Indians, bank robbers and even prisoner's black and white stripes complete with a ball and chain. (Know anybody that would look perfect in a size 60 Extra Large?) But don't feel tied down due to high prices because most costumes edge out the competition for $35-$55 a day. Children's costumes run less and rent for $25 (with lots for sale at $39.95). Discover the undercover world of Hale's Costume and wear what's on your mind.

★ ★ ★ ★ ★ Ragwear   214/827-4163
2000 Greenville   Mon-Sat 11-7; Sun Noon-7
Dallas, TX 75206

Got a date that needs some special something? Try setting a world's record in making a bee-line to Ragwear. Jazz it up. Snazz it up. Steppin' out with your baby does require an outfit that turns heads. Imagine not saying for once, "I've got nothing to wear!" Like a good wine, these clothes get better with time. Wind up with a few outfits that reflect the good ole days gone by. If it's authentic and 20 years or older, you'll find it hanging out with other older garments. Older is better. And better yet, find good old-fashioned prices, most items under $40. If they're trendy enough to make the cut, you might even find new fads that are all the rage. Ragwear is wearing out the competition and feeding the fashion frenzy next to Lula B's restaurant and located across from the Arcadia Theater.

★ ★ ★ ★ ★ Rose Costumes   940/566-1917
521 N. Elm St.   Mon-Sat 10-5:30
Denton, TX 76201   www.dentononline.com/rosecostume

A rose by any other name just wouldn't smell the same. Plant yourself here, it's going to be a while. Tons and tons of styles from basic costumes to duds you might not want to dig up. Avant-garde to vintage to just plain funky. Pick an era, any era. But make no mistake about it, Rose Costumes is the place to get fitted from head to toe. Did you know you can complete just about any costume with socks, shoes, hosiery, jewelry, wigs, capes, purses, ties, suspenders, parasols, wands, canes and props for propping up what ever poops out of ya? It might just be your wallet with costume rentals starting at $45 and up. But what a great way to remember the day with a 1970s sherbet-tinted tux or zoot suit from the 1920s. Get in the game with knights in shining armor, fair maidens, scoundrels and gypsies. Maybe Elvis is really not dead. He was last seen hanging out with Captain Hook and Cher. Was that Minnie Pearl or Minnie Mouse? Sherlock Holmes has requested the assistance of the Keystone Cops while he apprehends Zorro, Darth Vader, Godzilla and Santa Claus. Clown around with royalty. Let the fireman put out the flames from those old-time bathing suits. Just what you needed...a bag lady and belly dancer! Go calypso with other costumes including Rhett Butler, Wizard of Oz, Pinocchio, Flintstones, poodle skirts, cheerleaders, Easter bunnies, pilgrims, gamblers, can-can dancers, a beer can, witch doctor, devil, rabbit, chicken, cow, wolf, pink elephant and much more. Make new friends and keep the old...one is sacred and the other old. Stroll down Memory Lane with MM and Joe DiMaggio, a Dallas Cowboy cheerleader and Troy Aikman, Lucy and Ricky Ricardo, John and Lorena Bobbit (yep, you read that one right!) Father Mulcahey and Hot Lips Hoolihan. Just look for the palm tree awning out front and flamingo mural. Hey, there's nothing too bizarre for Rose's Costumes.

Apparel: Women's

7th Avenue Plus Size Outlet
214/638-9033

1331 Inwood Rd.   Mon-Wed 10-6; Thu- Fri 10-7; Sat 10-6; Sun Noon-5
Dallas, TX 75247

Best **100** SHOPPING DESTINATIONS

No need to mark up an outfit just because it's a plus size. No siree. Shop where the stars shop for designer fashions (accessories and hats, too) where styles are chic and prices are cheap. Pardon the expression, but this is the largest plus size outlet in the Metroplex, in the State, probably the Southwest, maybe the world. Over 11,000 square feet of the best for less. One whopping step for womankind, no ifs, ands or butts. At last, get covered in a fashion-forward wardrobe without robbing Peter to pay Paul. From embellished suits to career suits, from tailored suits to sequined suits, from sportswear to eveningwear, being big is a BIG plus here!

★★ A & A Fashions
972/241-8588

11363 Denton Drive
Dallas, TX 75229
Mon-Sat 10-6

Giddyup gals if you're ready to hit the trail. This outlet gets an "A" in selection, and "A" in prices but they flunked English. (Fortunately, they can make change from a $50 bill.) Nothing un-Americanabout that, now is there? So, look and ye shall see a round-up of women's sportswear including lots of denim at wholesale prices. Hours are flexible, just ask them. ***Call toll-free: 800/590-6888***

★★★★★ Amazing Fashion Outlet
214/688-0466

1505 Wycliff Ave.
Dallas, TX 75207
Mon-Fri 10-8; Sat 10-6

Just when you think this town's got enough retailers, another amazing one opens their doors. Name brand women's apparel and shoes at "amazing prices" means just that. Sizes 4-16 in fully-lined career suits that retail as much as $230 for $29-$78; shoes and boots, $10 (regularly $40-$90); dresses with values as high as $139 for under $40 and thousands of bottoms, pants, shorts, skirts, $8. Now, how much more amazing can you get? On Wycliff, behind the Wilson World Hotel at the corner of Stemmons and Wycliff. Another one of Byrd Jessup's collection of apparel outlets that are springing up everywhere.

★★★ Avenue, The

3701 W. Northwest Hwy.
Dallas, TX 75220

214/358-5642
Mon-Sat 10-8

Bigger sizes usually means bigger prices at this store formerly know as Plus Sizes, Plus Savings. As we say, bigger is better as long as the discounts tag along. Why not strut down The Avenue in their private label clothing and boast of being just one of the smart shoppers who are dedicated to saving money? Hello…good buys for the fuller-figured woman. Take a walk down The Avenue in your new sportswear, dresses, coats and separates in sizes 16-32. Now we're talkin'! Get pampered by informed personnel that help put it all together, at the best possible price. The only thing small about this store is…well, there's nothing small about any of their stores. Visit their other Avenues in Red Bird Mall, 3265 W. Camp Wisdom and across from Vista Ridge Mall on I-35 in Lewisville.

★★★★★ Bierner & Son Hat Factory Outlet

3120 Commonwealth
Dallas, TX 75247

214/634-1286
Mon-Thu 8:30-4; Fri 8:30-Noon

Bluebonnets may be the state flower but picking any color bonnet from the field of dreamy hats is a different story. Pick out your bonnet from the factory and you'll automatically score a home run. Up the outside steps to Bierner & Son's Factory Outlet and see a sea of designer and department store hats with discounted prices on every lid. See how they grow 'em in Texas and why you'll be proud to tip your hat that's half off from the biggest hat factory in the state, if not the country. Brims are everywhere. There are over 300 hats to try on, just for size. Felt to feathers, buttons and bows, derbies and straws, organza, fedoras, caps, boaters, sunhats and panamas. If the season calls for it, it's hat's off here at half off. Go to the head of the class and show off some class by saving big bucks on hats to compliment any outfit. See why all the men turn their heads when you walk in any parade, down the aisle, through the crowd, or around the table.

★★★★ Bon Worth

4321 I-35 N., Suite 245
Gainesville, TX 76240

940/668-0777
Mon-Sat 10-8; Sun 11-6
www.bonworth.com

Comfortable, wrinkle free, carefree clothing at factory direct prices is what's in store—the **BON WORTH** store, that is. This nationally-known manufacturer and retailer has over 100 stores throughout the country. Closest to the Metroplex is their Prime Outlets of Gainesville location catering to misses and petite sizes in SM-XL and 6-20. Find lots of comfy separates to relax with at across-the-board 40 percent off savings . Their specialty is embroidered-decorated apparel so don't ever think, "Plain Jane." Lots of appliqués and other embellishments appear generously on everything, from denim to knit sweaters. Find big deals on their clearance racks offering an additional 20, 30, 40 even 50 percent off. Don't expect to eat bon bon's but you will find some mouth-watering deals at their outlet, off I-35 and Exit 501.

★★★★★ C'est la Vie!

2267 Vantage St
Dallas, TX 75207

214/631-4446
Mon-Fri 8:30-5

C'est la Vie to high prices and high tail it to one of the contractors who make clothing for the Coldwater Creek catalog. Oh me. C'est la vie! Living the good life at half the price, however slim the pickings, is the way to the promised land. Racks and racks of samples and overruns in sportswear, pant sets, jackets, separates and fun dresses available in sizes 4-14 and SM-XL. You can say fare 'thee' well to this outlet if you're a plus size but their catalog and online clearance store have plenty (www.coldwater-creek.com). They've said C'est la Vie to their old location and now have set up shop on what is becoming a serious invasion of specialty stores' high prices on Vantage Street. So, what are you waiting for?

★★★★★ Career Outlet 214/637-7702
1331 Inwood Road
Dallas, TX 75247

Tues-Sat 10-6

Plus Sizes, Amazing Dresses, and now the Career Outlet join the line-up of power outlets with a similar bent, though different in their intent. Save 50-75 percent off on suits and dresses in sizes 4-16. That's right. Fully-lined suits at up to 75 percent off can help you not only climb the corporate ladder, but lett you do so without going broke. That's a nice perk, when you think of it. After all, as you move up in the company, make more money, it means you've got to always dress the part. But, if you have to pay more for your career wardrobe, it'll eat up all your salary increases, and that's not a good thing. Be smart. Shop smart. Enroll in Dressing 101 and get your outfits here.

★★★★★ Clothes-Out 817/731-0086
3710 W. Vickery
Fort Worth, TX 76107

Thu-Fri 10-6; Sat 10-5

Just about a decade later, Clothes-Out is still closing the deal on great values. The *Fort Worth Star-Telegram* called it one of the top 15 places to shop in the Metroplex. Not too shabby. And neither are the styles with designer dresses, suits, separates, sportswear, sweaters, denims and more arriving weekly. This fashion broker broke the mold on retail prices. Reject those imitation outlets and find lots of designer closeouts to choose from in sizes 2-26. Then let them dazzle you with more great prices on purses, vests, belts, accessories, silver jewelry, costume jewelry and the like. You'll like shopping here or their Arlington location at 4201 W. Green Oaks Blvd. Suite 400, 817/483-7418. Thousands of other fashion-conscious shoppers make it a regular stop each weekend.

Designer Group, The 972/335-9176
6991 Main
Frisco, TX 75034

Tue-Sat 10-5; Thu 10-6

North Dallas socialites know where to shop for just the right fashions, for just about any occasion. Meander through 4,000 square feet of designer clothing and accessories, gifts, antique accessories, collectibles and decor for home and garden. Whatever the occasion, The Designer Group can outfit you and your home. Apparel selections range from casual to dressy-country. Mix and match with lots of separates in cottons, linens and blends for comfort and easy care. Have fun trying on **BARBARA LESSOR, FAITH & SURYA, FRESH PRODUCE, IRIS SINGER** and **SOFTWEAR** for your next outing. Raise the standards with accessories, gifts, shoes and assorted special buys. And those great buys change often but at least the savings will never go out of style. The Designer Group is now where the action is. (Suppose they had a crystal ball?) Frisco is the emerging real estate 'boom town' for retailers and The Designer Group was already there. Just north of Plano, drivr past Hwy. 121 and when you hit Main Street, take it all the way to the end. Find the cream and green building on the corner of Fifth and Main and you've hit the designer lode.

★★★★★ Discount Dresses

214/634-3366

Inwood Trade Center
1304 Inwood Rd.
Dallas, TX 75247

Mon-Fri 10-6; Sat 10-7
www.discountdressesonline.com

Hallelujah, Baby! Time to do up the town, don your dancing shoes and shimmy on down, downtown. Or uptown, if you prefer. Shop at Discount Dresses—if you're looking to dress up with something special at a store just for swingers. They have one of the largest selections of special occasion dresses and suits in town, this town or most any other. Dressy suits from $39.99 to formal dresses as low as $59. Just think of the five-course meal you can now indulge in, as well as be dressed for the occasion. Church suits, embellished suits, cocktail suits, plus coordinated jewelry and top it off with one helleva hat. Now you're cookin'. What a looker you are—besides, you're saving up to 75 percent on dresses and suits in sizes 6-26. OK, they also have casual dresses, too, for $15 and up, but who's looking to dress down when the time is ripe to kick up your heels and let loose? Shop also at 4118 W. Camp Wisdom Rd., between Westmoreland and Cockrell Hill. Layaway available.

★★ Dress Barn

972/437-0967

1361 W. Campbell Rd.
Richardson, TX 75080

Mon-Fri 10-8; Sat 10-7; Sun 1-5
www.dressbarn.com

Leave these barn doors open for business and steer us in the right direction. Don't be chicken; pecking through these racks of both name brand and private-labeled apparel is half the fun. Rake in savings of 20-50 percent on sizes 4-24. A stable selection of career and casual wear along with a few trendy styles from **ARIUM** (a **KASPER** knock-off), **ISAAC HAZEN**, **LEE DAVIS**, **SIGNA** and **WESTPORT** (their private label) can make for a very interesting blend in your wardrobe. Separating us from the animals is our ability to accessorize. So go for it. A selection of necklaces, earrings, pantyhose, belts, socks and occasional gift items will keep you humanizing. It's no bull—charge it on a new Dress Barn account and save an additional 10 percent on your first purchase. Stop stall-ing and race over to one of the Metroplex's 16 locations. This Dress Barn is also a Dress Barn Women offering plus sizes and is located in the Pavilion One Center.

★★★ Escada Co.

972/355-8186

3000 Grapevine Mills Pkwy.
Grapevine Mills Mall
Grapevine, TX 76051

Mon-Sat 10-9:30; Sun 11-8
www.escada.com

One of the most sought-after designer labels has found themselves outlet bound. You will, too, once you know that there's an Escada Outlet at Grapevine Mills. Others will say, so what! Made for a tall and lean model figure, if that describes you, then their suits, dresses and separates will suit you to a T. Head to their website for a visual treat; from fashions, accessories, jewelry to fragrances, it oozes romance, intrigue and allure. For a sampling of last season's styles, their outlet will beckon, your budget will smile. Talk about "sticker shock!" Let's hope they have a defibrillator handy. These items cost thousands at the retail level; expect outlet prices to be less but if you perspire, you'll be dripping wet. Let's hope you don't sweat! Even at half price, its only redeeming factor is that it reeks snob appeal. Okay, it's beautiful clothing, agreed. But c'mon, why blow a down-payment on it?

★★★ Inlook Outlet, The
1431 Regal Row
Dallas, TX 75247

214/630-5320
Mon-Sat 9:30-5

Drop anchor in this Inlook Outlet. This may not be the Titanic in size but savings are a true 50 percent and more. Hit the deck and get decked out in moderate missy dresses and sportswear from size 2 to 24 from the Jerell Company (now a part of **HAGGAR**). Wave bon voyage to high prices on denim, khaki, handkerchief broomstick skirts, vests, dresses, pantsuits and accessories. Sail on in for sale prices on first-quality samples and irregulars. A dinghy of a selection is located at their corporate offices. Visiting their yacht-sized inventory is more enjoyable at either 6245 Rufe Snow, Watauga, 817/428-0115, or in Waxahachie at the corner of Highways 77 and 287.

★★★★ L'eggs-Hanes-Bali-Playtex
Grapevine Mills
Grapevine, TX 76051

972/724-4910
Mon-Sat 10-9:30; Sun 11-8
www.hanes.com

Love it, or leave it empty-handed, but then you'll be going out with naked underthings. That's the way it goes. If you want the latest in popular brands, get a **L'EGGS** up on the competition and shop this outlet store. They cover those legs for less, whether you're a guy, a gal, or a kid. Sock-it-to them in both first quality and irregular men's, women's and children's socks and pantyhose, including those with fuller figures. Save 20-50 percent each time you put your foot into one of these. But then, you've got to keep abreast of the top things, and lingerie and bras are not ignored, either. Get moving. Your underthings are not to be ignored otherwise you'll fall flat on saving money on all those unmentionables. Even if you can save $1 or two off Wal-Mart's prices, isn't that what life's all about? **HANES** and **HANES HER WAY** are part of the **SARA LEE CORPORATION** family of brands. They just happen to be the largest brand of apparel in the world, in case you didn't know, and they're headquartered at 1000 East Hanes Mill Road, Winston-Salem, NC 27105.

Lilly Dodson Designer Outlet
The Corners Shopping Center
Central and Walnut Hills Lane
Dallas, TX 75231

214/696-1381
Mon-Sat 10-6

Well, if I'm lying, I'm dying. Look what I found—Lilly Dodson's got an outlet store. *Lilly Dodson's got an outlet store.* Alas, we're talking right out of the pages of *Vogue* magazine. We're talking about designers who are so snooty, they wouldn't be caught anywhere near a department store. We're talking couturiers with names like **ANNA SUI**, **CAROLINA HERRERA**, **CHRISTIAN LACROIX**, **DINA BAR-EL**, **FENDI**, **GIVENCHY**, **HERGE LEGER/PARIS**, **ICEBERG**, **LAFAYETTE/NEW YORK 148**, **MUGLER**, **LEONARD**, **MICHAEL KORS**, **MUGLER**, **PEGGY JENNINGS**, **RENA LANGE**, **RICHARD TYLER**, **TAPP/NEW YORK**, **SONIA RYKIEL**, **TOM AND LINDA PLATT**, **VIVIENNE TAM**, **VOTRE NOM/PARIS**, **ZANELLA**, **ZANG TOI**—didn't I say, couturier from A to Z? Well, one visit and you'll be hooked. Can we talk? Not everybody's welcome. Smaller sizes from 2-14 have their wardrobes down pat. Though I have my eye on several (racks), I'm hoping one day to be their best customer. For the lunch bunch, the country club set, the After 5 gals, those who want to look chic without paying the full fare will fall hook, line and choker for Lilly Dodson's Designer Outlet. To accompany the outfits, they also showcase companion jewelry and handbags. You didn't expect something tacky to join these stars, now did you? Tari and her crew is in charge of providing bend-over- backwards service, so why not say you've been there, done that? Your wallet will be forever grateful. They're across from Kozlow's Furs and next to Red, Hot and Blue, how appropriate. Delicious deals at ever corner.

★★ Pursley Discount Fashions   972/298-3384
208 N. Main   Mon-Wed, Fri-Sat 9:30-6:30; Thu 9:30-8
Duncanville, TX 75116

Not necessarily a source for Purses, but this Pursley is a name that is recognizable to anyone from the 50s who remembers it well. Almost 50 years young and still going strong, this mature and seasoned veteran of the bargain business is still a mainstay on Main Street. First quality and some irregulars (well marked) line the walls and racks of this Duncanville legend. With prices on dresses as low as $5 and up to $125, imagine averaging $60 on some of Dallas' favorites like **ANN TOBIAS, JENNIFER JEFFRIES, LESLIE LUCKS, MELISSA** and others that make it from the Apparel Mart to here at a savings. Locations in Lancaster, West and Hubbard, small towns, big savings is their business plan to date.

★★★★★ Rhodes Collection   214/342-9400
1621 S. Jupiter, Suite #102   Wed-Sat 10-5:30
Garland, TX 75042

Travel the Rhodes less traveled and you'll wind up saving money. That's correct. If you don't believe me, then shop at this manufacturer's outlet and see first hand, first-quality garments at wholesale prices. Eliminating the middleman equals saving money, it's just that simple. This local manufacturer provides "climbing-the-ladder" fashions to the corporate career gal. When you buy direct, you'll be saving at least 50 to 80 percent because the overhead and all of the other retail amenities are a forgone conclusion. Save even more during their periodic warehouse sales and fulfill your dreams as well as your closets in sizes 2-34. For suits, try on petites, misses, talls or plus sizes and never hold a pink slip. The styles won't set any fashion trends, but they're basic and deliver a much-needed corporate wardrobe from the executive to the secretarial pool. Located across from E-Systems, exit LBJ and Jupiter.

★ Sheryl's Basement   214/630-9499
9011 John W. Carpenter Frwy.   Mon-Sat 10-7; Sun Noon-6
Dallas, TX 75247

The bottom line descends to the basement of this chain of stores. That's where the action is, make no mistake about it. This veteran retailer, like the Diva, returns in many different reincarnations but what worked once, generally works again, regardless of the name. If you're a working stiff, working 9-5, you'll find Sheryl's Basement offers relief from the high price spreads. Sizes 4-24 have the opportunity to dress up in work clothes or play clothes, whichever the occasion, in misses, juniors, petites and plus sizes. The inventory changes like the wind, blowing hot and cold. Some days they're swell; other days, they're not. Check directory for additional locations.

Special Occasion Dresses   972/732-8900
19009 Preston Rd.   Mon-Thu 10-8; Fri-Sat 10-6
Dallas, TX 75252   www.specialoccasiondress.net

Got a special occasion? Any of the following count: Wedding, Anniversary, Mother's Day, Birthday, Graduation, Prom...get the picture? Don't show up in your same ole, same ole. Pull out all the stops. Add glamour. Put on the glitz and still save up to 70 percent. Check it out. Pick it out from more than 30,000 dresses in stock per store. Among their three locations and their one outlet store at 1314 Inwood Road, 214/638-2900, they can outfit you in style within your budgetary limits. In fact, their outlet store makes the "Guinness Book" of most-number of sequins in any one store in the world. Count them. Millions of them, sewn meticuluously onto many of the dresses——strapless, oneshoulder, backless, low-cut, high-neck, every designer name and style is here. Where else in the Metroplex could you get decked out in a $300-$400 designer gown for $49.99-$99.99? Think about it. There's isn't a competitor out there. Then, just when you think they couldn't possibly go any lower, you check out the "back room." Seeing is believing. Yes, there are dresses there for $19.99. Special Occasion Dresses gives new meaning to "chic is cheap." There's no better time to hit the night life and save on dinner dresses, evening dresses, semi-formal wedding dresses, dresses for that black-tie soirée, even the non-occasion where you get dressed up for the fun of it. Why wait for the Prince? Prince Lewis already offers the fullest (pardon the expression) selection to fit any size, any occasion, any shape and style. Deck out in beaded tops to long flowing gowns. Dresses for under $100, no problem. Mothers of the Bride, forget looking elsewhere. Special Occasion Dresses has the largest selection of "After Five" in the Metroplex. And if you want that extra "lift" to that barely there dress, they have those special "inserts" to keep them up when everything else has failed. (No more explaining. Just look at the jewelry cases and see what lies above.) Add in all the frou-frou jewelry, satin and beaded handbags, shoes dyed to match and have an *Affair to Remember*. More Special Occasions in Arlington in Lincoln Square, 817/226-0100, and in Dallas at the southwest corner of Walnut Hill and Central Expressway, 214/691-1300 as well as Atlanta, Charlotte, Houston and Kansas City. Denver, Nashville and San Marcos, TX coming soon. Then, nationwide, according to the rumors.

★★★ Suzanne's   214/638-8429
1335 Inwood   Mon-Wed, Fri-Sat 10-6; Thu 10-7; Sun Noon-5
Inwood Trade Center
Dallas, TX 75247

Familiarity breeds savings and this ole-time name brings out the best. Some days, the labels are impressive—**ANNE KLEIN** and **DONNA KARAN**, for example. Other days, the labels were unfamiliar but still impressed us. Whatever day you hit Inwood Trade Center, you might find yourself captivated by the hundreds of moderately-priced to higher-priced garments that will get you to the church and back on time and in style. Suit up at $75 and start your day off on the right foot (Shoe Fair's across the street). Also, slip into some casual sportswear and separates. If price is a consideration, you can take these to the bank!

Talbot's Outlet   972/315-5900
500 E. Round Grove Rd., Suite 101   Mon-Fri 10-9; Sat 10-6; Sun Noon-5
The Shops at Vista Ridge   www.talbots.com
Lewisville, TX 75067

If you're a fan, start the cheering now because here's the outlet for one of a mall's favorites. Save 50 percent and more on Talbot's last season's unsold inventory. But last year's sure looks like this year and if you want that au natural look in natural fibers, there's none better. Keeping a low profile and darkened windows allows them to sell their outlet merchandise without slapping the full price stores in the face. Tailored and well-made slacks, the kind you'd see Kate Hepburn wear, man-tailored shirts, shirt-waist dresses, suits and appropriate shoes make for a well-rounded "preppy" kind of look. Think **ANN TAYLOR**. Think **RALPH LAUREN**. Think **HAROLD'S**. But shop Talbot's. Then, when they have a clearance sale, run, baby, run. Most things were 75 percent off; and then, they took another 30 percent off at the counter. A wool crepe jacket was under $20 bucks; saw it in their catalog for $178. Then, we slipped out wearing a pair of black ballet flats that retailed for $64, for $12. They also have baby apparel in matching fabric and looks. A full size range is one of their claims to fame and every dame, from infants to size 24W should find them very appealing. Other stores in Houston and San Marcos.

Terry Costa   972/385-6100
12817 Preston Rd., Suite 136   Mon-Thu 10-8; Fri-Sat 10-7; Sun Noon-6
Dallas, TX 75225   www.terrycosta.com

Terry's the berries when it comes to celebrating that special occasion, be it a prom, a wedding, a Black Tie affair or a debutante's debut. Terry Costa not only has a sense of style and the merchandising hand of a maven in women's retailing, she also has the savoir-faire to develop a Teen Board consisting of 75 young women from over 40 area schools and universities. The group focuses on poise, self-confidence and self-esteem, and it's open to all girls ages 13-21. The group produces two fashion shows annually and maintains an inventory that may even be the largest selection of designs, prices and sizes in the southwest. If they don't have the gown you want, they can most likely get it for you. Then accessorize, accessorize, accessorize! They carry **ALFRED ANGELO**, **EDEN**, **GALENA**, **MAGGIE SOTTERO**, **MON CHERI**, **MORI LEE** and more bridal gowns. They also carry exclusively a line from Spain called **PRONOVIAS**. Then to finish the ensembles, there's lots of rhinestone jewelry, handbags, tiaras and faux pearls for all those gearls! A sea of straplessness, sequins and satin luxury in sizes 2-18 means you can be dressed to the nines and still feel like you've gotten your money's worth.

Tiny Thru Plus Size Outlet   817/265-3737
705 Secretary Drive   Tue-Sat 10-5; After 5 By Appt. Only
Arlington, TX 76015

Whatever they call themselves, Dress Outlet, Traveling with Jane, or Tiny Thru Plus Sizes, as long as you call upon them for your fashion wardrobe, that's all that counts. And believe me, it's where you shop that counts when you're looking for variety, selection, service and price. This outlet represents over 500 different manufacturers that are sold in department and some specialty stores. In fact, they may even be the largest sample buyer in the southwest. If you're looking for garments in all the wrong places, turn around and head to Arlington. You'll probably not want to ever shop anywhere else. Thousands of outfits and so little time. Head 1.5 miles north of I-20 off Matlock, and turn left at the Texaco. Dresses, suits and pantsuits in sizes 2-34, plus petites to choose and who are you kidding? You prefer to pay retail??? Average expenditure, $29-$69 instead of three or four times the price. Be sure, though, to verify they're open before you head out the door. They hit the road (Jane's Traveling Dress Show) in a semi and travel to small towns for sales on regular weekends, so please call ahead. Out-of-towners in Waco, Athens, Belton, Nacogdoches and Marshall get in on the act, too). Listen to the Diva and watch newspapers for their twice annual sales, the second-third weeks of January (2002 sale is closed Jan. 14-18; sale Jan. 19-26) and July (closed July 3-9; sale July 10-21) where everything is marked down to practically nothing. This is la cremé de la cremé of women's outlet stores in the Metroplex.

★★★★★ Wycliff Dress Factory Outlet   214/634-8444
1305 Wycliff   Mon-Fri 10-5:30; Sat 10-5
Wycliff at Monitor
Dallas, TX 75247

Though they may answer their phones, "Immediate Resource" (that's their wholesale operation), you can still shop at this dress factory outlet. If you've got a taste for the good life and plan on partying, you can choose from hundreds and hundreds of dresses, suits and separates with savings up to 75 percent off. Samples, overruns, and irregulars in sizes 2-14 at down and dirty prices is why Wycliff Dresses has a stronghold on women's purses in the Metroplex. No, no, they don't sell purses, just clothes for a paltry pittance.

Appliances

★★★★★ **Allen's Wholesale Appliance Outlet**   **972/727-4798**
103 N. Austin Drive   Mon-Fri 8-5:30; Sat 8:30-3
Allen, TX 75013

Appliances, unlike jewelry, do not have the margin of markup potential. That's why you don't see half off prices, unless used. The big box stores buy in such volume, they can afford to manipulate the prices downward. But this is where it gets interesting. Ver-r-r-y interesting. How does a little mom 'n pop shop beat the pants off of them? Well, head to Allen and see for yourself. What you see is 15-30 percent off brand new, name brand appliances—wholesale prices. At Allen's Wholesale Appliance Outlet, it doesn't get much better than this. Next door is their retail operation, Rodenbaugh's Appliances, but when they want to move an item, it relocates to their outlet from their showroom display for a quick sale. If it's a refrigerator that came in scratched, or a washer that has a knob missing, or the color of the stove just struck out, whatever, it's moved to their outlet, it's just that simple. But, that's where it gets good. When they make that move, the price descends. Now we're cookin'! If you are looking for a name brand appliance such as an **AMANA**, **JENN-AIR** or **WHIRLPOOL** in any of the sought-after home appliances such as cook-tops, ovens, refrigerators, dishwashers, washers and microwaves, then you're headed in the right direction. Shop both stores, outlet and retail, as even at retail, their prices are often hard to beat. Either location, full warranties are provided on all their products.

★★★★ **Arrow Appliance**   **817/860-4263**
2902 W. Pioneer Pkwy.   Mon-Fri 9-5:30; Sat 10-4
Arlington, TX 76013

Even a used arrow does the trick. So, when making an "Overture," make sure you "Tell" them the Diva sent you—especially if you want to hit a bulls-eye. Arrow is one place to strike while the iron is hot. Often they have products that no one else does. In fact, when we were searching for a 30-inch built-in stove-top and microwave, we found it here for $399 while elsewhere, it was priced at $1,100. Now we're talkin'! All appliances come with a one-year warranty; rest assured, if it's used and reconditioned, you will get a lot of mileage out of one hit. Even if you don't know owner Chuck Friberger, let me introduce you. He's been buying and selling used appliances (washers, dryers and refrigerators) for years and he only carries the best brands like: **GE**, **KENMORE**, **MAYTAG**, **WHIRLPOOL** and more. Washers started as low as

$99 and refrigerators $159. Whether you need appliances for your second home or your first, consider used where you can come clean, for less.

◆◆◆◆◆ Broward Factory Service   817/640-1772
1225-F Corporate Drive E.   Mon-Fri 8-5
Arlington, TX 76006

Though Broward County covers Ft. Lauderdale, Florida, you can participate in their warranty program living in the Metroplex. An important element when buying a home that has been lived in, is to insist it comes with a home warranty. Sellers should throw it in because don't you know, the minute you move in, the heating coil breaks, the **JACUZZI** goes kaput, and the dishwasher leaks. Protect yourself for $199 a year. That gets you insurance to protect you from both an appliance breakdown and nervous breakdowns on appliances, central air conditioning, refrigerators, heating (gas or electric), wall thermostats, ovens/ranges, water heaters, freon recovery, dishwashers and disposals. When you think about it, you'll rest easy and life will continue to hum smoothly at least for a year.

Factory Builder Stores   817/410-8868
512 E. Dallas Rd.   Mon-Fri 8-5; Sat 9-Noon
Grapevine, TX 76051

 A decade in business does count for something. Originally, Factory Builder Stores began selling to builders and remodelers, but you, too, can participate since the price is right. If it's an appliance, here is a source for them all. Though they specialize in **KITCHENAID** stainless appliances, you can also find an impressive lineup: **ASKA, BOSCH, DCS, DYNASTY, JENN-AIR, MAYTAG, SCOTSMAN, SUB-ZERO, THERMADOR, WHIRLPOOL, U-LINE, VIKING** and more. They just moved into their new location in Grapevine, but their warehouse/showroom is just a hint of bigger better bargains to come. They've spread their wings through the state and make Texas really cool with all their haute cuisine. Other locations in Houston, Dallas, San Antonio, Austin and Bryan.

Ferguson Bath & Kitchen Gallery   817/261-2561
2220 Duluth Drive   Mon-Fri 8-5
Arlington, TX 76013   www.ferginc.com

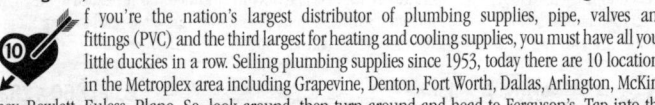 f you're the nation's largest distributor of plumbing supplies, pipe, valves and fittings (PVC) and the third largest for heating and cooling supplies, you must have all your little duckies in a row. Selling plumbing supplies since 1953, today there are 10 locations in the Metroplex area including Grapevine, Denton, Fort Worth, Dallas, Arlington, McKinney, Rowlett, Euless, Plano. So, look around, then turn around and head to Ferguson's. Tap into the faucets and fixtures for the bar, bidet, kitchen, lavatory, roman tub, tub and shower. Sinks with pedestals, wall mounts, bar, kitchens, new toilets, shower pans, tubs or tub and shower units, whirlpools and shower doors, are all displayed artfully in their showroom. Any of these names ring a bell? **ALSONS CORPORATION, AMEREC PRODUCTS, BALDWIN BRASS, DELTA FAUCET CO., DUPONT CORIAN SURFACES, ELKAY MANUFACTURING CO,,GROHE AMERICA, INC., JACUZZI WHIRLPOOL BATH, JADO, KALLISTA, INC., KITCHENAID, KOHLER CO., KWC FAUCETS, MOEN INCORPORATED, NUTONE, ONDINE, PRICE PFISTER, PHYLRICH INTERNATIONAL, ROBERN, ROCAILLE, SEA GULL LIGHTING PRODUCTS, INC., STEAMIST CO., INC., ST. THOMAS, WHIRLPOOL**—well, don't settle for less. Now why don't you "Skip to my loo!"

★★★★ Oliver Dyer's Appliance   817/244-1874

8201 Hwy. 80 West   Mon-Fri 9-6:30; Sat 9-6
Fort Worth, TX 76116

If you're in the market for a Dryer, think Dyer. Then again, you may be already washed up and the only thing that will cool things down is a refrigerator? Then again, it might be a room air-conditioner? But now you're cookin'. Onward to the stoves, ovens or cook-tops that are required to transform that deal into a meal. In that case, Oliver Dyer is the place to go—especially if you're patient enough to wait until their final days when prices are slashed up to 50 percent. Whether it's seasonal products, or models that have been used for display or demo, or got scratched or dented, it's all in the plan for saving you money. Every brand is represented, five-year guarantees are issued, plus a small charge for delivery and installation, if needed. The line-up includes **CARRIER**, **JENN-AIR**, **KITCHENAID**, **MAYTAG** and others you can trust. All makes and models of appliances are sold and serviced and used appliances come with a one-year limited warranty. The parts division closes at 5:30 while the store remains open until 6:30.

★★★★★ Robert Kent Television & Appliance/Repairs   817/923-1973

4944 James Ave.   Mon-Fri 8:30-6:30; Sat 9-6
Fort Worth, TX 76115

From appliances to electronics, these folks are a mainstay in the Fort Worth metro area. No relation to Clark Kent, they are, nevertheless, the supermen of appliances and electronics. Expect to be electrified by the selection of TVs and VCRs, washers, dryers, refrigerators, stoves, microwaves, dishwashers—they sell them, service them, warranty them, and know about them. Now, all they need is you— to buy them! They'll even service them whether you buy it from them or not. Since 1953, Robert Kent has been turning hot and cold and on and off all the major players: **CARRIER**, **GE**, **KITCHENAID**, **MAYTAG**, **RCA**, **WHIRLPOOL** and **ZENITH** alongside bedding and furniture to complete the home scene.

★★★★★ Sears Appliance Outlet   972/428-8445

1927 E. Belt Line @ Josey   Mon-Thur 10-6; Fri 10-8; Sat 10-6; Sun Noon-6
Carrollton, TX 75006

Living the good life...at a great price is as close to my own trademark, "Living the Good Life at Half the Price," as they can get. But rather than fight it, just think, I thunk it first. Nevertheless, there are some commonalities and a definite synergism between us. And if truth be known, they do have some of the best prices in the Metroplex on washers—as low as $371.99, dryers, $239.99, side-by-side refrigerators, $699.99, top mount refrigerators, $399.99 and electric ranges, $399.99. Keep this posted when you're ready to take the plunge. They not only carry their own private label brand **KENMORE** but also **AMANA**, **FRIGIDAIRE**, **GENERAL ELECTRIC**, **MAYTAG** and **WHIRLPOOL**. Isn't that a good beginning to living the good life for less? And you'll see for yourself, they are indeed the best source for Kenmore appliances and other brand names plus big screen TVs. That's right. Even big screens. Big screens, big screens, we all scream for big screens. And there are not many stores that can save you 15 to 50 percent as well as similar savings on other home appliances. It's nothing to ignore, even if you have to watch the commercials. Shop often as the merchandise moves in and out as stealthily as an agile quarterback during a football game. Weekend warriors, arm yourself. Weekends are whoppers. Bumper to elbows is typical when they've marked anything down 50 percent off the original price. Visit also in Grand Prairie at 2985 S. Hwy. 360, 972/988-3036. But keep in mind that the Sears Outlet in GP sells only furniture.

Texas Appliance & Builders Supply
3401 W. Pioneer Pkwy.
Arlington, TX 76013

817/469-6644
Mon-Fri 8-6; Sat 9-6

This Tarrant County landmark has been home to the most famous back room since Loehmann's. Bypass the impressive front showroom, go through the back doors to the warehouse where there are literally hundreds and hundreds of scratched or dented appliances just waiting on final adoption papers. Prices are cut to the core just because there's a nick in the door. Can't even see it, yet prices are slashed. All the top brands are represented including stainless steel commercial models such as **SUB-ZERO** with a scratch in the back. Now, who's going to notice? Lots of odds 'n' ends, one-of-a-kinds, freight-damaged, display units and close-outs from major manufacturers are there at substantial discounts. All they need is your love and commitment. Say "I'll take it" and make arrangements for delivery. That's all it takes. All manufacturer's warranties are included. You'd be hard pressed to find anyone who sells refrigerators, washers, dryers, freezers, microwaves, cooktops, dishwashers and ovens—for any less. Call for prices before shopping anywhere else. They service any brand they sell, and maintain a substantial parts inventory at all times. Shop where the contractors and builders have been shopping for years. And if you need a little help from your friends, ask for their 90-day, interest-free financing. You'll be spoiled once you've been there. Look for the white, two-story building in southwest Arlington, just one mile west of Bowen.

★★★★★ Thompson's Appliances
2408 S. Cooper
Arlington, TX 76015

817/277-1131
Mon-Fri 8-7; Sat 9-7

Apply every ounce of good sense and see if this doesn't sound yummy. Appliances at retail prices can eat your lunch. So if you've got a healthy appetite, head to Arlington where Thompson's Appliances can ease the temptation. All the brand names fit to print with the prices suitable for buying. Have it your way with **BOSCH, KITCHENAID, SHARP, SUB-ZERO, THERMADOR** and **WOLFE**, it's just the beginning. Then mix in such ingredients as **AMANA, FRANKE, JENN-AIRE, MAGIC CHEF, MARVEL, MAYTAG, WHIRLPOOL** and you've got the beginning to a wonderful repast. If you are flush and want to buy the whole kit and kaboodle kitchen package, you'll be allowed to do some wheeling and dealing, They expect it. So, have at it! Builders do it all the time. The minute you walk through their doors until the appliances are in your home, you can expect service every inch of the way. Expect, too, a three-year warranty on everything they sell. Why? Because they also service them. We wound up buying a front-loading Maytag washer and dryer because we learned it uses half the water, is much gentler on your clothes, and has a delayed timer so you tell it what time to go, washer, go. Then, if you're building your home from scratch or just remodeling your kitchen, you'll want to call upon their designers for advice (at builder's pricing, of course). They will orchestrate the job from start to finish that includes such custom features as hoods, built-in refrigerators and freezers, wine cellars, under-counter ice makers, blenders or coffee makers, hot water dispensers, commercial sinks, ice machines, beer taps, commercial-style ranges, cooktops/hoods, built-in ironing centers, toasters and can openers. Rumor has it that one famous doctor had a **DIET COKE** dispenser installed, but it's just a rumor. (Not a bad idea the more I think about it.) Just south of Arkansas Lane and west of Cooper. The parts department is open Mon-Fri 8-6; Sat 9-6 while the sales department is open Mon-Sat 9-7.

★★ Vac-Mobile, The   972/247-5838
12895 Josey Lane, Suite 122   Mon-Fri 9-6; Sat 9-5
Farmers Branch Shopping Center
Farmers Branch, TX 75234

There was the Smutzmobile (my old jalopy), then the **OLDSMOBILE**, and now the Vac-Mobile. Two were cars, and one is a seller of vacuum cleaners. Which one is it? Almost as old as my books, these folks (not the original owners, but who can stay in such dirty work for long?) have been selling vacuums cheap and making vacuums run and hum. H-m-m, it doesn't take much to make my carpets and floors happy. They know what they're doing and make a clean sweep of it. Buy used commercial vacs at lower than new residential models and see how much more dirt you can accumulate in your neighborhood. All the best brands are available for sale as well as some of those you covet but can't afford like **ELECTROLUX**, **KIRBY** and **RAINBOW**. All elaborate, heavy-duty and expensive and frankly, hard to operate. Some of the newer Hoovers, in my opinion, are hard to beat; and their prices are, too. Suck up to Kirk, the owner, and he'll pass on a terrific deal on a **DIRT DEVIL**, **EUREKA**, **HOOVER**, **PANASONIC**, **RAINBOW**, **SANYO** or **SHARP**. Pick up a used model for as low as $39. Trade-ins are welcome because they can fix them up like new. Whether it's new or used, this small neighborhood shop often snags great deals and passes them along to their customers. Tucked away at the southwest corner of Valley View and Josey in the Farmers Branch Shopping Center.

Walt's Appliance   972/263-3751
2336 E. Main   Mon-Fri 9-6; Sat 9-4
Grand Prairie, TX 75050

Walt's and Rick McDonal are synonymous with appliances beyond their territorial roost in Grand Prairie. Folks from hundreds and hundreds of miles schlep to this unremarkable site of 35,000 square feet of brand name appliances, both new and used. With 40 years of experience, what do they have going that others do not? Well, low, low prices is one. About 10 percent off on new appliances and more on closeouts and last-one-on-the-floor model deals. Well, so be it. Not bad. But it's their acres of rebuilts that have built their reputation. The choices include **AMANA**, **FRIGIDAIRE**, **HOT POINT** and **MAGIC CHEF**...all in working order and all can be delivered to your kitchen practically overnight. So, if you need to replace your appliances, think Walt's, especially for second homes, student apartments, and those who want to save plenty of money on an appliance that looks good, works good, and is good. Walt's also maintains a service business for repairing home appliances and a parts department.

Arts, Crafts, Kits

★★ American Needlewoman
2944 SE Loop 820
Fort Worth, TX 76133

817/551-1221
Mon-Sat 10-4

How many needlecraft project kits have you bought this year from Wal-Mart? One, a few, hundreds? Well, have I got a deal for you. I hate to needle you with my money-saving wisdom, but this manufacturer has been supplying Wal-Mart with craft supplies for years. Now, say goodbuys to dear ole Uncle Sam (Walton) and introduce yourself to this outlet store. They've been around and needling folks since 1976 with their catalog. Now, they've opened a 2,500-square-foot outlet attached to their warehouse fulfillment center and offer whatever they sell in their 72-page, full-color catalog. The only difference...the price. If an item has been discontinued, the price is half off their already low prices. If you're a senior citizen, take another 10 percent off. Choose from a variety of projects to work your fingers to the bone...craft kits, supplies, yarns, books are ready to make your day. Then for cross-stitchers, try your hand via a kit that's ready to sew and go, European needlepoint tapestries, latch-hook kits, even wood paintings and supplies. Don't wait until the last minute to start those crafty projects. If you snooze, you'll lose out on some of their best deals. Get with the program by signing up for their quarterly catalog mailings. Or, the more adventurous head there in person. Where Loop 820 meets I-20, go west to the Wichita exit (if you get to the Campus exit, you've gone too far), go under the freeway to the first right after the Fina station (across the street from the TCJC campus) to the second row of warehouses. If you get lost, like I did twice, they're very patient with directions.

★★★ Beadworks
7632 Campbell Rd., Suite 309
Dallas, TX 75248

972/931-1899
Mon-Sat 10-6; Thu 10-7; Sun Noon-5
www.beadworks-dallas.com

Get her in a choker hold and string her along until she's green with envy. How? Take a jewelry class at Beadworks. If you want to establish yourself as the next Ying Yang, learn the ropes. Every kind of bead imaginable is waiting for you to pick up. You don't even need a line. They're willing to go along, next to others of a like kind. crystal, glass, wooden, bone, seed, pearls, quartz, it's up to you and your artistic inclination. You don't need a crystal ball to project your next avocation. You might even find yourself next displaying your works in a craft mall, in a retail store, on the internet. Who knows, you may even get a choke-hold on the competition. Learn to make the latest jewelry designs, from a lariat necklace to a flat peyote. Maybe tansform old lampshades with a few glass beads added to the trim or fringe. Let Linda Hoffman guide you every step of the way. Located on the southwest corner of Campbell and Coit.

★★★★ Binders Discount Art Center   214/739-2281

11661 Preston Rd.   Mon-Fri 10-7; Sat 10-6; Sun Noon-6
Dallas, TX 75230   www.bindersart.com

Paint this new location as the spot for starving artists. Creativity starts with supplies and there's no getting around it unless you paint with your toes or sculpt with your mouth. Shop at this Atlanta-based catalog art store which just happens to have a brick and mortar store in Dallas. Now located in a bigger better space, how fitting that they offered grand opening specials of 50 percent off **NIELSEN** readymade frames and 40 percent off all paints, brushes and canvas. Too bad you missed it. But they are the best place to buy professional art supplies in the city. For paint like **NEWTON** and **WINSOR**, brushes, canvas, paper, poster board, mats, **X-ACTOS**, ready-made frames and presentation binders, Binders sells them for 30 percent less. They also handle custom framing, whether it's a museum-mount or not.

★★★★★ Coomers Craft Mall   972/554-1882

900 W. Airport Freeway   Mon-Sat 10-7; Sun Noon-5
Irving, TX 75062   www.coomers.com

Often imitated, but never duplicated, Coomers is the originator of the crafts mall craze. They are the largest (30 malls and growing) retailer of unique gifts, handmade crafts and home decor but while they're at it, they are providing an outlet for America's crafters and artisans who had nowhere to go...nowhere to show. Thousands of talented hands are putting their creativity to work, turning hobbies into full-time businesses. Doctors, lawyers, teachers have turned their after-hour activities into full-time works of art and are finally putting their heart where their art is. Hop aboard their online site to learn why you, too, could be their next major display artist. Shopping any of the Metroplex malls is like shopping in hundreds of artsy-crafty people's hobby rooms or garages. Imagination at every turn. If you're a do-it-yourselfer, they carry a complete line of **AILENE** craft supplies. Work your way across the Metroplex to view how the crafty creators are working their fingers to the bone. Additional Coomers Malls are in Carrollton, Plano, Arlington, Fort Worth and Richland Hills. Online, they even reveal how you, too, can open a craft mall, tour their stores, sign up for a crafter's newsletter and more. ***Call toll-free: 888/362-7238***

★★★★ Garden Ridge   972/681-5006

2727 Towne Center Drive   Mon-Sat 9-9; Sun 9-7
Mesquite, TX 75150   www.gardenridge.com

This ridge is so big, you get dizzy looking down the aisles. But, if you're looking for home decor objects, surely you can find something here. Sometimes the prices are good enough to bring home to Mother. See, Mom, look, Mom, buy, Mom. There are more mothers here than at a Mother's Day march, doing wheelies around the corners, kids in tow, baskets screeching, but never ceasing to amaze me. Love their ficus trees, their baskets, their file crates, their waste baskets. Why spend a fortune getting organized at The Container Store? You can get twice as much for your money here and still be able to put things in their place. Add artwork and picnic totes, porcelain bowls and bean bags, ornaments and ordinary wrapping paper, and if at the holidays you can't get your shopping done within a normal 12-hour period, they'll keep the doors open 24-hours, just for you. Whether it's a marathon shopping experience you're after, or just need a lot of "stuff" at good prices, put a dent in Garden Ridge and save your collision insurance for another day.

★★★★★ **Hobby Lobby**   **972/772-5021**
2004 S. Goliad   Mon-Sat 9-8
Rockwall, TX 75087   www.hobbylobby.com

No, this is not some politically-savvy representative in Washington lobbying for your artistic rights. In fact, it's not even close. But if you have a hobby, chances are this company has all the tools to win your vote. This is one way you can control costs—do-it-yourself. Significant savings on everything you've ever thought of making in the arts and crafts venue. Supplies of every kind to satiate your creative urges. Splurge on all the little doodads and whatevers that will result in a one-of-a-kind home decor element or perfect gift for mankind. A beautiful masterpiece can be arranged with silk or dried flowers, a tree can be planted in Brooklyn or your own backyard with nary a drop of water. Put them in a vase, a basket, a pot, a myriad of containers; they're all waiting to be dropped into your basket and whipped into shape. Into needlepoint? Got just the project for you. Can't wait to crochet? Dying to decoupage? Frankly, is it a faux finish or not? They're always cheaper than elsewhere and when their sales are on, expect shopping with savings up to 90 percent. Load up with picture frames and furniture, wallow in wicker baskets and paint the town any color you want with their aisles of paints. You will not be "underwhelmed!" And if you sign up for their own credit card (**VISA**), you can expect an additional three percent off all your purchases at Hobby Lobby and one percent on any other purchase. Remember, every little bit helps. Check directory or their website for multiple locations.

★★★★★ **Marshall Moody**   **214/631-5444**
2910 N. Stemmons   Mon-Fri 8:30-5; Sat 8:30-Noon
Dallas, TX 75247   www.marshallmoody.com

Say Happy Birthday to Marshal Moody, Inc. They're celebrating 75 years in business so they've finally hit their stride. What started as an art supply company in Fort Worth, Texas selling brushes, paints and sign painting supplies evolved into a mega display source for local department stores. Today, they are one of the biggest suppliers of quality display materials, and lucky for us, visible from Stemmons Freeway. You can see their handicrafts all decked out in store windows from Dillards to Macy's, Bloomingdales to Sak's Fifth Avenue. So, why not yours, too? They also offer custom designs for decorators, interior designers, and florists. If you're looking for seasonal decor, think beyond Christmas because what about Valentines Day, Easter, Mother's Day, Father's Day, Independence Day, Back-to-School, Mardi Gras, St. Patrick's Day and Halloween, too? Santa would be disappointed if you thought only of his day and not of all the other times you want to decorate. Then, what about those "theme" parties from luaus, casino nights, western days, Mardi Gras, the rockin' '50s or the rollin' '20s? From Hollywood to retail display helpers like mannequins and clothes racks, you can see that if the occasion calls for decorations, MM is the place that'll do it up right. Online, you can secure a 10 percent discount, ask for their catalog, and see what's in store. From topiary forms to display turntables, artificial foods to spray paint, photographic supplies to giant flowers, ooh, la la. Let's have a party tonight! Exit Inwood, on the service road of Stemmons. *Call toll-free: 800/627-0123*

Metro Home Warehouse   **214/426-4663**
2234 Cockrell Ave.   Thu-Sat 9-6
Dallas, TX 75215

First, you've got to find the place. Secondly, you've got to find the place. And third-ly, *when* you find the place, you'll then walk up a marble-like stairway, enter a break room, and ultimately see a work table where you can lay out stuff to frame. Now, we're getting closer to the meat and potatoes of Metro Home Warehouse. Once you've walked through another door, you'll heave a Hi, Ho, Silver. You've made it. You're not the weakest link. You have survived. Now we're cookin'. Samples of art, frames, end tables ($10-15), posters, frames of every description are waiting to assuage your hang-ups. Ready-made frames from desktop to wall size, decorative frames, gold leaf frames, faux finished frames, wood frames...like I said, "There is nothing like a frame!" Like I've told you before, they're the largest manufacturer of frames in this part of the country, and I mean it. But there's still more. There's another room with accents and antiques, moldings for a mantle, or moldings for an imaginative headboard, lamps and...well, you never know what lies behind those doors. Since they're a manufacturer, there's always something leftover, or some-thing new they're testing before rolling out to retail stores. Decorators will have a field day. Ever hear of kokopelli? It's Southwestern/Indian-type furniture that you see all over Arizona and New Mexico. It's inter-estingly carved black furniture and mirrors, predominately, and priced for a lot less wampum than retail. Like I've said, once you've found it, never let it go. The prices will remain imbedded in your brain even if the location doesn't. Maybe nows the time to install that tracking device. Terrible location, limited hours but the area surrounding them supports several art warehouses close to Deep Ellum and is worth getting acquainted with.

★★★★ **Michaels**   **972/691-1355**
2705 Grapevine Mills Circle   Mon-Sat 9-9; Sun 10-6
Grapevine, TX 76051   www.michaels.com

You can't fool with Mother Nature or Michaels. Both are here to stay. This Dallas-based mega-empire is the country's largest craft purveyor. We're talking billions of dollars of nifty little craft projects being worked on, somewhere on some kitchen table, in some town across America. Here in the Metroplex, at most corners, in most counties, if you want to engage in an arts and crafts project, the world is your oyster. Without stringing you along, the list of possibilities is endless. Even the artful dodger could-n't evade the projects here: floral arrangements, silk and dry flowers, decorative decor, wall hangings, wearable art, party supplies, framing materials, painting, gluing, decoupaging, sculpting, beading, draw-ing, there aren't enough hours in the day to support the over 36,000 items waiting for you to explore. You know Michaels. Just open your wallets wide and let your creative spirits soar. If you're artistically-challenged, take a class. There are plenty of them side-by-side with demonstrations, kids' activities and enough tools to make Bob Vila a convert. Lots of brushes to paint the town any color of the rainbow, frame-it-yourself or let them do it for you (their legendary FREE framing is a great come-on). Get into making scrapbooks or other kinds of books, then throw a party with all the trappings—streamers, strings, rib-bons, candles, face paint and lastly, bake a cake. Check directory for multiple locations. ***Call toll-free: 800/MICHAELS***

★★★★ MJDesigns　　　　　　214/696-5491

810 Preston Forest Shopping Center　　　Mon-Sat 10-9; Sun Noon-6
Forest at Preston　　　　　　　　　　　　　www.mjdesigns.com
Dallas, TX 75230

The Creativity Store is credited with giving birth to the craft store phenomenon and Michael Dupey, its leader. But that has all changed now and new ownership brings about a whole new era of egalitarian opportunities. Leaner. Meaner. Though the name remains the same, ten area locations (two up from last year), with the newest in Frisco, means things are on a slow and deliberate climb. A great place for home decor, silk and dried flowers, wicker items, vases, rockers, cushions, frames and more. Then, turn the corner to their party supplies and wrap yourself up in balloons, cards, art supplies, ribbons, wrapping paper, needlework, T-shirts (and paint to apply). One of the best sources for balloon bouquets and bigger, better bargain bows. What about recording your life story in a memory book that'll last for generations? Maybe crafting a piece of bisque pottery? Learn the art of crafting it yourself by way of their many "how-to" classes. Save money and give the gift of yourself that will be treasured forever. Check directory or their website for all three locations.

★★★ Old Craft Store, The　　　　972/242-9111

1110 W. Main St.　　　　　　　　　　　Mon-Sat 10-5; Thu 10-7
Carrollton, TX 75006　　　　　　　　　www.flash.net/~oldstore

For the dedicated Queen Bee, this is the hive to flock to. After nearly 30 years in business, their philosophy remains the same: offer the latest items at the best prices while educating customers with all the current trends and timely traditions in the art of quilting. They have a knowledgeable staff, a quarterly newsletter filled with new patterns and swatches and a calendar of classes and tips. Expect down-home, old-world service and a warm, "Y'all Come In" welcome. That alone is sweet enough to tweak anyone's interest, but the "Discount Quilting Club" will really have you buzzing. Join for $25 a year and receive discounts of 20 percent off the prices of all fabric and notions, plus 25 percent off patterns, magazines, books and most classes. During your birthday week, enjoy savings of 30 percent, honey. *Call toll-free: 800/576-4251*

★★★★★ Rock Barrell, The　　　　972/231-4809

13650 TI Blvd., Suite 104　　　Mon-Tue, Thu-Fri 9-6; Wed 9-8; Sat 9-5
Dallas, TX 75243　　　　　　　　　　　www.rockbarrell.com

Since 1972, the first year the Rock Barrell opened its doors, it has been on solid ground. Rock around the clock in this 4,000-square-foot, one-of-a-kind store whose premise is to "Sharon the Stone" (semiprecious, of course). Cabachons, glass beads, African tribal beads and more are available to string along. They can offer incredibly low prices because they are direct importers of much of their merchandise. Secondly, they buy closeouts all over the world and you know what that means. Why not stretch your imagination without having to stretch your budget? Dig in to their stretch bracelets made from 4mm bicone glass crystals with your choice of a large assortment of colors. They can either be used as bracelets or the beads can be used for other jewelry applications. Ever hear of stone cross beads? These beads are drilled top to bottom and are great additions for either bracelets or necklaces. They can also be used as individual beads. Use a head pin and attach them to an ear wire or for drops on a necklace. You won't have to scrape the bottom of the rock barrell, either. Choose Silver Leaf, Fancy Agate, Yellow Jasper, Poppy Jasper, Picture Jasper, Unakite, Blackstone, Lapis Howlite, Howlite, Leopardskin Jasper, Flourite, Green Moss Agate, Red Jasper, Red Adventurine, Turquesite. Impressive, eh? Looking for precut, polished, or raw stones or cabochons? Don't look under a rock. These are all in plain view. Agate, Aventurin, Carnelian, Goldstones, Hemitite, Malachite, Mother of Pearl, Onyx, Paua, Quartz, Rhodonite, Snowflake, Sodalite,

Tiger Eye and Unakite are available in sizes 5 by 3 mm up to 38 mm. Hey, what's wrong with owning a big piece of the rock? Then, if you want to learn the art of the rock, they have all the supplies to tempt you.

★★★★★ Squadron Mail Order

972/242-8663

1114 Crowley Drive
Carrollton, TX 75011

Mail Order Catalog Sales Only
www.squadron.com

For over 30 years, Squadron Mail Order has been the oldest and considered the most reliable mail order firm in the United States specializing in military models, books and modeling supplies. They scour the world to find just the best of modeling supplies, maintaining an inventory of over $2 million within their 50,000-square-foot warehouse in Carrollton. If you order it from their catalog, orders are shipped with 24 hours - really. While they cannot accommodate shoppers, you can order from their catalog or by phone or fax. Their 88-page 2001 catalog is known around the world. Once you're on board, you'll be kept up-to-date with 12 monthly reports that keep customers in high gear with new products and the latest bargain offerings. Listen to this: the catalog lists over ten thousand modeling items. It only costs $5 per year, which includes the 12 monthly supplements that contain 3,000-plus new and sale items. Super sale priced items can also be found which makes the subscription price a real bargain. Over hill, over dale, why not hit the dusty trail, as the model airplanes, motorcycles, bombers, battleships, tanks and other "militaria" come rollin' along. If you want to dig yourself out of the trenches and win the war on prices, here's the place to shave 30-70 percent off the wingspan.

10

Art & Collectibles

★★★ Art & Frame
304 S. Park Blvd., Suite 200
Grapevine, TX 76051

817/329-8500
Mon-Fri 10-7; Sat 10-6

This shop has more names than a leopard has spots. Formerly Warehaus Gallery, then Kangoo Gallery, and now Art & Frame, yet they're still the same ole, same ole. So be it. What's in a name anyway? Still, if you're tired of searching the outback for an outlet just for in-stock custom framing as well as framed art at good prices, park your fram here. Take a few hours to wander through their stock of thousands of prints by **G. HARVEY** and **KINCADE**, to name drop a few popular ones. Then have it framed at prices lower than fair on all frames and framing materials, including matting, glass, etc. Custom framing also is available. Art & Frame works almost entirely in wood frames, with a wide variety available. Low prices and good workmanship keep the customers coming back.

★★★★★ Art Encounter
230 Spanish Village
Dallas, TX 75203

972/726-7220
Mon & Sat Noon-5; Tue- Fri 10-6
www.artencounter-dallas.com

It's not The Louvre, it's not the Metropolitan Museum of Art, it's not the Kimball, but it is the Southwest's largest gallery with over 2,000 works of art from over 150 emerging artists waiting to be discovered. One step before the big time, it's up to you to make them or break them. At the intersection of Arapaho and Coit in far north Dallas, tucked away in the corner, is this gathering of talent in an informal but stunning gallery. Original works of art, sculpture, pottery, jewelry and custom framing make this an encounter of a creative kind. Prices are higher than a traveling art show but less than an uptown gallery. Somewhere in between, it's a fair and happy medium. Home is where the art is, so from theirs to yours, help keep them all from starving. Most mediums represented—oils, pastels, modern, Southwest, ethnic, jewelry, pottery, wood carvings, sculpture and bronzes. Prices began as low as $10 for a hand-crafted bracelet, $42 for pottery and around $50 for art. It then goes up, up and away. As Degas once said, "A painter out of Monet is worth supporting!"
Call toll-free: 800/340-1194

★★ Art USA   972/491-2441
7000 Independence Pkwy.   Mon-Tue, Thur-Fri 10-7; Wed & Sat 10-6; Sun 12-5
Plano, TX 75025

See the USA in your **CHEVROLET**, but America is also calling you to stay home and hang out. In that regard, the framers of the constitution would be pleased to note that this chain (some franchised and some not) is located at the northeast corner of Independence and Legacy (next to Kroger), and it's here you can save 25 percent on framing. So, if you're looking for proof of your Frame and Fortune, check out other framers, bring in your quote and Art USA will match the materials, then cut the price by 25 percent. When a promotion's going on, that's the time to strike it rich. There are plenty of posters and framed art for sale, so don't miss a trick. Multiple locations in the Metroplex for your critique.

★★★★★ Art-Frame Expo   214/824-1214
5620 E. Mockingbird Ln.   Mon-Sat 10-7; Sun Noon-6
Dallas, TX 75206

There is nothing like a frame, and here's one dame who found this gallery and went artistic! Frame a poster for $34.95, or use their "buy one, get a second at half-price" policy as a beginning to the end of framing elsewhere. There are also thousands of oil paintings, mirrors, prints and posters to reflect on this country's competitive spirit. Low prices offered similarly at three other locations: 3501 E. McKinney Ave., 214/219-2242; 17390 Preston Rd., 972/373-8449; and in Plano, 1725 N. Central Expressway. Go, Expo, Go!

★★★★ Dallas Visual Art Center   214/821-2522
2917 Swiss Ave.   Tue-Fri 10-8:30; Sat 10-5
Dallas, TX 75204   www.immedia.net

Leave it to the Swiss to be culturally enriched. This non-profit art center is located in the hub of the Wilson Historic Buiding and houses some of the best cultural bargains in the Metroplex. The center is free and open to the public. See original works of art by up-and-coming Picassos and Monets. Don't miss their annual Critic's Choice Juried Show that features artists from all over the state of Texas. Seeing is believing at this Visual Art Center in Dallas. Literally hundreds of artists participate with the hopes that their works will be shown at the Center. Many mediums are presented, from pottery to photography, oils to water colors, from '40s retro images to minimalist abstract paintings, it's all a visual treat to behold. Circle their summer hours to be Tue, Wed, Fri 10-5; Thu 10-8:30; Sat 10-5 and make a trip to East Dallas where you'll find this Swiss location much easier to climb than the Alps.

★ Florence Art Gallery   214/754-7070
2500 Cedar Springs@ Fairmount   Tue-Fri 10-5; Sat 11-5
Dallas, TX 75201   www.florenceart.guidelive.com

To the Max, **PETER MAX** and Florence Art are quite a pair. When he's in town, you can expect special goings-on at the Gallery where his work is often shown. But man does not live on Max alone. There's also other artists' work of the original kind that is shown here. Specializing in paintings and sculpture, Florence Art Gallery is wall-endowed with 4,000 square feet of artistic endeavors. Both contemporary and traditional works are represented. Consignments, buying or selling and appraisals are part of this gallery's distinctions. Occasionally, they offer furniture and other special offerings that reflect the gallery's particular bent. The artists are varied, including **HENRIETTA MILAN**, **J. MILLER** and of course, Peter Max. Their consignment service can help you take home a painting or sculpture, regardless of your price range. Whether you're a buyer or a seller, consider maximizing every inch of empty space with a work of art and your home will appreciate accordingly.

★★★★★ Framing Warehouse   972/416-3626
2760 E. Trinity Mills   Mon-Fri 10-6; Thu 10-8; Sat 9-5
Carrollton, TX 75006

Framing Warehouse claims their frames are priced, "wholesale to the public." Now we're talkin'. And if you want it fast, they will deliver in one hour (or a week, depending on your request). Located at the corner of Trinity Mills and Marsh Lane, the choices include both metal and wood frames custom-fitted to the particular work in question. They do both residential and commercial framing and tailor each work to the wall in question. They recognize that diploma, that "Hole-in-one," that "Medal of Honor" or that First Dollar Bill earned came with sweating bullets, so each is handled with precision and care.

★★★★ Helene's Fine Art and Framing   972/867-1733
2001 Coit Rd., Suite 305   Mon-Sat 10-6
Plano, TX 75075

Helene's is supreme when you're looking for original fine art, paintings, limited edition prints and custom framing all rolled into one. Her sense of adventure and taste for the sublime result in an eclectic mix of artistic intentions. What a fun turn to take when your cupboards are bare and you're looking to fill it with collectibles. For example, if you want to start with collectibles and objects d'art, consider **GIUSEPPE ARMANI** sculptures or **MARK HOPKINS** bronzes. No, not your type? Then gaze at some **SWAROVSKI** crystal, or smile at some **WALT DISNEY CLASSIC COLLECTIONS**. For Dad, dear **LARRY DYKE** is America's most collected golf artist. If he's good enough for Pope John Paul II, Ronald Reagan and Jack Nicklaus, it should be good enough for your Tiger wannabe. Helene's also shows many local and national artists' original oils, water colors, lithographs, sculptures and bronzes and can be considered an expert custom and museum-mounted framer. If you've never heard of a local wunderkind artisan who has created a series called "Pocket Dragons," you will. Their little faces are enchanting and sure to be in demand as a work to be collected. Pay attention—eBay, remember? *Call toll-free: 800/410-4278*

★★★★ JW Sports Cards & Collectibles Superstore   972/788-5487
14902 Preston Rd., Suite 410   Mon-Fri 10-8; Sat 10-6
Dallas, TX 75240

SPORTS memorabilia is one category that has slipped by me. I didn't collect trading cards as a child, nor even consider them as an adult. That's, of course, until my son met Mickey Mantle and started collecting them himself. On eBay, he has supported himself buying and selling them...so who would have thought they would someday save his day? That's where JW comes in. At the southeast corner of Preston and Belt Line, here's where it all begins and...ends. Whether you're buying or selling trading cards or collectibles, JW is there. Autographed sports memorabilia include all-time favorites like Babe Ruth, Pudge Rodriguez, Troy Aikman, Michael Jordan and others who are found trading back and forth. Then for the non-sports crowd, you can fill in the gaps with **POKEMON**, **STAR WARS**, **G.I. JOE** and other collectible figures. Before you head to an online auction, however, see for yourself why JW is the ultimate collector's Nirvana.

★★ Lone Star Sportscard Co.   972/245-8884
2150 N. Josey, Suite 100   Mon-Fri Noon-7; Sat 10-6; Sun Noon-5
Carrollton, TX 75006   www.lonestarsportcard.com

All alone and far away lies a whole other world of sports card fanatics. And where do they go when they want to "collect" their thoughts? To Lone Star Sportscard Co., that's where. Oh where, oh where did those Mickey Mantle cards go? Oh where, oh where did they go? Well, check it out. Located at the northeast corner of Josey and Keller Springs in Carrollton, if it's sports cards you covet, you'll love it here. Sports cards, **POKEMON** mania plus autographed memorabilia is the stash that'll bring you increased cash one of these days, mama. Let them have at it. Whether you're buying or selling major trading cards such as **STADIUM**, **TOPPS** or **UPPER DECK**, young or old, male or female, there's something of value here. Too, if you're the kind that likes to don the memorabilia such as jerseys, or memorialize the actual sports equipment that made history, here's another reason to head to the mound of the Lone Star Sportscard Co. Can you imagine owning one of the original Troy Aikman jerseys this year? It should be worth a fortune.

★★★★★ Moses Gallery   214/528-7983
4253 Cedar Springs Rd.   Wed-Fri Noon-6; Sat 11-6; Sun 1-5
Dallas, TX 75219   www.mosesart.com

Now open Wednesday through Sunday, Moses Gallery has nothing to do with leading more than a half million shoppers through the desert of the Metroplex. Actually this Moses has other talents. He can paint. Yea, though we walk through the valley of other galleries, there is none so impressive online or in person. A one man art gallery, he is an empire all unto himself. Think a combination of Andy Warhol and **PETER MAX**, only less expensive. Well, I hate to ascribe such an unworthy characteristic as less pricey, but in this book, that's what it's all about. Forget starving artists. This one probably eats but at least we don't have to sing for his supper. At the southwest corner of Cedar Springs and Wycliff, one block off the Dallas Tollway, you have the privilege of entering the walls of Moses, a one-man gallery. Moses paints. And one of his specialties is a **GICLÉE PRINT**. Like offset lithographs, Giclée prints start with an original painting that is scanned into a computer where it can be color corrected and stored digitally. A series of tiny nozzles spray the paper with a fine stream of ink - more than four million droplets per second. Because there are no screens involved, Giclée prints have a higher resolution than offset lithographs. The inks are sprayed as droplets rather than dots; each droplet bleeds into the paper creating more of a continuous tone than dot pattern. Moses chose Giclée prints over other forms of reproduction because he felt it best reproduced his works. The Giclée process, because of its high resolution and color range, captures the subtleties of each stroke of the artwork. Prices range from $650 (36"x36") to $750 (36"x46"), shipped in a tube and unframed. Well worth every stroke of genius. Okay, so I like his stuff. What's it to ya! I also like that he paints animals, retro, foods, abstracts, flowers—things that I dig. So there.

★★★★ Nostalgia Crafts and Antiques   972/613-6622
971 W. Centerville Rd.   Mon-Fri 10-6; Sat 10-8; Sun Noon-5
Garland, TX 75041   www.nostalgiaca.com

Ah, memories, of the days gone by and of times past. Memories of the time when your grandma rocked you in your cradle and your mother put an afghan over you at night. Memories of ice cream sundaes in those special sundae glass cups and memories of lace cloths draped over the piano top. Here it all comes together. The combination of things from the past and hand-mades of today. Antiques to original art, bird houses to blue suede shoes, collectibles to cookie jars, dolls to doilies, silk flowers to silver spoons— if you weren't born with one in your mouth, then take a trip down Memory Lane. Three locations in the Metroplex (Lewisville and Plano, too), you will love them and hate to leave them. For example, at the location above, there's a fab '50s diner and an old-fashioned soda fountain; in Lewisville, dine in splendor at the Cameo Tea Room. In the Plano and Lewisville locations, you laugh at the first ever store to specialize in "I Love Lucy" collectibles. You don't even have to collect her to love her. There's something for everyone up and down the aisles of styles, antiques and ceramics, hand-painted apparel to hand-made jewelry, soaps to stained glass, porcelains to potpourri, woodcrafted items to yard ornaments, variety is the spice of life. Nostalgia Crafts and Antiques in Lewisville at Highway 121 at I-35, 972/434-8004 and in Plano (in the back of Plano Market Square Mall, Central at Spring Creek), 972/424-2995.

★★★★★ Sandaga Market   214/747-8431

1325 Levee St.   Mon-Fri 9-6; Sat 10-6; By Appt.
Dallas, TX 75207

If you want a taste of African, then head to the Levee...where you'll find Darrell Thomas' Sandaga Market. This is one show of artistry. The African imports are intoxicating. One dose, and you're drunk with pleasure. Unless you travel the continent, you'll never see such tribal tribulations west of the Congo. It's like being on a safari, capturing a bird's eye view of jungle artisans and craftsmanship. It's certainly the best selection of such African imports in the Metroplex. Taste the distinctive array of tribal art and textiles from Ghana, the Ivory Coast and Mali. Savor the dogon stools, masks, mud cloths, sculptures, fetishes and fine art. Whether it's one piece or a hundred, accent your home with a little local color from Africa. At these direct prices, you might be able to outfit an entire house. To get to Sandaga Market, take I-35 E. southbound to Continental, turn right, turn right again at Industrial, go four blocks to Cole, then turn left to the end of the block and look for a big white sign with red letters...To Market, To Market, you've found "Sandaga Market".

Tapestries & More   972/781-2434

Lakeside Market   www.tapestries-more.com
5813 Preston Rd., Suite 554
Plano, TX 75093

First, call this Plano place a treasure. Then hang up on them. That's right. Their tapestries are the perfect artwork to hang up on your walls. You'd never see a castle without one, so why not have a good knight for a change? This newcomer to town joins their parent company from Atlanta, GA to offer every imaginable type of tapestry with history or without. Custom installation, reproductions and custom handwoven royal crests, tapestries from England, France, Dutch Masters, Belgium and medieval floras, traditional hunt scenes, medieval crests, scenes of history, Italian landscapes, Renaissance scenes, maps, Oriental, mythology, religious and more. If it was made to be a tapestry, you can find it here—for less. *Call toll-free: 888/827-0527*

★★★★★ Weber's Nostalgia Supermarket   817/534-6611

6611 Anglin Drive   Mon-Fri 9-5
Fort Worth, TX 76119

Since 1917, Weber's Nostalgia Supermarket has known there are many things in life that are too good to be threw. Thanks, Weber, for the memorabilia. It's probably the largest repository of gas pump restoration supplies, globes, signs, decals, photos, books, clocks, magnets, novelties and gifts all related to the good old days. Nostalgia continues to play an ever-increasing role in Baby Boomer home decor (or for any age group, come to think of it). From game room to garage, these are great items for a conversation piece, a movie prop or a restaurant decoration. Ever wonder where all these trendy restaurants get their wall and shelf decor? Weber's is the place. The price of the catalog will be deducted from your purchase. Returns are accepted with a receipt within two weeks on catalog items. Mailing charges: 10 percent of purchase with a $3.50 minimum (but that's subject to change, so be sure to check).

Zozza Gallery

972/889-0440

2260 Promenade

Mon-Fri 10-6; Sat 10-5

Coit Rd. (Between Belt Line and Arapaho)

www.zozza.com

Dallas, TX 75080

When the passion of its owners meets art where the heart is, that's when you separate the ordinary from the extraordinary. Joe Raphael and Carole Altman have carved out an unusual niche in the Metroplex. Their gallery glistens with dazzling art glass and their jewelry displays a comparable reflection. From buying exquisite engagement and wedding bands to buying a wedding gift that's perfect for the couple in question, it might be "From your lips to God's ear." Hey, if it's a Jewish couple, their selection of Judaica gifts, for example, is the best in the Metroplex. Mezuzahs, for instance, the miniature 10 Commandments that Jewish couples hang in their office or home door jam to welcome each and every entrant, are often signed works of art with history accompanying the purchase; or just plain and simple, but a welcomed gift nonetheless. Choose from appropriate Jewish gifts from $30-$300 in glass or in metal. Why honor the couple with the ordinary? Surprise them with the extraordinary. Their motto, "Where the Unusual is Usual!" And they mean it. Raphael and Altman travel the globe ferreting out the artisans who have not yet entered the marketplace with their work at untenable prices. Instead, you can buy the newest collectibles at the start of the curve and watch them appreciate. Special lighting accents the glass sculptures and vases, many of them signed by artists from across the globe. Then look in the jewelry showcases to see many hand-crafted works of art for your fingers, wrists, neck or ears. Don't expect anything but the experience of four generations of jewelers. How else could they have achieved such buying power to be able to sell diamonds at below wholesale prices? They showcase one-of-a-kind pieces that are not only dramatic but conversation pieces as well. Once you've shopped Zozza's, you'll never shop anywhere else. Zozza's is the exclusive distributor for the **HUBLOT.** Watch how can words describe the most beautiful and technologically-enhanced watchpiece in the world. Of course, you pay for it, but then, who could ever show you up? (Unless, of course, they bought a Hublot from Zozza's, too!) Nobody else sells them in town and that's exactly what Zozza is all about. Each location offers different merchandise, so you have to do double duty to experience the whole megillah. You can get another taste of Zozza across from NorthPark, next to the Cheesecake Factory. Forget dieting—then again, the carats at Zozza's are non-fattening. ***Call toll-free: 800/992-2728***

11

Baby & Mom

◆◆◆◆◆ Baby Bedding
3415 S. Cooper St., Suite 102
Arlington, TX 76015

817/419-0088
Mon-Sat 10-6; Sun Noon-6

For the custom look in baby's room, this is the hand that rocked the cradle. Expect custom fabric, yours or theirs, and let them sew it up. Next door, you'll see sewers needling every project as they cater to every mother's dream. Nobody beats their prices on baby bedding and matching accessories. Welcome your li'l one to a room laden with the finest matching linens, lamps, wall hanging, pillows, cradles and cribs, highchairs and changing tables, gliders and rockers. What makes this outlet so enticing is its ability to pull the entire room together with fabric. Whether you buy one piece or the entire ensemble, your baby will enjoy being in the "lap" of luxury—for less. Their prices often beat those in resale shops and these items are all brand new, in the box. Shop their weekend location at Traders Village, 2600 Mayfield Rd. in Grand Prairie.

★★ Baby Delights
610 Cedar St.
Cedar Hill, TX 75104

972/291-7844
Tue-Fri 10-6; Sat 10-5

This shop is beyond conception. When the time comes to welcome baby into this world, mommies and daddies will be delighted with the hand-made bedding and bumper pads here. It doesn't stop with the delivery, either. They offer adorable apparel, furniture, and nursery doodads for infants through 6X. Make sure your baby sleeps tight while visions of sugarplums dance overhead. Cribs in the $250 range available in traditional finishes like oak, white or natural. Everything can be mixed and matched from the line **MILLION DOLLAR BABY**. At least, you can believe yours is, but they shouldn't have to send you to the cleaners. Calling all girls, ages 4 to 9 for their infamous "dress-up tea parties." What a great idea for a birthday celebration.

★★★★★ Baby Depot @ Burlington Coat Factory   972/613-1333

2021 Town East Blvd.   Mon-Sat 10-9; Sun 11-6
Mesquite, TX 75150

Ooh, baby, ooh baby, ooh! Choo-choo your little caboose over to this offspring within Burlington Coat Factory. One-stop shopping for the expectant mom, infants and toddlers at its bargain best. In fact, shopping here should carry you through your baby's needs for several years, at best, without a pregnant pause. There's a huge selection of car seats, cribs, bedding, bumper pads, strollers, play yards, swings, dressers, changing tables, rockers, layette items, infant apparel, baby gifts and more from all the leading manufacturers. Check out **APRICA**, **BASSETT**, **CHILDCRAFT**, **GRACO**, **LAMBS & IVY**, **NOJO** and **SIMMONS**—there's not too many others out there to consider. In fact, we heard through the grapevine that Simmons hand-makes all of their furniture. If true, it sure beats the assembly line. Baby, let's face it, a wonderful wicker bassinet and matching lace skirt caught our eye and it soon went "Buy, Buy!" If you're expecting, don't forget to sign in, please, to the gift registry. See, even with discount prices, you can expect all the little extras which make shopping a pleasure. Other Baby Depots located at Burlington Coat Factory outlets at Webb Chapel and Forest; in Plano, Central Expressway and Parker; in Euless, Industrial Blvd. and 183; at Grapevine Mills Mall; and in Arlington, at I-20 and S. Cooper St.

★★★★★ Baby's Dream, A   817/795-2366

2205 W. Division St., Suite A-6   Mon-Sat 10-6
Arlington, TX 76012

Fairy tales do come true, they can happen to you, if your babies dream. And why not? Isn't that what saying, "Night-Night" is all about? So while they're nodding off to dreamland, make sure you've got all the right stuff. That means, custom bedding. And that leads me to A Baby's Dream. This custom workroom sews everything for the baby's nursery—from bedding to wall hangings, chair cushions and cradles, dressing tables, window treatments, lamps, mobiles, gliders, if it's the best for baby's room, Pearley Terry has got them covered. Whether you're wanting a circular crib or a more traditional model, both are available with your fabric or theirs. Either way, chances are baby will not know the difference (but her grandma will!) Once mom rocks her little babe in arms in a **TOWNE SQUARE** glider-rocker, she'll never go back to rockin' in another. It's the one that most moms request. So, start thinking about your color schemes and start transforming baby's dreams into reality. Located in an industrial business warehouse district, you'll be able to peek next door into the workroom while the sewers are busy as bees. Fortunately, orders do not take nine months to materialize.

babysheaven.com   866/343-2836

4870 Santa Monica Ave 2D   24/7
San Diego, CA 92107   www.babysheaven.com

Everything you've ever needed, wanted or wished for in a baby store is here—heaven on earth. Bassinets, bedding, bicycle trailers, breast pumps, car seats, carriers, changing tables, cradles, cribs, crib mattresses, furniture sets, high chairs, jogging strollers, monitors, play yards, potty trainers, rockers, safety gates, strollers, swings, toddler beds, walkers and bouncers, wicker/wood—everything but the nanny. Great editorial features include "Ask the Doctor", downloading coupons, a baby contest, a baby newsletter, the ability to track your order online, your 100 percent satisfaction, a great return policy and FREE shipping. Oh, did I also mention the lowest prices? How does every name brand in the business at 25-75 percent off and no sales tax? See first-hand and stop whining! 🇺🇸

★★★★ Beary Cute Kids   817/370-0058

5352 Wedgmont Circle N.   Tue-Sat 10:30-5:30
Fort Worth, TX 76133

Okay, so the clothes are beary, beary cute. What did you expect? Moms clamoring to buy ugly ones? No siree, this store sells cute clothes for cute kids and sends ugly clothes down the street. So, if you're looking for quality childrenswear, from newborn through pre-teen in girls and size 14 in boys, this is a beary, beary bundle of joy. Head to Trail Lake Drive and Wedgmont Cir. N. behind the credit union building if you're looking to outfit your children in style, in sync and in season. Though small in stature (700-800 square feet), what they lack in size, they make up in savings and selection. Their most joyful addition is their toys—both new market samples and gently used models. Do your kids know from one toy to the next if that **L'IL TYKES** tricycle is new or not? Why spend a fortune, then? For $4, they can put the pedal to the metal, or dine on a picnic table for $20 or cuddle up with a new **BOYD'S BEAR** for $13. Sales are common—winter duds discounted off their already low prices during the spring; and vice versa. Summer things are slashed in the winter. So, maybe you're going on a cruise in December or skiing in the Andes in the summer? So be it. They're still very cute kids in very cute clothes.

Better Maternity Outlet/BeBe Maternity   214/742-2229

1644 Irving Blvd.   Mon-Fri 11-6; Sat 10-5
Dallas, TX 75207   www.bebematernity.com

Better save it while you can. At Better Maternity Outlet, you'll find all the maternity fashions you'll need in Tencel denim and linen and Pima cotton. Why suffer any more than you need to by wearing too tight jeans and scratchy Angora sweaters? Just how comfortable can you be—especially while toting your two year old around while awaiting his baby sister? Pretty darn comfortable. Then add in the savings of 50-70 percent over comparable items, and maintaining the family life starts to look pretty darn affordable. Find it all—from tops and pants for work or play to undergarments including nursing bras. All wonderfully made by BeBe Maternity. Get going, you only have nine months to wear 'em out. ***Call toll-free: 887/740-2323***

★★★★★ Diaper Mart Superstore Warehouse   214/358-1499

2600 W. Mockingbird Lane   Mon-Fri 9-6; Sat 10-6; Sun 11-5
Dallas, TX 75235

On your way to Love Field, if your water breaks, don't worry. Diaper Mart's right there to answer the call. Factory-direct diapers, the perfect handi-wipe for your baby's needs 24/7. Regardless of size, newborn diapers sell for $10.99 (case of 96) and Ultras (with liner and gathered waists) were $16.99 for the large size. Sure could have fooled Mother Nature. They looked like a Pamper, responded like a Pamper, so why pay top dollar for the brand name and marketing campaign? It does the trick, regardless of the name. And they beat Wal-Mart prices. Since all of their diapers are disposable, make sure you have a **DIAPER GENIE** (or a very large trash can) and life will be almost bare-able! Stacks of diapers are co-mingled with racks and stacks of baby and children's clothing, some of their own making and some department store excess. As they grow into "I can almost do-it-myself," disposable training pants were $13 for a 50-count and diaper bags were snagged for $4. Then, it was hard to resist completing the wardrobe, so we added shoes, T-shirts, infant dresses and unisex jumpsuits for $2-$5. What grandparent can buy just one? Next door, you'll grow attached to their accompanying children's bedding and furniture department, all discounted, and all winning parent's applause. Complete the baby's room with a layette: the crib, changing table and all the little nothings mom and dad will need to keep baby dry and smelling baby-powder sweet. We wrapped up boxes of baby wipes and added up the savings. Then, when all was said and done, we had enough money left over to celebrate with a champagne flight to Cancun—without baby. Circle back and check out their Grand Prairie outlet called Diaper Mart II at 2424 S. Carrier Pkwy., 972/606-0180; Diaper Mart III, 2825 Valley View Lane in Farmers Branch/Carrollton, 972/484-2880; or Diaper Mart IV in Garland at 1030 W. Centerville Rd. Now when they can sell online, they will finally be able to deliver the goods without any epidurals.

★ iMaternity/Dan Howard

13323 Montfort Drive
Dallas, TX 75240

972/233-4077
Mon-Sat 10-6; Thu 10-8; Sun Noon-5
www.imaternity.com

Don't be confused. iMaternity and Dan Howard Outlet have now joined like conjoined twins. Not easily separated, in this case, you now have the benefit of double the pleasure. Hey, the more the merrier. At least for the next nine months, you can tolerate the expansion plans, right? Look what you get in exchange. Even if they feel like the longest nine months of your life, the savings, if you can find them, will make it all worthwhile. Every li'l bit helps when you're outfitting the carrier. Jump out in jumpers for $17 and shorts for $9, for starters. *Call toll-free: 800/966-6847*

★★★ Kid to Kid

1201 W. Arbrook Blvd., Suite 115
Arlington, TX 76015

817/468-1995
Mon-Sat 10-8; Sun 1-5

Can we talk—kid to kid? Face it, clothes don't make the child, but we can't go to school looking like a ragamuffin, now can we? Why spend a fortune on kids' clothes when for a few bucks, you can outfit them in style, including their rooms when they start out. This Arlington resale shop has a finger on the pulse of quality used kids' clothes, furniture, toys, even equipment (but call ahead, equipment moves fast!) They accept both consignment resale as well as buy the clothes outright, it's up to you. And moms-to-be are not left out in the cold; they can get covered in maternity wear. Gifts for babies include infant toys, baby furnishings, nursery sets and linens, car seats and strollers, cribs, cradles, bassinets, play pens and port-a-cribs, infant swings and walkers, swimwear, shoes—the list is exhaustive. Look for great prices on the popular **TEXAS TOWN SQUARE** gliders which are considered the only brand safe for children. They buy used children's items six days a week, just make sure they're clean, pressed and on hangers, if required. Right across from The Parks of Arlington Mall, have yourself a field day if you want to save serious money. Also visit their other locations in Fort Worth at 4750 Bryant Irvin Rd. (817/263-4660) and in Bedford at Highway 183 and Central Drive (817/283-6364).

★★ Kids Too

8214 Grapevine Hwy.
North Richland Hills, TX 76180

817/656-2919
Tue-Fri 11-6; Sat 11-5

If you've got kids, too, you know that they cost a pretty penny. How to outfit them in style is as easy as learning the ABCs. Start at the very beginning with resale shopping. Two lights north of I-820 on Grapevine Highway just before Harwood Rd., begin your lesson in frugal shopping 101. Babies, kids, and moms-to-be can be outfitted in someone else's wardrobe and nobody will know the difference. Consider resale in uniforms, too. Why buy new, when someone else's will do? Department store labels, worn once or twice, look new to me and you. So, who are you kidding? Girls' sizes 0-16 and boys' 0-12 can expand your children's wardrobe by a mile. You'll smile, too, if you recycle what's in their closet, make a few dollars, and apply it to something else. Keep the ball rolling. That's what it's all about via the resale network. New and used maternity clothing alongside shower invitations and custom birth announcements, all at discounted prices. Nursing moms can rent or buy **MEDELA** breast pumps from Lactation Connection.

★★★ Lik-Nu   817/428-9400
8053-A Grapevine Hwy.   Mon-Wed, Fri-Sat 10-5; Thu 10-6
North Richland Hills, TX 76180

Smart shoppers know if it's as good as new, why do you need to spend twice as much to buy new? Welcome aboard the gravy train. Resale shopping is as good as new. Of course, it's got to look like new, or Lik-Nu won't even allow it through their doors. Consider that the average price of each item is around $5.99 when I ask you, "Where will you find prices like this unless you turn back the clock twenty years?" Expect everything to be clean and steam-pressed before it's displayed. An occasional crib comes through the door but prices were higher than average, so bid a good night. From infants to size 12 and a large selection of children's shoes makes for an impressive lineup. Lik-Nu is always in the market to buy used baby furniture like high chairs, strollers, walkers, dressers, changing tables, swings, and of course, toys are always high on their priority list. Lik-Nu is just north of I-820 on Grapevine Highway between Bedford-Euless Rd. and Harwood. It's easy to find because it's near Chuck E. Cheese's Pizza, which you'll have plenty of opportunities to get acquainted with considering the number of birthday parties your children will be attending.

★★★★★ Motherhood Outlets   972/539-2154
3000 Grapevine Mills Pkwy.   Mon-Sat 10-9:30; Sun 11-8
Grapevine Mills Mall   www.motherhood.com
Grapevine, TX 76051

Let's vote for motherhood. Whoever you campaigned for, all women, regardless of their affiliation, deserve a break today. At this outlet, you can save more on your wardrobe. This outlet store has retail stores all over the city, so its name should be a familiar one. Some are located in regional malls, others are inside Babies R Us or anchoring strip centers. Anyway, they're everywhere. Their outlets, however, showcase their castoffs, closeouts, discontinued styles, last season's merchandise yet still with mileage left. Brands such as **MATURNITEE**, **MIMI**, **MOTHERHOOD** and **PEA IN THE POD** are potential candidates for the next nine months. At the end-of-their-rope, we saw skirts as low as $1.50, some ensembles as low as $3-$9 and designer private labeled Motherhood dresses for $138. No, this was not a miscarriage. There were also cotton knit dresses for $19, a two-piece career knit dress with short sleeves with a matching long jacket for $49—all at a savings of 30-75 percent. From conception to birth, this is probably as good as it gets for your maternity wardrobe. Visit their other outlets at Katy Mills, outside Houston, Gainesville Factory Shops, Prime Outlet Center in Hillsboro and San Marcos Factory Shops for savings throughout the state or shop online for everything, from accessories to sundresses, jumpers to swimwear. It's all available without waddling out of the house. Website easy to navigate and lots of content provided for the mother-to-be. FREE newsletter and camaraderie available.

★★★★★ Neighborhood Diaper Delivery   817/652-0477
1226-B Corporate Drive   Call to set up deliveries
Arlington, TX 76006

What goes wee-wee all the way home? You guessed it! At last, the time has come for all good parents to stay put when they run out of diapers. This disposable diaper service delivers anywhere in the Metroplex and the delivery is free. Wee! If you live outside of the Metroplex, deliveries are handled by independent dealers or by mail. When you run out, you won't have to run out ever again...even if your baby has the runs. Stock up with a few extras, just in case, and buy your diapers by the caseload. Small, medium, large and extra large diapers are available along with the necessary baby wipes and the potential training pants. By the case, newborn diapers were as low as 14.6 cents each. Day care deliveries, too. This national concept has got expansion on their mind, so if you've got a friend elsewhere, it may provide some additional income or the start of something big. They'll even pay you for the referral. Small diapers were $22.95 for a package of 136, extra large diapers were $31.99 for 120 and training pants were $32.99 for 90. Not bad, considering the alternative. For babies out for the swim team, they even carry swim diapers plus baby gifts, too, to round out their sweet smell of success. ***Call toll-free: 888/391-1356***

★★★★ R.B.J. Manufacturing   888/566-LITE
PO Box 353   www.johnny-light.com
Burleson, TX 76097

Remember, we found it first. The invention called the **JOHNNY-LIGHT** was first discovered by one frustrated mom with three little boys in our office. What a clever idea, we thought. Then before we knew it, the Johnny-Light was being touted on national talk shows, from "Regis" to "Leeza" and in magazines and newspapers everywhere. We thought we were letting you in on our little secret, but no, in 1966, this Burleson group called R.B.J. (Richie, Bill and Jack) had to promote it everywhere. Don't blame them, though. When you've got it, flaunt it. They're the originators who thunk it up. DHC (domestic harmony commodity) can be achieved with the Johnny-Light, an easily installed light to help eliminate late-night fall-ins and help in toilet training. This battery-powered device lights up when the seat is down, to remind users to return the seat to its full down position after late-night use. The light also reportedly helps potty-training efforts by giving a visual aide. Also a handy reminder if you sleep walk or are groggy when you first wake up. You know the old saying, "We aim to please, you aim, too, please!" You don't have to be flush to afford it, either. It only costs $12 and is available through the mail only (batteries included). It's simple to install, no tools necessary.

★★ Wee Resell It   972/446-8189
2150 N. Josey Lane, Suite 316   Mon-Wed 10-5; Thu 10-7; Fri-Sat 10-5
Carrollton, TX 75006

Wee Resell It is for wee ones who outgrow their wardrobes, some as often as monthly. Why invest lots in their clothing when you turn around and they've shot up another two inches? Instead, recycle it to a reseller. This one's always got something exciting going on. Hardly the Tower of Babe-l, children are everywhere babbling like a broken record, while moms are negotiating with the store's personnel on what they can get for their **HEALTH-TEX** and **OSHKOSH B'GOSH** items sans spit-up and formula stains. There are also all the other accoutrements children demand while growing up, even though they claim "I won't grow up!" From infant seats to cribs, walkers to high chairs, shoes, books and toys will keep them out of stitches. There's also discounted new clothing for the well-endowed. They cost a tad more, but still less than retail. Ah, music to our ears!

★★★★★ You & Me Babe   972/669-2110
870 N. Coit Rd., Suite 2651   Mon-Fri 10-6; Sat 10-5
Promenade Shopping Center   www.youandmebabe.com
Richardson, TX 75080

The theme song of Sonny and Cher probably was never intended for a children's resale store. But, who cares as long as it's a winner. And this one is. You've Got Me, Babe, lock, stock and bargains. Thank heaven for little girls and boys who wear sizes 0-10 because everything here can save you 50-75 percent off new. So what else is new? Well, maternity clothes, that's what's new. Sizes 2-26 in petites to size 3X can get covered. You go, girl. While you're shopping for the baby (with perhaps your other children in tow), you can load up on undergarments, lingerie, hosiery and more. Those items can often be ignored in other outlet stores so it's a welcomed sight. Need a bathing suit for the pool? A cruise? A swim class with baby? Don't worry, be happy 'cause they've got these too, but new. And lastly, for those nursing moms, you can buy all the necessary apparel and supplies (like the **MEDELA** breast pump) or rent it as the case may be. Like your bosom buddy, this store will become your best friend. And when it comes time to outfit the nursery, you must opt for the latest in cribs, bedding and accessories. You can't bring the baby home to riff-raff and expect them to make it through the night! *Call toll-free: 888/258-4552*

12

Bath & Linens

★★★★ Bed Bath & Beyond
5100 Belt Line Rd., #1000
Dallas, TX 75240

972/991-8674
Mon-Sat 9-9; Sun 11-7
www.bedbathandbeyond.com

This New Jersey chain of bigger better bed and bath items was founded in 1971 but today is one of the dominant forces for better quality domestics and home furnishings. With more than 300 stores, ranging in size from 30,000 to 80,000 square feet, trust me, they leave no room for you to shop elsewhere. Offering a huge selection at what they call everyday low prices, they provide everything you could ever need or want when it comes time to living the good life....for less. Kick back and relax with coffee, me and a tall, cool glass of iced tea. Such a deal. This set comes with eight 17-ounce glasses and one 60-ounce pitcher. It's perfect for Texas year 'round. In fact, I have discovered that when I order icedtea in New York City, they cock their heads and give me "that" look. But the BB&B inventory list exhausts even the doyenne of domestics herself: air purifiers, blenders, coffeemakers, cookware, cutlery, dinnerware, down comforters, duvets, espresso machines, flatware, food processors, glassware, heaters, humidifiers, irons, mattress pads, pillows, scales, sheets, stand mixers, tablecloths, toasters, toothbrushes, towels, vacuums, water filters, window treatments—did I miss anything? Their national computerized bridal and gift registry makes it easy to buy the perfect gift with the vow of matching any competitor's prices. Still, don't expect cheap sheets....just lower than department stores. More than 70,000 items are within their confines with customer service a priority. Some of the brands highlighted include everything from **ALL-CLAD**, **CALPHALON**, **FARBERWARE**, **LE CREUSET**, **JOYCE CHEN** and **T-FAL** cookware to dinnerware by **DANSK**, **MIKASA**, **PFALTZGRAFF** to linens by **BAY LINENS**, **CROSHILL** and **WAMSUTTA**. Couldn't resist the towel warmer for $49.99 and the gold leaf charger plates, four for $19.99. Now we're talking turkey! Weekends are like visiting a cooking school, Farmers' Market, and State Fair—demonstrations everywhere and crowds circling like cattle. Seven area locations besides Village on the Parkway above: Caruth Plaza on Park Lane, 214/692-1778, Creekwalk Village, 801 West 15th Street, Suite D, Plano, 972/881-7273, Grapevine Mills, 3000 Grapevine Mills Parkway, Suite 253, Grapevine, 972/ 355-0820, Arlington Park Plaza, 3803 South Cooper Street, Arlington, 817/784-9795 and Southlake, 2930 East Southlake Blvd., Southlake, 817/748-3000. *Call toll-free: 800/GO-BEYON*

★★★★★ C & E Custom Bedspreads   817/485-4422
4209 Clay Ave.   Mon-Fri 8-5
Haltom City, TX 76117

Get the look you've been looking for in your bedroom. C & E will custom make your bedding with your supplies. Bring in those yards of fabric and notions and the wizards at C & E will zip (or sew) your comforter and bedding for you. One price includes labor and batting. Strike up a good deal with their nimble fingers to make you a match. It's a sham if you don't! From twin to king size, they can cover you from head to toe for less dough. Listen to these prices for labor only: $174 (twin), $180 (full) and $215 (king), dust ruffles from $51-$73 and pillow shams ($31-$39.50). Trust me, it doesn't get much better than this. Cording, ruffles and extra stuff costs more, but that's standard operating procedure. Allow three-four weeks for turnaround time; then it's time to go undercover.

Draperies & More   972/353-2672
1565 W. Main St., Suite 220   Mon-Fri 10-6; Sat 10-4:30
Lewisville, TX 75067

When you wish upon a star, don't forget to include Draperies and More in your dreams. After thumbing through enough decorator magazines to earn a place in the Guinness Book, pick your favorites and dream on. Then take those dreams and have Karen Moore (though she does more than others in her field of dreams) whip up a drapery treatment or a bedding ensemble that looks just like those retailing for thousands, for a fraction of the price. 'Tis true, 'tis true, there is a fabric fairy that can make dreams come true. Whether you shop her Lewisville shop that will WOW you when you walk in, or her Carrollton location at 3733 Josey Lane, Carrollton, Texas, 972/394-4893, you can expect the most window treatments and matching or coordinating ensembles in the Metroplex. This is it. Don't even look elsewhere. Head to the corner of Garden Ridge and Main, where you'll see horizontal and vertical blinds, shutters, carpet, custom furniture, reupholstery, custom draperies and shades. Hang out with brand names from **CAROLE**, **GRABER**, **HUNTER-DOUGLAS**, **KASHMIR**, **RALPH LAUREN**, **ROBERT ALLEN** and **WESCO**. Deck the walls with grand names such as **IMPERIAL** and **YORK**. Discounts soar to 70-80 percent off list price on wood blinds, PVC blinds, mini-blinds, vertical blinds, pleated shades; up to 30 percent off fabric/lining on valances and window treatments; 10 percent off comforter sets; 30 percent off carpet and wallpaper. Shop 'til you drop off to sleep in either custom or readymade spreads (even her ready-mades are to die for!) Here, you've got it made in the shade!

★★★★★ Home Elements   214/637-0011
7900 AMbassador Row   Mon-Fri 8-3:30
Dallas, TX 75247

A rose by any other name would have to be called Rose Tree if you shop at this outlet. This manufacturer produces linens and things for department and specialty stores. They sell their leftover finished products like comforters, duvets, place mats & napkins and excess fabrics, pillows, table and bed linens, decorative pillows, runners, fringe, trim, and cording. They can be yours for a song. In their annual "Take It Away Sale," we saw comforters priced as low as $35, fabric at $2/yard and place mats for 50 cents. How low can they go? This is it but during the rest of the year, prices are almost as good and worth a regular visit. Adjacent to their manufacturing site, you'll find a wealth of upscale opportunities for very little budgetary considerations. Located between Mockingbird and Regal Row, just west of Stemmons.

★★★ Kayan's   972/238-9835
102 Dal-Rich Village   Mon-Sat 10-5:30
Richardson, TX 75080

This Kayan is the salt of the earth. If you don't want to pepper your decor with mismatched and unmatched items, this is the place to accessorize. Since 1985, Kayan's has been sewing up a storm, creating award-winning bedcoverings. Want to make Pillow Talk? Then let them spread the word—at 25 percent off. Everything to mix and match for your bed and bath including comforter and duvet ensembles, bedspreads, daybed sets, headboards, benches to fit at the end of your bed with matching window and wall treatments to complete the picture-perfect room. Any style, pick it out and it's made in your choice and color. Upholstery, too. Expect delivery to take about four weeks. Instant gratification is only in the movies. These sew-and-sews want every stitch to count. That's why they win awards.

★★★★ Linens 'n Things   214/265-8651
10720 Preston Rd., Suite 108   Mon-Sat 9-9; Sun 10-7
Dallas, TX 75230   www.linensnthings.com

Since 1975, Linens 'n Things has been just that, Linens 'n Things—a leading home textiles, housewares and home accessories superstore coast-to-coast. As of March, 2001, they had 293 stores between 35,000 and 40,000 square feet and you'll hear no complaints at this end. No siree. They are a favorite amongst frugal fanatics who want high thread counts at great prices (25-50 percent off, and more during sales). With over 28,000 stock items, where else do you need to shop? Linens (bedding, towels and pillows) and "things" (housewares and home accessories) with names that have made America famous: Brand names like **ALL-CLAD, BRAUN, CALPHALON, CUISINART, HENCKELS, KRUPS, LAURA ASHLEY, ROYAL VELVET, WAMSUTTA** and **WAVERLY** to name-drop a few. Say beddy-good buys to their increasing presence of private labels which supplement their brand name products yet give shoppers more bang for their buck. Of course, "we won't be undersold" is their everyday low pricing strategy with almost 40 percent of their sales now coming from the "things" such as frames and area rugs, candles and small electronics. Check directory for nine other area locations.

★★★ Luxury Linens @ Burlington Coat Factory   972/613-1333
2021 Town East Blvd.   Mon-Fri 10-9; Sat 11-9; Sun 10-6
Mesquite, TX 75150   www.bcfdirect.com

How do I love thee? Let me count the ways. Burlington Coat, as we all know, sells more than just coats. They sell ladies, men's, children's apparel and shoes, plus, fragrances, baby, home decor, luggage, and at this particular store, linens. Some brand names you've come to love over the years and their newest offering exclusively by Christopher Lowell of HGTV fame. Besides his decorating "How-to" books, his collections are garnering rave reviews. With his designer eye, he coordinates the entire bedding ensemble for you making it easy to deliver a decorator look, without the decorator. With almost 300 stores nationwide, it all began back in 1924 when Abe Milstein launched a successful wholesale outerwear business. Then, when Monroe Milstein joined his father in the '50s, they began selling retail. When I caught up with him in my first book in 1972, they had just acquired a coat factory and outlet store in Burlington, New Jersey—hence the name Burlington Coat Factory. But you should see them now. Save up to 60 percent off department and specialty store prices on more than one thousand (yes, 1,000) designer and name brand fashions for the entire family. All locations feature an extensive and impressive selection of the latest, first-quality ladies designer dresses, suits, sportswear and accessories; top name men's suits and sportswear; and famous-label clothes for children of all ages. Each store stocks 10,000 to 20,000 outerwear garments every day, year round, even throughout a typical Texas summer (I guess if you're embarking on a ski trip to the Andes, you'll need to keep warm)! Another feature that has been lost by Marshall's and TJMaxx is the "hard to fit" customer, from petite to plus; short to big to tall to big and tall. They will even special order merchandise from manufacturers to meet special sizing needs. Within the majority of Burlington Coat Factories is their Baby Depot and Luxury Linens Department—offering a one-stop shopping experience for specialty merchandise. Savings of up to 60 percent off there, too. Check directory for multiple area locations or log on to their website and shop online at www.bcfdirect.com.

★★★★★ **Peacock Alley Outlet Store**   **972/490-3998**
13720 Midway Rd., #203   Mon-Sat 9:30-5:30
Dallas, TX 75244

Count the Pope, Oprah Winfrey and Bruce Willis as fans of these linen products. (I wonder if that was before or after Demi?) Well, if you're looking for demi-prices, shop their outlet for luxurious bed and bath linens. This Peacock Alley store is divided into two sections: retail and outlet. On the retail side, you will find a full line of the most luxurious bath towels, bed linens, comforters and bathrobes. On the outlet side, you will find similar items that are samples, discontinues or slightly flawed. The outlet prices, however, are a dramatic 50-60 percent less. Egyptian cotton towels and sheets with thread counts up to 350 were drippingly discounted. This is living life on the right side of the tracks. Bring in your own fabric and they will custom-make a duvet, pillows or shams for you. Once you've dressed your bed and bathroom, it's time for a spritz of some of Peacock Alley's best-selling home fragrances. *Call toll-free: 888/822-7016*

★★★★★ **Westpoint Stevens Factory Outlet**   **940/565/5040**
Denton Factory Stores   Mon-Sat 10-8; Sun 11-6
5800 North I-35, Suite 508   www.westpointstevens.com
Denton, TX 76201

Even if you haven't an appointment to WestPoint, you can graduate to this outlet for savings on things for your kitchen and bath. Forget department stores and paying full price. Here's some of the best brands in the business: **GRAND PATRICIAN**, **LADY PEPPERELL**, **MARTEX**, **RALPH LAUREN**, **STEVENS**, **UTICA** and **VELLUX**. Too, they also maintain quite a line-up of licensed brands such as **DESIGNERS GUILD**, **DISNEY HOME COLLECTION**, **DR. SCHOLL'S**, **GLYNDA TURLEY**, **JOE BOXER** and **SERTA PERFECT SLEEPER**. They are also the manufacturer for **MARTHA STEWART'S** bed and bath lines. Here you can save up to 70 percent on everyday popular brands in this 10,000-square-foot emporium. Get back into snuggling. Whether you need to cover up with a light wrap or dry yourself off with the heavy-duty towel, they can accommodate. The inventory's extensive: towels, bath sheets, duvet covers, comforters, pillows and pillow shams, shower curtains, bathroom accessories, blankets, throws, kitchen towels and dish rags, pot holders and table tops, you can buy the works without getting short-sheeted. Directions: I-35 North to exit 470 or I-35 South to exit 471. For more than 187 years, West Point Stevens has been a giant in the textile industry. They are the nation's largest producer of bed and bath fashions so you can imagine why we would lay down and cover up with something from here. There are more than 50 outlets primarily in Alabama, Florida, Georgia, Indiana, Louisiana, Maine, Nevada, North and South Carolina, Texas and Virginia plus Canada and Great Britain. *Call toll-free: 800/533-8229*

13

Beauty & Drug Stores

◆◆◆ Academy of Healing Arts, Inc.   940/566-1880
531 Londonderry Lane   Mon, Wed, Thu 10-7; Tue, Fri 10-5; Sat By Appt. Only
Denton, TX 76205

A good massage can heal what ails you. Go weak in the knees with full body massages by fully licensed therapists for $45 an hour. If you're lucky, you can cash in on the learning hands of a student intern and pay just $25 for that same massage. And if $25 is all you can squeeze from your checkbook and no interns are available, that will get you at least a partial body rub for a half hour with a licensed therapist. Just expect to "knead" a good long nap afterwards. Knot able pay for it yourself? Manipulate those loved ones of yours and stress upon them that a gift certificate would make a perfect present. Be sure to decide at least a day in advance because walk-in appointments are rarely available.

★★ Aladdin Beauty College   940/382-6734
407 Sunset   Tue, Wed 10-5; Thur-Sat 8:30-5
Denton, TX 76201

Here it is ladies, Hair 101. Let Aladdin work their magic on you, Genie. Learn a few tricks from those who have just learned them, too, all while taking advantage of great prices. Conjure up a whole new look and cut out high prices with perms setting the standard at $36 and under. But fear not, there's no mistaking. All work is carefully supervised by Masters of the Art(teachers) and performed only by the senior class. Look for specials during the week or nail down other great deals on manicures. Sculpted nails and overlays were just $10-$15. Tweak your new look with eyebrow sculpting. Pull it all together for less than a single service at most salons. Cut time into your schedule for these deals since last customers are taken at 4 PM each day. Nail services on Thursday and Friday don't begin until 10:15 AM. Check directory for additional Metroplex locations.

◆◆◆◆◆ Beauty Brands Salon Spa Superstore   972/231-4573
2060 N. Coit   Mon-Sat 8-9, Sun 10-6
Richardson, TX 75080   www.beautybrands.com

Fray the frizz with professional hair care products at amateur prices. Over 10,000 spa and salon quality products line the shelves of this beauty mega store. Relax, or perm with everything from rods and rollers to hairbrushes and combs. Decorate with barrettes, beaded bobby pins, scrunches, hair bands, bandanas, clips and more. Clean up with **FUDGE**, **GRAHAM WEBB**, **H2O**, **MATRIX**, **REDKIN**, **SEBASTIAN** and all the shapes and styling products you need to create salon looks at home. Don't want to go home? Hop into a chair at the spa and salon where waxing, massaging, manicuring nails and facials are all part of the process. Expect to pay $35 for hair cuts but only $15 for manicures. Either one will cure the blues. Visit their other locations at Park Blvd. and the Tollway in Plano (972/248-1480) or their newest in Frisco at 3211 Preston Rd. (972/668-4290)

★★★★ Beauty Smart   972/596-2673
3100 Independence Pkwy.   Mon-Fri 9:30-7; Sat 9:30-6; Sun Noon-5
Plano, TX 75025

Banish those blemishes. With savings of up to 40 percent, they just might get you to blush. Bob Berliner's new gig is called Beauty Smart, the official new name of the former Beauty Mart. Carrying an oasis of mainstream beauty products, as well as some new ones you might not know; at these prices, you should be willing to give them a try. If not, stick to **L'OREAL**, **PAUL MITCHELL**, **REDKIN** and **TONY & GUY**—all with fabulous price tags. But if doing your own thing is not your style, try their full service salon. That should "do" it!

◆◆◆ Beauty Store & More   972/867-6888
1900 Preston Rd.   Mon-Fri 9-8; Sat 9-7; Sun Noon-6
Plano, TX 75093

We are the world, we are the children and we can look our best by shopping at Beauty Store and More. Why more? Because this location is not only concerned with preserving your natural beauty, but the environment as well. Save $1 each time you recycle containers and bring them in for refills. Set out for a barrage of beauty supplies from **BAIN DE TERRE**, **BIOLAGE**, **BROCATO**, **JOICO**, **MATRIX**, **NEXXUS**, **PAUL MITCHELL**, **REDKEN**, **SCHWARZKOPF**, **SEBASTIAN** and **VAVOOM**. In this jungle of beastly beauties, we found some new additions such as **JINGLES**, **LANZA**, **TRI** and **UPPER CANADA**. And if you've heard the latest buzz about the **BUMBLE & BUMBLE** line, they've got it, along with cosmetics, hair accessories, brushes, nail products and more. More? You want more? Okay, line up—their full service salon is a force to reckoned with. Take a stand at this location near Preston and Park Boulevard or make-up at the store in the Willow Bend Market on the southeast corner of Parker and the Tollway in Plano, 972/608-4444.

◆◆◆ Beauty Store & Salon   972/608-4444
5964 W. Parker   Mon-Fri 9-8; Sat 9-7; Sun 12-6
Plano, TX 75093

Want to turn heads? Then get the look that gets you noticed. Beauty Store and Salon has services for men and women. Get transformed in the rear (of the store that is) or do-it-yourself with products available for purchase. Find it all from wall to wall. From the bath to the vanity, head to toe, you can look smart as well as shop smart. The buzz is, they're even carrying the **BUMBLE & BUMBLE** line. Sweet as honey. Look fresh and renewed while the rest of the world is frazzled. Beauty Store & Salon is located just east of the Tollway and Parkwood Boulevard.

★★★ Beauty Supplies, Etc.
972/231-8848
718 Lingco Drive
Mon-Fri 9-5
Richardson, TX 75081

Mirror, mirror on the wall, who's got a great selection and fair prices on nail and hair salon products, after all? Beauty Supply, Etc. is this fair lady. Think about all the Dragon Ladies you know who love long nails? Add in those who like the polished look. And don't forget those who want to be painted in stars and stripes. Count on saving 10-20 percent off, no biggie, but at least you're not paying full price. If you're suffering from Manicure Depression, try on **ALPHA 9**, **DEVELOP 10**, **JESSICA** or **ORLY**—all the nail salon products around can be brought forth at this warehouse. We barely scratched the surface of nail care products when we ran across **CALVERT** nail dryers, polish, nail tips and accessories from **ESSIE**, **FORSYTHE**, **OPI**, **PRO FINISH**, **STAR** and more. No doubt about it, Beauty Supplies, Etc. is hands down the largest supplier in the Metroplex. Bring in a beauty license and save an additional 25 percent off their already discounted prices. Then, if nails are not your stock and trade, trade in your old school of thought for some "mane events". Choose brushes, rollers, hair colorings, shampoos, conditioners, frosts and highlighters, clips and pins—well, hair today, gone shopping tomorrow. Delivery and shipping during regular working hours and wax ecstatic over their vast inventory. Three blocks east of Central Expressway. *Call toll-free: 800/783-8898*

★★★★★
Discount Mail Order Pharmacies

Here are some discount mail order pharmacies for consideration:

www.DrugPlace.com
2201 W. Sample Road, Bldg. 9,
Suite 1-A
Pompano Beach, FL 33073
800/881-6325

www.RXusa.com
28-28 13th St.
Long Island City, NY 11101
800/798-7248

www.RXUniverse.com
5090 North Dixie Highway
Ft. Lauderdale, FL 33334
800/794-6490

www.USmedication.com
524 Clarkson Ave.
Brooklyn, NY 11203
877/624-5879

★★★★ Big State Drug
972/254-1521
100 E. Irving Blvd.
Mon-Fri 8-7; Sat 8-4
Irving, TX 75061

Texas is a Big State that makes a statement in itself. And so does this 50-year-old drugstore in downtown Irving. Remember a simpler time when sitting at the soda fountain with friends was a highlight of your day? Now, use this stop as a great break from the hustle and bustle, or kick back after a long day of shopping and unwind. You'll flip over the selection for breakfast, lunch or dinner (but make it an early supper since the grill closes at 5:45 during the week and 2:45 on Saturdays). Sip on old favorites including ice cream floats, malts and bottled sodas in cream-ale, orange cream, key lime and root beer. Now that's a refreshing change of pace. If you're still not energized to head out for another round of shopping, browse their great gift and card selection along with easy to find pharmaceutical items. Then head home for a nap in the hammock.

CBI Laboratories Outlet Store

972/484-3500

2055-C Luna Rd., Suite 138
Carrollton, TX 75006

Thurs-Sat 10-6

What woman would turn her back on a bubble bath? Not too many in my book, especially when they can get their bath products at up to 90 percent off. Want beauty—at the least? CBI is the warehouse that delivers the suds. Manufacturers of private label bath products for department and specialty stores across the country, their outlet will indulge your every fantasy. Be it skin care or bath gels, gift sets or shampoos, you can double the bubble without getting soaked. Save 50-90 percent off with products that retail for $15, for just 50 cents. No kidding. No dirty tricks. At the corner of Luna and Valwood Parkway, load up for gift-giving; or just load up for those private moments where lotions and potions, oils and bath salts, shampoos and gift baskets are scentsationally price. Add in the sister gift, paper and bag outlet and what you see is what you get! Note the reduced hours.

★★★★★ Fragrance World/Fragrance Outlet

972/241-9696

2588-A Royal Lane
Dallas, TX 75229

Mon-Sat 9-6:30

"A rose by any other name wouldn't smell this cheap," so says one happy customer. Probably the best smelling outlet in the Metroplex, expect an around-the-world cosmetics counter ride for a lifetime of fragrances and cosmetics at the closest thing to wholesale prices. If you're playing the Face Card, then you'll want to save 25-60 percent on cosmetics and skin care products from **CLINQUE, ELIZABETH ARDEN, ESTEE LAUDER, LANCOME, LA PRAIRIE, YSL** and more. Then, add on layers of perfume at up to 70 percent off from **ESCADA, GIORGIO, PASSION** and **WHITE DIAMONDS** (how do you think Liz got eight husbands going on nine?) For girls who love sweet-smelling guys, dab a little **ARAMIS, LAGERFELD, JOOP! PHOTO**, even old **MACKIE'S** back and see what spell can be cast. Be careful, there's even **POISON** lurking on a top shelf. Stop, I want to get off Stemmons, east of Harry Hines. Sure smells like a sweet deal to me. Great for gift-giving. Great for yourself. Why pay department and specialty store prices? Are you ready for that face-off yet?

◆◆◆◆◆ Makeup by Teisha

972/223-2646

Dallas, TX

By Appt. Only

This former back-up singer to Prince has as many talents as colors in Joseph's coat. She wears them all well, too. Add make-up and styling for photo shoots, TV appearances, wedding days and other special occasions to her list of credits. Talk about making even chubby cheeks herself look chic and sleek on TV despite the jowls, and I say, this woman's makeovers are magic. Call her, you'll love her inspirational get up and go and her makeup wizardry.

★★★★★ Medicine Program

573/996-7300

PO Box 520
Doniphan, MO 63935

www.instituteedc.org/pd370r4.txt

Looking for a way out of paying for prescription drugs if you really can't afford them? Well, download this book published by the Cost Containment Research Institute and find out which drug companies will fill your prescription for free. This publication offers an A to Z listing of manufacturers who have patient assistance programs. Most manufacturers do provide free medications but rarely publicize it. Since 46 million Americans lack health care insurance, if you're sick, you need a prescription. Of course, you can't proceed without your doctor's assistance. You can't just call in your **PAXIL** yourself. Make sure you check the manufacturer's shipping policy. Try to anticipate your needs in advance since shipping times vary. Another cost saver, if you're currently seeing a doctor, is to ask for samples.

★★★ Ogle School of Hair Design 214/821-0819
6333 E. Mockingbird, Suite 201 Tue-Fri 8:30-5:30; Sat to 5; Appt./Walk-ins
Dallas, TX 75214

For less pomp and circumstance, primp and take your chances at the Ogle School of Hair Design. If you've survived the school of hard knocks, then take a chance and have your locks done here, for less. Senior students, ready to make the grade and go out in the cruel, real world and triple their price, offer manicures, haircuts, perms, facials, pedicures—the whole nine yards. Expect services to start as low as $6 to about $30. Save at least 50 percent over the full salon menu. Teachers hover overhead so they're not left alone with the scissors.

★★★★ Oriole Barber Shop 214/651-0019
1923 Commerce Mon-Fri 7-5:30
Dallas, TX 75201

Return to the days of the buzz of the razor and a price for a good old-fashioned hair cut for under $10 bucks. Dream on, this is just for the cut but no facials, no manicures, no day spa procedures. Just plain vanilla snip and go. A decent haircut but if you want a shampoo, expect to shell out some more money. This barber shop has defied the 21st century sophisticated marketing campaigns and all the ambience you've come to expect in the unisex salons of north Dallas. Definitely a step back into a time warp and particularly popular with the no-frills downtown executive. Sing your own tunes and get yourself a haircut for a song.

◆◆◆◆◆ Parfumelle 817/731-6633
6441 Southwest Blvd. Mon-Sat 10-6
Fort Worth, TX 76132 www.parfumelle.com

If your favorite fragrance has been discontinued, lost for years, changed its packaging or name and you are hooked, who can you hire besides a Private Eye to track it down. Well, why not a Private Nose? They are the folks who specialize in finding those long lost scents that have gone by the wayside. Even if they've gone stateside, they can find it. You won't be saving money, it's the fact that you want it and can't find it, that you'll pay the price for gratitude alone. Their selection of perfumes and colognes is astounding. Almost every brand known to man (and woman) is available. Variety is the spice of smelling good, just the way you like it. This beauty tracer takes time, but it's worth it if they find it. After all, love is where they find it. Shipping's free. Now, for the new stuff that smells like a winner. It's called the **LAMPES BERGER**, magnificent crystal, porcelain and ceramic objects d´art miniature bottles/vases that capture and destroy odors with the addition of perfume. It also purifies the atmosphere and I predict an elegant replacement for pot pourri and **GLADE** plug-ins. The exquisite nuances of floral scents, sweet, spicy, classic or contemporary satisfy all tastes and can create the right ambiance to your home or office. And, too, they're now carrying an exquisite line of handbags that are both luxurious and egalitarian. Large bags, small bags, shoulder bags, bags of all shapes and sizes... bags for all uses and for all occasions and priced accordingly. *Call toll-free: 800/874-1118*

★★★★★ Perfumania
4321 I-35 North, #285
Gainesville, TX 76240

940/665-4124
Mon-Sat 10-8; Sun 11-6
www.perfumania.com

It's always nice to have your perfume precede you when you walk into the room and it lingers on after you've gone. If you want to smell your very best, you need to shop at the very best. And that means Perfumania and Perfumania.com. Online, it's the premier discount fragrance retailer and wholesale distributor specializing in the sale of genuine (not copycat) designer fragrances, bath and body products, cosmetics and skin care treatment and related gifts and accessories for men, women and children. The three S's are very much the operative words at this company: service, selection and savings on quality perfume, fragrances and related products. So, if you're not practicing safe scents, you better start with this scent-sational experience. You can shop in Gainesville, or online and save 20-60 percent. Bet you can't buy just one. There are hundreds, no thousands, to choose from. You won't have the benefit of biting on a coffee bean between whiffs, but then again, if you know what you like, stay home and smell the roses instead by shopping online. I did and saved on women's "NOA" by **CACHAREL**, "Theorema" by **FENDI** (to match my handbag), "Ferre" by **GIANFRANCO FERRE**, "Animale" by **ANIMALE PARFUMS** and "Cabotine" by **PARFUMS GRÈS**. Then, for the bath, I had to have a pair of bath gloves and a long back brush by **JEROME PRIVEE**…who else is going to scratch my back if I scratched yours? Here's to "Smelling the good life…at half the price!" *Call toll-free: 800/927-1777*

◆◆◆◆◆ Star College Of Cosmetology
120 N. Main
Grapevine, TX 76051

817/329-0222
Tue-Sat 8:30-5 (Appt. Suggested)
www.starcollege.com

Stars are born here and then they go off in the real salon world and charge two and three times what they charge right before they graduate. Grab 'em a month or two before they go out to the cruel, curl world. Experience a "do" here and other spa procedures at a fraction of the price. In fact, when comparing other beauty college prices against one another, Star College came out a-head! (pardon the expression!) Consider this your first lesson in cost-cutting! Who's doing the best for less? Start here.For a decent haircut, supervised by teachers, get out for a song. Sing $5 (thats with a shampoo included!) or $20 for a perm, and you'll carry a tune with a sparkle in your eye and rosey cheeks to boot! Facials, manicures and more are available by appointment only. They were rated as the number-one cosmetology school in Texas in 1998 and for good reason. **CORNELLA** and **REFLECTIONS** products are used and sold. If you're a student, they help you get a job once you've graduated. And, of course, they are licensed by the Texas Cosmetology Commission.

◆◆◆◆◆ Tip Top Nails
1071 W. FM 3040, #400
Lewisville, TX 75067

214/488-5292
Mon-Sat 9:30-7:30; Sun By Appt. Only

Once I get hoisted up into the spa pedicure chair and my feet feel the rush of the jacuzzi-like waves, I drift off to never-never land. When I awake, my feet, bunions and all, actually look presentable in public. I have reminded you for 30 years never to step foot outside your house without your toe nail polish on. You never know who you may run into and that little extra effort elevates you to the upper crust of society. For $15-$20 bucks, be a sport. You can look rich and your feet will be forever grateful. Since it's almost as cheap as what I used to do (glue and go), I now have beautiful nails thanks to Laura at Tip Top Nails. They do all the latest techniques, do it cheaper, faster, and as good if not better than the fancy salons. So, why not? The only thing I won't let them do is paint stars on my pinkie. There's a limit to my beauty regime.

◆◆◆◆◆ Toni & Guy Academy   972/416-8396

2810 E. Trinity Mills
Carrollton, TX 75006

Mon 9:30-5; Tue-Sat 8:30-5
www.toniguy.com

The only way to achieve "Beauty and the Least" is to get your name on their Academy's special hair sessions. Otherwise, you'll pay an escalating schedule for their services depending on the level of training of your stylist. Is he a Creative Director or an Apprentice? Their services are priced accordingly. You may even curl up and "dye" when you see what the real world spends at Toni & Guy's beauty empire worldwide. You will pony up no less than around $40 at the lowest end of the totem-pole hierarchy. Color for medium length hair can run $50-$80 and that's for partial color (a few strands here and there.) For full color, well, $65 to well over $100. Now, take a look again at that Clairol box and know that's your only solution (well, the Beauty Colleges are another). But never fear, there's the Toni & Guy Academy, located at Marsh and Trinity Mills in the Mills Point Shopping Center (look for Tom Thumb and Mr. Gatti's). Here, you can be dis-tressed for less by talented stylists who are still learning the Toni & Guy methodology. Since the academy has grown to such proportions, it is now open full-time. For a hair-blowing experience, haircuts are $15, $21 for highlights, $41 for coloring short hair, perms are $44—but for chemical treatments, you need to make an appointment for a consultation first. Dye jobs are priced upon request, after the review session. Call for appointment and wash those retail prices right out of your hair.

◆◆◆◆◆ Top Secrets 2000   214/363-0611

Studio Salons #34
10455 N. Central Expressway
Dallas, TX 75231

By Appt. Only
www.topsecrets2000.com

Jackie Harriel is a hair replacement specialist. You might even refer to her as a Hari Krishna. Turn to her if your life is filled with nothing but bad hair days. Let her work her magic, for men, women, even children. You have your choice—stock system or custom, but always at affordable prices. In fact, she prides herself on offering only discounted maintenance supplies which you'll need to keep it up...and on. No contracts, all hair problems welcome, ethnic hair care and professional styling means you can add oomph and volume to your existing baby fine strands, or if you have an absence of hair, they can make a really tressful contribution. If you feel like you're being held hostage by the Hair Club, give Top Secrets a call. You'll need to visit every two-four weeks for maintenance depending on how oily your scalp is and how often you shampoo. But then again, if you're not blessed with a Farrah Fawcett mane attraction, why not go for it?

★★★★ Ulta   972/612-6031

2432 Preston Rd., Suite 320
Plano, TX 75093

Mon-Sat 10-9; Sun 11-6
www.ulta.com

There's always a flier in my mailbox that lures me in the door with a free gift. Am I not their target audience, or what? Never mind, my last trip netted me a $20 sterling silver frame that was soon given as a bridal gift. I'm no fool when it comes to sharing my Beauty Secrets. Secret #1. Shop at Ulta (although I wished they would have called it Ultra because it's a whole lot easier to spell.) #2. Buy at Ulta. From all your favorite cosmetics, fragrances, skin care, hair and salon care products, bath and body stuff, small appliances...if it's related to keeping your up-do's up and your nails and toes polished down and smelling good all day long, consider one of the more than 1,500 products that are displayed along the aisles. But not all is good at Ulta. A big negative is their lack of shopping carts. Those little canvas bags don't cut it. Forget trying to duplicate the department store ambience and no shopping carts like at a discount (pardon the expression) stores. Shopping carts help load up on **CALVIN KLEIN**, **CONAIR**, **COTY**, **ELIZABETH ARDEN**, **FREEMAN**, **GIVENCHY**, **HOMEDICS**, **KNEIPP**, **MAYBELLINE**,

MURAD, NEUTROGENA, REMINGTON, SALLY HANSEN, SASSOON, YVES ST. LAURENT, well, everything we need at one time instead of schlepping to and from the check-out counter with armloads. Looking for a best friend in the beauty business? Make friends with Ulta. From nail polish to tips, lipsticks to **Q-TIPS**, there's 1,500 items to choose from. Lather up a storm with **GOLDWELL, IMAGE, JINGLES, NEXXUS, PAUL MITCHELL, PETER HANZ, TIGI, TRESSA** and more. Then give yourself a hand with **CREATIVE NAIL, POI, PEAU DE PECHE** or **ZOOM**. Mix in a few other brands like **FRANCIS DENNY, ULTIMA II** and more and you get the pretty picture. Most of the staff were knowledgeable about the vast products, what they do, and at least, where they are. And if it's a salon treatment that would "do," I won't split hairs here. You can get moderate hair cuts and manicures, but certainly not like a Super Cut and Go! Watch for periodic news inserts for great specials and gifts with purchase. Check directory or website for location nearest you. ***Call toll-free: 800/968-5823***

14

Beds & Mattresses

★★★★★ **A Fuller Mattress**
3305 Dallas Parkway, Suite 343
Plano, TX

This factory-direct clearance center (**FULLER** Manufacturer) carries several brand names besides their own, all sizes, at savings of 50-70 percent off. They even have custom sizes, 3/4 beds and antique beds to fill out their fuller, rounder selection. Fuller is the operative word, though, as their skills include updating your current mattress, or repairing it, which is the cheaper alternative than buying one new. They use the same "innards" as the national companies, such as the springs and coils, offer factory warranties, home delivery and all this with discounts, too? That's how the cow ate the cabbage at their other locations, too: 1614 E. Irving Blvd., 972/579-3261 and Traders Village on Daniel Dale Rd., Grand Prarie 214/535-4065.

★★★★ **American Wallbeds/Off the Wall**
2530 Electronic Lane, #702
Dallas, TX 75220

There's a lot of secrets hiding behind these walls. Looking to conceal a few notches in your bedpost? Putting together an affair of do-yourself wall bed parts can only happen at the **AMERICAN WALLBED**/Off the Wall store. No beating around the bush, or bed, getting down to the basics is what matters most. What you see is what you get with full size wall beds including frame and bunkie mattress starting at just $499. *Call toll-free: 800/223-1820*

★★ **Bedroom Shop, The**
2012 W. Pioneer Pkwy.
Arlington, TX 76013

Since 1966, top of the morning to you beckons that little ole man in the stocking cap. Bedroom Shop, with eight retail stores in the area, has been making mattresses so they can control the quality. They even own their own trucks so delivery standards are maintained. In addition to their manufactured mattresses, they offer adjustable electric beds (some with massagers) oak furniture, juvenile furniture (a much-overlooked segment) including those bunk beds with full-size futons that kids clamor for, brass headboards, footboards, frames even special frame fittings, waterbeds and specialty linens. Heads up! The adjustable beds here are moving out the door for $749 (compare that to Beds Galore in Arlington.) If you're still restless, try their own premium line of bedding. First-rate customer service is a priority here with their offering of a full 20-year, non-prorated warranty where most other manufacturers simply offer only ten. Not the cheapest, but not the most expensive either. Other locations in Duncanville, Fort Worth, Richardson, Hurst, Wichita Falls, Temple and Longview. *Call toll-free: 800/433-5360*

City Mattress Factory   817/834-1648
900 S. Haltom Rd.   Mon-Fri 8-5 ; Sat 9-4
Haltom City, TX 76117

It takes a Ph.D. in cartography to find this place (off 121, exit Haltom Road and go south for a 1/2 mile—across the railroad tracks, then around a curve) but your back will be forever grateful. Look for the second warehouse on the left, home to this Fort Worth renowned manufacturer of mattresses. Choose from their versions of the natural latex European mattresses that they call the **DUNLOPILLO SLEEP SYSTEMS** or consider the possibility of an adjustable bed that you can raise and lower at whim. Some of the bed names in Dallas society sleep on these custom mattresses (considered state-of-the-heart). 'Course, I'm not of the society that can afford anything I'd like. However, I do have an adjustable bed from City Mattress and they'll never get it "back." Why? Because it's the best mattress/bed system I have ever slept on. Up and down I go, like that old black magic called love. Save plenty of restless nights on any of **ROYAL SLEEP**'s products. Sleep like a king on a pauper's pay. You'll also be lulled to sleep on a vast variety of pillowtops, air mattresses (the kind Gary Collins promotes), even futons for as low as $159, the newest sleep sofas, soft-side waterbeds, inner spring mattresses for at least half the price at twice the value. Buy direct and save up to 70 percent. Are you still awake? *Call toll-free: 800/834-2473*

★★★★★ Dallas Mattress   972/423-7173
301 W.Parker, #118   Mon-Sat 10-8 Sun Noon-5
Plano, TX 75023

When you're sent to bed without dinner, it won't matter if you get to sleep on a Dallas Mattress. You'll be dreaming about a 12-course feast before you know it. Even on an empty stomach, these folks fill you up with a quality eight hours. For more than 16 years, they've been keeping the Metroplex snoozin' without losin' a good night's sleep. Brands like **KING KOIL**, **SEALY** (the futon collection) and **SERTA** fulfill all the requirements on your journey to dreamland. Listen to this one dream that came true——a Serta or King Koil queen pillow-top set for $299. Oops. Sorry. You snoozed, you lost out on the deal. So, pay attention next time you see their ads. Six locations to bed down with: Lewisville, N. Central Expressway in Allen, Irving, Dallas, Northwest Hwy. at Jupiter and in north Dallas, Frankfort at the Tollway.

★★★★★ Factory Mattress Outlet & Futons   817/346-4893
6236 McCart Ave.   Mon-Sat 10-6; Thu 10-8; Sun 1-5
Fort Worth, TX 76133   www.factorymattressoutlet.com

Not even a princess could feel a pea under these mattresses. Even if some of them are showroom samples, this gal will sleep sound just knowing we got a good deal. Say foo to other futon dealers that can't hold a candle to the selection of futons here. Don't be left in the dark, find it all, rest assured, from major mattress manufacturers, bunk beds, daybeds, iron beds, brass beds, kid's beds, all kinds of beds. Add those final touches with lamps and accessories to complete any ensemble. Bounce back with inner springs and more from **SEALY POSTUREPEDIC**, **SERTA** and **SPRING AIR**. Leap for joy with savings of

30-60 percent. Now, turn the lights off and go to sleep. One mile south of I-20 on McCart (second exit pas I-35 South, go over the bridge for one mile) and by that time, you should be pretty sleepy.

★★ Heavenly Sleep Shoppe   817/595-4205
1133 W. Pipeline Rd.   Mon-Sat 10-6; Sun 1-5
Pipeline at Melbourne
Hurst, TX 76053

Pull up a cloud or grab one of these mattresses, not much difference in the comfort. Drift off into a good nights sleep with **SEALY POSTURE PREMIUM** mattresses. Prices may not be exactly what you expect to find at these pearly gates, even if they do claim that "nobody sells for less." So what if they're pennies from heaven and not quarters. After all, a penny saved is a penny earned. And the angels here will go out of their way to provide divine customer service.

★★★★ Lone Star Mattress   214/630-0798
2348 Irving Blvd.   Mon-Fri 9-6; Sat Noon-6
Dallas, TX 75207

The one and only place to find a Texas-size deal on name-brand mattresses. OK, so nobody is perfect but who cares when you're saving big on mismatches, floor samples and discontinued lots? Do you really care if your box spring is the same pattern as the mattress? Sure hope not. Then you, too, can take advantage of **BASSETT**, **EASTMAN HOUSE**, **KING KOIL**, **SIMMONS**, **SPRINGWALL**, **THERAPEDIC**, **THOMASVILLE**, well you get the idea. But stock gets carried off quickly in this part of the country, so if you want a good nights sleep, get up early and head over to Lone Star Mattresses. You might even grab a deal on twin sets for $99, full sets for $129, queen sets for $149 and king sets for $199. Now that's a king size deal, even if you're a queen!

★★★★ Mattress Firm Clearance Store, The   972/401-9665
10699 N. Stemmons Frwy.   Mon-Fri 10-9; Sat 10-8; Sun Noon-6
Dallas, TX 75229   www.themattressfirm.com

Nobody sells **SEALY** for less. Certainly not this Sealy-owned chain of stores. Their low price guarantee, remember, is not the lowest price guarantee. Nevertheless, this is just one of 275 stores nationwide and growing. Print out $25-$75 coupons from their website and shop their more than 22 stores in the Metroplex. **STEARNS & FOSTER** is Sealy's high-end line and is available in the $899-$1,999 range for queen and king-size, sometimes less at their Clearance Store. Other more moderate models such as the Sealy Posture Premium cushion firm queen set was further reduced to $399 and got our attention on the day we visited. free delivery or bed frame with premium set purchase. One-year free financing with approved credit available. And all with three-hour express delivery, same-day, next-day, any day you want delivery. Join the many other firm believers in this mattress kingpin.

★★★ Mattress USA   972/424-0474
811 E. 15th St.   Mon-Sat 10-7; Sun Noon-6
Plano, TX 75074   www.mattressusa.com

If you've been shopping for mattresses lately, you know how difficult it is to compare "apples to apples" since manufacturers produce the same mattress under different labels. It's a challenge when every one of them claims to be offering a "low price guarantee." Well, we guarantee you'll bite into a good deal at Mattress USA. With 50 percent and more off, it's as American as apple pie. Top it off with a large selection of futons, daybeds, bunkbeds, iron beds, canopy beds, even futon and sofa accessories. Create your own comfort with custom-made mattresses that are available upon request. Choose from the readymades such as Chiropractic by **SPRINGWALL**, **KING KOIL**, **POSTURE BEAUTY** and **SIMMONS BEAUTYREST**. Take Central to 15th Street in Plano, one red light east to old town in Plano. See the USA at the northeast corner.

★★★★★ Mattressland

972/423-5656
Mon-Fri 10-7; Sat 10-6; Sun 12:30-5

6000 N. Central
Plano, TX 75074

In a world all their own, Mattressland will lull you sleep with their dreamy prices. Just because they're factory seconds, closeouts, liquidations or blemished doesn't mean they'll induce nightmares. Instead, take advantage of the savings. Believe me, a slight discoloration on the underside will not keep you awake all night. Hey, dreams are in black and white anyway and so are the prices. It's clear to see that when **BASSETT** pillow-top sets start at just $250, your dreams are finally coming true. But this is no fairy tale with **KING KOIL**, **SIMMONS BEAUTYREST**, **SPRING AIR** and **SPRINGWALL** stacked high in a plain Jane showroom. That's how a star sleeps well without worrying about paying a fortnight for that good night's sleep.

★★★★ North Texas Mattress & Futons

817/274-1266
Mon-Sat 10-7; Sun Noon-6
www.ntxmattressfuton.com

1615 W. Park Row
Arlington, TX 76013

Get into the z-z-z-zone at North Texas Mattress & Futons. Leave all those big players in the dust. This is where the game is played. Score big with savings on top-quality mattresses for beds and futons. Even the Cowboys couldn't break the frame on a "Sleigh Arm" futon. Toughest in the industry but so versatile, if folds into three positions. We gave big cheers for the "Portafino" futon available in golden oak, American oak, dark walnut and black finishes. There's a reason why the settlers proclaimed, "Go west young man, go west! It's how the war on high prices ended in North Texas. *Call toll-free: 888/652-8436*

★★★★★ Rest World Mattress Center

972/306-5555
Mon-Sat 10-8; Sun Noon-6
www.restworldinc.com

3920 Rosemeade Pkwy., Suite 180
Dallas, TX 75287-2443

Remember the prayer your Mommy taught you? Well, my version goes something like this: "Now I lay me down to sleep, I pray the Lord my soul to sleep." And boy do I! You, too, can "rest" assured. Hunker down for a peaceful night's sleep with a quality mattress from Rest World. They are a mattress outlet center offering brand name mattresses at a much lower price. You're guaranteed a better night's rest (or if you work nights, it could be a better day's rest) for much less. Of course, if you have a new born, well, you just may never get any rest for a while. Some of the best names in the mattress world, such as **BEAUTYREST**, **COMFORT-AIRE**, **FUTON COLLECTION**, **SEALY**, **SIMMONS** and **SPRING AIR** are waiting for delivery. And speaking of delivery, it's free. Wake-up fully rested after spending a night on their queen-sized pillow-top Beautyrest for $1,900. Yikes! Also known as the "do not disturb mattress." What about a **FOUR SEASONS** queen set for $700? Or a **SIMMONS BEAUTYREST** queensize pillow-top set for $699? For those on a budget, get the low down on a comfy Spring Air Champion for $230. Now we're talking cheap! Not only is Rest World a great mattress source, you'll also find headboards, bunk beds, daybeds, futons and more. They have one of the largest selections of futons in the Metroplex with prices starting as low as $99. If you don't see what you want on the showroom floor, browse through their extensive catalog, and they will have it ready for you within five business days. With six months interest free credit and no money down, there's no reason for not getting a good night's sleep! Sleep on it also at their other location at 2301 N. Central Expwy. Suite 182 in Plano (972/509-0555).

★★★ Rick's Bedrooms   972/840-3000
3010 S. Jupiter   Mon-Fri 10-8; Sat 10-7; Sun 12-6
Garland, TX 75041   www.ricksbedrooms.com

At Rick's Bedrooms, it's more than waterbeds but that is certainly what brought them fame and fortune. Now, shopping for budget bedroom furnishings is part of his empire of options. With four stores in the Dallas/Fort Worth area, you can do some window shopping online, and then shop in person. From futons, waterbeds, waterbed accessories, bedroom furniture and name-brand mattresses, you should be a sleeping beauty in no time. Inexpensive bedroom furniture, **SIMMONS BEAUTYREST** mattresses and more are available in any of their four locations; Addison, 15300 Midway, Plano, 901 W. Parker and Mesquite, 3501 Gus Thomasson. *Call toll-free: 866/RICKS BEDS*

★★★★★ Sweet Dreams Bedding Co.   817/790-8510
4125 S. I-35 W   Mon-Fri 9-5
Alvarado, TX 76009

No need for soothing lullabies, **SWEET DREAMS BEDDING COMPANY** is all the comfort you'll need. No need to fuss over several labels because Sweet Dreams is the manufacturer of futons as well as mattresses used in the hospitality industry. Your questions and comments are always welcomed since production of these mattresses both meet and exceed the industry standards of quality name brands. If you remember having a good night's sleep while staying at a Marriott hotel, you've slept on a Sweet Dreams mattress. See, I told you. When you're tired, you don't look for the designer name before you get some shut-eye. The quality of their mattresses generally exceed industry standards established by the major brands. Have any mattress delivered FREE in the Metroplex. Just call for a price quote.

World of Sleep/Simmons Mattress Outlet   214/631-3257
1290 Conveyor Lane   Mon-Fri 10-7; Sat 10-6; Sun Noon-5
Inwood Trade Center   www.simmons.com
Dallas, TX 75237

Hopefully, you're lucky in love and lucky in…bed with a good night's sleep. Well, I can guarantee if you shop at the Simmons Outlet now called World of Sleep Mattress Outlet, off Inwood and Stemmons, in the Inwood Trade Center, you will rest easy. After all, they've been making mattresses for more than 125 years. This company has been manufacturing bedding and inventing products we consider commonplace today, including the Hide-A-Bed sofa in 1940. In fact, during the war, they made 2,700 different items, from parachutes to bazooka rockets. They are also credited with being the first mattress company to introduce a super size mattress in 1958. Now basketball players can sleep comfortably, too, without having half a leg hang over the side. Two years later, Simmons began manufacturing both queen and king-size mattresses that today outsell twins and doubles. Now, you, too, can have the benefit of all their innovation and industry "know-how" at outlet prices? Don't re-coil; these are all genuine Simmons mattresses that often appear at 60-70 percent off retail. They offer their "Do-Not-Disturb famous "Beautyrest" mattress as well as their other models such as the "Back Care", "Maxipedic" and "Ultimate Supreme" where it's common to see savings of hundreds of dollars. Queen sets started as low as $199; king sets started at $350. Visit their second location at 1144 Plano Rd., Suite 100, Richardson (Arapaho Station), 972/690-4270. Same hours and same great products.

15

Boats & Supplies

★★ Barber Boats
10220 Harry Hines Blvd.
Dallas, TX 75220

214/357-8294
Mon-Sat 9-6
www.barberboats.com

Some of us always end up in the same boat. The wind has been let out of our sails or there's no more gas in our "gitty-up." If this sounds familiar, the perfect place to sail is Barber Boats. They are true life-savers offering quality boats and boating accessories along with a parts and service department that provides excellent service with better than starboard prices. Prices and service are appealing to even the most discriminating a-fish-ionado. Anybody can learn to go boating. Nothing much has changed over their 49 years in business, but then again, they've never had a "Hitch in their Gitty-up." It's full throttle ahead with Barber Boats if you are looking for quality boats, boating accessories, and repairs at better than excellent prices to his customers. The parts and service department maintain the standards that fishing folks are accustomed to when traveling by boat. Keep yourself afloat on the high seas by not paying retail. You can get cookin' in a **BAYLINER**, **MISTY HARBOR**, **RANGER** and other brand name boats. Want something a little different? Maybe a pontoon for the company picnic would be fun? Check out the outboard collection, too, for out-of-the-water prices that won't drown your budget.

★★★★★ Defender Industries, Inc.
42 Great Neck Rd.
Waterford, CT 06385

800/435-7180
Mon-Fri 9-5; Sat 9-3 EST
www.defenderus.com

The defenders of the sea since 1938, if you're an *Old Man and the Sea*, you might as well set your sights on saving on over 100,000 products for sailboats, powerboats, water lovers and outdoor explorers. Try fishing through the sea of brand names including **ANDERSON WINCHES**, **BOMAR**, **CANNON**, **DOUGLAS GILL**, **JENSEN**, **KEEP ALIVE**, **LEWMAR WINCHES**, **MERCURY**, **NIKON**, **PENN REELS**, **PIONEER**, **POMPANETTE**, **PUR**, **SEA**, **SCANDVIK**, **TIMEX**, **UNIDEN**, **VILLAGE MARINE**, **XM YACHTING**, **ZODIAC** and more. Land ho—jump aboard for **MUSTANG** floater vests and drop anchor with **SIMPSON LAWRENCE**. Then again, there's no need for a life raft with their low price guarantee, which simply states that if for some reason you do find it for less, they will match it or even beat it. The categories are oceanic: Boats & Motors— Inflatable Boats, Outboard Motors; Clothing— Foul Weather Gear, Shoes, Boots, Gloves; Computers (huge savings on **PANASONIC** & **IBM** computer packages; Computer Software including accessories, navigational software); digital charts, inverters (hey, I thought those were belly buttons?), computer cases; electronics (GPSs, VHF, chartplotters; electronics); Entertainment like stereos, speakers; fishfinders; fishing gear— **DAIWA** reels, **KEEPALIVE** tanks, pumps; fishing gear—**MILLENNIUM GROUPER** rods, fish bags, squid strips (ever seen a squid strip live?), Fishing gear like **PENN** Reels, **MILLENNIUM** offshore rods, custom reel engraving; fishing gear-reel clamps, battle stix, trolling rods; galley—dishes; water heaters; marine toilets; binoculars, BBQs, coolers, cameras, bikes; safety equipment, man overboard modules, PFDs, first aid kits, rigging bags, riggings, knife ladders, tethers; sailing-cordage, mooring pennants, winches; ventilation-fans, air conditioners...if you can't find it here, you might as well forget walking on water! If you prefer, they'll even download their catalog without drowning in overload. Visit their special clearance center for even bigger bargains on discontinued, overstocks and one-of-a-kind items. And if naming your own price floats your boat, than visit their online auction area. Even insurance can be arranged by visiting Defenders Industries—a trusty guardian against today's wave of high prices.

◆◆◆◆◆ Holloways   214/823-5888
4221 Ross Ave.   Mon-Fri 9-3; Sat 10-2
Dallas, TX 75204-5199

Don't want to be ripped off if your car or boat's got a rip in a seat? Don't shed alligator tears just for a little tea and sympathy. Here's your remedy for those wounds. Ask for Ronnie, as he's the expert. He'll come to your location if it's not too far (and Carrollton was OK from his shop on Ross). Or, you can bring the car or boat to him. No charge for estimates and they'll be very accommodating around your schedule for an appointment. They can really sew it up right. For an eight-passenger boat, it would cost approximately $50 a seat (and that included a moderate yet appropriate fabric) and would take only about five days start to finish. Now, how's that to buoy your spirits. The price would go up if you chose a more expensive fabric or if the seats needed reconstruction with new plywood. But if ever there was an easier guy to work with, we haven't found him. He prefers to leave by 3 PM to avoid that downtown jam, but he's flexible, especially if he comes to your location. Sew, what are you waiting for?

★★★★ Marine Max   817/465-9595
808 W. I-20   Mon-Sat 9-6
Arlington, TX 76010   www.marinemax.com

With more than 50 stores coast-to-coast, it's time for you to join the Marine's. No, not that kind, the kind that doesn't send you to boot camp. After all, if they don't have a boat for you to float, then sit down, sit down, you may be rockin' the boat! Choose from **BAJA**, **BOSTON WHALER**, **CENTURY**, **HATTERAS**, **LOWE**, **MALIBU**, **SEA PRO**, **SEA RAY** and **STRATOS**—from fishing boats to yachts, they have something that you can launch, I guarantee it. No hassle trials at sea or on water can be arranged if you're not too sure of your favorite make or model. And the sale's not complete just because you've signed on the dotted line for a boat. These folks include with the sale, fenders, dock lines, PFDs (life jackets), fire extinguishers, flare kits and anchors which go hand and hand with a full tank of gas. They'll even go so far as to put your name and hers on the appropriate place. If you buy a Sea Ray Sport Cruiser, Sport Yacht or Yacht, you also get a two-year preventative maintenance agreement. Boats can be picked up and dropped off for service but they also provide mobile dockside service right to your floating doorstep. Now that you're a member of the Marine Max family, editions of *Gateways* will be sent to your home throughout the year. If you can't afford a new boat (or crew), why not take advantage of the great rates on used boats or check them out online for frequent boat auctions. (And I'll be happy to sign on board to steer!) Launch a deal from their other location, too, at 1491 E. Hill Park Road Route 3, Lewisville, TX 75056, 972/ 625-9979. Anchors away!

★★★ Pro Bass Shops/Outdoor World
Grapevine Mills
Grapevine, TX 76051

972-724-2018
www.basspro-shops.com

Without a doubt, the design, style, and ambiance of Outdoor World will make a visit here worthwhile if all you want to do is walk through. However, lest we forget, they sell stuff as well. A lot of stuff. So much stuff, you need a field trip pass for an all-day outing. There is virtually everything for every outdoor activity known to mankind. This includes boats and boating/watersport accessories, camping, hiking, fishing, hunting, bowhunting, golf (complete with putting green and driving range), footwear, general outdoor clothing, specialty clothing, supplies and gear, and a gift section with artwork, books, audio and video tapes. It's one serious destination location, located in the land-locked center of the Dallas/Fort Worth metropolis. Bass Pro Shop Outdoor World is convenient to get to and escape from city life surrounded by other great attractions, dining and lodging. Of course, neighboring Grapevine and Lewisville Lakes are incentives to think water sports. Folks fly in, drive in, sail in and even drop in since it's so close to the airport and Grapevine Mills. Opry Land and a string of more hotels are on their way. Don't leave town without at least taking a shot at this incredible blend all of the spending money modalities: entertainment/education/shopping. Money saving, well, we've never landed a big one here to either brag about much less exaggerate!

★★★★★ Show Me Fly Shop
1301-B Rayce Drive
Greenwood, MO 64034

816/623-9460
www.showmeflyshop.com

Fly me to the moon or show me the fly shop, either one's a must stop. If you're reeling from the high cost of fly fishing equipment, the Show Me Fly Shop is your one-stop, online discount source. Why buy at Show Me Fly Shop? It's simple. You'll save up to 40 percent. In fact, show them a better price at another fly shop, and they'll beat it, guaranteed! What a selection! Fly rods, fly reels, breathable waders, boots and other fishing equipment at unbeatable prices. Accessories are another plusincluding flies, fly samplers, floatant and dressing, fly boxes, fly fishing outfits, fly lines and backing, fly tying tools, leader and tippet, library nets, rods, traveling cases, vests, waders, wading boots, wading gear and more. They only sell quality products from the most reputable manufacturers: Fly fish with **CORTLAND**, **DIAMONDBACK**, **FLY-TECH**, **GRIFFIN ENTERPRISES**, **HARDY**, **STH REELS** and others with a 100 percent money-back guarantee. Of course, their site is both secure and user-friendly with a hassle-free ordering experience. They provide flexible payment options should you choose and a toll free hotline. Same day, flat rate ($4.50) shipping on all orders received during normal business hours. Once your order is received, an e-mail is sent with a tracking number so you can check the order status directly from their home page. They do it up right so isn't about time you fly right! Stay tuned as their product line will soon be expanding with products from **J.W. OUTFITTERS**, **SCIENTIFIC ANGLERS** and more. *Call toll-free: 866/FLY-RODS (866/35* 🇺🇸

★★★★ Travis Boating Center
1320 S. Stemmons Frwy.
Lewisville, TX 75067

972/436-BOAT
Mon-Fri 8-5:30; Sat 8-5
www.travisboatingcenter.com

Bigger better bargain boats, that's Travis Boating Center all right. When you're the biggest discount boating chain in the country, you've got a right to boast. When the water gets chopping, you can feel secure in the knowledge that you haven't gone overboard in spending too much for the boat. No wonder they brag about giving you a line. They carry **BAYLINER**, **FISHMASTER**, **LARSON**, **LOGIC**, **PROMASTER**, **RANGER**, **SEA-ARK**, **SILVERTON**, **STARCRAFT**, **WELLCRAFT** and more. How could you ever go on without a **BEACHCOMBER** or **CREST** pontoon? What about a **CARVER MOTOR** or

CRUISER yacht? Then again, life is pretty dull without knowing a few Basses or two. So what about a **SPRINT** bass boat? I brag about going out with a **BASS**, you can, too. Travis also powers up with **EVIN-RUDE**, **JOHNSON**, **MERCURY MERCRUISER** and **VOLVO** stern drives. Whether your looking for a yacht to take you into the deep blue sea (although that would be quiet a ride from Dallas) or duck boats, fishing boats, bay boats or a ski boat, you can expect Travis to be your onboard pass. Located just south of Bennett Lane. An additional location in Arlington, 1900 E. Division St., 817/265-3232 but hours at this location changes seasonally so call ahead.

16

Boots & Western Wear

Beads Beautiful/Wanted
106 W. Walnut
Decatur, TX 76234

940/627-7394
Mon-Sat 10-5

Wanted—bred or alive! **WANTED!** is the label that has made Beads Beautiful a name that opens doors in Southwestern circles. If you're looking for the perfect western outfit to wear to the Cattle Baron's Ball, look to Decatur-for the look that separates the women from the girls. Shop Beads Beautiful's outlet store for factory pricing on ladies' dresses, skirts, jackets, vests, fringed outfits and silk broomstick skirts, all hand-painted or decorated by on-site artists. In front of their factory, there are other labels hanging around promenading out with their own factory overruns, discontinueds, overstocks and last-season items. Look for **BRIGHTON**, **MICHAEL LOO** and handcrafted Indian jewelry, for example, that will indeed add that extra oomph. Watch heads turn as you make your grand entrance. And, if you're clamorin' for a western wedding, they make custom bridal ensembles, too, from the white dresses to the tuxedo shirts or hats for you and your beloved. Expect to see these clothes in specialty stores that cater to high-fallutin' rodeo queens. Save up to 75 percent and since you've probably not visited Decatur recently, here are some recommended cafes if you've worked up an appetite: The Courthouse Cafe and Mattie's Buffet are almost worth traveling to just tor the cheap eats. Beads Beautiful is a multi-million success story started by two women 18 years ago in a garage. See, anything's possible with a little grit! *Call toll-free: 800/959-WANT*

★★★★★ Boot Town
2821 LBJ Frwy.
Farmers Branch, TX 75244

972/243-1151
Mon-Sat 9-9; Sun 11-6
www.boottown.com

Kick up your heels and move 'em on out. Boot Town is the premier discounter in this part of the woods. Snuff out the competition with snuff can lids for $19. Or buckles as low as $30. If you really are out doing the town, consider a **COMSTOCK** buckle for $725? (Over my dead body!) **ACME**, **DAN POST**, **DURANGO**, **JUSTIN**, **LAREDO**, **LARRY MAHAN**, **LUCCHESE**, **NOCONA**, **RIOS**, **TONY LAMA**—over 30 top brands: belts from plain to exotic skins (lizard, snake, ostrich, antelope, cowhide and more) in sizes that'll knock your socks off! Clothing and accessories from key rings to outerwear, watches to wallets, wrist bands and hats, even snuff (oops, I mean stuff) for kids. Let 'em play the part with their own sized hats, toy gun sets and collectable **BREYER HORSES**. Dress up a room with western sculptures or show your true colors with a 16-piece set of western dinnerware for $99. Then, back to the basics. **TRINITY RIVER** snake skin boots, $99, **HORNBACK** alligator boots in your choice of skin or tail, only $299. JUSTIN calfskin and bullhide western boots were $99 and full-quill ostrich ropers were $369. Sizes 6 1/2-13 for men, 4-10 for women and children's sizes, too. Tip your **RESISTOL** hat alongside other major brands and western shirts and jeans by **LEVI'S**, **PANHANDLE SLIM** and **WRANGLER**. Ever worn a pair of **WOLVERINE** durashocks? They're guaranteed to be the world's most comfortable boot—you be the judge, old bunion toes. Boot Town has been kicking up their heels for the past 21 years, with seven locations in the Metroplex. To rope your boots and westernwear by mail, order from their FREE catalog. Locations throughout Texas, in Houston, San Antonio and Austin. ***Call toll-free: 800/222-6687***

★★★ **Cavender's Boot City**   **817/589-7311**
857 W. Pipeline Rd.   Mon-Sat 9-9; Sun 11-6
Hurst, TX 76053   www.cavenders-boot-city.com

Little did James Cavenda know when he started his westernwear store in 1965, it would grow to become the world's largest boot company in Dallas. With over 40 stores, you wouldn't be caught dead without getting dressed in true Texas fashion. Still family-owned and operated, they have it all: boots, westernwear, jeans, home accessories, purses, wallets and stuffed animals. Somehow, too, there's usually a Bennigans, Fridays or Olive Garden nearby. There's always something on sale. Whether it's 20 percent off all **WRANGLER** oxford shirts or **TONY LAMA** smooth ostrich boots, $178. You won't have to be a scavenger when you look for boots at Cavender's. Though huge, it's easy to pick a pair or two from their well-organized racks. You'll find **ACME**, **ARIAT**, **DAN POST**, **JUSTIN**, **LUCCHESE**, **NOCONA** and **TONY LAMA** starting as low as $49 and up, and keep going. **DAN POST** lizard boots were $219 and a pair of bullhide western boots were $99 (retail $129). Racks and racks of western duds like shirts and jeans by **CINCH**, **LAWMAN**, **PANHANDLE SLIM**, **ROPER** and **WRANGLER** as well as women's duds by **LAWMAN**, **ROCKY MOUNTAIN** and **WRANGLER**. Straw hats, belts and buckles and workboots by **DOUBLE-H**, **DURANGO** and **WOLVERINE** made our work day fly by. Selection rates a big "Hee Haw," but their prices are a yawn, except during sales. Check the directory for multiple Metroplex locations. It's been rumored that if you make them an offer, they usually don't refuse. (No horse's head on my pillow, please.) (They are big Elvis fans)Basically....they have everything!.

★★ **Circle C Western Wear**   **817/237-7111**
7640 Jacksboro Hwy.   Mon-Wed, Sat 10-8; Thu-Fri 10-9; Sun Noon-6
Fort Worth, TX 76135

You can circle the Metroplex but you'll land a square deal at Circle C Western Wear in Fort Worth. Their men's department and boots (**COWTOWN**, **DIAMOND J**, **DOUBLE H**, **JUSTIN**, **REDWING**, **RHINO** and **WOLVERINE**) make it worth your while. But they've also surrounded themselves with western home accents, Montana jewelry, belts, buckles, hats and a hat bar that creases hats right on the spot. Lest women think they've been forsaken, there's women's' clothing, purses, western furniture and a line-up of restaurants to keep your appetite satisfied. So, if you're looking for clothes in all the wrong places, this may well be the place to head. Turn down Jacksboro Highway just northwest of I-820 if you want a detour from high prices on westernwear. Not only that, they sure are friendly in them thar parts!

★ **Foster's Westernwear/Saddle Shop**   **940/383-1549**
6409 N. I-35   Mon-Sat 9-6:30;
Denton, TX 76207

Located just north of Denton Factory Stores and Loop 288 on I-35, while heading north to the ranch, stop by and say "Howdy, pardner!" Foster a relationship with this family-owned ranch store especially if you're living, learning or ropin' in Denton County. When classes resume, there's usually a line outside their door. **DOUBLE D** and **WRANGLER** clothing takes a front and center position for the entire family. Leather coats and jackets, a must. And of course, you've got to have a pair of boots that were made for walkin'. From **DAN POST**, **JUSTIN** and **TONY LAMA**, be it a pair of ropers, lace-ups or full quill ostrich, it's your call. Add in the saddles and tack for a well-rounded ride and lastly, bring out your western jewelry. You can't leave home without it. What will the neighbors think? Look after those feet and cultivate an entirely new western look from Foster's Westernwear and Saddle Shop.

★★ **Just Justin**   **214/630-2858**
1505 Wycliff Ave.   Mon-Fri 10-8; Sat 10-7; Sun Noon-6
Dallas, TX 75207   www.bootsforless.com

Did you know that when buying boots, you take a half size less than you normally wear in street shoes? And that's without even dieting! Don't you just love it. **JUSTIN** boots for kids started at $39, though most ran $49 and $59. You just can't get away cheap. Same with grown-up models. Lots to choose in the same price range. Expect discounts to range anywhere from 40-70 percent off list. More than 20,000 pair in stock so they mean business. Don't expect any other brand other than **JUSTIN**. Ask for their FREE catalog and try your hand at ordering for your feet. They know how to fit you site unseen just by knowing your shoe size. Returns are accepted if you are dissatisfied—just don't scuff the soles. If you wear them and there's a defect, they will gladly accept returns or exchange them. Shipping's preset at $10 a pair regardless of where you live. Expect to be out two-stepping in about a week to 10 days, if ordering by mail. *Call toll-free: 800/292-2668*

★★★★★ **Justin Boot Outlet Store**   **817/654-3103**
717 W. Vickery Blvd.   Mon-Fri 9-5:30; Sat 9-5
Fort Worth, TX   www.justinboots.com

W4hen this hometown favorite shut down their manufacturing site in Fort Worth, we were a little nervous they'd move the outlet store to El Paso, too. Thank goodness they didn't. Right off I-30 in downtown Fort Worth, exit Commerce to Jennings, then turn left. Continue on to West Vickery and turn right. You'd think they'd make it easier for us die-hards, but no. Bargain shopping does have its drawbacks. But then, once you've found them, you'll see that life is good again. You'll get a kick out of their brick building with a big red boot that beckons you inside. Buy boots for the entire family. And the prices, well, it just doesn't get better than shopping at the outlet.Slip into a stupendous selection, but there's nothing but irregulars, small blemishes and defectives. Still, who can see? Sure could have fooled me. Their motto, "For wherever life takes you," supports their Justin Cowboy Crisis Fund (a non-profit organization that helps injured rodeo athletes) whereby they give 100 percent of all donations to this group. And that's straight from the horses mouth—George Strait's, that is. What started by H.J. Justin in 1879 is still going strong today. **JUSTIN** boots are handcrafted today with each pair built and inspected one at a time to ensure quality with every stitch. Justin boots is Texas!

★★★★ Justin Discount Boots   940/648-2797
101 FM 156   Mon-Sat 9-6
PO Box 67
Justin, TX 76247

JUSTIN has become a discount town with Justin Discount Boots leading the way. If you're ready to boot, scoot it to Justin—they're ready when you are. Check out their FREE color catalog for probably the most extensive western collection of apparel, accessories and boots in the country - maybe the world. See how the West was really won—from work boots, ropers or exotic skins (bullhide, lizard, ostrich and shark) in men's, women's and children's boots. Have your Just-in desserts and save money but not on them all. Now hear this. In this one store, it is estimated that they generate more than $60 million in revenues from a worldwide audience of westernwear devotees. If you head west, young man, to Justin, Texas, you, too, can see first hand how they continue to "rein" supreme. Since 1978, this Texas bastion has been rustling up the boots-by-mail or in person at their historic old Wallace Building in the town of Justin. The whole family can get in on the act. Westernwear, including all the famous brands and styles, from jeans, belts, jackets, purses and boots give you a leg up on the competition. Tip a **STETSON** hat, wear a **WRANGLER** shirt or pair of jeans, keep warm in a **COMFY** or **TEMPCO** goosedown jacket and wrap it all up with a silver buckle, belt tip and more. Note: not everything is discounted, I'm sorry to report. Some first-quality items are full price, though some irregulars are 30-60 percent off. Everything's all under one roof and you can check out prices by mail, phone or letter before heading west. If you don't wear it or scuff the soles, you can return it within 30 days for a refund or exchange. *Call toll-free: 800/677-BOOT*

★★★ Lone Star Boot Outlet   972/445-0277
3209 E. Carpenter Frwy.   Mon-Sat 10-9; Sun Noon-6
Irving, TX 75062

Swing your pardner to and fro, dosey-do and away we go. Let your partner take a rest, then it's to Lone Star Boot Outlet for some of the best. Footwear that is. With over 15,000 pairs of boots, Lone Star children can find their roots. Men and women will stomp their feet, when prices like these are such a treat. (On the wallet that is.) Ok, enough of the ho-down, here's the lo-down on prices. Boots are priced as low as $39 and all the family favorites are here, too. Rope in a good deal on traditional and trendy western wear. Paint on a pair of jeans, lace up those boots and head on out in button-down-long sleeve shirts by the bushels. Glitter and shine with buckles, hats, jewelry, gifts, accessories and more. Swing on in with **CODE WEST**, **DAN POST**, **DURANGO**, **JUSTIN**, **LAREDO**, **NOCONA**, **RESISTOL**, **ROCKY MOUNTAIN**, **ROPER**, **STETSON** and **WRANGLER** and line up for special orders on even **ARIAT**. You can boot and scoot your way through these doors near Texas Stadium or visit them in Dallas on I-30 just west of Buckner Blvd. and in Hillsboro near the Prime Outlet Center on I-35.

★★ Master Hatters   972/276-2347
2355 Forest Lane   Mon-Sat 10-6
Garland, TX 75042

How many hats could the mad hatter have if the madhatter bought his from the Master Hatter? Well, at these prices, twice as much. Please don't be mad but this is a family matter. The Cook family offers the perfect topper for a sunny day. Straw hats for men and women are their forté, starting as low as $24.95. But if you want to call out all the big guns, they also carry a variety of cowboy hats in sizes 6 3/4-7⅞. Whether you've got a big head or not, you can protect your scalp with a sun shade made in Texas. You'll also go wild for the westernwear selection. From the **WRANGLER** brand to less familiar names, you'll find that all of their jeans come from good genes. All are first-quality and sell for $20-$25, with irregulars as low as $15. Just look for them through the forest on Forest just east of Shiloh.

★★★★★ Mistletoe Boot Shop   214/946-0049
942 E. Jefferson Blvd.   Mon-Sat 9-5
Dallas, TX 75203

Give me that ole time religion and pair of boots from Mistletoe Boots and kiss paying retail good by. Of course, the good buys are good riddance with prices starting as low as $20 in a variety of sizes, styles, shapes, colors and brands. This Oak Cliff shrine is a throw-back to the '60s when life was easy and the men all wore cowboy boots because they liked them instead of wanting to be a fashion plate. Mistletoe Boot has been in my book since 1972 and they remain a stalwart in the world of bargain shopping. Since World War II, they've been a cowboy's last stand. You, too, can win the war on high prices if you're in the market for babies', children's, men's and women's boots. Mistletoe Boot has been right out there in the trenches, selling closeouts, discontinueds, seconds, going-out-of-business liquidations and manufacturer's rejects in brands such as **ACME**, **DAN POST**, **JUSTIN**, **LAREDO**, **PANHANDLE SLIM**, **TONY LAMA**, **WRANGLER** and more, even an occasional **DOUBLE-H** work boot. Don't expect the brands to always be there, or that you'll find more than a few choices in your size (especially the larger sizes). Call ahead so you won't be disappointed. And I'm warning you. This is not an elegant setting. Expect each of the rooms to be outfitted in different flooring materials, wood rotting in places, lights dim, rickety benches to sit on, after all, you're not shopping on Fifth Avenue. But this Oak Cliff beige building has been around for ages, and the rock of ages doesn't come tumbling down easily. You will be on firm footing so have at it. There are hundreds and hundreds of boots to try on so unless you prefer the boxes, surely you'll find one that's half price or less. Take I-35 south going towards Waco; cross the Trinity River bridge; take the second exit which is Jefferson. Bear right. It's one block down on the left hand side at the corner of 7th and Jefferson. It's a trip, but worth it.

★★ Rowan's Western Wear   903/887-3618
Highway 90 at 175   Mon-Sat 9-5:30; Fri 9-7
PO Box 571
Mabank, TX 75147

Being a proud sponsor of the Texas Wildfire Express Drill Team, Rowan is still goin' and growin' and staying involved in the Mabank community. They've just moved down the street about ¼ of a mile up the road on the right. You can't miss it. They still have the same big sign with the horse on it. Since things were moving right along, they decided to move to bigger and newer digs. Instead of being satisfied with a new store, though, they bought the entire shopping center instead, and leased out the excess space. These Rowan's are smart. And you can benefit from their sharp buying power. Head down scenic U.S. Highway 175, turn onto Highway 90 and you're practically there. Westernwear is the specialty at this house including **NOCONA**, **TEXAS** and **TONY LAMA** boots at a savings of 20-25 percent. **JUSTIN** lace-ups were placed at the check-out counter for $89.95 and ropers were just $79.99 (at least $20 less than most Dallas stores.) It pays to shop away from the maddening crowds that attract those big city slickers. Instead, head to the outskirts and snag straw hats for $29.95, a pair of **RED WING** work boots for $99.95 or a pair of **WRANGLERS** for $19.95. Lots of casual wear as they cater to lake goers in the area. Donnie and Sheila Rowan are still firm believers in the meaning of a fair and square deal.

★★★★★ Sergeant's Western World   972/406-9464

13600 Stemmons Frwy.   Mon-Sat 10-8; Sun 11-5
Farmers Branch, TX 75234   www.sergeantswestern.com

Get out the iron and brand this name on the closet doors. Sergeant's Western World has a huge
selection, great prices and nobody comes close to good old fashion customer service. Who would have
thought this Sergeant would have turned out to be such a softy. Lucky for us there was everything from
western apparel to show clothing, saddles to tack, horse equipment and everything in between. With
guaranteed low pricing, we'll take that. There's just far too much to list. But make a list and head on
over. You'll be sitting in the winner's circle with **SILVER MESA** saddles. And only available at Sergeant's
is the official saddle of the Appaloosa Horse Club. Looking for something a little different? We found
a sale on a **WILD WILD WEST 6** corner saddle for $4,999 that was originally $5,999 and a **JUSTIN**
peanut caiman cream crepe was $399 but originally sold for $699. Take a trip or make a day of it. Either
way you'll come out a winner in the war on high prices. Sergeant's Western World also has a
superstore in south Arlington just south of I-20 at 4905 S. Cooper St. *Call toll-free: 800/383-3669*

★★★ Sheplers Westernwear   972/270-8811

18500 LBJ Frwy.   Mon-Sat 10-9; Sun Noon-6
Mesquite, TX 75150   www.sheplers.com

Even if you're a "shlep," you can still shop at Sheplers Westernwear. With 50 years under their belt buckle, this westernwear department store has some of the best buys west of the Pecos River. Brands include
**ARIAT, BAILEY, CARHARTT, CINCH, DAN POST, DURANGO, LAREDO, LAWMAN, LEE, LEVI'S, LUC-
CHESE, JUSTIN, NOCONA, RENEGADE, RESISTOL, ROCKIES, ROPER, SAGE,
STETSON, TONY LAMA, WRANGLER** and many more. From top to bottom and everything in between,
you'll never have to rack your brain lamenting, "I've got nothing to wear," to the rodeo, to school, for
casual day, or to the ranch. The name Sheplers is synonymous with both the old and new West. From its
humble beginnings as a single store in Wichita, Kansas, Sheplers has an international reputation. If
you're a modern day cowboy or a gal who's a rugged individualist, you will find Sheplers a place to be
seen and outfitted. It's surely one of the largest western stores online. Off line, their bricks and mortar
stores have over an acre of selling space under roof so as to accommodate Sheplers' enormous inventory of boots, jeans, hats, western decor and apparel. But when you see racks of $10 shirts, jeans, closeouts
on hats and boots, that's when you become the leader of the pack and rack in the savings. Accessories,
too, make the man (and woman.) Recently, they were rated among the top 10 of all catalogs in the U.S.
for customer satisfaction. So, jump aboard. The stage coach is leaving soon. Giddy-up and laugh all the
way home. Call toll-free to order their catalog if you prefer to shop via the pages rather than online. Visit also at 2500 Centennial Drive in Arlington, 817/640-5055. *Call toll-free: 888/835-4004*

★★★★ Western Warehouse   214/634-2668

2475 Stemmons Frwy.   Mon-Sat 9-9; Sun Noon-6
Dallas, TX 75207   www.boottown.com

Different names, same folks. It's all in the family, so who cares? And when you know that the
family's in the Pink, you think, what a hoot! Another Boot Town in disguise owned by the Pink
family, a legendary boot and westernwear retailer. Downtown visitors coming to Market love to make a stop at this
Western Warehouse. It's geographically desirable and priced to pack away. Check it out. Savings on jeans,
westernwear and boots, well, do they have boots! We found **ABILENE, ACME, ARIAT, JUSTIN, LARRY MAHAN,
LUCCHESE, NOCONA, PANHANDLE SLIM** and **TONY LAMA** boots ready to roll out the barrel. Next, it's western
apparel. You can't walk out naked, so pick out a pair of jeans likes **LEVI'S** and **WRANGLERS** or **ROCKY
MOUNTAIN** jeans for women in every color imaginable. They go perfectly with **DIAMOND J** ropers at $39. Our

cowhand snagged a smooth ostrich Nocona boot for $179 rather than having to pay retail elsewhere at $249. We never counted, but there are claims of more than 50,000 pairs of boots in stock. Let me know if that's an accurate accounting. Rope other good deals in Dallas at 10838 Central Expressway in Dallas (214/891-0888), 2501 Centennial in Arlington (817/640-2301) and Grapevine Mills (972/355-8312). *Call toll-free: 800/222-6687*

★★★★★ Western Wear Exchange

817/738-4048

2809 Alta Mere
Fort Worth, TX 76116

Mon-Sat 10-6

You can count the consignment westernwear stores on one hand—no, with one finger. This is the one and only and for that reason, give them a round of applause. If you have something western and want to turn it into cash, there's no need for an appointment, just bring them in—in good condition, freshly laundered or cleaned and on hangers. This is the "Cadillac" of resale stores that specialize in westernwear. You'll make some money on those items that are still hanging in your closet and going unworn. Then, with the money you've made, grab somebody else's clothes and come home with a whole new wardrobe. Whether it's that pair of jeans or that leather vest, duster coat to Ropers, hats to shirts, boots to zoot scooters (isn't that something that cowboys wear on cattle drives or something like that?) Anyway, I grew up in Detroit and I still don't know a lot about cowboys except that I like them, they're handsome and rugged and have cute tushies. Whether you're a kid or a grown-up, there's something here for you. They've also expanded into home decorative western accents and jewelry. Still, the big deal is on the clothing, hats and boots. Rustle them up and tote them home. Your wardrobe and your budget will yell, "Whoopee!"

★★★★★ Wild Bill's Western Store

214/954-1050

West End Marketplace   Fri-Sat 11 AM-Mid.; Mon-Thu 11-10; Sun Noon-6
603 Munger St., Suite 321
Dallas, TX 75202

www.wildbills1.com

Meet Bill Dewbre and his wife, Drewe. Bill's the Wild Bill in the name and has been at the helm since 1977. Anybody that locates on the third floor of the West End Marketplace and guarantees the lowest prices in writing, even after the sale, has got to be worth noting. At least that's what they said, once. "Whether you need a $5 souvenir for your Aunt Martha or a pair of custom-made-to-measure boots, you'll find what you're looking for at Wild Bill's. Prior to opening in the West End, they were located across from Neiman Marcus in downtown Dallas for ten years, specializing in the convention, visitor and tourist business, which included supplying merchandise to meeting planners, associations and corporations and gifts to the VIP's. So, they've got a feel for the tourist as well as the local yokels. Enjoy a huge dose of Texas hospitality when you visit their store. Out-of-towners appreciate that Bill knows how to ship an eight- foot Texas longhorn or longhorn furniture anywhere or in-towners can trust to have it delivered to the suburbs. Wild Bill loves to also grab some media attention every once in a while. For one, they custom make boots for some famous celebrities such as Sylvester Stallone, Arnold Schwarzenegger, Bruce Willis and Chuck Norris. Now that's kickin' booty! They also can outfit your home or your car with a western motif. Go online to print coupons off. Examples: $5 off a purchase of $25 or more; $10 off a purchase of $96 or more and $20 off a purchase of $175 or more. Also buy one, get one $\frac{1}{2}$ price on T-shirts. The store's a great backdrop for a western photo, or the site for a deal on anything western, dude. *Call toll-free: 214/969-0134*

17

Bridal

★★★★★ **All for Less, Wedding Invitations and More**　　972/509-5368
Dallas, TX　　　　　　　　　　　　　　　　　　　　　　By Appt. Only
　　　　　　　　　　　　　　　　　　　www.allforlesswedd.cceasy.com

If I have but one party to plan, let me call Sharon Nichols at All for Less to help me make it through the night. Her attention to detail, the savings of 25-30 percent off every kind of invitation and all the extras that she makes available in person or online, you shouldn't plan a party without her. Leave your name and she'll return your call. She'll even give you the week you can expect to plan on getting together. Check your order online (even to see what it looks like before it's printed) so you won't get nervous wondering if you'll make it to the church before the invitations. Expect only the finest invitations and accessories at the best discounts in town. Take a walk down her aisles of wedding products: invitations, accessories, engagement announcements, bridal shower invitations, rehearsal dinners plus the full spectrum of greeting cards including, anniversary, birthday (for kids and grown-ups), calendars, congratulations, a new line of Courage Cards, get well, sympathy, thank you and more. Then, for personal or business use, what about letterhead, business cards, envelopes, mailing envelopes, customized stamps, advertising labels, **POST-IT**® notes, shipping labels, personalized labels, memo pads, well, make a note to call Sharon ASAP! And if you are looking for specialty and premium items, don't forget to peek at her selection: address books and planners, pens, T-shirts, mugs and cups If you want to promote your business, here's the place to place your bets.

★★★★ **Anderson's Schmalzreid Formal Wear**　　　972/423-4233
1201 E. Plano Pkwy.　　　　　　　　　　　　　　　Mon-Fri 8:30-6; Sat 9-1
Plano, TX 75074

Though it may be an even longer name to remember, you can still get the groom to share in the spotlight without looking too shabby. Great designer tuxedos from Anderson's Schmalzreid Formal Wear can make his day. Don't worry about pronouncing it, just remember that the price is right. And the styles are up there with the best of them. Whether you're walking down the aisle or taking a trip down the red carpet, don't forget to strut your stuff. This star-studded cast hangs around in **CHRISTIAN DIOR**, **PIERRE CARDIN** and **OSCAR DE LA RENTA**. If your looking for a stunt double, then you'll be equally impressed with **ANDREW FEZZA**, **PERRY ELLIS** and **RALPH LAUREN**. One mile east of Central Expressway on

Plano Parkway, pull up in the front parking lot and start thinking penguins! *Call toll-free:* **800/729-3718**

★★★★★ Anonymously Yours   214/341-4618
204 Abrams Forest Shopping Center   Mon-Fri 10-6; Sat 10-5:30
Dallas, TX 75243

Now that your secret admirer has revealed his true feelings and "finally" popped the question, pop on over to Anonymously Yours for big savings on resale gowns. Lets remember, these gowns have only been worn once. So why not take advantage of saving 50 percent or more. Put the savings towards your honeymoon. Who's to know at Anonymously Yours that the gown of your dreams was also the gown of someone else's dreams. Lots of styles to fit any occasion and just about any waistline with sizes ranging from 4-24. A perfect 10 (or at least a size 10) can walk away in their large selection of sample gowns.

Bridal Co. Outlet   940/484-2660
Denton Factory Stores   Mon-Tue, Thu-Sat 10-7:30; Sun 1-6
5800 N. I-35, Suite 505   www.bridalco.com
Denton, TX 76207

What's in a name...but everything you've always wanted to know but didn't know who to ask. Here it is. A bridal outlet with a name you won't forget. Styles, service, selection, savings...talk about a grand slam, thank you ma'am. Don't even think....Aisle, Alter, Hymn. Designers that line up include: **ALFRED ANGELO, MARY'S, MORI LEE BRIDALS, SINCERITY BRIDAL, SWEETHEART GOWN** and many others that specialize in both bridal and evening wear. Does it matter they're 20-70 percent off retail? In my book, it does. For better or worse, right? Well, it just keeps getting better and better. Okay, the problem? Try deciding which one from the selection of 20,000! Take the walk for less. Don't worry, be happy. Sizes 4-44 should cover any woman who has decided on the state of matrimony.

★★★★★ Bridal Fashions Unlimited   817/589-1272
7290 Glenview Drive   Sat 10-6; Sun Noon-6
North Richland Hills, TX 76101

There are no boundaries with Bridal Fashions Unlimited. Whatever type of wedding you're planning, there's bound to be something from their vast selection of designer gowns that meet your criteria. Those same ones you've seen between the pages of all the leading bridal magazines but didn't think you could afford. Well, fancy this. All gowns are not created equal. Some are discounted 40 percent while others soar to 70 percent below retail. From satin to beads, there are racks and stacks for all your bridal party's needs. Sizes 2-28 should fit the group to a T with over 500 styles ready to be chosen. Hand-in-hand, down the promised land, be sure to check their clearance racks before you take off. Otherwise, you may miss the huge selection of gowns for just $99.99. This weekend-only event is closed Mon-Fri.

★★★★ Bridal Secrets   817/346-4848
6138 Westcreek Drive   By Appt. Only
Fort Worth, TX 76133

Shout it from the mountaintops, big mouth. Bridal Secrets like these are too good not to share. So what's all the fuss? Big savings on big dresses, little dresses, all size dresses from 1-44. Since you can rent everything for that bridal day—the limo, the hall, the tux, the band, why not the dress, too? An idea whose time has come. But if you want to keep it because maybe you'll have a daughter and she may want to wear it (right, as she elopes to Vegas), then go ahead and buy it during their semi- annual clearance sale where savings can soar to 80 percent off on those gowns that have previously taken the walk. Now you know. So much for being a secret! During those annual clearance sales, each spring and fall, gowns retailing up to $1,800 are grabbed for $200-$400. Though they also accept gowns on consignment, their specialty is still rentals. You can also rent or buy prom and formalwear dresses just for black tie affairs. Alterations available on site.

★★ Bridal-Tux Shop   972/303-9022
6527 Duck Creek Drive   Mon-Thu 10-7; Fri 10-6; Sat 10-5
Garland, TX 75043

It's very simple. Shop at Bridal-Tux shop for, you guessed it, bridal wear and tuxedos. But what you didn't imagine were prices that were rock bottom. Make this wedding a no-brainer with gowns starting at just $149 and racks of dresses for the bridal party and mothers-of-the-bride for only $39. Feeling lucky? Then you might just walk out of here with one of these great names at a great price including **ALFRED ANGELO**, **AMY LEE**, **BILL LEVKOFF**, **BRIDAL ORIGINALS**, **FOREVER YOURS**, **MA CHERIE**, **MORI LEE**, **T.R. THORNTON** and more.

bridesave.com   806/826-5500
PO Box 421, 807 North Main Street   24/7
Wheeler, TX 79096-0421   www.bridesave.com

 Talk about a one-stop shopping environment when planning for that wedding day. It's mind-boggling. Bargains at every click of the mouse. And selection? Well, gigantic. Over 3,000 bridal gowns alone. Add in more than 1,200 bridesmaids' dresses, 650 flower girl dresses, plus veils, headpieces, shoes, bras, gloves, handbags, hosiery, shoe accents, invitations, books, I mean there's nothing like it on the web. And insured shipping is FREE. Spend hours as a voyeur browsing through thousands of hits and slicks. In the shoe department alone, there were hundreds to choose— from slides, pumps, sandals, even boots. With over 640 styles, the only option left is to wear the box. Some can even be dyed to match. Then, not to be outdone, consider a honeymoon to Vail. Pick the perfect finishing touch from over 70 Bridal Classics headpieces and veils, and over 1,100 headpieces and veils by other designers. Their gift registry is one of the best when ease is a consideration. Planning for your wedding starts with a trip to bridesave. If your Mother told you, "You better shop around," you can forget it. This is the place that Mothers have been looking for. Now it's time to teach Mother a thing or two. ◆

★★★★★ BridesMart   817/784-1171
4648 S. Cooper St.   Mon-Thu 10-8; Fri-Sat 10-6; Sun Noon-5
Arlington, TX 76017   www.bridesmart.com

Bride smarts is what you don't need here. All the work's done for you already. As corny as it sounds, you don't want to write the Bridal Book for Dummies, now do you? Get the skinny on real deals on real designer dresses starting at just $199. Find occasional clearance dresses for any occasion at just $30 and up. I know one bride who got dressed with shoes, slip, veil and dress for under $100. Now we're talking smart! Inflation won't stop the deals at BridesMart. For years they've offered the same great names like **ALFRED ANGELO**, **BRIDAL REPLACEMENTS**, **FOREVER YOURS**, **ILISSA** by **DEMETRIOS**, **MON CHERE**, **MORI LEE** and more at savings up to 70 percent off. No matter what shape your wedding budget is in, you'll fit into these dresses sized 1-44.

★★★ David's Bridal

5525 Arapaho Rd.
Dallas, TX 75248

972/458-2211
Mon-Fri 11-9; Sat 10-6; Sun Noon-6
www.davidsbridal.com

You'll love David's Bridal. Maybe even more so than your betrothed. But he doesn't need to know about the other man in your life. David's will pamper you with a huge selection of over 1,400 bridal gowns. Save big on designer show-offs from just $99. Wait around for their $99 sales and put the savings towards your veil, shoes, flowers, hat, headpiece, jewelry, gloves, purse, card pouch, hosiery, garter...wow, do you really need all this stuff? You bet. So why not save while the savings are hot. Something borrowed? Something blue? Something old (besides your new mother-in-law)? Now you're set to go buy something new. *Call toll-free: 800/399-2743*

★★★ Designers Encore

8216 Grapevine Hwy.
North Richland Hills, TX 76180

817/656-9354
Mon-Sat 10-5:30

We show our appreciation with a standing ovation for Designers Encore. More, more we want more. Greedy aren't we? But when savings on previously-worn gowns, veils, bridesmaids' dresses and more averaged 65 percent, being needy means you've got to be greedy. On these racks you will find plenty of **ALFRED ANGELO**, **BIANCHI**, **DEMETRIOS**, **ILISSA** and **JORDAN** hanging around. We fell in love with the prices and Designers Encore is in love with their customers. It's a match made in heaven. Nobody has to know that most of these dresses have been matched (or mis-matched) before. Most items in the shop are resale but a few new can be found hanging around in sizes 0-24. You may need something old for the walk anyway. Let guests think it's your handbag (or your intended, that's old) and not the dress. Besides gowns, expect to don handbags, shoes, veils, jewelry and more for that once-in-a-lifetime special day.

★★ Discount Bridal Service

2616 Abercorn Drive
Grapevine, TX 76051

817/424-1559
Mon-Fri 10-6 By Appt. Only
www.discountbridalservice.com

Press two to leave a message for owner Sandra Thrash if you're a bride-to-be . This is really a home-based business, though from this day forward, you can love, honor, and save 20-40 percent on bridal gowns, veils, bridesmaids' dresses, mother's gowns and more by calling on their services. The original and probably the largest "Personal Buying Service," in the country catering to the bride, through their enormous buying power, you can purchase first-quality wedding attire and more and more at a discount. You can save hundreds of dollars on the same gowns that you ogled in the major bridal magazines. But to buy them, you'll order through a local representative, like Sandra. If she's not the closest rep, corporate will refer you to one that is. She is also a bridal counselor who will help you in selecting dress styles, material, fabric colors and dress sizes. You tell her the manufacturer's name, style number and color name...or simply tell her which issue and page number the dress appears on the bridal magazine, then she'll quote you a price, shipped directly from the manufacturer. For more than 15 years, DBS has been putting brides into gowns of their choice, saving them time and hassles. You can even inquire via their website for an online quote. There are some caveats, though, such as holding your breath hoping the gown arrives at the designated time and that it leaves you plenty of time for alterations, etc. Sandra, however, is used to smoothing out all of those wrinkles. She's done it all. *Call toll-free: 800/874-8794*

★★ First Impression Formals   817/459-3773
2304 W. Park Row Drive, Suite 21   Tue-Sat 10-6
Arlington, TX 76180

First Impressions always make a lasting impression. When the occasion calls for it, you've got to dress the part, from head to toe. Brides and bridal parties can make this trip eventful with everything you'll need from dresses to jewelry, purses, gloves and additional accessories. Go all out this prom season with fabulous looks from **DAVE & JOHNNY**, **JESSICA MCCLINTOCK**, **SCALLA** and now **SCOTT MCCLINTOCK**. Better than the names are the prices. We love the slogan "Never Pay Retail" and those words hold true as one takes the vow of "salebacy" at First Impressions.

★★★ Gladis Bridal Boutique   972/783-9643
1617 Centenary Drive   Mon-Sat 10-6; After 6 By Appt.
Richardson, TX 75081   www.gladisbridalboutique.com

The lessons to be learned here are as easy as A-B-C. See Gladis and her bridal boutique. Dressing only the most elegant brides and preparing the wedding party for that special day is the specialty of this house. Although other occasions including communion dresses and proms are also available, here you'll be indoctrinated into Pre-Nuptial 101. Learn how to create a beautiful ensemble including bouquets, photo albums, unity candles, garters, cake tops, flower girl baskets, gloves, ring bearer pillows, toasting flutes and more to make the day memorable. But the top de resistance is their custom-made headpieces. They're simply stunning.

★★★ Invitation Warehouse   214/381-6367
PO Box 570368   By Appt. Only
Dallas, TX 75357-0368   www.invitationwarehouse.com

Lois knoweth the invitation business and can save you 30 percent across the pages of a myriad of albums. Wedding invitations and all the other printed matter can be etched into the occasion without gouging your budget. More than 35 albums to choose from in all the popular brands. **CARLSON CRAFT**, **CHECKERBOARD**, **CLASSIC**, **KREPE KRAFT**, **MASTERPIECE**, **REGENCY**, **STYLEART** and others are waiting to be engraved R.S.V.P. Graduations, anniversaries, thank you notes, bat/bar mitzvahs, quinceaneras, birthday parties, anniversaries, greeting cards, graduations, rehearsal dinners, birth announcements—if it's a paper invitation or announcement, all that is yet to do is address the invitees. Monogrammed stationery, too, available online or by appointment. With so many albums to browse through, you may miss the party. Delivery, if it's coming from a Waco-base company, takes three to five days; engraved invitations from the finest factories take three weeks, so plan accordingly. *Call toll-free: 866/381-6367*

★ Isis Bridal & Formal   972/681-5939
1032 Town East Mall   Mon-Sat 10-9; Sun Noon-6
Mesquite, TX 75150

Simply say, "I do" to the array of formal wear from Isis. To have and to hold, from this day forward, hold any dress for just a $20 deposit. For richer or poorer, either way you'll get a deal on gowns over $500. Consider this a gift of a lifetime because the headpiece, veil, gloves, petticoat and shoes are FREE. Have you ever tried to add up all the extras? Not a bad deal. Bridal packages included tuxedos and/or bridal party wear. Plenty of quinceaneras dresses and coronas. The cup runneth over in this store. So get over to Isis Bridal and Formal before getting to the church this time.

★★★★ Lasting Impressions Bridal Boutique   972/991-7498

15056 Beltway Drive   Mon-Thu 11-7; Fri 11-6; Sat 11-5
Addison, TX 75004

Since the day only lasts for a moment, make the memories last forever. Every bride wants her day to be special, unique and truly her own (oh yeah, and the grooms, too). But why buy? After all, it only lasts a few minutes. Rent beautiful gowns from $185-$500. They make a statement all of their own. Or get the entire wedding package for $300 and up. You only wear it once. Would you rather spend up to $500 on a so-so gown you'll just store away; or rent a fabulous, to-die-for gown for the same price and save the storage area in your closet for something else? It's all up to you! And now, where are you going on your honeymoon?

★★★★★ Le Renaissance Wedding Facility   214/692-8442

8041 Walnut Hill Lane, Suite 820   Mon,Tue,Thur &Fri 11-6, Wed 1-7:30
Dallas, TX 75231   www.lerenaissance.com

Want to create your own backdrop for your wedding day? How about a beautiful courtyard garden, quiet, secluded and intimate. A charming chapel, crystal chandeliers, warm candlelights, twinkling stage lights and an elegant bride's room with double mirrors. No, you're not seeing double. But you will hear the bridal march on their website. View the dramatic balcony where you can throw your bouquet. Entertain guests in a separate reception area. Choose some of the finest chefs, bakers, uniformed wait staff and all because you've chosen the Le Renaissance as your wedding facility. This is one of Dallas' favorite little secrets. So while you're making that list and checking the price, consider this first on your "To Do" agenda. Prices are generally 30-60 percent under the going rates of your traditional hotel facilities and your event will be handled by experienced bridal consultants. Whether it's a small gathering of close friends and family or up to 200 guests who crawl out of the woodwork, this family-owned business can supply everything to make your day. Let them handle all the details. Order a carriage or leave in a limo, it's your day. You've got enough to worry about. Let them do their thing and arrange it all—from caterers, bakers, limos, florists, paper products, make-up experts, musical and video artists—whatever it takes to make "Memories" of your special occasion. And if you want to feed the brood, then have them bring on the food! Food, Glorious Food! Your menu can be extensive or limited; from barbecue, chef carving stations, pasta stations or the deluxe south of the border bar—enough to make your day or evening affair as delicious as possible. Check out their website with photos of days gone by but please, no crying. Your mascara will run all over the keyboard.

★★ Milliners Supply Co.   214/742-8284

911 Elm St.   Mon-Fri 8:30-5
Dallas, TX 75202   www.milliners.com

You've got the guy of your dreams, you've got the ring you've always wanted and the gown your friends won't forget. So what's missing? Complete the picture with a trip to Milliners Supply Co. Take the stress out of any wedding ensemble by stepping through these doors and back in time. Good old-fashioned prices (wholesale and clearance items at least 35 percent off in dozen lots.) Right for the pickings are shelves of bridal ribbon, flowers, hats, headbands, tiaras, boas, petticoats, garters, ring pillows, accessories and even hoop skirts. That should make for an interesting removal of the garter. Everything you need from wall to wall and floor to ceiling, except the bridal fabric itself. Walk softly. The floors still creak. *Call toll-free: 800/728-3962*

★★★★★ Resale Gallery

724-A E. Pipeline Rd.
Hurst, TX 76053

817/285-0633
Mon-Sat 10-6

Prince Charming will fall to his knees and bless the ground you walk on when he learns that you were smart enough to save some extra cash for the honeymoon and shop for your dress here. The dresses may have made their debut elsewhere but a grand entrance is still in order. Think of how many times a new gown has been tried on in the bridal shop? Now realize that it just means higher price tags. So, what do you have against saving money for the honeymoon? Hwy. 183, south on Brown Trail to Pipeline, left two blocks. It's behind the Grandy's in the Village Square Shopping Center. You found it. You might as well enjoy it.

Saleplace, The

3641 Shepherd Lane
Balch Springs, TX 75180

972/557-7747
Mon-Fri 10-8; Sat 10-6; Sun Noon-5:30
www.weddingsuperstore.com

You've got the church, the hall, the caterer, the dress, the bridal party. What more do you need? How about confetti, bubbles, ring pillows, flower baskets, unity candles, pew bows, veils, garters, gloves, cake toppers and charms. Trinkets for your guests and thank you's for the bridal party. And you thought you were done? Weddings cost forever. But don't worry. They've got it all somewhere within their 22,000 square feet of wedding needs, essentials and "I wants!" You'll find something antique looking (old), something new (everything), something borrowed (certain traditions) and something blue (the blue lace garter was eyed). The Saleplace has it all—from heart-shaped bubble bottles (instead of rice) to wands (the no-mess trend) to ring pillows, flower baskets, gloves, veils, headpieces, canopies, unity candles, cake decorating elements, the cake knife, the guest book, confetti, and all the other little things that make the big event a hit. Do your shopping here and end up finished with the entire event. Since 1977, the Reid family has provided the only one-stop wedding store in town. "I'll drink to that!" Not as difficult to find as you might suspect, it's a hop, skip and a jump off LBJ (I-635) and the Elam Road exit.

★★★★★ Sample Shop

718 W. Pipeline Rd.
Hurst, TX 76053

817/268-0311
Mon-Fri 11-7; Sat 10-6

While Mrs. Williams is recovering from a broken hip, you can stay hip by shopping for all your bridal needs here. Daughter Annette is keeping watch on the store and all the gowns in sizes 2-44. The entire bridal party is considered, even the groom. Tuxedo rentals start at $39.99 and bridal gowns were as low as $150. Mothers-of-the-bride, bridesmaids and matrons-of-honor can be outfitted with a little help from the experts here. You'd expect perfection after 33 years in the bridal business, no? They also sell prom, party, debutante and quinceañera dresses starting out as low as $99. Then, complete the ensemble with shoes and accessories and you can say, you're dressed to the hilt. As they say, "They supply everything but the groom!" Now for additional cuts to the quick, don't overlook their closeout department. Wander from room to room and don't miss a thing. This is one-stop shopping at its best. Go from room to room, dour to darling, plain to perfect and all at decidedly discounted prices. Whether it's for your wedding or any other formal occasion, they can dress you up. In fact, the entire bridal party will be able to participate in the savings. Wade through rack after rack, room after room of formal, prom and flower girl dresses, then wind your way to the special-order and bridesmaids' dresses, select from the mothers-of-the-bride collection if that's who you are, deck out in the sequined pageant collection (behind glass) and, of course, the wedding gowns and veil salon. You won't even need a pre-nuptial agreement. Both will concur, this is one of the best for less.

★★★★★ **Timeless Blooms**   **972/530-1909**
Garland, TX   By Appt. Only
                                            www.timelessblooms.com

Your wedding is a special occasion that you'll remember (or want to forget) for a lifetime. For those sentimental souls who want to keep those special memories alive with, if nothing else, the flowers from your wedding, meet Timeless Blooms. This home-based business will freeze dry your flowers for a few weeks after your wedding and then return them to you decorated in an attractive framed acrylic dome with other mementos from your wedding (if you choose), such as your marriage license, an invitation, garter, photo or any other special item. If protected from dust, humidity, insects, inclement weather or any other damage, your flowers should last for many, many years. The folks at Timeless Blooms are proven pros at flower freeze drying, so you're in good hands here. Frame displays are available in a variety of shapes in sizes starting at around $70. This price includes pre-treatment of your flowers, freeze-drying, post-treatment, designing, ribbon and display container. Plus, if you don't want to take your flowers to Timeless Blooms yourself, you can ship them. Be sure to call before you do, because the shipping location is different from the business location.

◆◆◆◆◆ **Wedding Cottage, The**   **972/771-2340**
730 S. Goliad St.   Tue, Wed, Sat By Appt.
Rockwall, TX 75087   www.theweddingcottage.com

Even if you decide to hold your wedding at the City Dump, I'd still think you were beautiful. (And I'd still cry.) But, let me propose a more perfect setting. Why not consider the bright and airy chapel of The Wedding Cottage. It's like being amidst an indoor garden of Eden, flowing with an arbor of flowers and greenery, Victorian flower baskets, candelabras and aisle candles. You have your choice of an intimate ceremony or one of their complete packages which includes the ceremony and reception. On staff, there are wedding specialists to guide you every step of the way. The Wedding Cottage can accommodate up to 150 guests. So when push comes to shove and the guy says, "Your place or mine," pick theirs. You'll love it...and I won't have to say I'm sorry!

★★★★ **Yvonne's Bridals**   **214/467-2870**
2550 W. Red Bird Lane, Suite 410   Mon-Fri 10-7; Sat 9:30-5:30,
Dallas, TX 75237

The belle of the ball rings here. Now that you've found your prince, what are you going to do? Cinderella could have made it to the party on time if she'd just stopped by Yvonne's Bridal first. This little gem will make any girl sparkle in beaded, satin, chiffon, taffeta and silk dresses. Prices begin as low as $200. A diamond in the rough will have you stepping right out of the pages of your favorite bridal magazine. Immerse yourself in the warm, friendly, pampering service that's been perfected by Yvonne's for nearly 20 years. Yvonne provides all the accessories, too. Then, if you decide to rent, you'll save 40-50 percent. Even flower girl dresses, mothers-of-the-bride and formal selections are ripe for the picking. Want to save up for that perfect day? Layaway's available with a 25 percent deposit.

18

Cameras & Optical

★★★★ Arlington Camera
544 W. Randol Mill Rd.
Arlington, TX 76011

817/261-8131
Mon-Sat 9-6
www.arlingtoncamera.com

Arlington Camera has focused on keeping one of the best selections of cameras in the Metroplex for over 13 years. New or used, co-owner Bill Porter can make taking great pictures a snap—whether you want a high-end **NIKON** or **MAMIYA**, or just want to take snapshots with a little **KODAK** or **POLAROID** disposable camera, or anything in between. They also carry **HASSELBLAD**, **BRONICA**, **CANON**, **OLYMPUS**, **MINOLTA**, **PENTAX**—the list goes on. A complete selection of films and darkroom supplies and the knowledge to go along with it makes you shutter at the thought of shopping for cameras elsewhere. ***Call toll-free: 800/313-6748***

Competitive Cameras
2025 Irving Blvd., #107
Dallas, TX 75207

214/744-5511
Mon-Fri 9-5:30; Sat 9-4
www.competitivecameras.com

Eugene and Ramsey Jabbour click. Their store is notorious for being the resource for serious shutterbugs or those just starting out. Since 1982, they have been delivering the goods with the name-brand lens as opposed to substituting a lesser quality lens to cut costs. Yes, here you can expect the lens to be what the manufacturer intended. Personalize service by knowledgeable photographers makes it easier to buy the camera that is right for the job. Located in the "photographic district" where many professional camera buffs have their studios, CC continues to direct you to the camera that gives you your money's worth. Name brands are the best: **BRONICA**, **CANON**, **CONTAX**, **HASSELBLAD**, **KODAK**, **MAMIYA**, **MINOLTA**, **NIKON**, **OLYMPUS** or **PENTAX** including cameras, film, lenses, flashes and lighting supplies. They have a complete line of darkroom equipment and carry Kodak and **FUJI** professional film and paper. If you're looking for video cameras or high-tech anything relating to cameras, this is the place to target your shoot. Even Olympus underwater cameras won't drown your budget. If you want information on the latest and greatest, or a deal on a pre-owned model, just say cheese to Competitive Camera, the best in the metroplex. They also buy, trade and sell your cameras.

★★★ Warehouse Photographic

972/416-7110

2255 E. Belt Line Rd., Suite 301
Carrollton, TX 75006

Mon-Fri 9-6; Sat 9-5
www.warehousephoto.com

Just about everything you need or want for your camera and darkroom can be secured at this 30-year veteran of the photo business. Equipment and supplies, cameras and accessories, lenses, camera bags, darkroom equipment and supplies, filters, negatives, slide storage, studio lighting, ink jet paper, books and more. They straddle the fence serving both the professional and amateur photographers with both new and used camera equipment and supplies. They pride themselves on carrying cameras and accessories that most camera stores don't carry. Shop online through the pages of their *Photo Equipment Catalog*, used equipment, film processing and more. Consign your equipment and let them sell it for you. And they'll even try to answer all of your photography questions. Great prices on used equipment such as the **CANON** AE-1 for $219, a **KODAK** digital camera for $299, an **OMEGA** D-2 lens board for $29.95 and a **PELOUZE** darkroom scale for $49.95. Lots more such as an **ELMO** T-3 slide timer for $15 and a **MAESTRO** meter for $399. How about 80 different models of point and shoot cameras by Canon, Kodak, **KONICA**, **MINOLTA**, **NIKON**, **OLYMPUS**, **POLAROID**, **VIVITAR** and more? Prices run anywhere from $7.49-$399.99. Prices may vary between the store and the website, so be wary. They also carry some excellent digital cameras and equipment. Commercial photographers and hobbyists alike recommend this source because of the vast darkroom supplies, plus there's a full-service photofinishing lab on the premises. The Kodak Create-a-Print machine lets you do your own enlargements in minutes, and the latest machine from Kodak does "picture-to-picture" up to a final image of 8 X 10, all in seconds, no negative required. How slick! *Call toll-free: 800/400-8203*

★★ Wolf Camera Clearance Store

972/241-0582

11171 Harry Hines Blvd.
Dallas, TX 75229

Mon-Fri 9-6; Sat 10-6; Sun Noon-5
www.wolfcamera.com

The Harry Hines Superstore is a sight to behold. Prices occasionally lower than mail order are available during most promotions at the Wolf's Clearance Store between Walnut Hill and Royal Lane. Don't expect consistency though, the inventory ebbs and tides. A brand new 550si **MINOLTA** camera was snapped up faster than a New York minute for only $169.95. A refurbished **NIKON** N60 Camera Body was $299.95. Buy it when you see it; if not, you'll be shuttered out. Trade-in your old camera and apply the credit towards another. Demos and cameras that have been opened are as good as new, so don't let your pride get in the way. They buy and sell used equipment but even so, on some models, you'll save as much as 50 percent; while others, maybe $50. And that's a big deal!

19

Carpets & Floors

★★★★★ American Tile Supply

2839 Merrell Rd.
Dallas, TX 75229

972/243-2377
Mon-Fri 8-5; Sat 9-2

This manufacturer/distributor is open to the public and it's a goodie. Then, they have tent and parking lot sales, which are also dandy. If you are looking for top-quality slate, granite, or limestone at exceptional savings, then consider their Natural Stone Division and for sure, take them for "granite". Prices started at 59 cents a square foot, hot-ziggety-dog! All current sizes including delivery makes even a stone cutter crack up. Their huge distribution center at 2244 Luna Road in Carrollton (972/620-1866) is impressive in itself and occasionally they, too, will open up to the public. Keep your eyes peeled for newspaper announcements. Second outlet open on a regular basis is in Richland Hills, 7412 Baker Blvd., 817/589-1252.

★★★★ Bargain Carpets

200 N. Lancaster Ave.
Oak Cliff, TX 75203

214/948-9449
Mon-Sat 9-5

Cheap rugs is not just his email address, it's his way of life. This Oak Cliff area bastion of bargains is still one of the best places to digest bargains on carpets. After all, if it's your name, why play any other game? Over 40,000 yards of closeout carpet acquired through bankruptcies and liquidations as well as mill overruns, irregulars and discontinueds start as low as $2.99, but that's where the story ends. If you want an installer, they will recommend several good contractors and you will be billed separately for installation. Carpet, and nothing but, baby. Ralph Cole is the "King of Karpets"; there's no denying his turf has been carved out for years. Call if you need help in getting there. On Lancaster, near 8th Street in South Dallas, Mapsco 55-A. Special orders welcomed but nothing special in the way of ambience. They keep their overhead low, way low, and pass the savings directly on to you without any frills just to thrill.

★★ Belt Line Carpet   972/399-1033
1224 N. Belt Line Rd.   Mon-Fri 9-5:30; Sat 9-3:30
Irving, TX 75061

To save money on carpet and other flooring, you have to hit below the belt. On Belt Line, that is. Hugh O'Neal is the purveyor of carpet, tile, and vinyls that are the envy of the neighborhood. Just south of Airport Freeway, Berber carpet starts at just $10.99 per square yard and includes installation. But, if you've got furniture in your house that needs moving, expect to have $1/square yard tacked on—making your outlay $11.99. Aren't I smart? You'll be smart ,too, if you recognize that the price comes with a four-pound pad. But if you really want to sink your toes into the plushest of plush, upgrading to a six-pound pad will cost you another $1 a square yard. It all adds up. Count your blessings and the add-ons before calling this dealer a deal.

★★★ Carpet Exchange   972/385-3545
4901 Alpha Rd.   Mon-Thu 9-7; Fri-Sat 9-6; Sun Noon-5
Dallas, TX 75244

Customer service has never been a priority in discount stores until we did business with Carpet Exchange. Lovelier than thou...from one of Texas's largest carpet stores with good, old-fashioned, "Welcome, y'all. Come back real soon, ya hear?" service. Love it or leave it, Texans are just plain proud to boast they're the biggest and the bestest, and in this case, they're not just whistlin' Dixie. Yee-ha! Choose from all the big names in carpeting, tile, vinyl, wood floor coverings, area rugs and laminates. Nary a brand is left unturned. Their 96,000-square-foot showroom will leave you huffing and puffing. Their prices are so good, they'll "floor you". Sales provide the best prices, though, and installation and padding are always extra. So, consider that when doing your comparative pricing.

★★★★ Carpet Mill Outlet   817/481-3551
401 N. Kimball   Mon-Fri 9-6; Sat 9-3
Southlake, TX 76092

Southlake is one of the only mini-cities to hold a mayor and the mayor's furniture store all in the same metro-environ. But man does not live with furniture alone. He's got to have something underfoot to keep the furniture in a proper setting. This 15,000-square-foot white metal building holds the title of Numero Uno Carpet One dealer in the country. They must be doing something right. You'll discover their strength the minute they cushion the blow of walking on cement. Instead, choose your comfort level and then line-up the players: **CORONET**, **MOHAWK**, **QUEEN**, **SHAW** and **TUFTEX** will be your odyssey of walking on air, including **SUTTON'S** new couture line (just like in better dresses, one step up). Prices are quoted just the way you like them, with or without padding, installation, furniture moved or not, so you are able to compare apples to apples. Hardwood flooring started at $6.25/square yard installed for 3/8-inch wood. Though they do carry quarter-inch thickness, too, they don't recommend it. Vinyl flooring started at $6.99/square yard with installation an additional $7/square yard. That price includes embossing or removal of old flooring. In laminates, choose from some of the best by **MANNINGTON**, **SHAW** and **WILSONART**, or perhaps you prefer it the hard way with hardwood floors by **BRUCE**, **HARTCO**, or others. Their motto, "Large enough to compete but small enough to care". Life in the fast lane wears you out, as well as wears thin on your budget. In this case, it pays to shop around.

★★★★★ Carpet Mills of America   972/283-9241

4353 Gannon   Mon-Fri 10-7; Sat 10-6 Sun 12-4
Dallas, TX 75237   www.carpetmillsofamerica.com

Talk about being on an expansion plan! Carpet Mills of America is now part of a 40-store master plan with stores throughout Texas and Phoenix, AZ. (Think retirement, the owner must have thought.) In any state, though, if the state of your flooring is in need of an uplifting experience, here is where to start. From Berbers to trackless, tract home carpeting to those in million-dollar hideaways, expect this carpet magnate to have you seeing green with any of the red carpets here. Of course, they also carry laminates, wood, tile and vinyl. Since 1989, there's a reason *D Magazine* named them the best. Now you can add the BBB (ours) endorsement, too. When a customer experienced a "bubbling" problem, none other than the president of the company responded to our inquiry. Now, talk about customer service. I'd say he laid out the royal treatment. Check directory for location nearest you.

★★★★ Carpet Town Discount Center   972/438-4056

3309 E. John Carpenter Fwy.   Mon-Sat 8-5
Irving, TX 75062

Nothing much new to uncover here this year. In fact, I'd say they were in kind of a rut but in this case, it could help keep you out of a hole. If you want to replace your carpet from the ravages of time, kids, pets or people, this is a place for some heavy-duty overhauling. Premium padding, though (that's the 6-pound kind) was $2/square foot and, considering prices elsewhere, a steal. Commercial-quality carpeting (the kind that gets a real workout) was priced at $7.95/square yard while residential carpet came installed with padding for around $9.95. They maintain their own installation crew, and that is very, very good. Paint the town red, roll out the red carpet, and red is the color of my true love's hair. You can't deny they're on to something.

★★★★ Ceramic & Marble Tile Outlet   214/951-9525

909 Regal Row   Mon-Thu 8-7; Fri-Sat 8-5; Sun 10-3
Dallas, TX 75247

Part of the Seconds and Surplus mega store complex, these guys are the ones to dote on when it comes to laying tile. They carry grades four and five; in fact, lots of grade fives were available—which is the same as being able to scratch a quarter on the floor and not leave a mark but the ridges on the quarter will be smoothed out. Put another way, this tile is good—real good. These thin settings will cost about $5.11 a bag for do-it-yourselfers; add $3.25/square foot for professional installation. They also stand on what they sell, and deliver. Also at 5200 Gus Thomasson, 972/681-1300 and in Denton at 216 W. University at Elm, 940/243-9000.

★★★ Ceramic Tile International   972/243-4465

2682 Forest @ Josey   Mon-Fri 9-5; Sat 9-1
Dallas, TX 75237   www.interceramic.com

This showroom is the ultimate showplace for ceramic tile for both public and contractor/retailer consumption. Talk about getting an eye full from this giant ceramic powerhouse. It all began south of the border in Chihuahua and found its way up to their headquarters in Garland in 1995. Since arriving, they have been helping you save up to 70 percent on ceramic tile in the center of their retail showroom. What is closed out, discontinued, seconds or otherwise unsuitable for sale to their wholesale customers is discounted to their BBB customers. Handyman hopefuls can attend special "how-to" clinics on the weekends. Learn how to install floor tile, wall tile and counter tile plus learn all the little tricks of the trade. Discontinued, closeouts and seconds give you plenty to choose from even though you've got to stay away from the perimeters of the showroom—they're strictly full price. Recently they've added several new lines, including the **PASSPORT** line, in a wide array of shapes, colors and textures. Some of the most interesting tiles included the **RIVER ROCK** line which are actual river rocks giving an authentic feel of a medieval castle. They have some of the most unusual tiles for even the most discriminating tastes. The nature collection, for example, had worn edges, uneven textures that looked so real, you'd think you were stranded on a desert isle. Learn about their tiles on their website, but no shopping there. Can you imagine delivering a house full of rocks to your mailbox? Check directory for their Fort Worth and Plano locations.

♦♦♦♦♦ Charles Sharp's Carpet Creations   214/749-0216

1515 Dragon   Mon-Fri 9-5
Dallas, TX 75207   www.charlessharp.com

Greet your guests at the front door with a signature piece of your very own. Charles Sharp is the creator of custom carpet and rugs, with discounts "to the trade" and savings to the non-trade, you, me and the fence-post. For over 40 years, this artisan has been making one-of-a-kind carpets and rugs that can tell a story in a million ways, with zillions of threads, hoop-de-loops, creative designs and patterns, a logo for your office entryway...what an impressive welcome to your corporate world. From stair runners to custom colors and borders, this company is sharp from the ground floor.

★★★★★ Dungan's Floors/Blinds & More   972/562-9444

1434 N. Central Expwy., Suite 109   Tue-Fri 8:30-5:30; Sat 10-4
McKinney, TX 75070   www.ccvm.com/dungan's_floors/index.html

Explain the phenomenon where a husband and wife can stay happily married for more than 20 years, raise a family, and corner the McKinney market for window and floor coverings, too. What is their secret? They should be packaging those secrets, too. They certainly have the bull by the horn and can put a wrench into any merchant trying to horn in on their territory. They're one of the originators of custom tile on both floors and counter-tops, laying imaginative patterns that you'd see only in million-dollar mansions. Let them install **ARMSTRONG**, **BRUCE**, **MANNINGTON**, **PHILADELPHIA** and **SALEM** carpet and hardwoods. Choose adobe, brick, ceramic tile, hardwoods or laminates. It's a never-ending cascade of options. Then, there's the newest stain-resistant fibers, custom ceramic tiles to match your wallcoverings, to match your back-splash, to match your...whatever. Then, if you're not satisfied showing your flooring to your neighbors peeking through the front windows, cover those windows up with a myriad of window coverings. Whether you choose blinds, shades, Duettes or other decorative accessories, expect Dungan's to be at your service. Another plus, they maintain their own installation crews and Lou Jenkins is a master craftsman himself. Lennie's the decorator and together they make quite a team. FREE estimates and doing it right the first time out of the box will ultimately save you time, money and aggravation. Bruce hardwood flooring started at $6/square foot, but that includes installation. Allow for waste, so an 11 x 11-foot room would run just under $800.

Factory Outlet Rugs   817/417-7847

3605 S. Cooper   Mon-Sat 9-6; Sun 12-5
Arlington, TX 76015   www.bstrading.com

FOR stands for putting your foot down on area rugs without the high price tags. Consider Factory Outlet Rugs as your answer to bare floors and cold feet. Keep both the room and your feet snug and cozy with your choice of the largest selection of area rugs in the Metroplex. Their 6,000 square foot showroom in Arlington is just the beginning to savings of 20-50 percent. Thousands of options from around-the-world are possible at prices that are out-of-this-world. Rugs from Belgium, China, Egypt, India, Pakistan, Spain and of course, the good old US of A. Rugs are stacked practically floor to ceiling and are also hung out to dry. It's like turning the pages of an area rug wishbook. Then, when a closeout is on the floor, don't waste any time cutting a rug. They even have rugs that are theirs alone, including a favorite called the "Texas collection", the boot, the state's outline, lariats, the whole nine yards. Adorable ones for your front door, back door, entry way, baby's room, in front of the sink, in the bath—if it's not wall-to-wall, it's an area rug from here. They no longer carry runners but they do carry samples of runners that average 26-inches wide and cost approximately $10-$28 per linear foot. Shop also at their Plano location, 1717 E. Spring Creek Pkwy. at the Plano Outlet Mall, 972/423-0745, open Mon-Sat 10-9 and Sun Noon-6. ***Call toll-free: 800/554-0910***

★★★★★ Feizy Clearance Floor   214/747-6000

Feizy Center   Mon-Sat 9-6; Sun Noon-5
1949 Stemmons   www.feizy.com
Dallas, TX 75207

For almost a quarter of a century, John Feizy has been bagging the carpets like nobody's business. This bastion of imported rugs has been a decorator's secret all that time. But when the 4th Floor Clearance Center opened, it was a welcomed stop-and-shop. Now housed in a 100,000 square foot, multi-story tower on Stemmons, this fourth generation organization continues to lay out the red carpet with their innovative, cutting-edge designs. As a dealer, manufacturer and collector of fine Oriental rugs, from its humble beginnings in a strip shopping center to the eight-story building it occupies today, the company has remained family-owned and run. Near the Design District and across the street from the Dallas World Trade Center, you, too, can mingle with the best of them. With two America's Magnificent Carpets awards under the belts, they don't have to boast much, it's pretty obvious. From fine hand-knotted rugs and the Feizy Home Collection of hand-hooked, hand-tufted, and machine-made rugs, choose from thousands of authentic, imported, hand-made, new and antique Oriental rugs in every size and color imaginable—all clearance priced. You won't find a selection at prices like this anywhere else in the country. From a Chinese Needlepoint to a Persian Tabriz, go ahead, take that magic carpet ride without being taken. ***Call toll-free: 800/779-0877***

★★ First Floors/Carpet One   214/340-8611

10771 Estate   Mon-Thu 8-8; Fri-Sat 8-6; Sun Noon-5
Dallas, TX 75238

Being a member of the buying empire of Carpet One means you've got the combined buying power of over 1,400 carpet dealers nationwide—hence, some of the best prices possible. Then if **LEE** carpets is behind you, you've got a double whammy. With a 25 year, "no-excuses" warranty, it's probably the best stain- or wear-protection guarantee on the market today. Now, you may ask. "What happens if the stain DOESN'T come out? Then what?" No problem. They will replace the carpet, no questions asked. Prices start as low as $2.20 square foot (but tack on pad and installation). Make sure you're not getting the rug pulled from under you. Most carpet is priced by the square yard, not the foot, and if you didn't know better, you'd think they have the cheapest carpet on earth. Never mind, this is a good deal for all concerned. In Southlake, the Number 1 Carpet One dealer is located at Highway 114 at the Wall Street exit, 817/421-2539, and in Denton at 420 S. Bell Ave., Metro 940/243-2131. Check directory for locations in Plano and Fort Worth, too. And, I suppose, if Chris Madden says so, it must be true. ***Call toll-free: 800/CARPET-1***

★★★★★ Ged's Carpets   817/275-7631
2633 S. Cooper   Mon-Sat 10-7; Fri 10-5
Arlington, TX 76015

Ged's my kind of guy. If he wasn't so gracious about serving the Metroplex, you'd think his next assignments would be to carpet the runways at DFW Airport, maybe the new **AMERICAN AIRLINES** stadium, and if things really get going, a shot at carpeting Mark Cuban's house. Now we're talking big. Anyway, even the rich and famous are prudent shoppers and this guy really can deliver the buys. Some of the brands highlighted included **COLUMBUS**, **MOHAWK** and **SHAW INDUSTRIES**, but don't expect to be nickel and dimed to death. No hidden charges, period. Prices, at first, appeared to be a bit higher. But everything's included in the price including moving of furniture and the removal of your old carpeting. Furthermore, all prices include the better six-pound grade of padding. Then, if you need prices slashed to the bare floors, shop their outlet store on Hwy. 360 and Mayfield in Grand Prairie where they still roll out the royal treatment even though you're only looking for the cheapest price on first-quality mill close-outs in carpet, ceramic tile, vinyl, laminates, or wood. See, you get the whole nine yards, without sacrificing the quality. The money you save...may be your own! Note, they close at 5 on Fridays and now, Sundays they put their feet up and rest.

◆◆◆◆◆ J.M.P. Tile Co.   214/762-7107
Plano, TX 75023   By Appt. Only

Don't expect instant gratification. This company takes days to return messages, but if you want an installer for ceramic tile or hardwood floors, his prices are a throw-back to the 80s. Besides, he's an expert, fourth generation floor installer who's been on his hands and knees practically since birth. Instead of a breach birth, he probably came into this world as a beech birth. This master craftsman has been installing tile, marble, granite, hardwood, (hard surfaces, in other words), so don't even think about asking him to install carpets. His price for installation is $3.25/square foot for ceramic tile and $2.74/square foot on hardwood floors (I paid $2.25 in 1985). Book three-four weeks in advance. This guy's as busy as a bee.

◆◆◆◆◆ Kiwi Services   972./934-1234
3230 Commander Drive   By Appt. Only
Carrollton, TX 75006   www.kiwiservices.com

Looking to make a clean sweep, without having to lift a finger? Then here's the dirt. Give Kiwi Services a call the next time your carpets are oozing with grape juice, lipstick stains, coffee grounds, bread crumbs...or whatever else is lingering on your carpets. Has stuff fallen on your carpets and you can't get it up? Angela Eideh had a better idea. About 12 years ago, she started a company that would clean carpets and upholstery and would be both affordable and trustworthy. Now, how is that different from any other company? Well, for one, they come back as many times as necessary during your year's contract. That's right. Whether you need some emergency clean-up right before the holidays, or you have an "oopsie" just before your mother-in-law decides to pay a visit, the cost is only $15 plus $3 per area. Talk about getting the royal treatment! Each carpet cleaning includes vacuuming, moving and replacing furniture, pre-spotting and conditioning, raking to prevent matted fibers and a one-year warranty when you spend $88 on any carpet service. (And that's easy to do.) They also do floors. And if your air ducts are clogged and begging to be cleaned out, this company is right on it. Dallas and Fort Worth (and Houston) areas covered. Here's a company that performs one giant step for womankind...by being the "cleaning lady".

★ Lee's Carpet

116 W. Jefferson
Dallas, TX 75208

214/941-5521
Mon-Fri 8:30-5; Sat 9-Noon

This old-timer can really pull up the rug and lay a new one in its place. What a delightful-**LEE** interesting experience this can be. Bill and his wife Hazel represent all the famous brands you've grown accustomed to: **ALADDIN**, **ARMSTRONG**, **LD BRINKMAN** stand out while **STAINMASTER** for $7.99/square yard plus $2.50/square yard for installation (you move the furniture) are reflective of the prices that the Lees have faith behind. Now, why they don't carry Lee's Carpet is anybody's guess. Then again, they don't carry Lee Jeans either. Parquet flooring can stand up to the wear and tear alongside tile, ceramic, vinyl, laminates, wood..."If it's flooring, we have it," says Hazel Lee. Work can usually be completed within a few days. FREE in-home estimates complete with samples are another plus. So, even though they don't move your furniture for the price quoted above, there's not much they don't do when it comes to flooring. Even if they don't answer the phones, they're probably there working with a customer. *Call toll-free: 800/717-5521*

LumberLiquidators.com

1620 N. I-35
Carrollton, TX 75006

972/323-5077
By Appt. Only
www.LumberLiquidators.com

Lay one on at this Lumber Liquidator by the name of **HUSKY**. As the name implies, if you are looking for hardwood flooring and are considering oak, exotics, prefinished, then start the ball rolling at 99-cents square foot. All grades of oak are available and they will beat any price, anywhere, anytime, don't you worry. They also carry in-stock the Husky brand of pre-finished woods with a 50-year warranty and exotic woods like maple, oak and cherry for $2.95 square foot. LumberLiquidators was named #50 on *Inc. Magazine*'s list of fastest growing companies. Woodn't you like to see why? *Call toll-free: 877-Mill-Direct*

★★★★★ Massey Distributors

911 N. Mill St.
Lewisville, TX 75067

972/394-7617
Mon-Sat 9-5, By Appt.

Being on the run, in this case, means Massey's on the move. With 15 mobile showrooms on the road at any given time, someone, somewhere is being shown the carpeted side of life. With no overhead costs except gas and a truck, they can save you about 40 percent on all kinds of flooring options: carpet, vinyl, laminates, wood and ceramic tile. Everything that is available at their local showroom is available through their mobile units at no additional charge. This is convenience at its best, with distributor-direct prices at the very least. Nothing down, no interest and 90-days financing with approved credit; what more do you want? Let them bring the store to you, put your foot down on high prices, and sink into the luxury of a new floor. If you're lucky, a same-day appointment is even possible. Too, they are also a distributor for **HOWARD MILLER** clocks. Clocks and carpet. What a grand time for singing—be it a grandfather model, marine, mantle clock or a wake-up gong, tick-dock, tick-tock, it's time to call it a night. Buy it right and keep time counting the ways you've saved the day.

◆◆◆◆◆ North Texas Bomanite

11107 Morrison
Dallas, TX 75229

972/484-8465
Mon-Fri 6 AM-7 PM
www.bomanite.com

Cool. Complete. Concrete and **BOMANITE** is the name and their products are the ones you can bank on. For more than four decades, The Bomanite Corporation has offered a variety of exceptional, high-quality concrete paving and flooring products. So, like we say in the biz, if you want the best, and you want concrete, see what it looks like by visiting their corporate offices right off Stemmons and Walnut Hill, between Ables and Shady Trail. It's amazing floors. It's an amazing floor surface. Choose from countless textures and designs. Transform your back patio or your inside floor surfaces into a unique and dramatic presentation. Be it commercial or residential, inside or out, you've come to the right ingredients. Try it. You'll love it. My garage and my patio have never looked so pristine. Learn more on their website and the longest working day in the book. ***Call toll-free: 800/492-2524***

★ Oriental Rug Gallery of Texas   972/991-5757

4519 LBJ Frwy.   Mon-Wed, Fri-Sat 10-6; Thu 10-8;
Dallas, TX 75244   www.rugstudio.com

Hundreds of Oriental rugs are waiting for you at The Studio. Here, they have all the right stuff—the right size, the right pattern, the right colors...and the right price. As a matter of fact, they have been a significant supplier of Oriental rugs for almost 70 years. Not quite an octogenarian, but no doubt, they'll make it to 80 with their buying power of every kind of hand-tufted rugs, handmade rugs, all wool rugs, all kinds of round and unusual-shaped rugs, and all at prices less than taking a first class carpet ride. Rugs begin under $100 and escalate to several thousand. Even as wall hangings, rugs are a fabulous wall-endowment for the arts. Change a boring room into a showplace utilizing different patterns compatible with your color scheme. Watch the conversation flow from everyday chatter to "Kilim Time" with a purpose. At The Studio within the Oriental Rug Gallery, learn about the art of Oriental rug making, explore the various countries in the Oriental rug-making world, and find out what you should know before purchasing one. Get a lesson before you become some fly-by-night carpetbagger's next victim. They'll help with decorating ideas and answer questions about what to look for when buying an Oriental rug. Furthermore, if push comes to shove and you prefer to shop from home, just head to their website and click away. Full refunds are given within 30 days of purchase, so you can shop absolutely worry-free. Not the lowest prices in town, just one of the most knowledgeable and consumer-friendly. ***Call toll-free: 800/944-4428***

★★ Persepolis Oriental Rugs   214/599-9966

3926 Oak Lawn   Mon-Sat 9:30-6; Sun Noon-5
Dallas, TX 75219

If you're interested in a floor show across from Park Place Mercedes, this may be the opening act in Uptown circles. This direct importer cuts out the middle man and delivers prices on Oriental rugs at particularly worldly-less prices. Talk about a Turkish delight...more than 7,000 of them are laying around at prices guaranteed to be the lowest. It's a difficult price-checking challenge, as anybody, even armed with some sophistication, finds difficult. No doubt, their selection is awesome. Master-crafted rugs from China, India, Pakistan and Persia (Iran) can take you around the world without having to lift a foot. Another plus is their professional rug cleaning and repair. (Note: thus far, they have lived up to their promise of being able to fix anything.) Expect to be sans (without) rug for 7-10 days. Other showrooms at 4100 Oak Lawn (where their office is located) and 19129 Preston Rd. in North Dallas, 972/732-8400.

★★★★ Rems & Rugs Carpet Outlet   214/630-8005

8888 Governors Row   Mon-Fri 9-5
Dallas, TX 75207

If Rems stands for remnants, does rugs stand for ruglets? Well, in the scheme of things, it probably doesn't matter, unless you are looking for curls to add to your area rug. Rems & Rugs is really carpeting, wall to wall, or a room full. Besides, when you can save up to 50 percent, who's counting square yards? Take any of the remnants and make your own area rug, carpet a door, a room, a garage, a work-out area or any other smaller than normal-size carpet area. Leave it to this eager beaver located at the intersection of Governors Row and Profit. Shows you where their motive lies!

★★★★★ Royal Rug Gallery   214/696-6669
10759 Preston Rd.   Mon-Sat 9:30-6; Sun 12-5
Dallas, TX 75230

Wholesalers since 1955, they have decided to open to the public and see what deals they can have you ride out on. Enjoy the magic of it all. Showing at their retail location were over 5,000 genuine Persian rugs in all shapes and sizes, including Antique and Masterpieces. Don't expect a $1.99 ride, that's for sure. But pay the same prices as the dealers do. Pay less, yes. How much less, that's up for grabs. Most of our research team felt confident these were the real McCoys. Experience counts when you also offer cleaning, repair and appraisals. Surely, they know which knot is not! If you're a dealer, call them at the World Trade Center, 214/696-8275. Watch this space. They could blanket the Metroplex with the next royal flush.

★★★★★ Rug City   972/488-0101
11111 Harry Hines   Mon-Fri 9-6; Sat 10-6; Sun Noon-5
Dallas, TX 75229

Hit the streets. Harry Hines is the strip that's fit for most shopper's needs. If money is a consideration, walk the streets just north of Walnut Hill. Rug City is at the northwest corner at the light at Southwell. There, you'll see a thousand or more area rugs—where they're expecting you to walk all over them. Though they don't custom-make area rugs, they can alter them. Need it cut down? Need two to marry? Want fringe added? Removed? Need an unusual shape or size? What about a runner that needs to be cut down to size? Well, let the doctors perform their surgical precision and with very little money, you can have yourself a new rug that will fit the bill. The selection provides adequate "roll models", believe me. Take a trip around the world and bring back a rug from this country or Belgium, China, Egypt, Russia, Saudi Arabia, Turkey and countries whose names had too many letters to type. Expect all of the rugs, though, to be machine made with inexpensive price tags. Rug City actually manufactures many of the rugs they sell, as well as being direct importers, so they're in a position to provide "Persian-to-Persian prices". They will match any competitors price but it's doubtful you'll be able to bring in a competitor's rug. Delivery is free on rugs too heavy to carry inside your Miata convertible...a nice service when needed.

S & H Carpet Distributors   214/638-3311
8717 Directors Row   Mon-Fri 8-5:30; Sat 9-3
Dallas, TX 75247

Not as well known as green stamps, but when it comes to carpet, it sure takes the licking out of paying full price. This warehouse is home to S & H Carpet Distributors, a well-known carpet supplier who started their business distributing direct from the mills to various carpet retailers around the state. As they grew, they discovered the public was also intrigued about how they, too, could get in on the act of buying "wholesale". (It beats paying retail!) And when they finally made the switch, they discovered a lot more folks wanted to buy carpet and other floor coverings at the same good prices that retail stores and contractors were buying at. The seeds of a runaway success story began to germinate and today, it's just a matter of being at the right place at the right time. They're one of the largest carpet dealers in town, and you can expect savings of 40-70 percent off. It's just another low blow to the high brows in town. In fact, you might even say they're "beyond wholesale" and beyond anyone's wildest dreams. Almost 45,000 square feet of warehouse wonders with the guarantee to have the lowest prices anywhere. So wonder why you would shop elsewhere? The brands line up row after row, followed by the fork lifts to cart it off to their final destination and installation trucks. **ANSO**, **COLUMBUS**, **CORONET** and **MOHAWK** carpet, for starters; **PERGO**, **PICKERING** and **WILSONART** for laminates come in a close second. Add in ceramic tile and vinyl, and it is why they're one of the area's favorite flooring finds. Speaking of a find, ask them about the "ODOR-EATER" pads if you have pets who have an occasional accident. But finding their warehouse is a close encounter of another kind. Pay attention. Exit Mockingbird off Stemmons, or Hwy. 183. They're between Regal Row and Mockingbird. Go west to Ambassador, then north to Dividend. Turn south over the railroad tracks and past several four-way stops. Soon, you'll see Directors Row. Turn right and it's the second building on the left-hand side. They are a free-standing building with maroon trim. Commit these directions to memory as you'll need to have an extra-sensory receptor or a sensitive homing device to land the first time out. Shop also in North Richland Hills, at 7395-A Grapevine Hwy., 817/581-7777, open Mon-Fri 9-6 and Sat 9-3. Ninety days same as cash. *Call toll-free: 800/880-1717*

★★★ **Stone Mountain Carpet Mill Outlet**   **972/219-2221**
1165 S. Stemmons, #130   Mon-Thu 9-7; Fri-Sat 9-5
Lewisville, TX 75067   www.stonemountainflooring.com

Capital B.I.G.E.L.O.W spells bigger better bargains on carpet but don't expect them to be the only player. This outlet represents over 50 different mills where you can save up to 70 percent, including **BIGELOW**. Large selection with most priced in the 20-30 percent discount range. But who's counting those percentages when laying one on? First-quality, heavy trackless carpeting as low as $6.99 square yard (but be sure to check if prices quoted include installation, padding, moving of furniture, etc.). Hidden charges can add up. Besides carpet, SM also sells ceramic, wood, vinyl and laminate flooring, so bring your measurements and see how far you can stretch it. (They promised a FREE gift if your measurements came with you. No, not THOSE measurements, silly.) Shop also their Mid-Cities location at 825 Airport Fwy., in Hurst, 817/590-2113. Over 2,000 colors and styles are available leaving nary a Stone Mountain unturned.

★★★★★ **TB's Home Decorating Center**   **817/731-8355**
6213 Sunset Drive   Mon-Thu 7-7; Fri 7-6; Sat 8-6
Fort Worth, TX 76116-5505

Fortunately, you're immune from paying full price at TB's Home Decorating Center. Their 9,000-square-foot warehouse is your prescription for establishing a wellness program for your home decor's fiscal health. Ward off paying full price on name brand carpeting, tile, hardwood floors and paint from **LAMBERT**, **PORTER**, **PRATT**—though paint was in very limited supply and is on its way out once all in-stock supplies are gone. Wall-ow around their selection of in-stock **SCHUMACHER/WAVERLY** and **YORK** wallpaper at 50 percent off. Located in the "old" Mott's Building on Camp Bowie, take a bite out of their Big Apple selection with small town prices. In-home estimates are FREE. If you pull up that old carpet and discover a hidden treasure underneath, call Brad and he'll see that your old hardwood floor gets refinished and restored! With a six months, no interest, no payment policy available, how can you beat it? So, beat it—and participate in some fiscal home improvement.

★ **Texas Discount Carpets**   **972/484-8051**
11265 Goodnight Lane, Suite 1012   Mon-Fri 10-6; Sat 10-3 (By Appt. Only)
Dallas, TX 75229

Talk about a clandestine rendezvous with your carpet destiny. When calling this company, ask to speak to Pete or Mindy and don't be scared off if you simply get a cell phone recording saying, "Hi, you've reached my cell phone. Leave your name and number...". They are really wholesalers (you know the kind) and don't particularly go out of their way to accommodate a retail customer...especially those of a bargain-shopping kind. But if you tell them the Diva (that's me) sent you (though the name Underground Shopper did have a nice ring to them), they'll gladly pay homage to you by opening their showroom/warehouse. But don't get greedy. **Hours are by appointment only**. They're just about ready to open wide so you can say, "Oh-h-h!" and soon they may be ready to throw abandon to the wind. For now, though, their customer base is still general contractors and one-on-one referrals. As far as I'm concerned, you have just been referred. Lay it on: **CABINCRAFT**, **LD BRINKMAN**, **SHAW** and other brands are waiting for your point and shop. Off Stemmons, two blocks west on Walnut Hill, prices ranged from 99 cents a yard on up. A luxury 63-ounce carpet was going for $16/square yard. A 55-ounce carpet was less, $14/square yard. And 30-ounce carpet and builders' grades all came in stain-resistant. FREE delivery, installation, repairs and restretching available.

Tile & Marble Clearinghouse & Brokerage Firm   972/221-8453

600 N Stemmons Fwy.   Mon-Fri 8:30-4:30; Sat 9-Noon
Lewisville, TX 75067

The move across the freeway to a huge floor show leaves tongues and tails wagging in its wake. Anticipation is finally realized with their new showroom where multi-colored ungaged slate was just $1.99/square foot with installation $4/square foot for slate and $3/square foot for tile. All installation, by the way, includes the setting materials (basically, it's $1 more per square foot if the job is more difficult, such as if you wanted the tile laid in a diamond pattern). Delivery is available for $25-$35 depending on distance, but, other than that, all products are sold at manufacturers' price or below contractor's price including custom-granite countertops. Tile was 85-cents/square foot and marble was $2.50/square foot. Expect all the hard surfaces to surface: marble, granite, slate, ceramic tile, porcelain, Saltillo, Cantera, limestone and more. If it was meant to be stepped on and remain beautiful the older it gets, you might as well save the money while it's still young.

★★★★★ Tile America   817/595-7900

7337 Dogwood Park   Mon-Fri 8-5; Sat 9-2
Richland Hills, TX 76118

See the USA while standing on the ground floor of luxury. This showroom is waiting for your touch, where putting their tile on your floors will separate the weak from the cheap, the cheap from the chic. They represent all the major and minor tile manufacturers in the world wide universe, some even out-of-this-world. Selling direct from manufacturers in Europe, Spain, Italy and Indonesia, for example, and eliminating the middle man, is it any wonder why shoppers leave with a foot-long smile on their faces? The prices are particularly pleasing with no allergic reaction even in the middle of the dogwoods. Their selection encompasses both wall and floor tiles at 89-cents a square foot, with their own brand of all-glaze tile that run squares around the competition. Though they do not maintain their own in-house crews, they will recommend contractors who are capable of doing the installation. Not only are their prices consistent with a manufacturer's outlet, but when they're having a sale, take the road into Dogwood Park and blow the whistle on the lowest prices in town. Count the number of tiles in stock and you'll go bonkers. There's over 3,000,000 square feet to navigate. So, if you're thinking about remodeling, refurbishing, or building new, this should be one of the first sources to turn to for tile, porcelain, glass blocks, marble, granite...and yes, the most requested item in my book, a granite countertop. One block north on Hwy. 121 off Handley.

★★★★★ **Verona Marble Co.**   **214/381-8405**
8484 Endicott Lane   Mon-Fri 8-5; By Appt. Only
Dallas, TX 75227

Marvel over exquisite marble in all colors and shades. Verona Marble Co. supplies some of the Metroplex's finest interior designers. Want your home to look like those featured in Architectual Digest? Then here's the scoop on finding affordable marble and granite. Close-outs in various sizes, starting at just $1.90 a square foot, should bring any home up from rags to riches. This factory outlet is everything it should be if you're wanting an impressive floor covering. Since these are all close-outs, huge quantities in any one style, color or size are hard to arrange. But if you're not as picky, you can marbleize your entry for as low as $1.90/square foot. Pick your project area and make sure it's small. All tile is imported directly from Italy, so by eliminating the mean-ole middleman, those savings are passed along to you. Plus, if you try and lay it yourself, they sell all the supplies. Let's hope none of it will lean like the Tower of Pisa. Hours are by appointment only; don't just show up and expect to be welcomed with the arms of Verona.

20

Cars & Parts

◆◆◆◆◆ A-1 United Transmissions
2201 W. Kingsley
Garland, TX 75041

972/278-9807
Mon-Fri 8-6; Sat 9-Noon

Family-owned and operated since 1976, the Easley's have the staying power when it comes to fixing up your auto power. If yours has a transmission, and you aren't accused of any transgressions, they will willingly take on the problem. Dealing in both American and foreign models, (not the ones that make a living posing on the runways), all of the mechanics assigned to your car are ASE-certified. They have access to all the computerized diagnostic equipment, so no stone goes unturned. Bring it on in, take a FREE road test and evaluation and I expect you to be in good hands. They even know the difference between a muffler problem and a transmission problem when inadvertently, we asked about fixing our catalytic converter. In fact, they even recommended a few muffler shops in the area who could fix it. If you bring the problem in, Mike, after driving the car for a few minutes, can usually tell you what's wrong. At least there's no trial and error waste of time here.

★★★★★ All Truck Tops
3305 W. Division
Arlington, TX 76012

817/461-7000
Mon-Fri 9-6; Sat 9-Noon
www.all-pickup-truck-tops.com

With as many requests as I get for truck toppers, it didn't take long to find just the right place. This company's specialty? Manufacturing custom truck toppers and selling to retailers. Bypass the retailer and shop direct here. Buy truck tops, tool boxes, toppers, canopies, tonneau covers, fiberglass camper shells, snugtops, tuck caps, truck bed linings, running boards, aftermarket accessories, RV parts, mini-dump truck conversions, tow trailers and more. Save 40-60 percent on it all. Don't expect them to quote prices online but they'd rather give you a price by phone so as to not offend their retailer customers. Financing available.

★★★★★ **Atomic & Import Auto Salvage**   **214/371-6020**
8835 S. Central Expressway   Mon-Sun 8-6:15
Dallas, TX 75216

Looking for carburetors in all the wrong places? What about a missing tooth for a **POSRCHE**? An engine for your **EDSEL**? Well, try searching here for the cheapest link. If you bring in your old transmission, for example, to buy a new one (or reserve one with a $10 deposit until you can), they will make the exchange for about $96.95 on an automatic front wheel drive tranny or $69.96 on a standard. Even though they don't handle antique parts, they were willing to hunt it down through their hotline. And if all else fails and you want your car to go to hell, they do provide car crushing.

◆◆◆◆◆ **Auto Critic**   **FW 817/460-8388**
Mobile Service   Mon-Sat 8-5; and By Appt.
Fort Worth, TX   www.usedcarinspections.com

Don't drive off the lot with a lemon. That's not the time to discover there's a little clink in the clutch while they're claiming, "It won't cost much to fix!" Make your first call to Auto Critics (Dallas or Fort Worth offices). They'll come to your home, office, seller's home or car lot with their 150-point diagnostic checklist, bumper to bumper, examining that vehicle from top to bottom. Let the experts review the body, frame, electrical and all the major systems; then you'll know for sure exactly what is the "real" condition of the vehicle you're buying. Auto Critic provides a comprehensive, unbiased written report by one of their certified ASE mechanics. They even take it out for a spin to detect any performance or operational problems. Then they compare the odometer reading to how the car actually handles. It should be pretty equitable; otherwise, the odometer may have been turned back, way back. And read on. Next is the most important credential of Auto Critic's service. They have no vested interest in finding anything wrong with your vehicle as there are never any referrals to mechanics, even if asked. Learn all the "do's and don'ts" when buying a car through the paper— never pay by cash, always by check or cashier's check and do ask if the seller is a dealer. Did you know that kicking the tires comes from the settlers kicking the spokes on the covered wagons to see if they were lose before buying a used one? What does it cost? Only $98.50—a small price to pay to avoid a lemon squeezing you somewhere down the road. Same day or next day appointments available. Franchises available if you're interested by calling 800/765-1857. ***Call toll-free: Dallas 972/386-8388***

★★ **AutoZone**   **972/221-1433**
1106 W. Main   Mon-Sat 8 AM-11 PM; Sun 9 AM-10 PM
Lewisville, TX 75067   www.autozone.com

Since 1979, this national chain has 3,000 stores operational so I guess the zone is a much bigger area than one store in Lewisville. In fact, since they bought out Dallas-based Chief Auto Parts, they are blowin' and goin' straight to the top. Prices on auto parts are their everyday low prices. All stores offer FREE testing of batteries, starters, alternators, voltage regulators and control modules. You can also bring in your used engine oil to the stores for recycling. Now we're talking ecologically-correct. All purchases, whether online or in store, can be returned to any location. You'll never need to worry about calling the manufacturer for warranty info when the part wears out. If it's under warranty, just bring it back to the AutoZone you bought it at and they'll take care of the rest. If your battery's kaput, have it recharged in 30 minutes, for nada. Often times, they're the ones giving basic repair tips to customers so they can avoid costly labor charges. Check directory for location nearest you.

★★ Avalon   **972/238-8884**
13539 Method St.   24 hrs, 7 days, 365 days
Dallas, TX 75243

Precept Transpotation is now called Avalon, but Frankie is not one of their drivers. Prices are a throw-back to the '50s, though. They have three limos at their disposal but can always acquire more if need be. Usually, you can book a few days in advance for weekends and a few hours in advance for week-days. Enjoy the ride. Prices are good. A six-passenger limo runs $65 hour and an eight-passenger limo runs $85 an hour. Both have a three-hour minimum. All limos come equipped with TV, VCR, phone, bar, the works, but it's strictly BYOB. No liquid spirits provided.

◆◆◆◆◆ Bergman's Paint & Body   **972/247-0925**
2316 Havenhurst   Mon-Fri 8-6; Sat By Appt. Only
Farmers Branch, TX 75234

Thirty plus years in the business gives Phil a solid foundation for his 5-diamond rating. Known around town as the Picasso of paint for your cars, trucks, vans or SUVs, no appointment is necessary, just come on in. But make sure you've made arrangements for another form of transportation. It could take two-three weeks from start to finish. Then again, the word "body" also appears in Bergman's name and that spells dents, dings and all things related to your car's exterior. If you need color matching, replacement of auto glass, frame or body straightening, fiberglass or plastic repair, here come the plastic surgeon, without a scalpel! Furthermore, even if you don't have insurance, your vehicle will come through the surgery pretty as a picture without significant losses to your budget. Whether foreign or **AMERICAN**-born, they can handle the dents, dings, scratches and hail damage with aplomb. Though you can see them from Stemmons Freeway, it's wise to call for directions.

★★★★★ CarQuest Auto Parts   **972/790-4775**
115 S. Belt Line Rd.   Mon-Fri 8-6; Sat 8-3
Irving, TX 75060   www.carquest.com

Your quest for car parts is over. Today, there are over 4,000 stores in North America to connect you to what-ever you need for a four-wheel moving vehicle. Since 1974, this chain has been the strongest and the cheapest link to car parts. As a proud sponsor of the Special Olympics, they deserve your patronage for that commitment, too. You get the additional warranty protection and convenience that is part of your purchase . If something goes bing-bong-gone before their time, simply return it to the store with your receipt within the warranty period and they will exchange the part for FREE, no questions asked. It's that simple. Now the best part, the price. Most parts are available at CarQuest at a fraction of what a dealer would charge you. And guess where the dealers' shop? For example, a price for a coil pack at the dealers was $259—that's just for the part, remember? We bought it at CarQuest for $48. Everything's computerized, so be patient on the phone or in line if you want to know if they've got what you're looking for in stock. They also can access, just as extensively, remanufactured, rebuilt as well as new parts for any car, truck, van or SUV. Too, you can also pick up discounted oil, filters, spark plugs, the everyday stuff. Check directory for the location nearest you. Each location is a separately-owned fran-chise but all have access to the same inventory. ***Call toll-free: 800/492-7278***

◆◆◆◆◆ City Garage   **972/434-4340**

475 N. Valley Pkwy.   Mon-Fri 7-7; Sat 8-5 Sun 9-4
Lewisville, TX 75067   www.city-garage.com

Two dozen garages in our fair city and still ready to go and tow. That's right. They offer FREE towing if you're within a 10-mile radius if you allow them to work on your car. How's that for service? If you sign up online, they'll even e-mail maintenance reminders, weekly specials and valuable coupons and discounts. Now, for somebody who doesn't keep track of those things, it's a boon to keep my car purring. City Garage has FREE pick-up and delivery with an offer for a FREE 30-point inspection. Not only do they look like a high-class garage, they are one. One-on-one personalize service reminds you of the days of Texaco's commercials on the "Milton Berle Show". They'll roll up their sleeves and get to work just like the good old days. You can even talk to the mechanic as he's working on your car. No problem has stumped them yet. From simple tune-ups, oil and lube jobs, heating and cooling jobs, transmissions and brake system snafus are an everyday challenge. Sunday hours are 9-4 (except for the downtown location which is closed on Sundays).

★★★★★ Classic BMW Clearance & Trade-in Center 972/918-1100

415 Greenville Ave.   Mon-Sat 7:30-5:30
Richardson, TX 75081   www.classicbmw.com

Want a Beemer? No, not a **BEANIE BABY** but a Beemer Baby. Maybe you'd like to collect them as a hobby? If so, you'll want to pay as low as they'll go. Current deals included a '99 **BMW** 528i touring wagon for $34,900 or a '99 BMW 328 for $27,000. Looking for one even lower? Then how about a '95 BMW 325iS for $15,500, with 24,000 miles? That should do it. Maybe buy two. Take advantage of service specials, too, that include a wash and vac package of six car washes and vacuums for $59.95 or get the complete detail package for $125 (regularly $150). You gotta keep the machine clean, you know, or the car attendant at The Mansion will park yours incognito. How embarrassing. This is the only Clearance and Trade-in Center for new or pre-owned BMWs in the State, so check 'em out. Find deals online for service and maintenance as well as monthly BMW car highlights.

◆◆◆◆ Comedy Defensive Driving School   **See numbers below**

Dallas, TX   Reservations Only
                                                  www.txdriving.com

By the time we got to the bottom of this school, it was no laughing matter. The number we had listed in last year's edition was kaput. So, we wound up finding one in Lubbock that was alive and well, only to be told there was indeed a Dallas operation. They gave us the following number to call: 972/671-6216. Then, we called that number, only to be given two options. If you wanted to take the course in a classroom, you need to call 214/341-9668. By this time, I was fuming. Such a runaround just because I got a ticket changing lanes over the double line. I never even saw the single line, let alone the double. Then, with this rigmarole, I was ready to take the bus. Finally, I did find out there are over 10 locations throughout the Metroplex offering the class at various times and dates. Cost, $37. Expect to be bored for approximately 6 1/2 hours but that includes lunch. But here's the other side of the coin. Heads up! All classes are taught by a professional comedian. Yuck! Yuck! Better than Comedy Central, you'll need reservations to be schooled and entertained at least a few days in advance. Don't have time for a good laugh? They also have courses online. Call 888/595-1911 and it costs $40 to register and then they will instruct you to go to www.txdriving.com. You'll be able to rent a video at Blockbusters and it may be worth it to not have to sit in a classroom. But the government is sneaky and you'll not be able to pull a fast one. Believe me, they know if you're sleeping during questions or not following the instructions to the letter.

Pay attention. These courses will help forgive tickets, reduce fines or reduce auto insurance rates. And it's worth it, even for a few laughs.

★★★ CycleSmart   972/712-0712
6427 Main St.   Tue-Fri 10-6; Sat 10-4
Frisco, TX 75034

Are you cycle dumb? If you are, get some lessons from CycleSmart where motorcycles and other bikes of the same persuasion are taken on consignment. You'll be buying a used bike but saving some money. Bring your bike down for a close inspection. See the full spectrum of name brand bikes: **BMW**, **HARLEY-DAVIDSON**, **HONDA**, **KAWASAKI**, **MOTO GUZZI**, **SUZUKI**, **YAMAHA** and others. From street or touring bikes (as opposed to dirt or ATVs), this company can propel you to greater heights at lower prices. So, if your bike is taking up space in your garage, or you want to trade it in so you can trade up, get going oh Wheelie Dan, you. New and used parts and accessories, too, are either in-stock or special ordered. Bob Sutton's one of the men on the scene; the other is a full-time seasoned mechanic/racer. Between the two of them, they will show you the Blue Book value of your bike. You must be willing to sell it below the *Blue Book* price, or they will recommend you sell it in one of the trader magazines. On average, they negotiate 10 percent for themselves for their efforts. On the way out, we noticed a '99 **HARLEY-DAVIDSON** Sportster for $9,995 and we almost weakened. But we thought twice. Driving to Channel 5 in my wig or costume-of-the-day would cause too much of a driving hazard.

★★★★★ Dallas Can! Academy (Downtown)   214/824-4226
2601 Live Oak   Every Sat at AM; Special Auctions Last Sat/monthly
Dallas, TX 75204   www.dallascan.org

If Dallas Can!, so can Fort Worth (817/444-5437). Now held every Saturday and with a special auction on the last Saturday of the month, auctions are conducted to raise money to help at risk students, ages 16-21 achieve a high school education and become a productive member of society. Your donations help create this sale and your purchases put money in their coffers and tax credits in your pocket. Sales include regular and antique cars, boats, RVs, motorcycles, riding lawn mowers, large box cars, golf carts, and various other equipment. Dallas auctions open at 8 AM and start at 9 AM and held at the location above. The special auction for Fort Worth is held the first Saturday of each month and regular auctions are also held every Saturday. Fort Worth auctions open at noon and start at 1 PM (so you can make it to both) where there are always at least 50 cars for sale on the auction bloc. The only difference is there are no boats sold at the Fort Worth Special auctions. The Fort Worth auctions are held on the Treasure Island Trade Days lawn. Each auction is open to the public and requires a $200 cash deposit and current driver's license. For a list of cars, go to their website the Friday before each auction. You will be paying wholesale prices and below if buying at the acution; creating a tax write-off if you're donating. Dallas and Fort Worth Can! Academy helps non-traditional, student-centered education programs. Dallas Can! Academy has three locations, all of which are located on or near a Dallas Area Rapid Transit system route. The other locations, besides Fort Worth include Dallas Can! Academy (Oak Cliff), 325 W. 12th Street, Suite LL, Dallas, TX 75208, 214/943-2244 and Dallas Can! Academy Families For Learning, 325 W. 12th St., Dallas, Texas 75208, 214/943-6073. Come on, you Can! do it!!

◆◆◆◆◆ Dent Doctor   972/434-2254
808 E. Hwy. 121   Mon-Fri 9-6; Sat 9-2
Lewisville, TX 75057   www.dentdoctorusa.com

Since 1986, The Dent Doctor has been like my chiropractor for my car. On call and ready to take care of those dings and dents. No major surgery here. Just quick repairs including hail damage. Question: Hey

Doc: I've got a boo boo on the driver's side of my car and one of my fenders was keyed. I hate hospitals and can't afford the services of a plastic surgeon. Any advice? Answer: Yes, Diva. Call me. I'm like the Doctor of Dents without the high cost of hospitalization. Chances are your insurance wouldn't cover my services anyway. The average repair cost of what I do is under $100. It's a quick fix and I'll come to you. It's painless. I'll even give you a free estimate. *Question*: Sounds good, Doc, but do you guarantee your work? *Answer*: Yes, ma'am. I offer a lifetime guarantee as long as you own the car. And, if you're not satisfied, you pay me nothing. Now, ask your plastic surgeon if he's willing to do that? Dents and door dings are their speciality, without painting. Same day service, though appointments are necessary. And now, they have a truck accessory store with bed rails, bed mats, bumpers, hitches, tool boxes, running boards, vent shades and can spray a bedliner protection coating like PERM-TECH to keep your truck looking really cool. If you're interested in a franchise, call them at 800/946-3368. If not, check directory for other doctors in your area. *Call toll-free: 800/946-3368*

★★★★★ Discount Tire Co.   817/571-2341
3233 Harwood Rd.   Mon-Fri 8:30-6; Sat 8:30-5
Bedford, TX 76021   www.discounttire.com

America's largest independent tire company with over 450 locations in 16 states is a fact. But what they don't tell you is that they're also the best. Customers sing their praises as their wheels go 'round and 'round. Their "fix your flat FREE" policy is just one reason customers are so loyal. No matter where you bought the tire, or which location you shop at, service is superb. Then, when it comes time to buy a new tire, bet you'll give them your business. Oh, there's another plus. You'll save 25-40 percent on all tires. The lineup of makes and models of tires include: **ARIZONIAN**, **BF GOODRICH**, **CENTENNIAL**, **CONTINENTAL**, **DUNLOP**, **GENERAL**, **GOODYEAR**, **KUMHO**, **MICHELIN**, **NITTO**, **PIRELLI**, **UNIROYAL** and **YOKOHAMA**. Speedy service with a smile on all of them. Custom wheels from **AMERICAN EAGLE**, **FITTIPALDI**, **ROH** and many others are available, too. Special orders, no problem. Their FREE fix flats policy still boggles our mind, but it certainly keeps me coming back for more. Superb customer service in spite of discount prices is what the BBB book is all about. And I promise, you'll never want to throw a tire through THEIR window. Used tires, too, are part of their inventory, some as low as $5. Ninety days same as cash. Check directory for one of the 20 locations in the Metroplex alone, besides those on the fringe. Search online for inventory and sign up for their tire newsletter. Just keeping up with the **FIRESTONE** controversy is enough to flood your mailbox.

◆◆◆◆◆ Fred's Foreign Car Service   214/350-6787
5915 Peeler St.   Mon-Thu 7:30-6; Fri 7:30-5
Dallas, TX 75235   www.dwfnetmall.com/freds

If you car's started to sputter in another language, it's time to take 'em to Fred. Though the website was not working during our research time, he was. Busy as usual, working on some fine European mobile machine such as a **BMW**, **FERRARI**, **JAGUAR**, **MERCEDES**, **PORSCHE**, **RANGE ROVER** or **VOLVO**, they can afford to discriminate. They refuse to work on American-made vehicles. Hey, this is America! Here's some assurances: They will not remove and replace items until they determine the problem. First, they want to find the cause of the problem and fix it, instead of treating symptoms at your expense. Ultimately, that will save you money. Though not cheap by any stretch of the imagination, they're right the first time under the hood. Regardless of the repair, Fred takes it upon himself to treat each and every car as a patient and he'll fix it, no matter what. It's like an ER room for your precious children, only these come with four wheels and a horn. Calling all foreign bodies!

◆◆◆◆◆ Holloways

4221 Ross Ave.
Dallas, TX 75204-5199

214/823-5888
Mon-Fri 9-3; Sat 10-2

Don't want to be ripped off if you car or boat's got a rip in a seat? Don't shed alligator tears just for a little tea and sympathy. Here's your remedy for those wounds. Ask for Ronnie, as he's the expert. He'll come to your location if it's not too far (and Carrollton was OK from his shop on Ross). Or, you can bring the car or boat to him. No charge for estimates and they'll be very accommodating around your schedule for an appointment. They can really sew it up right. For an eight-passenger boat, it would cost approximately $50 a seat (and that included a moderate yet appropriate fabric) and would take only about five days start to finish. Now, how's that to buoy your spirits. The price would go up if you chose a more expensive fabric or if the seats needed reconstruction with new plywood. But if ever there was an easier guy to work with, we haven't found him. He prefers to leave by 3 PM to avoid that downtown jam, but he's flexible, especially if he comes to your location. Sew, what are you waiting for?

★★★★★ Hub Cap Annie

11648 N. Central Expressway, #B
Dallas, TX 75243-3840

972/669-9898
Mon-Fri 9-6:30, Sat 9-4

Laurie had a better idea when it came to Hub Cap Annie. She suggested if you can't find a hub cap that matches the other three, why not buy two that are similar? Put two on one side and two on the other. No one will ever know the difference since you can't look at both sides of the car at the same time, now can you? Boy, what a brilliant idea and something most folks have not ever considered. A set of four rims started as low as $30 but can go as high as $70 depending on the vehicle. They also carry rims starting around $10-$15 each. Chances are, nobody beats their prices. Go north on Central, exit Royal Lane and stay on the service road. It's one mile down the road and your absolute best source for hubba-hubba hubcaps. Didn't meet Annie, but Jerry sure was helpful.

★ Lewisville Auto Auction

1836 Midway
Lewisville, TX 75056

972/434-2020
Mon-Fri 9-4:30; Closed Wed (dealers day)

You don't need a brother-in-law in the business to get it for you wholesale. Now, you, too, can shop for cars just like the dealers do—only they shop on Wednesdays and you don't! Unless you know what you're doing, you buy the car "as is" but they do allow you to drive the car around the lot giving you a hint of things to come. You can also bring your mechanic (or a service like AutoCritic). If you like it, they will call who owns the car (if the car's on consignment) and if they like your offer, the car's yours. Though there weren't many cars we'd deem acceptable, you never know what will be coming in next. Most seemed like jalopies, but you will have the "pick of the lot." Other cars come from area banks, credit unions and dealerships whose cars have been repossessed, but who cares from whence they came? Both foreign and domestic models, from 1980 and up, were spotted. During their occasional live auctions, registration fee is $10. Otherwise, you can shop the other days at your leisure. When buying any mechanical apparatus, be as thorough as you can. As always, "buyer beware."

★★ Maaco

4103 Lindbergh Drive
Addison, TX 75244

972/702-8877
Mon-Fri 8-6 Sat 9-1; Appt.
www.maaco.com

Since Pete Rose is the spokesman for this 30-year-old company. You, too, can hit a homerun. Though well known for a variety of car services, they will try to work with you within your budget or customize the work upon request. If you're trying to accommodate the requirements of your insurance, these folks will try to be flexible. If you've got to repair the exterior of your auto body such as dings, dents, rust, collision repair, painting, Maaco can provide more than just a base hit. There are almost 20 locations in the Metroplex (18-20 depending on distance, to be exact). Each location offers the painting package, for example, that includes a chemical cleaning, a thorough surface sanding, machine sanding if more chips and scratches, priming and block sanding, feathered areas, if needed, the application of a full coat of primer sealer, refinished with durability plus catalyzed enamel, and finally, an integrated coat of gloss-extending UV sunscreen. Whew, that's quite a list. But your car's not finished yet. Now, it's time to bake. Help keep your vehicle a few more years or get it ready to sell just with a new coat of paint. Expect a warranty in writing that is honored from coast to coast. If you've got a high dollar, late model or antique car, you can request their custom service which will duplicate that "factory look." Maaco is the largest body repair shop in North America, over 500 franchises. Millions and millions of satisfied customers can't be wrong. Check directory for the location nearest you.

★★★ McClain's RV Superstores

I-35 E., Exit 460
PO Box 969
Lake Dallas, TX 76205

800/497-3586
Mon-Fri 9-7; Sat 9-5
www.mcclainsrv.com

Did you know that car dealers have to post the MSRP price (manufacturer's suggested retail price) while RV dealers do not? Yet, McClain's always posts the price to show you they do not inflate their prices and then take the mark-down. These folks sell them for less, in a no-haggle, one-price transaction and save you money, period! No doubt, this is the easy way out when shopping for an RV. So hit the road, Jack and don't come back for a while. In some cases, you may stay out forever. Save thousands of dollars on the best brands in recreational vehicles. They will also make you a trade-in offer you can't refuse even if you don't buy a new one from them, offering a written offer good for seven days. Customers of McClain's can take advantage of their "Customer Care Program" which includes emergency road side assistance and appointments set while you're on vacation for service in other areas. But it doesn't stop there. As part of your first year's service, they offer FREE trip routing and maps delivered to your door, FREE jump starts and FREE tire changes, fuel delivery and lock out service with every RV purchased from McClain's. You don't have to be Irish to get these deals. After that first year, it'll cost you around $150 to maintain this kind of yearly service plan. Some of the buys we saw included a 1995 **ALLEGRA BAY** 28' for $29,900 (list was $33,300) and a 1987 **WINNEBAGO** Chieftain 31' for $11,900 (list $19,300). Or go all out with a 1994 **LUXOR** 35' for $79,900 (list $125,000). What a way to see the USA!

◆◆◆◆◆ Oliver's Automotive

1244 S. Stemmons
Lewisville, TX 75057

972/221-5583
Mon-Fri 7-6

If your car has let you down and you're not up for getting into a row with a mechanic, here's a new Twist on car repairs. Oliver's Automotive in Lewisville is who I recommend, even if it's not on your way to work. Make an appointment just two or three days in advance, and put your vehicle in their hands (their ASE-certified mechanic's hands, that is). When something doesn't NEED replacing, don't expect them to tell you it does. Honesty is their best policy. They've been in the business for almost twenty years and have all the qualifications for both domestic and foreign vehicles, brakes, tune-ups, carburetors, fuel injection, A/C and heat and all electrical work. They don't work on depression, though, yours or your cars. Exit Hwy. 121 and stay on the I-35 service road going north into Lewisville. If you're close (within a few miles), they'll take you where you need to go (like home or the office). Don't put a monkey wrench into your budget, Oliver's is your RX for getting your vehicle in superb running condition.

★★★★★ Radiator Express Warehouse   800/252-1313

320 South Belt Line Rd., #112   Mon-Fri 7-5:30; Sat 9-4
Irving, TX 75060   www.radiator.com

You've got ste-e-a-m heat? Well, don't get hot under the collar, or hood. If you're steaming mad about a radiator that just doesn't seem to hold water, then call on the Radiator Express Warehouse. With over 20 years in the business, over 20,000 radiators & AC condensers in stock, this is the place to radiate. Have it shipped directly to you or to your mechanic to install. All new radiators come with a lifetime warranty. Brands include **AC DELCO**, **MODINE**, **VALEO**, **VISTEON** and more. Their low price guarantee means that not only will they meet a lower price but they will beat it by 10 percent and you'll have up to 30 days after your purchase to take them up on this offer. How about the right fit and quality? If there's a problem, they'll replace for as long as you own the vehicle. FREE overnight delivery when you order online.
Call toll-free: 800/RADIATOR

★★★★ Rent-A-Wreck   214/398-7368

2025 S. Buckner   Mon-Fri 8-6 Sat 8-3:30
Dallas, TX 75217   www.rentawreck.com

The name is cute but hardly describes their inventory or their mission. First, they rent both new and used cars, vans and trucks. And they aren't exactly wrecks. Most are two to four years' old. In the late 60's, Dave Schwartz's tongue-in cheek-name (but very viable concept) was born. Today, it has matured into the one of the leading franchises in the industry with numerous awards and impressive rankings in the franchise business. Named the fourth most successful franchise, for example, out of 2,800 surveyed by Success Magazine. So, if you only need some plain get up and go, nothing beats a vehicle from here. Choose from a wide range of reliable, clean cars, trucks, vans (great for a weekend of bargain shopping) and convertibles (for a leisurely drive to the lake.) Rent-A-Wreck provides FREE local pick-up and delivery and is even recommended these days by some insurance companies. There are locations in Plano, 972/881-8142; Lewisville, 972/420-6305; Irving, 972/258-8260; Garland, 972/840-6531; Richardson, 972/669-2450 and Northeast Dallas, 972/620-1505. Another plus is that these folks accept a rental with cash and lots of "ID." Can you believe you don't need a credit card?
Call toll-free: 800/398-2544

★★★★★ Self Sell Auto Sales   972/219-1803

1035 S. Mill St.   Mon-Fri 8:30-6; Sat 8:30-6
Lewisville, TX 75067

FORD had a better idea. But Self Sell has a better idea for selling your Ford. For a flat fee of $50, why risk having some pervert coming to your house at all hours just to take a look at your car "for sale?" Take the risk as well as the hassle out of selling your car yourself. Let Self Sell unload your car for you instead. Figure how much you want for it; then they'll add on their fee for the negotiations and all the other elements to make that sale happen. They usually charge a minimum of $300 for themselves, but who cares? Get real. You'll get what you want, regardless. They even offer buyers a warranty on cars (but then you know how I feel about extended warranties. See www.warrantysuperstore.com and save 40-60 percent.) Choose from a variety of cars with several financing options if you're a buyer. But consider trading in your car, too. Now get a load of this! They will pay you what you want for your car if you trade it in, as long as its reasonable. Expect your car to sell in 30 days, the average selling time. In a world of doing-it-yourself, sometimes it pays not to. And at this auto lot, you auto let them do it for you. For your monthly fee, they show it, handle all negotiations, advertise it in the local papers, offer multiple in-house financing options, take trade-ins and offer warranties. But here's the bad news. If they think your car's unsuitable to sell (like being too old or too fat), they tell you right up front. It hurts to be rejected, but business comes first. Isn't that just like a man?

★★ Southwest Ford   817/596-5700
3001 Fort Worth Hwy.   Mon-Fri 9-7; Sat 9-6
Weatherford, TX 76087   www.southwestford.com

Whether you're shopping for cars or not, you've got to hear this. Head to Weatherford, where the living and shopping is easy. Look for the blue and gray building, home to Southwest Ford. Exit 414 from I-20, then past the first red light. Look for it about half a mile on your right. New cars, of course, but they also have used cards and rentals. That's a new one. In case you need wheels for a special occasion, trip or family event, here's a place to rent one. Or maybe you want to haul some stuff and need a truck? Or maybe you just need a temporary replacement due to an accident or service/body work? Special rates available for daily, weekly, or weekend rentals. Used cars are listed on their web page and separated by price. Take a look at their website to view the current inventory before you make the long drive. They also have cornered the market on **TOYOTAS**, **JEEPS** and **EAGLES**. Stop at the first light to take a look at Southwest Toyota Jeep Eagle. Looks like they've taken Weatherford by storm! On their site, there's even a link to the **FORD /FIRESTONE** updates.

★★★★★ Texas Mustang Sales   972/243-3400
2718 Forest Lane   Mon-Fri 10-6
Dallas, TX 75234   www.texas-cars.com

If a **JAGUAR** in on your dream list of cars, why not consider a late-model pre-owned model and drive off living the good life at the best prices in town. Since 1981, Pete and the guys have been at your service. Located on Forest Lane in an industrial showroom/warehouse, this is the way to buy cars. Have them fax you their current inventory list, or view online. There are no salesmen to contact you, follow you around while you're looking, or even follow-up with a courtesy (Ha! Ha!) call. Unless you request a call back or assistance, you'll get neither. View the numbers in the ID# column which are the last four digits of the Vehicle Identification Number (VIN). The VIN is usually located on the driver's side dash or inside the door. But once you have the VIN #, you can log on to www.carfax.com and get the lowdown on that car's history. With the Vin #, too, you'll be able to secure bank financing on site, by fax, phone, or now online, with their credit application, with terms up to eight years with approved credit. Bumper-to-bumper extended warranties on most vehicles up to 100,000 miles are available but check with www.warrantysuperstore.com before you buy their warranty and save 40-60 percent. Trade-ins are welcome. Besides **JAGUARS**, see late model **MERCEDES**, **LAND ROVERS**, **CADILLACS** and **LINCOLNS**.

★★★★ Tire Factory Outlet   817/735-8061
3021 Alta Mere   Mon-Fri 8-6; Sat 8:30-3
Fort Worth, TX 76116   www.michelindealers.com/tirefactoryoutlet/

Are you tired of paying full price for tires? For over 25 years, Tarrant County drivers have supported the concept of saving money and shopping here. Since 1975, though they've been discounters, they've never sacrificed quality of service. Just ask the BBB (us) and the BBB (Better Business Bureau). They have a flawless record. They offer a full line of competitively priced **BF GOODRICH**, **MICHELIN** and **UNIROYAL** passenger, performance and light truck brand tires. When you buy a tire from them, the price includes FREE mounting, balancing and valve stems, all those hidden costs that other shops might try to sneak in. They also offer alignments, front end service, shocks/struts, wheel balancing, oil changes, air conditioning repair, batteries, electrical system service, headlight/bulb replacement, cooling system work, light engine repair, tune-ups and more, including state inspections. Work is always done by certified technicians and alignment specialists. Vehicle pick-up and delivery is available and 90-days is the same-as-cash. Other locations at 1901 West Berry, Fort Worth 76110, 817/924-9191; 3300 Mansfield Hwy., Forrest Hill 76119, 817/534-4964; 6516 McCart Ave... Fort Worth 76133, 817/292-0957; 1441 N. Plaza Drive, Granbury 76048, 817/579-1210; plus San Marcos, Seguin, Lockhart, Graham and Tyler.

★★★★ Vehicles-in-Motion

1000 W Crosby, Suite 100
Carrollton, TX 75006

972/242-BIKE
Mon-Fri 9-5
www.v-i-m.com

For the true Biker Babe that coos over a good deal, here is where to go to rev up a good deal on a **HARLEY**, **HONDA**, **KAWASAKI**, **SUZUKI**, **YAMAHA** and more. Hundreds of them go on the auction block. Repossessed motorcycles, all terrain bikes, personal watercraft and more. Bid for a bargain and cruise out on a Nighthawk, Rebel, Virago or Vulcan. Take a tour on a Goldwing, Valkyries or Voyager. Public inspections are the day before the sale. Call or check their website for times. Public buyers (Non-Dealers) must give a $300 cash deposit plus $35 registration fee. Bidder fee of $35 is refundable towards purchase only. Also, there's a $45 buyer's fee added to each vehicle sold. Arrangements and assistance for overseas containerization and travel are available upon request. Trip the bike's fantastic and watch them roll out of there: sport bikes, dirt bikes, ATV's, snowmobiles, golf carts and more. Call or go online for times and dates.
Call toll-free: 800/292-7376

21

China & Crystal

★★★★ China Chasers
Grand Prairie, TX 75052

972/660-4760
24 Hours Online
www.swchinasilver.com

I hate to be a "Beveled Advocate", but when it comes to breaking bread or breaking a piece of glass china, it's wise to call upon this China Chaser. That's right, they chase down lost or broken pieces of your china pattern so you'll have the complete set. Why set out your finery at the dinery when you've got to substitute a few jelly glasses instead of your **LENOX**? All of the better brands of crystal and china can be replaced at this place. Just make sure to goes ping a ching-aling. This home business tracks down your cracked or lost pieces including **FLINTRIDGE/GORHAM**, **MIKASA**, **PFALTZGRAFF**, **ROSENTHAL**, **ROYAL DOULTON**, **ROYAL WORCESTER**, **STUDIO NOVA**, **WALLACE** and **WEDGWOOD**. Too, they will even help identify any pattern for FREE with a photo. So, chase the blues away with that missing piece of famous blue Wedgwood. Now, all's right with the world.

★★★★ China Teacup, The
509 Texas Ave.
Mart, TX 76664

254/876-3453
Mon-Sat 10-5:30
www.chinateacup.com

"I'm a little teapot, short and stout. Here is my handle. Here is my spout." Now, we're ready to read the tea leaves from The China Teacup. Charter members of IADM (International Association of Dinnerware Matchers), this company provides a FREE listing and search of patterns. Other companies charge for the search, but not here. Aside for the fact they belong to such a prestigious professional organization, they do hold the key to making a match. Since moving out of the Metroplex, this family-owned business continues making the connection to lost china, crystal and silver. From **ANSLEY**, **CASTLETON**, **DANSK**, **DENBY**, **FIESTA**, **FLINTRIDGE/GORHAM**, **FRANCISCAN**, **JOHNSON**, **LENOX**, **MIKASA**, **MILTON**, **NANCY CALHOUN**, **NIKKO**, **NORITAKE**, **ONEIDA**, **OXFORD**, **PICKARD**, **ROSENTHAL**, **ROYAL DOULTON**, **ROYAL WORCHESTER**, **SPODE**, **SYRACUSE**, **VILLEROY & BOCH** and **WEDGWOOD**, just to highlight a few. Whether you were born with a silver spoon in your mouth, or you've lost your favorite **WALLACE** spoon, The China Teacup can be your conduit to filling in the blanks. They not only provide replacement parts, they also buy your heirloom collections as well. Bottoms up!

★★★★★ Dishes from the Past   817/737-6390
3701 Lovell Ave.   Mon-Sat 10-5
Fort Worth, TX 76107   www.dishesfromthepast.com

Looking for the perfect "Dish Fulfillment?" Then call on Dishes from the Past——the menu for a perfect re-past. Dine in from an entire collection displayed in their 6,000 square foot store if you're looking to buy china or crystal. This company not only replaces broken or missing pieces, they offer a bridal registry, and a table is already set up for mixing and matching the different patterns, or designing wall arrangements. What a novel idea. Owners Jennifer Marcell and Ida May Fleet know the difference between a gravy boat and a tureen, from **SPODE** to **WEDGWOOD**, and every blue plate special in between. If they don't have the piece you are missing, they can put you into their database and notify you when they've located it. C'est la vie. Surely your company will understand if one plate doesn't look like the rest. It's on its way. *Call toll-free: 800/984-8801*

Fitz and Floyd Company Store   972/458-1471
5100 Belt Line Rd., Suite 400   Mon-Sat 10-6; Sun Noon-6
Dallas, TX 75240   www.fitzandfloyd.com

New name. New store. New location. But still the same incredible savings. Save as much as 60 percent off retail on everything from **FITZ AND FLOYD**. This whimsical manufacturer's company store is one of Dallas' home-town favorites. Save cash with lots of panache. Fine china and fanciful fare is presented with flair, you wonder now why you ever paid retail? Load up your "gift" closet with distinctive home decorative items. Then when the occasion calls for a gift— (birthday, house-warming, Mother's Day, whatever) you'll have just the right thing stashed away. The only difference, you didn't pay full price. That's right, turkey neck. You'll gobble up their wonderful turkey or chicken casserole dishes, present your next Easter banquet on an adorable bunny platter, you'll never run out of special occasion options. Choose from hundreds of closeouts, discontinued lines, rejects, last year's models, one-of-a-kinds,——whatever they can't sell through their regular retail channels winds up here at a substantial savings. Holiday favorites are not forsaken. Halloween, bring on the pumpkins, Christmas, bring on the Santa's, get the picture? Easter, bring on the bunnies? Bargains bring on the shoppers!

★★★★★ House of 1776   800/989-1776
Loehmann's Plaza   Mon-Sat 10-6
11411 E. Northwest Hwy.   www.houseof1776.com
Dallas, TX 75218

Here you can have your cake and eat it, too. Before they were just a mail-order resource to save on china and crystal, except for an occasional windfall clearance sale which was held during the pre-holiday season in their parking lot. Load up on brands such as **FIESTA**, **JOHNSON BROS.**, **LENOX**, **LUNT**, **MIKASA**, **NORITAKE**, **ONEIDA**, **REED & BARTON**, **ROYAL DOULTON**, **TOWLE**, **VILLEROY & BOCH**, **WALLACE**, **WATERFORD** and **WEDGWOOD** at their showroom at Loehmann's Plaza in Northeast Dallas. See Suzy run. See Suzy run after china and crystal. Their 12,000 square foot showroom resides at the northeast corner of Northwest Hwy. and Jupiter Road and yes, they were founded in 1976. Selling fine tableware, collectibles, jewelry and home furnishings at the lowest possible prices is their claim to fame. And speaking of prices, it is still their policy to never be undersold by any authorized dealer of the same factory fresh, first quality goods. They will beat any advertised price that happens to be lower than theirs on same first quality goods. It is that simple-they will not be undersold. Online, you will relish the **SPODE'S** World Famous "Christmas Tree," a five-piece place setting, retailing for $82/online price was $38.99. Now, do you get the picture? Sterling frames, crystal frames, lucite frames all make beautiful shower and wedding gifts, or the perfect gift for the grad or dad.

★★★★ Mikasa Factory Store   972/881-0019

6100 Ave. K, Suite 100   Mon-Wed 10-6; Thu-Sat 10-9; Sun Noon-6
Plano, TX 75074   www.mikasa.com

It's hip to be square and square dishes are in, just ask any savvy shopper who's been to Mikasa's Factory Store lately. In fact, they offered six new styles in square dishes alone. Dish it out and enjoy the savings. Step right up, ladies and gentlemen, and head to the back for even bigger, better bargains. If you dawdle, you'll lose out on those deals as they'll expire before you've even worked up a sweat. Strike fast if you want to gratify your every wishful thought. The same patterns you see in department and specialty stores are at their factory store for 30 percent off and more. Registries are even available online. It's a cinch to shop with ease and in an extravagant environment, though they're discounting every step of the way. Test the "ping" at Grapevine Mills, Tanger Outlet Center in Terrell, Prime Outlets in Gainesville and in Hillsboro. During clearance sales, it's possible to retrieve placements for 99-cents from the pile that once retailed for $3.49, stemware for $2.99 instead of $11, casual fine china service for four for $39.99 instead of $290 and bone china service for four for $79.99 instead of $460. It pays to wait it out until the sales begin. ***Call toll-free: 800/833-4681***

★★★★ Oneida Factory Store   254/582-7449

Southwest Outlet Center   Mon-Sat 10-8; Sun 11-6
I-35 South, Exit 368   www.oneida.com
Hillsboro, TX 76645

Interesting facts about **ONEIDA**. First, they are the largest manufacturer of stainless steel and silverplate flatware in the world. Secondly, they started in Oneida, New York during the 1840's when a religious group of "Perfectionists" started making among other things...flatware. Now look at them! Oh, my, how that silver baby spoon has grown. They became an official company in the 1880's so it's official, they're here to stay. Frankly, their flatware's almost flawless, bite after bite. At their outlet stores, expect discounts of 25-75 percent on every last item. Serves you right if you bought Oneida elsewhere. It's just last season's merchandise, discontinued lines and some seconds in silverware, flatware and crystal. Believe me, if there's even a flaw, it is undetectable to the naked eye. Now, put that on your "to do" list when it comes time to entertain, buy a wedding or shower gift, congratulate the grad, whatever, because you will look like a most generous fella. Keep your dinner list to a minimum and the same with your dining budget. Just "send in the tureens". Sorry to say, though, that you can only buy full sets at their outlet stores, not individual place settings. Their Denton location has closed, so you'll have to visit the Conroe Outlet Center outside Houston or the Tanger Factory Outlet Center in San Marcos for additional locations. The good news, though, is they accept mail orders by phone.

★★★★★ Oriental Outlet   214/638-8382

2250 Monitor   Mon-Fri 10-6
Dallas, TX 75207

Confucius says, "Wise man who saves money for a rainy day, finds a reason to shop here." Nothing is written in the wind saying just because it's at a sizeable discount, doesn't mean it can't be in sync with the latest fashion trends. See the Orient express itself in 20,000 square feet of warehouse. That means, they're a deal. From authentic Chinese craft and gift items to cloisonné and silk screens. The popular four-panel screens, for example, were tagged $65. Though there's often a language barrier, the walls of China came tumbling down when we saw the prices on figurines, antique porcelains, wood-crafted items, furniture, jade and more. Now, you want to be a sport and ship it anywhere in the country as a gift? No problem, they can do it. Yes, again and again, those who speak the language of savings don't have to speak Mandarin, they only have to have the desire to save a fortune, Cookie. Some items are even manufactured in their own factories. And if you're looking for a planter or urn with a Far Eastern bent, bet on any one of the thousands here.

Replacements, Inc.
Greensboro, NC

336/697-3000
Mon-Sun 8 AM-9 PM (Showroom); Mon-Sun 8 AM-Midnight
www.replacements.com

To see it with my own eyes confirms my original premise. Replacements, Ltd. is irreplaceable. It should be listed as one of the "Greatest Wonders of the world." Founded in 1981 by Bob Page, Replacements, Ltd. (located in Greensboro, NC) houses the world's largest selection of old and new china, crystal, silver and collectibles. Imagine four football fields, approximately 225,000 square feet and that's where their inventory resides. Over seven million pieces in 150,000 patterns, some over 100 years old is just part of the story. They add items (new and old) to their website so they can reach out and touch ever last potential customer. Thousands and thousands of broken hearts are eased via the phone lines, online or in person making a match with something from here. You, too, can replace broken or missing pieces to your china, crystal or silver set, or add to your collectible collection. How embarrassing to finally have your in-laws in for a formal dinner party only to use jelly glasses or Slurpee cups in place of those two **MIKASA** crystal glasses that broke last Thanksgiving. They receive up to 10,000 telephone calls each day and are ready when you are to take your inquiry and start their "seek and find" mission. Every item is carefully inspected and entered into their computerized inventory system—a site to behold. It's like maintaining dossiers on each and every person's request and they're not satisfied until they find every one's missing relatives. Having visited their beautiful 12,000-square-foot-showroom, it's worth a trip to Greensboro just to see the "Museum" inside with contains Bob Page's 2,000 rare pieces of china, crystal, silver, collectible plates and figurines. A free tour of their warehouse is also conducted every half hour from 8:30 AM to 8 PM, 7 days a week. Located between Greensboro and Burlington, NC, at exit 132 off Interstate 85/40, just in case you're packed and ready to go. Don't be surprised if you run into a dozen or so dogs when visiting. They were the originators of the "Take your dog to work" campaign. How can you not love them? In china alone, they offer the top 3,000 patterns. You can register online to begin receiving FREE inventory availability and pricing lists via e-mail, FAX, or mail for your pattern(s)! If that doesn't do it, there's even a larger list of up to 150,000 patterns available just by calling the toll free number above. And get this? Their average answer speed is seven seconds! And to add just one more incentive, prices are always discounted for new and old. ***Call toll-free: 800/REPLACE***

★★★★ Southwest Gold & Silver Exchange
5722 Locke Ave.
Fort Worth, TX 76107

817/735-1451
Mon-Fri 10-6:30; Sat 10-2

The rush is on! This pan handler's going to town with sterling deals on well known sterling merchandise. So, why be up the creek without a paddle? If you're looking for just a piece here and there to complete a set, here's where you can make a perfect match. In fact, if you've got a sterling piece you want appraised, there's no charge for appraisals. Southwest Gold & Silver is a sterling example of specializing in one niche of the market and becoming noted for your prices and service. If you're looking for flatware and serving pieces, the Pewter Principle has taught us to look for discounts on only the better brands: **GORHAM**, **LUNT**, **REED & BARTON**, **TOWLE** and **WALLACE**, for starters. For individual estate items, you can complete your set or just settle for an exquisite serving piece, platter or tray. In fact, most things here are "Tray Chic!" For coin collectors, just for old dimes sake, they still buy and sell rare coins, gold and silver (domestic and foreign.) Lots of little silver things, a 90-day layaway program, and other kindly incentives makes shopping here a slam dunk. ***Call toll-free: 817/735-4696***

22

Computers & Online

♦♦♦♦♦ Ace Computer Camps 2002

Allen, TX

800/386-4223
www.ComputerCamp.com

At 90 of the top college campuses around the country—MIT, Stanford, UT Dallas, Rice, SMU, for example—weekly computer camps are held for boys and girls ages 7-16. Offering both overnight and computer programs, all age-appropriate classes and activities, see what Johnny or Jill can create on their own. Websites, digital movies and more are being churned out by emerging talents discovered while going to camp. Nightly seminars and tournaments are planned with 24-hour supervision, when necessary. Could the next Bill Gates be looming behind some 17-inch monitor? Who knows? Well, you won't know, if you don't make these kinds of activities available to your children. Call for reservations.

♦♦ Advanced Electronic Sales & Services

2305 Belt Line Rd., Suite 100
Carrollton, TX 75006

972/418-7505
By Appt. Only

Since 1987, this company has been running circles around computers, networks, upgrades, accessories, printers, software, supplies, technical services and consulting. In other words, they are your back door into your front page. Since they are an authorized repair center for most brand name printers, why not consider their preventative maintenance program that schedules routine cleaning and maintenance. If truth be known, most computers and printers are just too dirty—even if they aren't talking to each other. Extend the life of your printer, and see if you aren't seeing things in a much cleaner way.

★★★★ Altex Electronics

3215 Belmeade
Carrollton, TX 75006

972/267-8882
Mon-Fri 8-6:30; Sat 9-5
www.altex.com

Everything from A-Z is part and parcel of the Altex Electronics inventory. From A/V cables to Zip drives and everything in between, including CD-Roms and DVD drives, batteries and hand carts, motherboards and mouse pads, power supplies and network switches, whatever turns you or your computer on, it's all waiting for a pick-up. Services include in-house and on-site technical and upgrade services, custom cable manufacturing, and on-site cable installation, to name a few. They've been in business since 1980; if you want to keep up with changing technology, take advantage of their lease plans. Altex works with Deutsche Financial Services and can provide in-house leasing as well as repairs. If you carry your problem in, rates are $45 an hour; on site, it's a $60 per hour charge with a $55 trip fee. Appointments available within 24 hours. Be sure to ask for their FREE catalogs. *Call toll-free: 800/531-5369*

◆◆◆◆◆ CCLIK- CCLIK   972/934-2545
3961 Belt Line Rd.   Classes available seven days a week
Addison, TX 75001   www.cclik.com

CCLIK-CCLIK, gee whiz, oh what a relief it is to know there's a school where it's possible to advance one's career. That's right. And it's not in Silicon Valley. To achieve certification in a variety of networking and computer arenas, think about it. Is e-commerce in your future? Are your skills current enough to wiggle your way into the IT department when there are plenty of unemployed dot.com has-been's? Get certified for instant credibility, respect and self-confidence. Expand your window of opportunities. Explore additional assignments and job options. And most importantly, command more money. Hear ye, hear ye! Be it a gigabyte or a slow DOS, it's time to CCLIK and Shout. Sign up for the **A+**, **CCNA**, **LINUX**, **MICROSOFT MCSE** and **NOVELL'S CNE5** certification classes. See how interactive and hands-on teaching points you in the right direction. Learn the ropes of theInternet and the Intranet. Pass all the tests the first time around (97 percent do) and practice-until-perfect labs ensure your success. Classes are usually held in the evenings or weekends. If you're interested, schedule a free meeting with a CCLIK Career Consultant! Life is a series of choices. CCLIK ("Computer Certification Learning Institute for Knowledge") is a good one!

★★★★ Clone Computer Corp.   972/934-2200
14839 Inwood Rd.   Office Mon-Fri 9-6; Showroom Mon-Sat 10-5
Addison, TX 75244   www.clonecomputer.com

Almost a quarter of a century doing what they do best, cloning. After all, when you do it right the first time, you want to do it again and again. At Clone, you simply start with the best computer and add from there. Keeping up with the Joneses is similar to keeping up with the latest technology: it's no small feat. Take the leap of faith and get 30-40 percent off published **MICROSOFT** manuals and training kits. Expect to see brand names including **HANDSPRING**, **NETBURST**, **PENTIUM**, **VISOR**, **XEROX** and more,including their own personal brand, **CLONE**. All service is done on-site. We condone it, so clone it! *Call toll-free: 800/388-6636*

★★★★★ CompUSA   972/233-4510
15250 Dallas Pkwy.   Mon-Sat 9-9; Sun 11-6
Dallas, TX 75248   www.compusa.com

From digital cameras to web cams, telephones to MP3 players, wireless phones to video games, you'll find more than just computers here. CompUSA sells a wide selection of digital cameras from the amateur to the professional, AND they sell all the supporting memory for the cams. Ooh Fah, and the MP3 players you'll find—well, they have one of the widest varieties of brands, types and accessories for these little musical jobbies anywhere. Video game systems, surround sound speaker systems, cordless and wireless phones—you can choose from many pre-built packages, or build one yourself at a HUGE savings. If you're thinking, "build one myself, yeah right!," no need to worry. With such competitive prices, hire a geek to build it for you. They also have one of the best translations from a bricks and mortar store onto a website. Check out their multiple locations in the Metroplex, visit www.compusa.com, and don't delete these guys yet. *Call toll-free: 800/COMPUSA*

★★★ Computek Systems

10703 Plano Rd., Suite 300
Dallas, TX 75238

214/503-6500
Mon-Fri 9-6:30; Sat 11-4
www.zdsparts.com

Off 635 at the Plano/Miller intersection, see what computes as the ultimate savings on both new and pre-owned computers and peripherals. This full-service computer resource specializes in **ZENITH DATA SYSTEMS**, and has been an authorized dealer and service center since 1990. Whatever you're looking for—from adapters to batteries, boards to cables, drivers to LCDs, keyboards, manuals, memory, mice, modems, power supplies, even laptops and software—these guys aren't lame in any category. How about learning a new language for just $10 or preparing your child for kindergarten for just $7? Be prepared with Project Manager, Day Planners, Calendar Makers or Resumé Design software for only $6 each—a real steal. They carry titles in business, children's, cooking, education, games, Internet, publishing, medical, music, religion, shareware, space, travel, utilities and so much more for PCs and **MAC** computers. Shop early, especially for consignment properties; otherwise, you'll come home empty-handed. They move out fast.

★★★★ Computer Recycle Center

303 E. Pipeline Rd.
Bedford, TX 76022

817/282-1622
Mon-Fri 9-6
www.recycles.com

I'm always a little suspect of a computer company whose website looks me in the face with a blank stare. Soon, they say, their order forms will be working again—just a temporary glitch. Well, we shall see. Certainly if you've found this computer pipeline for both new and refurbished computers, you are well acquainted with the dramatic savings. **PENTIUM'S** were selling for a song, and what a solution to your home, office or school work load! If you don't want to buy new, consider an upgrade or a refurbished model. Prices will soon be back up on their website. But for now, you can sell your usable computers to the specialists who can refurbish them to like-new status. And if you're looking to buy (or sell) software, they'll take you on. But if you are simply looking to toss an old computer or monitor away, rethink your options. Computers and their components contain aluminum, plastics, glass, cathode ray tubes (CRT's), liquid crystal displays (LCD's), solder, lead and other materials that are not environmentally-friendly, so don't just dump them anywhere. Drop them off here or arrange for a pickup of unwanted computers and parts. Doing your part in not polluting the environment is your contribution to recycling. It makes good sense all the way around. ***Call toll-free: 888/282-5944***

★★★★★ Computer's Worth

120 Lavon Drive
Garland, TX 75249

972/487-8922
Mon-Fri 9-5:30
www.computersworth.com

No, not in Fort Worth, this is Computer's Worth and it's located in Garland. Get acquainted, bargain shopper. Say hello to the good buys via excess inventory that they buy as surplus or liquidation and never pay full price on software, hardware or accessories again. This is it as far as CD-ROMs go. Look at some of the best software and applications in the business: **ACT**, **ADOBE**, **BORLAND**, **COREL**, **LOTUS**, **WINDOWS** and more. Software is available for **MAC**, Windows '95, '98, NT and Millennium. Software titles start at just $3.99, like the popular "You Don't Know Jack/ Sports" and "You Don't Know Jack/ Movies". Save money and get "Your Wedding Consulting Software" for just $15.99 or, if you'll looking to remodel your house, do it with "Floor Plan Suite 4.0" for just $24.99. Their website is extensive and easy to shop. No need to leave home to enhance your computer's worth. Shop in person or online, or visit them during "First Saturday" sales. (See First Saturday write-up.) ***Call toll-free: 800/838-7884***

◆◆◆◆ **Computize**
1365 Glenville Drive
Richardson, TX 75081

972/437-3100
Mon-Fri 8:30-5:30; Sat 9-5
www.computize.com

This company came upon the scene in Houston in 1983, just when the revolution was beginning to surface. Since that time, they have been leaders in selling over 90,000 IT products. Those in the Information Technology departments will think they have died and gone to high-tech heaven. Companies and brands that they work with not only span the globe but also the alphabet: **ACER**, **APPLE COMPUTERS**, **CANON**, **COMPAQ**, **HEWLETT-PACKARD**, **HITACHI**, **IBM**, **IPLANET**, **KODAK**, **LEX-MARK**, **NEC**, **OKIDATA**, **SUN MICROSYSTEMS**, **TOSHIBA**, **VERITAS**, **XEROX** and **ZEBRA** are just the first course. From soup to nuts, the main course includes computers to printers, plotters to monitors, storage devices, power equipment, video boards, scanners, networking, modems, memory, software and accessories. Financing and leasing options are available as well as service, repair, extended warranties, networking and onsite IT support. If you're the government or an educational institution, special prices will be considered. Though they specialize in corporate accounts, don't shy away from them if you're an individual user or small business. Online shopping seems to be the direction they're going, consolidating all of their retail locations into one as online sales becomes more and more predominant.

★★★ **Cyber Exchange**
360 East FM 3040, Suite 850
Lewisville, TX 75067

972/316-3030
Mon-Sat 10-8; Sat Noon-6; Sun 1-4
www.cyberexchangedfw.com

When it comes to grabbing a burger, you know you can always pull up to a Sonic and have your order ready in a few minutes. Well, next time, eat and run next door to CyberExchange where they buy, sell and trade preowned software and hardware. Have a good deal and digest the helpful service. Here they can do it your way—repairs, upgrades and networking services are available. For in-house PC upgrade and service, expect to shell out $99 plus parts. This national franchise is making lots of headway as folks fed up with old games, video titles or how-to applications can trade in, up or away for a percentage of the original price. Then, you earn credits toward the purchase of something else. Hundreds of both new and recycled titles for both the PC and the **MAC**, including hard-to-find software for older computers and "Apples". All the software has been checked for viruses and guaranteed not to be defective. You, on the other hand, have not. Lots of variations on the theme of getting you and your business off the ground, from leasing to upgrading and convenient to the Vista Ridge community in Lewisville. *Call toll-free: 800/601-2999*

◆◆◆◆ **Doctor PC**
209 W. Main St.
Richardson, TX 75081

972/235-3772
Mon-Fri 9-6; Sat 10-6

If your computer is experiencing those "senior moments," it's time to call the doctor. Whether you're suffering from a slipped disc or your hard drive has gone soft, this Doctor of PCs can fix 'er up. Maybe it just needs a good cleaning? Or there's not enough memory to hold all your thoughts. He's got a remedy for most any problem you're experiencing. Labor prices are not per hour but run instead from $65-$85 to a maximum of $125 per problem plus parts. No house calls. You bring your computer in for the Doctor to execute the prescription. Insurance is not accepted but emergencies are.

Electronic Discount Sales   817/548-1992
908 E. Pioneer Pkwy.   Mon-Sat 10-7
Arlington, TX 76010   www.electronicdiscountsales.com

No, laptops here are not kitties purring in your lap, but rather the brands that will make you feline fine. Input these: **3COM**, **ACER**, **APPLE**, **ASUS**, **BELKIN**, **CISCO**, **CYRIX**, **DIAMOND**, **DIGITAL**, **EPSON**, **FUJITSU**, **HEWLETT-PACKARD**, **HITACHI**, **IBM**, **INTEL**, **JVC**, **LOGITECH**, **MATRIX**, **MICROSOFT**, **MITSUBISHI**, **MOTOROLA**, **OKIDATA**, **PANASONIC**, **PHILLIPS MAGNAVOX**, **QUANTUM**, **SAMSUNG**, **SEIKO**, **SONY**, **SUN MICROSYSTEMS**, **TDK**, **TOSHIBA**, **VIKING**, **XEROX**, **YAMAHA**, **ZENITH** and hundreds of others. How about a factory-refurbished **LEXMARK** 1100 color printer with $30 rebate, final price $59.99, or a case of 50 CD-Roms for $49.95 and software titles as low as $2.99? Then maybe the inDELLible 17" monitor for $229 will get your goat? Even phones, accessories, surround sound and car stereos are available here at sensational prices. Service and repairs, too. Look for special reconditioned and used items not only in-store but also posted on eBay. Then, if you'd rather shop online at their site, go forth and ye shall prosper. The items represented online are but a fraction of the inventory that's in store. But they select certain items because of "price," "hard-to-find parts" and "Super Buys" that they deem worthy of distributing around the world. They have very lofty goals, but those more down-to-earth can visit their store in Irving at 4070 N. Belt Line, 972/570-7393. How can they sell so low while others are selling it at twice the price? Their philosophy is based on "turns." In other words, how fast can they turn (sell) the item so they can invest the money into more great deals? Since the computer market changes so rapidly, not holding on to inventory very long is a very wise decision. They are smart cookies. Just look at their initials (EDS)!

★★★ Electronics Boutique   972/783-6416
501 S. Plano Rd.   Mon-Sat 10-9; Sun Noon-6
Richardson, TX 75081   www.ebworld.com

There's a boutique for clothes, a boutique for home furnishings, and now an Electronics Boutique...with bargains to boot. Play the game correctly and you'll wind up a winner. Here you'll find video and software titles looming from wall to wall: everything for **PLAYSTATION**, **PS2**, **XBOX**, **GAMECUBE**, **GAME BOY**, **GAME BOY ADVANCED**, **NINTENDO 64** and **DREAMCAST**, as well as your PC and **MAC** computers. Save big on preowned titles like "Playstation's Tenchu", "Tony Hawk Pro Skater", "Metal Gear" or "Final Fantasy 8" for only $14.99. For that same price, get "Nintendo 64 A Bugs Life", "Battle Tanx" and "Asteroid Hyper" or "Dreamcast Aero Wings" and "Evolution". Need the whole system? Get a used Nintendo 64 for just $54.99 or a used Game Boy for $49.99. Even pre-owned Playstation 2 titles are available from just $17.99 (and that's a real steal!). If you're playing on your computer, bring the games to life with new Sound Blasters, Micropoint ll Mice (mouses?), GeForce3 graphics controllers and more. And, if you've never heard of any of these, welcome to the club.

★★★★★ First Saturday   214/720-9054
2632 Ross Ave.   Fri 10 PM-'til Everyone Leaves
Dallas, TX 75201   www.firstsaturdaysale.com

Expect a recording to give you the poop to scoop up some of the best bytes for your computer dollar. On the First Saturday of the month, expect the parking lots at Ross Ave. and Routh St. to swell to a combination shoppers' bazaar and flea market, full of hams (the radio kind) and the balance overflowing with cyber-geeks. Thirty years ago, ham radio operators congregated under the bridges of North Central Expressway to swap and shop. Today, it's a place where 250 or more merchants show up regularly and temporary booths are set up à la a garage sale at two distinct locations, selling a plethora of computer, radio and electronic supplies. On the north lot, it's more a garage sale than a serious vendor operation, run by former State Senator John Leedom, who owns the Wholesale Electronics Building. Spartan surroundings, no electricity, just a bunch of enthusiastic guys out to make a buck. Vendors can rent space for as little as $40. Bring your flashlight because the deals are negotiated in the dark. The south lot is the computer mix and match where deals are tabled starting the minute you start a conversation. You'll need a vendor table on the south side plus a resale certificate. It's much more serious than the more ethereal vendors on the south side. Bring cash, just in case the merchant in question doesn't take credit cards, but don't flash the cash, even in the dark. Parking across the street, $5.

★★ Gateway Country Store   817/788-2979
4900 Oakridge Terrace   Mon-Sat 10-9; Sun Noon-6
North Richland Hills, TX 76180   www.gateway.com

Well, even **GATEWAY** may want to moo-ve over. Things may not be so ducky down at the farm. What started strictly as a mail order company has now morphed into retail brick and mortar stores. Chairman and CEO Ted Waitt actually started Gateway on his family's cattle farm. He took it public in December, 1993 and it is now headquartered in San Diego, California. They pioneered the build-to-order PC business but have since expanded, offering peripherals, accessories, software products and related services like training, financing, high-speed Internet access and networking solutions for home and business. The Holstein dairy cows on the Waitt farm inspired the distinctive and nationally-recognized patterns on their boxes. In fact, you may want to take a look at the cow-spotted Gateway-branded merchandise online. Gateway also offers classes, called clinics, which are FREE. So, if you're still standing back from hopping aboard the super highway, you can learn "How to Get Started with the Internet," or "Technology for Seniors" or "Intro to Digital Music" or "Educating Your Children". These are but a few of the learning possibilities. Check local stores for times. Service on your computer and trade-ins are welcomed. If you bring in any brand **INTEL** Pentium-class PC, they'll give you cash back to use toward the purchase of a new Gateway PC. They will even pay you to recycle your old computer. Also, there are locations in Plano at 1300 N. Central Expressway, Suite 601 and in Lewisville at 2240 S I-35 E, Ste. 300 (although the one in Lewisville does not have a business center).

★★★★★ Half Price Computers   972/250-3332
124 E. Arapaho   Mon-Fri 9-7; Sat 9-6
Richardson, TX 75081   www.halfprice.com

It's all in the name and what's in the name here is the whole story. Used and rebuilt PC's are just as good as the originals—maybe even better, once all the bugs have been worked out. And they're half price. So why not sell your working computer components, trade your old PC for a new one or just come in to buy the whole shebang from keyboards to printers? Get a 15" monitor for $38 or 17" monitor for $68 in your choice of **COMPAQ**, **DELL**, **HEWLETT-PACKARD** or **IBM** brands with a 30-day warranty. Reduce the byte and increase your revenue stream. Get an **HP LASERJET** for $105 or 32 megs of RAM for just $10. Get new parts like a **TOSHIBA** 12x DVD was $79. On the way out, we noticed a great looking oval conference table, cubical partitions and some metal desks, so it looks like they've expanded into office furniture as well. Why not? Even with a half price computer, you need more than the floor to work on. Occupying almost one block in the heart of Richardson's own Silicon Valley, enjoy the flea market atmosphere and haggle all the way down the line.

★★★★ ICS Computers   972/509-8000
2301 Central Expressway   Mon-Fri 9-6; Sat 10-6
Plano, TX 75075   www.icspc.com

And the shelves came a-tumbling down. With over 50,000 name-brand products (and services) on their shelves, it's no wonder there's an occasional fall-out. But in general, ICS Computers sells hardware to software, supplies to setting up a network, technical training to launching a professional website. These are the guys to call. If the chips are down, like they were when I went to their website, don't give up. Their server could be the problem. Once I was able to connect, I headed right for the clearance merchandise and wound up buying a port replicator for my **IBM THINKPAD** for $80 and a **MICROSOFT** Office Word 2000 training video for $86. Now, I need to find the time to view it so I can learn it. Then, I contemplated the **TOSHIBA** Protege ultra-thin notebook computer that was $1,200 but thought twice because there was a **CANON** Multipass with printer, fax, scanner and copying capabilities for $81. Seeing is believing. Located between Park and Park Boulevard in Plano, connect to this computer company and you'll be able to purge your files, surge to greater heights, network to your office, or call upon them to make an on-site service call. Whether you want to jump aboard a DSL or ISDN line to ensure you're connecting at rapid-fire speed, you don't want to fall behind or you'll be left out in the cold.

◆◆◆ ImagiNet Communications   817/516-0040
PO Box 172977   Mon-Fri 9-5; Internet Access 24/7
Arlington, TX 76003   www.imagin.net

Just exactly what do they imagine at ImagiNet Communications? Well, imagine providing Internet access and associated services to individuals and small- to medium-sized businesses. Does that explain it in general terms? If you need technical support, it's available 24/7 with a guaranteed two-hour turn-around time. Now how's that for service? Since 1996, they've done their due diligence to find out what people in the business really wanted, used and needed when it came to the Internet. They opened their doors (though they don't really have doors, just modems) and began offering one of the fastest access networks to the Internet. For Plain Old Telephone (POTS) access, ImagiNet uses only the fastest analog modems available in the marketplace. Choose from plain old telephone dialup to ISDNs and 56kbps up to a full T1 access. Some clients of their web pages include Rick Akin Realty, American Media Services, The Candle Lady, Elizabeth's Cake Supplies, Fort Worth Boat Club, Mercedes Boot Company, Net Auctions, North Texas Tollway and many more. Well, if it's good enough for NetAuctions (Felix-Holland), why not for you, too? If you don't, you might be going, going, gone!

★★★★★ IMS Computers   972/416-4000
2741 Belt Line Rd.   Mon-Fri 9-6; Sat 10-5
Carrollton, TX 75006   www.imscomp.com

IMS is to computers what a Motrin is to PMS: a quick fix for when you're in pain. The Carrollton location has a substantial service center and state-of-the-art repair facility. Though the rates are steep, they're so good that they can probably solve the problem in half the time it takes others. Labor rates are $65 an hour with priority service at $95 an hour. They offer flat rates for monitor repairs at $49 for a 14", $59 for a 15" and $85 for a 17". But they can also provide solutions for networking, video conferencing and streaming, too. If you're looking for a deal on motherboards and CPU's, then pick up an **INTEL CELERON**-2 700 for $159 or an **AMD** Duron 900 for $215. Don't overlook the CPUs, monitors, video cards, motherboards, printers, input devices, back ups, memory, hard drives, modems, cases, controllers, accessories and more. Start with the shell if you'd like to build your own system, then add name brand parts that are top-notch at the lowest prices, guaranteed. They even design web pages. No stone is left unturned when the subject is computers and all that they can be.

★★★★ Micro Center

972/664-8500
Mon-Sat 10-9; Sun Noon-5
www.microcenter.com

Keystone Plaza
13929 N. Central Expressway
Dallas, TX 75243

In 1979, Micro Center was just a micro-mini store in Columbus, Ohio, but today, they're one of the largest computer retail companies in the United States. First, they sold books, magazines and one **DYN-ABYTE** computer, and to make matters worse, their first customer was looking for a microwave oven. So much for selling computers. Today, it's a whole other company. Departments were created for accessories and peripherals, classrooms were added (computer training is available with class sizes averaging 8-10 students with approximately 150 different classes available), curriculum developed to educate customers, racks and racks of software (one of the largest selections in the country), then a furniture department was added, and walk-in, technical support was established in-store and more. To further meet customers' needs and demands, all stores now offer a digital imaging department. Stores are large enough to support a substantive selection of technical and computer books, PCs, **MAC**'s and accessories. Choose: **APPLE**, **COMPAQ**, **EPSON**, **HP**, **IBM**, **IOMEGA**, **NEC** or **POWER-SPEC** for all your PC needs. There are more than 700 product categories and sub-categories and nearly 36,000 products, including more than 6,500 software titles alone. Their staff know their Ps and Qs. Next to the Loew's Theater at Spring Valley and Central, there's only one Micro Center in town.

◆◆◆ PC House Call

972/234-0655
Mon-Fri 8-5:30; Sat 10-2
www.pc-housecall.com

14001 Goldmark Drive, Suite 101
Dallas, TX 75240

Don't worry if you don't have Medicare yet. You won't need it if the doctor is in. At least this one still makes House Calls. If your PC is experiencing a breakdown or any other mechanical ailment, you've turned to the perfect provider. Relax and take a load off. They can handle all the troubleshooting, network integration, DSL installations, upgrades, system setups and data transfers and recovery as well as phone support that any PC would ever need. Trip fees are $29 in their service area of Dallas to Frisco and Bethel to Wylie, then billed in half hour increments thereafter. Now, that's a deal! But it will cost $69 in extended service areas like Lake Dallas, Lewisville, Cockrell Hill, Irving and Lucas. Sorry, Flower Mound and Grand Prairie residents. If the doctor is in, emergency services will add an additional $30 to the trip fee and double the labor costs. Now, that's a real labor pain! Try to get your PC to cooperate and not have a nervous breakdown after hours. Drop-off service for in-House Calls are also available at $79 per hour. The cost of PC health care doesn't come cheap; but usually your whole (business) life depends on it. Too, what if you lost all your e-mails? You'd feel naked. So pay up, sucker, and hope that your computer stays in shape!

Resource Concepts

972/245-5050
Mon-Sat 9-6
www.outletcomputer.com

2940 Eisenhower, #130
Carrollton, TX 75007

Best **100** SHOPPING DESTINATIONS

Waste not. Want not. If you thought you couldn't afford the industry leaders (**COMPAQ**, **DELL**, **HEWLETT-PACKARD**, **IBM**, **MICRON**, **TOSHIBA** and others), think again! Resource Concepts sells computers and all the extras at "as low as they go" prices. They move factory-refurbished and excess inventory from major manufacturers at a substantial savings to the public. All the latest technology with one difference: the price. They also sell returns. These are known as "open-box returns", meaning just that. Only the box has been opened, but they have to be sold as "used" products, even though they're not. They offer end-of-product cycle and demonstration models as well as special deals and bulk-packaged products that

are new, too. In other words, they find the best deals and pass them on to you, me and the other smart shoppers in the Metroplex (and the world, online). Now, should you worry if the computer's been refurbished? Nope. Expect them to be stringently checked and tested to exceed industry requirements for new machines. Then again, they may have a slight blemish, but who cares? It may have been demonstrated at a trade show, who cares? It came back to the manufacturer as an exchange, who cares? All computers come with a one-year or three-year RCI warranty. Truckloads of product arrive daily at their 150,000 square foot recycling warehouse and showroom facility. When you see it, buy it, or tomorrow you'll be sorry. See Jack run to the outlet. See Jack buy everything he needs for his office and home office at outlet prices. See Jack save on servers, systems, notebooks, accessories, monitors, displays, printers, scanners, cables, CPUs, memory, modems, motherboards, multimedia, networking, software, storage, video cards— well, I told you, the inventory's extensive. What I haven't revealed yet, though, are some of the prices. How about a Dell Optiplex PII 350, 6.4G HD, 64 meg RAM and 24X CD for $369? Call for the latest prices because inventory flies out like Raid spray at a picnic. Shop online and call for prices, too, for the same reason. See why Resource Concepts wins all the ecological and economical awards in the industry. Folks like Ike! They're located at the corner of Eisenhower and Frankfort in Carrollton; take I-35 to the Frankfort exit and go east approximately one-half mile. They're on the corner and occupy the whole block.
Call toll-free: 800/588-9468 🇺🇸 ✒

★★★★ Software, Etc.

801 S. Greenville Ave.
Allen, TX 75002

972/727-9695
Mon-Fri 10-8; Sat 10-5; Sun Noon-5
www.software-etc1.com

Consign your old software and hardware for up to 30 days with a 60/40 split and you'll come out with the bigger half. Just agree to their simple terms (which is the only thing on their website). Deliver the merchandise in good working condition and they'll handle the rest. Over 30,000 different software products on consignment. Find software like "Easy Family Tree", CAD packages, virus scanners, games and screen savers for a fraction of their retail cost. Both software and hardware are available on consignment, as well as a selection of video games. If you're a dummy, read any one of their "how to" books to learn the ropes. If you're cyber-challenged, they may come in handy. Most software is priced in the $7 range but would have cost $35-$40 new. Their 3,500 square foot facility is filled to the brim with software and more, complete with a fast check-out and point-and-find sales personnel.

◆◆◆◆◆ Verio

214/672-RAMP
24 Hours
www.verio.com

Imagine our surprise when our previous Internet provider OnRamp was sold to our current Internet provider, Verio, the leading provider of Internet solutions aimed at helping businesses of all sizes grow and compete in the new online marketplace. At least, that's their mission statement. I won't challenge their size. I won't challenge them on providing lots of Internet support and service. I won't belittle them or deny that you can register domain names for $19 with a .com, .net, or .org. Internet dial up is available for $19.95 per month. Well, that's par for the course. But more than likely, signing up with Verio is a best bet for small to large businesses. That's the good stuff. But calling them...that is a nightmare. When our server goes down, I hate them! But fortunately that's not everyday; most days, I am their biggest fan. Check them out yourself. On a good day, I might give them a reference. Online, you'll find all the support telephone numbers; some I know by heart! I'm going to give them 5 diamonds anyway, just in case they decide to take it out on my website for speaking my mind! *Call toll-free: 800-GET-VERIO*

23

Department Stores/Off Price,
Online & Catalogs

★★★★ Big Lots   **972/889-9815**
1400 W. Spring Valley Rd.   Mon-Sat 9-9 PM; Sun 10-7
Richardson, TX 75080

Big Lots is part of America's bigger broadline closeout retailer Consolidated Stores, so expect their buying power to be formidable. With annual sales of over $3 billion and more than 1,300 stores (Big Lots, Odd Lots, MacFrugals and Pic 'n Save), their stores offer a myriad of merchandise at closeout prices as well as everyday basic and seasonal goods. All merchandise is priced 15 to 35 percent below most discount retailers and up to 70 percent below traditional retailers. This former grocery store site offers housewares to sporting goods, gifts to jewelry, comforters, hard candy, name-brand toys, lawn and garden equipment, tools, furniture, cleaning products to sundries. A solar AM/FM was $29.99 compared to $79.99. Stay tuned. You never know what shows up on their bargain-laden shelves. From **PLAYTEX** bras for $4.99 to $5.99 to a 20-piece assortment of bungee cords. What a mix! *Call toll-free: 800/269-9571*

---

biggerbetterbargains.com   **469/293-7467**
PMB 428   www.biggerbetterbargains.com
1079 W. Round Grove Rd., Suite 300
Lewisville, TX 75067

Head to our website and find the click 'n shop button. Then, you're practically home free. Sasha Deal is the name of the store where the living is good and the prices are even better—as much as 80-85 percent off, no kidding. Only the best brands are represented and unlike some of your "other friends", when Sasha Deal finds an extra special something, she wants to share it. Quantities are limited, so if you snooze, you lose. Pack away an authentic **COACH** "Puggie" makeup accessory bag that retails for $38 at the Coach specialty stores for only $20.89 (almost 50 percent off). Then hide behind the full spectrum of designer sunglasses from **CARTIER**, **CHRISTIAN DIOR**, **GUCCI**, **SERENGETI** and **MASSIMO** if you really want some behind-the-scene deals. Then for the ultimate power trip, guys can get a load of a **MAKITA** table saw priced to sell at $263.91/retail price, $619. What about a pebble-grain three-piece leather luggage set marked down over 75 percent? Retail $229/your price, $53.88! Everything's first quality, no seconds, no imitations, period! Pack it all up and be the envy of the airline's check-in counter. For more, seeing is believing. How about the Cartier "Glamour" sunglasses that retail in department stores for $328, your price, $131.95. That's over 60 percent off. See what I mean? The categories are endless. Shop for Apparel, Collectibles, Dolls, Fragrances...oh, let me tell you about one of my absolute favorites—**FRED HEYMAN'S** cologne called "Hollywood"—a three piece set that sells for $69.99 was only $13.07. Sucha Deal from Sasha Deal!! Needless to say I bought four sets for the price I paid for one bottle at a discount perfumery in New York. Then, take a look at the jewelry. Probably nobody sells it as low as Sasha Deal. A gorgeous **CITIZEN** chronograph watch that retailed for $395 was $54; all **EBEL** watches were 65 percent off!! "Watch out!" Here's the lineup: antiques, appliances, art, audio, automotive, collectibles, computers, crystal and pottery, fragrances, furniture/home decor, hobbies, home and garden, home/office, household, jewelry, memorabilia, movies, posters, promotional items, sporting goods, sports memorabilia, stamps, telecommunications, toys, videos and TVs and watches. What a deal from her Lowness, Sasha Deal! 🇺🇸

★★★★ Burlington Coat Factory   817/571-2666
1201 W. Airport Frwy.   Mon-Sat 10-9; Sun 11-6
Euless, TX 76040   www.coat.com; www.bcfdirect.com

One of the few off-price powerhouses that offers an opportunity to shop online as well as on site, Burlington Coat Factory is anything but just coats. Women's, Men's, Children's, Coats, Shoes, Linens and Home Fashions, Baby Furniture and Accessories, Fragrances and Luggage. Couldn't resist leaping over to the "Cheetah" ensemble for my bath. Transforming a plain vanilla guest bath with jungle effects was the cat's meow. What's next? Their **MARTHA STEWART**-clone niche, the **CHRISTOPHER LOWELL COLLECTION**. This HGTV decorator has his own collection of bed and bath ensembles at Burlington with detailed decorating recommendations on bringing the entire look together. Hop on to this bargain train and save 20-60 percent. See also Luxury Linens and Baby Depot Departments within most stores. Hop on board the online train and save even more in time and energy. Check directory for location nearest you. 🇺🇸

★★ Clearance Center, The   972/387-0700
5812 LBJ Frwy.   Mon-Fri 10-7; Sat 10-6
Dallas, TX 75240   www.clearancecenter.com

Leaving no stone unturned, The Clearance Center searches far and wide for the best deals on closeout merchandise. It's like a garage sale for manufacturers. This place is a warehouse to be reckoned with, so be prepared for just about anything. Get charged up over electronics at rock bottom prices on VCRs, computers, camcorders, stereos and even TVs. Dig up a fantastic deal on lawn and garden equipment or pick up just what your pantry needs with grocery liquidations. Pour on the good stuff and treat yourself to a new sweater or whatever apparel may be on the shelves that day. Buy it when you see it as tomorrow's another day, another deal.

★★★★★ Costco   972/244-0000
3800 N. Central Expressway   Mon-Fri 10-8:30; Sat 9:30-6; Sun 10-6
Plano, TX 75074   www.costco.com

Happy days are here again. The creator of the warehouse club concept has moved in and the ground shook. It's electrifying what a few well-priced gourmet food baskets and name brand appliances will do. And you thought this town had too many stores aready! Well, think again! There's always room for **JELLO**—say Hello to Costco. Five locations (Arlington, Southlake, Fort Worth and East and West Plano), life is good on this side of heaven. Join the club. Get with the program. To describe Costco as cost-effective is like describing Mt. Kilimanjaro as a molehill. It's the apex, the pinnacle, the peak in wholesale ware-house shopping. Finally, it's indeed one-stop shopping for the family that has (or wants) everything; ditto for small businesses. The line-up includes appliances (both large and small), electronics, cameras, audio/video equipment, automotive accessories, digital cameras, video games and systems, musical instruments, books, movies and music including new releases, family fashions, sunglasses, briefcases, handbags, luggage, computers, furniture, wine cellars, gift baskets, houseplants, desk accessories, golf clubs, pens, sports memorabilia, hardware, outdoor furniture, pet supplies, barbecue grills, plumbing supplies, sauna and spas...whew, I'm exhausted. Let's face it. Costco has everything. Gourmet food, house-wares, kitchen accoutrements, tabletop, storage containers, jewelry, diamonds, wedding bands, jade, office supplies, sporting goods, toys...it's literally an A to Z madhouse. Oh, did I forget to tell you we booked our vacation package here, too? *Call toll-free: 800/774-2678*

★★★★★ **Depot 42**   **940/648-3344**
1429 West FM 407   Mon-Sat 9-6
Justin, TX 76247

Closeout carnivores will feel right at home. Depot 42 is a 25,000 square-foot monster for food and house-wares. Expect gadgets galore with popular grocery-store names like **RUBBERMAID**—how can you not buy a ton of stuff for the kitchen here? Or what about a coffee maker by **MELITO**? Stir around the pots and pans, cookware, stainless steel mixing bowls, storage containers, school supplies, stereos, luggage, purses, knives, tools, well, maybe. This is a closeout place, so if you see it today, you better buy it today, else you'll be sorry. One day it might be **SEIKO** watches, or a sports watch, even a kid's watch, you just never know. But what I do know, everything's at wholesale prices or below. You'll be astonished at the assortment of new and notable. Pottery to glassware, handbags to T-shirts, vases to vaseline...what, now you're telling me there are sundries? What about food? Okay, they've got some of that, too. Maybe it's a box of cereal with Christmas characters. Well, who eats the box anyway? Then again, Christmas cereal made for December to be eaten in May? No May to December recommendations here. (I wouldn't touch it with a ten-foot spoon!) The Justin store closes at 6, but the Fort Worth store is open until 8. The Fort Worth store also goes by the name of Bargain City but claims they are one and the same.

★★★★★ **Dillard's Clearance Center**   **817/649-0782**
Festival Marketplace Mall   Mon-Sat 10-7; Sun Noon-6
3000 E. Pioneer Pkwy.
Arlington, TX 76010

Spice things up with Dillard's Clearance Center. Take your wardrobe from "blah" to "ahh" with discounts on designer labels including **ANNE KLEIN, CAROLE LITTLE, CHRISTIAN DIOR, DOCKERS, ELLEN TRACY, KASPER, LITTLE ME, LIZ CLAIBORNE, LEVI'S, PERRY ELLIS, POLO** by **RALPH LAUREN, TOMMY HILFIGER** and more. The list is endless and so are the savings with up to 75 percent off. How about occasional sales that offer another 30 percent off the lowest marked price? Do we have your attention? Stop monkeying around! If you like shopping at Dillard's, you'll go ape at their clear-ance store.

★★★ **Dollar Tree Store**   **817/461-6899**
Pioneer Plaza Shopping Center   Mon-Sat 9-9; Sun Noon-6
2212 S. Fielder Rd.   www.dollartree.com
Arlington, TX 76013

If only it grew on trees. Well, even if money doesn't, the stuff here is ripe for the picking. This national chain is rooted in good old-fashioned greed. A buck's a buck, and let your buck stop here. Buckle up, knuckle-head, and head on out to your closest Dollar Tree. Closeouts, overruns and repackagings from major and generic manufacturers of housewares, seasonal goods, candy/food, toys, health/beauty care items, gifts, party goods, stationery, books, accessories—it's almost overwhelming and certainly dis-arming. My arm got a workout grabbing item after item, all for $1. Load up on things you could live without but don't want to. From a sports team logo yo-yo to wrapping paper, **LOONY TUNE** keychains, hair spray to cologne, crépe paper to candy, yum-m-m, it's all pretty delicious for a buck. Like a modern-day version of the 5 & 10, expect to see general merchandise in a variety of categories. Since they operate over 1,720 stores in 36 states, they are big and they're getting bigger. By the way, they also operate stores under different names such as: Dollar Tree, Dollar Bill$, Only $1.00, Only $One and Dollar Express. Check directory for the store nearest you.

★★★★ Horchow Finale

3400 Preston Rd.
Plano, TX 75093

972/519-5406
Mon-Fri 10-7; Sat 10-6; Sun Noon-5
www.horchow.com

You know the name Neiman Marcus, but do you know Horchow? Roger Horchow, founder of the Horchow Collection (now owned by Neiman's) and now the New York producer of Broadway revivals, well, Roger's out and the Finale Shops are in. This step-child to the giant mail order mogul's catalog sells the remains of the day. Chi-chi fashions for the home and closet are temptingly displayed between the gorgeous pages of their catalogs. Log on to their website if you want to place your name on their mailing list to receive them. Then, when you get them, dream on. But that's where the Finale Shop comes to the rescue. What doesn't move fast enough winds up at the Finale Shop at a fraction of the price. Maybe it was a wrong size and returned or maybe the item just didn't sell. Lucky you. Does it really matter if you can save 30-70 percent off the catalog's prices? That makes it worth waiting a season or two. Drool on. Unfortunately, some of the items are so outrageously over-priced and with limited appeal, it still doesn't make sense to buy, even at half price. On the other hand, sometimes that pair of sterling earrings or that velour robe is the perfect gift at full price and even more perfect at half the price. So be it. Each of us have our own reasons for buying. And that's what makes this store successful. Beautiful merchandise with meaningful bargains gives us all a pause that refreshes. Second location's at 3046 Mockingbird Lane (at the northwest corner of Mockingbird and Central Expressway in Dallas), 214/750-0308. *Call toll-free: 800/456-7000*

★★★★★ JCPenney Outlet Store

Grapevine Mills Mall
3000 Grapevine Mills Pkwy.
Grapevine, TX 76051

972/874-0578
Mon-Sat 10-9:30; Sun 11-7
www.jcpenney.com

A penny for your thoughts? At their outlet, you get more than you bargained for. Often, they're running a sale with an additional percentage off, and discounts of 75 percent off the original price is commonplace. That's when it's time to call out the troops. Strike up the band. Load up the truck. Reward yourself with closeouts, discontinueds, returns or overruns from their retail stores or catalog. The usual savings? At least 40-60 percent off. Just look what your pennies will buy: family apparel, athletic apparel, family shoes, athletic shoes, petites, misses, and tall women's fashions, home furnishings, home accessories, electronics and even big and tall men's apparel. The warehouse environment presents the merchandise without any distractions of fancy displays or colorful vignettes. Plain and simple. Shop and Go. Even if you're not a full-fledged Penney's shopper, give it a look-see and you might be persuaded to join the Penny Brigade—where every penny counts!

★★★★ Kohl's   **972/939-2887**
4120 Old Denton Rd.   Mon-Thu 9-11; Fri-Sat 8-11; Sun 10-7
Carrollton, TX 75010   www.kohls.com

This Kohl not only won't burn you on high prices, but they won't make an ash out of you, either. Fan(s) flock to this neighborhood discount department store concept while department store's flames are flickering in regional malls across the country. Bet you're going to see some of those department stores emulating Kohl's success. Watch them try to clone Kohl's. We shall see. But I can see why they are making their way across America. Founded in 1962 in Milwaukee, Wisconsin, they carry all of the popular brands that a value-oriented family wants: **ADIDAS**, **CANDIES**, **CARTERS**, **CHAMPION**, **DOCKERS**, **HAGGAR**, **HEALTHTEX**, **GLORIA VANDERBILT**, **JOCKEY**, **KEDS**, **KRUPS**, **LEE**, **LEVI'S**, **NIKE**, **PFALTZGRAFF**, **PLAYTEX**, **REEBOK**, **UNION BAY**, **VANITY FAIR**, **VILLAGER** and others. Who can resist running to the corner store and filling the shopping cart when you need something NOW? Well, therein lies their only serious drawback. They don't have any. A store without shopping carts is a store where I buy one thing! When I complained, they said, "You don't see shopping carts indepartment stores, do you?" Hello! Why do you think consumers are flocking to TJMaxx and Marshall's? Anyway, their inventory, besides clothing for the entire family, will sometimes burn a hole in your pocket so beware: fill up the "no-cart" arms with shoes, housewares, home decor, jewelry, toys, cards and more. They offer their own credit card and there's always a great sale going on. Twenty percent is their usual discount but more during frequent sales. Check directory for the nearest location. ***Call toll-free: 800/837-1500***

★★★★ MacFrugal's   **972/484-4821**
2865 Valley View Lane   Mon-Sat 9-9; Sun 10-7
Farmers Branch, TX 75234

When you see the word c.l.o.s.e.o.u.t., grab yourself a big one at MacFrugals. A closeout on a six-piece patio set with umbrella was $79.99, a hand truck, perfect to lug around all those hard-to-carry items, was a paltry $19.99, an eight-slat wooden park bench sat two of us for a five-minute break from shopping for $19.99, baby wipes for $1.49...ok, so we don't need them now, but we did grab a few bottles of **MAALOX** for $1.49. You would have indigestion, too, if you just bought it for $1.99 elsewhere. That's 50-cents too much. We left with 20 pounds of **GRAVY TRAIN** for $5.99, a cast iron birdbath fountain for $39.99 (compared to $66.99) and we chirped, "Cheep, Cheep" all the way home. Check directory for the location nearest you.

★★★★★ Marshall's   **972/248-8494**
7609 Campbell Rd.   Mon-Sat 9:30-9:30; Sun 11-7
Dallas, TX 75248   www.marshallsonline.com

Let me introduce you to the Marshall's plan. No doubt, it's soon to overtake the world of discount shopping. Going strong for longer than I have, it's now part of the TJ Maxx family. Even in the off-price world, mergers and acquisitions are an everyday occurrence. This Boston-based giant is headed by a old friend, Bernie Cammarato, who helped orchestrate TJ's buy out of his old alma mater, Marshall's. Now it's one big happy family doing billions of dollars one item at a time. Always save 20-60 percent and more when there's a sale going on. Currently, they're expanding their gift department, bed and bath world, housewares and Women's World for plus sizes since TJ decided to exit that niche market. Desirable name brand fashions for men (one of their strong suits), sportswear for women, children's apparel and lingerie plus shoes and accessories, gourmet food items, jewelry, hosiery and more. What would I ever do without my designer knee-high's at half the price? Designer fragrances for $19.99 such as **CHLOE**, **FENDI**, **PALOMA**, **PASSION**, **POISON**, **SHALIMAR**, **SUNG**—popular favorites for the scent set. Selection ranges from staggering to skimpy, but that's typical in the off-price arena. Check directory for nearest location. And on a charitable note, I want you to know that Marshall's is a big supporter of the National Violence program, United Way and Juvenile Diabetes. ***Call toll-free: 888/333-5447***

NV Neiman's Last Call

Grapevine Mills
Hwy. 121, Exit Bass Pro Drive
Grapevine, TX 76051

972/724-4900
Mon-Sat 10-9:30; Sun 11-8
www.millscorp.com/grapevine

It was only a matter of time before **NEIMAN MARCUS** brought their clearance store to the Metroplex. It's about time. Opening in the Spring of 2002, it is anticipated to be approximately 32,000 square feet of outlet bliss joining their other Texas location in Austin and eight other locations around the country. No doubt, home-based fans of Neiman's will probably be holding their bargain breath until the doors open. Apparel and accessories are what you'll see marked down 40-80 percent from their 32 regular stores, NM Direct, and one of their sister stores, Bergdorf Goodman. Now we're talkin'! What you'll see will be past season's merchandise, but how different is last season's **DONNA KARAN** black skirt from this season's? Nobody will ever know how low you would go just to bring home an outfit or two from N-M. When asked where you shop, at last, you can say Neiman's. Unless you're like me and brag how little you paid! Last Call will be built on the mall's east side, near Rainforest Cafe and Books-a-Million. Welcome home. What is Stanley thinking now?

overstock.com

www.overstock.com

When it comes to writing RAVE reviews about a shopping site, this is one name that stands head and shoulders above the rest. Founded by wunderkind Patrick Byrnes, this is one of the dot.com success stories of the century. It doesn't get better than savings up to 70 percent everyday, seven days a week, 365 days a year with a guarantee that they will refund the difference if you ever find the same item for less anywhere on the web. A 100 percent, 240 thread-count down comforter that retailed for $199 was $69.96—that's 65 percent off right there. The endless stream of categories and products will boggle your mind. Search by brand or by product. A few brands to brag about include **ADIDAS, AMERICAN TOURISTER, ANNE KLEIN, AVIA, BETTY CROCKER, BRAUN, BVLGARI, CANON, CASIO, COMPAQ, CONAIR, CUISINART, DKNY, DISNEY, ESPRIT, EUREKA, FARBERWARE, FILA, FOSSIL, G.E., GORHAM, GÜND, HAMILTON BEACH, HASBRO, HOOVER, HUMMEL, KODAK, KRUPS, LENOX, LLADRO, MIKASA, MILTON BRADLEY, NASCAR, NIKON, NOKIA, ONEIDA, OSTER, POLAROID, RCA, REVEREWARE, RICOH, ROLLERBLADE, ROWENTA, ROYAL VELVET, SAMSONITE, SEGA, SERENGETI, SMITH & HAWKEN, SONY, SUNBEAM, TRAVELPRO, UNIDEN, WALLACE, WATERFORD, WEDGWOOD, XEROX, YAMAHA, ZENITH**—yep, from A to Z, they can keep you shopping for a lifetime. Well-organized, shipping flawless (each item comes in a sturdy box, well wrapped, and within days), easy to communicate with, and every category under the sun: bed and bath, decorative accessories, furniture, kitchen, lighting, rugs, window treatments, small appliances, cookware, crystal and china, gourmet, health and beauty aids, tabletop, costume and fine jewelry, sporting goods and gear, luggage and handbags, collectibles, baby items, crafts, dolls, games & puzzles, toys—I told you, once you've made your first purchase, you'll be hooked!

★★★★★ Sam's Wholesale Club

751 W. Main St.
Lewisville, TX 75067

972/436-6684
Mon-Fri 10-8:30; Sat 9:30-8:30; Sun 11-6
www.samsclub.com

You don't need me to tell you about Sam's. (Uncle) Sam needs you! Even with a Super Wal-Mart nearby, you might find the prices compatible with the club. Occasionally, though, I've found some prices at Super Wal-Mart to be less than Sam's Club but not all items are available in both places. It's like talking out of both sides of your mouth. You feel like you're taking candy out of one hand to feed the other. Why they compete with themselves is beyond comprehension, if not to strengthen their stranglehold in the marketplace. Oh well, just remember, competition may breed contempt, but consumers may be the benefactors. Just in case you need an introduction, this is Wal-Mart's division for wholesale shopping. You'll need to be a member and get a card to get in the doors; a tow truck to carry you and your packages out. Forget the amenities, just shop and never look back. Though you may be buying **FRITOS** in bulk, you either do it and die-t later, or forget it. That's how it comes, take it or leave it. You may even find some of your favorite vending snacks (like **ELIOS** pizza which was a great lunch during one shopper's visit.) It's also a great place to buy tires. Those were the days, my friend, when the new guys on the block couldn't break through the Wal-Mart power chain. Well, watch Costco go. Let them fight it out to the bitter end. The bigger the fight, the better they both get. Now adding more services such as a photo-developing desk, an eyeglass counter, a pizza kitchen, a fresh bakery, car sales, mobile phone service, travel, DirecTV and satellite TV and more. Wear comfortable shoes. It sometimes takes an afternoon of shopping especially, if you're buying for the office. Load up on TVs and TV dinners, bargains in best-selling books and blue jeans, food and furniture, office supplies and equipment, faxes and floorcare, carpet and Christmas wrap. Check directory for other locations throughout the Metroplex, most located next to a Wal-Mart. When shopping for a new car, pull out your Sam's Club Membership and there's a chance they'll negotiate. They did when we tried it. Soon you will be able to join, renew or upgrade your membership to elite status and also be able to shop online 24 hours a day. Just what I need.

Saturdays Only   **972/681-7766**
4702 Saturn Road   Fri Noon-9; Saturday 9-9; Sun Noon-6
Garland, TX 75041-5754

We're off to see the Wizard, the wonderful wizard who's open on Saturdays Only but is now open on Fridays and Sundays, too. What a find! You'll find electronics, housewares, clothing, toys, shoes, even boxed and packaged food—at 50-75 percent off regular retail. From lawnmowers to candy bars, and everything in between. You don't even have to be mow-tivated. Look what I've found within their 13,000 square feet that has come from major retailers around the country. Now open three days a week, it's like being on a treasure hunt. You'll never know what you'll find next but this store's already making waves. Check all merchandise carefully, as they do accept damaged goods and sometimes a lid is missing or a screw is more than just loose. Saturdays Only is weekend only and who doesn't look forward to the weekends? Shop, shop and shop some more for overstocks and closeouts by the truckloads that are unloaded hourly in this plain vanilla self-standing brick building. Eighteen wheelers pull up to this former office environment and unload a stash for a whole lot less cash! One **HITACHI** DVD player was $119 instead of $299; **SONY** VCR $54.95 instead of $159; **DREAMCAST** Tomb Raider game and Book $22.95—retail $79.99 (movie about to come out); **PIONEER** CD car stereo with speakers, $99 instead of $299. Then when our little scout spied the **STAR WARS** action figures for $3, the walls came a-tumbling down. The $499 for a 36-inch **TOSHIBA** TV is my next dream purchase but will probably be gone by the time I get to my piggy bank. Take LBJ to the Northwest Highway exit. Go left over the freeway and travel a mile or two to Saturn; turn right. It's across the street from Winn-Dixie.

★★★ Service Merchandise   **214/361-1202**
11250 N Central Expressway   Mon-Sat 10-9 ; Sun 12-6 (EST)
Dallas, TX 75243   www.servicemerchandise.com

Their restructuring, their repositioning, and their smaller and more targeted niche stores appear to finally be paying off. And their new logo, @Your Service, is one of the best campaigns I've seen in a long time.

Must be a woman at the helm? Now a more manageable specialty store catering to being America's largest jewelry store, expect to shop for diamonds, bridal and wedding bands, gold and silver jewelry, pearls, gemstones and name brand watches. Even children's jewelry will make an appearance in one of the many cases on display. Then, it's on to the kitchen for small appliances like toasters and roasters, mixers to matching appliance covers. Looking for a massager or something to relax your back? What about your aching feet? Doesn't everyone need a foot bath now and then? See the world through the lens of a camera, or see the planets through a telescope? Where to buy a pair of binoculars to get a close-up of Jerry Jones calling the shots and his new face? Stir up a dinner in a set of cookware, bakeware, place it on a new set of china, accompanied by a water or wine glass. Note, all of these items are not only perfect for yourself but make for great gifts. Check out the bridal registry and help the bride and groom pack for their honeymoon with a new set of luggage. Grill it, thrill it, kill the full price and you're getting a taste of the new Service Merchandise, @ Your Service. Over 200 locations nationwide, I think they've got it!. At last. I think they've got it! Checkthem out in Arlington, Dallas, Lewisville, Mesquite, N. Richland Hills, Plano, Richardson, Tyler. *Call toll-free: 888/764-4387* 🇺🇸

smartbargains.com

866/MY-BARGAINS
www.smartbargains.com

Having the Gordon Brothers Group as their strategic partner doesn't hurt this power shopping website called smartbargains.com. Gordon Brothers is the company that is generally behind the "Going Out of Business" sales where "Everything Must Go!" Well, guess what? Some of it filters through to smart bargains. You don't want to be called ill-informed, ignorant, out-of-it, behind-the-times, or any other name that would be construed you're NOT smart, do you? Sign up for their Bargain Alert. Watch for their clearance items. Save money like you've never saved before on enough categories to put the department store to shame. Why wander the aisles looking for just the right "buy"? Buy it online without the wandering. Save wear and tear on your feet and de-feet the high cost of paying full price. Names like **CALVIN KLEIN, NICHOLE MILLER** and **TODD OLDHAM**. How many pearl necklaces have you bought recently for $39.99 and saved $210? What about saving 66 percent off on a **PIERRE CARDIN** cardigan sweater for $20, a **JOSEPH ABBOUD** polo shirt for $30, a set of **ROYAL VELVET** towels for $19.99, a **PRADA** bag for $259.99 or a **TOSHIBA** 2.4 GHz portable phone for $79.99? They even tell you if there's only a few of those items remaining so you can get in on the horn. Women's and men's apparel, fashion accessories, home decor, games, jewelry, watches, fragrances, luggage and more. Be smart, shop smart. This is your smartest link! Say hello to these good buys. 🇺🇸

★★★★★ Stein Mart
6385 Camp Bowie
Fort Worth, TX 76116

817/735-4533
Mon-Sat 10-9; Sun Noon-5:30
www.steinmart.com

No relation to Goldstein, this Stein is still golden for discriminating shoppers. Designer and well-known brand apparel for men, women and children, it's the real McCoy. And, it's where the Diva and Tammy Faye shop when together in Charlotte, NC. The Boutique ladies hover over their selective turf, with all these upscale favorites. Guys can don luxury fiber sport coats, classic khakis and designer shirts and the all-important golf sportswear bearing golf hero's names. SteinMart also caters to Petites' and Women's Sizes and a Big & Tall men's department. Shoes for both, and more accessories and gifty housewares, gourmet food stuff, bed and bath items; it's like a miniature Saks Fifth Ave. But it's the jewelry department that sends my heart a-flutter. Love it. Clasp it. Dangle it. Hang it. Wear it. I dare you to buy just one! Check directory for other locations if you want to save 30-50 percent off and more. *Call toll-free: 888/SteinMar* 🇺🇸

★★★★ Syms

4770 W. Mockingbird Lane
Dallas, TX 75209

214/902-9600
Mon-Fri 10-9; Sat 10-6:30; Sun Noon-5:30
www.symsclothing.com

Go online and print off a coupon worth an additional 10 percent off. Then go shopping at Syms. Shopping there is like being at a candy store with all the many flavored tags. Don't be a sucker. Once you get the hang of it, you'll find it delicious. Italian men's clothes starting at just $99 for sportscoats and $59 for dress pants. Start panting up the ladder of success. Here's your wardrobe ticket. You can't exude success if you look like a schlump. (Figure it out, Bud!) Start the climb early and dress the part. Save on young men's wardrobes such as blazers, $59 and dress pants, $29. Remember, they retail for almost 40 percent more elsewhere. That's why you need to get an education, says Marcy Syms. She's right. "An educated consumer is their best customer." Syms selection is complete, just like being in a department store, without the full price tags. Save 25-40 percent on clothes for the entire family, luggage, leather goods, lingerie, linens, shoes, coats, furs, and more. Names to consider include **BALLY**, **COLE-HAAN**, **PERRY ELLIS**, **REEBOK**, **STANLEY BLACKER**, **RALPH LAUREN** and others that you could fill the pages of *Fashion! Dallas* with (well, before the *Dallas Morning News* dropped that section). The fun begins as soon as the automatic markdowns get posted. The price descends as time goes by. The men's department, though, remains their forté and occupies 60 percent of the store's merchandise in sizes 36S-54XL. They also have another location in the mid cities, in Hurst on the Airport Freeway (Highway 183) just west of Precinct Line Rd. near Abuelo's Mexican Restaurant. Muy bueño! The merchandise is often superb but the sales personnel are both lax and disinterested. So now, an educated sales personnel should be taking the next course in customer service.

★★★★★ TJ Maxx

12 Richardson Heights
Richardson, TX 75080

972/437-1842
Mon-Sat 9:30-9:30; Sun Noon-6
www.tjmaxx.com

Here we go again. To think I knew them when. Back in 1973, I was sitting on the floor of the founder of TJ Maxx who was then with Marshall's. They invited me to their offices to discuss the potential of the new, fledgling "off price" industry. Did I think they were on the right track? Is the world ready for a bargain? Is the Pope Catholic? Today, the same gentleman is the head honcho and founder of the biggest off-price retailer in the nation. It started out as small potatoes in Massachusetts and now it's stuffed with cheese and bacon bits—mashing prices to what has become the standard in the industry. Shoppers can expect 20-60 percent off everyday and during sale time, prices hit rock bottom. Though you may have to forgo a few buttons now and then, or a pair of pantyhose with one leg six inches longer than the other, you can't ignore the thrill of it all. Since the opening of their first stores in Worcester and Auburn, MA in 1977, they have grown to be the nation's largest off-price retailer with over 660 stores in 47 states. TJ Maxx sells brand name and designer fashions for the entire family and home decor at up to 60 percent less than department and specialty stores. And some values are astounding. Over 10,000 new items are received each week, which makes me want to check them out hourly. On many Saturday Nights, Live a group of the girls descend upon the Old Denton Road location in Carrollton where we meet up with the North Dallas crew for a little round of shopping. See Sue shop. See Sue shop for bargains. See Sue at the checkout counter. For men's, women's, or children's clothes, I somehow manage to inch my way down the aisles with a smile. I smell the latest fragrances, try on a pair of shoes, find a matching handbag, grab a few pairs of big hoop earrings (or are those out of fashion already?), find some new duvet covers and placemats, well, what else is better than that on the lonliest night of the week? Give me a few bargains for a few bucks and I'm not lonely, ever. Even watching others at the checkout counter is like people-watching at the airport. Instead of thinking, now where are they going? I'm thinking, how much are they saving? It makes for interesting fodder at the water cooler on Mondays or on my talk show on Saturdays. I've seen local TV anchors, a Dallas cowboy, a society matron, and the President of a public company doing it, so why shouldn't you? Check directory for additional locations or hop online and they'll direct you to the closest one. But bring cash. You're apt to maxx out your credit card. ***Call toll-free: 800/2-TJ-MAX***

Tuesday Morning
14631 Inwood Rd.
Dallas, TX 75247

972/991-2996
Major Sales Throughout the Year
www.tuesdaymorning.com

Not just another day of the week, when their doors open, run for your life (style.) Expect closeouts on a laundry list of everything that has gift potential at prices of 50-80 percent less. How do they do it? Where do they get their merchandise? Well, let me count the ways. Closeouts and excess inventory from manufacturers, department and specialty stores, Trade Mart samples, mail order catalogs, even failed dot.com sites are now fair game. When they bought out the inventory of pet.com, for example, I bought a dozen of their logo keyrings (with that wonderful little dog trademark) for all my pet lover friends for $4.99 instead of $10. It's like being in boutique heaven with an ax. Cut out all the fat, pare it down to a warehouse sale environment, close the doors during times when shoppers don't traditionally buy gifts ("Closed for restocking" is a customary sign in their windows coast-to-coast) and there, you have the beginnings of this almost 30-year old veteran of the bargain biz. Go online to find the dates they're open and their seasonal hours. Once in the store, be sure to pick up a wallet-size calendar with dates clearly marked. Ranked the biggest closeout gift chain in the country, and to think I knew them when. Satisfaction is guaranteed or your money back—for any reason. Some regular brands include **AMERICAN TOURISTER, BILL BLASS, CIAO, CUISINART, FARBERWARE, LARK, LEGO, LIMOGES, MADAME ALEXANDER, MARTEX, MURANO, PIERRE CARDIN, REVERE, ROYAL DOULTON, SABATIER, SAMSONITE, WEDGWOOD** and more. If you are looking for name-brand gifts, housewares, linens, fashion apparel, crystal and stemware, luggage and small leather goods, electronics and gadgetry, paper goods, toys, dolls, flowers, party decorations, furniture and accessories, jewelry, hair accessories, bed and bath, one-of-a-kind samples in categories all by themselves, area rugs, brass, games, cards, books—there isn't a close-out in the world they won't eventually get. More than 300 stores nationwide. Meet me Tuesday Morning; I'm sure we'll bump into each other one of these days .

UCC Total Home of Dallas
850 N. Dorothy Drive, Suite 502
Richardson, TX 75081   www.ucctotalhome.com; www.interiorhome.com

972/952-0226
By Appt. Only

With over 16 years in the Metroplex, UCC is a name you can bank on. It's a members-only organization, part of one of the largest private buying groups in the country. In fact, they are party to more than 100 locations in 30 states and Canada. With membership, you get privileges such as being able to buy direct from the manufacturer at the same prices as a store would—without the markup. You'll have access to literally hundreds of manufacturers for furnishing your entire house, for your bedroom, living room, dining room, baby and youth furniture and more. In fact, they can provide just about everything from the floor up. Yes, floor coverings, kitchen and bath cabinets and fixtures, wall units, patio furniture, office furniture, lighting fixtures, exercise and sporting goods, bedding and mattresses, appliances and electronics, jewelry and giftware. And to top it off, artwork and window treatments. What don't they sell? By appointment only. It's the only credible buying service we've found in the Metroplex. So have at it!

24

Electronics & TVs

★★★★ Best Buy
4255 LBJ Frwy.
Dallas, TX 75244

972/239-9980
Mon-Sat 10-9; Sun 11-6
www.bestbuy.com

If you haven't shopped Best Buy, you probably haven't bought a best buy. These are the big box bargain players for everything that relates to Electronics & TVs and then some. Everything you've ever needed or wanted that would add a little learning or fun and entertainment to your life can be found off their shelves. From PC's to software, VCRs to DVDs, car stereos to home theaters, big screens to movies, boom boxes to cell phones...along with a vast array of music CDs plus now, you can buy it all–online. In some instances, nobody can touch their selection and prices. Looking for a desktop, notebook, monitor or printer? What about a scanner? Or a disc drive? Need a graphics or sound card? What about a handheld computer? Need more memory? What about a digital camera? Or a portable MP3 player, a modem, a keyboard mabye even sign up for internet services? And that's just in the computer department. For audio products, they carry audio systems, components, compact systems, speakers, TVs, VCRs, DVD players, camcorders and media furniture. Of course, you'll also need your own personal boombox, portable CD player, mini-disc recorder/player, stereo, clock radio, headphones, hey, what about musical instruments? Oh, I'm tired. This bricks and clicks retailer allows you to buy it both ways. So go online and shop 'til you drop. Over 400 stores throughout the U.S., they are the largest volume specialty retailer of consumer electronics, personal computers, entertainment software in the country and appliances and headquartered in Eden Prarie, Minnesota. Their plan is to have more than 550 stores nationwide by 2004. Their online selection is almost unparalleled. Check directory or their website for the store nearest you. *Call toll-free: 888/BEST-BUY*

CAM Audio
2210 Executive Drive
Garland, TX 75041

972/271-0006
Mon-Fri 8:30-5
www.camaudio.com

Until their website is completed, this is the place to call for personalized video tapes with your name customized on the labels FREE or white with a green sleeve.) If you're going to duplicate a tape, get 50 for $1.29 each. Now do you see why they have 5 stars? And listen to this. No charge for freight shipping, if necessary. Located near Jupiter and Miller Rd., CAM is a distributor of **3M** audio products. Over the years, they've expanded to other audio, video and sound amplification products such as tapes, albums, storage units, video cameras, decks, monitors and blank videotapes. If you're looking for the best in sound equipment, including microphones, speakers, mixers and amps, CAM is the man! Tune-in to such brand names as **AMPLI VOX, ASTOUND, BOSE, BRAVO, BRETFORD, BUHL, DA-LITE, DOLBY, DRAPER, EIKI, ELECTRO-VOICE, ELMO, GEM, HAMILTON, JVC, LUXOR, MARANTZ, MAXWELL, MOTOROLA, OTARI, PANA-SONIC, PELICAN, SANYO, SHARP, SURE, SONY, TDK, TEAC, TECHNICS, TELEX, ULTIMATE SUP-PORT** and **VIDEONICS**. Discounts are offered off manufacturers' suggested retail price and even more from their "house" brands. They also discount bulk audio cassettes at substantially less that retail. Well, you read about the video tapes? Everything is at the best prices in town. For professional users, shop here for supplies if you want custom boxes, labels or albums. You'll also find high-speed cassette (16x) duplicators, audio and video recording equipment and sound amplification. Returns are accepted if in new condition. Merchandise is shipped via UPS within 24 hours. If you prepay with a check, the freight is FREE as is their catalog. *Call toll-free: 800/527-3458*

★★ Circuit City
4820 W. I-20
Fort Worth, TX 76132

817/738-1796
Mon-Sat 10-9; Sun 11-6
www.circuitcity.com

Some times I feel short-circuited when shopping here. Each time, answers are mostly guesses, prices are not always visible and products are not always plentiful. On two or three occasions, looking for a print cartridge, they sent me on a wild goose chase. Finally, I bought them elsewhere—they seem to always be out of my particular model number anyway. Tells you something about their inventory control, doesn't it? Though they offer no interest and no payment due for six months on the big ticket items, their prices are not always the best to begin with. I lose track of all the items with rebates, because you have to buy additional purchases or services—particularly in the instance of cell phone and computer/internet providers. They will match any advertised price and refund the difference up to 30 days but that's already another trip I don't care to make. Products include digital cameras, PDAs, wireless phones, computers, cameras and imaging, computer peripherals and accessories, TVs, video and camcorders, portable electronics, home audio, phone, fax, and pager equipment, satellite TV systems, electronic games, broadband, car audio and security systems, office furniture and desk accessories. A recent deal that was tempting was the **KENWOOD DOLBY® DIGITAL** Home Theater System for $499.99. Lots of High Definition Digital TVs throughout the store, but before you buy, remember, there's a 15 percent restocking fee if you return it within 14 days. Other merchandise, though, is given a 30-day return policy with no restocking fee. Since this is the parent to CarMax, maybe CC is just too broadband. Their technical service hot line still leaves much to be desired. They're always busy. We give up... Check directory for location nearest you. *Call toll-free: 800/284-4886*

★★★★★ Ed Kellum & Son
4533 Cole Ave.
Dallas, TX 75205

214/526-1717
Mon-Sat 9-6; Thu 9-8

Here they've been leaders in the electronics, TVs and appliance business for 50 years, yet there's nothing on their website; go figure? Well, don't hold that against them. Since 1948 they've been busy doing other things like installing built-in kitchen appliances to the new **DOLBY DIGITAL** home theater rooms with High Definition 52-inch big screen for $2,599. For any size TV, for that matter, Ed Kellum can deliver. From a nine-inch to 80-inch, they can make you see straight. Buy everything that makes your house come alive! From VCRs, DVD players, DSS dishes and receivers and camcorders as well as video cabinets, stands, remotes, tapes, cables and batteries. The line-up of brands is celestial: **CANON, DENON,**

ELITE, FUJI, GO-VIDEO, INTEGRA, JBL, JVC, M & K, MAGNAVOX, MB QUART, MIRAGE, MIT-SUBISHI, MONSTER CABLE, NILES, OMNI MOUNT, ONKYO, PANASONIC, PETRA, POLK, QUASAR, RCA, SONY, TOSHIBA, UNIDEN and others. They'll pay you $1,000 cash on the barrel head if they don't beat another's deal. (Well, you know they're never going to let someone beat their price!) Pump up the volume and not the price tags with amps, pre-amps, home theater receivers, speakers, CD players, mini-disc players, and cassette decks. Appliance brands include AMANA, BOSCH, FRIGIDAIRE, GENERAL ELECTRIC, JENN-AIRE, KITCHENAID, MAYTAG, MAGIC CHEF, RANGE AIR, SCOTCHMAN, SUBZE-RO, THERMADOR, U-LINE, VENT-A-HOOD, WHIRLPOOL and WOLF. One-stop home enhancement at the best prices is how to wrap up their products and services in one neat bow.

★★★★ FuncoLand   972/385-0422
Forest Village Shopping Center   Mon-Fri 11-9; Sat 10-6; Sun Noon-6
12817 Preston Rd.   www.funcoland.com
Dallas, TX 75230

What game are they playing with their website? When you go to funcoland.com, it defaults to GameStop. Well, as long as you land in the right place, this is the used game mecca for a garden of savings. If you're bored with the old Mario Brothers, check out Funcoland for the latest and greatest. New and previously-played video games that have been reconditioned, all come with a 90-day warranty and are guaranteed to work. Let someone else take the test drive while you pay the depreciated price. Even the "Playstation2" is already being sold used. Get discounts by buying used bundle packs that include the game console, extra controllers and games of your choice. Get all of this for the price of a new one, $299. Used "PS2"games started as low as $17.99. Other used games available for "Playstation","Playstation2", "Nintendo 64", "Game Boy", "Game Biy Advanced" , "Dreamcast", "Sega Genisis" and PCsoftware. Even hard-to-find games for the old "Super Nintendo"were available and started at $9.99. Overall, used games start as low as 95 cents and used consoles are usually always on hand. But if you must be the first out of the gate, there's also lots of new in the hottest titles and new release categories. If it's your "Final Fantasy" to "Test Drive" the "Twisted Metal," then there's no need to sit "Alone in the Dark;" instead, "Pokemon" around here for the "Greatest Arcade Hits."

★★★★ Kenwood Factory Outlet   972/243-7524
13990 N. Stemmons Freeway   Mon-Fri 10-7; Sun 12-5
Farmers Branch, TX 75234   www.kenwood.com

Tune in, tune up, turn off full prices on any KENWOOD product for eventually they will wind their way to their outlet store. Choose your pleasure from car, home or marine electronics. Whether factory refurbished or new, the savings don't sound too bad to me. Expect everything at their outlet to be refurbished except for receivers. Those, you'll only save about 10 percent. Others items, though, you'll save 30-40 percent, up to 50 percent during sales. KENWOOD manufactures receivers, DVD players, CD players, cassette players, amplifiers, home theaters-in-a-box, full and mini-systems, micro-systems, portable players and speakers. If that's not enough, throw in a pair of equalizers, a turntable, head-phones or accessories and your hearing will either improve or diminish as the case may be. This 40-year old world company started by designing and manufacturing Japan's first FM tuner and solid-state ampli-fier. Credit them with creating the most popular stereo receiver ever sold in the U.S., the world's first audio/video amplifier for home theater use, and the first anti-theft car cassette deck. Not bad by the time they reached 40! You never know what will end up inside their outlet store, so check back often. *Call toll-free: 800/KENWOOD*

★★★ Panasonic Factory Service Center   972/385-1975
13615 Welch Rd.   Mon-Fri 9-4:30; Thu 9-6
Dallas, TX 75244

Don't expect any of this merchandise to gather dust. It's in and out, faster than a speeding bullet. What you can expect, though, is for the products to all have the name **PANASONIC**, **QUASAR** or **TECHNICS** embedded. A DVD player was $149 and a plain paper fax machine with copying capabilities was $74. Remember, these are all refurbished or new that have been returned, dropped, scratched or dented, but a 90-day warranty is given to ensure your satisfaction. Again extended warranties can be bought (but better to do so at www.warrantysuperstore.com at 40-60 percent less.) Some categories are rarely in stock. For examples, camcorders. Same with large screen TVs. They haven't seen any in four-five months. When they do come in, it's two or three at a time and then they're out the door in minutes; it's another six months or so before more make it to the sales floor again. Bring your **PANASONIC** in for repairs; most take about three days (longer if they need to order the part but most small electronics, take two-three days.) Other products seen included small TVs, bread machines, microwaves, console and portable stereos, boom boxes, telephones and more. Like I said before, if you see something you want, grab it now or forever walk in silence. *Call toll-free: 800/545-2672*

★★★★★ Radio Shack Outlet Store   817/654-0337
900 Terminal Rd.   Mon-Sat 9-8; Sun Noon-6
Fort Worth, TX 76106   www.radioshack.com

Listen to this return policy: Anything over $20 has a seven-day return policy; but anything under $20, that's it. It's a final sale and sold as-is! Some items come with a warranty and some warranties are voided for various reasons, so ask before you buy and be sure to plug it in and kick the tires before your seven day return is up. Once the eighth day arrives, there's no turning back. This is Radio Shack's outlet and merely a portion of their regular store's inventory. But at their retail stores, they do offer a full 30-day return policy, warranties and repairs (Radio Shack, by the way, will also repair any make and model of electronics no matter where you bought it!) How's that for service? Their outlet, though, is a fully-stocked store that includes scratched and dented (mostly the boxes), seconds, imperfects, discontinued and overproduced items where savings of 50 percent can be realized. Located near the Fort Worth Stockyards, bring those tourists to Fort Worth and visit both. Lots of fun and lots of frugality on TVs, computers, CD players, car stereos, mobile phones, scanners and more. At Christmas time, it's a mad house, so shop early. In the off-season, you can often see goodies marked 50-80 percent off retail, particularly batteries. So stock up for that stocking-stuffer now. *Call toll-free: 800/223-8344*

◆◆◆ Satellite Guy, The   972/243-3838
Dallas, TX   By Appt. Only

Mike Allen's either "up on a roof or under the house!" Leave your message and he'll call you back and work you into his regular satellite set-up schedule for some of the big electronics store in town. He's fast, knows what he's doing and can even help with surround sound installation as well as satellites. He's so busy that you can expect a wait. When you hear his message, you'll smile. When you hear his message ten times, you'll probably look elswhere for installation. He's swamped!

★★★★ Tweeter

9100 N. Central Expy. @ Park Ln.
Dallas, TX 75225

214/373-0600
Mon-Fri 10-8; Sat 10-7; Sun 12-6
www.tweeter.com

Tweeter is Home Entertainment's new name but the game's the same. High end audio and video equipment at the best prices or so they say. Then, they pass on that power buying clout to you, the customer. Audio, video and a lot of other high-tech toys for sophisticated boys in both departments. Great names if you're an audiophile; otherwise, they won't mean a thing. But for those looking to hear a song and (pay a song,) consider the price tags that **ALPINE**, **ACOUSTICS**, **NAD**, **PHASE TECH**, **VELODYNE** and **YAMA-HA** command. Whistle a pretty penny. But what a store. **DOLBY®** sound everywhere, divided into spacious areas where you can hear for yourself the sounds of music. For me, it's all melodious minutia but you've gotta have what you gotta have. Then, call in the gang for a **JVC DVD AUDIO** player that offers a format that is superior to a lowly CD. Double the resolution. Hear every bead of perspiration. Hear every wrinkle in their brow. And note, throughout the store, their Price Guarantee provided by Automatic Price Protection. Hey, that's better than the Price Patrol! Hear this: If it's advertised for less in a major local newspaper within 30 days, they'll automatically mail you a check for the difference. That means, you don't even have to confront them. They do the shopping. You don't even have to do the talking. It's a courtesy done automatically. But it doesn't hurt to keep your eyes peered to the advertised prices, as a back up! Shop also at the Gallery, 3rd Level, in Plano at Preston at Parker Rd., and in Lewisville, I-35E north of Main.

◆◆◆◆ U-Edit

1002 N. Central Expwy., Suite 689
Richardson, TX 75080

972/690-3348
Mon-Thu 9-8; Fri 9-6; Sat 10-4
www.u-edit-video.com

U-see what you can duplicate at U-Edit. Video services include editing, dubbing, titles, sound recording and special effects. Got a favorite French film you want to convert? How about a new twist on photo albums? Place up to 75 pictures on video for $75. That includes five-second viewing and music. Nice. Change any video to include your own narration for just $20 an hour. The equipment and the expertise is all here and if you don't bring your own tape, they can sell you one. Add titles to your video library for $5 each. Machines are also available to convert 8 mm film to VHS videotape. They'll also make copies of tapes and copying charges start around $8. Editing charges run $18-$75 an hour depending on how complicated and sophisticated. Visit also in Lewisville on FM 3040, 972/459-0086. Appointments are preferred

25

Eyewear

★★ 20/20 Eyecare Center
4721 W. Park Blvd.
Plano, TX 75093

972/596-2250
Mon, Wed, Thu 9:30-6:30; Tue, Fri, Sat 9:30-5

Speed sometimes is next to Godliness. Not only does 20/20 offer one-hour service, their one-hour service is often only 30-45 minutes! Designer frames like **ARMANI**, **FISHER-PRICE** (for kids), **GUESS?**, **JORDACHE**, **LIZ CLAIBORNE**, **NINA RICCI** and **VOGUE** are part of Bonnie Noyer's claim to frame. For more than 10 years, she has been discounting frames less than the average and Dr. Haislip has been providing eye exams in 15-20 minutes for $59. If you're wanting contact lenses, that exam takes longer and costs $104. Of course, you might like to hold off and buy your lenses through some of the mail order companies ('cause they're cheaper, old four-eyes!)

★★★ Contact Lens Center, The
6921 Snider Plaza
Dallas, TX 75205

214/739-2020
Mon-Fri 9-5; Sat 9-3

Be a good pupil and center your sights on this location. Just down the street from SMU, prices have remained stable. **ACUVUE**, the kind you can dispose of everyday are $28 per box and eye exams are still $99. What's particularly noteworthy is most lenses are in stock, so there's no waiting or down time. See through your final exams with gas permeable, colored, soft-lenses, the works. Other locations to peek into: Carrollton at Belt Line between Josey and Denton Drive and off North Central Expressway in Richardson between Belt Line and Arapaho. Whichever way your turn, you'll see the same good prices.

Fashion Discount Optical
1912 E. Belt Line Rd.
Carrollton, TX 75006

972/416-8200
Mon-Fri 9-5:30; Sat 10-4

When it comes to seeing the bottom line, Mark Schanbaum is the man to see. Born into the business (his family founded Royal Optical), his own Fashion Discount Optical locations can complete your high-fashion eyewear wardrobe with most brand name frames (without feeling you're getting framed in the process.) Now, for the big bang theory of bargain shopping. Save 50 percent on them all with almost instant gratification. Delivery time generally one to two days. More difficult prescriptions usually are delivered within a week. Frames start at $49, but the average is $89. Seeing is believing: **CHAPS/POLO**, **ESCADA**, **GUCCI**, **KENNETH COLE**, **OLEG CASINI** and many more that can not be divulged. At least 100 different designers that can be ordered at huge savings. Do you have to read between the lines? This is the best discounter in town, with generations of experience and service beyond compare. And if you don't own those Magnetic Sun Clips by "Innovative Eyewear," you've been living under a rock. This is the newest thing to turn your regular glasses into sunglasses without needing to purchase another frame. Choose Progressive no-line bifocals at unheard of prices like I did. At last, the perfect computer prescription glasses. Choose **KODAK**, **VARILUX COMFORT**, **VIP**, **ZEISS** and many more for $159. And lastly, don't miss seeing their *Super Saver* section for a one-stop source for complete glasses for only $79. Now, do you see what I mean? Visit also their Oak Lawn location at 3430 Oak Lawn Ave., at the corner of Oak Lawn andLemmon, 214/526-6006.

★★★ LensCrafters

Valley View Center
13331 Preston Rd.
Dallas, TX 75240

972/991-9940
Mon-Sat 10-9; Sun Noon-6
www.lenscrafters.com

LensCrafters was one of the leaders in the one-stop eyewear business, bringing the eye doctor, frames, lenses and the lens-making lab all under one roof. Now, you don't have to wait long to see the light of day. Since 1983, it doesn't take a mental giant to understand why they've been such a success. Delivering a wide selection of frames, competitive prices and superb customer service, today they're the largest chain of optical superstores in the country and in Canada. Brands we saw included: **ANNE KLEIN**, **AVANT GARDE**, **BANDOLINO**, **BROOKS BROTHERS**, **CAPEZIO**, **ELIZABETH ARDEN**, **EMANUEL UNGARO**, **ESPRIT**, **FEATHERWATES**, **FILA**, **LAURA ASHLEY**, **LAUREN MICHAELS**, **LENSCRAFTER FLEX**, **MODA**, **MOSCHINO**, **PERRY ELLIS**, **PC**, **POLICE** and others. **RAYBAN** and **REVO** sunglasses were also waiting in the shade. The **LUXOTTICA** frame company bought LensCrafters in 1995 and today, they do well over $1 billion in sales in over 850 stores. LensCrafters' doctors and associates work closely with the Lions Club by collecting and recycling old glasses and sending them to developing countries, offer vision screenings at health fairs, and provide new glasses to the needy. Another plus is their mobile vision vans that go out into the community to serve those who can't afford an in-store visit. Just recently, they signed a U.S. blind Olympic track and field star to be their company's spokesperson for their "Give the Gift of Sight!" Being philanthropic doesn't always mean *you're* getting the best deal, but you can't ignore their generosity.

★★★★★ Luck Optical

7108 Camp Bowie Blvd.
Fort Worth, TX 76116

817/738-3191
Mon-Fri 9:30-6:30; Sat 8:30-5:30
www.luckoptical.com

When you've been in the same business for over 60 years, it's sort of in your blood. They, of course, think of it as THEIR family taking care of YOUR family. Exam rates for children's (12 & under) only $34 and $39 for adults. Contact lens exams are $79 and broken down as follows—$44 for the exam, $15 for the fitting and $20 for the follow up. If you're in the know, you know these are very good prices. There are six doctors on staff, so no appointment is necessary. Since their earliest beginnings in downtown Fort Worth on Houston Street, we have been in luck, thanks to Dr. L.H. Luck. Believe it or not, he was the first to come up with "glasses in one hour" when he decided to add an in-house lab to his practice. Offering the latest technology and the guarantee to beat the competition by 10 percent—including prices on eyeglasses, exams, and contact lenses, it all adds up to a value-enhanced experience when shopping for eyewear. Keep your eyes wide shut! No, I'm not "cruising" to "kid you, man". They are Tarrant County's finest. ***Call toll-free: 800/613-8117***

★★★★★ Lux Eyewear for Less   972/686-0595

1020 W. Centerville Rd.   Mon-Fri 9-6; Sat 9-575041
Garland, TX 75041

Lux be a lady tonight. And if you want to enjoy the luck of the Irish, why not take a chance here. See clearly with two pairs of single-vision glasses or two pairs of flat bifocals starting at $44.95 from their SmartBuy frames. Now, smarty pants, what if you want those no-line models? Two pairs of no-line bifocals, with clear plastic lenses, were $102.95. A pair, a spare and all frames from their SmartBuy selection, this is your lucky day! Eye see. You're cheap. So here's the place to act on your genetic disposition. Check directory for the location nearest you. Glasses are ready in five working days (or sooner.) Bring in your current prescription and you'll be seeing the light at the end of the tunnel in no time. They can do some repairs on eyeglasses but most are sent out so you might be better off sending them somewhere else. Seeing dots before your eyes? That's their sign of savings—that's if the dots are red, yellow or green. Since the two pairs of single vision or flat bifocals cost $44.95, they'll have the red dots. If you're seeing yellow dots, the frames will cost $64.95 and green dots will cost $84.95.

★★★★ Optical Dispensary   972/285-8941

3914 Hwy. 80   Mon-Fri 8:30-5:30; Sat 8:30-1 (Walk-ins on Sat)
Mesquite, TX 87150

Now hear this so you'll be able to see this. An exam at this Optical Dispensary is just $39 whether you're a kid or a grown-up. There's always a special going on. On this particular day, it included the exam for contacts, the contact lens and a pair of glasses. This dispensary can save you up to 50 percent on frames and more on contacts. One day the deal was: daily-wear contacts plus glasses (including the exam) for $88! Another day, single-vision lenses were $29 and $10 tacked on for an eye exam. What a deal. Almost too good to be true but it was. Bifocals as low as $44. But how do they do it? By eliminating expensive over-head, designer and brand-name frames. But somehow, most frames all look alike anyway. At least you'll be able to see straight when it comes time to ante up at the check-out. Same-day service has an upcharge and walk-ins are taken on Saturdays, but only the first 20 patients with appointments are booked every 20 minutes. Dawdlers, big mouths, and shufflers need not apply.

★★ Optical Mart   972/669-9648

804 University Village   Mon-Fri 9-6; Sat 9-4
Richardson, TX 75081

Be smart and take the savings to heart at the Optical Mart. And why not? You got something against keeping costs within seeing-eye range? Here, the styles are staggering. Over 400 styles and colors to choose from with single-vision glasses only $28.95 (same as last year's). In fact, prices have remained constant for more than three years. Now, that's a record. Ask the gas company if they might like to share a few pointers? If you want a tint, UV coating or scratch-proofing, add another $25. Still not out of the line of duty. Extras do add up so consider seriously if you really need them; don't get duped into buying them. Lightweight or oversized lenses do not cost more. However, you'll be forgoing, for the most part, designer names. Let's face it. The name **LAUREN BACALL** is probably not the most requested designer out there (unless you're a Bogie fan!) So, one way they can keep costs under control, give up the designer names, plain and simple. No eye exams available, so you must bring in a current prescription. Located across from Richardson Square Mall, check directory for the one nearest you.

★ **Pearle Vision Express**   972/239-8585
5549 LBJ Frwy.   Mon-Fri 9-8; Sat 9-6; Sun Noon-5
Dallas, TX 75240   www.pearlevision.com

"Nobody cares for eyes more than Pearle" is quite poignant if you knew this little gem. Dr. Stanley Pearl's idea was born back in 1961, and if you agree with his mission, you will be seeing crystal clear in no time. One-stop shopping for eyecare was his contribution to the eyewear industry and he can certainly be credited as a pioneer. No wonder Pearle became an overnight success! His idea? Provide convenient locations, expanded hours, competitive prices and a better selection of frames, and the consumers would come. And they did. Go online to print out money-saving coupons or check the*Dallas Morning News* or *Fort Worth Star-Telegram*. Exams for glasses were $45 for adults and children. In this particular location, Dr. Boyles is right next door and appointments can be made directly with him at 972/490-4849 with same-day appointments. You can save money periodically during sales but it varies based on the frames in question. Their formula? The more desirable the frame, the less drastic the discount. You can see names like **JOAN COLLINS**, **LIZ CLAIBORNE**, **SILHOUETTES**, **WRANGLER**, some popular brands indeed, but they may not be the most sought after. Be sure to separate the frames from the lenses when comparing prices. One way to "getcha" is to price the frames for less, and mark-up the lenses. It's all part of the game of discounting. But at Pearle's, there are some positives that should be pointed out. Great service. Great selection. Great pearls of wisdom spewing from their sales personnel...sure to make Stanley proud.

★★★★ **Reading Glasses To Go**   972/392-3111
5411 Belt Line Rd.   Mon-Sat 10-6
Dallas, TX 75240

Up and down they go, where they stop, nobody knows. But if you want to buy a pair of reading glasses on the go, here is the place to go. What a selection! Though they are non-prescription glasses, they do come in varying strengths of magnification. Prices have gone down from last year, if you can believe. Starting out as low as $18 to one that's all decked out for those After 5 occasions for $65. Use these glasses to read the menu, find the place for the tip, see the advertising on the bathroom door, or really anything that requires a hint of reading. You don't want to pull the wrong plug or turn off the wrong switch, do you? Sun readers are also available for the beach, the boat, the garden or pool. They even come in progressive lenses. To figure out which strength suits you, do not be insulted but you will have to take a little reading test. That way, the staff will know whether you need bifocals, no-lines or even progressive lenses. Since you don't need an RX to buy a pair of glasses here, if you lose or break your glasses on the road, you can always use one of these for an emergency. Check directory for multiple locations. A quick fix for a fashion plate who wants a pair of glasses for every outfit; or an extra pair, just in case.

★★ **Southwest Vision Center**   817/281-3386
7728 Mid Cities Blvd.   Mon-Fri 9-6; Sat 9-2:30
North Richland Hills, TX 76180

This will make your brown eyes blue. For just $169, you can pick two pairs of **DURASOFT** colored contacts (chose from blue, green, hazel and grey.) You want more? Then for $199, you can get a pair of clear and a pair of colored. But these Durasoft contacts come in many more colors. If contacts aren't your cup of tea, then glasses and frames can be picked out for $99.95-$109. Between great prices, they have lots of "gimmes" such as little gifts with promotions. Plus they have more than 1,000 frames in stock at prices that have not risen at all at the top (same as last year) and only $30 more at the bottom. Appointments book up a week in advance and Saturdays are strictly walk-ins from 9-2:30. Bring in your current prescription or they can also duplicate your current prescription. Medicaid/Medicare and most insurance programs are accepted.

26

Fabrics & Upholstery

★★★★★ A Cut Above Fabrics and More   214/748-7106
2920 Taylor Street
Dallas, TX 75226-1908

What is this world coming to? Is there no sacredness left in just selling wholesale? To the Trade? Nope. Everybody's got to make a living and more and more strictly wholesale operators are opening their doors to the public. Whoopee! Now we're talking. Though these folks have been in business for more than 45 years wholesaling their fabric to other upholsterers in a five-state region, you can well imagine, their fabrics are most definitely "a cut above." It's sew mahvelous, dahling. Visit their warehouse just south of Deep Ellum and know that you're getting a cut above the rest. Just don't expect to stay cool. You'll probably "sweat it" without the A/C but that's how all the great discounters began—in a sea of hard work and lack of retail amenities. Give me fabric, and give me a dearth! See home fabrics, trims, beads, silks, prints, and the ability to create one-of-a-kind custom furniture or have your favorite furniture reupholstered. They're two blocks south of Commerce, between Hall and Good Latimer; once you find them, your next trip will be "seamless".

★★★★ ABC Textiles   214/357-8700
2623 Perth St.   Sat 8-1
Dallas, TX 75220

A stitch in time saves nine; but a stitch of mine better be a stitch in time. This is an old "Confusion" saying but if you want to dive into an ocean of fabrics priced from a low of $1/yard, take your chances and swim only on Saturdays. Off Harry Hines, between Walnut Hill and Royal, new fabrics arrive knee deep at the reef of the Fabric District. Dressmakers unite. Get a great deal on gabardine, the finery of wool, gingham, velveteen, sateen, crepe de chine, challis, silk, cotton, toile, batik, denim, linen, so many you could patchwork a quilt across the Metroplex. Find many moderate to better dress fabric overruns from local manufacturers piled high. You will have a field day!

★★★★ Bargain Fabric Outlet
2601 Perth St.
Dallas, TX 75220

214/351-0107
Mon-Sat 9-3

Talk about having a yard sale! Add this bargain fabric outlet to the Fabric District on Perth Street. No confusion over what they sell...they sell it and tell it like it is. Drapery and upholstery fabrics from $2.99-$4.50 (values up to $20/square yard); and all dress fabrics a buck, one dollar, uno dinero, plain and simple. Choose satins, brocades, cotton prints and solids, Lycra®, suitings and more. Sew, how many outfits can you make for a dollar?

★★★★★ Best Fabric Outlet
10901 Harry Hines Blvd.
Dallas, TX 75229

214/350-2583
Mon-Sat 9-5

I hate name-calling, but this company is redundant. They are the best. And their name's the best. Like a bustling flea market in Hong Kong, there is fabric flying from bolt to bin, shelf to shelf, hand to mouth, so to speak. It's wild and furious, especially on Saturdays, but then, since they have some of the best prices and the best selection of dress and upholstery fabrics in town, you put up with the tumult. It's like doing the "Hokey Pokey". You put your left arm in. Then, pull your left arm out, you put your left arm in and you pull it all out. You pick a bolt of fabric and you turn it all around, that's what it's all about! When you've made your decision, one of their helpers will cut it and bring it to the register. Chinese is spoken at the check out counter but they count every penny in English.

Childress Fabric Outlet
2517 Ferris St.
Dallas, TX 75226

214/565-0900
Mon-Fri 9-5; Sat 9-3
www.childressfabrics.com

Barbara Childress is one feisty lady with an eye towards the future. Little did she realize when she opened her shop in 1958 in a small warehouse in downtown Dallas, that today she would be the matriarch to over 70,000 square feet of fabrics, frames and furniture for less, with a second location in Frisco. With over 10,000 fabrics in stock and more coming in daily, she is the queen. Since they buy in such quantity from the mills, (all of the big ones, and can special order from any of them), they have the buying power to pass on the savings to you. In their showrooms you will see hundreds of different furniture frames, rooms dedicated to just one mill like **ROBERT ALLEN**, **WAVERLY**, or whomever, and a selection of trims, tassels, pillow forms—so many, you'll probably need a **DRAMAMINE** not to get dizzy. Wade through more than 4,500 designs in stock, running from $5 and up, with a stupendous 50-70 percent off and 30 percent off special orders from the fabric books. Furniture, drapery and bedding can be custom made to coordinate an entire house full of fabrication. But now, let's talk Frisco. Fabulous "Frisco and Fabrics" are now synonymous because Custom Upholstery Mart and Children Fabric Outlet are finally together in this fast-forward northern metropolis called Frisco. See for yourself by visiting 8760 7th Street, 469/633-1180.
Call toll-free: 800/821-6463

★★★★ Current Fabrics
2655 Perth St.
Dallas, TX 75220

214/353-2766
Mon-Fri 9:30-4:30; Sat 9-2:30

The tides were changing from retail to discount as we bolted out of this fabric warehouse. Head to the current fabric district on Perth Street and see what's current on the horizon. If you'd rather not buy last year's dogs anyway, you can bark when you see the selection of whites in the eye-lets. From cotton prints, plaids, florals, geometrics all the way to the delicacy of bridal toile, taffeta and lace, you might find out it's now cheaper to say, "I do" than to say, "you didn't!" Buy it by the bolt and your buy gets an even deeper discount. Off Walnut Hill and Harry Hines, there're more than 15,000 yards to wander through. But to land in Perth, you don't have to fly Quantas Airlines. From dressmaking to upholstery, you can even fabric the front yard, if that's your pleasure.

Custom Upholstery Mart

2512 Ferris St.
Dallas, TX 75226

214/821-4444
Mon-Fri 9-5; Sat 9-3
www.customupholsterymart.com

Sew what's new? How about a second location in Frisco at 8760 7th Street, across from Abbey's Restaurant (469/633-1180), for this fabric and furniture powerhouse. Since 1958, Barbara Childress and Family have operated out of an expanded 70,000 square foot facility and continue to make mince meat out of the competition. With over 10,000 fabrics in stock and more coming in daily, there isn't a piece of furniture that can't be reupholstered, recovered, repaired or built from scratch. Take that "to-die-for" chair from your favorite *Elle Decor Magazine* and have them make a lookalike at a fraction of the cost. That's Custom Upholstery Mart, for starters. Then cross the street to The Fabric Outlet and if the thousands of fabrics don't send you into a tizzy, then the thousands of trims and tassels will. Where else could you find beaded or feather trim? You can literally find enough fabric to redo half of the Metroplex and maybe even the American Airlines Center. And now with their Frisco outpost, you have your choice of uptown or downtown. This is like the Trade Mart for interior decorators if a transformation is on the drawing board. For their fabrics online, go to www.childressfabrics.com. *Call toll-free: 800/821-6463*

★★★★★ Cutting Corners

13720 Midway Rd., Suite 200
Farmers Branch, TX 75244

972/233-1741
Mon-Sat 9:30-5:30; Thu 9:30-8; Sun Noon-5
www.cuttingcorners.com

Another family tree that has branched out into a forest of fabric, Cutting Corners has been up and in a family way for the past 20 years. Two organized showrooms (Dallas and Fort Worth) make shopping here a breeze. At the corner of Midway between Alpha and Spring Valley, you do not need a bolt of lightning to get fired up about how they don't cut corners, just prices. This quality mills outlet is a fixture in the Metroplex. They also have their own line of window fixtures called "Iron Designs", in your choice of metallic finishes, at really great prices: adjustable rod, $4.99; extendable brackets, $2.99; ball finials, $5.99; clip rings, $5.99. Fab new fabrics found hanging around: pleated "Fortuni" silk, $7.99/yard; bronze-colored sheers, $11.99/yard; print and solid chenilles, $12.99/yard; and that old stand-by, chintz, $5.99/yard. They custom-make sofas and chairs, too; just pick your style and fabric, and they'll deliver in six weeks. Cut another good deal at another corner in Fort Worth at 5525 S. Hulen St. (817/262-6834), just south of Hulen Mall.

★★★★ Fabracadabra

5370 W. Lovers Lane
Dallas, TX 75209

214/357-3555
Mon-Fri 9:30-5:30; Sat 10-4
www.fabracadabra.com

Hocus-Pocus, and presto, you'll even have money left over. Even in the Park Cities, money doesn't grow on trees (well, maybe on a few crepe myrtles, it does). Still, you can magically transform your plain and boring yard with yards from **FABRICUT, P. KAUFMAN, ROBERT ALLEN, WAVERLY**, and still maintain your integrity. Depending on the deal they cut from the manufacturer, you could save 20-30 percent, but more like 40-50 percent. Voila! Abracadabra! Watch the wand whip up some gorgeous drapery treatments, coordinated accessories and bedding, and even if you want to lock yourself up in a padded bathroom, they can do that, too. (Pad your walls, that is.) For interior decorative purposes, count on them doing all the transformation a room might need except the paint and carpentry work. Since the labor is not discounted, every material effort made to save you money is appreciated.

★★★★★ Fabric By The Pound   972/287-5447
203 N. Kaufman St.   Wed-Fri Noon-5; Sat 10-3
Seagoville, TX 75159   www.fabricbythepound.com

If crafting is your notion, then get all your portions for braiding rugs, making crochet rag rugs, crochet rag baskets, quilts, toothbrush rugs, or other fabric rugs at Fabric By The Pound. So what will you find here? Warehouse prices on mill end strips, textile remnants, lace, craft patterns and an assortment of trims for curtains, draperies, and upholstery. Get all the accessories you need with P, Q and S size crochet hooks, fabric holders, patterns and more. Not sure where to start? How about their FREE classes. Call in advance, since space is limited to six participants per class. And if you're looking to go larger than life, then wholesale pricing is also available on orders of 300 pounds of more. That's a lot of fabric. So grab hold of a lot of books and get started on those projects. From rugs to hats to fun projects for the kids, everyone can benefit from the creative ideas and savings from Fabric By The Pound.

★★★★ Fabric Source, The   972/267-3400
2385 Midway Rd.   Mon-Fri 9:30-5; Sat 9:30-5
Carrollton, TX 75093

Still experiencing growing pains, this company can be your source for fabric in the coming years. Their expansion only means one thing...more fabric, more savings, more opportunities to blanket your household with fabric new cover-ups. Within 7,000 square feet, you can surely transform one piece of furniture and enhance your lifestyle with the whole nine yards. David was our guide, knowledgeable and friendly. He recommended the 100 percent nylon fabric for $8.99, claiming it was very durable and washable. He also gave it rave reviews as a great value even though shoppers pass it by in favor of polyester. Actually, he said, it's really a better deal. For $8.99/yard, it could be a smart buy. Polyester, on the other hand, starts around $15/yard. One block north of Keller Springs on the west side, you can get it all sewn up and that's the end of the story.

★★★★★ Fabric Yard   972/774-1740
15319 Midway   Mon-Sat 9-7; Sun 1-5
Dallas, TX 75244

"The Planet of the Drapes" is heating up in the North Dallas corridor. This newcomer has opened its doors recently, offering some of the most beautiful fabrics in town. We bolted out of our complacency and thought we'd roll up our sleeves and dig in. Thousands of yards of upholstery and drapery fabrics at up to 75 percent off are laying around neat as a pin in this 9,000 square foot showroom. Star struck names stuck out, including **BARROW**, **BROOMCRAFT**, **KRAVET**, **SCHUMACHER**, **WALDOLF** and **WAVERLY** creating their own red carpet. No washed up has-beens, just big bins filled with hundreds of bolts at deeply discounted prices. No need to call in the officials or ask for autographs, though some of their prices are a steal. Uncovering the wealth of opportunities here makes the Fabric Yard a big plus in the decorating genre. Though you won't need a "hoe" to get it "hoesale," fabric is priced dirt cheap here.

★★★ Falk Fabric Outlet   214/855-0636
2633 McKinney Ave.   Mon-Fri 9-5:30; Sat 10-5
Dallas, TX 75204

This is no Falk lore. Falk Fabric Outlet is larger than life and is the source for one of the largest decorative fabric inventories this side of the Mississippi. Since 1951, it's Falks like this that have given shoppers something to brag about. In the heart of the Uptown/Downtown resurgence, whether you'd like to ride the trolley, grab a burger at the Hard Rock Cafe or find gorgeous moir® taffeta fabric for your movie-star boudoir, start your journey of saving money here. Drapery and upholstery fabrics exclusively; the prices belie their exquisite detail. So if you are looking for all the "Fringe Benefits" of a bargain shopper, you can start with the savings on the right side of the tracks here.

★★★★★ Golden D'Or Outlet   214/351-6651
10795 Harry Hines Blvd.   Mon-Sat 9-4:30
Dallas, TX 75220

This is remnant heaven. If you've got the notion to get your wardrobe in motion, the buck should stop here. They've got the Midas touch when it comes to all the popular fabrications for dressmaking: linens and Lycra®, challis and cotton, poplin and denim, knits and twills. Thrill at the prices...everything's priced at least half off. Sew, start your star search for fabrics here as low as $1.99-$4.99/yard; drapery fabric, $4.50/yard, decorator fabric, $2.50/yard and remnants, oh there I go again, another senior moment. Oh dear, I am repeating myself. Remnants. Plenty of remnants. From denim to the deep blue sea, calicos to cats, poplins to prints, jungle prints to art prints, interlock to...well, they've got it all, from 99 cents/yard. The list of possibilities is exhaustive. Which one to pick? Well, one to the lady who wanted sequins, another chose **DUPIONII** silks, while two gals behind us chose a combination of satins and rayon. Yes, some day your prints will come, too! Fabric priced from 59-cents to $4.99/yard. Most choices are under $3. Shop around, dig around, pick a bale of cotton. Located on Harry Hines, between Walnut Hill and Lombardy, in what I refer to as "The Heart of the Upholstery Fabric District".

★★ Interior Alternative, The   214/637-8800
1305 Inwood Rd.   Mon-Sat 10-5; Thu 10-6; Sun Noon-5
Dallas, TX 75247

The secret is out on the streets, but at times the secret's a mess. Though this is the outlet for powerhouse **WAVERLY/SCHUMACHER**, on Saturdays the place looks like a tornado struck at mid-afternoon. Service is almost non-existent and it's not nearly as appetising as their beautiful ads. Now, that's the bad news. The good news, it's not always that way. Some days are quiet and serene and there's enough Waverly to wave the flag in all-American bargains. So there. Now you have the full picture. If you want to make a detour from paying full price, here's where they dispose of their overruns, closeouts, discontinueds and irregulars. At least, you can applaud the final curtain. Making it the last chapter of a good book, there are savings on their popular fabric and readymade comforter sets. Choose chintz, damasks or tapestries, velvets and moirs®. Choose matching wallpaper, trimmings and accessories. And it does spell savings. In store, there's also a sewing center for small projects like toppers or pillows. In the Inwood Trade Center, there's lots of activity to make a day of it.

★★★ Keeton Supply Co.　　　　　817/332-7888
912 E. Vickery Blvd.　　　　　　　　　Mon-Fri 8-5; Sat 8-Noon
Fort Worth, TX 76104

For the industrious kind, here's the place to stock up on upholstery supplies. Do-it-yourself not only saves money, but it allows you to exercise those fingers and your creativity. Zip your lip, button-up, and keep Keeton on your supply list for foam, dacron, padding, welt cord, burlap threads, staples, tools—everything you'd need for the future upholstery job. They carry a variety of veritable vinyl to velvet and everything in between. Stock fluctuates, so check back often. They will even special order if what you need is not in stock. The savings here are not in the actual material but in the fact that you're supplying your own blood, sweat, and in my case, tears (both the kind that you shed from your tear ducts, and the kind you create by ripping the fabric from its stitches three times in one hour!) ***Call toll-free: 800/792-8777***

★★★★★ M & M Upholstery　　　　214/391-4085
8337 Lake June Rd.　　　　　　　　　　　　　　Mon-Fri 8-5
Dallas, TX 75217

Bring your imagination when you shop here because the sky's the limit. This company's been around since 1857 and today, the third generation is in charge of the family business. The secret of where the decorators have brought their client's upholstery jobs for years too is about to be let out of the bag. It's name is M & M; they don't melt in your hands but in your heart. Today, they sell both to the trade and the public; bypass the middleman and save by shopping direct. One stitch at a time, their expertise is really in their craftsmanship. They shower you with the three R's: restoration, rebuilding, restyling, though they do sell fabric, too. Expect the fabric to be in the $15-$20/yard range for vinyl; other materials vary from $10/yard to...hold on to your seat, $2,000/yard. Of course, at that price, it better cover the yard. One of their unique fabrications is mixing and matching different fabrics like solid cushions with printed arm rolls and floral skirts. Somehow, when all it said and done, it works. And it's gorgeous. The proof is in the end product. For example, an antique sofa was restored to its original condition, with approximately 18 yards of fabric, for about $425. (Sure beats buying a totally new piece of furniture.) Wingback chairs, with approximately 7.5 yards of fabric would cost about $250 in labor. See, giving birth is not as expensive as you once thought. Just breathe deeply and take out your checkbook.

★★★★ Pete's Upholstery Shop　　　817/274-2431
2620 W. Pioneer Pkwy.　　　　　　　　　　Mon-Fri 8-4:30
Arlington, TX 76013

For a completely reupholstered deep-seated couch, chair, loveseat or anything that could use a good makeover, for Pete's sake, consider Bill Yeager. He's the perfect craftsman for a face lift or an uplift. Pick your fabric from his repertoire and consider it done. He's been doctoring furniture with fabric since 1963 and considers word-of-mouth his secret source of marketing 101. Repeat business is really how his business has grown exponentially. Expect to pay $395 for labor plus fabric and tax. Fabrics start at about $15 or $16 and go up from there. If you buy the fabric from him and live in Arlington, then pickup and delivery is FREE. If you buy the fabric elsewhere, expect to pay $40. Once he's gotten it all together, expect to be sitting on your throne in about three weeks. Yes, his fabric is a little more, but when you are good, very, very good, you can command it. (Or so the story goes!)

★★★★ Super Textiles Fabric Outlet   214/353-2770
2667 Perth St.   Mon-Fri 9-5; Sat 8-2
Dallas, TX 75220

Super Steve makes Super Textiles worth shopping just for his comedic delivery, if nothing else. He's hilarious and maybe has a second career in the wake. You never know—Letterman and Leno can't last forever. Ask him a basic question like, "Do you have any jacquards or denim?" and he'll wind up with a five-minute comedy routine. Just ask. You'll see. But you're really here because you want to buy some fabric, right? This Perth-Street fabric warehouse showcases fabric from the apparel manufacturers in town. When it lands here, prices are cut accordingly. If he doesn't have what you're looking for, he does send you to one of his sworn enemies up and down the street. Bring your credit cards, he admonished, all of them. You'll bolt out eventually with better womenswear overcuts, closeouts, discontinueds or last season's castaways. Prices on challis, prints, jacquards, poly-cotton, interlock and denim (at a low $3/yard) were all discounted. While stock was great and prices low, this year the reception was definitely sterling. Now they've earn those gold stars. Warning: If you're not careful, not only will you buy fabric, you might buy Steve's recruitment pitch and wind up changing jobs.

★★★★★ Upholstery Place, The   972/271-6669
2406 S. Jupiter Rd., Suite 2   Mon-Fri 9-5
Garland, TX 75041

What are the Seven Wonders of the World that you'd like to cover? Let me count the ways. Bed, chair, pillow, windows, ottoman, shower and tub, and matching toilet seat? Not to worry. Teresa Garner can custom cover it all in no time. As a matter of fact, she prides herself in being able to deliver the "redo", looks like new, for example, in three-four weeks (not months or years). So why not get the ball rolling and reupholster that favorite old chair or treasured sofa? Prices, well, they're a whole lot better than buying new. Whether a slipcover or a complete make-over, you can expect savings of 20-40 percent. And like the old-fashioned family doctor, this gal makes house calls. The fabric selection is limited, but as they say, their "Superior Service Sets Them Apart!"

27

Flea Markets & Bazaars

★★★ **First Monday Trade Days**   **817/421-1778**
303 Palo Pinto   Fri-Sun 7 AM-Dusk
Weatherford, TX 76086   www.firstmonday.com

Weatherford is where it's happening the weekend before the first Monday of each month. It's a city that treasures their western traditions and heritage, but Saturdays, whether you're back in the saddle or not, are still the best days to shop. For over a century, vendors have been packing it up on Fridays, and packing it in on Sundays. When they sell out, they're out and ready to call it a wrap. On days when the temperature's not in triple digits, you can really enjoy the crafts, the food and the fun. You can buy anything here, including animals, so why bark up another tree? Too, if you've been laid off or retired early, think second careers. Lots of new-found money has been generated by wheeling and dealing at a flea market. In November, reservations are in order if you would like to rent a space—and should be made the first week of the month prior to the month you want to open shop. Call 817/598-4215 for reservations, or fight City Hall, 303 Palo Pinto St. in Weatherford. Mailed payments should be addressed: First Monday Reservations, PO Box 255, Weatherford, TX 76086. Ask about their "Intent to Reserve" policy for ensuring the same place every time. To set up a food booth, it costs $150 for a hookup for wagons and $5 per day for electricity. A maximum of 10 spaces can be reserved by an individual/group/company, etc., and walk-up customers are accepted for $15 per day as long as space is available.

★★★★★ **First Monday Trade Days**   **903/567-6556**
I-20 East to Hwy. 19 and Kaufman Street   First Mon Weekend 7 AM-Dark
Canton, TX 75103   www.firstmonday.com

No other day of the month is as important as the first Monday in Canton, Texas. If you're a shopper who loves to walk the beat, this is the beat to Beat it! If worse comes to worst, try doing the Moon Walk over the worldly walkways, the ups and downs of the hillside blues, and consider there being no rest for the weary. During the summer, it's nothing more than one big Hot Flash—bring cash and carry it off to bigger, better places! First Monday Trade Days in Canton is the largest outdoor flea market in the world. Born in 1873 as Canton's Court Days when the town folks started selling their wares by "horse trading", today it's home to thousands of dealers who sell both new and used items, arts and crafts, antiques and collectibles, computers and electronics, food stuff to musical instruments and everything in between. Acres and acres that will boggle your mind, make for sore feet and swollen carry-alls. Admission is free; parking is not—$3.

★★★★★ **Old Mill Marketplace, The Village, & The Mountain**   903/567-5445
542 Highway 64 East   Weekend prior to First Monday 8AM-Dusk
Canton, TX 75103   www.oldmillmarketplace.com

Going to build a mountain! Welcome to the wacky world of First Monday, where "The Mountain", the "Old Mill Marketplace" and "First Monday" are all lying in wait for the onslaught of 20,000,000 bargain hunters. Be there during the first Monday weekends where you'll be shopping until you're dropping, not only a bundle, but to your knees with exhaustion. The Old Mill Marketplace has over 800 shops, and they joined First Monday in 1994 as the "Newest" First Monday shopping area in Canton. Each First Monday weekend, 200,000 folks descend upon this sleepy East Texas town. Come rain or come shine, shoppers are shopping, with umbrellas and all. At the various pavilions, at least you can get out of the sun or the cold. There, you'll be able to shop under several rooftops offering a large variety of unique gifts, bargains and antiques. And, if someone says, "Don't sweat it," you won't have to. There are restrooms and showers to help you make it through the night. Then, for convenience, there are shuttle buses running every 20 to 30 minutes to cart you to other areas. The seven covered pavilions offer some respite from the weather, and an opportunity to browse and shop for unique crafts, the latest designs in home decor and a wonderful selection of antiques. The 800 shops are all located within the "Old Mill Marketplace", "The Village" and "The Mountain". "The Mountain" is the pioneering town with shops with a western motif, cowboy shoot-outs, a petting zoo, demonstrating artists, and live local entertainment with a FREE "Saturday Night Live" musical showcase. Bed and Breakfasts are even located on "The Mountain". Man does not live by shopping alone—even the best of them gotta sleep. Now, we're off to "The Village" for a flavor of the "Texas Hill Country". And don't forget to stay late on Saturday for their "Chinese Quarter Auction" held every Saturday during market in the Village Food Court. Doors open at 6:30 PM. Join others who park their RVs and spend the weekend. Lastly, we wind our way to the Old Mill Marketplace on the Friday, Saturday and Sunday before the First Monday of every month. Some shops are even open on Thursday. Check out the website for a complete calendar of events and dates. And if you've got any room to shop anywhere else, I bet your feet will scream out, "No!"

★★★ **Second Monday Trade Days—Bowie**   940/872-1680
304 Lindsey   Fri-Sun 7 AM-Dusk
Bowie, TX 76230   www.morgan.net/~a2ndmonday

This is not the town where David Bowie was born, but rather it's where shoppers converge on the rodeo grounds on East Wise Street in Bowie, Texas, the second Monday of each month. Get a whiff of fresh country air and put the airs of the citified folks behind you. Mosey in and out of the antique shops around the Wise County Courthouse Square, where about 350 vendors set up shop on Saturdays, the Second Monday of the month. Better be an early bird if you want to gather the most moss without building up a sweat. If you want to get into the act as a vendor, booths go for $20 for the weekend plus $4 for electricity. Take 287 north, exit on US 81/Waurika Exit—you can't miss it. You'll find a plethora of prices and products, from TVs to livestock, handbags to cantaloupes. And food, well, you gotta eat, don't ya?

★★★★ **Third Monday Trade Days—McKinney**   **972/562-5466**
4550 W. University   Fri-Sun 7 AM-Dusk
Hwy. 380   www.tmtd.com
McKinney, TX 75069

Find it all from Mr. Brown who sells reconditioned vacuums to Fred and his tools for sale. That's the fun of participating in one of the oldest county-wide markets this side of the Mason-Dixon Line. What began more than 100 years ago when judges rode the circuit, from county seat to county seat, is now the hub of contemporary horse trading. The difference, of course, is that today there're paved roads to travel. Head north on the Saturday and Sunday before the third Monday of the month. Gee, you've got to have your calendar in hand to figure that date, for sure. Treasure hunt your way up Highway 75 to Highway 380 and go west for two miles to the historic Buckner Community where, since 1966, McKinney's Third Monday Trade Days have been a major happening. More than 800 vendors are scattered throughout the 30 acres, making a believer out of a discontent. The market has undergone many changes under its present ownership, so be sure to visit the new Trading Post section and the large pavilion. Have yourself a feast—from snacks to full meals. Open-air space rentals are $35 for the first lot and $25 for each additional lot. There's a price tag on everything and some of the best buys are things someone else discarded. Western paraphernalia, hats, blankets, saddles and spurs to antiques, videos, **HARLEY** collectibles, toys, sporting goods and more. And when all is said and done and you've worked up a he-man's appetite, sink those choppers into juicy hamburgers, hot dogs, barbecue, corn-on-the-cob, turkey legs, funnel cakes, snow cones, popcorn and more. One of the nicest features this year is delivery to your car. FREE parking on Friday; $2 on Saturdays and Sundays. Restrictions are laudable: No alcoholic beverages, tobacco or pets allowed. (Husbands are welcomed on a leash, please, as they have a tendency to wander!)

★★★★★ **Traders Village**   **972/647-2331**
2602 Mayfield Rd.   Sat-Sun 8 AM-Dusk
Grand Prairie, TX 75052   www.tradersvillage.com

Since Traders Village opened in the Dallas-Fort Worth area (Grand Prairie, specifically) in 1973 and then in Houston in 1989, millions of people have browsed, shopped, haggled, picked through the bric-brac and landed quite a few deals. Hundreds and hundreds of dealers offer a little bit of everything, all at bargain prices. From the days of the Trading Post in the Old West until now, here is one gigantic step(s) for mankind. Who doesn't like to wheel and deal? There's so much being offered that, unless you've got your equilibrium in check, you could fall flat on your face in the frenzy. Up and down, in and out, over and around the miles of aisles trying to cajole the vendor into believing you've only got your last $200 bucks for that boudoir. The atmosphere's like the State Fair rather than Barnum and Bailey...some serious transactions, some with an air of frivolity. But just like some folks like to gamble for a few hours knowing that they have $100 to play with, and that's it, shoppers, given the same mind-set, will have a whale of a good time and just maybe come home a winner. It's a great way to have a family outing, and a whole lot more fun than going fishing (though there are some similarities). Only at Traders Village can you stroll through literally thousands of shops where you can wheel and deal with the store owners themselves and maybe secure the bargain of a lifetime. From paper clips to bulldozers, on any given weekend you can find it at Traders Village. There's an R.V. Park, kiddie rides and games, ATM machines, stroller and wheelchair rentals, snack stands, restaurants, mobile beverage carts, covered rest areas, modern restrooms, and all types of special amenities—all making for a pretty comfortable and all-around shopping experience. No foot reflexologists standing by, which is all that's lacking for a perfect day.

★★ Vikon Village Flea Market

2918 South Jupiter
Garland, TX 75041

972/271-0565
Sat-Sun 10-7
www.vikonvillage.net

One reason to intersect Kingsley and Jupiter is to land at Vikon Village. Just two blocks north of LBJ, this indoor flea market is as old as the hills. In fact, if my memory serves me correctly, it was the first flea market I ever shopped when I moved to Dallas. Find it all, from sporting goods to computers, bicycles to cameras, rare coins to gifts, and swords. Do they have swords? Their prices are slashed, too? Then move down the next aisle to sewing machines, dinnerware, area rugs, jewelry, baby buntings, furniture, and lo and behold, even a TV repairman. Stock up on feed, grain and farm supplies, then mosey on over to the pool supplies. Jump in. Dive in. It's a sink or swim world. Somewhere in this maze of about 300 dealers, you will be introduced to trash or treasures and a lot of kitsch, some kaboodle and everything in between.

28

Food Stuff

★★★★ Addison Coffee Roasters
15012 Beltway
Addison, TX 75240

972/404-1145
Mon-Fri 9-5

At the intersection of Belt Line and Midway, there's a secret little stash of coffee beans just waiting to be ground. So, if you're looking for a ground-floor opportunity, enjoy your next cup of java from here. They roast their own beans in the back of their showroom. It's impossible to avoid the aroma and almost impossible to find them. Once you do, you'll probably be addicted. The bean itself looks vanilla-like, but what's plain and simple, is to tell them the Diva sent you so you'll pay 25 percent less. Try their two-week-old coffee (tastes the same to me), and save 50 percent. Shop where the restaurants shop for coffee and specialty teas. Ah, the hazelnut creme, the Columbian French Roast, the many blends that are all roasted in small batches to ensure freshness. It's now coffee, tea and me—what a combination!

★★ Blue Cottage Herb Farm
8050 FM 4030
Kaufman, TX 75142

903/498-4234
Mon-Sat 10-6

Still waiting for their machine to answer, but as far as we're concerned, Blue Cottage is still alive and kicking. Take Hwy. 175E past Kaufman to FM 2860 and turn left. Three miles, you'll come to a stop sign. Stop. Then look for the first gate on the right. If you've got a hankerin' for herbs, and consider yourself an Herb-an Cowboy, you'll see the herbs growing on site. How green is their valley? Well, you can see for yourself during a tour of their greenhouses and then a stop over in their herb shop to buy the dried and fresh herbs, including those that are recommended for what ails you. An apple a day may keep the doctor away; but the doctor's probably loading up on herbs during his off-hours. 'Tis better to be healthy than sorry. Call ahead before you depart on your journey.

◆◆◆◆ Candy in Bloom   214/363-2399
728 Preston Forest Shopping Center
Dallas, TX 75230
Mon-Fri 10:30-5:30 Sat 10-2   www.candyinbloom.com

Candy is dandy, but what good is it if it lies in state? Forget flowers. Soothe my savage taste buds and send me something to satisfy my sweet tooth (that was before my surgery). This company puts it all together, ties it with a bow and sends it post haste. Even if the recipient's on a diet, they can create a masterfully decadent low-cal, low-fat, sugar-free basket. Tsk-tsk. Cookies, chocolates, hard candies, if you're craving for something sweet, consider these as an alternative for: House Warmings, Corporate Gift-Giving, Kiss and Makeup Baskets and other important occasions; they can be all wrapped up in any price range. Order by phone or online, it's sublime. *Call toll-free: 800/37-CANDY*

★★★★★ Cheesecake Royale   214/328-9102
9016 Garland Rd.   Mon-Sat 8-6
Dallas, TX 75218

Dino, Dino, Dino makes cheesecakes, cheesecakes, cheesecakes. Just don't expect to eat just one. When times are stressful, there are a few of us who've been known to down a whole one in one sitting. Do we have taste, or what? These cakes are sold in the finest specialty stores and catalogs but are half price at the source. This bakery makes other things besides cheesecake, but trust me, I know cheesecakes. Forget The Cheesecake Factory, Lindy's Cheesecake, The Stage Deli—no matter, you've never eaten a cheesecake quite like this. Everything's natural—real cream cheese, whipping cream, hand-squeezed lemon juice, dairy butter, sour cream and fresh fruits—with absolutely no added preservatives, artificial flavors, flour or gelatin. There is one problem (well actually several). Which one to choose? Do I want key lime or white chocolate? Amaretto or Black Forest? Raspberry or just plain old New York cheesecake? To solve that problem, order one of each. They make a sampler which is individually pre-cut with tissue separating the 16 large slices. And I mean large like in ten-inches in diameter. The cake itself weighs approximately four-five pounds which probably corresponds to the number of pounds you gain upon eating. Pick up or if you want to send a gift, delivery is overnight by FedEx. Other cake varieties besides cheesecakes that are Dino's delicacies include chocolate mousse, Kahlua, rum, Black Forest, rum raisin, chocolate, three-layer cake and carrot cake...all waiting in line for conspicuous consumption. And at prices good enough to eat, what are you waiting for? "Since life is uncertain, eat dessert first!" *Call toll-free: 800/328-9102*

★★ Chicotsky's Liquor Store   817/332-3566
3429 W. 7th St.   Mon-Sat 10-8
Fort Worth, TX 76107-2781

Chicotsky's has raised the bar on service, price and selection. Just let those big chains try to compete with this hometown favorite. With down-home pride for the small businessman and a lot of sassafras to fill the ole gut, don't wine over the details for your next party. Let Chicotsky's Liquor Store deliver those cases right to your front door. This Fort Worth chain is one of the oldest liquor stores in the city. Ask about their party kegs while they bite the bullet of the competition around them. They continue to wage a war themselves on high prices, come "hell or (Scotch) and water." Check directory for other locations.

★★★★★
Cupboard Natural Foods & Cafe
940/387-5386
200 W. Congress
Mon-Sat 9-7; Sun 11-5
Denton, TX 76205
www.cupboarddnaturalfoods.com

Denton can be mighty proud of its universities, its horse farms, and the Cupboard Natural Foods & Café. Maybe that's why Whole Foods has stayed away from Denton County. This home-grown treasure is a creatively-ensconced favorite of the academic community and those who are organically-inclined. And no wonder. They've been voted "Best Veggie Fare/Health Food Store" three years in a row by readers of the *Denton Record Chronicle*." Now they can add, voted "Best" by Bigger Better Bargains. (By the way, they've also been featured in *Southern Living*.) It's a real treat for your health buds and a visual treat for your eyes. Their deli is a feast for both. The "Burrito Meal" for $4.95 was fabulous, black beans and brown rice with all the fillings; plus your choice of a mild or spicy sauce, chips and a **BLUE SKY** natural soda. Yu-m-m! No artificial anything. The real stuff. Enough! Then there's the selection of imported, specialty and micro-brewed beers and wines (including those from North Texas). The bulk food department is a money-saving emporium. Bulk up! Herbs, spices, freshly roasted coffee beans, oils, syrups, honey, whole grains, flours, pasta and granola. And the Trail Mix, well, I could live on it for years. At least when you're having a snack attack, you're eating whole foods that are good for you. Organic produce is lush and dewy, their café is roomy but there's no chopped suey...but their roasted, nitrate-free chicken breast, roasted red bell peppers, basil pesto and feta cheese crumbles served upon an herbed focaccia roll is...well, one bite from heaven. Tums not needed. Prices are extremely reasonable but don't hesitate to sign up for their discount programs for your frequently-needed vitamins and supplements, and if you're a Senior Citizen, you're granted special price dispensations.

🎯 Gourmet Meats by Mail

Meat me all the way since I too joined the ranks of satisfied customers. If you're ready for Prime Time meat, and I mean the best that money can buy, restaurant quality and all that, here are a few top places to indulge:

Superb Veal
Summerfield Farm
Culpeper, VA
540/547-9600

Superb Lamb
Jamison Farm
Latrobe, PA
800/237-5262

Superb Lamb, Beef and Pork
Niman Ranch of California
www.nimanranch.com
510/808-0340

★★★★★ **Dallas Farmers Market**   **214/939-2808**
1010 S. Pearl Expwy.   Mon-Sun 7-6
Dallas, TX 75201

With the addition of cooking classes and facility rentals, I wonder when couples will be requesting taking their wedding vows amongst the eggplants? This downtown legend is alive and healthy selling basketfuls of fruits, vegetables, meats, cheeses, plants, who knows what else will ensure a real "Food Awakening". They shine heads (of lettuce) and shoulders (pork loins) over all the other Farmers Markets because they are the biggest (may they "Rest in Peas!"). Direct from grower, this metro-gopolis attracts even the world-famous Rio Grande grapefruit and oranges, just minutes away from being picked. And nuts, do they have them every which way but canned. For example, there were more than seven varieties of pecans, in the shell, out of the shell, cracked, salted, unsalted, hot, cold, well, nuts if I remember them all. Come Christmas, the trees line up like an army gearing up for battle. Have them your way, flocked or unflocked. Add in gift baskets, fruit baskets, filler up with all the gourmet goodies down in the wholesale market district where you'll rub elbows with restaurateurs, celebrities and those just waking up with the dawn. From Daniel's Gourmet Coffees to Paula Lambert's famed Mozzarella Company, very few palates are sent out to pasture. Open 363 days (closed Christmas and New Year's Day), this farm-to-you source is the one to take for the trip to bountiful. They have the freshest fruits, vegetables and florals in the area. Call the Produce Hotline to check the day's specials. True farmers are few and far between. Most of the stands are run by dealers who buy produce wholesale and resell it. But if you're a purist, look for the signs at each stall identifying whether the sellers are "farmers", "dealers" or "farm merchants" (farmers who purchase and resell produce). Shed No. 3 (the orange shed) is *all* dealers. Shed No. 4 (red) primarily holds dealers selling watermelons. For *real* farmers, head for shed No. 1 (yellow). My favorite, hands down, is Shed 2. On weekends only, they bring out the gourmet foods and decorative gifts. It's a contemporary "Stand and Deliver" taste event. Enjoy it all—fresh vegetables, fruits and flowers all within an environment that is like a produce symphony complete with music, children's activities and craft demonstrations. FREE parking. A Dallas institution on the brink of being the hottest place in town to live, work, shop and be happy.

★★★★ Dallas Tortilla   214/821-8854
1418 Greenville Ave.   Tue-Sat 8-7; Sun 8-6
Dallas, TX 75206

They don't call me Guacamole Goldie for nothing. Add in a few tortillas, and you can vote me your newest ambassador to freshly made tortillas. Made daily in their Oak Cliff factory, if you are looking to throw a real Mexican bash, get it all from here. I'd like to give them a "pizza my mind", though, they also make tamales, tostados, chips and taco shells by hand. Now for those entertaining in a big way, let them prepare fresh (or frozen) tamales, beef, pork or chicken filling with or without jalapeños, and pop them in your oven. Nobody will ever guess you didn't make them yourself. (After all, you have been taken cooking classes for years, haven't you?) Serve it hot today, or it'll be chili tomorrow! Located at the corner of Greenville and Bryan, shell out $4.75 for tamales per dozen or less if you order by the 100s. I didn't ask for a price by the gross because I thought they wouldn't believe me. Holy molie!

★★★★ Dolly Madison/Wonder Hostess   972/399-0770
584 S. Belt Line   Mon-Sat 8-6; Sun 11-5
Irving, TX 76060

Jan led us through the wonders of shopping this day-old outlet, but good grief, Charlie Brown, when we run of out "ZINGERS", what shall we do? Well, shopping here is one of the solutions to buying on the cheap all of the unsold **DOLLY MADISON** sweets and **HOSTESS/WONDER** bakery treats. Great place to feed the neighborhood gang, the soccer team, the Brownie troop with dozens of cupcakes that you pop into the freezer and retrieve when necessity calls. Hotdog and hamburger buns (eight-pack) were $.59 each (or 2/$1.09) and **LAY'S** potato chips were off the block for $.99. We couldn't help but wink for the "Twinkie" multi-packs for $1.59. Of course, when there's a coupon, imagine how much more cents off are accepted even at their outlet. Check directory for more Dolly Madison and Wonder Hostess stores. Don't forget to ask for the 10 percent off if you're a senior citizen (save more dough, sister). And for anyone younger, they also offer free cards they call the "Snacking Card" at the Dolly stores and the "Sweet Treat" card at the Wonder Hostess stores. Check your directory for additional locations of Dolly and Wonder Stores. Isn't it nice to be kneaded?

★★★★★ Entenmann's/Oroweat Bakery   **972/231-3487**
1419 E. Spring Valley   Mon-Fri 10-6; Sat 10-5
Richardson, TX 75080

So, what's your favorite **ENTENMANN'S**? Doesn't matter 'cause you can find most (if not all) varieties of your favorites at this one and only remaining Entenmann's/**OROWEAT** Bakery Thrift Store in the Metroplex. (Their former location at 3068 Forest Lane is now a Mrs. Baird's Thrift, but believe it or not, you'll still see some of Entenmann's products for sale there.) Now owned by the Best Food Baking Company, their no-fat coffee cakes are still on my replace weekly shopping list. The cheese Danish makes you want to return to "Home, Swede, Home". Calling all gluttons, eat your heart out without having an attack of the guilties when you check out. Save up to 50 percent on products right-from-the-ovens to maybe a day or so old. This hippie baker is nothing but our favorite Flour Child! *Call toll-free: 800/356-3314*

★★ Farmers Market   **817/838-8781**
5507 E. Belknap   Mon-Sat 8-6
Fort Worth, TX 76117

After 27 years in business, Fort Worth's Farmers Market is a hand full of fruits and vegetables, including some exotics that you may not see everywhere. In-season papayas, pineapples, guava and plantains make the world go around at this original Fort Worth's Farmers Market. Wait with baited breath for the Sweet Vidalia or 1015 Onions...they're worth crying over. They're also great for making your own Bloomin' Onion, just like those at Chili's. Melons are ripe and waiting for yourspecial touch. You don't even have to get up at the crack of dawn to beat the farmers unloading their trucks. But an occasional scuffle will ensue if you and someone else grab the same quart of three-inch strawberries. Stand your ground. You got there first. Though not as large as the Dallas Farmers Market, by a longshot, they are big enough to deliver the variety, but not so large as to let a bad apple spoil the apple cart.

★★★★ Fiesta Mart   **214/944-3300**
611 W. Jefferson Blvd.   Mon-Sun 7-11
Oak Cliff, TX 75208   www.fiestamart.com

Since 1972, this Houston-area institution has grown to include Dallas/Fort Worth and Austin on their area roster. Though catering to an ethnic audience (Hispanic, African-American, and the Asian shopper), their 50,000 square foot grocery store with an entertainment flair offers the highest quality meat, groceries, fresh produce, seafood, a world class delicatessen, beer and fine wine, as well as a variety of international and specialty foods and products. The authentic "Fiesta" atmosphere transforms shopping into a buffet of food options liken to a supermercado. And is it super! Now, with six area locations, is it any wonder other grocers are trying to compete with the introduction of ethnic foods and catering to a Hispanic marketplace? Online, you can even download a page of coupons that are redeemable in their stores. The menu of Hispanic favorites include it all, from camellias to mangoes, shitake mushrooms to radicchio. Then belly-up to the taco and fajita bar where the aroma alone makes you stop and smell the "flours". Services beyond the typical grocery store amenities include paying your utilities, purchasing license tags, buying concert and sporting event tickets, and the usual like money orders, lottery tickets, cashing checks or sending money via Western Union. At various locations, you'll see fresh seafood departments, a fresh deli, Taquerias and Salchichonerias (Mexican-Style Hot Deli), an in-store bakery providing fresh baked goods daily and an International and Specialty Foods Area which offers products from around the globe. Also, you'll be taken aback by the offerings of soft goods, clothing and natural foods, too. Fiesta is also a huge supporter of local charities, educational programs and special events, as well as working with community leaders and citizens in a variety of programs and projects. I loved them in Houston; ditto in Dallas/Fort Worth. You will, too.

★★★★★ Fresh Express Dallas   214/421-1947
2500 S. Good Latimer   Mon-Fri 5-5; Sat 5:30-11
Dallas, TX 75215

Who doesn't like the freshest fruits or the best of vegetables packaged for commercial use by restaurants at fabulous prices? Of course, prices fluctuate with the seasons, the droughts, the heat waves and such, but as we speak, a five-pound bag of fruit salad (cantaloupe, honeydew melon and grapes) was $11.55 and a five-pound bag of pineapple cubes was $12.55. Want to throw a party and have them do up the veggie trays so all you have to do is whip up a dip? Easy does it, $7.50. Price list changes, but calling in advance for your orders hasn't. Why chop 'til you drop? Let these folks do if for you. They know their stuff and will suggest what's in season, what looks good, what IS good.

★★★★★ Gene's Fruit Stand & Patio   972/247-7301
2508 Forest Lane   Mon-Sun 9-6:30
Dallas, TX 75234

If it ain't broke, Gene's won't fix it. For more than 30 years, they have been doing it right in front of everyone's eyes. Their very visible LJB/Forest Lane open-air emporium is laden with hanging baskets and trellises, gazebos, bird baths, fountains, willow lawn furniture, concrete benches and tables; it's your backyard's best friends. But as fresh as the day is long, don't overlook from whence they came—in fruits, herbs and vegetables, all plums when it comes to quality. Seven days a week, you can pick from the shelled peas brought in from East Texas or squeeze the succulent squash when the season dictates. Just don't expect to squeeze the **CHARMIN** or the delicate Swedish Ivy or Airplane plants. See some of the biggest pots in the city hanging from the eaves or swing on their swings; either way you'll be in the "Garden of Eaten".

★★★★ Georgia's Farmers Market   972/516-4765
916 E. 15th St.   Mon-Sat 8:30-6:30; Sun 9-5
Plano, TX 75074

Georgia, Georgia, if you've got Georgia on your mind, perhaps its the same Georgia Machala Massey that is owner of this peach of a Farmer's Market. What began as a downtown family enterprise with her father and brothers at age seven, now has evolved into a budding establishment in Plano as well. The Machala family is still rooted in the downtown Dallas Farmers Market, operating a stand in the No. 2 shed, but in 1997 some of Georgia's brothers followed her to Plano to continue in the family tradition. Everything that Georgia sells is a peach. But just try eating one of those plump seedless grapes. Bet you can't eat just one! But with grape prices being so high, $3.29 a pound, looks like you might have to forego even a cheap glass of wine (or start stomping your own in your back yard). Nevertheless, you're not getting "graped." You can hardly believe that this bastion of produce was once home to a body shop, complete with roll-up doors. Today, it is an open-air marketplace, reminiscent of those in Europe. Exit 15th Street off Central Expressway. Turn right and go approximately 1/2 mile, across the street from City Park.

★★★★ Goody-Goody Liquor Store   972/701-8475
14851 Inwood Rd.   Mon-Sat 10-9
Addison, TX 75247

Oh, you met your match with a Golden Cadillac, Goody-Goody. Ride 'em cowboy and round up a thirst-quencher if the spirits move you. If you really want something to wine about, let's talk prices. Here, they're about as competitive as it gets: **ANDRE** Champagne for **$2.95** right up to the **DOM PERIGNON** for $115. Drink up and salud the savings. Prices are on the rocks, best on moderate liquors, but still pretty good on top-shelf brands as well. Center yourself in the middle of their stores for their specials including exotic liquors and domestic beers. By the bottle or by the case (or even by the paper bag), Goodie-Goodie is a formidable liquor store (but don't expect to toast their laurels on the premises). No drinking. Check directory for other locations, as they are spreading their cheer across the Dallas area.

★★ Grapevine Farmers Market   817/410-3185
701 S. Main St.   Sat 8AM - Sellout; Wed 3PM - 6PM (Seasonal)
Grapevine, TX 76051

This Grapevine moves in very healthy circles and wraps its tentacles around the heart of this community. With its historical bent, the look of Main Street and its Gazebo and antique stores, add this small Farmers Market to its charm. About 15 farmers roll up their sleeves and roll in their carts usually twice a week towards the end of May to entice you with their fresh produce. Presenting a seasonal exchange of earthy tales and mouth-watering peaches, plums, tomatoes and corn, the season starts the weekend after Main Street Days in late May and runs through November when the frost hits the pumpkins and gourds. Another nostalgic contribution to shopping in small towns and its merchants who have a unique and personal hands-on approach to selling one-on-one. "Cheese Whiz", what's next? *Call toll-free: 800/457-6338*

★★ Homemade Gourmet   972/712-1885
6943 Main Street   Tue-Sat 9-5
Frisco, TX 75034   www.homemadegourmet.com

Here's the answer to contemporary fast food. Faster than a New York minute, add a few ingredients to any of Homemade Gourmet's mixes and you can serve up a hearty party in no time. Doesn't everybody want their fair shake? Just add an egg, some oil, water, milk, maybe a dollop of sour cream, voilà! You don't even have to add the eight spices to their Taco Soup Mix, they've already done it for you. For dessert, what about an old-fashioned apple crisp? Better than even grandma's favorite. Your guests will think you've been slaving over a hot stove for hours. Serve a delicious tomato basil bread right from the oven (from a mix where the sweet basil and dried tomatoes have already been added). I'm telling you, this is the way to cook. You can even fool your mother-in-law. Dump, stir, heat and eat! That's what I call livin' the good life, for a lot less wear and tear on your already busy day. Shop online, in person, or call one of their distributors. (Debbie Diaz, 972/712-1885, is one.) Distributors all over the country ensure there's something coming from your oven. Online you'll be introduced to kid's stuff, marinades, shakes, hot cocoas, vegetable and chip dips, barbecue mixes and entrées. It doesn't get better than homemade gourmet. The mixes are the creation of Tami Van Hoy, who was prompted to form a business after garnering rave reviews from family and friends. Many of her recipes are adaptations from old family recipes from her grandma's days. She has carefully preserved the rich flavors and "homemade" taste of them. Once you've tried them, you will go back for more.

★★★★ IWA-International Wine Accessories   214/349-6097
10246 Miller Rd.   Mon-Fri 9-7; Sat 10-4
Dallas, TX 75238   www.iwawine.com

IWA stands for International Wine Accessories, Inc. and if you are dedicated to the red, white and brewer, this may be your liaison to fine wine accessories. If you pride yourself on being a wine connoisseur, this mail order company, formed in 1983, is the brainchild of Robert S. Orenstein, an ex-corporate tax specialist who just happened to love wine more. When he founded his company, it was so it could obtain quality, wine-related items that were not readily available elsewhere. In 1999, he went online and after seventeen years experience in the traditional bricks and mortar catalog business, IWA was prepared for the web shopping customer. First, they already had a highly-trained and knowledgeable customer service department that could handle the questions. Secondly, their purchasing department was prepared to maintain stock and a warehouse the size of a football field. Shop direct, from home or office, by phone or mail, by fax or web—they make sure they can do it your way. Trade and wholesale programs are open to volume purchasers such as wineries, retail establishments, wine stores, hotels, and restaurants but the public can sip and save because they're importers and their prices are highly competitive. For gift-giving, they'll even be able to private label your company's name and logo. Although they specialize in wine cellars, they also carry all the wine accoutrements: corkscrews, stemware, books, videos and more. Described as The Horchow Finale of wine, the closeout section features beautiful items from previous catalogs, samples, one-of-a-kinds, overstocks, blemishes/imperfections and canceled orders, all at prices that are 10-50 percent below original cost. There are antique bottles, glassware, crystal, decanters, room dividers, sculpture, tables, rotisserie grills, books, videos, ties, wine-cellar units and racking systems, even dining room tables— all themed with the fruit of the vine. Espresso machines were a little steep, $999-$1,500, but remember, these are the finest commercial/home models. (If you buy one, it may wind up to be grounds for a divorce.) We finally toasted our good fortune and called it a day. L'chaim! *Call toll-free: 800/527-4072*

★★ La Spiga Italian Bakery   972/934-8730
4203 Lindbergh   Mon-Fri 7-3; Sat 8-3
Addison, TX 75001   www.whitepages.com

There's no loafing off at this company. They're up at the crack of dawn, baking breads as fast as they can. Do you think **MRS. BAIRD** started this way? Since 1994, Donato Milano and Carolyn Nelson have been whipping up their breads and pastries and selling them to many of the major hotels and restaurants in town. Then, the public got a whiff of their focaccia, their famous Italian Milano bread, or their menus of other breads like Calamata Olive, Jalapeño Cheese, Pumpernickel, Baguettes, Sweet Basil and Rye. Oh me, oh rye! And for the Jewish holidays, their Raisin Challah is scarfed down like it was the last supper. Their Biscotti Cookies are a dunkers' delight. Come to think of it, so are the Ciabatta and Panini rolls. Their early morning power Italian breakfasts, their daily lunch specials, their home-made breads and rolls, their chocolate eclairs for dessert, their Caesar salad with a light yet hearty quiche or lasagna— what a nice change of pace. Catering orders are accepted with 24-hours advance notice. Enjoy.

★★★★ Margarita Masters   972/641-7926
PO Box 540502   Call to Reserve
Grand Prairie, TX 75054

When was the last time you hit Margaritaville? If you're due, then take time to chill out with a frozen drink machine that you can rent for your next party. Margarita Masters is the oldest and largest company of its kind in the Metroplex. Their service, their attention to detail and reliability, not to mention their price, are the reasons party planners, both professional and amateur, seek them out. For a rental fee of $95 (down from $125), you get FREE delivery and set up (they'll even mix the drinks for you), 50 plastic nine-ounce cups, salt and straws. For the average size drink, this should serve 71 drinks, give or take a few. Add $15 per Margarita mix (serves approximately 80) and three liters of tequila per package of mix, and you're in business. Go exotic with frozen specialty drinks like a Bellini, daiquiri, piña colada or a swirl. Prices ranged $15-$20 for the mix. Different drinks call for different liqueurs. If in doubt, call Carl, the friendly Margarita man. He's the bartender-on-call. You'll need about a week's notice to reserve your machine. (Did you know the first tavern to open in Alaska was a polar bar?)

Metro-Webb Foods
1411 W. Randall Mill Rd.
Arlington, TX 76012

817/261-2260
Mon-Fri 8-6; Sat 9-3

When it comes to food, glorious food, gluttons are often found hovering around Metro-Webb Food. This salvage operation buys closeouts from area food distributors and then sells them wholesale to the public. Everything's delicious, from pre-made foods like lasagna to hamburger patties. Add in sauces, salad dressings, desserts—just about anything for the pampered purveyor of food can be found here. Maybe your next soccer hop or church social needs a celebration? Find something scrumptious to bring to a pot luck supper, and if your luck holds out, you'll be eating in for a whole lot less. They've been in business for 20 years (owners name is Ken). Wouldn't you just love to eat restaurant-quality food at wholesale prices? They are well-known and sought-after for their pre-cooked chicken fajita meat which is all white meat chicken. But wait 'til you taste their cobbler. It's the berries! Try their soups, eggs, tomatoes and more—need I repeat myself, at wholesale prices.

★★ Mrs. Baird's Thrift Store
3068 Forest Lane @ Webb Chapel
Farmers Branch, TX 75234

972/247-2392
Mon-Sat 9-5

Boy, oh boy, the Dough Boys will have a field day at this hometown favorite thrift store. Save some bread even on dinner rolls—you knead it! Shop a day or so later for Mrs. Baird's fresh from her oven to yours with just a matter of hours' lag time. Pop them in the freezer and when you take them out, they'll taste just like fresh. From split-tops to dinner rolls, load up for your next dinner party (they all taste the same) and it will then look like you're the perfect "Roll Model". Check directory for other locations including South Dallas, McKinney, Plano, Richardson and Sherman.

★ Omaha Steaks
10854 Preston Rd.
Dallas, TX 75230

214/368-7597
Mon-Sat 10-6; Sun Noon-5
www.omahasteaks.com

"One of life's affordable indulgences", if you're mad at the cows, give it up. If not, stake your claim to a great steak for at least the thrill of the grill. Meat-eaters have been ordering a piece of the beef from Omaha Steaks since World War I. Corn-fed, Midwestern beef is considered the best. (Just ask me, I've a Midwesterner who prefers it over Texas beef.) Do not make an issue out of it, however. So, where's the beef? Locations in Dallas, Lewisville and Plano, that's where. But wait 'til coupons shave 50 percent off the price. Occasional discounts like these are when you load up. Beef, sauces, seasonings, kosher foods, poultry, seafood, veal, pork, lamb and desserts. There're even some cookbooks to start you on your way.
Call toll-free: 800/228-9055

★★★★ Pendery's

304 E. Belknap
Fort Worth, TX 76102

817/332-3871
Mon-Fri 8:30-5:30; Sat 9-5
www.penderys.com

Remember, if it's chili today, it'll be hot tomorrow. This adage may be as old as the hills but so is Pendery's. Since 1870, they've been spicing up the town with their custom-blended chili powders and spices via their beautifully-crafted catalog, and they're now online. Why pay for the fancy bottles when all you really want are the spices themselves? From generation to generation, the Pendry family has produced an innovative and vast collection of spices. Whether you cook with them, or ingest them for medicinal purposes, start with the first family, where chili began! Their expanded inventory now includes candy, fruits, nuts, sauces, teas, jams and jellies, plus things that you can't eat like utensils, flowers, plates, jewelry, peppermills, posters, spice containers and racks, lights, cookbooks and more. The only caveat when shopping their catalog or online, when you finish shopping, you're hungry for more! *Call toll-free: 800/533-1870*

★★★ Rainbo Bakery Stores

2914 Centerville Rd.
Dallas, TX 75228

972/686-2330
Mon-Fri 9-7; Sat 9-6

Somewhere over the Rainbo Bakery Stores, they didn't pass spelling, but they sure know a thing or two about baking bread. Day-old or otherwise, tastes the same once you've popped them in the freezer, or warmed them in the oven. The prices you save may be your own. **EARTHGRAIN** is how they answer the phone. (Or is it Earth Green with a Southern accent?) Large hamburger buns were two packs for $1.89 and five packs of hot dog buns were $2.99. Hot dog! Yes, they still carry donuts, but keeping up with their daily specials is worse than keeping up with the Joneses. Well, now that you know how the other half lives, do as the Roman's do, and do it. It's cheaper. Check directory for other area Rainbo Bakery Stores.

★★★ Red Coleman's Liquors

7560 Greenville Ave.
Dallas, TX 75231

214/363-0201
Mon-Sat 10-9
www.redcoleman.com

Since 1946, Red Coleman's is still family-owned-and-operated. You'd think they've already had too much to drink by now, but instead they've managed to stay sober along with their 10 liquor stores and 20 convenience stores in the Metroplex. You'll see red, white, and probably blush since they're always on the lookout for a closeout on wines. On a regular basis, you can sip a brew or two as much as 50 percent off or more. Then, too, if you buy by the case during their quarterly sales, you can expect to shave another 20 percent off (12 bottles or more). Make sure to try their French Bordeaux and Burgundy selections—très bien. With their expanded inventories of beer, wine, spirits, micro brews and lots of hard-to-find cigars, there's not much they've missed. Pick-up and delivery, also available. They're located between Meadow and Walnut Hill on Greenville, so take a shot. Other Red Coleman locations throughout the Metroplex. Check directory for one nearest you but remember to toe the straight line. And don't drink and drive or I'll get MADD!

★★★★ Russell Stover Candies   972/563-8227

Metrocrest Industrial Park
200 Apache Trail
Terrell, TX 75160

Mon-Sat 9-6; Sun Noon-6
www.russellstover.com

Since 1923, they've been finger-lickin' good. When traveling to the Tanger Outlet Center, don't bypass one of the best little chocolate houses in Texas. Besides, they're the biggest candymaker in the USA. It just so happens that their Southwest distribution center has a little outlet store that is open to chocoholics. Take the FM 148 exit in Terrell, or order a catalog from the toll-free number if you'd rather stay home and pig out. When the holidays are over, that's when you'll never sleep owing to too much chocolate. Or mabye you'd rather wait until the holidays are over and store up on leftovers. That's when you can really achieve a rush. Christmas, Valentine's Day, Easter, Mother's Day, Father's Day and Halloween are all candy-giving feasts. Get them for a lot less all year round but especially the morning after. (Not the pill, silly.) *Call toll-free: 600/477-8683*

Spirits Liqueur Store   214/748-2459

2825 Canton @ Malcolm X
Dallas, TX 75226

Mon-Sat 10-9

Now it's time to sip the savings in any number of spirited liquid pleasures from a wholesaler in downtown Dallas. Deep in the heart of Deep Ellum, this 15,000-square-foot warehouse is open to the public and was voted best liquor store in several different publications. More than 8,000 different items from A to Z (**ABSO-LUT** vodka to **ZIEGENBOCK** beer) can be found standing or sitting on their sides. Other spirits are at your fingertips in this expansive warehouse, where you don't even have to leave a little tipsy for great service. Celebrate with champagne from **DOM PERIGNON** or a less expensive though notable **VEUVE CIQUOT** Brut Yellow (this French champagne is from one of the world's most respected champagne houses, founded in 1772). Toast any special occasion with sparkling wines such as **MARTINI & ROSSI'S** "Asti Spumanti" (the #1 premium imported sparkling wine from the heart of Italy and a gold medal winner at the New England Wine Festival) or "Opera"—a real zinger! Heaven knows, when you're ready to get into the spirit of things, or are planning a party, start here. Great prices, great selection, lousy location. Except now that downtown is happening, it's probably a great location for some. From domestic to imported, from France to Oregon, Texas to Germany, there's something for everyone. Remember, you don't have to sacrifice quality to sip the savings. Just don't get "snookered".

★★★★★ Texas Pecan Co.   972/241-7878

2850 Satsuma
Dallas, TX 75229

Mon-Fri 8:30-5

Are you nuts? Are you paying retail prices for pecan halves or pecan pieces? Why? You can buy them here for $4.95 a pound. Of course, the prices vary by time of year and crop production, but you're still paying a shell of the retail price. You'll crack up with the selection: Almonds, Spanish peanuts, walnuts, filberts, Brazil nuts, pumpkin and sunflower seeds, pine nuts, trail mixes and roasted/salted nut mixes. Go directly to the source. Do not pass Go. Do not shell out $200. Your taste buds are like the salt of the earth. Satisfy the urge to splurge. Off Stemmons between Forest and Royal, whether for cooking, for baking, for the candlestick maker as a gift, or just for yourself, you're nuts if you don't shop here. Orders by phone accepted.

★★ Tony's Wine Warehouse & Bistro   214/520-WINE

2904 Oak Lawn   Mon-Thu 10-10; Fri & Sat 10 AM-11 PM
Dallas, TX 75206

How many bottles of wine on the wall, how many bottles of wine? If one of them falls, how many are left? Well, at Tony's, we're talking more than 2,000 bottles off the wall and stocked at their warehouse/bistro. Don't even think of them running out on a Saturday night. A nice touch, wines are offered by the glass, and I'm talking an extensive menu. They offer open wine classes for $30 once a month (meaning they are open to anyone and not just to certain groups). So with a jug of enthusiasm and thou, toast to learning the art of fine wine. Imbibe and indulge excellent French-Italian cuisine at the Bistro, choose a bottle of wine from the store, have it opened and brought to your table—each bottle is extremely affordable that way. The owner is from the wine valleys of France and has been honing his craft in importing fine wines for almost 35 years. In the heart of Oak Lawn, between Cedar Springs and Congress, lunch is served from 11-2:30, and dinner 6-10. For a special night out on the town, enjoy a jazz dinner for $69.44 which includes a five-course meal and wine tasting (tax and gratuity included). It begins at 7:30 PM and includes, you guessed it, a live jazz band. Bid adieu to pretentious dining—this one wins the Tony. Gift certificates, a nice aperitif. Our only complaint is on our last visit, our waiter really really pushed us to BUY the whole bottle.

★★★★★ Top Line Warehouse Store   972/262-5326

433 E. Church St.   Mon-Sat 9:30-6
Grand Prairie, TX 75050

Top shelf and premium brands line the aisles of this warehouse. A little of this and a little of that, all well-organized and priced low. That's how Bud Bobbitt started his company 25 years ago and it's how he continues to maintain the "Top of the Lines" today. No membership fees needed. All that's needed to be affiliated with this store is the mere knowledge of their existence. After that, you're hooked. We reeled in good deals on pet food and supplies like **NATURE'S RECIPE**—a five-pound bag was $1.99 and a 40-pound bag was $12.95. **WALTHAM** eight-pound bags were $8 and **IAMS** canned food was a mere 89 cents a can—and our critters wolfed them down. Other brands included **ALPO**, **CYCLE** and **PEDIGREE**, but brands come and go around here. From pet supplies to paper goods, groceries, office supplies (paper, pens, binders), trash bags and paint to occasional supplies of large and small appliances and furniture, it's all here at big savings. Though most items are considered freight-damaged, the fact is that most, about 90 percent, are simply mis-marked, mis-loaded or mis-routed. If it's been handled and shipped by motor carrier, it might wind up here. All is well in the war on high prices but should you be feeling a bit under the weather, be sure to stop in their pharmacy at the front of the store. Simply find your way to the corner of Church St. and 5th St. But don't forget to look across the street to their other store. Top Line Select specializes in clothing, fabric, toys and books. This location is at 208 N.E. 5th St. and open Tue-Sat 10-5.

★★★★ Wonder Bread Thrift   817/534-3152

5609 Wichita Ave.   Mon-Sat 8-7; Sun 11-5
Fort Worth, TX 76119

I **WONDER** where the **HOSTESS** went? If she's smart, she went shopping here. Be the Hostess with the mostest when you buy your day-old Wonder bread stuff from here for the leastest! After all, isn't that the staff of life? So what if it's a day late or a pound less? Saving money is what it's all about. Chomp into hot dog or hamburger buns in the eight count, two packages for $1.09; 12-count were 99 cents. Then, for dessert, add in the **TWINKIES** and Chocolate Cup Cakes in the eight-count packs that are usually $1.99 (ask any mother), but were three for $5. Wait for sales, and they're often 99 cents. **DING DONG**, Wednesdays and Saturdays are bargain days, where prices are slashed even more. Though promoted as day-old, some are right from the ovens. My nose sure doesn't know the difference. Check directory for multiple locations.

★ ★ ★ ★ ★   World Food Imports   972/480-9911
13434 Floyd Circle   Mon-Sun 10-8
Dallas, TX 75243

If you're a galloping gourmet, and want to command attention at your next soirée, here's a warehouse full of worldly food imports that are waiting to be digested. One Israeli gourmet cook revels in their international foods and imported cheeses. Step into this warehouse environ and get a great whiff of delicious foods from around the world that you don't see at your typical grocery store. They also have restaurant-quality meats with prices that are hard to beat. (Hey, I'm a poet—and I don't know it!) And some of their breads were like Long Fellows. Once you've found them, you'll make a mad dash on a regular basis, especially if you're a gourmet cook or an "Ainsley Harriott" fan. You don't even have to be a "Naked Chef" to shop here!

Yes! Less   972/494-3389
1518 Buckingham Rd.   Mon-Fri 9-8; Sat 9-7; Sun 12-6
Garland, TX 75081   www.yesless.com

Coming to a location nearest you, Yes! Less—is so simple, it's shameful. You get so much more for so much less, even I'm impressed. I hope they consider one in my neighborhood soon 'cause six Roma tomatoes for $1 and four of the most delicious avocados for $1 is just the beginning to something big! With locations now in Arlington, Athens, Hurst, College Station, Longview, Denison, Sherman, Killeen, Shreveport, LA , Garland, Waco, Dallas and Wichita Falls, TX, watch for all hell to break loose when they open their doors in your neighborhood. Yes! it's less, much less. But don't for a minute think you're having to sacrifice the quality of the food you're eating. Not! You'll save up to 50 percent, that's true. You'll save on both brand names and private labels (top quality, the same as the brand name), that's true, too. Owned by the wholesale food giant Fleming Foods, this is the start of something huge. I predict this is the next retailer to jump start in the fast tract. But they also carry merchandise like you'd see in the Everything's a Dollar, Just a Buck, or Dollar General kind of store. You might say they're a limited assortment superstore. Save money, honey buns, on everything from hamburger buns to hot water bottles, meat to produce, bakery goods to **AMERICAN TOURISTER** luggage (when it's gone, it's gone), snacks to toys, cereals to candy, ah, the sweet smell of success. How do they do it? By limiting the number of skews (that means assortment). Instead of handling every kind of ketchup, for example, you'll only see one kind. They make a "power buy", you save and say "buy, buy" to high prices. It's as simple as that. And if that were the only thing they were selling, they wouldn't necessarily be so unique. Instead, they are also selling a company based on family values and respect. Yes! Isn't that special? Fun, fast-paced and integrated with integrity. Yes! This small company with big company benefits and big company thinking is on its way. Yes! Less—coming to a location near you. The store at 5828 Abrams in Dallas is 18,000 square feet (smaller than your traditional grocery store) with over 1,000 items at $1 or less. Yes!Less.

29

Furniture & Home Accessories

5th Avenue Dinettes & More
14000 Stemmons Frwy.
Farmers Branch, TX 75234

972/241-5565
Mon-Fri 10:30-7; Sat 10-6; Sun 1-5

Man does not live by food alone. Man needs a table to eat on. Man needs one that will look great but cost little. Man needs durability and name brands. Man needs to shop at 5th Ave. Dinettes. Man, oh man, when it comes to satisfying all of the above, there's no better street to travel than 5th Avenue. You buy your clothes on 7th Avenue, now sit down and enjoy them at your casual dinette sets. Only the best names like **CHROM-CRAFT** can be found, so shimmy up to hundreds of choices including all the popular and funky bar stools. I bought a pair of chrome and purple leather ones for $100 apiece. Such a conversation seat! Then, when it comes to playing games, they also have a large selection of game sets. OK, poker-face, you can let down your guard. Everything here is a winner. The combination of service, selection, styles and savings is like being dealt a "Royal Flush!" Going north, exit Valley View and stay on the service road.

★★★★★ Adams Furniture
417 N. FM 156
Justin, TX 76247

940/648-3145
Mon-Sat 9-6; Thu 9-7

Stroll down Memory Lane, especially if you're a fan of small town prices on uptown furniture. Adams Furniture in Justin is just the place to make you homesick. Two of the most popular lines represented are **LANE** and **BROYHILL**. One hometown favorite is Broyhill's casual styled collection called "Fontana". What a home run! This grouping is made of a distressed washed finish in solid pine. Another grouping in oak scored a triple. The base price on a queen sleigh bed with wooden rails was $799 and the dresser and mirror was $899. Not bad, wouldn't you say? Certainly, a trip here is Justin-fied. They've been around since the days of the Depression of 1929, so they must be doing something right. You won't be depressed, though, about their prices or selection. Today, they're still not extravagant with their overhead but they do maintain an ample inventory in popular name brands besides Broyhill and Lane including **CORSICANA**, **EAGLE INDUSTRIES**, **ENGLANDER**, **MAYO**, **SEALY**, and one they're well-known for called the "Texas Western" collection. It's no wonder they've been getting rave notices for years, especially on furniture made by Texas artisans and craftsmen. You're a Texan now and you'd better look the part. FREE delivery, folks, so giddy-up and head north, young man.

★★★★★ AFFORDIT Furniture   940/566-3222
1802 Alice   Mon-Sat 9-7; Sun 1-5
Denton, TX 76201

Muy bueno, amigos. Let's get this show on the road. Affordit Furniture is the way to go for your first home away from home. Starting right out of the gate, escape from the humdrum of jelly glasses and bricks and sticks bookcases. Enjoy real furniture for unreal prices. Students love it here because they can outfit their entire abode for less than one rental's lease payment. This family-owned enterprise has settled into their bigger location across the street from their original University digs. Hop aboard a futon bunk bed, complete with twin mattress and regular mattress, for under $300. Plus, choose your color. Give up the boxes for tables and the cartons for chairs. A nice farm table grouping with four chairs in your choice of three finishes was $168. Prices are pitifully low with styles that are perfectly contemporary. If it looks good, wears good, feels good...then it must be good. Great starter shop for students, second homes, RVers and folks who like to keep their budgets mean and lean. Visit their other location in Watauga at 6535 Watauga Rd., 817/281-9140, Mon-Sat 9-7; Sun 1-5. If you need to confirm if you can affordit or not, call Don or Eldon Nicholson for your credit report.

★★★ American Furniture Warehouse   972/988-0303
2000 S. Great Southwest Pkwy.   Mon-Sat 10-9; Sun 10-6:30
Grand Prairie, TX 75051

Wave the flag when you've landed an all-American deal from here. Let the world know you're both smart and born in the USA. Sing the praises of this warehouse merchant who promises good prices and makes good on that promise. Circumnavigate the globe in search of that elusive bargain, or turn your car around and head for the northwest corner of Great Southwest Parkway and Pioneer Parkway. It's a lot closer to shop Grand Prairie than to fly cross-country to North Carolina. Located across from a bowling alley, you won't strike out on lanes of moderate furniture here. **ASHLEY, CLAYBROOK, MAYO, PIONEER, SOUTHERN TRADITIONAL** are just a few of the pillars of the community. The prices will "bowl" you over. Sofas and loveseats by Ashley were under $500. Dinettes were over $100 or just under $1,000. You'll not land in the gutter, either. These lines appear in retail furniture stores across the Metroplex. The difference between here and the other places is the prices! Financing can be arranged through Norwest with 90 days same as cash. Their other location is just down the street from Gabbert's Outlet, at 4554 McEwen Rd. in Dallas (972/866-6600).

★★★★★ American Leather   972/296-8016
3700 Eagle Place Drive, Suite 400   Tue-Thu 1-5; Fri-Sat 10-6
Dallas, TX 75236   www.americanleather.com

The demand for leather has never been greater 'cause we want what we want. President Bob Duncan should know. Since 1992, American Leather has been manufacturing high-end leather furniture, generating $29 million in sales last year alone. With 250 employees, you can expect to see their products in department and specialty stores. Then, if you're smart, you'll find their clearance showroom for factory returns, samples and distressed merchandise. Sink into the seat of high-end leather sofas, chairs, recliners, loveseats or ottomans at 50-70 percent off retailers like Cantoni and Macy's. What you see is what you can buy. Showroom samples only. ***Call toll-free: 888/254-9758***

★★★ Arabella's

114 E. Louisiana
McKinney, TX 75069

972/562-0607
Mon-Sat 10-5, Sun 1-5

There's an air about Arabella's, which spells shopping for clothing and furnishings for weekend retreats to the Hamptons, the Cape or the Hill Country. Offering a complete interior design service with hundreds of faded cabbage rose fabrics, for example, if you're smitten with the craze of mixing florals and stripes on the same chair, well, you've come to the right shoppe. Breeze through the new painted furniture, over-sized finials, braided rugs, silk flowers, candles, topiaries...the **TRACY PORTER** iron ribbon drawer pulls for $8 were tugging at our purse strings. The Lost Cow whitewashed tin birdhouse for $130 moo-o-ed and coo-o-ed. Upstairs, the balcony beckoned us to snare one of their sweet, pastel needlepoint throw rugs. Downstairs, it was all chatter about this and that. We left with a pair of well-heeled ladies in Great Gatsby garb who were also loaded down with parcels. We bought a bundle, too. LeAnn is very helpful and she'll even stay open late if she knows you'll be there.

★★★★★ Armoire Store, The

10745 Preston Rd.
Dallas, TX 75230

214/696-2684
Mon-Sat 10-6; Sun 1-5
www.armoire-store.com

What was once just an afterthought as a second job for Pete Markward in 1992 is now his passion...and business is booming. Store managers Jamie Ray and Ryan Elmore are shaking up the town of San Miguel de Allende in Mexico on a regular basis, since that's where most of their armoires come from. Don't let the world, or this store, pass you by. It's sometimes a little hard to see from the street as it's tucked away like a buried treasure, but once you've spotted their narrow brick pathway, you'll be on the road to ruins (lots of antiques are waiting to be discovered). Choose from hundreds of high-quality wood armoires such as French, country French, art deco, Chippendale pine, Louis XVI, even Queen Anne—their artistic reformations are imaginative and functional. From wine racks to computer stations, bookshelves to a pantry, armoires can take on a whole new meaning. Expect prices to range from $600-$2,000 but can be configured to meet your specifications from their own in-house cabinet shop. When in San Antonio, visit their historic store at 355 West Sunset Road, San Antonio, TX 78209, 210/805-9004 or their warehouse at 901 East Houston St., San Antonio, TX 78205, 210/885-8862. Online, you can see their wonderful array of expanded furniture besides armoires, though armoires are still their forté alongside some other unique furniture and accessories. Shipping anywhere in the continental USA, consider these pieces worthy of your home or office or both. Interesting Eastern European pine reproductions were priced right on the money, $299. Other reproductions from India, such as a Royal Swing, were a little more pricey, $1,995. And for those who like to keep their antiques protected from the wear and tear of everyday living, **FIDDES** furniture wax from England should do the trick. Why look to them for armoires? Well, consider their quality: made with thicker doors, solid backs, dovetailed drawers and other above-standard features. Some even included pocket doors and extra depth for TVs. None yet fit the large screens, but those may be custom ordered soon, you never know. ***Call toll-free: 800/5-FURNISH***

★★★★★ Artistic/Design Resource and Remodeling 214/742-1996

1308 Dragon St.
Dallas, TX 75207

Mon-Fri 8:30-5

Without working weekends, this studio can help slay the dragon of full-price design prices. Tucked away in the heart of the Design District, eliminate the middleman and let Casey be your guide to her 6,000 square foot warehouse. Worm your way into her good graces. Let her help you eliminate the middleman and work through most any interior design project (layout, construction, draperies or interior finish, for example). Everything except the roofer, the plumber and the electrician. Everything to get the job done efficiently and effectively is woven into their methodology. Selling wholesale services such as drywall and painting, draperies, both fabric and labor at 30 percent less, 65 percent off wood blinds and 20 percent off interior design, carpeting and remodeling is really a one-stop trip to a bountiful transformation. Watch the workers right in front of your eyes create a project from scratch. Browse through their sample books if you're plumb out of ideas. From Neo-classic to contemporary, Gothic to Oriental, all they need is your go-ahead.

PS Baker's Furniture & Accessories Warehouse Store   972/221-3252
1036 S. Jupiter Rd.   www.bakersthomasville.com
Garland, TX 75042

Their warehouse store in Garland, just north of LBJ, between Miller and Forest, may be the cash and carry dream come true. Though they have retail stores throughout the Metroplex, and are one of the largest dealers of **THOMASVILLE** furniture, this is the location where they get down and dirty. Bring your own ropes, blankets and trucks and don't expect the white glove treatment. Or like me, hire Around Town Moves and let them do the hauling. Though periodic in nature, watch newspapers when much of what is offered at their warehouse store is at or below cost. Save on sofas, loveseats, chairs and more from an incredible selection of **FLEXSTEEL**, **HOOKER**, **LANE**, **LEXINGTON**, **MASSOUD**, **RIVERSIDE**, **THOMASVILLE** and more. Dining rooms and bedrooms were more than half off. Designer floor samples and discontinued items were all reduced to near give-away prices. Saving 50 percent and more on all the Thomasville curios and display cabinets gave my library some breathing room. (I never realized how much space I had when I got the dozen or so knick-knack boxes onto the shelves and off the floor!) Then there were recliners. Lots and lots of recliners, perfect for Father's Day. What you don't see at the warehouse store, check for at their retail locations where the newest Hemingway collection (inspired by Papa's travels to Havana, Kenya, Ketchum, Key West and Paris) gives credence to a bold, dramatic look in wrought-iron, wood, metal, stone and leather. Check directory for the location nearest you, where prices ascend accordingly. Special financing packages are also available. All sales are final, quantities are limited, there's no layaways, holds or COD's. Nada. Nothing. Furniture. Half price. Sold.

★★ Bar Stools Plus, Inc.   817/589-7055
2220 A-Delante Ave.   Mon-Fri 9-5; Sat 9-3
Fort Worth, TX 76118

On your way to Gravel Furs, drive by Bar Stools Plus if you're in the market for a bar stool. This is the manufacturer's outlet, so unless you want to drink yourself under the table, the least you can do is sober up on the stool. Great for the game room, the breakfast bar, or the plain ole bar. Saunter up to the bar and choose either a wood or metal base, 24 or 30-inches, and then cover with your choice of hundreds of fabric, vinyl and naugahyde options. Don't be barbaric. You can't sit on pins and needles, you know. Call for directions if you're unfamiliar with the Fort Worth area—Hwy. 121 between Minnis and Carson. ***Call toll-free: 800/817-8665***

★★★★ Bassett Furniture Direct   972/315-9988
1915 S. Stemmons Frwy.   Mon-Sat 10-9; Sun Noon-6
Lewisville, TX 75067   www.bassettdfw.com

In 2002, Bassett will celebrate its 100th year, but not only are they getting older, they're getting better. This year, they introduced HGTV's decorator/author Chris Madden's collection as well as continuing to make shopping for an entire "look" easier by the vignette. These well-made, good-looking and affordable home furnishings were the original mission of the founders a century ago. And going direct couldn't have been better for bargain hunters. Six locations in the Metroplex

(Arlington, Garland, Lewisville, Mesquite, North Richland Hills and Plano) make it a cinch for penny-pinchers, especially when you can take up to 60 months to pay while setting up housekeeping or redoing an entire house full of dated or worn contents. With approximately 23,000 square feet of home furnishings, **BASSETT** has hit a home run.

★★★ Bent Tree Resale Furnishing   972/250-2060
17610 Midway Rd., Suite 144   Mon-Fri 11-6; Sat 10-6; Sun Noon-5
Dallas, TX 75287

If you can bend the rules, then here's a good excuse for bypassing paying full price. At Bent Tree, the tree's been planted on solid ground. Trade in the old; trade up to something new (even if it isn't). Though they do acquire occasional model home furnishings that a decorator brings to them, it's limited and usually gone in a day or two. So settle for the consigned goodies of furniture and accessories, some antiques and collectibles, throw in a mix of artwork, real and reproductions, and office furniture and see how far a dollar will go. Arrange to have your castaways picked up, for a fee, but discuss it ahead of time. Do not show up with a semi to unload some Saturday when you've decided to clean house. Expect to pay about a third of what the item cost new. Lots of decorator touches. If you're in the mood for love (seats) or prefer a one night (stand), this shop is not filled with Horrors.

Best Seat in the House, The   972/458-7655
12300 Inwood Rd., #150   Mon-Sat 10-6
Dallas, TX 75244

A woman's place is in the House, so take a seat and take in all the glory. Wave good buys at every nook and cranny. From small, eclectic accents and accessories to custom comforters, cushions, chairs—whatever seats your fancy. It's best to "Leave it to Marcy" to make your dream house a dream come true. A mixture of hand-crafted and hand-picked home accessories (artwork, lamps, sofas and chairs) can transform any home into a *House Beautiful*. The options are limitless. Pick your fabric and be awash in style. Custom draperies and upholstered furniture set the scene. Then it's off to accessories to create the conversation groupings. Add an antique or a reproduction, an iron piece, a trunk, an armoire, from whimsical to traditional, from more than 80 different manufacturers who are not what you see at every furniture store. Coordinate with window treatments, custom bedding (duvets, bed skirts, comforters), slipcovers, pillows and more from their in-house workroom. Then, all that's left to do is "ooh and aah!"

Bombay Co. Outlet, The   817/485-3151
6039 Precinct Line Road, Bldg. C   Mon-Sat 10-9; Sun Noon-6
Fort Worth, TX 76180   www.bombayco.com

Do you have to travel to Bombay to purchase something from the Bombay Company Outlet? No! But you will need a long memory if you want to remember the depth of their products. Beds, bedroom furniture, bedside tables, cabinets, coat racks and caddies, coffee tables, console tables, dining room tables, chairs, storage and display cabinets, end tables, hallway furniture, home entertainment centers, furniture, occasional tables, office chairs, office desks, office storage, plant stands, screens, small bedroom furniture, wall systems, mirrors, plaques, prints, sconces, shelves, baskets, blue and white porcelains, candles and home fragrances, ceramics, chandeliers, clocks, collectibles and keepsakes, crystal and glass, decorative accents, fireplace accessories, games, garden and florals (individual stems and some in pottery), jewelry boxes, lamp shades, desk accessories, pens, photo frames, rugs and pillows, silver serving collections—the list has already given me carpal tunnel symptoms. What I'm saying, in a nutshell, this Tandy-owned company is the place for gifts for you, your home and for others, lock, stock and barrel. It may appear to be bombastic of me to write any more; suffice to say, their outlet disposes of their overruns, discontinueds, returns, last season's flops, whatever at least 50 percent off. And since many are reproductions to begin with, they already look more expensive. So, this is really some kind of fun. They not only feature classic and traditional styles, but they coordinate with matching accessories and wall decor. Too, they not only look to represent reproductions, but they're now manufacturers themselves...and selling direct via their over 400 retail stores in malls across America. Other outlet locations in Texas include Allen Premium Outlets, Hillsboro Outlet Center and San Marcos Outlet Center. Shop online 24/7 if you get the urge after hours. ***Call toll-free: 800/829-7789*** 🇺🇸

★★★★★ Brad's Factory Direct   972/986-0365
1718 N. Belt Line Rd.   Mon-Sat 10-8; Sun Noon-6
Irving, TX 75061

With cowprints everywhere, Brad's no cad. He's just a good ole boy who's gone from bad to Brad since opening his cavernous 100,000 square foot showroom and manufacturing site. You can't hide behind his hides because they're just plain good deals. If you buy one of his cool leather, top-grain sofas, for example, you'll get the love seat FREE. See, this free spirit is a love. Choose from six different cool colors and pay a measly $888. Now, how bad can Brad be? Just south of Hwy. 183 on Belt Line, he "moo's" a lot of product in his factory-direct location. Just don't rope him in because he likes room to roam. And he needs it because they also build lodgepole beds and matching pieces for as low as $488. See them muscle their way into your house with iron futon groupings with six-inch mats for $138; or a pine, three-in-one futon lounge love seat and bed for $218. For a custom-built estate bed in all sizes, just say where and when! But man does not live 24-hours a day in bed. Man has to eat. And on what? That's where Brad delivers a five-piece country dinette set that's a puny $138. Talk about cheap eats. No more financing specials, though. You just fill out the finance application for Wells Fargo (formerly Norwest Financial) and the rest is between you and the credit bureau. The actual manufacturing and bedding site is next door at 1414 N. Belt Line Road, and if you're escaping the heat travel east, where you can visit their Tyler store at 3717 S. Broadway, 903/509-2150.

★★★★★ Brooks Weir Furniture Outlet   972/503-3503
4515 McEwen Rd.   Mon-Wed, Sat 10-6; Thu-Fri 10-8
Dallas, TX 75244

I love it when they run their sale, "Every third item is $1"! Then you'll save up to 75 percent off the old-fashioned way, three pieces at a time. That's right. Whether you're buying a center TV armoire for $798, a left-side unit for $349, a fabulous hand-carved premium hardwood, hand-rubbed cherry king sleigh bed for $998, or one of over 200 area rugs, it's all the way you buy it. Just imagine, though, two are discounted and the third costs $1. Open now six days a week, they continue to price their furniture with the ripple-down effect. In spite of the name, this is not a watered-down offshoot of the Weir's familiy of stores. This Weir does it his way and sells discounted furniture like **BASSETT**, **BERNHARDT**, **RIDGEWAY** and others that are good-looking and priced right without the Weir's mark-up. One block north of LBJ off Midway before you reach the Gabbert's Outlet Store. Oh dear, I just read where they had a two-drawer file cabinet for $29 (retail $198) but you had to buy the 60-inch cherry computer roll top desk for $798. (See, it pays to read the fine print.)

★★★★ **Cargo Factory Outlet**   **817/294-5717**
Hulen Shopping Center   Mon-Sat 10-8; Sun Noon-5
5000 S. Hulen Street, Suite 100   www.cargofurniture.com
Fort Worth, TX 76011

If your bill of lading says, F.O.B Fort Worth, it might be coming from the Cargo overstocks that have landed here. Cargo Furniture is a Fort Worth-based designer, retailer and wholesaler of casual lifestyle furniture, including children's furniture and accessories. Founded in 1981, it is owned by Tandycrafts and is well known in most circles for its children's furniture with a common-sense approach—casual, simple, safe and durable. Solid wood craftsmanship should spell kid-tested longevity. Its look is a combination of Shaker, Country French and Mission designs. Though its original lines were aimed at children, over the years they have broadened their reach to include master bedrooms, family rooms, dining, home entertainment and more. Still, their emphasis is on fun, flexible and expressive children's furniture and accessories, including bedding and framed art. Their unique 4-in-1 approach includes models for sleep, study, storage and safety. They expect kids to grow into their products, not out of. They're all full-sized and designed to mix and match and combine seamlessly with a broad selection of companion pieces. When you think of bunk beds, think Cargo. Their one outlet store is now in Fort Worth where they sell their display products, scratch and dent, discontinueds or closeouts. Expect to shave at least 20-30 percent off, and sometimes more. They operate a chain of 22 company owned stores but also sell through a nationwide network of dealers, contract sales and a toll-free ordering division.

Carolina Furniture Co.   **972/988-8560**
2920 N. Hwy. 360, Suite 100   Mon-Sat 10-8; Sun 11-6
Grand Prairie, TX 75050

Since they've move to the front and center of Hwy. 360, their name tells it all, and now in a bigger, better way. Their 40,000 square foot warehouse/showroom is like being in North Carolina, without jet lag. When they first came onto the scene, they sold only wholesale to the design trade. Then, they opened to the public, and it was like a floodgate, with bargain shoppers pouring in like a dam had busted. With 50 percent off retail, you can expect to save on all the popular names like **AMERICAN DREW**, **BROYHILL**, **HOOKER** and **STANLEY**. A Clearance Section is carved out with further reductions, if you can believe it. Period antique reproductions are another of their specialties, such as Queen Anne and 18th century four-poster rice beds, sleigh beds, china cabinets, dining room suites, bedroom ensembles, occasional tables—nothing could actually be finer than to shop at Carolina. Now for a good night's sleep, think like a queen on a **KING KOIL** mattress set. Queen sets were $248; king sets under $400. Not bad. Recliners for $399 move out of the warehouse as fast as they can uncrate them, so if you see one in your color or fabric, sit down on it and make it permanent. It's like Squatters Rights. If it's occupied, it's sold. Ninety-days same as cash is another incentive to start assembling a house full of furniture from Carolina by way of Grand Prairie.

★★★★★ **Casa Bonita Mexican Imports**   **214/651-8284**
905 Dragon St.   Mon-Fri 9-5; Sat 10-3
Dallas, TX 75207   www.casabonitamexicanimports.homestead.com

If you want to slay the Dragon and shop direct for Mexican imports, you've hit the bullseye! (Oh, how tragic.) No, this isn't some bloody sport, unless you call bargain shopping a sport. Well, I do and here is where to start for clay pottery, containers, chimeneas, home accessories, lots of gorgeous wrought iron chairs, railings, gates, table bases, stands, beds, candelabras—even custom work is available. Now, what about carving those deals in **CANTERA** stone? What about fountains, columns, balustrades, flooring, molding, table bases and custom work carved in stone? All at direct-import prices from south-of-the-border. Mi Casa, Su Casa, right? But make sure it's coming from Casa Bonita—Mucho Bonita. Surely you can find something wonderful to drag home from this 6,000 square foot designer showroom that decorators have been keeping a secret for way too long. Now, it's your discovery, too.

Changing Places
101 S. Coit Rd., #82
Richardson, TX 75080

214/570-0077
Mon-Sat 10-6; Thurs 10-8; Sun 12-5
www.changingplaces.net

Now expanded to 11,000-something square feet, talk about the "coil" boom. Who cares if gas goes to $3 a gallon? Not to worry...you'll make up the difference in the money you save here. The business of consigning castaways, even if they didn't win an Oscar, is busting at the seams. Now in their bigger, better showroom, Louis and Sue Ring have hit paydirt. Dirt-cheap prices, that is, on consignment furniture—from folks just starting out to those to whom money is no object. Approximately 85 percent of their offerings are consigned from overextended households—or from couples who have called it quits. The balance is new items. Sorry, they're only furniture brokers, not marriage brokers. So, is it "Your place or theirs?" Either way, you'll want to buy it all.

★★★★★ Circa Design Center
Inwood Trade Center
1311 Inwood Rd.
Dallas, TX 75247

214/630-5185
Mon-Sat 10-5; Sun Noon-5

Formerly Oak Lawn Antiques & Consignments, they are now Circa Design Center, and what a glorious transformation. Next to Crate & Barrel, expect to ogle designer names seen only at the finest retail stores and pay 75 percent less. Everything's drop dead gorgeous, circa 2001. Consigned antiques, lighting, furniture (both new and consigned) and accessories make any house a home worth writing home about. Owner Carl Lowery has really done it up right, from contemporary furnishings to some of the most sought-after traditional and contemporary designs. See **CENTURY**, **DREXEL HERITAGE**, **GRATALE**, **HICKORY**, **HENREDON**, **MULHOLLAND BROTHERS**, **PALACEK**, **PERCZEK** and others, at sizeable savings. My entryway looks like "The Mansion" with a floral arrangement in acrylic water sitting proudly on a pedestal. Sure fooled my neighbors. I paid $99—it looks like $500. They also house a second location of Peacock Alley's Linen Outlet. Don't miss their original Dallas location, either, at 2914 Oak Lawn at Cedar Springs.

★★★★ Consignment Collection
12300 Inwood Rd., Suite 116A
Dallas, TX 75244

972/788-4444
Mon-Sat 10-6

Whether you need to get a toll tag (on one side) or a taco (Mexican restaurant on the other), there's always room for more. Look for the large 4,000-square-foot beige stucco building with the blue awning that sells furniture and accessories on consignment. More than 5,000 items are on the floor with 200-300 new ones set out every day. Now the best part...the average price of a sofa was $295. For an eclectic mix of furniture, antiques, gifts, accessories and more, with lots of fun in store, this is like scrounging around your grandma's attic! Whether you're buying or selling (they split it with you 55-45 percent), you'll wind up a winner. This showroom houses furniture and antiques wall-to-wall, but some of them needed collagen injections. What you see is what you get—sofas, chairs, dishes, dolls, tables, lots of home accessories and bric-a-brac, all priced accordingly.

★★★★ Consignment Galleries
5627 W. Lovers Lane
Dallas, TX 75209

214/357-3925
Mon-Sat 10-5:30

Hang on to this one. A wrought-iron chandelier with eight candlestick bulbs and approximately 24 inches in diameter was $125 and perfect for the rustic dining room or the casual dinette. Located between Inwood and the Tollway on the north side of the street, how's saving 75 percent from some Highland Park estate castoff? No names are included, but the quality of the furnishings speaks for themselves. From traditional to antiques and the accessories to fill in the blank spaces (area rugs, china, sterling, wicker, lamps, crystal, mirrors, paintings, objects d'art, copper and bronze figures, and all kinds of collectibles), why not outfit your home from the million dollar mansions you drive by at Christmas time? Gee whiz, oh what a relief it is not to pay full price. Once it arrives on your doorstep, who would ever guess it's origin began somewhere else? Consigned pieces split 55/45 with you coming out on top. This isn't like your typical consignment furniture store, though, as prices are much higher to begin with since they've come from such"exclusive" homes.

★★ Consignment Solution, The
1904 Skillman
Dallas, TX 75206

214/827-8022
Tue-Fri 11-7; Sat 10-6; Sun 10-5

I hate answering machines. I hate voice mail systems. I hate phones in general, especially when I get a recording. Well, the solution is perhaps to get rid of them all, because this store's recording is always on. I guess it means, get in your car and head to Skillman Ave. (an exit off LBJ), and choose from a pot-pourri of home furnishings...from vintage to traditional, ordinary dinette sets to vintage 50s, and a mixture of everything in between. You won't be sorry. Their pick-up day is Monday but make sure you get their approval first. Rejection at your front door is hard to take.

★★ Consignment Store, The
5290 Belt Line Rd., Suite 122
Dallas, TX 75240

972/991-6268
Mon-Sat 10-6; Sun Noon-5

Don't even think of bringing anything in on consignment without Maryann O'Neil's blessings. Make an appointment as she's not only very busy, but very particular. Why buy new when you can save up to 50 percent on someone else's home furnishings? Nothing far out—like bunk beds, canopy beds or futons. This store is serious traditional. Once your household furniture is accepted, there's a 60-day contract with a 50/50 split issued. That mean's if it's not sold in that time, either it's donated or you get it back. Pick-up and delivery's extra, $45, and can be scheduled around your schedule. Samples from the Trade Mart are also co-mingled within the gently worn items, but who can tell the difference? All artfully arranged whereby you wander through the maze of used furniture, mirrors, Oriental rugs, pictures and frames, flower arrangements, birdcages, quilts, potpourri and more. A wonderful aroma greets you at the front door along with the vast expanse of possibilities. It's like being in a candy store. Which is your favorite color? Shape? Size? I still love chocolate and that chocolate leather sofa was perfect for my low-calorie diet. But still way too pricey in my book.

*

Cort Furniture Clearance Center
250 W. Airport Frwy.
Irving, TX 75062

972/445-2678
Mon-Fri 9-6; Sat 10-5
www.cortfurniture.com

After one visit for residential or office furniture, you'll want to Cort them for a permanent live-in relationship. As America's only national furniture rental company, imagine the savings on brand name furniture for your home or office that lies in wait at their three clearance center outlets in the Metroplex. Any style or budget can be satisfied. What home or business does not consider the bottom line? If that's your concern, you'll be impressed with the substantial savings on previously-rented furniture. For business purposes, renting furniture makes sense. It's flexible, you save on capital, and there are, of course, tax benefits. Imagine, though, saving 30-70 percent on what has been returned. For more than 20 years, they've been courting the home and office customers. Now, you can participate in the collective bargaining that's available here. And don't overlook their online catalog which features color pictures and specs for office furniture. At least, you can shop from home—even for the office. Besides, there are discount coupons online to print out and use. But it's the clearance centers that really get my fiscal side on red alert. Support the other Cort Clearance Centers at 14215 Inwood Rd., Dallas, TX, 75244, 972/386-2981 and 2208 N. Collins, Arlington, TX, 76011, 817/274-2717.

★★ Custom Oak Furniture Mfg.
10660 Plano Rd.
Dallas, TX 75238

214/340-6656
Mon-Sat 10-6

Here's the closest thing to the unfinished symphony for the do-it-yourselfer. If you've got an inkling to whittle away a few hours during the weekend, here's the place to exercise the all stain/all gain theory. Whether it's a bookshelf or an armoire, you have your choice—finished or not. If you take it upon yourself to add your elbow grease, you'll save about 30 percent. During specials, the prices are shaved even more. Since this is a factory, you could have them carve out a final creation that is priced direct-from-maker. It's an option to consider with plenty to choose from: in-stock bookcases, tables, chairs, wall units and more, some already with the Midas touch; others are left in the nude. Pick your finish, your color, your stain and call it a day. Then wait a few weeks for the end product to be delivered. Original and imaginative projects are a challenge and, as a matter of fact, encouraged. They prefer to start from scratch and will save you some scratch, natch! A hope chest could be made from beginning to end in four weeks, instead of the usual six or seven. Well, it was tempting. Only problem, my dog Hope wouldn't have fit. No website yet, but they're working on it.

★★★★★ De La Garza Furniture Services
2901 National Drive
Garland, TX 75041

972/864-1933
Mon-Fri 9:30-5

These true artists speak to the spirit of ingenuity. Custom furniture is this family's claim to fame. Since 1960, they've been providing FREE on-site estimates (don't even try asking for a quote by phone, the answer is NO, NO, a thousand times NO!) Located just off Kingsley, between Jupiter and Shiloh, De La Garza will transform a piece of furniture from the ground up. Stay put—they pick up and deliver for FREE, and will be happy to bring a large selection of fabrics to your home or office for your pick of the lot. Re-dress your favorite chair or sofa. After all, even yours is entitled to a change of wardrobe. Now, what about a face-lift for furniture that's made of wood? Refinishing is another specialty at this house of De La Garza. This lost art along with carpeting is on their menu of services with a turnaround time of about two or three weeks for both upholstery and refinishing. Speed does not supercede quality. These folks are artists with a brush, with a level, with a staple gun. They really do work their fingers to the bone.

And listen to this. They don't accept payment until the job is done. If you're in the neighborhood, stop by the shop as they often have completed projects (that were never picked up) for sale and Jessie prices them to move fast. The Black Forest Cuckoo Clocks can also be special ordered, all sizes and models, at very good prices along with carpet at $1 above cost. These guys aren't kidding. They mean business.

★★★★★ Decorator's Reserve   972/620-8999

13970 Stemmons Frwy.   Mon-Thu 10-7; Fri, Sat 10-8; Sun Noon-6
Farmers Branch, TX 75234

Bargains for millionaires couldn't cut it in the Big Apple, but they're still reserving the bargains for their two stores—Orlando and Dallas. (In Orlando, though, they're called Liquidation Station.) They changed the name so as to not offend the Dallas shopper when they pulled up in their circular drives with a truck named Liquidation Outlet. Unbeknownst to them, being a bargain shopper is the badge of honor in this city. You're not cheap...you're smart. And nobody's ashamed of being called smart that I know of. Anyway, this is a very interesting haven for the oddball decorator item. Expect the unusual, the eclectic, the economical—though some items will give you sticker shock. It's definitely a fun foray into some of the latest and greatest. From life-size replicas to carved wood and painted statues, bronze mermaids to lions and tigers and bears, oh my. For about five grand, get a statue to thy arboretum. Etch their wrought iron and bronze items into your memory, table the issue of display shelves, plant stands, columns, candelabras or decorative art objects. Walk the baby in a rattan and iron baby carriage or center your entire decorating scheme around the Far Eastern reproductions or English Tudor manor house replicas. The walls are alive with mirrors, sconces, art (unsigned "original" oils sell for less than $200), Tiffany-like lamps starting at $29, and an art-deco mirror was $225. The lawn ornaments and the gigantic urns are beckoning you from the freeway. How can you resist? The novelty items and conversation pieces are worth spreading the word.

★★ Dinette Center   972/235-7626

2250 Promenade Center   Mon, Thu 10-8; Tue-Wed, Fri-Sat 10-6; Sun 1-5
Richardson, TX 75080

Casual dining is intended to be less expensive than a dinner at The Mansion or 111 Forks. So expect this place to lay it on, slick. Dinettes started as low as $299, barstools were as low as $49, so what can I say? If you want to save 30-45 percent on dinette sets, game and party sets, barstools and such, belly up to the Dinette Center and say, "Grace"—there are more than 200 sets to choose from. Ratt-on casual rattan for a popular sunroom, family room, or porch all the way to more formal polished oak sets from **ASHLEY** to popular patio/dinette combinations from **CHROMCRAFT**, **ELITE**, **JOHNSON CASUAL**, **PASTEL**, **PACIFIC**, **RATTAN SPECIALTIES** to name a few. Don't expect to serve filet mignon on some tacky card table. Consider one that retails as much as $7,000 to do justice to prime beef. The best buys, though, are to be had in their clearance department. And for competitive purposes, they guarantee to meet or beat any price. Delivery charges average around $25, but can escalate depending on distance traveled.

★★ Elegant Casual   972/669-9098

1621 N. Central Expwy.   Mon-Sat 10-7; Sun Noon-6
Richardson, TX 75080

If you can't find it here, it's not been made. Between Arapaho and Campbell, this 25,000-square-foot superstore is just what Texas is all about. Big. Bold. Beautiful. All the elements for success in outdoor living: teak, wicker, rattan, wrought iron, cast aluminum, steel...what else is there? The selection is celestial but the savings are more down-to-earth in the 10-30 percent range (70 percent during sales). Bragging rights are held for brands such as **HOMECREST**, **LANE/VENTURE**, **MALIN**, **RATTAN SPECIALTIES**,

WINSTON and **WOODWARD**. Not a bad beginning for the sunny season. Hammocks and birdbaths set the scene for casting abandon to the wind. Then, when the temperature drops, they hit the fireplace and dinette scene and fans come running like a blaze of fire. *Call toll-free: 888/240-6936*

★★★★ Eurway
4720 Alpha Rd.
Dallas, TX 75244

972/386-0389
Mon-Fri 10-7; Thu 10-9; Sat 10-6; Sun Noon-5
www.eurway.com

Since 1980, Eurway has been offering contemporary designs at direct-import prices. Not discount, mind you. Just affordable. All circa modern furniture, office furniture, lighting and accessories from all over the world. Really cool and inexpensive, these items function in a number of ways, from curl up and relax, to get down to business and work. Everything really coordinates with everything else but it's still the storage components that continue to garner rave reviews. If it's sophisticated yet simple, functional yet fun, this 35,000-square-foot showplace represents almost 100 different manufacturers—that you can have Eurway.

★★ Expressions
2900 South Hulen, #10
Fort Worth, TX 76109

817/921-4100
Mon-Sat 9:30-6; Sun 1-5
www.expressionsfurniture.com

What was once one of the hottest custom furniture concepts since sliced bread has now limited their expression in Texas to one lone store in Fort Worth. The Dallas location has closed, so it's either there or nowhere. As we say in this part of the woods, if it ain't Baroque, don't fix it. But if you want to express yourself, this franchised store has enough fabrics so you'll never see the same one twice. With over 1,000 fabrics and 150 different sofa and chair frame styles, which one is YOU? The only designer name they revere is yours...so dig into your lifestyle questionnaire and discover your own personal signature line. Since 1978, their collection is the perfect solution for families with kids and pets. Their high-traffic fabrics can take the wear and tear of rough riders. Just add stain-resistance and round edged frames and you've probably saved many of those potential bumps and bruises of modern day life. Expect a finished product in about 45 days. A lifetime warranty is offered on springs and frame, so rest assured, you can sit for a long, long time. Compared to others of the same ilk (Norwalk and Fabric and Frames,) they win in the price department.

Finfer's Furniture Outlet
4145 S. I-35 E, #104
Denton, TX 76210

940/484-1818
Mon-Sat 10-7; Sun Noon-6
www.finfers.com

Nothing could be finer than to be in finer furniture at Finfer's, that's for sure. Settled comfortably into their new, self-standing building on I-35, you will not go wrong with anything you pick from their 9,000 square feet of fine furniture. Join the F-troop (FFF-Finfer Fine Furniture) and go to the head of the class. An "F" here means you've got the best grades in the class. Only top grade furniture at bottom of the barrel prices. If you thought twice about buying name brand furniture because you couldn't afford it, these guys make you eat your words. Perish the thought! This is where dreams are built. Why do you think I call them the "dream team"? As the one and only outlet for **AMERICAN LEATHER**, you can sit on easy seat. One of the finest leather furniture manufacturers in the country, nothing but the finest hides from Europe are used (called **ELMO BOUTIQUE** hides). Each piece is eight-way hand-tied (a lost art but a detail that should not be overlooked), down cushions (yes, once you've sunk down on down, you'll never want to get up), fully aniline hides (which means the color is soaked throughout so there's no bleed-through) and how much? How does up to 65 percent off sound? What does it cost? Well, up to 65 percent off. Add in a lifetime warranty on the frames with more than 700 color options and this spells S.O.L.D. Now don't overlook all the other furniture practically from A (**ALEXANDER JULIAN**) to U (**UNIVERSAL**) and **POSTUREPEDIC** mattresses in between. At last, sleep tight, too. If you're looking for a custom sofa or chair, pick from over 250 fabrics and go from plaid to mad about denim, velveteen, suede, cotton— you name it, they've got the books. And in my book, when you can save up to 70 percent, I say, Cheers! Mazel-tov on your new store, Scott (Finfer).

Freedom Furniture Design Studio
13810 Welch Rd.
Dallas, TX 75244

972/385-7368
Mon-Sat 10-7
www.freedomfurniture.com (under construction)

Flea from the strangle-hold that retailers have on name brand furniture prices. Here, they're rewriting the book and the best just got better. Escape from following the crowd. Declare your independence and reroute your thinking to Freedom Furniture. This 25,000 square foot expanse of showroom is the perfect place to reaffirm your loyalty to the spirit from which this country was founded. Oh dearly beloved, let me count the ways. Competition is good for the soul and Freedom Furniture solely represents some of the best brands in America: **BERNHARDT, BROYHILL, LANE/VENTURE, PULASKI** in many different finishes and fabrics. It's also a full-service interior design firm with additional case goods proudly displayed. (Case goods, by the way, are wood furnishings like tables, wall units, armoires, china cabinets, etc.) Bet your bottom dollar that Diana and Danny Beck and their team of full-service interior designers will set the record straight and contribute to the revolution currently being waged in furniture retailing in the 21st century. Just north of LBJ between Midway and Inwood. *Call toll-free: 800/256-HOME*

Furniture Buy Consignment
1340 W. Main St.
Lewisville, TX 75067

972/436-4389
Tue-Sat 11-6

If you've got a piece or a household full of furniture to sell, your best bet is to take a photo and bring it in for review. Don't drag in your has-beens or dregs. You will be rejected no matter who you are. Though this consignment store is for cheapskates, it passes for the finest decorator boutique in town. They cater to the hoi polloi at prices 50 to 75 percent off; buy it when you see it, otherwise you'll end up empty-handed. I got lucky first time in when I bought a $12,000 custom smoky-glass dining room table and eight leather chairs for $1,200. That's 10 percent of the retail value and who would have ever suspected how low I go? See for yourself what $100 can buy in accessories like crystal, iron sculptures, floral arrangements and pictures. Would you like to see entire dining room suites for under $500? Leather chairs and ottomans for $299? Floor lamps for $49? It's almost sinful how far your dollar will go. Owner Jeannie Verastique is the epitome of the designing wife, mother and entrepreneur. The whole place reeks of fun and frugality. Same with their second Lewisville location at 201 S. Mill St., 972/221-3878. Consignors get a 60/40 split; after 30 days, you can either pick it up if it hasn't sold or go another 30 days but the split changes to 50/50. Pickup and delivery are offered for a nominal fee, though they prefer you pick up and deliver the items yourself to keep costs down. You do your part, they'll do theirs. This year their Main Street location has doubled in size. Business is booming, deservedly so.

★★★ Furniture Source   **972/243-8311**
11545 Reeder Rd.   Mon-Fri 10-7; Sat 9-6; Sun Noon-5
Dallas, TX 75229   **www.furn.net**

Sorry, my nerves (sciatica, that is) can't make it to the second floor of this 20,000 square foot showroom. Plus, you've got to jump around and turn around to get there to begin with. Facing Stemmons, exit Royal, go east under the overpass and there you are. It's much faster to eat on the run at the McDonald's or the Wendy's if shopping during the noon hour is your bag. However, if you're a die-hard, and you find saving up to 50 percent an appealing enticement, you'll find moderate to better furniture for the entire house, plus carpet and everything in between. Dinette sets, bedroom suites, occasional tables, recliners, and accessories are represented in brands such as **AMERICAN DREW**, **ASHLEY**, **BROYHILL**, **BENCHCRAFT**, **BERKLINE**, **FLEXSTEEL**, **KIMBALL**, **LANE**, **LEXINGTON**, **MAYO**, **PULASKI**, **SEALY**, **VAUGHN BASSETT** and more.

★ Futon Factory Outlet   **817/379-6921**
2225 N. Pearson Lane   Mon, Fri 11-7; Thu 11-8; Sat 11-6; Sun Noon-6
Keller, TX 76262

Make sure you don't get the urge to shop for a futon on Tuesdays or Wednesdays. They take those two days off for some peace and quiet. Then, the other days, it's full steam ahead. This manufacturer can sell you futons at wholesale prices (anywhere from 20 to 90 percent off) because they're the maker. Voted best futon store by the *Dallas Observer*, we found them first. Just finding them is a chore, but once you do, you'll be sleeping on firmer foundations with a natural airflow. If you sit, sleep or chill out on a futon, you'll be cooler in the summer and warmer in the winter. More than 50 are in stock at all times and custom orders are available at no additional charge. Choose from over 600 fabrics for either beds, couches, lofts/bunkbeds—from as low as $99 complete all the way to a twin-over-full loft for over $500. Lifetime warranties issued from head to toe so no part of your body goes unattended. This family-owned business also manufactures custom furniture, offers refinishing, frame repairs, entertainment centers, platform beds, bunkbeds, custom wall units, tables, lamps and more. It's kind of like a Phoenix rising out of the dessert in Keller. Call for directions. It's a lot bigger than you'd imagine. Between Keller and Southlake, fee, fie, fo, futon, my how creative they have become.

★★★★★ Gabberts Furniture Outlet   **972/385-9666**
4612 McEwen Rd.   Thu Noon-9; Fri 10-9; Sat 10-6; Sun Noon-5
Dallas, TX 75244

Two blocks east of their retail showroom, it's no wonder they were named the numero uno furniture retailer in the country by *House Beautiful*. Even with Robb & Stuckey entering the marketplace, Gabbert's has held its own. Imagine what decorator wannabees think about their outlet! Though only open four days a week, they pack a lot of punch and p-jazz into a shortened shopping week. But what you lose in days, you make up tenfold in other ways. Shop for chairs, sofas, loveseats, recliners, bedroom suites, dining room suites, bedding, area rugs, Oriental rugs, mirrors, lamps, pictures and objects d'art in this warehouse environ, all priced at 40-80 percent off retail. Whether it's a showroom closeout, a manufacturer's sample, a model home display, discontinued or returned from their main line store at LBJ and Midway, don't you bat an eyelash. You'll save plenty of cash. Who cares from whence it came? They all look, feel, sit, show the same in the...end! Enjoy popcorn in the snack bar and the casual sales consultants who provide bend-over-backwards service. Since they spent over $4 million renovating their main store, expect the outlet to be equally appealing. Though they sell about 1,000 items a day, their leftovers are what bargain shoppers wait for at the outlet. Delivery is available seven days a week. And now in the Fort Worth Gabbert's store, 6301 Oakmont Blvd., one mile south of Hulen Mall, 817/346-5600, don't miss out on their Odds & Ends room. That's how the Dallas stand-alone outlet began, so watch out, they may be on to something.

★★★★★ Globetrotter

1601 Dragon St.
Dallas, TX 75207

214/744-4732
Mon-Sat 10-6

Be a world-class globetrotting shopper without leaving the Metroplex. Just land here at Globetrotter. Located at the Design District, shop where the decorators shop and pay less. Better brands. Bigger selection (17,000 square feet) and bargains every step of the way. Get on a first name basis with **AMERICAN DREW, BROYHILL, HOOKER, PARKER SOUTHERN, PULASKI, MILLENNIUM, RIVERSIDE, ROWE, SAM MOORE, VAUGHAN BASSETT** and more. Choose from hundreds of sofas, chairs, lamps, dining sets and area rugs, mirrors and framed prints. Not to worry, they offer a lifetime guarantee on all their eight-way hand-tied sofas and chairs with more than 200 different frames and hundreds of fabrics and leather (at no additional cost).

★★★★★ Goodfellow Furniture

17194 Preston Rd.
Dallas, TX 75248

972/248-3062
Mon-Sat 9:30-6

Just a plain old everyday mom and pop furniture shop for less than retail is how they describe themselves. Not particularly exciting, but then again, maybe it's hard to toot your own horn. These are all goodfellas who will make you a deal you can't refuse. A rocking chair by **JEFFCO** was priced over $1,000 but had a cane finish and silk creme and black seat. There are some things in life that just should be negotiated. The store's a dream house to navigate, and the pool of manufacturers would win the American Cup race to the finish: **BERNHARDT, HARDEN, HEKMAN, HENKEL-HARRIS, HICKORY CHAIR, JEFFCO, LA BARGE, MAITLAND-SMITH, NATIONAL MOUNT AIRY, SHERRILL, TOMLINSON, WOODMARK** and others flank the promenade deck, ready to take the world by storm. Who would have imagined that they discount, across the board, 30-50 percent and throw in decorator design service. Now you know the truth about "The Importance of Being Furnished!"

★★ H & K Furniture

303 E. Camp Wisdom Rd.
Duncanville, TX 75116

972/709-8989
Mon-Sat 10-8; Sun Noon-6

Handsome and kid-proof, H & K was right on the money when it came time to buy that little girl's canopy bed for just $88 (plus $49 for the canopy rails). Then, for the finishing touches, add the matching dresser, mirror and nightstand for another $229. What a dream come true, rather than a "Knight in Shining Armoires". Any age group, any financial bracket can get hooked on this family's retail stores. For more than 13 years, their 43,000 square foot store in Duncanville has been home to furnishing every room in the house. Expect Wisdom to rule on brands like **ASHLEY, MILLENNIUM, SEALY** and **UNIVERSAL**. Rocking chairs for $49 and plant stands as low as $19 sealed their fate. Then we eyed a cafe table with two bars stools by Ashley for $149 and decided to toast our good fortune. Low prices, six months FREE layaway with 10 percent down, and now you can see why we're hooked on their looks. Furnish the living room, dining room, bedroom, even baby's room—all's fair in love and shopping. Fair game at fair prices. Shop another location at 11055-B Harry Hines Blvd. in Dallas, 972/484-8986.

Habitat
13615 Inwood Rd.
Dallas, TX 75244

972/701-9800
Mon-Thu 10-7; Fri-Sat 10-6; Sun 1-5

Enter laughing. The door itself is an entry to the artistry inside. Take a group of talented artisans, put their works on display at the corner of Alpha and Inwood, and what do you get? An interesting mix of contemporary and unique furniture and decorative items that are not of the same old four legs and two arms mentality. Don't expect their creativity to come cheap. Designers will work with you while you shop in the store, or come to your house for an in-house assessment. Top-of-the-hide leather furniture at the lowest leather-grade price can cut some of the fat. Though there are 20 styles and over 70 leather colors to choose from, life in the fast lane doesn't come cheap, just chic. Expect upholstery pieces to take six-eight weeks to deliver with some taking up to 12 weeks, depending on the level of funk. Choose works of artware in iron, marble, murals, wall hangings, gifts, headboards, media centers, floor surfaces and more. A favorite still remains the stained concrete that looks like leather—for walls or floors. Just don't take their service for granite.

★ Home Concepts
2900 Main St.
Dallas, TX 75226

214/761-1872
Tue-Sat 11-7; Sun 1-6
www.homeconcepts.com

A little birdie told me cheap, cheap, cheap...but not to expect some fly-by-night operation. Perched in the heart of Deep Ellum, you can't miss them. They're the ones in the grey building with a big red sign. The common denominator is that everything's retro and contemporary in style. Over 30 different fun and funky CD holders from towers to wall racks. Minimalist furniture and accessories are their modus operandi, with full-size eight-foot futons with black or white metal frames priced at $159 (same as last year). There are hundreds and hundreds of futon covers ranging from $39-$99 (most were $99), but choices included velvet, textures, prints and even throw pillows starting at $9. Now, where else are throw pillows so cheap? Several retro and modern dinettes for $299 were perfect for that little house uptown. Lamps, TV stands, foam chairs and even shower curtains were seen hanging around. Loiterers are welcome. Lots of barstools, étagères, wall units, adjustable shelving, divider screens, multimedia storage units, corner desks, steel rockers, desks, tables and chairs, head boards—you can furnish that loft from top to bottom and fill in with everything in between.

★★★★★ Home on the Range
110 E. Louisiana St.
McKinney, TX 75069

972/562-9877
Mon-Sat 10-5

If you're back in the saddle again and ready to take a ride to McKinney, don't forget to return to Home on the Range. Oh, give me a home where they specialize in hand-crafted rustic, western and Southwestern furniture at prices that won't create a stampede. If you love the look of pencil post beds and leather seating, consider the look here. How else do you think the West was won? The range is massive. Whether it's fabric or skins, tables and chairs, cabinets and armoires, rugs and pottery, you can incorporate the look without the mark of Zorro.

★★★★★ Iguana
Grapevine Mills Mall
Grapevine, TX 76051

972/691-0403
Mon-Sat 10-9:30; Sun 11-8
www.iguana-mexico.com

From the "Night of the Iguana", there still may be a few remaining remnants of furniture and accessories reminiscent of the steamy side of the border. But to make the grade, rustic furniture must be priced right. Enter this Iguana. Nothing slimy, either. Iguana Ameramex is one of the largest direct importers of Mexican furniture, pottery, glassware, ceramics, folk art and wrought iron. Now, Grapevine Mills' shoppers have a place to shop on the wild side. Scouring the back roads of Mexico, finding the little-known cottage industries of artisans and craftsmen and then buying everything direct is how this company eliminates the middleman to keep prices under wraps. In their massive warehouse showrooms, you will find items the casual visitor to Mexico would never encounter. From the versatile Mexican Colonial furniture of Puebla to the one-of-a-kind Michoacan carvings, Iguana offers the largest collection of hand-made home decor anywhere north of the border—at the lowest prices in town. Most of the home items resemble those produced during the Spanish colonial era—and some even are produced the same way they were 200 years ago. Everything Iguana sells is made by hand. Hardware is hand-forged, glassware is hand-blown, pottery is pressed into molds by hand and hand-decorated before firing in wood kilns. The wood furniture is primarily made of pine and all carvings are laboriously hand-done. Often, you'll see old mesquite and pine doors salvaged from haciendas. Then, if the door's no longer suitable for use as a door...guess what? They're transformed into a specialty table with framework and legs made from hand-hewn timbers, wrought iron or oxen yokes. An occasional armoire or bookcase was seen crafted from a door, another from a shutter. One rustic-looking pine armoire was $399 and folks were lined up placing orders. That's what makes this a place of least resistance...you want it all!

★★ Infinity Leather

972/866-6700

4901 Alpha Rd.
Dallas, TX 75244

Mon-Thu 10-8; Fri-Sat 10-6; Sun Noon-6
www.infinityleather.com

If you have an affinity for leather, this may be the your manna from heaven. It was also time for them to make a move to bigger, better quarters. In fact, they're now residing in 18,750 square feet at the corner of Alpha and the Dallas Tollway. Business is booming. Even with the threat of "Mad Cow Disease" when leather may be in short supply, it's still the choice covering for many a homeowner. Hide and go seek skins in 35 different styles, 17 kinds of leather and more than 100 different colors. Another location is in Plano at the NW corner of the Tollway and Parker, 972/781-2800; in North Richland Hills at 7927 Grapevine Hwy, 817/427-5850; and in Arlington, 629 W. Pioneer, 817/299-9141.

★★★★★ Inside Out/Clearance Outlet

972/931-0626

17390 Preston Rd., #120
Dallas, TX 75252

Mon-Fri 10-8; Sat & Sun 10-6
www.insideandout.net

Next To Texas Land & Cattle Restaurant, rustle up some grub and then steak out next door to Inside Out and their Clearance store. After 26 years in the Metroplex, there is no excuse for a barren patio or fireplace with these folks. Printable coupons available on their website with deals changing monthly. Patio brands to consider include **BROWN JORDAN, HOMECREST, JENSON JARRAH, KINGSLEY BATE, MALLIN, O.W. LEE, SAMSONITE, WINSTON** and **WOODWARD**. Choose from lots of different styles, including aluminum, wicker, wood, accessories and umbrellas. Then, when the temperature drops, it's time to snuggle by the fireplace with brands such as **BECKWOOD, GOLDEN BLOUNT, HARGROVE, HEATALOR, MAJESTIC, PETERSON, PILGRIM, RASSMUSSEN, SUMMER CLASSICS** and **UNIFLAME**. Keep the home fires burning on both fronts. Next door is their outlet. Two lights north of Campbell, this furniture dampens the slings and arrows of everyday living. Though the store passes the savings of their volume buys on to the customer, it's their clearance outlet that is where the "have-to-buys" are. *Call toll-free: 800/329-0626*

NV Iron Works
13465-B Inwood Rd.
Dallas, TX 75244

Mooving out, Leather Leather; mooving in, Iron Works. Finally, they're making their move back to Dallas where they belong. Noting that their location at the Festival Marketplace was not meeting their expectations, their movie-star sales person (Don Johnson) is the one to talk to when they finally get settled into their new digs. Not related to any Miami vices, their furniture is way cool and way cheap. Iron works is the operative word here, but it's up to you to track them down. We've given you at least some of the perameters, but we were going to press when the move was on!

Isabella Designs
Lakeside Market
4017 Preston Rd.
Plano, TX 75093-7362

972/781-0500
Mon-Sat 10-6; Sun 12-5
www.isabelladesigns.com

Don't let the name, upscale store front or the high-end merchandise fool you into thinking this is a shop you could only dream of being able to shop. Ooh, la la! These former wholesalers may have gotten out of that game and into the retail marketplace, but they haven't left the good pricing behind. They import a lot of their stock themselves from around the world, pricing it not only below expectations, but also below the competition as well. They've filled their 5,000-square-foot store with imaginative and unique gift items, furniture, home accessories, crystal chandeliers, lamps, some clothing, handbags, fine art glass and porcelain, hand-carved home accessories, garden items, jewelry, silverware, custom drapes and more, including, of course, interior design services. They've left one world and entered another without missing a beat. They're the epitome of a "To Die For" store. Congratulations!

J. Douglas
3301 Oak Lawn Ave.
Dallas, TX 75219

214/522-8100
Mon-Sat 10-6; Sun 12-5

What is this world coming to? J. Douglas does not discriminate between the public and "the trade". Everybody gets in on the act and receives 40 percent off. If I'm lying, I'm dying. It's time to call in all the markers and shop where there's the absolute best selection of furniture, art, accessories and lamps available, without having to have a designer in your back pocket. Anything goes. Everything's gorgeous. Then, when you're tired of saying, Ooh-lookie here, or Ahh-lookie there, grab a delicious bite next door at Parigi's or across the street at Nuevo Leon. Oak Lawn has never been this cool. This is a "to die for" store with discount prices. Don't expect to see the traditional fare; most items appear to be one-of-a-kind and guaranteed to thrill.

★★★★ Kirkland's
Grapevine Mills Mall
3000 Grapevine Mills Pkwy.
Grapevine, TX 76051

972/724-1426
Mon-Sat 10-9:30; Sun 11-8
www.kirklands.com

Kirkland's has been in business for more than 30 years, bringing the best in home accessories to you and me, babe. With more than 220 stores in 27 states, having an outlet at Grapevine Mills is a definite coup for area shoppers. Shop online, then run and see if this store has it on sale, or when it might be coming in. Expect to save up to 75 percent off art, frames, decorations and seasonal items for inside and out. Tabletop water fountains from $19.95; pot perchers, three for $9.95; copper garden sprinklers, $79.95 retail, $49.95 here; chiminaria with candle, $9.95. Actually, there were tons of candle gardens and centerpieces for the same price. Then, add in the stained glass and hummingbird rain gauge for a drop in the bucket, $5.95, and you can see why everyday we feel like we've hit the lottery. As we've said before, one of their strongest lures is table lamps —expressive monkey figures, textured art deco, elegant metals. From front door mats to floating candles, wall sconces, vases and more, take advantage of their additional savings at this unique outlet. Design professionals can receive an additional 10 percent off. ***Call toll-free:*** ***877/208-6668***

PS Kreiss Collection

214/698-9118
1628 Oak Lawn
Dallas, TX 75207

Mon-Fri 9-5; Sat 10-4
www.kreiss.com

Take a seat. Any seat. And experience the Kreiss Collection of fine furniture, accessories and luxury bed linens. Shop their special sales in the Design District (preview their collections online to get a wishful hit list). Their linens alone will put you in a heavenly sleep, crafted from pure Egyptian cotton in 320, 500, 540, and 600 thread counts. There are 100 different designs to choose from. When you finish, your ensemble will be a magnificent one-of-a-kind boudoir beauty. The look of Kreiss furniture is a unique blending of classic styling and contemporary comfort that is both elegant and, well, the envy of my greedy little eyes. From custom sizes to fabrics and dozens of finishing choices, Kreiss is really living like the hoi polloi for those who are only on the second rung of the ladder of success. Showroom on the left off Stemmons and Oak Lawn.

★★★★★ Leather Center

972/458-0885
13460 Inwood
Farmers Branch, TX 75244

Mon-Thu 10-8; Fri-Sat 10-6; Sun Noon-6
www.leathercenter.com

Moo-o-o-ve over, cowtowners. The pioneer who made owning a piece of leather furniture in families with children is none other than The Leather Center, a legend in its own town. From their humble beginnings in 1982, they now boast 11 Metroplex locations and over 100 around the country. Today, they do about $100 million in sales and, in spite of the economy, there's no lack of takers. For more than 18 years they have produced custom-made leather: chairs, recliners, ottomans, sofas, love seats, theater seats, sectionals and chaise lounges, but it's their recliners at The Ballpark in Arlington that are the coup d'etat. Well, there's always the **MARILYN MONROE** line. M-m-m-m! Check directory for multiple locations.

★★★★★ Legacy Furniture

972/272-8427
626 Easy St.
Garland, TX 75042

Mon-Fri 9-5

Anybody looking to relocate to easy street may want to create a legacy. And the only Legacy on Easy Street that is known in this neck of the woods is Legacy Furniture. Get a rock-solid piece of furniture from some of the finest craftsmen around. At first, they were only selling wholesale to the trade; today, they sell to the public at wholesale prices. Woe is me. Life with so many possibilities can give a girl a headache. But now, you can pick and choose to your heart's content. Furniture, draperies, bedcovers, wall upholstery and slipcovers, too. Want to copy a sofa you saw in *Architectural Digest*? They can do—just ask Sue.

Lone Star Trading Co.
6443 W. Main St.
Frisco, TX 75034

972/712-1669
Tue-Fri 10-6; Sat 10-5; Sun Noon-5
www.lonestartradingco.com

Feeling like you want to get away from it all? Need to take a trip South or North (depending on your starting point)? How about to Lewisville? You won't even need your birth certificate to shop down Mexico way. They don't even accept the other green card (American Express.) But when you see the mix of merchandise, you might need a translator or a guide. The assortment of wrought iron, cast aluminum, wicker, PVC, rustic cedar and pine furniture, pottery, patio sets, bird baths, chimeneas, piñion wood, statuary, bakers' racks, bar stools, gargoyles, topiaries, trellises, arches, gates, bird cages and accessories are enough to backdrop an entire Home and Garden segment. A wrought iron bistro set for $139 was just one taste of Mexico that served breakfast tortillas at el cheapo prices. Choose from little wrought-iron baskets or a Cowboy hat and coat rack for just $19. Come holiday time, hang up icicle Christmas lights for the holidays for $9.99 in white or blue. A white wicker rocker for $129 and footstool for $39 were perfect for the porch at the lakehouse, and a full size chimenea with wrought-iron stand was $139. Add finishing touches with ceramic parrots, snake walking sticks and wooden boat shelves; baby giraffes were just "deer" for only $19 each. (Now I'm really sticking my neck out!) *Call toll-free: 888/883-9971*

MF Industries
2110 W. Division
Arlington, TX 76012

817/795-2368
Mon-Fri 9-5; Sat 10-2
www.mfteakwood.com

Shop the warehouse way and get it wholesale. Teakwood products and sleek teakwood furniture for the great outdoors are right at your fingertips. Their designs epitomize fine craftsmanship and beauty that will last a lifetime. Teak is probably the most versatile hardwood used in furniture making today, requiring little or no care; so choose the style and have yourself a field day. Theirs is harvested from plantations established by the Dutch in the Mid-19th century in Indonesia. The Indonesian government allows a limited amount of teak to be harvested yearly, which ensures an equal amount of reforestation. All of their products, then, are created from sources that can be recycled—making them ecologically-and- politically correct. As a manufacturer, they hold the benchmark for bargains in benches. Get them with backs, without backs, benches that fold or are extra large. If all else fails, have yourself a seat—a love seat. Add coffee tables, end tables, big tables, small tables. Cover up with an umbrella or add planters, teacarts, swings, arbor or poolside bars—there's an endless array of choices. And don't forget the kids, because they even make miniature versions of the grownup benches and chairs to size. Then, to make an even smaller statement, let's do up a line for Barbie. Even she has her own line of teak and mahogany doll-size furniture. Shop online or in person.

★★★★ Neal's Unfinished Furniture
2760 Trinity Mills
Carrollton, TX 75006

972/418-7329
Mon-Sat 9:30-6; Sun Noon-5
www.nealsunffurn.com

Though they don't violate any obscenity laws by selling nakedness, you can buy nude furniture without looking over your shoulders (or any other parts of the body). At the southwest corner of Trinity Mills and Marsh Lane, get ready to add some of your own personal touches. There isn't a room that is left out in left field. They have dining room tables (with or without leaves), pub tables, arm style tables, barstools (with or without backs), rocking chairs, coffee/lamp/sofa tables, entertainment centers, TV stands, oak bookcases, computer desks, writing desks, juvenile bedroom furniture, baby changing tables, chairs, child's rockers and horses, footstools, pine bookcases, toy boxes (with safety hinges), high chairs, vanity tables and stools and over 30 varieties of chairs. Whoa! Of course, they will sell you all the tools of the trade to finish what they don't. Knock on wood, you may even have the rudiments of a second business. Painted furniture is not only hot, it's haute! And Neal's has the best prices in town. Visit also in Plano at Independence and Parker. Other locations in Houston and Austin. And now, shop online for a limited selection. Stay home. Stir those creative juices. And go with the faux.

★★★★★ **Nearly Home**   **214/855-0255**
3300 McKinney Ave.   Mon-Sat 11-7; Sun 11-5
Dallas, TX 75204   www.nearlyhome.com (Under Construction)

When you come from being a senior buyer for Pier One, then a consultant to major retailers, what is there left to do except to do your own thing? Will Holland is one happy fella. Like a good neighbor, he and his partner have created a nicer home away from home. Nearly Home is the place to go when you're feeling blue or empty. Five minutes later, you'll be jumping for joy. It's an experience, just like Pier One, only more intimate and individual. Their showroom is overflowing onto the sidewalk, where sidewalk sales are a daily event. See one-of-a-kind items, market samples, manufacturer's samples, closeouts. But if you wait, there'll be no tomorrow. It's out of there. Gone. Sold. Went bye-bye. Merchandise changes daily. Save 25-75 percent off retail prices of decorative accent pieces for the living room, prints, lamps and florals. If you must shop retail, go down the street to their retail shop called Near and Far at the new West Village Shopping Center. Though some of the inventory comes from their brotherly-loved retail store, there is no sibling rivalry. Expect both stores' items to be value priced, with more of a designer atmosphere than Pier One's, but at their outlet, Nearly Home, the savings can be the difference between night and day. Shop and go around-the-world with them, without the jet lag. Buy it when you see it. If you snooze, as they say, you lose. At the corner of McKinney and Hall, this 1,800 square foot emporium for nifty and neat accessories just can't be beat. (Except when it rains, the sidewalk sales pull up and go—inside.) *Call toll-free: 800/655-2264*

★★★★★ **Newport Furnishings**   **972/219-7667**
Lewisville, TX   By Appt. Only
                                          www.newportfurnishings.com

If you love the look of Crate & Barrel or Restoration Hardware, why not consider this as your best-case scenario alternative? If you're fed up with self-serve retailers, try Leslie and Andrea's way of doing business. By appointment only, they will meet you at their private warehouse and show you quality at up to 50 percent off. And that's just the beginning. Why pay for a fancy showroom? Let the furniture and accessories speak for themselves. Eliminate fancy overhead, a million dollar ad campaign and pay for what you get, period. Listen up, bargain breath! Order direct from the manufacturer and save tons of money. It couldn't be any easier. Trendy furniture selections include sofas, leather couches, handcrafted mirrors, iron tables and more. Shop from samples. Shop from catalogs (there are over 100 to choose from). Shop from the showroom floor. This is a new wave of retailing that is sweeping the country. Why not? It's great furniture, with great variety, at great prices. You may find it so appealing you'll want to start your own store! Who says you can't find hidden treasures in the Metroplex?

★★★★★ **O'Neal Furniture**   **817/337-0068**
1711 Keller Pkwy.   Mon-Sat 10-8; Sun Noon-5
Keller, TX 76248

You've gotta have hope (chests), and for only $79 you can buy Faith and Charity one, too. Hope chests by **LANE** are just one of the items on the showroom floor. Home, cheap, Home-r O'Neal. He and his family have spent their every waking hour making sure Fort Worth and nearby furniture shoppers have something to sit on, relax on, sleep on. They've been doing so since 1935, so they aren't going away any-time soon. In fact, they're going and growing. Specializing in traditional, colonial and country furniture designs, they don't ignore accessories, either. See art. See art on the wall. See furniture alongside the art on the wall with names like **AMERICAN DREW**, **DREXEL HERITAGE**, **FAIRFIELD**, **HFI**, **KIMBALL**, **LANE**, **RIVERSIDE**, **STANLEY**, **SUMTER CABINET** and others at decidedly discounted prices. Any room in the house is fair stomping grounds. They stand (by) and deliver. You don't have to be Irish to love this O'Neal. Savings are substantial on sofas, dinettes, bedroom suites—this Homer is a home run!

★★ Rishers Furniture   817/274-7187
108 N. Collins   Mon-Sat 9-6; Sun 1-5
Arlington, TX 76011

Talk about staying power—this company's been delivering furniture since 1956. In fact, delivery's avail-able within 24 hours of purchase and if you don't mind having it delivered Tuesday through Saturday, delivery is even FREE. What? You mean just like the big boys? And at a discount, to boot! At the corner of Division and Collins, this store's an institution, saving you at least 35 percent on name brands like **BASSETT**, **CORSICANA**, **HIGHLAND HOUSE**, **QUALITY**, **STRATALOUNGER** and others. The full spectrum of household furniture and accessories is included in their repertoire. Beds, sofas, chairs, tables, bookcases, entertainment centers, the whole nine yards of inventory including accents like art work, glasswork and other table accessories. Listen to this: returns are accepted even if you don't like it, changed your mind, it doesn't fit, it doesn't matter. Just say the word. And, if there's something wrong with it when you get it home, give them a call, and if there's a button missing or a drawer pull off, don't fret—Mr. Rishers makes house calls. A dinette table with four chairs was $229; an oak dining room table by **MASTER DESIGNS** was $499 complete with table, four side chairs and leaf. Add a matching hutch for another $859. Not bad. Look for a 10 percent off coupon in the Yellow Pages if the discount isn't already low enough for you to say, "Charge it." Don't expect any retail amenities such as carpeting or air-conditioning. These folks cut their overhead to the bone. Try not to sweat it...even though you will.

★★★ Rita's World Clearance Center   817/831-9250
384 NE 28th   Fri-Sat 10-6
Haltom City, TX 76111

Rita's the Queen of Haltom City with her furniture store's triple hitter. Starting on a shoestring in 1986, Rita Wilson gave up her marketing job in favor of opening up her first retail store in Haltom City. Hmmm...and the rest is history. The Clearance Center opened the first weekend in April and is as up front and personal as their warehouse, making distribution of merchandise they want to close out an easy tac-tical move. This woman deserves credit for creating the small Belknap Street business community near Fort Worth and being their most ardent supporter. If it's furniture, Rita's a real solid performer. If it's at a discount, don't miss her two-day-a-week event.

Room Service   214/369-7666
4354 Lovers Lane
Dallas, TX 75225

Imagine yourself propped up in bed laden with ruffles and pinstripes, florals and plaids, dripping in fabric and trim in every direction. Order in Room Service and expect rave reviews. From upholstery to slipcovers, furniture to accessories, their periodic sales bring the prices down to 25-75 percent off. But if price were the only object here, we wouldn't be telling you to indulge. Room Service is a nice touch every once in a while, don't you agree? In fact, lay-ing in a bed of roses has made this retailer famous. Stock up when the beautiful robin's egg blue display is swashed in the colors of blue, vanilla, coffee and rose. Why not? Read all about it in *Country Home Magazine*, where owner Ann Fox often is asked to write stories or is cited for her wonderful and imaginative creations. You don't have to wait until Mother's Day to enjoy Room Service. You may even get used to it. Fill up to capacity with one-of-a-kind, oversized and stuffed chairs in damask or denim. Enjoy lots of upholstered furniture to whet your appetite. Sink your teeth into delicious slipcovers, a large selection of luscious fabrics, picture frames and mirrors, doormats, unique architectural accents and antiques. And imagine, you don't even have to leave a tip!

★★★ Rooms to Go Showroom & Kids Store   214/513-8550

2905 E. Grapevine Mills Circle   Mon-Sat 10-9; Sun Noon-6
Grapevine, TX 76051   www.roomstogo.com

No smart go-go girl would turn her nose up at this sleek one-stop shop for outfitting most any room in the house, including the often-overlooked kids' room. Easy does it. And easy on the pocketbook. The savings when you purchase all five pieces is another 10-20 percent, no big deal. Furniture, though, is not expensive to begin with. An entire bedroom suite can be had for as low as $750 to an average, about $1,200. Sure looks good and fills the void. But remember, it wasn't intended for a lifetime. Nothing heirloomish about it. Just good looking and inexpensive. And sometimes even cheap but good looking. Cute accessories like wall décor and rugs, for additional color. Expect a youthful housekeeper to be your guide. Three other locations besides Grapevine Mills include Plano, 2600 N. Central; Mesquite, 1233 Town East Blvd; and one in Arlington. Rumor has it that the Mesquite store may be their clearance store, if not already (and that means it will move to the head of the class!) ***Call toll-free: 800/ROOMS-TO***

★★★★ RoomStore Clearance Store   214/358-7287

3546 Forest Lane @ Marsh   Mon-Sat 10-8; Sun 12-6
Dallas, TX 75234   www.roomstore.com

Factory overstocks, discontinueds, showroom samples, one-of-a-kinds and some scratch 'n dents all add up to one big furniture outlet from one of the giant discount furniture retailers. Add in a catchy song, and it spells s.a.v.i.n.g.s. Odd mirrors for as low as $28, lamps starting at $18, cocktail and end tables beginning at $38—but most cost more. But for an inexpensive addition to your home life, you could find a real steal on an odd headboard for $68 or an **ASHLEY** bunk bed for $198. Save 40-50 percent on all shapes and sizes of dinette sets. A kingsize **SEALY** mattress set was $288 and 100 percent leather couches were $578 instead of over $1,000. Don't expect to overpay; then again, you'll get what you're paying for. Moderate furniture at lower prices...that's what they're all about!

★★★★★ Sam's Furniture & Appliance   817/838-6991

5555 E. Belknap St.   Mon-Fri 10-7; Sat 9-6
Haltom City, TX 76117   www.samsfurniture.com

Founded in 1946, Sam's Furniture and Appliances has come a long way, baby. From a small corner grocery store to an interesting business twist on a one-stop shopping experience, see what lies in store. The two sons of the founder, Sam Weisblatt, run the place now: Paul runs Sam's Video and Herb is the president of Sam's Furniture and Appliances. Even their mother handles the accounts payable. What's interesting about their approach is their ability to offer two different ways for you to buy their merchandise. Buy it the old-fashioned way and pay cash (though they do accept checks and credit cards, or choose outside financing for larger purchases). Or, try their unique "Lease-to-Own" program. They even call it a five-star lease program for anybody who may not be credit worthy enough for a credit card. But it's their rates that are outstanding, much lower than the typical "Rent-to-Own" stores whose interest rates are outrageous. It's also their way of helping customers rebuild their credit while still being able to afford some of life's luxuries. At Sam's, they pride themselves on personalized customer service. Currently, they operate three locations in the Fort Worth area. Their main store is located at 5555 E. Belknap but is also home to their corporate offices. Right across the street is Sam's Annex, which is their Lease Return outlet, offering terrific values on their entire line of lease returned items. When an item is returned from a lease, it is restored and repaired if necessary and then sold in the Annex for a lot less. Same with the jewelry lease returns. Then there's their Grapevine Store and warehouse, which is located on Highway 26 in North Richland Hills. Expect to find: appliances...Sam's only carries those brands that provide outstanding customer service. Considered one of the most successful independent appliance dealers in the Fort Worth area, Sam's is a member of MARTA, a buying cooperative for appliances. This association enables them to compete with the chains and the category killers by being able to purchase merchandise at low prices and directly from the manufacturer. Service policies are an important part of their success story, too, selling them at less than half the price of the bigger stores. Soon Sam's entered the television business, too, offering bigger and better TVs at the lowest prices in the area. But it's furniture—that they consider to be their future. Today, furniture occupies over 70 percent of their current floor space. Many different price points are offered. They use a furniture cooperative called SAFBI located in Terrell where they can access millions of dollars worth of inventory. They sell fine jewelry, too, at their Belknap location, but listen to this: their jewelry is available for lease, too. Can you imagine—rent-to-own an engagement ring? Then, if it doesn't work out, let's hope you don't have too many more months to honor on the lease . But back to the furniture—we eyed the **BROYHILL** "Fontana" dining room table and chairs that retailed new for $1,295 but were marked $799 (with four chairs) when it came back off of a lease. Wow! If you don't see something you like, browse through their catalogs and place your order. Delivery available within seven days. Go to their website and get a coupon for $25 off a lease. Additional brands for appliances and electronics included **AMANA**, **DISH NETWORK**, **FRIGIDAIRE**, **RCA**, **TOSHIBA** and **WHIRLPOOL**, just to name a few.

★★★★★ Select Collections
3733 N. Josey Lane, Suite 100
Carrollton, TX 75007

972/492-2491
Mon-Fri 10-6; Sat 10-5
www.angelfire.com/biz/antiqueman

Being a little selective means a lot in the consignment business. That means, just because you want to rid your house of furniture and antiques doesn't mean Selection Collections wants them. They are picky, picky. Located at the northwest corner of Josey and Rosemeade, this neighborhood consignor has something for everyone, but is highly selective in laying out the welcome mat. Furniture to antiques, new to reproductions, at least every era has an equal opportunity. Consignments are taken for 90 days on a 50/50 split. But after 30 days, the price drops 25 percent. For larger items that pictures do not provide justice to, they will go out to your home to appraise; or they can appraise an antique from a picture. A trés bien French dining room set with two armchairs and four side chairs was a drop-dead $1,295. Oui, Oui! amour. Then we accepted our "calling", which was a 1930 telephone stand for $119 (now that has a nice ring to it). Lots of new stuff, too. Inventory moves fast, so shop often. Charles and Barbara Holland and Associates are still the purveyors with the eagle eye. Visit their second location at the corner of Coit and Campbell, 972/248-7021, same hours as their Carrollton store.

★★★★ Sell It Again, Sam!
10233 E. Northwest Hwy., Suite 401
Dallas, TX 75238

214/340-6897
Mon-Sat 10:30-6; Sun 1-5

Love it, trade it, buy it! This eclectic paradise is seasoned with just the right stuff. If you're dancing through the aisles as fast as you can, you'll be able to see quite a pot-pourri of items. Let Sam "Sell It Again", Ma'am. Besides the Book Rack, this entrepreneur continues to amaze shoppers from miles around with her mix and match collections of individual and unique mixtures. Over 20,000 square feet of store surprises you at every turn. Watch for the big yellow sign and see what luck brings next. Furniture, housewares, accessories and accents—like a giant garage sale where it's cool in the summer and warm in the winter. Garden furniture and furnishings, not to worry, dig in—all was dirt-cheap. Consignments are still a 50/50 split but bring your own truck or arrange for your own delivery.

★ ★ ★ ★ ★   Shortell Bros. Intl.   214/748-4233

122 Howell St.   Mon-Fri 8-5; Sat By Appt.
Dallas, TX 75207   www.shortell.com

For over seven years, they haven't gotten the itch yet, but what started as a hobby for Joseph Shortell has emerged into a full-fledged specialty store for handmade Mediterranean, Southwestern and Spanish-colonial style wooden furniture and accessories. If the big guys can shop here, you and I can, too. Why not? You got something against paying wholesale prices? Their clients include restaurants, hotels, interior designers, architects, landscape architects and retail stores. All custom work is done on the premises and artisans in Mexico and Central America supply the rest. Products include: handmade wooden furniture, wrought iron, pottery, hand-carved stone fountains, table bases, figurines, tile, marble and stone pavers, pewter, glazed and unglazed ceramics and lots of decorative accessories. They're even concerned with the environment: all supplies used are earth-friendly. One particularly coveted product line is made from cantera stone that is found in central Mexico. This quarry produces four colors of stone: rose, white, grey and umber. The artisans then chisel each piece by hand, producing a variety of stone products that include fountains, statues, columns, moldings, table bases, fireplaces, benches and more. They also offer stone pavers that can be used indoors and out. They are available in a variety of beautiful colors and are very reasonably priced. Many pieces have a story behind them. One in particular was the one that evolved from the stone found in a quaint village in Guatemala. Manuel hand-carved the stone into angels, painted them and stored them in his personal residence. Now they're on display at their showroom where you will no doubt want to buy them. Howell is located just south of where Irving and Market Center Boulevard come together. *Call toll-free: 800/628-0437*

★ ★ ★ ★ ★   Showplace On The Square   214/742-6523

1645 Stemmons Frwy., Suite 200   Mon-Fri 9:30-4:30
Dallas, TX 75207

They've thrown open the doors to the public and the lines form on the right. Please, no unruly shoppers. You won't need a permission slip to shop here. To the Trade Only signs have disappeared, and now this Showplace has opened its showroom to the public. Me, you, and everybody in between. Take a walk on the wild side: one-of-a-kind barstools and chairs from the showroom are priced to sell, and did they sell fast. Forget paying $700 for one. They were taking the walk for $25-$75. Talk about having the right stuff at the right price! Who wants to save hundreds, maybe thousands on one-of-a-kind accessories? Well, I do. You can, too. Tell them the Diva sent you and see what happens. Exit Oak Lawn Ave. and help cure those decorator blues.

★ ★ ★ ★ ★   Simple Things   817/332-1772

1540 S. University Drive,   Mon-Wed, Sat 10-6; Thu-Fri 10-7; Sun 12-5
University Park Village
Fort Worth, TX 76107

It's very simple. No catalogs, no websites, just a simple notion that true customer service is the best advertising around. So in order to find out about this shop, you're gonna have to come on down. Simply put, you choose the fabric and frame, then wait about 6-10 weeks, depending on which of their two lines you pick, and presto: for a $35 delivery charge, you'll find it sitting on your doorstep. Simple is as simple gets. Just south of I-30, you'll find, simply put, incredibly soft, washable slip-covered sofas, deep sumptuous cushions, impressively constructed and generously-sized frames. Like your favorite pair of jeans. Choose from over 600 fabrics and then the rest is simple.

SimplyFurniture.com   **800/424-1304**
701 W. Ward Ave.   24/7
High Point, NC 27260   www.SimplyTogether.com

 Just one visit to this furniture website and you'll have an entirely new perspective on modular furniture. Assemble custom furniture in four easy pieces with only four bolts, in less than five minutes, and when it arrives, carry it yourself up a flight of stairs. Too good to be true? Well, let me introduce you to one of the most inventive and cost-effective lines of furniture to come down the pike in a decade. Randy Hoover is the classic entrepreneur, holding a ton of patents on all his creativeness, especially his furniture line. Located in the hub of the furniture capital of the world, High Point, NC, you don't have to travel there to see their line—up close and personal. Just shop online. It's simply terrific. Find out why they've been featured in newspapers like the *NY Times*, the *Washington Post*, and the *San Francisco Chronicle*. The furniture, simply put, brings fashionable and well-made designs together with the price and ease of ABC. The furniture actually fits through a narrow passageway or doorway in those older homes that are the rage of urban dwellers. It's even GSA-rated "Heavy Duty". Try it, you'll like it. It's a snap. Just choose whether you want a sofa, a chair, an ottoman, a sleeper-sofa or a kid's chair, then pick your choice of fabrics and it's on its way. The furniture is shipped in modular units, and I promise, no tools are necessary to assemble (four bolts,that's it!). When was the last time you carried a brand-new, custom sofa for under $500 up to your apartment on the second floor? See their website, don't overlook their clearance center, and say hello to Randy for me.

★★★★ Stacy Furniture   **817/424-8800**
1900 S. Main   Mon-Sat 10-8; Sun Noon-6
Grapevine, TX 76051   www.stacyfurniture.com

Hissoner, Rick Stacy, has finally settled into his brand new Grapevine location where the colors of burgundy and white catch your eye miles away. If you're burning money, you haven't shopped Stacy Furniture. Pull up under the porte-cochère, circle the driveway and remember, it's no longer politically correct to pay retail. Acres and acres, all tastefully appointed in a SoHo kind of way. Shop all under one roof if you've got the stamina to endure close to 300 manufacturers, like **DUCKS UNLIMITED**, **HUNTER'S RUN**, **KINCAID**, **PULASKI**, **RIDGEWAY**, **ROWE**, **SINGER**, **UNIVERSAL** and mattresses by **RESTONIC** and **SIMMONS**. For example, the Simmons Queen-size mattress started as low as $329. Shopping here, though, is like training for a marathon. Get into shape before you tackle the feat. And wear comfortable shoes for the agony of de-feet. Every room in your house is covered, including all the decorator touches from sofas to chairs, recliners, bedroom suites and dining room suites. Delivery averages $45 with most scheduled between one and seven days, depending on where you live. (By the way, each area has specific delivery dates.) Prices are discounted off retail, but they are not the lowest prices in town. They are, perhaps, the biggest, in size, in inventory, and in advertising. Well, somebody's got to pay those big salaries for Channel 8's Investigative Reporters. Website looks like it's just getting started.

★★★★ Sunnyland   972/239-3716

7879 Spring Valley Rd.   Mon-Sat 9-6; Mon-Thur 9-9 ; Sun Noon-5
Dallas, TX 75240   www.sunnylandfurniture.com

Take a walk on the sunny side of the street and shop Sunnyland Furniture, one of the largest outdoor/patio resources in the Metroplex. Their 30,000 square foot showroom is located at the intersection of Spring Valley and Coit Road. For over 30 years, this family-owned operation has provided not only patio sets but a complete parts, service and umbrella repair facility. They display over 300 outdoor patio sets and umbrellas and lots of accompanying accessories. Save at least 30 percent on such brands as **ALLIBERT**, **ARLINGTON HOUSE**, **DAYVA**, **GROSFILLEX**, **HOMECREST**, **LLOYD FLANDERS**, **LYON-SHAW ACCESSORIES**, **MALLIN**, **MEADOWCRAFT HAMMOCKS**, **SAMSONITE**, **TROPITONE** and **WOODARD** to test your sunny disposition.

Tommy Snodgrass Discount Furniture   972/262-1507

505 E. Main St.   Mon-Sat 10-7; Sun 1-5
Grand Prairie, TX 75050

Don't expect your best friends to spill the beans. Typically, they've shopped here but give you the silent treatment when asked, "Where did you get that gorgeous art deco chair?" Since 1945, Snodgrass Furniture has been kept under-wraps. After all, if everybody knew where YOU shopped, then maybe they'd get greedy and raise their prices. Nope. Not Tommy Snodgrass. After all, if you knew where to get name brand and designer furniture at half the price, would you be quick to share it? Simply put, this store garners rave reviews because they deserve it. Though they won't win any prizes for elegant surrounds, they do win hands down in selection, service and prices. Remember, they're the ones pulling up to mansions in their unmarked trucks so neighbors won't know where the furniture's coming from. Let them always think its Robb & Stucky. Expect stellar names like **AMERICAN DREW**, **ASHLEY**, **FENTON** (Hand-Blown Glass), **GEORGIO LEONI**, **KIMBALL**, **MAYO**, **POWELL**, **PULASKI**, **RIDGEWAY CLOCKS**, **RIVERSIDE**, **SPRING AIR**, **UNIVERSAL** and **VAUGHN BASSETT**. Newest to brag about is **VINEYARD**, one of the most gorgeous and solidly crafted bedroom lines on the scene. Leather couches for as low as $699. Tick off the savings on clocks, from cuckoos to contemporary, traditional, curio, grandfather or anniversary. Choose from their stock or special order—be it living room, bedroom, dining room furniture, mattresses, lamps, recliners...if it's to cushion the blow of high prices, you will find it here. And listen to the Snodgrass legendary layaway plan: "Pay whatever you can, whenever you can, and pay no interest, period!" Combine old-fashioned, unpretentious surroundings with down-to-earth country charm and see first-hand why folks from miles away shop here. It's the prices and service that draw shoppers who live in million-dollar houses to shop here...in dark glasses. First they send in their decorators, then their husbands, and lastly, they walk in with checkbook in hand. Cunning but cute!

★★ Ware Thomasville Home Furnishings   817/274-5521

222 W. Main St.   Mon-Wed, Fri-Sat 9-6; Thu 9-7; Sun 1-5
Arlington, TX 76010   www.warethomasville.com

Ware oh Ware has their clearance store gone? Well, here they are in Arlington. If you prefer to shop their other locations, go to their website to see what sales are running that week. (Saves time cutting out ads from the paper before anyone has even read it.) This family-owned business has been "waring" their furniture hat since 1948. They specialize in high quality bedroom, dining room and living room furniture. In addition, they have a **THOMASVILLE** leather gallery. But what really gets our goat is the clearance center across the street. Located two blocks east of Cooper St., why not get a deal while you're at it? Choose your financing plan of 12 months with no interest or get a Thomasville revolving account with a nine percent interest rate. Delivery is free up to a 50-mile radius.

★★★★ Weir's Clearance Center   972/445-6427
4510 Buena Vista   Mon-Fri 10-5:30; Sat 10-6
Dallas, TX 75205

Just around the corner from their Knox Street Furniture Village, see what bargains lurk for your inspection. No phone orders, holds or CODs, and a $35 delivery charge within the Metroplex, but who cares if you're going to save substantial dinero? You'll find factory seconds, "as is" merchandise, clearance and discontinues which all adds up to less money. For example, a dining group crafted of hardwood solids and veneers in a heavily distressed walnut brown finish with black iron strap work was $299 for the table (instead of $699). Add an arm or side chair for $99 (instead of $179-$199). Besides dining room furniture, take your pick of select bedrooms, sofas, loveseats and chairs in leather or fabric. A classic wing chair sent us flying to the truck without a wing and a prayer, only $199.

★★★★ Wholesale Furniture & Bedding   972/247-8990
2470 Joe Field Rd.   Mon-Fri 10-8; Sat-Sun 10-5
Dallas, TX 75229

Spend as much as you want, or as little. Buy from a full range of manufacturers as you wind your way through the mixture of budget to moderate furniture. From inexpensive particle board to well-made models—items that may indeed last longer than I will. Chests of drawers ranged from $89-$700, which goes to show you, their demographics are all over the map. But one thing is universal: you won't pay retail. Wrought-iron furniture was a standout, while furniture by **ASHLEY**, **BENCHCRAFT**, **CLAYBROOK**, **HARDEN** and **SOUTHWEST** gave us a sense of security. Look for the sign of the times to lead you to the front door of their 20,000 square-foot pebble and masonite building. Joe Field Road is one block south of Royal Lane, go west approximately three blocks.

Wickes Furniture Budget & Clearance Outlet   214/365-9494
9358 N. Central Expressway @ Park Lane   Mon-Sat 10-6; Sun 12-6
Dallas, TX 75231   www.wickesfurniture.com

Wicks and sticks may break my bones, but this Wickes won't break your budget. Say hello and welcome Wickes Furniture Budget & Clearance Outlet to the family of shaping how America REALLY shops. Where else but Wickes Outlet can you save 30-80 percent off their already "Compare-At-Prices". Granted, their retail stores are already price-conscious, so imagine what their clearance outlet can deliver—it's mind-boggling! Turn promises into reality and what you see is what you can get delivered on a limited basis. If not, as they say in the biz, bring your own truck. Where else but Wickes could you find all of their floor samples, cancelled special orders, one-of-a-kind returns and bedding at such low, low prices? Behind Just for Feet, now you can defeat the high cost of furniture and step aside from the high cost of decorating. It's a mighty improved collection since last year. Save hundreds, sometimes thousands, on furniture that looks good, feels good, sits good, and is good. From entertainment centers for under $500 to sofas in the $300-$500 range, their outlet can have you stretched out without maxing out your credit cards. It's pretty tempting, especially if you want a complete makeover but your budget says, "Whoa." Now, you can do it practically on a dime. Ask my dinette? A whitewash farmhouse grouping that included a 39 x 65-inch tile-top hardwood table, six hoop-back side chairs for under $500. Seeing is believing. They've been selling furniture and accessories around the country since 1971, but it was in 1998 that they put out the "I'm just looking, thank you" button. That's a button shoppers wear to ensure their shopping experience is hassle free. When you need help, just ask. (You know how I feel about them asking me, "Can I help you, honey?") If they say anything but hello or welcome, they're down for the count. They also have a coffee cafe and it's okay that it's not a Starbucks. They offer a 7-day risk-free return policy, a 30-day lowest price guarantee and an optional 5-year warranty. (And that's in their retail stores!) You won't get a headache by shopping at Wickes B and C Outlet! Located in the Home Place Square Shopping Center.

★★★★★ Woodbine Furniture

8705 Davis Blvd.   Tue-Sat 10-5:30; Thu 10-7; Sun Noon-5:30
North Richland Hills, TX 76180   www.woodbinefurniture.com

Shaker-up baby, let's rock and shop. Looking for that **RALPH LAUREN** look? Then look no more. Here's the source for Amish-made furniture made in small individual woodshops, built from scratch one piece at a time. From country armoires to five-piece cherry wall-units, what makes this furniture so unique is that everything is crafted utilizing hand and medium-sized stationary tools. No assembly lines here. Choose from many different styles where seeing is believing. Country, Mission, Queen Anne, and the sought-after Shaker styles abound or, if you prefer, custom-made is available made to your specifications. Add many interesting extra features such as lighted cabinets, beveled glass, glass shelving, mullion doors, claw feet, metal hardware and more. Then, if you think you don't have room for anything more, build an addition. These are too good to pass up. Every room in the house can be accommodated: dining room to toys, bedrooms to entertainment centers, children's furniture, wooden toys to more than 750 items to choose from. In fact, some of these pieces may be the antiques of the future. Most furniture is available in oak, cherry, hickory and walnut and available in 12 finishes. They also offer hardware and ornamental touches. Delivery is available for $35; financing is with American General with six months, no interest. Not bad. From the time you place your order, expect delivery in 8-12 weeks (remember, it's made by hand). Your payments will not start until after your furniture is delivered so you really have eight-nine months to save up before interest starts accruing.. Oh, I hate being practical!

★★★★ Wooden Swing Co./Children's Furniture   972/386-6280

13617 Inwood Rd.   Mon-Sat 10-6
Dallas, TX 75244   www.woodenswing.com

For the active tykes, get them the tree house in the August moon. Imagine keeping them up a tree, without costing a fortune. Just think what a pool costs? Sleep-a-way camp? A trip to Grandma's? For a fraction of the price, build them a vacation in the backyard and keep them looking up. Or keep them occupied indoors with lots of space-saving bedroom suites such as modular bedrooms that grow with them through their teen years and beyond. What kid wouldn't dream of bunk beds complete with a slide or canopy beds, trundle beds, captains beds, and lots of imaginative twin beds? Then, add in all the matching furniture and accessories to complete their sweet dreams. Lots of styles from big to bigger to keep them out of your hair and having fun in the sun. **BRIO** toy railroads are always 10 percent off suggested retail. Since 1978, this company has been building their business while building their market share selling market samples of children's furniture, taking over about half the store. Children's furniture has definitely been a void in the marketplace and now it's here, often at the lowest prices. Novelty beds will bring a smile, from racecars to bunk beds. And of course, outdoors they can be swingers in wooden swing sets, or on the lookout inside the fort. Imagination and safety are always paramount in their strategy.

★★★★ Your Furniture Connection

733 Fort Worth Drive
Denton, TX 76201

940/382-0690
Mon-Sat 9:30-6

Looks like they got out of the website business, and decided it wasn't for them. Still, what you no longer see online is still proudly displayed on their showroom floor. And more importantly, all at discounted prices. Samples, samples, and more samples on the showroom floor plus catalog orders are still an important component to their overall approach. They also carry fun and functional furniture by **LEE** that only takes approximately two weeks for delivery from the time ordered. Delivery is just $25 and financing includes 90-days same as cash. But now that you know the bottom line, what else can I tell you about YFC? Well, it's no KFC, that's for sure. But the deals here are finger-lickin' good. Going on almost 50 years, they've figured out all the "ins and outs" of discounting furniture. You also can custom-order from catalogs at equally appealing prices. Names that connect-to-you include **ASHLEY**, **HAMMARY**, **LA-Z-BOY**, **PULASKI**, **RIVERSIDE** and others—actually, almost 40 different manufacturers are represented. Savings run the gamut—from 20-80 percent...so you're not going to feel the pinch. ***Call toll-free: 800/658-8814***

30

Gifts

◆◆◆◆◆ Action Trophies & Awards
1600 N. I-35 E., Suite 100
Carrollton, TX 75006

972/245-0105
Mon-Fri 8:30-6; Sat 9-2
www.atawards.com

This is one of the largest trophy dealers in the Metroplex, so why not award yourself with some just rewards? After all, who will know you're the best cook and bottle washer in the neighborhood if you don't get some recognition? Looking to reward your top salesman or the winner of the soccer team's playoffs? Their 3,900-square-foot facility in Carrollton can create an acrylic, glass or marble award for that special honoree. They also carry trophies, medals and ribbons. If you need your trophy or award engraved, they've got the tools to do it. And if you need something in a hurry, they can deliver a special one-day turnaround on custom-designed awards when requested. Check them out online at www.atawards.com. Why do we recommend them? Because what's good for the goose is good for the gander. They do incredible engravable work, promptly, at very competitive prices. They even send custom awards across the country. They have on hand a large inventory of in-stock supplies, too. It doesn't have to be custom. But whether you need trophies (and not a Trophy Nissan) or medals for an individual, team, or league, a plaque for the salesman of the month, or other promotional products for advertising, you can get more than just engravings with logos—they have a full graphic design team, too. For hot deals like a Rosewood pen and box set with a laser-engraved monogram, how does $18 sound?

★★★ Basket Case, The
700 University Village
Richardson, TX 75081

972/231-5100
Mon-Sat 10-6
www.thebasketcaseonline.com

Twenty years in business and they're still a basket case. What did you expect? A valium-laden packaged plan? No, this is baskets full of specialty items handpicked and put to good use. Why bring a gift of the same ole, same ole? Fill-er-up with **CAMILLE BECKMAN** lotions and bath products, stationery, candles, tea and cookies for just $35. Make your out-of-town friends jealous with a Texas basket including **ADOBE HOUSE** dips and chips, pralines and candies from **LAMMES** or better still, delectable treats from **JARDINES**. Price? How does $28 sound? That's what I said. Woe is me. I can afford that. Lots of great smelly stuff from lotions to candles and potpourri. Order online or toll free, from baby gift baskets to something to bring to a guest's dinner party. You don't want to walk in empty-handed, do you? *Call toll-free: 866/231-5100*

★★★★ Creative Gift Baskets & Balloons   972/516-2940

Plano Outlet Mall   Mon-Sat 10-9; Sun Noon-6
1717 E. Spring Creek Pkwy. www.smartpages.com/home/creativegiftbasketsandballoons1
Plano, TX 75074

With a website this long, you'd think it was worth going to. It is, but only if you want a map on how to get to Plano Outlet Mall. Well, they might be working on a new website as we speak, so I won't disparage their efforts. They're creative and imaginative, especially if you have a budget that squeaks. Only $7.50 for local delivery, which is quite a bargain in and of itself. So, if you're tired of saying it with flowers, consider the alternatives: not sending a thing, or going Creative. From balloons to gourmet gift baskets, something dedicated to brides and grooms for their wedding, or a candlelight basket for them a year later. Need to butter up the boss? Or you can send an "I Love You" (let's kiss and make up) basket. They've got it all. Expect to pay an extra $9.95 if your needs require a cross-country delivery.

NV Ergo Candle Outlet Store   214/905-9050

1302 Motor Circle   Saturdays 10-4
Dallas, TX 75247

Banker's hours come drippingly shorter and shorter. Take Ergo, for example. Exit Motor Street, and they're one block west of Stemmons. Tell us what you think. Are they a drip or not?

★★★★ Mark & Larry's Stuff   214/747-8833

2614 Elm St.   Fri-Sat 11-9
Dallas, TX 75226   www.mark-larry-stuff.com

It's all in the name...of fun. And that's exactly what Mark Sonna and Larry Groseclose have in their Deep Ellum repository. So, what kind of stuff do they have? "Stuff" is the operative word here. A plethora of products to sift through, including toys, antique-oriented items, books, jewelry, toiletries, home furnishings and more. But this is no ordinary general merchandise store, thank you very much. Keeping in stride with the hip, eclectic atmosphere and attitude of Deep Ellum, you won't find these aforementioned items just anywhere. Quick, name all the places where you can find a 60th Anniversary **MADELINE** ragdoll in a velvet dress for $55, or a **FLYNN** clock that looks as if it's being suspended in mid-air for $60? Thought so. We had trouble, too. Glycerin soap with a rubber frog inside for $8.95, along with a cinder bowl for cigar fans. Save those ashes for $12. Over 3,000 items are all here to feast your eyes upon, with most items under $35. Thumbs up for their pocket shower curtain that holds over a hundred items for $29; but if you'd rather get the rubber ducky, it will float for $3.99 (or $4.99 if you want the one with the squeaker). Whatever floats your boat. The rather unusual store hours attract a rather unusual crowd. Expect to see quite a few "Little Shoppers of Horror" wannabes who prefer shopping in the dark. Returns and exchanges are permitted up to seven days after purchase with a receipt. All sales are final on jewelry, discounted merchandise, bath accessories, artist pieces, custom orders and seasonal items. Nothing they carry, you need, just fun to have. Although they stick to their basic under-$35 ceiling price on most, sometimes they go sky high. Need a hand? How about a chair shaped like one for $195? They also offer gift-wrap and worldwide shipping (at an additional charge, of course). And get a load of the card selection. It's the largest in the city with over 2,500 choices. They're a card, too!

Index

J. Douglas		Furniture & Home Accessories
Jack Whitby Piano		Musical Instruments
Jeans Warehouse		Apparel: Family
Jewelry Exchange, The		Jewelry
K & G Men's Center		Apparel: Men's
Kiva Pottery		Housewares
Kiva Pottery		Pools & Yards
Lights Fantastic	A5	Lighting & Lamps
Lilly Dodson Designer Outlet	A10	Apparel: Women's
Little Red's Antiques	A67	Antiques & Auctions/Pools & Yards
Lone Star Trading Co.		Furniture & Home Accessories
LumberLiquidators.com		Carpets & Floors
Men's Wearhouse, The		Apparel: Men's
Metro Home Warehouse		Arts, Crafts, Kits
Metro-Webb Foods		Food Stuff
MF Industries		Furniture & Home Accessories
Mudpuppy		Apparel: Children's
overstock.com	A64	Department Stores/Off Price & Catalogs
Patio One/Fullrich Industries	A44	Pools & Yards
Patti Lee @ Five Star Hair Studio	A26	Beauty & Drug Stores
Pier 1 Clearance Store		Housewares
Pool & Patio Landscaping		Pools & Yards
Pet Love Mobile Dog Grooming	A13	Pets & Vets
Rainbow Custom Shutters		Windows & Walls
Republic Industries/Cabinet Outlet		Home Improvement
Resource Concepts	A38	Computers & Online
Rose Petal, The		Pools & Yards/Plants & Gardens
S & H Carpet Distributors	A6,A72	Carpets & Floors
Saleplace, The		Bridal
Sam Moon Luggage & Gifts/Handbags & Jewelry		Handbags & Luggage
Sam Moon Trading		Jewelry
Saturdays Only	A42	Department Stores/Off Price & Catalogs
Seconds & Surplus	A24	Home Improvement
Small Fry	A71	Apparel: Children's
Solitaires	A54	Jewelry
Special Occasion Dresses	A66	Apparel: Women's
Spirits Liqueur Store		Food Stuff
St. Bernard Sports Outlet		Sporting Goods
Stone-Tec	A32	Home Improvement
Sunshine Sunrooms		Home Improvement
SW Canvas Products		Home Improvement
Sword's Music Co.		Musical Instruments
Talbot's Outlet		Apparel: Women's
Tapestries & More		Art & Collectibles
Texas Appliance & Builders Supply		Appliances
Tile & Marble Clearinghouse & Brokerage Firm		Carpets & Floors
Tiny Thru Plus Size Outlet	A19	Apparel: Women's
TM Century		Music & Books
Tommy Snodgrass Discount Furniture	A20	Furniture & Home Accessories
Tour Line Golf		Sporting Goods
Tuesday Morning		Department Stores/Off Price & Catalogs
UCC Total Home of Dallas	A56	Department Stores/Off Price & Catalogs
Vantage Shoe Warehouse	A22	Shoes
Venture Pools		Pools & Yards
Wallpaper Source & More	A16	Windows & Walls
Walt's Appliance	A48	Appliances
Wickes Furniture Budget & Clearance Outlet	A49	Furniture & Home Accessories
World of Sleep/Simmons Mattress Outlet		Beds & Mattresses
World Traveler		Travel/Handbags & Luggage
Yard Ideas		Pools & Yards
Yes! Less		Food Stuff
Zale Lipshey Hospital		Medical
Zale's Outlet	A50	Jewelry
Zozza	A34	Gifts/Jewelry

★★★★ **Third Monday Trade Days—McKinney**   **972/562-5466**
4550 W. University   Fri-Sun 7 AM-Dusk
Hwy. 380   www.tmtd.com
McKinney, TX 75069

Find it all from Mr. Brown who sells reconditioned vacuums to Fred and his tools for sale. That's the fun of participating in one of the oldest county-wide markets this side of the Mason-Dixon Line. What began more than 100 years ago when judges rode the circuit, from county seat to county seat, is now the hub of contemporary horse trading. The difference, of course, is that today there're paved roads to travel. Head north on the Saturday and Sunday before the third Monday of the month. Gee, you've got to have your calendar in hand to figure that date, for sure. Treasure hunt your way up Highway 75 to Highway 380 and go west for two miles to the historic Buckner Community where, since 1966, McKinney's Third Monday Trade Days have been a major happening. More than 800 vendors are scattered throughout the 30 acres, making a believer out of a discontent. The market has undergone many changes under its present ownership, so be sure to visit the new Trading Post section and the large pavilion. Have yourself a feast—from snacks to full meals. Open-air space rentals are $35 for the first lot and $25 for each additional lot. There's a price tag on everything and some of the best buys are things someone else discarded. Western paraphernalia, hats, blankets, saddles and spurs to antiques, videos, **HARLEY** collectibles, toys, sporting goods and more. And when all is said and done and you've worked up a he-man's appetite, sink those choppers into juicy hamburgers, hot dogs, barbecue, corn-on-the-cob, turkey legs, funnel cakes, snow cones, popcorn and more. One of the nicest features this year is delivery to your car. FREE parking on Friday; $2 on Saturdays and Sundays. Restrictions are laudable: No alcoholic beverages, tobacco or pets allowed. (Husbands are welcomed on a leash, please, as they have a tendency to wander!)

★★★★★ **Traders Village**   **972/647-2331**
2602 Mayfield Rd.   Sat-Sun 8 AM-Dusk
Grand Prairie, TX 75052   www.tradersvillage.com

Since Traders Village opened in the Dallas-Fort Worth area (Grand Prairie, specifically) in 1973 and then in Houston in 1989, millions of people have browsed, shopped, haggled, picked through the bric-brac and landed quite a few deals. Hundreds and hundreds of dealers offer a little bit of everything, all at bargain prices. From the days of the Trading Post in the Old West until now, here is one gigantic step(s) for mankind. Who doesn't like to wheel and deal? There's so much being offered that, unless you've got your equilibrium in check, you could fall flat on your face in the frenzy. Up and down, in and out, over and around the miles of aisles trying to cajole the vendor into believing you've only got your last $200 bucks for that boudoir. The atmosphere's like the State Fair rather than Barnum and Bailey...some serious transactions, some with an air of frivolity. But just like some folks like to gamble for a few hours knowing that they have $100 to play with, and that's it, shoppers, given the same mind-set, will have a whale of a good time and just maybe come home a winner. It's a great way to have a family outing, and a whole lot more fun than going fishing (though there are some similarities). Only at Traders Village can you stroll through literally thousands of shops where you can wheel and deal with the store owners themselves and maybe secure the bargain of a lifetime. From paper clips to bulldozers, on any given weekend you can find it at Traders Village. There's an R.V. Park, kiddie rides and games, ATM machines, stroller and wheelchair rentals, snack stands, restaurants, mobile beverage carts, covered rest areas, modern restrooms, and all types of special amenities—all making for a pretty comfortable and all-around shopping experience. No foot reflexologists standing by, which is all that's lacking for a perfect day.

★★ Vikon Village Flea Market
2918 South Jupiter
Garland, TX 75041

972/271-0565
Sat-Sun 10-7
www.vikonvillage.net

One reason to intersect Kingsley and Jupiter is to land at Vikon Village. Just two blocks north of LBJ, this indoor flea market is as old as the hills. In fact, if my memory serves me correctly, it was the first flea market I ever shopped when I moved to Dallas. Find it all, from sporting goods to computers, bicycles to cameras, rare coins to gifts, and swords. Do they have swords? Their prices are slashed, too? Then move down the next aisle to sewing machines, dinnerware, area rugs, jewelry, baby buntings, furniture, and lo and behold, even a TV repairman. Stock up on feed, grain and farm supplies, then mosey on over to the pool supplies. Jump in. Dive in. It's a sink or swim world. Somewhere in this maze of about 300 dealers, you will be introduced to trash or treasures and a lot of kitsch, some kaboodle and everything in between.

Best 100

SHOPPING DESTINATIONS

Dallas • Fort Worth

BIGGER BETTER
bargains

www.biggerbetterbargains.com

★★★★★ **Tuesday Morning**   **972/991-2996**
14631 Inwood Rd.   Major Sales Throughout the Year
Dallas, TX 75247   www.tuesdaymorning.com

It's not just another day of the week—when their doors open, run for your life (style.) Expect closeouts on a laundry list of everything that has gift potential at prices of 50-80 percent less. How do they do it? Where do they get their merchandise? Well, let me count the ways. Closeouts and excess inventory from manufacturers, department and specialty stores, Trade Mart samples, mail order catalogs, even failed dot.com sites are now fair game. When they bought out the inventory of pet.com, for example, I bought a dozen of their logo key rings (with that wonderful little dog trademark) for all my pet lover friends for $4.99, instead of $10. It's like being in boutique heaven with an ax. Cut out all the fat, pare it down to a warehouse sale environment, close the doors during times when shoppers don't traditionally buy gifts ("Closed for restocking" is a customary sign in their windows coast-to-coast) and there, you have the beginnings of this almost 30-year-old veteran of the bargain biz. Go online to find dates open and their seasonal hours. Once in the store, be sure to pick up a wallet-size calendar with dates clearly marked. Ranked the biggest closeout gift chain in the country (and to think I knew them when). Satisfaction is guaranteed or your money back—for any reason. Some regular brands include **AMERICAN TOURISTER**, **BILL BLASS**, **CIAO**, **CUISINART**, **FARBERWARE**, **LARK**, **LEGO**, **LIMOGES**, **MADAME ALEXANDER**, **MARTEX**, **MURANO**, **PIERRE CARDIN**, **REVERE**, **ROYAL DOULTON**, **SABATIER**, **SAMSONITE**, **STEINBACH**, **WEDGWOOD** and more. If you are looking for name-brand gifts, housewares, linens, fashion apparel, crystal and stemware, luggage and small leather goods, electronics and gadgetry, paper goods, toys, dolls, flowers, party decorations, furniture and accessories, jewelry, hair accessories, bed and bath items, one-of-a-kind samples in categories all by themselves, area rugs, brass, games, cards, books—there isn't a close-out in the world they won't eventually get. More than 300 stores nationwide, so why not meet me Tuesday Morning? I'm sure we'll bump into each other one of these days.

RosesGiftWorld.com   **972/496-0207**
2305 Emberlee Drive (Office Only)   24/7
Garland, TX 75040   www.rosesgiftworld.com

A rose is a rose is a rose, but this Rose has it made in the shade. Shop at home from the big book, the really big book of Rose's Gift World, home to thousands of gifts and home accents that are perfect for any home decor. Based in Garland, this worldwide catalog company is unlike any other. Expect it to be your bargain-shopping wish book when thinking of a gift—for yourself or someone else. Where else would you be able to choose from more than 2,100 items of this quality and at these prices? It's like uncovering the Holy Grail. A one-stop shopping Nirvana for those who can never find just the right gift. Page after page, it's click and shop 'til you drop from finger overload: jewelry, art and decorative accents in styles from African to Asian, garden accents, collectibles like dolls, teddy bears, wizards to dragons (hello **HARRY POTTER**), **NASCAR** stuff, gifts for both little and big boys (knives, tools, electronics) and more. Well, seeing is believing, and I guarantee you'll be a believer after one trip online. Get a preview taste in person at Rose's Gifts at the Dusty Attic's sister location, The Attic Too, 2140 E. Belt Line in Richardson, 972/671-9577; or stay home in your mumu and have at it online.

★★★★ Stoney's Wine & Gifts   **214/953-3067**
2701 Harry Hines Blvd.   Mon-Fri 11-6; Sat Noon-6
Dallas, TX 75201

They've done it! I found it! And the record books will soon add another round of applause to Stoney and Diana Savage's menu of credits. Displaying more wines in the smallest square foot space is now their claim to fame. In what was formerly a 1937 gas station, this talented and creative couple has spread their wings to another gig that gives shoppers a taste of the finer side. More than 115 selections of wines for under $12 are available in this 300 square-foot space, constructed of quarried stone and a nice backdrop to inexpensive libations and gift baskets. That's where Diana comes in, wrapping up interesting soaps, sachets, candles, and packaged pastas with the wines to go. Bring a gift. Never show up empty-handed. And that's one of the new "Rules" for girls from the 21st century.

Surprises   **214/360-0900**
208 Preston Royal Village   Mon-Sat 10-6
Dallas, TX 75230

Hand-made surprises to die for are waiting for you at Surprises. And who doesn't love a surprise? I don't mean the kind that the IRS might send you, but the kind that brings a smile to your face and a rush to your heart. Gifts, accessories and functional art are waiting to get drafted for your gift-giving list. One of the best selections of American crafts—I guess that's why they've been named one of the "Top 100" retailers of American crafts ever since they opened in Houston in 1996. In fact, that's where we first were "surprised!" If you are looking for hand-blown glass, don't pass them by. The selection is stupendous. But it's their "Poupee Dolls" by **ISABELLE** that are a favorite on one shopper's shelves. Whimsical and wishful, perfect for the woman who has everything. This just may be my next major collection. How surprised I was to discover frequent-buyers certificates. That should help escalate my collection immediately. What fun, funky and festive additions to an ordinarily dull curio cabinet!

lilly dodson
Designer Outlet

DINA BAR-EL

CHRISTIAN LACROIX

TAPP
NEW YORK

HERVE LEGER PARIS

Peggy Jennings

VOTRE NOM...

MICHAEL KORS

VIVIENNE TAM

ZANG TOI

GIVENCHY

RENA LANGE

The Corners Shopping Center
Central and Walnut Hill Lane
214-696-1381

Where Smart Women Buy Their Couturier Wardrobe

CAROLINA HERRERA

MUGLER

LÉONARD

Zanella

Fendi

TOM AND LINDA PLATT

LAFAYETTE 148

Richard Tyler

BERNARD ZINS

Iceberg

SONIA RYKIEL

Anna Sui

Smart Savings
From Office-Chic
To Dazzling After-Five

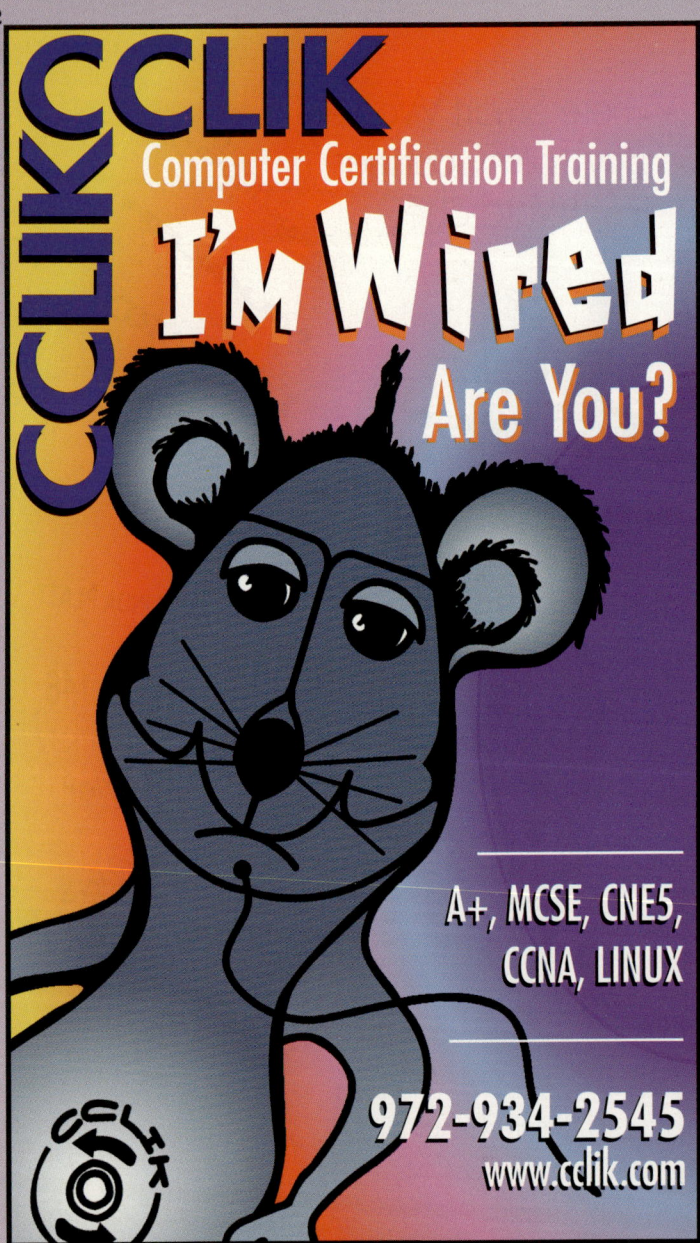

Mobile Pet Grooming

We Come To You

All Bathing And Grooming Performed In Our Vans

- ♥ Your Pet Never Leaves Home
- ♥ 35 Vans Serving Dallas, Mid-Cities And Surrounding Areas
- ♥ In Business Since 1977
- ♥ Professional Groomers
- ♥ All Breed Dogs And Cats
- ♥ $5 Off Initial Grooming For First Time Customers

972-243-8331 • 817-318-8336

Monday - Saturday By Appointment

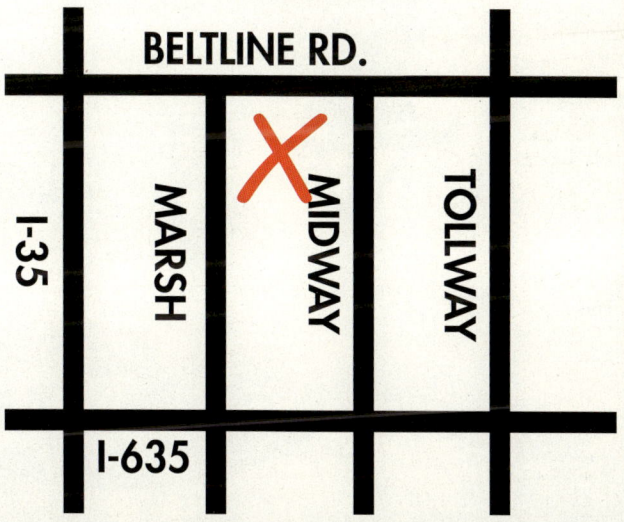

Wallcoverings by: Brewster

Binford FENCE Supply Co.

WHOLESALE FENCE SUPPLY

Serving The Metroplex Since 1950

PUBLIC INVITED

- **WOOD and CHAIN LINK**
- **ORNAMENTAL IRON**
- **PICKETS • RAILS • POSTS • GATES**

ASK ABOUT OUR NEW "CONTRACT IT YOURSELF" PLAN

LET US HELP YOU DO IT YOURSELF

2915 Hickory Tree Mesquite, TX 75180

Lake June Rd.

Hickory Tree Rd.

635

Elam Rd.

972-286-2881
FAX 972-286-6500

Tiny *thru* Plus Size Outlet

Designer Dresses, Suits & Pants, Casual & Career

Wholesale Prices Or Less

1000's Of Name Brands:
FROM
$29 - $69
REGULARLY
$90 - $250

Direct from the Manufacturer

Call First For Hours & Days Open

Please Call If Traveling By Distance

Regular Hours
- OPEN -
Tues thru Sat 10-5 • Tues. & Thurs. till 7

Always Closed Sunday - Monday

- Road Show Weeks -
OPEN - Tuesday - Wednesday -Thursday

- ROAD SHOW TOWNS -
WACO • BELTON • ATHENS
MARSHALL • NACOGDOCHES

No Road Shows
December, January, June & July

Warehouse has approx. 6,000 square feet. 235 racks of clothes. We have off-season, pre-season, latest mark downs, sale items and separates. Sale items proced $5 - $29 and everything is always wholesale & below.

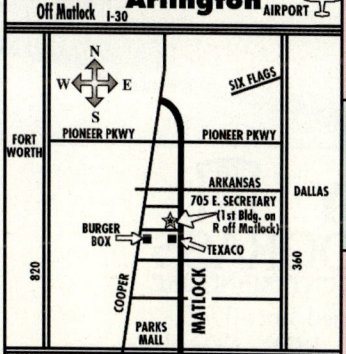

2 Miles North of I-20 Off Matlock

Arlington AIRPORT

I-30

N
W E
S

SIX FLAGS

FORT WORTH

PIONEER PKWY   PIONEER PKWY

ARKANSAS
705 E. SECRETARY
(1st Bldg. on
R off Matlock)

DALLAS

BURGER BOX

TEXACO

820   COOPER   MATLOCK   360

PARKS MALL

I-20

$5.00 OFF
First Time Customer
(purchase of $49 or mre)
Not valid at shows (In-house only)

705 Secretary • Arlington, TX • 817.265.3737

As Seen On Channel 11 and Channel 5 News ★★★★★ Rating - Underground Shopper

WE'LL BEAT ANYONE'S PRICES

American-Drew

Millennium

Pulaski

Riverside

Mayo

Standard

Kimball

Ashley

Powell

Segusino

Vaughn Bassett

Ridgeway Clocks

Spring Air and Fenton Hand-Blown Glass, Curios

Living Room

Bedroom

Dining Room

Mattresses

Featuring The
LAYAWAY OF DREAMS
Pay whatever you want down, pay whatever you can per month for as long as you need to & pay no interest!

VANTAGE SHOE WAREHOUSE

3 Locations

13410 Preston Rd.
Arnold Square
(across from Valley View Mall)

214.231.0027

Mon.-Sat. 10-9,
Sun. 12-6

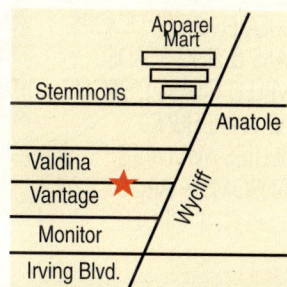

2222 Vantage St.

214.678.9928

Mon.-Sat. 9:45-6,
Fri. 'till 7, Sun. 12-6
Former location of
Vantage Shoe Warehouse

11255 Garland Rd.

214.328.3603

Mon.-Fri. 12-9,
Sat. 10-9, Sun. 12-6

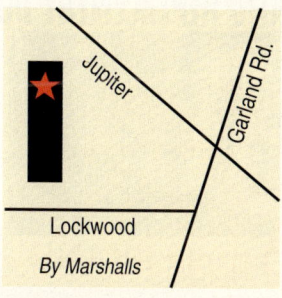

INTERIOR DOORS

SAVE 50%

Slabs Start at:

14.00-Colonist

19.00-Solid core

55.00-Pine 6-Panel

35.00-Metal Flat

40.00-Metal 6-pnl

35.00-Fiberglass

As low as:
$225
6068 Prehung
French Unit

As low as:
$60
2868 Modified
9-lite Slab

As low as:
$50
2068 Pine French
Door Slbs

As low as:
$50
2068 Pine 6-Pnl
Door Slbs

FRONT ENTRY DOORS

SAVE 50%

SOLID MAHOGANY DOORS
SOLID OAK DOORS
ENGINEERED PINE DOORS
INSULATED STEEL DOORS
BRASS & ZINC LEADED
BEVELED GLASS DESIGNS
SLAB & PREHUNG
SIDELITES AVAILABLE
TRANSOMS & ARCS
WE SPECIAL ORDER

Solid
Mahogany/Zinc
$AVE 50-60%
off list

List:299.00
$149

**WE HAVE
8' DOORS**

PATIO REPLACEMENT DOORS

SAVE 60%

6FT INSULATED STEEL FRENCH DOORS
Reg:$499.00 LIST   **$300.00**

6FT CLEAR LT-WOOD FRENCH DOORS
Reg:$2150.00 LIST   **$699.00**

Also available are Aluminum Clad Units in
Patio,French even Sliders! And we always
discount them 30% off list when ordering!

Atrium BRAND

Master Stylist To The Stars

Patti Lee
5-Star Hair Studio
972-966-6562
By Appointment Only Monday - Saturday

2920 F.M. 407, Suite 500
Highland Village, Texas 75077

Childress

Fabric & Furniture
Large Discount Outlet

Custom Built Furniture
Re-Upholstery
Draperies
Bedding
Large Room Trim

Furniture
And Fabric
By Top
Manufacturers
And Mills

Childress Family Since 1958

Largest Fabric Selection in the North Texas Area

**DALLAS
SHOWROOM**
2517 FERRIS ST.
DALLAS, TX 75226
PHONE: 214-565-0900
FAX: 214-565-8431

**FACTORY
LOCATION**
2512 FERRIS ST.
DALLAS, TX 75226
PHONE: 214-821-4444
FAX: 214-827-8752

**FRISCO
SHOWROOM**
8760 7TH ST.
FRISCO, TX 75226
PHONE: 469-633-1180
FAX: 469-633-1984

info@childressfabrics.com

www.childressfabrics.com

Nobody beats our deals

DALLAS
Gold & Silver
EXCHANGE, INC.

All Major Credit Cards Accepted.

City Mattress Factory

900 S. Haltom Rd. - Ft. Worth, Texas
1/2 mile South 121 & Haltom Rd.

Buy Your
"Mattress At The Factory"
Don't Pay Retail !!

Adjustable Beds
At Wholesale Prices!!

Dunlopillo Natural Latex Sleep Systems

Latex Will Out Last All Other Bedding Products

Conforms Perfectly To Your Body Contours

100% Dunlopillo Edge To Edge Greatly Reduces Pressure Points

Hypo-Allergenic

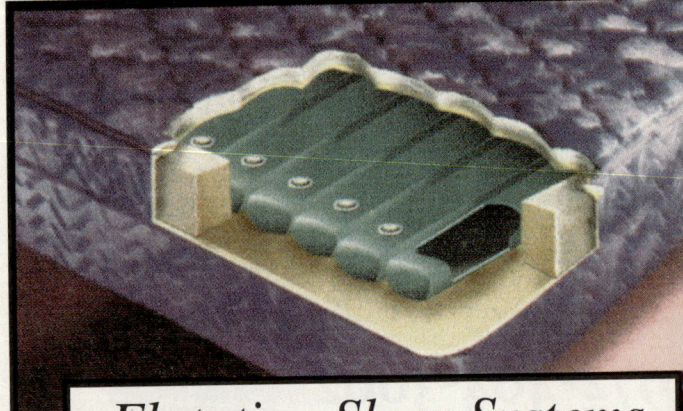

Flotation Sleep Systems

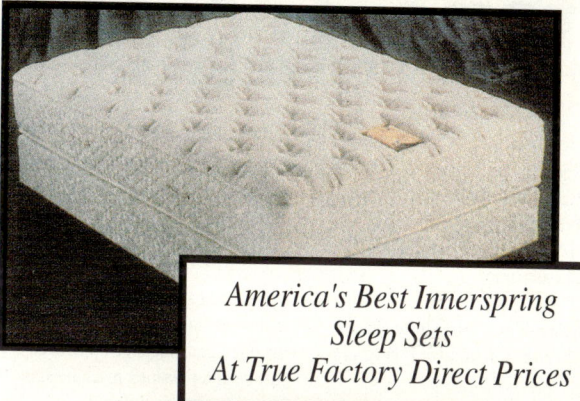

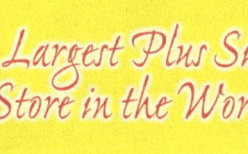

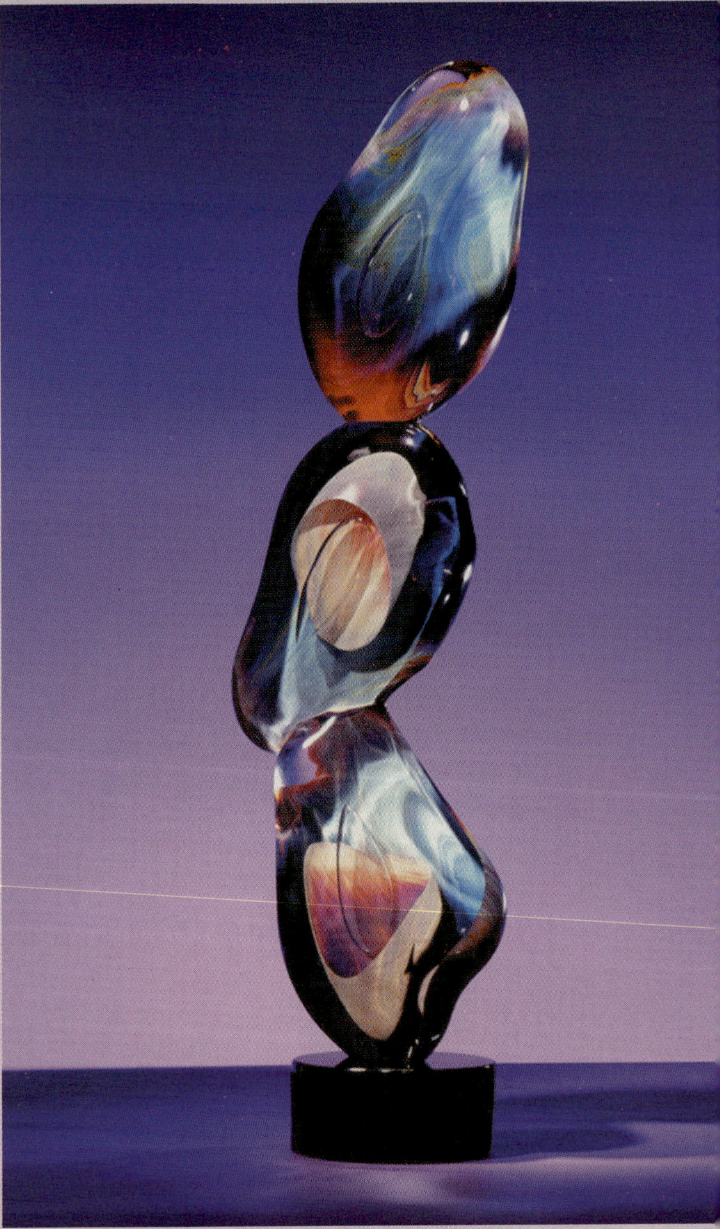

Fine Jewelry,

Loose Diamonds,

Hand Blown Art Glass,

and Luxury Gifts

Lincoln Park (Next to the Cheesecake Factory) • 214.691.0028

Dallas Galleria 972.490.6100 • Promenade Center 972.889.0440

www.zozza.com

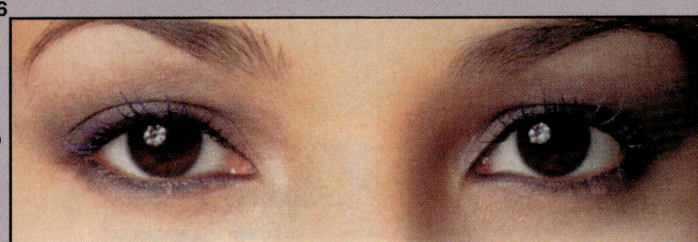

SAVE UP TO

50% OFF EYEWEAR

Name Brand Frames & Lenses at Discount Prices

FASHION
DISCOUNT OPTICAL

9:00am-5:30pm • Mon-Fri • 10am-4pm • Sat
All Major Brands • Fast Service

Progressive No-Line Bifocals $159.00
THE BEST FOR LESS

Everyday Low Prices
REGISTERED DISPENSING OPTICIAN
Prescription Required or Lenses Duplicated • Convenient Eye Exams Next Door

All Vision Care Discount Plans Accepted

3430 Oak Lawn Ave at Lemon • Dallas   1912 Beltline at Josey Lane • Carrollton

(214) **526-6006**   (972) **416-8200**

**Desktops • Notebooks
Workstation Servers • Monitors
Keyboards • Hard Drives •
Memory • Video, Sound and Network
Cards • Parts**

FURNITURE BUY

"Let Us Sell It For You"

★ FURNITURE

★ ANTIQUES

Furniture Buy Consignment
1340 W. Main St. • Lewisville
972-436-4389

CONSIGNMENT

Gently Used Quality Furniture

★ **HOME ACCESSORIES**

★ **ESTATE LIQUIDATION**

biggerbetterbargains.com

Furniture Buy Consignment
201 S. Mill • Lewisville
972-221-3878

Electronics • TV's • DVD's • VCR's •
Toys • Canned Goods • Cosmetics • Ho

WE BUY
OVERSTOCKS &
CLOSEOUTS
BY THE TRUCKLOAD SO
WE CAN SELL TO YOU AT
50-75% OFF
NORMAL RETAIL PRICES

BARGAIN HUNTING MADE EASY

SATURDAYS
ONLY

FRIDAYS: Noon-9pm

SATURDAYS: 9am-9pm
SUNDAYS: Noon-6pm

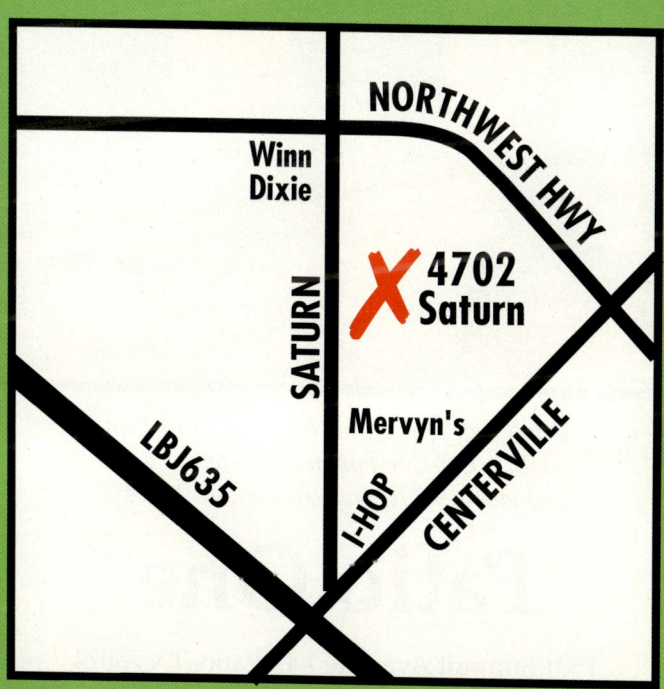

The place where North Texas comes to talk.

Ankarlo Mornings
Mornings 6-9 am

Glenn Beck
Middays 9 am-Noon

Scott Anderson
Middays Noon-3 pm

Greg Knapp
Afternoons 3-7 pm

Michael Savage
Evenings 7-9 pm

Clark Howard
Weeknights 9-Midnight

Talkradio 570 KLIF

The Dallas/Fort Worth Talk Radio Station

talk radio

570 KLIF

www.klif.com

Saturdays

Talkradio 570 KLIF
is Dallas/Fort Worth's interactive, informative and entertaining all talk radio station. Every time you turn us on, we're talking with YOU about today's news, real life events and pop culture-the things that affect YOU and the things that YOU and your friends and family are talking about. This is THE place where North Texas comes to talk.

Diva of Discounts with Sue Goldstein

Sue Goldstein, The Diva of Discounts, is live on Talkradio 570 KLIF. She can be heard Saturdays 2-4pm, Sue will take your calls, don't be shy, ask her anything—but only if it relates to her favorite four letter word—S.H.O.P. Call (214) 787-1570 or toll free (800) 583-1570.

For more information tune in to Talkradio 570 KLIF Saturdays 2-4pm or log on to www.biggerbetterbargains.com e-mail: askthediva@aol.com

Wheels with Ed Wallace

Ed Wallace Saturdays 8am-1pm

Wallace brings over two decades of knowledge working inside the automotive industry to his frank discussions on car manufacturers, new vehicles being released, and governmental issues facing the driving public. Wallace is both an automotive analyst and historian, who is often quoted in major newspapers across America for breaking automotive news and when historical background is needed on an automotive story.

For more information tune in to Talkradio 570 KLIF Saturdays 8am-1pm or log on to Ed's website: insideautomotive.aperian.com e-mail: ed-wallace@home.com

For a complete weekend line-up log on to www.klif.com.

$1299
Retail Value $2410
Bangle
1 CT. T.W.
14K Gold

$999
Retail Value $1850
Pendant
1 CT. T.W.
14K Gold

5TH AVE DINETTES & MORE

- Always Discounted 25% - 40% from Retail

- Featuring: Pastel, Whitaker, Ashley, Stoneville, Chromecraft and more

WHITAKER
FURNITURE COMPANY

biggerbetterbargains.com

ASHLEY FURNITURE INDUSTRIES, INC.

- Over 7,000 sq. ft. no pressure showroom

- No commission attitude

- Over 100 sets and barstools

- All styles and prices

14000 Stemmons Frwy.
(Between Valley View & Valwood Exits)
Farmers Branch, TX
972.241.5565

If you have ever dreamed of walking through the ornate doors of an elegant jewelry box filled with glittering diamonds, rubies and emeralds, all set in exquisitely designed settings of 14 and 18 kt. gold or platinum and at a price you can afford...your dreams can now come true.

Welcome to Diamontrigue where every man-made gemstone and fine piece of jewelry reflects the discrimination, pride and attention to detail of owner Judy Mason. Her passion and dedication to service and providing her customers with top-quality gems, chosen and separated from mass-marketed stones by their gemologist with nearly forty years of experience, is equal only to the excitement and mystique that jewels have evoked since ancient times.

Diamontrigue has dramatically increased their loyal following of discerning customers over the past twenty-three years. Their simulated gemstones are so close to perfection, expert gemologists have a difficult time distinguishing them from authentic gemstones. So will your friends?

Diamontrigue's clientele ranges from the newlywed couple with a $500 budget, to the business-woman wanting the image fine jewelry reflects without the added cost of insurance, to the wealthy client who wants duplications of their valuable pieces for travel and security.

If you want to look important, feel important and stay within your budget, enter the wonderful world of Diamontrigue.

biggerbetterbargains.com

Furnishing?
Decorating? Remodeling?

UCC

Total Home®

of Dallas

AROUND TOWN MOVES

All Trucks Are Maintained By Ryder Fleet Service

LOCAL & STATE WIDE MOVING
CALL FOR ESTIMATES & SERVICE NOW

✔ Free Use Of Wardrobe Boxes On Local Moves

✔ Expert Packing Services / Boxes

✔ Will Load & Unload Your Rental Truck

✔ Same Day Service - Throughout Texas

✔ Additional Cargo Insurance Available

✔ Exact Price Quotes On Apartment Moves

✔ Bonded & Insured

biggerbetterbargains.com

We'll Give You Something To

Talk About...

...by saving an extra $10 off your first purchase of $50 or more.

To receive this exclusive offer, just type:
www.overstock.com/bargains.html into your internet browser. The $10 discount will appear at checkout.

It's true! Now you can **save up to 70%** on thousands of your favorite **name brands**.

You'll find names like **Krups, Cuisinart, Fieldcrest, Mikasa,** and **Samsonite,** all at clearance prices that will leave your friends talking. **And shipping is cheap**—just $3.95 on all orders.

Brands & Bargains Happen Everyday at Overstock.com

At **Overstock.com**, we also help you **shop smarter**. You'll love how we help you find the perfect gift in our **Gift Center**. We **guarantee** that you'll find the **lowest prices** on the Web at **Overstock.com**.

Go ahead and share the secret with your friends. With the money you save, you're sure to be the talk of the town.

Name Brands at Clearance Prices.

ARLINGTON · ATLANTA · CHARLOTTE · DALLAS · HOUSTON · KANSAS CITY

ROMANTIC DRESSES!

The perfect dress, at the perfect price,
for your perfect special occasion.

Save up to 70% on over 50,000 dresses in stock!

Black Tie · Wedding · Dinner · Evening

Cruise Wear · Party · Mother · Pageant Gowns

Beaded · Sequin · Jackets · Tops · Evening Shoes

Jewelry · Handbags · Sizes 2-24

SPECIAL OCCASION DRESSES

Designer labels, not designer prices. Since 1987.

DALLAS	NORTH DALLAS	ARLINGTON	OUTLET
SW Corner Walnut Hill Ln. & I-75	19009 Preston Rd. 4 blocks N. of Frankford	Lincoln Square I-30 at Collins	1314 Inwood Rd. 4 blocks S. of I-35
214-691-1300	972-732-8900	817-226-0100	214-638-2900

Store hours: Mon.-Thurs. 10-8, Fri. & Sat. 10-6   Outlet hours: Mon.-Sat. 10-6   Visit www.specialoccasiondress.net

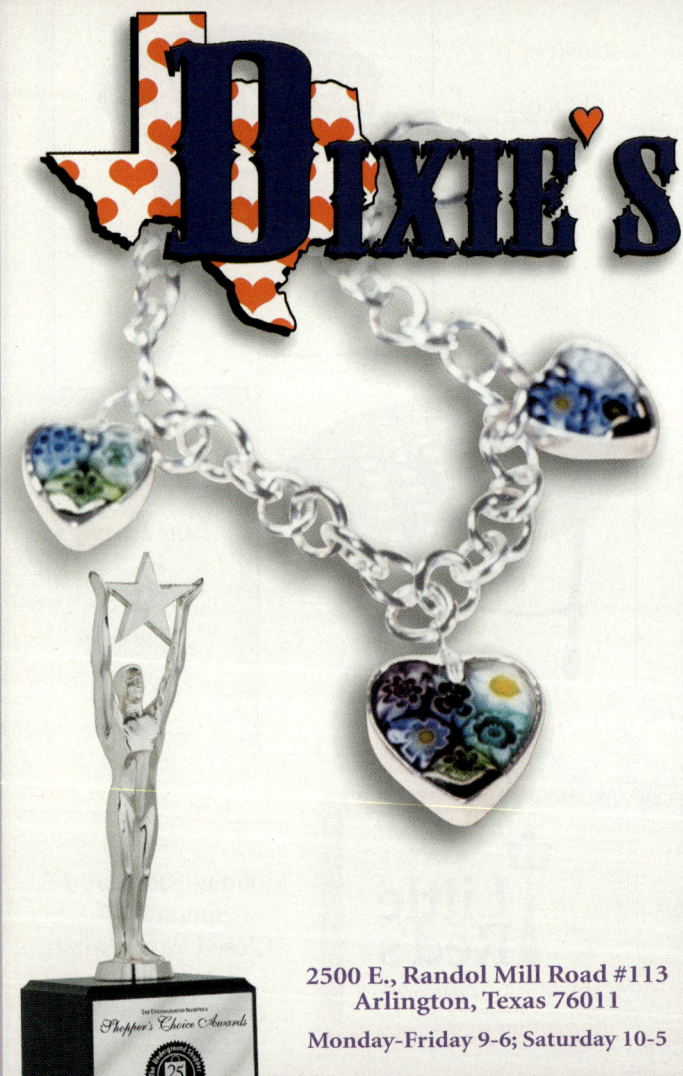

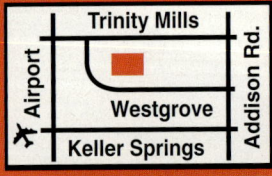

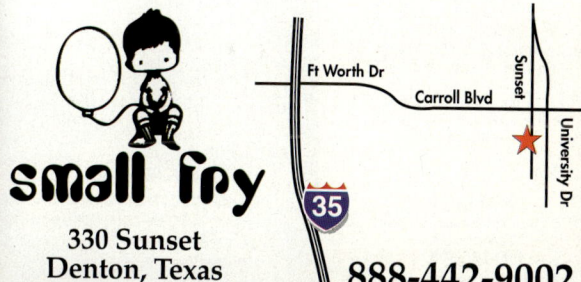

Unfortunately, wall-to-wall carpet is not machine-washable.

AVAILABLE THROUGH

S & H Carpet Distributing

800-880-1717

"We'll Beat Anyones Prices."

In Dallas:
8717 Director's Row
214-630-3311
(between Regal & Mockingbird)
Mon.-Fri. 9-5:30 • Sat. 9-3

In The Mid-Cities:
7305-A Grapevine Hwy.
N. Richland Hills
817-581-7777
Mon.-Fri. 9-6 • Sat. 9-3

In Temple:
4501 S. General Bruce Dr., Suite 60
Temple, TX
800-225-8083

For more information see our ad under flooring in your Southwestern Bell Yellow Pages.

Odor-Eaters™

Carpet Cushion System

FROM CARPENTER CO.

No Odors. No Stains. No Problems.

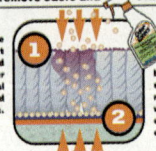

The Odor-Eaters™ Carpet Cushion System works both above and below the carpet to remove odors and stains

1 Above the carpet the Odor and Stain Remover treats topical stains and odors.

2 Below the carpet a moisture barrier prevents spills from saturating the cushion, while powerful enzymes eliminate offensive odors.

Now it's O.K. to breathe again.

✳ CARPENTER

Contact your Carpenter District Manager for more information.

www.carpenter.com

Handbags & Luggage

PS Bag 'n Baggage Outlet

11065 Petal St.
Dallas, TX 75238

214/355-3050
Mon-Fri 9-5:30; Sat 10-4
www.bagn-baggage.com

With 80 stores to date in eight states, I remember when previous owners came forth with the original Bag 'n Baggage Stores back in the mid seventies. They were the best retailers of luggage then and, with new owners, even better years later. With multiple locations in the Metroplex, there's always something on sale. Same with their store at Grapevine Mills. The Petal Street store is their service center, so quite often repaired pieces are left unclaimed and wind up in the outlet. Who cares from whence it came? Online, look for monthly specials that might include a FREE duffel bag with purchase of a two-piece set or money-saving deals on flasks, valets and **PALM PILOT** cases. You can also save with rebates, too. The complete lineup of brands sounds like the Red Book of Blue Bloods: **ANDIAMO**, **CROSS**, **DAKOTA**, **EAGLE CREEK**, **FOSSIL**, **FRENCH**, **GHURKA**, **HARTMANN**, **HUGO BOSCA**, **JACK GEORGES**, **JANSPORT**, **KENNETH COLE**, **KIPLING**, **LODIS**, **PATHFINDER**, **RETRO 1951**, **SAMSONITE**, **SCULLY**, **TIMBERLAND**, **THE SAK**, **TRAVELPRO**, **TUMI** and **ZERO HALIBURTON**. They also carry small leather goods and writing instruments from **MONTBLANC**, **WATERMAN** and others. They run periodic closeout sales at the outlet; that's when to take a trip.

★★ Cases Unlimited

10757 Mapleridge Drive
Dallas, TX 75238

214/343-3494
Mon-Fri 9-5:30; Sat 10-6; Sun Noon-5
www.casesunlimited.com

Case closed. This is a wholesale supplier of leather and vinyl attachés, briefcases, pens and accessories, so you won't have to travel the globe to find a world of difference. Find **AMERICAN TOURISTER**, **SAMSONITE** and **TRAVELWELL** luggage at sizeable savings, as well as **SEIKO** and **CITIZEN** watches. Shop in person or online, but head to their closeout section for substantial savings. And as if that weren't enough, they are also the Starwalk Party Rental Company that specializes in birthday parties, carnivals, church fundraisers and corporate events. And what exactly does Starwalk of Dallas do? They rent those giant inflatable slides, obstacle courses, fun houses, Joust, Bounce Houses (8' x 8' to 26'), castles, dragons, lions, ponies, clowns, sports games, carnival games, dunk tanks, concession stands—even generators. So if you're climbing the ladder of success, dress the part. If you're the boss and wanting to reward employees with incentive gifts, or if you want to take charge of your school carnival, this place has all bases covered. ***Call toll-free: 800/536-3496***

Dixie's Fashion Accessories Outlet
2500 E. Randol Mill Rd., Suite 113
Arlington, TX 76011

817/649-1112
Mon-Fri 9-6; Sat 10-5
www.dixieoutlet.com

You'll whistle Dixie when you cross over to this side of the Mason-Dixie's line. Scoring a home run is easy. Near the Ballpark at Arlington, you're but a hop, skip and a slide home to some of the best fashion accessories money can buy. When you dress-for-success, or just play dress-up in costume jewelry, the least you can do is buy it at wholesale prices (or below). Sterling silver is also a specialty alongside soft side bags and designer look-alike bags from such sought-after labels as **BRIGHTON** and **COACH**. Instead of paying hundreds, pay $30, $40, $50 and see if heads don't turn. When you see the **KATE SPADE'S**, you'll start loading up at the checkout counter. Choose from hundreds, no, thousands of accessories priced at 50-90 percent off retail. Who doesn't need another pair of earrings, anyway? For me, I've had to add another closet, just for handbags and jewelry. Create a priceless charm bracelet for grandma or a necklace of liquid silver. Say thanks to this family who rings in the New Year by not just getting older, but better. Now brace yourself. There's more. Lots of gift sets, bath products, leather accessories, sunglasses and more. Angel pins and seed beads are all the rage. Toe rings and bracelets...do they have bracelets. For the ankle, the wrist, charm bracelets, Christian bracelets, stone bracelets, name bracelets, glass bead bracelets, oh Dixie, how we love Dixie's. The Brighton-like sunglasses for $6.95 were snapped up two pair at a time. What a great gift. Sure looks like a $100 pair. I won't tell, will you? ***Call toll-free: 800/535-6825***

★★★★ J. Tiras Classic Handbags
5600 W. Lovers Lane, Suite 122
Dallas, TX 75225

214/956-8181
Mon-Sat 10-6
www.jtiras.com

Expensive handbags and fashion accessories are the classic inventory at J. Tiras. But it's online where the bargains are. There, you can really save 70-80 percent. During one visit to the store, I eyed those $60 tortoise-shell fold-up magnifying glasses, which I had seen earlier for $5 on Harry Hines. But that's not to say that their handbags are not good-looking (look-alikes from very famous designers) and trendy, that their jewelry is not glamorous and more expensive-looking than their price tags, or that every now and then you should abandon wisdom and blow your entire paycheck in one fell swoop. It happens to the best of us. Sometimes the items are just plain irresistible, like the leather bags with rattan handles, or the battery-operated curling irons, or the jelly band watches that match all those jelly-like flip-flops. Perfect for the beach and all your summer outfits. For $32, you can get the bands in clear, fuchsia, turquoise, smoke or purple. Well, you know my color's purple. But with the diamond-looking bezel, how could I resist? Online, you can see not only the jelly watches but jewelry, bags to do lunch with, fall classics, casual and evening bags, tote bags and more. Some were as low as $15 and some were just a tad under $500. But for a **JUDITH LEIBER** look-alike panda purse, it's worth every stare and compliment. (After all, at Neiman's, the real ones sell for thousands!) ***Call toll-free: 800/460-1990***

★★★★★ Leather Loft
3000 Grapevine Mills Pkwy. @ Hwy. 121
Hwy. 121
Grapevine, TX 76051

972/874-1695
Mon-Sat 10-9:30; Sun 11-8
www.leatherloft.com

There's a distinct smell of leather the minute you walk through the doors of this outlet store whose history is as rich as its feel. Find clothing, purses, luggage, small leather goods, belts and more, in leather and for all kinds of weather. Some of the best leather goods lines, including **BUXTON**, **NINE WEST**, **SKY-WAY** and **STONE MOUNTAIN** and all at 30-70 percent less. A 22-inch duffel, regularly $70, was reduced to $19.99. Belts were $4.99 each or three for $14.99, and wallets were as low as $4.99. If you're looking for leather, this is a great place to start. They travel the world in search of fine quality leather products and buy direct from the manufacturer. Leather Loft has roots that extend to Prussia over 100 years ago in conjunction with Shafmaster Leather Company. This family business, which was born with Levi Shafmaster handcrafting shoes in Prussia in the late 1800's, is steeped in deep discounts. After the sons immigrated to America in the early 1900s, they began shoe manufacturing in Lynn, Massachusetts. The foundation was laid and in order to continue manufacturing the best, they began their search for the best tanneries in the world. Today, there are over 120 Leather Loft Stores in factory outlet centers across the country. What a story! What a store!

Sam Moon Luggage & Gifts/ Handbags & Jewelry   972/488-1333

11429 and 11433 Harry Hines Blvd.   Mon-Sat 9-6:30
Dallas, TX 75229   www.sammoon.com (under construction)

Two stores and soon to be a block long, Sam Moon is flying high. Even extra-terrestrial beings have lined up to load up their space ships and return to sites unknown laden with the widest selection of handbags (next door), luggage, totes, briefcases, attachés, carry-ons and small leather goods that they have ever seen. Don't even think of traveling to any other place on earth without them. Here everything's discounted and only the finest names are carried: **AMERICAN TOURISTER**, **ATLANTIC**, **BRIGGS & RILEY**, **DELSEY**, **LEXI**, **SAMSONITE**, **TRAVEL GEAR**, **TRAVELWELL** and **TRAVEL PRO**. Get your boarding passes and get ready to ride first-class. Buckle up and return all trays to their full and upright position! Sam's your man. And since we're talking about this legendary Harry Hines honcho, you might as well know that, alongside their handbags next door, you'll probably see the largest costume jewelry selection in the Southwest. When the doors of their mega-showroom open at the northwest corner of Royal Lane and Harry Hines Blvd., I suppose you'll be there, in line, with miles of other bargain hunters behind you.

World Traveler   972/724-1638

Grapevine Mills   Mon-Sat 10-9:30; Sun 11-8
3000 Grapevine Mills Pkwy.   www.worldtraveler.com
Grapevine, TX 76051

If you have aspirations to be a world traveler, than look the part. Shop this Grapevine Mills outlet or hop aboard their website for all your travel needs. Pack 'em up, head 'em out, then fly away with the best of them. Save 20-70 percent and still get complete manufacturer's warranties, great customer service, and a lowest price guarantee. Excuse me, is there anything else you need to ask? Offering the largest selection of luggage I've ever seen and a 100 percent customer satisfaction guarantee, how can anyone not shop here? This is it! They didn't locate so close to the airport because they wanted to sell you a boom box! As an incentive, when you buy online you'll receive Double WorldPoints on your first order. Names that will go in the overhead compartments include: **AMERICAN TOURISTER**, **ATLANTIC**, **BRIGGS & RILEY**, **DAKOTA**, **DELSEY**, **HARTMANN**, **JANSPORT**, **KENNETH COLE**, **LARK**, **RICARDO/BEVERLY HILLS**, **SAMSONITE**, **SKYWAY**, **TRAVEL PRO**, **VENTURA** and **ZERO HALIBURTON**. Now to give you an example of why you need me, though I had an uncle who could get me Ventura luggage wholesale (but didn't), I found mine here at half price anyway. So there! You don't even need an uncle in the business to get it for wholesale! On another purchase, we found a Samsonite Aspire Expandable 30-inch upright suiter (not suitor—I've never met one that is expandable or was 30-inches anyway). That suiter retailed for $280 but was $118 here. I can't help it. That's their price. You got something against saving 60 percent? If so, you probably have something nice to say about flying in the cargo department! ***Call toll-free: 800/314-2247 (BAGS)***

32

Health & Fitness

◆◆◆◆◆ Abundant Life Health Foods
1130 W. Main
Lewisville, TX 75067

972/221-1210
Mon-Sat 8:30-7

Since 1975, this local health food store has seen the community grow by leaps and bounds—which only increases their reach to convert those aches and pains the natural way. The knowledgeable owner and other staff personnel take a real interest in your well-being and seem to know what nature had in mind as a remedy. Organic groceries, produce and herbs, grains and nuts, vitamins and minerals are part of their growing stock responses to what ails you. There's a real sense of camaraderie once you grab your cart and start down the aisles. Someone's always talking about the latest cure or the greatest skin cream. It's like over the garden fence, only it costs.

Breast Augmentation USA

www.breastaugusa.com

You've heard of a two-fer, but this is getting ridiculous. Using as their motto, "Get two boobs for the price of one," you may get the impression that their target audience is just babes. Au contraire. Any woman who wants to keep abreast of the most sought-after cosmetic procedure performed today would love, without sacrificing the quality, to get the job done for less. Enter these "board-certified" plastic surgeons who, like any other profession, have time on their hands (for use on other body parts). For example, when an appointment's cancelled, that time is wasted and every minute lost means lost revenues. It's money, honey, that makes the world go around and they'd rather book you than lose that operating room time. So, online, book your appointment and save a lot of money—probably 50 percent, as they imply. There's also a financing program where you can pay as little as $200 a month for the surgery. If you think you'd feel better and look better, this route is an option. And since these same surgeons perform the same kind of surgery on others who can afford to pay twice as much, who's going to ask you when you show up in your bikini? Like faux jewelry or shopping at an outlet store, no one's going to know the difference! If they ask, bust them in the mouth!

★★★★★ **Herb Mart**   972/270-6521
Market East Shopping Center   Mon-Sat 10-7; Thur 10-8
1515 Town East Blvd.
Mesquite, TX 75105

Spice up your life the natural "whey" at the Herb Mart. Get the popular **METABOLIFE**, 60 capsules for $6.95, or get the **MA HUNG** for $10.95. I almost fainted when they told me the price of Metabolife because the same bottle, strength and number of capsules was selling at Wal-Mart for $20. How could that be? Well, we shall see. Across from Town East Mall, savings of 50 percent on **NATURE'S WAY** is one of the reasons our blood coagulates when we see prices like this. Their everyday low prices make living an alternative life style almost worth living. Choose your poison:, **EMERGEN-C**, **GREEN MAGMAN**, **METABOLIFE**, **PRO-GEST CREAM**, **RICE DREAM** and dream on. Oh wellness, for goodness sake. Take the road less traveled, because soon, it won't be an alternative. It might even be mainstream medicine because many of the homeopathic and natural remedies actually work. Duh!

◆◆◆◆◆ **Natural Health Therapies/Dr. James Snow**   903/564-7600
Optimal Natural Health   By Appt./Thursdays Only
11661 Preston Rd., Suite 140
Dallas, TX 75234

Want the best massage at the lowest prices in town? What about a homeopathic session where Doc (Bachelor of Science in Anatomy, D.C., Doctor of Chiropractic Medicine, DNBHE —Diplomat of National Board of Homeopathic Examiners, RMT, Registered Massage Therapist...enough credentials to do most anything healthy) can tell you his secrets of herbs and minerals and why they work. (Need an endorsement? Just ask me.) Buy the kit of homeopathic remedies and every ache, pain and symptom I've experienced disappears with one little homeopathic pill dissolved under my tongue. I am a believer. You also can have Doc and his partner/wife Carolyn Jo, both registered massage therapists, provide any number of therapeutic massages on a weekly basis: $45 an hour for existing patients (that includes the wear and tear on his car from his hour's drive each Thursday from his new homeopathic clinic in Whitesboro, Natural Health Therapies, 2508 Highway 82 East, Whitesboro 76273) or $50 an hour for new patients. Get in a few chiropractic adjustments if you need them and you've just gotten the best deal in town. Be sure to drink plenty of water afterward because it works as a natural detox and you might be a little sore if you don't. Individual and couple massages work wonders for everyone. Whatever skill and power in laying on of the hands, they possess it. And don't even question its magic appeal—it works. Now, even insurance companies are recognizing its therapeutic benefits. Try it...you'll like it. Call for your Thursday appointment. See why folks fly in specifically for their regular sessions. They book up fast and as long as they save an hour for me, I won't hesitate recommending them forever. *Call toll-free: 877/485-8350*

◆◆◆◆ **Natural Silhouettes**   817/263-0014
Wedgewood Shopping Center   Tue-Fri 10-5; Sat 11-3
5316 Trail Lake Drive
Fort Worth, TX 76133

Natural Silhouettes understands that the search for breast prosthetics and bras is not only a challenging task but an emotional one as well. This staff is great. Not only are they certified but they will also offer their fashion consulting expertise, understanding and style to have you looking your best and feeling your best, too. Let them be the support you need, from bra fitting to wig design, hats and medical make-up. Donna's Wigs is located just inside their shop for added convenience. You won't have to go through the hassle of shopping around when it's this important. Make it a one-stop shop at this location or their other store at 1600 Central, Suite 157 in Bedford, located in the Respiratory Connection in the Oaks Shopping Center.

◆◆◆◆ Relax the Back Store   972/277-BACK

624 Lincoln Square   Mon-Fri 10-8; Sat 10-6; Sun 1-5
I-30 and North Collins   www.relaxtheback.com
Arlington, TX 76011

Lighten the load and relax your back. Unwind, loosen up, settle down and Relax the Back. Feeling more than just a knife in your back? Don't worry, be happy in a classic recliner for $995. Since 1984, they are now considered the largest and most innovative back store in the world. They also carry a wide selection of pillows, wedges and even motion beds for sleep problems. Find posture-pedic chairs for the office and lumbar support rolls and neck supports for traveling. If working out has you looking out for your back, then try your choice of heating pads, $30, back supports and magnetic gloves for just $30. Don't forget your aqua barbells and jogging belts, because what could be better than working out in the pool? Kind of your own in-house chiropractor. Relax at other locations: 5425 W. Lovers Lane across from the Inwood Theatre, Dallas, 214/357-3529; 6031 Camp Bowie Blvd., Fort Worth, 817/732-6797; and two Plano locations at 8612 Preston Rd., Suite 107, 972/668-2225 and the Texas Back Institute at 6300 W. Parker Rd., 972/943-1814.

★★★ SNS-Sports Nutrition Source   214/361-1328

5500 Greenville Ave., Suite 1105   Mon-Fri 10-7; Sat 10-5; Sun 1-5
Dallas, TX 75206   www.snsonline.com

Attention weekend warriors! Get all the fuel you need without spending that weekly paycheck. SNS-Sports Nutrition Source, along with their Frequent Feeder Cards ($20 annually), keep fitness buffs eating their cake and vitamins, too. Hey, sport, if you're looking for the edge and you need a washboard stomach, buff up here. You'll find knowledgeable sales personnel and supplements, a winning combination for success. Forget Phen-Fen or any other chemical enhancements. Get your vitamins, herbs, protein powders, meal replacements and sports nutrition products for less. Try their **FEM FIT**, **FAST FOOD**, **NORANDROGEN**, **ANDRO**, **BIG DADDY** and others at one-third off national products with your Frequent Feeder card as well as the SNS brand products. If you have a GNC card, you can trade it in for an SNS card—for FREE. Check directory for additional locations. ***Call toll-free: 800/583-6999***

★★★★★ Vitamin World   972/234-5030

607 S. Plano Rd.   Mon-Sat 10-9; Sun Noon-6
Richardson Square Mall #3607   www.vitaminworld.com
Richardson, TX 75081

How can you go wrong with a return policy that allows you to return the product for up to one full year if you are not completely satisfied? Okay, I give up. Vitamin World's a king pin in the world of vitamins—they also own **NATURE'S BOUNTY** and **PURITAN'S PRIDE**, their sister mail order business. Located off the food court by Ross, if you've outgrown your size 14, you might want to consider VW's weight control answer called **METABOSURGE** (compares to **METABOLIFE**) which sells for $14.95 a bottle or **CHITOSAN** (which has also become a hugely popular item, pardon the expression). For $12.94 a bottle, you might not lose a lot of money, but lose a lot of weight. If you're working out and need to gain weight (LOL—right!), power up with **PROTOPLEX** powder supplements. They were on sale for $23.99, and **CREATINE** capsules were $11.94. Don't let achy joints stop you with joint maintenance remedies starting at just $8.44. Even children's vitamins were as low as $1.49 a bottle, and that was for a two-month supply of 60 tablets. Beats putting them on Ritalin for a lifetime. Now for Fido. If she's having a little trouble getting around, hopping up on your couch, or jumping into bed with you, then get with their program of pet products. Something for everyone from vitamins and minerals to antioxidants, nutritional supplements, digestive aids, eye nutrients, nutritional oils, pain relief, teas and even books if you need help getting started on the road to good health. Plenty of locations in the 972 area codes: Town East Mall in Mesquite, Irving Square Mall in Irving, Allen Premium Outlets in Allen, Stonebriar Centre in Frisco, Valley View Mall in Dallas, The Parks at Arlington in Arlington, Grapevine Mills in Grapevine, Fort Worth Outlet Square in Fort Worth, Tanger Factory Outlet Center in Terrell. It's a Vitamin World after all...

◆◆◆◆ **Xpect First Aid**   **972/774-9777**
13766 Beta Road   Mon-Fri 8-5
Dallas, TX 75244

Got a boo-boo at work? Then get with the program. First aid supplies, kits, cabinets and van-delivery safety products are what you can expect from Xpect. This also includes safety glasses, hearing and respiratory protection products. Whether your business is large or small, if you've got employees' welfare to consider, then consider this company's services. Have employees lifting heavy boxes or equipment? Well, don't let them scream out in pain. Make sure they're wearing some kind of back support. Get those here, too. And if you want someone designated as a First Aid specialist, perhaps you want them to provide a CPR/first aid training class or the OSHA Compliance training program. I know, I know. You didn't know who to call. That's why you need me. And I love to feel needed. Bring in the emergency oxygen—I can't breathe. Be prepared. It's more than just the Boy Scout's motto. *Call toll-free: 800/878-7152*

★★★★★ **Years to Your Health**   **972/579-7042**
503 E. 2nd St.   Mon-Fri 10-6; Sat 10-5
Irving, TX 75060   www.yearstoyourhealth.com

Cheers to Years to your Health. They're alive and well after 17 years and seeing green. Learn the difference between kola and Coca-Cola.® Open your eyes to more than 500 botanicals at 30-40 percent less than traditional health-food stores. For the past 15 years, this company's got a healthy outlook on business. Serve up one of the largest selections in the country of bulk herbs, pot-pourris, spices, teas, candles, books, jewelry and vegetarian vitamins and then you'll be able to write your own ticket to retirement. At least you'll be alive and well. They also offer their own private label line to keep costs under control. Herbs are the spice of life, from powdered versions to capsules. They also have homeopathic aids, tinctures, essential oils and flower remedies, cosmetics and environmentally-safe products. Savor their medicinal arsenal before running to the emergency room. (But check with your doctor first.) Take Herbs 101, and get your Ph.D. in spices. Maybe an alternative to prescription drugs? A healing remedy? Quartz crystals and gemstones, tissue-cleansing, massage oils, astrology, flower essences, vibrational medicine, mysticism and herbs for health and spiritual use? Tea blends included Root Beer Tonic for $2.75/ounce, Fruit Tea for $1.75/ounce, Night-Time Tea for $2.60/ounce. Try natural cocoa butter, five ounces for $4.15; jojoba oil for $3.35 for 1/2 ounce; garlic capsules, $4.40 for 50; or bee pollen for $5.35 for 50 caps. Think you know it all? Well, get a whiff of Native American raw tobacco twists, braided sweetgrass or sage, crystals and gemstones in clusters, points, wands, spheres, eggs, carved animals or other shapes. There's always a special going on, and if you want to save more then consider buying in bulk. Then you can really save 30-50 percent off the usual and customary high-price health food store prices. Soak in the charms of beautiful crystals (rumored to cure headaches). Drink some aloe vera juice (a concentrate of Orange-Papaya was recommended) for an ulcer or upset stomach; or maybe order up some authentic fresh-squeezed, yucky-tasting aloe juice. Still not satiated? Then buy some oils, powders and homeopathic compounds, and have them brewed, ground or pureed. Want to create your own personal pot-pourri, or sip gingerly on a cup of tea blends or spices? Then have at it. They also sell individual herbs, empty containers with glass droppers, clear glass, amber glass and white plastic, herbal formulas, natural oils, pure cosmetic ingredients as well as gift certificates. If you start now, and buy some stuff, you'll live long enough to go back to buy some more. *Call toll-free: 800/860-7042*

33

Home Improvement

★★★★ Acme Brick
10550 Plano Rd.
Dallas, TX 75243

214/348-4978
Mon-Fri 8-5; Sat 8-3
www.acmebrick.com

Based in Fort Worth, this company is as solid as a ton of bricks. As the official brick of the Dallas Cowboys and the Kansas City Chiefs, I'd say it's a great line of defense. Besides, it comes with a 100- year guarantee which is more than Troy-bilt! Their Acme king-size brick is a best seller. Why? Because it's more economical due to lower labor cost, lower mortar cost and faster construction. Look for **ACME**, **MANNINGTON** and **PAVESTONE** bricks and tiles. While bricks and stones may break your bones, don't let them break your pocketbook. Expect factory-direct pricing and professional sales personnel to guide you down the path of least resistance. It's the source for creating a glass block window, a dividing wall, a skylight and a full line of masonry accessories, ceramic tile, fireplace systems, even pool coping. Enjoy Acme pavers and special brick shapes, and learn more about the Troy Aikman Foundation. Once you've shopped ACME BRICK, you see why this company's been paving the way into Metroplex homes since 1891. Since they're also connected to **AMERICA TILE**, you can spruce up your entry way, your kitchen, bath...well any room for that matter, with beautiful ceramic tile. They only carry the premium tile from **ENDICOTT**, Italian glazed tile from **CERIM**, **TERRA NOVA**, and their own Acme Quarry Tile. For do-it-yourselfers, tile away the hours with their stock of tile sealers, cleaners, setting materials and grout. It's not my fault your entry way looks like the St. Andreas fault, so get moving to ACME BRICK. Save money, save time, and get it done right! Check directory for other locations.

◆◆◆◆◆ Advanced Foundation Repair
5601 W. Jefferson Blvd.
Dallas, TX 75211

214/333-0003
Mon-Fri 8-5

They stand behind their work while you can stand inside their work (and not have the world crashing in around you.) Superior support from a company that stands behind their work. They'll even do more than repairs. How about renovations to your home? Want to convert your one-story ranch-style house to a two-story? They'll do a free estimate that you can bank on. They are the ones to tell you if your foundation can stand up under the strain, or if you'll need a little more support. Kind of like woman's undergarments. You don't want anything sagging—and these are the folks to set the record straight. Do not pay just any foundation repair company. These are the professionals who go the extra mile by backing their claims and their work with a $400,000 cash trust account in the bank for your protection. Besides, they offer a lifetime transferable warranty, which means, when you go, it stays with the new owners. Talk about a selling point. They do it all: steel pilings to bedrock, pressed pilings, drilled piers, pier and beam, pressure grouting and drainage corrections. Though pretty technical, don't worry. If you've got a foundation problem, they can rectify it. ***Call toll-free: 800/405-8880***

♦♦♦♦♦ Affinity Designs, Inc.   972/539-7380
Lewisville, TX   By Appt. Only

If you have an affinity for nice things, then consider adding this company to your roster. If you need quality decorating or storage solutions that meet your standards of excellence and beauty, this firm builds custom shelf-systems and cabinetry, entertainment centers and accent furniture. *From Here to Affinity*, everything will be in its place.

♦♦♦♦♦ Affordable Inspections   972/263-1007 (metro)
1601 East Lamar, Suite 210   By Appt. Only
Arlington, TX 76011

This is one service that's a no-brainer when buying or selling a house. Call these folks when you need a house or termite inspection. Around since 1985, their on-the-spot instant computer inspection is very impressive as well as thorough. Have piece of mind when buying that house that there's no bugs eating away at the rafters or faulty wiring that can lead to an explosion. These are experts in their fields who spend several hours going through your house with a fine-tooth comb. When they're finished, you can ask for a computer printout of the inspection. Affordable and immeasurable is the backbone of their service.

♦♦♦♦♦ Amazing Siding   817/329-8830
Grapevine, TX   By Appt. Only (Mon 1-8; Tue-Fri 9-8; Sat 9-1)
                                                   www.amazingsiding.com

Amazing grace is all we can say about Amazing Siding—the first company to offer a lifetime function of the structure warranty covering both the vinyl and the insulation in the siding business. With the reputation of an industry where siding salesmen are considered lower than low, this company also warrants their workmanship in writing—for a lifetime of the house (and yes, it's transferable to the next owner). Amazing! They also provide those efficient vinyl replacement windows with similar guarantees. Vinyl siding sure looks good and is available in a variety of styles, textures and colors. Select from many different clapboard widths in horizontal or vertical styles. Choose smooth or wood grain finishes along with a full line of accessories, including shutters, soffits, fascia, and trim. Just think, no more painting, ever! Save 30-50 percent over Sears' prices and consider your home to be your "vinyl resting place." They also do custom replacement windows, too. They have an impeccable rating with the BBB (unlike many of their competitors). They are based in Grapevine, but serve the entire Metroplex. In fact, they do the same Amazing Siding service coast-to-coast.

♦♦♦♦♦ American Eagle Builders   817/588-2050
401 Crowley Rd.   Mon-Fri 9-5
Arlington, TX 76012   www.americaneaglebuilders.com

Okay, so they're not selling storm/tornado shelters since they've discovered a problem with them floating out of the ground, everything else they do stays put. At least they caught the problem in time.

Otherwise, these remodelers continue to soar in the eyes of the folks at *Qualified Remodeler Magazine*. One of the largest home remodelers in the country, just take a look at the quality of their workmanship, with an eagle's eye. For the past 15 years or so, you can call upon them for exterior home improvement, siding, roofing, windows, carports, perma strait wall systems, patio covers, gutters, soffit, fascia and more. If you tell them you've seen it on their website, listen to this...you'll get your choice of a free storm door or three sets of shutters. Their slogan, "Made in Texas by Texans".
Call toll-free: 800/788-3245

★★★★★ **American Service Center** 972/681-2222

15330 LBJ Freeway, #210 Daily 7-7
Mesquite, TX 76150 www.americanservicecenter.com

Open sesame! This company is a **GENIE** and **LIFT MASTER** authorized dealer where you can get factory-direct, same-day service on your garage doors. Other brands are available too, like the **AMARR** 24-gauge steel garage doors that start as low as $299 installed. They offer several different sizes and qualities alongside the Genie Pro Screw Drive garage door opener. This garage door offers a direct drive for maximum lifting force, a one-piece solid-steel screw for added strength and security, fewer moving parts for more years of reliability, a quieter operation and an automatic 120-watt lighting system for safer evening entries and exits. It also has a high-impact, heat-resistant polypropylene lens cover for easy bulb replacement. Protect your cars, your garage contents, and the security to your home. FREE estimates for repairs, too. Like, do you need the springs, glass, cables, or chains replaced? Uniformed techs are in radio-dispatched trucks and can somehow magically appear to rescue you—if the garage doors do not open (not if you're in your car on Central Expressway.) Serving the entire Metroplex, but in Fort Worth, you need to call 817/436-3000 and in North Dallas, call 972/335-5885. Whether it's garage doors and openers, residential or commercial installation, repair or replacement, this center can get you up and down in no time. And new this year, are the retractable **DURASOL** awnings. Easy does it, maintenance-free design on these custom-made awnings. Available in a wide range of colors and designs, free consultations are also provided. Available in Dallas and surrounding areas only. Call the number above.

★★★ **Anchor Paint Co.** 972/699-0151

715 N. Central Expwy. Mon-Fri 7-5; Sat 7-Noon
Richardson, TX 75080 www.anchorpaint.com

It's anchors away if you plan on painting the town red with the paint from this company. Since 1962, you can shop where the professional painters shop but if you want a special color, expect a 50-gallon minimum. Flat, semi-gloss, oil-based glosses, latex enamel, undercoats, drywall sealer, water repellants, masonry sealer, primers, stains, varnish, stain killers and elastomeric coatings are available. Even specialty items like oil based Safety colors, hi-temp silicone, tar epoxy and communication tower paints can be found. But if you're a homeowner, I doubt if you're thinking about painting the towers of KXAS anytime soon. Special requirements for coatings can also be requested. Besides all this technical stuff, they carry a complete stock of paint supplies for the do-it-yourselfer. Since this paint is made in their own Tulsa, Oklahoma factory and sold via their own outlets, you can moor the savings because they've eliminated the middleman. Make sure you stay cool, though. I don't want you suffering from "brush stroke!"

★★★ Appliance Fixx
1311 E. Belt Line Rd., #3
Carrollton, TX 75006

972/466-0808
Mon-Fri 9-5:30; Sat 10-4
www.appliancefixx.com

If you were not born with a propensity towards being Mr. or Mrs. Fix-it, this place may be able to service you with a smile. But most of their business today is selling washers, dryers, stoves, wall ovens, side by side refrigerators and stand-alone freezers that they've fixed and can be bought for a lot less than new. Brands include **AMANA**, **DACOR**, **GENERAL ELECTRIC**, **HOTPOINT**, **JENN-AIR**, **KITCHENAID**, **ROPER** and **WHIRLPOOL**. Join the counter culture with counter top and under-the-counter microwaves, dishwashers and disposals, too. Looking for a part? This is part and parcel of their service, too. Make appointments online and save yourself a phone call. This company does it all. They service most makes and models of appliances, sell the parts, and sell you the appliances, too. Talk about meeting a need and filling it! Between Josey and Old Denton Road in Carrollton and another location at 629 E. Jefferson, Dallas, TX 75203; 214/946-WASH (9274)—just northeast of Zang Blvd. Trust these guys—they've got a decade of years in the business under their fix-it belts.

Around Town Moves
6700 Harry Hines
Dallas, TX 75235

214/350-3873
By Appt. Only

When it comes to getting around town with your life's worth of home furnishings, this is the company to call. Since 1994, this husband and wife-owned company (the Greg Mitchell's) have commandeered a crew of 15-20 able-bodied men who lend their helping hands (and back) in helping you make the move. Whether up or down, across town or down to the Rio Grande, this company can be trusted. Expect their prices to be extremely competitive (having come in several times as the lowest bid). They can move you from one place to the next, across town or around the state with men who know the difference between an armoire and an armadillo. Whichever you treasure most, you want them carried in compassionate hands. Well, this week they moved my lawyer, my next door neighbor, my niece and a friend of a friend. If I can trust them to move pianos, antiques, computers, and all of my friends and family, don't you want them to move you, too? They can put your stuff in their trucks, whether it's for a commercial or residential move. Then, to save even more, if you want to rent your own truck, they can still help you out by providing the manpower to load and unload. Same day service on most jobs, but if you're moving the 15th floor of your office or a 20,000 square foot estate, forget it if it's at the end of the month. They need a few days to squeeze you in because everybody likes to move at the end of the month. Why do mortgage companies and landlords like to start the clock running on the first? If you want them to be the movers while you're the shakers, that's fine with them. Call Greg or Sherman to schedule a moving date.

★★★★★ Bath-Tec
5142 Hwy. 34 W.
Ennis, TX 75119

972/646-5279
Mon-Fri 8-5
www.bathtec.com

Bath-tec manufactures a complete line of luxury acrylic whirlpool bathtubs, soaking tubs and shower bases for residential construction and the lodging industry. They offer factory-direct pricing (my favorite words) plus quality and craftsmanship all rolled into one. Soak in an acrylic whirlpool bath, invite a friend into a two-person whirlpool, or wash off in an acrylic shower manufactured from durable, easy-to-clean, high-gloss, cast acrylic that should get you spic 'n span. Lather up for years. Their shower bases have a slip resistant surface, built-in flange, raised dam to prevent water leakage over the threshold and they're easy to install. (Right!) They come in a variety of sizes and colors with optional chrome or brass drains. Want a whirlpool faucet set in polished chrome, polished brass with lacquer coating? Or if you're into the Hollywood lifestyle, what about the 24K gold-plated waterfall or Roman-fountain faucet? Buy more than one, and the prices go even lower. The tubs' standard features include choice of white or bone color (additional colors, additional charges), six adjustable jets, trim is color coordinated, commercial quality pump, deck-mounted air switch buttons, rubber pump pad and a safety suction system. Though there are many standard features, nothing is set in stone, just acrylic, and although standard is more than expected, expect to pay more for additional bells and whistles. Me, I had to have the mood lighting. What about you? They make 18 different whirlpool bath styles. Take 45 south towards Houston, to Highway 251 (the Ennis/Kaufman exit). At the stop sign, turn right and go to the third red light. Then turn right at the four-way stoplight. Follow that road over the reservoir approximately .8 of a mile to Bath-Tec. Fortunately, you don't have to do the backstroke back. *Call toll-free: 800/526-3301*

◆◆◆◆◆ BCS Foundation Repair   817/534-2192
6412 Crawford Lane E.   Mon-Fri 8-5
Forrest Hill, TX 76119   www.BCSfoundationrepair.com

Formerly Brown's Construction/Awning Co, it's now firmly planted in the ground of foundation repair with a lifetime transferable warranty. And this is no B(C)S. In business since 1970, thirty years later, they are one of the leaders in the foundation repair business where they operate from the same location in south Fort Worth. When Bob retired, his son-in-law, Corey Ingram, and Corey's partner, Craig Powers took charge. Though other competitors may promise a lifetime guarantee, read the fine print. They often have loopholes with no intention of ever being honored. This is totally unacceptable to BCS. They will survive because of their core values: The company has endured due to its three core values: Honesty, Trust and Integrity. It believes that foundations should be fixed one time, the right way. Foundation problems never fix themselves, so call a company that you can count on. Going above and beyond the local ordinance requirements, they ensure that the job is done right the first time. Taking on one repair job at a time, they've not wanted to spread themselves too thin and dilute their promise of superb customer service. If you've noticed a shift in your foundation, their company's solid as a rock. *Call toll-free: 888/282-7822.*

◆◆ Better Shelf Co., The   972/578-1760
Plano, TX   By Appt. Only
                                                   www.bettershelf.com

Founded in 1977 by Lee and Pat Pfoutz (and they're still running the show), why break your back bending and reaching for that sauté pan or that waffle maker somewhere in the back of your cabinet? If you had rollout shelving, life will be good. So, organize your cupboards, your cabinets, your drawers by installing their custom-made models, or do-it-yourself for less. All come with a 90-day guarantee even with the Do-It-Yourself manual. If you don't like it, send it back for a full refund. Featured on the Discovery Channel's, "Your New House," if it is good enough to be touted on national TV, imagine how lucky we are in the Metroplex to have the founders based here.

Binford Supply Co.

972/286-2881
Mon-Fri 8-5; Sat 8-Noon

2915 Hickory Tree Rd.
Mesquite, TX 75180

Not exactly "Tool Time" with Tim Allen but Binford Supply will put you on the right path to savings. Actually, they'll keep you fenced in so you can't get lost. How would like yours, pine or chain-link? Do you want your wood treated for the elements? Whatever, this wholesale fence supplier invites you to take the do-it-yourself challenge. Serving the Metroplex since 1950, this company has sold to fence contractors all that time. But now, you too can build yourself a fortress with a surround-around fence, gates included. You can buy the materials and let a fence company install it, saving you considerable money; or you can "contract-it-yourself" and save even more. Go ahead, and watch those fingers.

★★ Bosch Factory Service Center

972/241-5385
Mon-Fri 8-5

2457 Walnut Ridge St.
Dallas, TX 75229

Grab when you see the blue and don't let go. A Bosch power tool has a blue color around it and then you know you've got the real McCoy. Why buy **BOSCH**? Well, first, they're very quiet, comfortable in your hand, lightweight and easy to use. Designed differently than most other tools with an easy-grip handle. You can handle it. You don't have to be a member of the Vice Squad to put a stop to paying full price for power tools with the name Bosch or **SKIL**. Bosch drill, 18V, was $179 (new $249) or a 13V with just as much torque was $129. Now, we're striking pay dirt. A Skil saw was a drop in the bucket for $34. Rebuilt routers cost about $100, jigsaws from $30-$100. How do they sell them so cheap? Well, simple. They're all refurbished—though they look like, work like, and are new to you, so who's looking? So new? Off Stemmons and Walnut Hill, go east on Walnut Hill and left at the second light, Abels. Turn left. Look for it at the corner of Abels and Walnut Ridge.

◆◆◆◆◆ Brennan Enterprises

972/660-3106
Mon-Fri 8-5
www.brennancorp.com

608 Grand Ave.
Arlington, TX 76013

Serving the entire state of Texas, this lone star provider has many stars on their client list. Offering siding, windows, roofing and enclosures including accessories such as gutters, shutters, solar screens and other relevant exterior building products, you can expect a fair price for an excellent product installed without a hitch. The **CERTAINTEED** vinyl windows are practically maintenance free. Another brand to consider is **GREAT LAKES** for windows. Both are choices well spent. Over 50 years in the home improvement business, this is a second-generation family-owned contractors. If you need an exterior job done, call on the big boys at Brennan. References provided upon request. Do not scrimp on home improvement projects that require a sizeable expenditure. You want it done right the first time around and provided by a reliable company who doesn't hire its crews from the street corner's "work for food" job pool.

★★★★★ Builder's Surplus

817/831-3600
Tue-Fri 9-6; Sat 9-4

6016 E. Belknap
Haltom City, TX 76117

There could never be too many cabinets in my kitchen. When you're ready to remodel for lack of space, don't make one move until you've seen the likes of Builder's Surplus. Cabinets by **CDI** and **WESTERN** should give you a clue that they're cookin' with class. The bulk of their inventory is of the high-end caliber, though they do have one builder's grade of cabinet called **ARISTOCRAT**. Bring in your measurements (no lying, please!) and they will computer generate an entire layout for you, in color no less. This color rendition will show you exactly the coloring of your cabinets, appliances and walls, should you decide to paint them, too. What a "before" and "after" transformation. Of course, if they don't have what you're looking for, they will order it for you and still save you a ton of money. Other products abound for many home improvement projects: **ATRIUM** windows and doors, **H & R WINDOWS**, **STANLEY**, **WILSONART** and more. Then, consider bottoms up—how about ceramic tile and vinyl flooring at prices you can stand on? Then move on to other name brand doors, countertops, tools, locks…the list is endless. The service is down home and right on.

★★★★★ Cabinet Depot Inc. (CDI)   214/637-5514
3004 Irving Blvd.   Mon-Fri 9-5; Sat 9-12
Dallas, TX 75247   www.arrowwoodcab.com

Since 1997, Cabinet Depot has been selling **ARROWWOOD CABINETRY** direct-to-the-public via their showrooms in the Metroplex and San Antonio. You don't have to be a mental giant to get into the groove. If you lack design know-how, CDI offers a professional award-winning design staff to help create that dream kitchen or bath. Located between Inwood and Mockingbird, in the heart of the Industrial District, CDI sells fine cabinetry from **CARDELL CABINETRY** and **KITCHENCRAFT**. You won't run out of options since there are almost 6,000 in-stock cabinets to choose from within their 45,000 square foot expanse. Higher in quality than what you get at the typical Home Centers yet lower in price. Yippee! Choose from a wide variety of styles, unique finishes and accessories. They even offer computer generated drawings so you can visualize the final product. Consider, too, the variety of options to design your efficient home office, entertainment center, bookcases or other cabinetry for your home or office. Cash and carry or have their installers do it for you. Knock on wood, now you can shop where the professionals have been shopping all these years.

◆◆◆◆ California Closets   972/550-0409
4441 Lovers Lane   Mon-Fri 8-5; Sat 8-8
Dallas, TX 75225   www.calclosets.com

Let's face it, when you organize your home, you simplify your life. Discover space you didn't even know you had by adding racks, shelves, bins and baskets for the most versatile storage ever. Head to the top of the class with the luxury of their handcrafted Italian line, Paradiso. Truly an "A" in quality and design. See what design fits your lifestyle best. Just call for a free in-home consultation. Whether you need to organize the closets, garage, pantry, laundry room, storage shed or even make a custom unit for the den, it'll seem like hundreds of square footage has been added to your home in storage space alone. Now, what will you do without all that clutter? We shutter at the thought of a well-organized home but the idea is inviting. So invite California Closets in and put away more than just dust bunnies.

◆◆◆◆ Classy Closets   972/355-7687
1565 W. Main St., #208-233   By Appt. Only
Lewisville, TX 75067   www.classyclosets.com

These are some Classy Closets. Jerry and Andrew, at your service, will create the best-looking, most functional, user-friendly environment your home or office will ever know. Not only do they create a sight to behold, their on-site systems are something to behold. Maximizing every square inch of space——be it your closet, your office, garage or pantry, everything will then have a place and everything's in its place. What a deal! But the best is the way they customize your space, put in that Murphy-type bed that disappears into a closet, even give you a choice of laminates that look like wood grains. See for yourself why they're number 1 in my book. In home estimates and design ideas given freely, while keeping your budget in mind. *Call toll-free: 888-CLOSET8*

◆◆◆◆◆ Climate Works
101 E. Renfro St.
Burleson, TX 76097

817/426-3366
Mon-Fri 8-5 By Appt. Only
www.climateworks.com

Keeping their cool since 1985, you can expect both 24-hour emergency service and same day service if either your heating or air-conditioner has gone on the blink. Then, if you want to get them working again, call on Climate Works. Because they want to be the best, they have their own sheet metal shop in-house; at least the work is sure to be fast and done right. Carrying their own brand helps to improve the quality of air indoors with air cleaners, humidifiers and CO detectors. Financing is available if you're in a pinch. They can also service all makes and models like **FRIGIDAIRE**, **LENNOX** and **TRANE**.

◆◆◆◆ Closet Factory, The
3313 Garden Brook
Dallas, TX 75234

972/620-0606
Mon-Fri 9-5 (By Appt. Only)
www.closetfactory.com

When you factor in all of your purchases, shopping the BBB way, you'll need bigger and better closets. No doubt, you've already figured that your drawers are over-flowing and your closet poles are bowing in the middle with all that weight. So, call on The Closet Factory about making room for Daddy's stuff and yours, too. Though you won't pay for installation, you will pay for custom workmanship (though affordable). They offer a free in-home planning session, which can last as long as an hour in the planning stage. Custom-built garage organizers and modular office spaces are also part of their repertoire. And if you think white is the only color choice, think again. With the added features as their SafeDrawer for storing valuables and The Jewel, a Lucite marvel for displaying jewelry, how can you resist? We couldn't. *Call toll-free: 800/692-5673*

◆◆◆◆◆ Closets by Design
Dallas, TX

972/361-0010
By Appt. Only
www.closetsbydesign.com

And the winner please! With all the closet organizers in town, who is the fairest of them all? Is price the only object? What about quality of workmanship and products? Closets by Design was founded in 1982 by European developer Rafael Feig who specialized in condominiums and large custom home developments. He understood how to utilize space and what homeowners wanted most—the proper use of space. He customized the closets not only to maximize space, but to also add real value to the home, both in increased property value and the enhanced quality of life. After all, what woman on earth doesn't aspire to a hundred pairs of shoes? Closets By Design was born in LA and today has 27 franchisers around the country, including one in the Metroplex. Their products are not only superbly crafted but also come with a lifetime guarantee. Now we're talking. Chances are, though, you'll never have to call upon the guarantee. But rather call upon them next to transform your garage, your kid's playroom, your home office or your media room. They're the best. All installers are bonded and insured. And their price guarantee is your insurance that nobody will beat their prices. *Call toll free: 800/By Design*

★★ Dallas Plumbing & Air-Conditioning
11055 Plano Rd.
Dallas, TX 75238

214/340-6300
Mon-Fri 8-5; Sat 9-Noon

Whether it's coming through the vents or out through the pipes, Dallas Plumbing & Air-Conditioning can keep your flush. Since 1903, they've been providing 24-hour emergency service and installation of **CARRIER** A/C units or they will repair what you've got. The showroom glistens with chrome and glass fixtures for your kitchen and bath. Builders and plumbers have utilized their services for name-brand plumbing supplies that are laid to rest on their showroom shelves. If you're a pro, or in the know as a handy Andy and would rather do-it-yourself, you can save about 25 percent on products. Service calls, though, are no bargain, in fact, steep. Unless you want to put your finger in the dike, when you have a leak, don't think cheap.

◆◆◆◆◆ Dempsey Electrical Services   972/247-8995
11005 Indian Trail, #107   24-Hour Emergency Service
Dallas, TX 75229

So watt's up, doc? These are the guys to turn to when everything goes dark. Don't be a hero. Call them. They're fast and professional, whether your electrical snafu is of a residential, commercial or industrial nature. After 40 years, no job too small, or too big. In fact, they were out in no time just to install a single wall sconce. Licensed and bonded for your protection, call on them for an evaluation of how to save on electricity. Then expect to save on your utility bills, too. Don't get your wires crossed. From fuse and breaker replacements to the installation of light fixtures, room additions, security lighting, aluminum wiring repaired and replacement, computer wiring, swimming pools, parking lot lighting, maintenance and new construction, electrical issues, they mean business— citywide.

★★★★★ Denton County Surplus   940/365-2889
Off University and 377 Crossroads   Mon-Fri 8:30-5; Sat 8-2
Denton, TX

At last, you can capitalize on someone else's lost arch, or a French door at $250. Why would you spend twice the price if you could pick it up without needing any translation? Oui, Oui, Messieurs. Entry doors, well, they were as low as $75, and one low, low price for a carport should get your motor running. Now in their expanded warehouse, you can conclude your weekend seek and search mission with something from here. Always save 50 percent...on windows, doors...well, it's surplus and a whole lot more!

◆◆◆◆◆ Devard's Heat, Air, Electric & Plumbing   972/422-1506
2710 S. Rigsbee, Suite A   Mon-Fri 8-5; Sat 8-1 (or By Appt.)
Plano, TX 75074

Expect to pay a $69 check-up charge for their spring or fall check-up calls, but when there's a break-down in your air, heat, plumbing or electrical system, they prefer to quote by the job. Train yourself to call them for service on all **TRANE** heating and air-conditioning systems and units, though they service any make or model. Consider them, too, for any project left incomplete on your "honey-do" list. Whether it's hanging that ceiling fan or creating a French drain in your yard, these folks are available for many of life's little problems. Regardless of your home or office needs, they can be your conduit to maintaining the good life. Just don't sweat the small stuff!

DFW Windows & Doors   972/378-0188
Plano, TX   By Appt. Only
                          www.dfwwindows.com

Best 100 SHOPPING DESTINATIONS

Dan Miller is the doctor of windows and doors. Take the pane out of paying full price when your utility bills continue to soar to beyond triple digits. It's bad enough to weather the weather in Texas, you shouldn't have to bare the burden of supporting the utility company, too. With ten years in business, DFW Windows and Doors is the manufacturer of quality aluminum and vinyl windows at discount prices. Aluminum windows come with a ten-year warranty, and vinyl windows have a lifetime warranty against seal failure. Just think, your utility bill will show a savings of 25 percent to as much as 40 percent per month. True? Just ask the doctor! They also sell and install vinyl siding. With the best installers in the business, they take great pride in their work and have hundreds of references in case you want someone else's experience to prove their net worth. Multiple window colors are available to match or contrast brick or siding as well as a myriad of different types of glass and windows. Same day or next day installation guaranteed. With the best prices in the Metroplex, give them a call cause Dan's my man. Don't waste money; check with them first before making a decision. Phone quotes are available; or simply log on and take advantage of their Internet Special: "Free storm door with installation of 14 replacement windows." Such a deal!

★★★★ Discount Countertops   214/951-0313
4735 Almond Ave.   Mon-Fri 8-Noon, 1-5
Dallas, TX 75247   www.discountcountertops.com

Between Mockingbird and Irving Boulevard, look atop for Discount Countertops, a family-owned business since 1990. Join the counter-revolution and get yours custom-made. Get them discounted for your kitchen, bar, computer workstation, even an entertainment center. They even fabricate to your specs...and that's no lie. FREE estimates and measuring done in-house (in your house or office), including additional remodeling finish-outs where required. A one-stop shop for discountcountertops. Save 30 percent over Home Expo's prices, but expect to wait weeks. They're booked floor to ceiling, but especially in between.

★★★★★ Elliott's Hardware   214/634-9900
4901 Maple   Mon-Fri 8-6; Sat 9-5
Dallas, TX 75235   www.elliottshardware.com

Kneepads' deep and 120,000 items later, this 51-year business keeps getting better. Since 1947, Jerre and Kathleen Elliott probably never thought they'd wind up like this—one of the best hardware superstores in the country. While discount home centers strangle the competition, they're more like an "Energizer Bunny" that keeps multiplying. However, if it's not the lowest price, it's more than competitive. Besides, the inventory is so extensive, their personnel so knowledgeable and they're so targeted, there isn't a nut, bolt or screw that's not priced right for you. Combining the elements of an old-fashioned hardware store with the 21st century state-of-the-art inventory tracking system and parts list, its' one of the best places to go for a manly gift or housewares for the home. This is the store that holds more hardware and home improvement gizmos, gadgets and goodies than a leopard has spots. Get an Elliott's Key Customer Card for a buy one, get one free on every key you have made. Plus, you'll be eligible for monthly door prizes, in-store specials with key tags hanging for extra savings, a year-round paint sale, notice of new merchandise and easy check writing services. There are more advantages to joining, but it's a good place to start. Besides, it's free! Buy what you need and rent what you don't. Take the challenge in Plano at Coit Rd. and West Park Blvd. and in Grapevine at 108 W. Northwest Hwy. at Main, 817/424-1424.

◆◆◆◆◆ Fashion Glass & Mirror   972/223-8936
585 S. Beckley Ave.   Mon-Fri 9-5
Desoto, TX 75115   www.fashionglass.com

This company's a glass act. For over a quarter of a century, they have managed to stay clear of any "tarnishment" to their impeccable reputation. They're all trained professionals serving the Metroplex from three locations including Desoto (above—the main branch), their north branch in Justin and a southwest branch in Arlington. With 35 fully equipped trucks running their "gl-ass" around town, they not only provide the service, but they're fast, too. Glass appears magically from their stocked trucks with inventory from their 43,000-square-foot manufacturing plant. What do they sell? Well, let's start with custom mirrors, frameless shower doors, tub enclosures, special ½" thick frameless shower units, and mirrored bi-pass doors for starters. Add leaded glass, etched glass, insulated glass, glass tops for tables and as you can see, their specialty is glass. Ask no more questions. They're the ones to call. Since 1973, they will work within your budget, travel to any part of the Metroplex, and provide a one-year limited warranty on any mirror, shower door or mirrored wardrobe door they've installed. So, if you're glass-conscious about the best, Fashion Glass and Mirror is it! *Call toll-free: 800/289-8936*

Ferguson Bath & Kitchen Gallery
2220 Duluth Drive
Arlington, TX 76013

817/261-2561
Mon-Fri 8-5
www.ferginc.com

If you're the nation's largest distributor of plumbing supplies, pipe, valves and fittings (PVC) and the third largest for heating and cooling supplies, they must have all their little duckies in a row. Selling plumbing supplies since 1953, today there are 10 locations in the Metroplex area including Grapevine, Denton, Fort Worth, Dallas, Arlington, McKinney, Rowlett, Euless and Plano. So, look around, then turn around and head to Ferguson's. Tap into the faucets and fixtures for the bar, bidet, kitchen, lavatory, Roman tub, tubs and showers. Looking for sinks with pedestals, wall mounts, bar, kitchen, laundry or maybe just a new toilet, shower pan, tub or tub and shower unit, whirlpools and shower doors, all this displayed artfully in their showroom? Any of these names ring a bell? **ALSONS CORPORATION, AMEREC PRODUCTS, BALDWIN BRASS, DELTA FAUCET** Co., **DUPONT CORIAN SURFACES, ELKAY MANUFACTURING** Co., **GROHE AMERICA,** Inc., **JACUZZI WHIRLPOOL BATH, JADO, KALLISTA,** Inc., **KITCHENAID, KOHLER** Co., **KWC FAUCETS, MOEN INCORPORATED, NUTONE, ONDINE, PRICE PFISTER, PHYLRICH INTERNATIONAL, ROBERN, ROCAILLE, SEA GULL LIGHTING PRODUCTS,** Inc., **STEAMIST** Co., Inc., St. **THOMAS, WHIRLPOOL**— well, don't settle for less. Now why don't you "Skip to their loo!"

Fireplace & Grill Factory Outlet
4301 Westgrove
Addison, TX 75001

972/250-2006
Mon-Sat 10-6

Got gas and you haven't eaten any beans? Well, don't fret. **GOLDEN BLOUNT** has a solution for either a gas grill or a gas fireplace. That's their specialty. If you're looking for a "Good Grill Hunting," then target your sites on the Fireplace and Grill Factory Outlet. Load up on the most impressive, state-of-the-art grill (or slap-on-the-burgers on your own George Foreman version.) When all is said and done, you're getting the same rare, medium, and well-done fixin's but why not consider the best—for less? Located behind the Addison Airport, the **TEXAS SIZZLER** by **GOLDEN BLOUNT** is the ultimate in infrared cooking. Their manufacturing company is right next-door. The grill is all stainless steel. No flare-ups, has a convection oven with the highest technology in the market today. Besides, it's $2,000 less than the TEC model that they also sell. When the patent ran out on the TEC last year, they stepped up to the plate and made one that is almost identical—all except the price. It can even deep fry, steam veggies and be used as a griddle. It even looks like a grill that a restaurant might use that cost thousands more. Then when winter rolls around, cuddle up around the gasfireplace. They custom-make doors that are solid brass and are hand-made for your hearth. Vice President Steven Blount will even come out to provide a written estimate. But remember, if you have not had gas previously installed, then forget it. Sorry, the zoning ordinances about propane tanks out back are generally prohibited. But back to the gas logs. Theirs is called the "Texas Bonfire" and looks so real, you can wage a bet and win. If you're fed up with cleaning out the grate every time you fire up, then this version is ideal. Since 1970, they've been discounting their own products in their outlet. Stamp out forest fires and turn on the gas here.

★★★★ Fixtures of America   214/638-5990
2229 Valdina   Mon-Fri 8:30-5; Sat By Appt.
Dallas, TX 752-7

Get a mixture of fixtures at up to 75 percent off. That's right. Need extra shelving for the garage, your office, the kids' room? Though prices vary between individual fixtures depending on size, condition and where they acquired them, they know their stuff. For example, before they could show me some clothing rounders so we could display clothes for TV, we got the third degree. Was it to be stationary or moveable? What were our height requirements? Did we want one that was adjustable? See what I mean? Then, we moved on to the Z racks and although they rarely get them in, they did have some in stock. You don't have to be a store to shop here. Some of the fixtures make for great organizers for all the stuff that piles up over the years. Some of them are even good-looking enough to use as a display cabinet. Exit Wycliff off Stemmons and go west to Valdina. They buy and sell quality used fixtures, including a sizable selection of showcases. No one can outdo them on prices. Don't overlook items such as cube units, ètagere and glass gondolas, shelving, signs, showcases, double bars, bags, hat racks, slat and grid wall accessories, peg hooks, rounder and rolling racks, counters, two-, three-, four- and six-way clothes racks as they make great closet additions, garage organizers or accent pieces. Take your list and go for it. Call ahead if you've got some particular needs in mind.

★★★★★ Four Seasons Design & Remodeling   817/334-0367
710 S. Main St.   Mon-Fri 8-5; Sat 8-1
Fort Worth, TX 76104

Brett was all set to arrange for an appointment at my convenience, of course, to come out and discuss all of my remodeling needs (little did he expect I wanted a model's figure, too). Once they've determined the needs for a particular project, in a few days, you've got a written estimate. That's the quick part. With you're OK, they begin the process of building you that much needed sunroom? Patio room or any kind of room addition for that matter. What matters next is ordering the materials, which should arrive in approximately four to six weeks. Then, it's hammer away and who knows how long that will take? Any time of the year, you can add their glass enclosed, double-paned, argon gas-filled windows or choose wood or aluminum. Usually, they'll install a heat pump for heating and cooling, but if necessary, ductwork can be included. Stop moaning about not having your own private space. This could be the place!

◆◆◆◆◆ Free Construction Co.   972/613-4432
Garland, TX 75043   By Appt. Only

Free to be you and me. And if anybody can, Geary Free can. Not to be misconstrued as a Free service, though Free does provide the service. His reasonable prices for quality repairs may be closer to Free than you think. But let's face it; you can't stay in business at giveaway prices. You know the old saying, "You get what you paid for!" But if you can at least afford it, you'd be better off than before you started. Tile work, light electrical and plumbing, minor roof repairs, painting, fences, decks, sprinkler repairs, if it's broken, call and see if it's something for Free. Free estimates, for sure. Just don't call him to do any masonry work. That's where he draws the line. Free to do whatever you please from laying new floors to repairing the roof. Hey, don't fence me in unless of course you need a fence installed or repaired. His phone is often forwarded to his house; so don't be surprised if his stepson answers. A week or two in advance is how he prefers his appointment set, but if it's an emergency, he'll try to accommodate.

G & S Sales
4303 Hwy. 80 W.
PO Box 949
Terrell, TX 75160

972/563-7821
Mon-Fri 8-5:30; Sat 8-5
www.building-materials.com

Don't even think about it. Buying your home improvement supplies anywhere else but G & S Sales is like not buying candy at a candy store. There's a sucker born every day. But here, you can lick high prices away. Five acres of everything including the kitchen sink. Carpet, cabinets, whirlpools, shingles, portable buildings, sinks, exterior shutters (painted, $2.99 a pair). Holy Moley! They probably should be called the 8th wonder of the world. That's probably why homeowners come from hundreds of miles to pay cash and carry. They do, however, offer delivery. Offering a vast selection of doors, paint, flooring, plumbing supplies, windows, cabinets, lumber and more, seeing is believing. A white 60" corner **WHIRLPOOL** (complete with ¾ pump) was $649.95; **ARMSTRONG** Laminate Flooring was $2.49 square foot; white lattice was $9.95 (5/8 4 x 8; and 20-feet of sheet metal (22 gauge) was $19.95 a sheet. Surplus, seconds, overruns, discontinued products or products that the home centers didn't sell...who cares? It's all here under one roof. *Call toll-free: 800/926-9534*

◆◆◆◆◆ Garage Storage Cabinets
Richardson, TX

972/239-5850
By Appt. Only

Can't pull the old **JEEP** into the garage for fear of running over the baseball bats, balls, golf clubs, birdcages, cartons of the *Bachelor Book* and more? Then, get with the program and unclutter that garage. Are you afraid if you parked your car where it belongs, you'd never find it when you needed it? These and other garage problems are handled by calling on these doctors of garage-ology. FREE estimates gladly given with a five-year limited warranty on storage systems that include cabinets, hanging systems, shelves, bins and drawers, pegboards, workbenches and more. It means, though, if you don't load the kitchen sink onto one of the shelves and expect it to be standing in the morning? The best part of their service? Units are not permanent fixtures, so when you go, they can go, too. Just think what the neighbors will say! All construction is made of solid wood, not pressboard. So press on to your FREE estimate.

H2O Wholesale Plumbing
2324 N. I-35 East
Carrollton, TX 75006

972/242-2289
Mon-Fri 8-5; Sat 8-1
www.h2osupply.net

You're all wet if you don't shop at H2O for wholesale prices on all your plumbing supplies. No, we're not suggesting you see a urologist. This is plumbing for your home. Keep your budget dry when buying a **WHIRLPOOL** tub, or faucets, water heaters, toilets, showerheads, pipes, values, fittings, fixtures and more. Let this Katz out of the bag and reap the benefits of his niche——plumbing. It's an easy way to go and flow. After all, that's all they do and they are experts at it. Why settle for less? Get all the major brands, the latest variety of plumbing fixtures, expert advice and ease of shopping. Roll it all up with toilet paper and you'll stay flush. The walls are filled with artfully designed faucets from bold geometrics to contemporary styles made by **ELJER**, **GROHE**, **HARDEN**, **PRICE-PFISTER**, **RUNDLE**, **UNIVERSAL** and more. No ifs, ands or buts, for the discriminating kitchen or baths, they offer stainless and colored sinks and the most functional and sleek faucets. Save 25-50 percent off retail and forget throwing any more money down the drain.

Habitat for Humanity/ReStore
3020 Bryan St.
Dallas, TX 75204

214/827-9083
Mon-Sat 10-6
www.dallas-habitat.org

As they continue to look for bigger and better warehouse space, this building-materials store launched almost four years ago is goin' and blowin'. Habitat for Humanity is one of the most noble of charities. Now under the hands of Fred Foster, former general manager for the Dallas Symphony Association, their goal is to raise $4 million for new headquarters, thereby enabling them to serve more families, institute a home-buyer's education program and expand their volunteer program so they can build more homes. Their dream is to increase building from 65 to 100 homes. Their current 12,000 square foot warehouse is busting at the seams, the pipes and the boards are ready to relocate but until they find a new home, cheapskates can make hay while the sun shines. Thischaritable treasure is a virtual hotbed of bargains. They not only they sell stuff cheap, but the proceeds benefit a worthy cause. Habitat for Humanity, in case you need enlightening, provides low-income housing for the needy. So buying your next new or used appliance, doors, windows, floor tile, tubs, sinks, plumbing supplies, flooring, hardware, fixtures, wiring and more for your next home improvement project makes perfectly good cents here. Everything is 50-80 percent off. New lighting fixtures are half off wholesale. Read that again. Half off wholesale. Remember, all purchases are tax deductible; all donations are greeted with open arms. Fort Worth's ReStore sells surplus new and used building materials, too, at the same solid discounts. Their second location is another manna from heaven at 3420 S. Grove St., 817/926-3585, Fort Worth, www.habitat.org/restore. Double jeopardy, though, as Restore means a whole new life for someone in need and another in greed. Saw a brass chandelier for $3, door knobs for $1, grout and paint cans for $1, doors for $15, used appliances for $60, the list is endless, the bargains divine.

◆◆◆◆ Handyman Connection
2351 W. Northwest Hwy., #2122
Dallas, TX 75220

972/361-0009
By Appt. Only
www.handymanconnection.com

In 1990, Arthur Newman was in charge of his condo maintenance committee. When he discovered he couldn't find handymen to handle small repair jobs and minor remodeling, he founded a company that could. Filling a void in the marketplace and...a business is born. Soon they were franchising and now there's a connection throughout the US and Canada with expansion daily. Retired craftsman and other experts offer low-cost home repairs and remodeling with their guarantee in writing. From fixing that squeaky wheel on your office chair to laying ceramic tile in your kitchen, if it doesn't require a building permit (like roofing, concrete work, fences, siding, or anything complicated or competitive), they can get the job done for you. They will save you approximately 25 percent on small- to mid-range home repairs throughout the Metroplex, including painting, installing fans, hanging garage doors, carpentry, minor plumbing and electrical jobs. These handymen have a list a half-mile long of what they WON'T do, such as structural work, but at least you'll have someone who'll show up. They bid by the job and try to keep their costs low by not driving fancy trucks or wearing monogrammed uniforms. There is no charge for a service call to evaluate a problem and they're ready to go to work immediately with your acceptance of the job. All of their repairmen have more than 10 years experience and they guarantee their work for one year. However, they insist you buy the materials so you avoid that markup. Labor is their contribution to the job well done. If you're not married to a handy man, then hire one and live happily ever after. Here's their limits: Carpentry, electrical, plumbing, painting, drywall, ceramic tile, kitchen and bath remodeling—basically, small to medium-size handyman jobs.

★★★★ Harbor Freight Tools   972/231-1872

1704 E. Belt Line Rd.   Mon-Fri 8-6; Sat 8:30-5:30; Sun 10-4
Richardson, TX 75081   www.harborfreight.com

Where do all the boys go for their toys? Probably to Harbor Freight Tools, the popular mail order catalog company that has entered the Metroplex with an outlet store. For the tools of the trade, you've probably heard of Harbor Freight Tools. They're a huge mail order company that I've talked about for years. Well, they've opened an outlet store on Belt Line in Richardson and another in Fort Worth (5268 Trail Lake Dr., Fort Worth, 817/370-1892.) Hammer away with the guaranteed lowest prices. Her "honey-do" list is finally within the realm of possibilities: An 18v Cordless VSR Drill/Driver was $49.97 instead of $72.99; a 12 V Jump-Start System and Power Supply for $39.99 instead of $69.99; Tool Boxes for $24.99; Tool Belts for $16.99. Then load up on all the $1 tools like screwdrivers or $2.50 wrenches and you, too, can be a weekend warrior tooling around town. Everything that's a tool, you fool, for your workbench, garden equipment, car equipment, grill items, even some craft items with the savings of 40-60 percent off the "Big Boys" prices. Popular scooters were $16.99 and for $49.99, complete that project with either a 5-speed drill press or 8" compound miter. Dying for a tarp? What about an air tool? You can rest assred this store's not just filled with hot air. ***Call toll-free: 800/423-2567***

★★★★ Home Depot   972/869-0330

6501 N.E. Loop 820   24 Hours/7 Days
North Richland Hills, TX 76180   www.homedepot.com

Add a little water and watch them grow. After 25 years, they are now the world's largest home improvement retailer. Seven years in a row, Fortune Magazine has voted them "America's Most Admired Specialty Retailer". Could it be their orange aprons? Sign your kid up for a home crafts' project on Saturdays, and let them experience a home improvement project like building a birdhouse. They'll receive a kids' size FREE apron just for that effort. A do-it-yourselfer discount supermarket with fork lifts and miles of aisles, they also cater to the construction and buildingmaintenance professionals, each store stocks approximately 40,000 to 50,000 different kinds of building, home improvement and lawn and garden products. On the weekend, after a weather disaster, after a drought, men are lined up at the checkout counters ten deep. Classes for grownups, too. Ask in the respective department for schedule.

◆◆◆◆◆ Home Town Plumbing Co.   972/564-5151

Forney, TX   By Appt. Only

You're never plumb out of luck if you have Home Town Plumbing Co. on your speed dial. Don't even input any other plumber into your sewage system. They are the best and the most affordable. Trust me. Trust my toilet. I've stayed flush over the years because these folks, who are not only as handy as the day is long, but bring their snake just in case. They'll never let you go down the drain. They guarantee your complete satisfaction, 24-hour service (their beeper # is 972/585-6468) and seniors get an additional discount. Do you know where your plumbers are? On site with plumbing a new house or office, repairing or remodeling a home or office, installing faucets and other plumbing fixtures, putting in new water heater. If it's a plumb job...they are the ones to call. They can remove an old tub and install a **JACUZZI** in their sleep. But they're never sleepwalking. They're alert, reliable, trustworthy, capable and certified plumbers. Don't call for second best; these are my Home Town Plumbers. Make them yours, too. Lifetime warranties on workmanship, how can you lose?

★★★★★ IMC (International Marble Collection)   972/241-7796

11210 Zodiac Lane   Mon-Fri 7:30-5; Sat 9-Noon
Dallas, TX 75229

Top quality stone tile in marble, granite, slate and limestone plus marble fireplaces…just don't take this distributor for granite. Periodically, their weekend blow-out sales offer prices that are almost too good to be true (like 99 cents/per square foot.) Of course, all sales are final and expect cash and carry to be the norm. Nevertheless, this is where the contractors shop, so why not shop there, too and pay the price BEFORE their markup is tacked on? Great resource for island tops, vanity counters, even a gravestone for your departed best friend (your dog.) Located East of I-35 and south of Royal Lane, upscale your home with the contemporary look of the 21st century. Delivery service is available. *Call toll-free: 800/929-4462*

◆◆◆◆◆ J & M Glass Co./Thermal Windows   214/630-5885

1201 Empire Central   Mon-Fri 8-5; Sat 9-1
Dallas, TX 75247   www.thermalwindowsdfw.com

Since 1979, Thermal Windows has been custom-manufacturing some of the highest quality, most energy-efficient window systems for residential and commercial construction. That means—your house or your office. Few windows can match the performance, durability, security or ease of operation that is standard on all of their window systems. They were even discovered by Sabrina Smith for "Sabrina's Solutions" on Channel 5 (same station that the Diva's on!) I wonder who discovered them first? You guessed it. We found it. We shopped it. And we loved it. Here you'll find storm doors, exterior doors and sliding patio doors with beautiful and artistic glass options. Window selections range from solid vinyl windows and storm windows to thermal barrier aluminum windows. Looking for a wood windows or a patio door? No problem, they offer products by **VETTER** who has been making wood windows for over 100 years With a full fabrication facility and one of the most experienced in-house installation crews in the southwest, they do their own installation and service work,) give them a call and start saving today. FREE delivery within Dallas-Fort Worth area (100 mile area radius).So, if your A/C or heating bills are giving you a "pane in your pocketbook," consider the cost-saving ability of thermal replacement windows. You won't believe how much you'll save, regardless of which utility company you pick. *Call toll-free: 800/339-3697*

◆◆◆◆◆ J.J.'s Window Service   972/479-1302

705 N. Bowser Rd., Suite 102   Mon-Fri 8-5
Richardson, TX 75083

Can't see a thing through the fog or film on your windows? That's where J.J.'s comes into the picture (window). Serving the Metroplex for more than 10 years, J.J.'s really knows their stuff. Let them show you the world without seeing them through fog-covered glasses. Through thick and thin, let them do all the cutting up in the back of their warehouse. Then, all of your windows and doors can be replaced with new glass, insulated glass, storm windows, solar screens, utility screens and patio doors. Double and triple-plated glass only with a 10-year warranty. Make sure to ask, "How much?" They will not be undersold (they even give FREE estimates.) But don't bother asking about front screen doors—they don't do them. The more windows you buy the better the price! Whether you've got small windows, odd sizes windows…no problem! They will gladly come to your home FREE of charge and give you a price quote. Installation is always included in the final price. But since they are a small company, with big growing "panes," don't expect them to offer same-day service.

★★★★ Joe Wallis Co.   817/335-1295
401 Bryan Ave.   Mon-Fri 8-4:30
Fort Worth, TX 76104

This company's got a firm grip on lockers. You know, the kind that you used when you were in elementary or high school and taped your favorite pin-up to? Anyway, if you need one, this is the place to buy them since they're the ones who make them. Joe Wallis has been a major supplier of lockers to schools for decades. Now, you, too, can expect that the lockers runneth over and are available for sale to the general public. Overruns and used lockers can be adopted and put to many good uses. Adapt them for any number of uses for your home or office. Specially, a used locker painted to fit into the scheme of things for a child's bedroom or your garage can be the perfect storage solution to any crowded condition. Used lockers start at $35 and then escalate from there depending on size and condition. New lockers, too. Delivery is available for $30. If you're price shopping, simply fax Tim at the fax number above and he'll put together a list of prices and options to meet your needs. Ah, the possibilities are endless——great place to store sporting goods, toys, lawn equipment, office supplies, even doggie treats. Almost anything. And if you're looking for heavy metal (storage cabinets or metal shelving, that is,) they can help out there, too.

◆◆◆◆ Kelly's Air-Conditioning and Heating   972/436-4340
151 Ridgeway Circle   24 Hour Service
Lewisville, TX 75067

If they're out on a call, you'll have to leave a message. If it's an emergency, they're Johnny's-on-the-spot. If it can wait a day or two, they will set up a program to fix whatever's bothering you. Heater giving you a headache? Air-conditioner's got its own aches and pains? Well if you want a reliable, less expensive (lower overhead) and more responsive company to fix the problem, Todd Kelly is the man to call. His company's philosophy: They won't quit until the job is done and it's minor, they're not likely to run up unnecessary or extraneous hours just to charge you more money. Reasonable rates and keeping their service area limited to Carrollton, Lewisville, Farmers Branch, The Colony, Coppell, Double Oak, Copper Canyon, Flower Mound and surrounding areas is how I know about them. Got a company comparable in your area, let me know. I'll be sure to spread the word.

★★★ Liberty Safes   972/579-8914
1431 N. Loop 12   Mon-Fri 10-5:30; Sat 10-3
Irving, TX   www.gunsafe.com

With over 200 safes in stock, how can you possibly feel insecure? No longer Pony Express, Liberty Safes has taken over and all I can say is Oy-ge-vault! Never leave a gun unattended. All gun owners should know that already. Remember, gun safety is a primary role of a gun owner. Throw your "arms" into storage when you can secure it lock, stock and barrel. Or, maybe you need a secure place for important documents such as your passport, stocks and bonds, Life insurance policies, jewelry and more. It's better safe than sorry. Free yourself from the tyranny of high prices. Get a full size gun safe as low as $495. They also carry individual cases for long guns and pistols. Delivery and installation is also available. Look for **LIBERTY SAFE**, **NATIONAL SECURITY** and **SUN WELDING** safes, for safety's sake.

◆◆◆◆ **Lone Star Locksmith**   972/724-7233
PO Box 270248   By Appt. Only
Flower Mound, TX 75028

Knock knock! Who's there? I don't know cause I can't open the door. If this is your problem, then it's time to call in the Lone Star Locksmith for the taming of the screws. As a former security consultant, this guy can get down to the bolts and screws. Expect a house re-keyed for $45 and an installation of a handle set on your front door for about $55-$65. He recommends, however, buying the actual fixture at Home Depot because he can't buy them any cheaper than you can. Serving the entire Dallas/Fort Worth area, John Murphy can handle any residential, commercial or automotive lock request and be Johnny-on-the-Spot, even in emergencies. What's even more appealing is that he'll go out of his way to recommend cheaper alternatives that are available. Most jobs completed same day or next. I'd say he deserves more than a Lone Star.

★★★ **Lowe's**   940/320-1938
1255 S. Loop 288   www.lowes.com
Denton, TX 76205

Even though Wal-Mart has taken a financial interest in Lowe's, I have to tell you, Home Depots prices are still less in most cases (but only by a buck or two). Though they carry the same brands as Home Depot, you might find different makes and models available here (adding some variety to the cat and mouse game.) Lots of do-it-yourself workshops or go online and get the animated version of just about any project. (Neato!) Get absolute power with a long line of drills and drivers or tame your yard with mowers, trimmers, seeds and sprinkler systems. Now when you're ready to sit back and grill it, they've got those, too. Money will only drip out of your wallet if you repair the roof yourself and Lowe's has everything you need to do the job, except for the fiddle! Lots of 6-12 month no-interest offers on various departments monthly. Lowe's is an official recommended dealer of **DEWALT** tools and their home safety council provides consumers information on making their homes safer. Too, they are sponsors of many charities such as United Way, Red Cross, Disaster Relief, Special Olympics and others. So, when you're ready to tackle those home improvement projects, go after them "tooth and nail."

★★★★ **Makita Factory Service Center**   972/243-1150
12801 Stemmons   Mon-Fri 8-4:30
Farmers Branch, TX 75234   www.makita.com

If you want to make it on the moon, take the **MAKITA** cordless drills that NASA used in the construction of the International Space Station. This 80-year old company is one of the most respected in the industry. Their only Metroplex location is on the service road of Stemmons, exit Valley View, just south of the Exxon gas station. Filler up and then go cordless. Save money on the tools that are refurbished and prices up to 60 percent off. Rebuilt electric equipment and a hodgepodge of electrical tools that if you're not in the market for anything particular, you'll love to roll up your sleeves so you can dig in. For the casual home user or the heavy-duty contractor, you'll see circular saws, cordless drills, compressors, routers, rotary hammers, jig saws, reciprocating saws, grinders, miter saws and parts (not that I know what half of this stuff does.) If you've got a broken Makita, subject to parts availability, you can expect a 24-48 hour turnaround. You'll receive a seven-point safety certification, FREE estimates before repairs and a 90-day warranty on all repairs. They also repair **B & D**, **BOSCH**, **DEWALT**, **MILWAUKEE**, **PORTER CABLE**, **SKIL**, and other major brands. If you prefer, let your fingers do all the work and request their catalog.

★★★ Merry Maids   972/516-8955
3129 I-30, Suite F   Mon-Fri 8-4:30; By Appt.
Mesquite, TX 75150   www.merrymaids.com

When there's just not enough hours in the day, hi ho, hi ho, it's off to clean they go. The Merry Maids and their band of merry maidens provide all their own cleaning supplies and are compliant with all the OSHA regulations. It's a real business, with real protection against breakage while they're cleaning up your mess. Don't worry, they're used to it. Prices are customized to your individual needs but typically start at $75 per cleaning for twice month in a 3/2 home. If you rub your hands over the chest of drawers and it comes up dusty, they will return to do it again, no questions asked and at no additional charge. This company's been in business over 20 years, which means they have a pile of dirt on their resumés. You may do better price wise through the classifieds or word-of-mouth, but with this company, they pay all the workman's comp and treat the maidens like honest-to-goodness employees.

★★★ Mini Maids   214/350-0330
Dallas, TX   Mon-Fri 8-5; By Appt. Only

Maid in the shade, this mini version offers maxi-service for the busy homeowner. From a bachelor pad to a mansion, or an entire subdivision, these lean green cleaning machines have been sweeping the dirt, but not under the rug. Cleaning up since 1973, they have won numerous awards as being the best in the cleaning business in the Metroplex. They have limited geographic areas to which they travel: North Dallas and all the northern suburbs, they don't want to drive all over the place. FREE estimates based on square footage, number of rooms, and what your expectations are over the phone and they accept coupons from the *Yellow Pages*, with Mondays, Tuesdays and Wednesdays designated double coupon days. Providing their own equipment, they offer both occasional and regular services and are known to be dependable. Your satisfaction is guaranteed as long as you don't "bleach your end of the bargain."

◆◆◆◆ Modern Home Patio   214/349-0303
10550 Church Rd. @ LBJ & Plano Rd.   By Appt. Only
Dallas, TX 75238

If you want an attractive carport or patio cover, look to Modern Home/Patio Company. This family-owned and operated business got started when Bobby Sheridan back in 1970 began installing carports and patio covers. When the company expanded in 1975 to their current address above, they added experienced sales and installation crews. Stocking only quality materials that are maintenance free (from rain and sun, that is), they will last for decades. Their carports shelter your vehicle from the ever-changing Texas weather and are also maintenance free and should last a lot longer than your car, truck, RV or even your boat. Anchors away, my friend.

◆◆◆ Moisture Shield   214/638-0502
2912 Barge Lane   Mon-Fri 8-5
Dallas, TX 75212

If you're water retentive, you might want to consider Moisture Shield. Moisture Shield wants to rid your home of moisture if water's seeping in. (Do you think they landed on Barge Lane for nothing?) Soggy problems can make you knee deep in debt. At Moisture Shield, they do all the preventative and remedial waterproofing work that you may need. Too, they also provide masonry restoration to stucco, repairs to concrete and brick, stone and wood, tuck pointing, and power washing and cleaning. Then, if you need to coat or seal your walls, your floors, your deck, whatever, they're the ones to call since they are the source that wears many coats. Coatings, sealers/patching, paint striping/painting, dry wall, urethane, epoxy injections and they work on sheet metal, too. They will meet you on the job site or in your office; it's at your convenience. *Call toll-free: 800/766-3393*

★★★★★ Monarch Paint
701 S. Stemmons
Lewisville, TX 75067

972/436-2001
Mon-Fri 7-5; Sat 7:30-1
www.monarchpaint.com

If you're have trouble finding the right paint color because it's varnished, then try spreading your wings and shopping at **MONARCH** paint. Butterflies are free, but not the paint. In business since 1967, they migrated to Dallas in 1984 and have been painting the town in a multitude of colors since. My special eggplant color is a hit in my house. And, of course, they discount. After all, they're the manufacturer and they sell it factory-direct via their Houston facility. All paints, by the way, are specially formulated for the rugged Southwest climate. Rugged? What do you mean? Aren't four or five months of 100-degree weather the norm everywhere? Ever been to Pittsburgh? Well, they now carry **PITTSBURGH** Paints, too, apparently to give northerners an equal opportunity. Since Pulte and Jim Miller Homes get painted with Monarch Paint, get out of your cocoon and try it yourself. Paint contractors line up early in the morning but they do not discriminate if you sleep in late and show up around 11. They also manufacture their own stains, varnishes, poly-coats, enamels and latex. Check directory for multiple locations, online or through directory assistance.

★★★★★ Northern Tool & Equipment Co.
110 W. Campbell Rd.
Richardson, TX 75080

972/705-9545
Mon-Fri 8-8; Sat 8-6; Sun Noon-5
www.northern-online.com

This Minnesota chain is perfect for select home improvement projects. Northern-ers find them particularly appealing because they fill in the gaps left wide open from Home Depot, Lowe's and Ace Hardware. Their specialty—tools and equipment at some of the lowest prices in town. Mow, mow, mow your lawn with a two-cycle lawn mower. Mix and match a variety of machine screws, marine accessories, water pumps, go-carts, hunting gear, storage units and equipment for trailers and RVs. How about a titanium drill bit set that will ensure you drill faster for longer—for only $24.99? Or clean up with a **NORTHSTAR** pressure washer for $399? Generate some real power with a 5500-watt vanguard powered NorthStar generator for $869. Add in a TV spot paint sprayers for as low as $99 and settle the water pressure issue with a 3.5hp 8400gph, 2" water pump for $299. Big boys shop the big toys here. No tooling around. Northern's main product lines are generators, small engines, pressure washers and hand, air and power tools. But they also pride themselves on carrying hydraulics, pumps, trailer parts, seasonal equipment and more. Brands include **BOSCH, BRIGGS & STRATTON, CHANNEL LOCK, COLEMAN, DEWALT, FULLER, HOMELITE, HONDA, INGERSOLL-RAND, NORTHSTAR, STANLEY, VISE GRIP, YARDMAN** and others. Their own brand is also a money-saver. Looking for a 20-ton vertical/horizontal hydraulic log splitter—that splits logs up to 24-inch long? Get one for $829. Or how does a **WOODMAN** 16-inch chain saw, 34cc engine, fully-assembled, factory-refurbished (performs as good as new) for $109? Take a camping trip and sleep under the Northern lights in a heavy-duty 5 x 7-foot tarp, and yes, it's water-resistant for $99. And if you've searched every inch of the Metroplex looking for a go-kart, here we found a **MANOO** 3.5 HP Red Fox Pup go-kart with a 3.5 HP Tecumseh engine for $499. For Father's Day this year, we bought a Homelight gas-powered cordless blower, factory-refurbished for $79 and made one dad happy. See pressure washers, generators, small engine parts, laser levels and Honda lawn and garden equipment, (as well as being an authorized repair site for **HONDA, BRIGGS & STRATTON** and **TECUMSEH** engines.) Mow them down on Belt Line and I-30 in Garland. Ta Ta! *Call toll-free: 800/533-5545*

★★★★★ Orr Reed Wrecking Co.
1903 Rock Island
Dallas, TX 75207

214/428-7429
Mon-Sat 9-4

They might just be falling asleep on the job with their laid back atmosphere but if you're looking for salvaged building materials, then take the trip over to Orr Reed Wrecking Co. They have a large selection of used building materials that's constantly changing. A designer's paradise if you're looking to re-do your castle on a pauper's budget. From doors to a/c units, ceiling fans to tubs, sinks, telephones, cabinets, columns and door handles to small electronic items and more...at salvaged prices! They don't offer delivery but can recommend a few names if you're in need. Or you can Reed between the lines and demolish the notion that salvaged is more than recovering old building materials, it's also recouping your losses when it comes to the high expenses of home improvement and remodeling.

★★★ Overhead Door Co.
1800 Vantage Drive
Carrollton, TX 75006

972/416-7100
www.dallasdoors.com

Are you a fan of the Doors? If so, turn to the pros at the Overhead Door Company. No newcomer to providing homeowners and businesses with doors, windows, security gates and other products for construction and maintenance projects. Since the early 1920s, this company's been opening doors. In 1962, they opened in the Dallas/Fort Worth area and nothing's been the same since. Whether you're a homeowner or a business, if you've got a need for doors, windows, security gates, wood or steel garage doors, garage door openers, entry and patio doors and vinyl windows, start by looking overhead! And that is just for homeowners. For commercial users, you can choose from entry and freezer doors, office walls, dock equipment, locksmith services, even restroom facilities. There's always a special going on, so check into them. If you're looking for residential service, their Carrollton location is the number to call (above), the Fort Worth residential showroom is located at 840 Southway Circle (817/921-3641), and their two commercial showrooms can be found at 2617 Andjon Drive in Dallas (214/350-4621) and 1039 E. Dallas Rd. in Grapevine (817/481-5502). *Call toll-free: 800/275-3290*

★★★★ Pest Shop, The
2231-B W. 15th St.
Plano, TX 75075

972/519-0355
Mon-Fri 12:15-6; Sat 11-3; Morning Service Calls
www.pestshop.com

If you have any desire to make a reservation at the Roach Motel, why don't you shop here first and get acquainted with the species. Not only is this shop a do-it-yourself pest control armory, but they are home to the infamous Cockroach Hall of Fame Museum. Just because Michael Bohdan has a list of media appearances a mile long, doesn't mean he's not serious about controlling those darn little creatures (or big as you will soon find out.) As seen on *The Today Show*, *Regis and Kathy Lee*, *Good Morning America*, *CNN Headline News*, *To Tell The Truth*, *Joan Rivers*, *Donny and Marie* and more. Better dead than in your bed! It took 10 years to write about his 20 years of experience but his book "What's Bugging You" is now available. He also makes private appearances at parties (but he never crashes one. Invitations only) as well as media appearances if you should ever want to know everything you've ever thought about pests but didn't know who to pester. Michael also loves to show and tell at conventions, garden groups or homeowners associations. His bugs will travel with him and he claims that he might show up as "Cockroach Dundee," wearing his safari hat that has 20 large roaches on it. (Dead of course.) And his live 3-4 inch hissing Madagascar roaches are indeed live and "hiss" on command. Oh dear. On a serious note, The Pest Shop is still the place to learn the ropes and gather the products that will do the job and eliminate those unwanted guests. I hate to bug him, but when you see them, you'll want them dead, not alive. He's got the answers if you've got the problem.

★★★★★ ProStar Security
3033 Kellway Drive, #128
Carrollton, TX 75006

972/418-0600
By Appt. Only

Chuck Goforth is the man who can connect you to a standard security system, which includes one key-pad, motion-detector and three openings sensors. These are all free with a 36-month monitoring contract (about $25 per month). Not bad, but read the fine print. You're locked in for three years and chances are, this particular system won't come close to handling your needs. So, expect to be upsold with a hard sell since they only work one-on-one, at your home or office. The good part, though, since they use ADT, if you move or get transferred, if you're contract is not up, you can take it with you. Estimates are FREE but expect a strong closer to go from there. ProStar is the nation's largest ADT authorized dealer so they certainly are protecting enough people to pass the Litmus Test. They also offer the Protection One system, which is what elderly citizens living alone might consider. That's the rapid, reliable monitoring system for about $1 a day with a 96 percent customer satisfaction rating in this area of more than 50,000 monitored customers. You will receive a FREE lifetime service program for the length of your monitoring contract and for one year, you'll get a free SafetyNet guarantee. They will reimburse your homeowner's insurance deductible up to $1,000 if you suffer a loss due to a monitored fire or burglary. Now, that's like getting a guarantee etched in stone! *Call toll-free: 800/SMART-80*

★★★ Quality Surplus
1004 S. Stemmons Frwy.
Lake Dallas, TX 75065

940/497-3749
Mon-Fri 9-6; Sat 9-5

It's and open and shut case if your looking to unlock a new look for homes exterior. Who knows what you'll find when walking through these doors, well other than doors that is? Styles may change but metal and wooden entry doors, French doors and leaded glass doors keep this store grounded. Peek and peck your way through the large warehouse. Don't see what you're looking for? Then open up a catalog. Orders will be on your doorstep within a week or two, provided you pick then up since delivery is not available. Install it yourself-or you might be out the door on luck. They will recommend several handymen if you just can't get the job done alone. We welcomed the wealth of information and advice provided on installation, staining, painting and fixtures. **QUALITY SURPLUS** is an invited addition to any home improvement project.

◆◆◆ Rent-A-Hubby
Irving, TX

972/871-8696
Mon-Fri 8-5; By Appt.

Too bad we can't hire them to escort us to our high-school reunion. For the right hunk, it might be worth it. Charges of $55 per hour with a two-hour minimum are racked up for all those little annoying jobs that never get done. From a sticky door to a leaking faucet, these Jacks-of-all-trades are really Johnny's-on-the-spot. They are booked about two weeks in advance so call early especially if in Carrollton and surrounding areas since these are the only areas of coverage.

Republic Industries/Cabinet Outlet
11074 N. Stemmons Fwy.
Dallas, TX 75229

972/484-8899
Mon-Fri 9-5; Sat 9-3

Knock, Knock. Who's there? Woodn't you like to know. Okay, so you don't like my jokes. But what you will like is this outlet for **REPUBLIC INDUSTRIES** and **LEGACY CABINETS**. How do I know that? Because prices are 40-50 percent below retail. Whether you're buying cabinets at a store or through your builder, buying here makes sense. Choose oak, maple, cherry or laminate, whatever's your pleasure. Outfit a kitchen from $900 for laminated particleboard to about $3,400 for Shaker-style solid maple. Too, they can order from **WILSONART**, any color laminate you would like for countertops. Not to worry. Experts are on hand to help you with measuring instructions. If you're all thumbs, then consider hiring them for installation---about $20 per square foot. Look for their billboard near Walnut Hill on Stemmons. You're almost there. Call if you need help getting there. *Call toll-free: 877/KIT-BATH*

Seconds & Surplus   972/263-2661
909 Regal Row   Mon-Thu 8-7; Fri-Sat 8-5; Sun 10-3
Dallas, TX 75247

Open wide and say, "Ah." Nothing is ever quite the same after a trip to Seconds & Surplus. Shop where the contractors shop and enjoy the benefits of a labor revolution. In need of a tool to complete the next project? Consider anything made by **DEWALT**, tools for the contractor—even if you're a weekend workman, you'll want the tools that will do the job right at the first taming of the screw. Then, it's off to the doors, a front door, a side door, an atrium door. In fact, you might like the prices so much you'll buy a patio door for rooms that don't even have a patio. Artwork, cabinets, hinges, mirrors, sinks, well, keep that "Honey Do" list handy...even if he's not. Too, enjoy the benefits of Ceramic Tile and Marble Outlet and the Carpet Outlet in back, independent retailers who, though good all by themselves, join Seconds & Surplus to round out that weekend homeimprovement project. Kevin and Don are young, old pro's and are conductors of this home improvement orchestra. There's more than 50,000 square feet of industrious possibilities with savings of 50-70 percent. Doors, though, are their staple since they're tied into a door manufacturer. Any kind of door: exterior, interior, louvered, bi-fold, leaded, patio——it's open for discussion.

◆◆◆◆◇ Service Lane   972/560-4900
2711 N. Haskell Ave., Suite 2700   www.servicelane.com
Dallas, TX 75204

As they say, Service Lane is definitely "the address for reliable service people for home or for business. A much needed service for answering the question, "Who should I call?" Offering competent referrals for most every household task including: carpet and floor cleaning, furniture rentals, upholstery cleaning, wallpaper hanging, electricians, floor, glass or mirror repair, handymen, pest control, roofing, security systems, siding, roofers, movers, fencers, storage facilities, landscapers, tree services, party and event planners, party and event facilities, photographers, printers, accounting and tax preparers, health insurance and more. How do they work? They are like matchmakers connecting you with a Certified Service Professional in your area that best suits your needs. You can check how others in the Service Lane community rate them, too. In addition, they have great Buying Guides that provide useful tips on selecting and working within a select category. For exterior home improvement referrals, find a good roofing company, siding, gutters, windows and anything that relates to an outside repair project. Of course, FREE estimates and design assistance, material warranties, a personal project coordinator, on-the-spot financing, each repairman is locally licensed, insured, has good credit and legal standing, is in good standing with the Better Business Bureau, has provided three customer references and has been in business at least two years. Wow! Service Lane adds an additional five-year warranty that materials used are free from defects. Welcome to BBB, the book. *Call toll-free: 877/386-3848*

★★★ Skillful Improvements & Restoration   972/279-0119

2143 Gus Thomasson   Mon-Fri 8:30-4:30
Mesquite, TX 75150   www.skillfulimprovements.com

What started out in 1976 as a group of student painters and carpenters looking to get by on a little more than peanut butter and jelly has turned into a champagne and caviar business. In 1986 the reality came to life by Ray Dettmer, owner and a NARI-Certified remodeler. His four lead carpenters are also certified along with 7 other employees that are IICRC certified in restoration work and cleaning. An entire division of the company is dedicated strictly to insurance repairs for everything from water damage to fire and smoke clean up, drying out of the structure and more. But don't stop there. The newest division is dedicated to cleaning carpets and air ducts. But not your same old technique. Skillful doesn't just vacuum your ducts but rather runs the air through water, capturing the dirt and dust, then dumps the water into tanks on their trucks that prevent those dust bunnies and allergens from re-entering your home. For carpet cleaning, they also offer **TEFLON** stain resistance by **3M** that comes with a one-year warranty. If you weren't aware, it was formerly called **SCOTCHGUARD** by 3M but they upgraded the technique to Teflon stain resistance. Skilful employees do it all from adding new space in your home to restoring your home after loss, remodeling to updating homes or simply cleaning your carpets/air ducts. Bottom line, Skillful is here today, will be here tomorrow and consistently offers quality and integrity. There are some things money can't buy, but money well spent is spent here.

★★★★★ SolaTube by Totally Tubular Lighting   972/263-6033

1115 N. Windomere   Mon-Fri 8:30-5:30; Sat 10-3
Dallas, TX 75208-3506

This interesting alternative from Australia has emerged on the skylight scene and its known as **SOLATUBE**. Unlike the traditional skylight, this one comes with a ceramic dome top and a reflective tube that affords natural lighting without the usual heat loss in winter or the opposite side effect in summer. It brightens at least a 150-square-foot area without the construction mess. How neat! No structural changes to your ceiling or roof are needed. It's also waterproof, burglarproof and maintenance-free. And it is about one-third the cost of a regular skylight. Installation take about two hours and both the SolaTube, as well as the installation, are guaranteed for 10 years. That means NO leaks. Totally Tubular Lighting is the SolaTube dealer in this area, so if you want one, this is where to get it. **SOLAR STAR** is newest in the line-up. It's a solar-powered attic fan that will pay for itself in just a few years. Remember that breeze you felt during the days of the attic fan? Well, all good things someday return, new and improved. A few interesting facts about natural sunlight light. For example, Wal-Mart installed skylights in half of its environmental demonstration store in Lawrence, Kansas. Results were significantly higher sales per square foot in the store's day lit portion. Also the Alberta Department of Education did a study that showed children exposed to more sunlight grew more, concentrated better and had less tooth decay. Oh rot! Natural light is also being used to treat depression. So just think of all the places you could install a SolaTube—the kitchen, bathroom, shower stall, living room, dining room, hallway/stairwell, garage, laundry room, walk-in closet, home office, attic, well, and there's always *my* dog house!

◆◆◆◆◆ Southwest Interior & Design   972/620-8091

1740 Trinity Valley   www.swinteriors.com
Carrollton, TX 75006

One-stop interior design services is the reason Southwest Interior & Design has been kicking kabooties and taking names. Services provided: remodeling, kitchen and bath design, custom painting, faux finishing, drywall repair, resurfacing, interior design, window treatments, flooring, wallpaper sales and installation. The Southwest Team services include exterior painting, carpentry, stucco repair, repair and replacement of balconies, patios, fences, siding, carports and the team leader is Wes Werner. FREE estimates and color consultation along with a two million dollar escrow account, Nick Losole is the creative inspiration behind the company and is its President. One call, that's all it takes to get your home or office up to snuff. Since 1982, they've been one of leaders of the pack. Since they are a full-service design studio, they can really handle the whole shebang. And they're not happy until you are. All work is guaranteed. *Call toll-free: 800/248-8091*

Staz-On Roofing

10889 Shady Trail, Suite 102
Dallas, TX 75220

214/357-0300
Mon-Fri 8-5
www.stazonroof.com

No leaks in this write-up. Staz-on stays on. Since 1981, this company has been fiddling on the roofs of the Metroplex. With a flawless record at the BBB, now our BBB book says, these guys are top-notch. Let them fiddle on your roof as they offer the lowest price on roofing and repair in the Metroplex. Get a faxed quote within 24-hours. One satisfied customer extolled their virtues because they completed the job in three days flat. Most any kind of roof—metal, clay, shingle and copper—is part of their repertoire. Metal, by the way, is stronger than traditional roofing materials and offers a wide variety of shapes and colors, allowing them to resemble different styles and materials such as cedar shakes, tile, slate and even asphalt shingles. The advantage of clay tiles is that they combine durability with a really upscale and lasting appearance. Clay tiles mellow with age and are resistant to exposure to the wind, rain, frost and sun. They offer the latest technology and a full six-year workmanship warranty along with up to a 50-year manufacturer's guarantee. Check them out for competitive pricing and a full range of options including custom sheet metal, waterproofing and repairs. Since 1981, they've been covering the Metroplex from the top. Hop online and read the testimonials. Looks like my husband, Bob Blair has another wife...just kidding but a Bob Blair did write a glowing review.

♦♦♦♦♦ Stephen W. Jones

Dallas, TX

972/285-6415
By Appt. Only
www.connect.net/sjones

Looking for a carpenter without any holes in his resume? Stephen Jones is your man with the Midas touch. His expertise: Remodeling, decks, fencing, painting and just about any project involving a carpenter's know-how. With a decade of experience, it's so refreshing for any contractor to show up on time. Well, here's one that does. And when he's finished, he actually cleans up. He specializes in the smaller jobs that the big guys don't want to fool with. Decks, doors, painting, doghouses, fences, arbors, wood storage buildings, caulking, flooring, installing ceiling fans and building rocking chairs. In fact, he'll do most anything but plumbing and some electrical work. With over 500 references, you can rest easy. But he's so busy, you may have to wait a bit. Still, give Steve a call and get it all fixed-for-less.

Stone-Tec

2929 W. Kingsley
Garland, TX 75041

972/278-4477
Mon-Fri 8-5; Sat 10:30-3
www.stoneteci.com

Wouldn't you rather switch than fight? No counter-resistance here. Think Stone-Tec when it comes to remodeling your kitchen or bath counter tops. They're the tops. Formica's out. Tile is okay, but not the elegance or durability of granite or marble. Wood, well, forget it. Redo those counters with magnificent granite imported from India and Pakistan in a variety of colors and textures. Talk about resistance? It doesn't stain, burn or warp, for starters. Hot pots and pans, no problem. Maintain the look for a lifetime regardless of the wear and tear you inflict. And since Stone-Tec is a direct importer, the prices are very affordable. Not only do they maintain an inventory of the raw materials, they are also the fabricator (meaning they cut it to fit) and install. Eliminate the middleman when shopping at a retail store or through a decorator. A little slab will do ya! Pick your co ors from the actual inventory, rather than just some chip off the ole block. With the transformation, you will add instant desirability to your home's worth as well as a surface that is both beautiful and durable. Whether it's for countertops, accents or flooring, former interior decorator Rubi Shah's your liaison to never being taken for "grantite." And when it comes to granite, she's one of the most knowledgeable in the land. Another showroom opened this year at the Inwood Village Shopping Center, 5470 W. Lovers Lane, #333-A, Dallas, 214/654-9075

★★★★★ Suburban Door
10420 Plano Rd.
Dallas, TX 75238

972/414-6900
Mon-Fri 7:30-5; Sat 8-2
www.open-sesame.com

They can usually be out within 24 hours for installation and repairs if your garage door is broken, or you need a new one, you might as well shut the door on high prices. They also sell garage door accessories, circuit boards, keypads, remote controls, door hardware and wall controllers just to list a few. Brands that they carry and/or repair include **ALLISTER, ALLSTAR, CARPER, CHAMBERLAIN, CRUSADER, GENIE, HEDDOLF, LIFTMASTER, LINEAR, MARTEC, OVERHEAD, SEARS, SKYLINK** and more. Most brands, if you must know. Add in all of the garage door hardware, and this is like a superstore for just one category product. After nearly 10 years, you can't slam them for offering low prices, now can you? If you're suffering from a broken spring, your remote control is out of control, or you want a brand new one installed (Genie is sold here, but they can service all brands), this is your liaison to it all. And the best part? FREE estimates and FREE service charges plus the lowest prices are guaranteed. Check out their maintenance policies. It may be just what ails you. A Genie chain glider opener was $229 installed. Open sesame.

Sunshine Sunrooms
2410 Glenda Lane
Dallas, TX 75229

972/243-5390
Mon-Fri 9-5; Sat 10-3
www.sunshinesunroom.com

Barry has one of the sunniest dispositions in town alongside one of the best resources for putting an extended roof over your house. They can do it all from a simple screen enclosure to double-plated glass windows and doors with full central air-conditioning. Even vinyl windows that close off your screened patio during inclement weather are available. Whether it's a room addition (without the contractor's markup), patio room, plant room, extra room, just buy the room and let the sun shine in. You can see their display rooms from Stemmons, but you might pay attention to these directions: Exit Walnut Hill, turn east to the second light (Ables); then left to Glenda. You'll jog around the sausage factory, but when you finally arrive at the scene, you'll scream, "Hot Dog!" Once you place an order, depending on where the material is coming from, they can start within one to three weeks. Financing can take up to two to three weeks (state law says there's a 15-day waiting period for home improvement loans), which adds to the wait for materials. They will, though, try to help with financing.

★★★★★ Surplus Warehouse
104 Simonds Rd.
Seagoville, TX 75159

972/287-5190
Mon-Fri 8-5; Sat 8-1

With the sound of a slow Southern drawl, you'll be escorted around this warehouse but don't put the pressure on to rush. The keys to economic freedom may be just lying in wait. No ambush, though Seagoville is home to the federal pen. Don't worry, you won't be in any danger. Stay firm to your convict-ions of not paying high prices, and you will be singing the "Jailhouse Rock" when you leave. Unless you prefer to go the chair, you will find yourself wallowing in the finer things for home improvement projects. Siding, paint, doors, hardware, cabinets, countertops, light and plumbing fixtures, shingles and more. Exit Simonds off 175 and make sure you head to the right warehouse (the pen's on the opposite side.) Most items are first-quality closeouts, though some have been slightly damaged yet useable. Shop where the builders buy. Though prices may not be considered highway robbery (50 percent off retail), pay attention to further reductions during blow-out sales. Reduce your sentence even further by following the Diva's rules. Live by the discount rule and you'll never been imprisoned again. Unless it's your last meal, no one's watching your every move. Shop without salesmen breathing down your neck. You're on your own for installation and delivery. However, they will recommend a few reputable handymen. When you buy something, they tag it and separate it from the floor inventory until you can arrange for a pick-up.

SW Canvas Products   817/624-9932
2418 Clinton Ave.   Mon-Fri 8-5; Sat By Appt. Only
Fort Worth, TX 76016

Awnings, awnings burning bright, shelter me from my window's light. Who to call? SW Canvas, that's who. This family-owned business is up and running with the founder's son Carlos performing the day-to-day duties. Stop yawning for an awning. Here's where to buy both energy-protection as well as great drive-up appeal to the front of your house. Why look like every house or office on the block? Make your appointment for a free estimate, then be up and covered in about two to three weeks. This company hangs the moon and the sun as far as I'm concerned. If it's supposed to be made from canvas, this company's your stitch in time. They utilize the **SUNBRELLA** brand for awnings, canopies, tarps, tents, truck and boat covers. If you want it made-for-the-shade, call the canvas king of the road. Since 1956, they've been putting an awning over the Metroplex for as low as possible, without hiding behind any shady deals. An average window awning runs $200-$275 (average $225) installed with a steel-welded frame. Once a project is agreed upon, they require a 50 percent deposit with installation forthcoming.

★★ Texas Tool Traders   972/278-0049
2414 S. Jupiter Rd.   Mon-Fri 7:30-5:30, Sat 8-Noon
Garland, TX 75041   www.texastooltraders.com

In business since 1973, there are locations, in Garland (above) plus Arlington, Lewisville, McKinney and Watauga. But don't expect any PhDs at the store level. We called to inquire when their website would be up and running and it took three different men including the manager who didn't even understand the question to tell us they didn't know. Finally, we were referred to corporate—how endearing just to get the answer to a simple question. When we called the corporate number they gave us, they also had no idea if ordering by phone was available? Then, how could they be delivering online? Duh?? No clues. Corporate communication must be in the beginning stages. But what a surprise when we landed the big one at the 800 number above that we got from their own website. Someone actually knew the answer to our poignant question. Yes, they will take your order over the phone and then either check their stores to see if it's in stock so you can pick it up there or take a credit card over the phone and ship it UPS to your door. That's hardly online shopping but it's a start. Shipping rates (for now) are just the actual shipping rates. If you're still not anxious to visit one of their stores and just want to know which tool to buy, you might talk to one of their former store managers, Alan in Purchasing. He's really the dandy who is handy with the information. He'll give you the low down on what you'll need to get the job done and the best price for the right tool. Ah, now we can move on. If you need a hammer with a straight claw or smooth-face, they've got them—but that's elementary, my dear. Power tools, too. We didn't see much that was discounted, so be careful not to get nailed. Since the discounts were few and far between and their website is nothing to write home about, it's up to you to decide "yea" or "nay!" Selection and number of stores may be their claim to fame. ***Call toll-free: 800/998-7001***

★★★★★ Tile & Marble Clearinghouse   972/221-TILE (8453)
600 N. Stemmons Fwy.   Mon-Fri 9-4; Sat 9-Noon
Lewisville, TX 75067

With a move across the freeway, Tile & Marble has established itself as the premier source of tile and marble. Everything's sold at manufacturers' prices or below. Look up and down your house or office and see what materializes on your floors or counters, walls or wherever marble, granite, slate, ceramic, porcelain, Saltillo, Cantera, limestone or more would likely go. Then lay it on thick.

◆◆◆◆ Tile & Marble Installations   972/406-0677
12029 Denton Drive   By Appt. Only
Dallas, TX 75234

If I've been asked once, I've been asked a million times, "Where can I get a tub installed? A fireplace tiled? Granite or marble countertops? A patio laid? Well, all laid plans of nice shoppers can go astray with the wrong installer. Here's a company that actually specializes in it, so call for your FREE estimate. You've only got a lot of grout to lose. They specialize in tubs and showers, upgrading floors, countertops, back splashes, foyers and more. Watch for coupons in *Val-Pak* for additional 20-30 percents savings. ***Call toll-free: 877/806-0677***

★★★★★ Tile America   817/595-7900
7337 Dogwood Park Drive   Mon-Fri 8-5; Sat 9-2
Richland Hills, TX 76118   www.tileamericainc.com

Tile America boasts the largest in-stock tile in the Metroplex with over three million square feet of tile available. No one manufacturer stands alone. They represent hundreds from all over the world, including Spain, Italy and Indonesia. By eliminating the middleman (whoever he is?), their prices are exceptional. Try dancing around the issue of their huge selection of wall and floor tiles as low as $.89/square foot. They even offer their own brand of all-glazed tile, from an 8 x 8-inch square all the way up to 18 x 18-inch. Pay attention to their closeout sales—you'll be floored with even lower prices. Traveling to Dogwood Park is worth it, but you may have to call for directions. If you think shopping online would give you an edge up, forget it. They have so much inventory that changes daily, they just can't keep their head above the grout. For do-it-yourselfers who want to cut their own, you can rent a wet saw for $40 day (Mon-Sat) or $20 on Sunday. This family-owned business has been around since 1996 with a combined experience of over 100 years. Julie, the daughter, is a walking-talking conveyor of tile tutorials. She'll give you tons of advice, recommendations and help with problem solving if you're in the middle of a project and stuck. If you can't make it in during store hours, just tell them what your looking for, they'll describe some pieces that fit your description and if it sounds like something you're interested in, they'll leave some samples outside for you to take a look. Now, how's that for customer service and treating you just like family? They sell both regular thin-set and flex-set that they recommend for the shifts in foundations of Texas homes. Unfortunately, no installation is available. You're on your own. (Or call Tile Marble Installations - previous write-up.)

◆◆◆◆◆ Twin Crest Roofers   **214/967-4180 pager**
Dallas, TX   By Appt. Only
                                                   www.twincrest.com

Double, double, toil and trouble…well, it's not all bad. This company is owned by twins…hence the **TWIN CREST** name, but *their* names are Anderson. When hail damaged destroyed most of my sub-division's roofs, the "Architectural Committee" interviewed dozens of candidates to replace all of our roofs. One was chosen. Guess why?

★★★★★ Walnut Hill Paint Warehouse   **972/484-5800**
2720 Royal Lane, Suite 172   Mon-Fri 7-5:30; Sat 8:30-12:30
Dallas, TX 75229   www.walnuthillpaint.com

If only the walls could talk. First, they'd tell us that Walnut Hill Paint Company's not on Walnut Hill. What a misnomer. You'll have to brush up to Royal Lane for famous brand-name paints like **BENJAMIN MOORE, JONES-BLAIR, MARTIN SENOUR, MOBILE, PITTSBURGH, PRATT & LAMBERT** and **RALPH LAUREN** for your beginning palette. Per gallon, how does $6.15 per gallon for flat paint sound? Or no strain on the pocketbook with stains like **CABOT** and **OLYMPIC**. Seal your fate, then make a date to paint the town red, white and blue. Enjoy the variety of mixing and matching. Stand elbow-to-elbow with professional painters and handymen getting the tools of their trade. Faux finishes are the rage and they've got what you need to create the look, phony or not. The selection is stellar for paints, stains and coatings. They also carry metal effects and aerosols for touch-ups. Located just west of Denton Drive, climb the hill for success.

★★★★★ Western Door Brokers   **972/272-8733**
3814 Miller Park Drive   Mon-Fri 7-4:30; Sat 7-Noon
Garland, TX 75042

Garage Door Brokers has been effectively renamed Western Door Brokers. Go for these brokers, they're the best. Ask for Randy, who can help fix any problem, for any garage door, even come up with a new window design for your garage door. Prompt and efficient service, next day, for sure, on installation of garage doors and motor replacements. Don't be left out in the dark. Or be stuck in a rut. If yours has suddenly ground to a halt, it's not your fault. A new garage door with motor for a two-car garage was $389 installed (windows are extra) but these prices are practically the same as just for the remote elsewhere. What gives? Well, their 15,000 square foot showroom is where you can buy garage doors at wholesale prices. They have 20 years under their belt opening and closing the garage doors on high prices. They also sell the remotes, but that's a moot point. Open sesame on **LIFTMASTER** and **MID-AMERICAN** brands, some of the best in the industry. Choose from 300-400 garage doors at any given time. Expect remotes for new garage doors or for your old ones to get fixed. Expect service and installation like you've never seen before. Go for the brokers who can deliver in Fort Worth, too. Their showroom, though smaller (7,500-square-feet at 1653 Hickory Drive, 817/222-3667) can also deliver similar garage door deals.

34

Housewares

★★★★★ **Ace Mart Restaurant Supply**　　　　　**214/351-5444**
3128 Forest Lane　　　　　　　　　　　　　　　　　Mon-Fri 8:30-5:30
Dallas, TX 75234　　　　　　　　　　　　　　　　　www.acemart.com

Cook up a storm, without setting a blaze. Surely there's something from the oven that's worth serving for dinner. After all, with all of your new kitchen supplies and equipment from Ace Mart Restaurant Supply, when are you going to get going? Dress to impress (your kitchen that is) with any one of their 7,000 products. From their kitchen to yours, this is definitely your Ace in the hole. Their new home on Forest Lane is greatly expanded and easy to shop alongside the other amateur or professional chefs and restaurateurs. Of course, you can receive a discount if you buy in dozens or in case lots. Same price, though, whether you're a pro or a peon. It all tastes the same in the end. Whether it's the dinnerware or the commercial gas stoves (not approved though for home/residential use), "bur-ner" the midnight oil and get cookin'! What really turned us on, though, were the Platters (no not the singing kind) but great for everyday use right up to those special dinner parties. There's plenty of restaurant supplies on Belt Line Rd. in Garland, which is open on Saturdays from 9-1, and in Haltom City at 5600 Denton Highway (817/498-5900), too, to pick and choose, whip or sauté, blend or broil. Enjoy! Over 25 years in business and they haven't burned a dish yet. Choose from some of the best brands in the kitchen: **ABC**, **AMCO**, **AMERICAN METALCRAFT**, **CARDINAL**, **CARLISLE**, **EDLUND**, **HAMILTON BEACH**, **HOMER LAUGH-LIN CHINA**, **LINCOLN**, **PANASONIC**, **RUSSELL HARRINGTON**, **TOWN FOOD SERVICE**, **TRAEX**, **WARING** and more. Stock up on bar, bakery, buffet, catering, clean-up, concessions, furniture, glassware, janitorial, paper, disposal, storage and tabletop items. Everything you need in the kitchen including brushes, can openers, cutlery, food storage, gloves, mixers, oven mitts, pizza supplies, pots and pans, seasonings, scales, scoops, timers, trays, utensils, aprons and more. You might as well look the part as you stock the pot!

★★ **Case-Baldwin**　　　　　　　　　　　　　　　**972/434-8197**
890 N. Mill St., Suite 113　　　　　　　　　Mon-Fri 8 AM-Noon; 1-5
Lewisville, TX 75067　　　　　　　　　　　　　www.yourjanitor.com

If you want to make a clean sweep, don't bother during 12-1. That's their lunch hour and there's no business other than eating that transpires during that time. Other times, though, if you've got a notion to clean up with janitorial supplies and equipment, you might find something to make it into the clean team supply bucket. You don't have to be a janitor or a professional cleaner, either. Who can't use trash-can liners, towels, tissues, disinfectants, a good industrial mop, and a bucket that won't tip over with a gallon of water? Add soaps and detergents, carpet-care products and floor waxes, and you will wax ecstatic over the selection. They also repair vacuum cleaners and decided a while back to open to the public. Manufacturers of supplies include **CLOROX**, **EUREKA**, **FORT JAMES**, **GEORGIA-PACIFIC**, **NOBLES**, **PROCTOR & GAMBLE**, **PRO TEAM**, **RUBBERMAID** and others. But let's back up a minute. Pay attention to what I said earlier. These guys do carpet cleaning, refinishing of floors and janitorial services, too. Now that's where my hearth lies. *Call toll-free: 972/221-6868*

★★★★★ Clockery, The   817/261-9335
2401 W. Pioneer Pkwy.   Mon-Sat 10-6
Arlington, TX 76013

Fly like an eagle over to the Clockery before the bell tolls. What? Are you cuckoo? Don't shop anywhere else if it's a timepiece you're after. From Highway 360, exit Pioneer Parkway and go west for 4 1/2 miles. Keep that little mouse climbing and earning his keep. After you pass Fielder, it's only another quarter of a mile on the north side of the street. A selection that doesn't quit. More than 1,200 different of the best clocks are sold at this pioneer of discount clocks. My, doesn't time fly when you're shopping? Grandfather clocks alone practically rule the roost. Then, fill in the blanks with small clocks, mantle clocks, anniversary clocks, wall and floor clocks, every kind of clock is ticking away time after time. They have one of the largest clock selections in Texas including the popular **RIDGEWAY** and **SLIGH**. An AWI-certified clock-maker is on site and all floor clocks are sold with a one-year manufacturer's warranty.

★★★★★ Corning Revere Factory Store   254/582-7326
Hillsboro Prime Outlet Center   Mon-Sat 10-8; Sun 11-6
104 NE I-35
Hillsboro, TX 76645

Paul **REVERE** would have missed the Revolution had he ridden to this store (just so he could make life in the kitchen a little easier for the woman in his life). And wouldn't she be pleased to know he saved so much money? All right, so we're not trying to get "Corning" on you but to prove the point that this store is worth the trip. Even if it's with two left feet, deals like a six-piece **CORNING WARE** cookware set for $19.99 is worth a little extra effort. But don't over-extend yourself when savings average 30-60 percent off. Take a stab at bigger savings with a Purchase Plus card that gives you a little extra punch. Get one punch for every $20 spent and after 20 punches, you'll get $20 off your next purchase. That ought to have you seeing 20/20. Glasses to cookware, pans to cutlery, names include **BAKER'S SECRET**, **CHICAGO CUTLERY**, **CORELLE**, **CORNING WARE**, **ECKO**, **FRENCH WHITE**, **OXO**, **PYREX** and **REVERE ELECTRICS**. Get a charge out of saving money at this factory store.

★★ Crate & Barrel Outlet Store   214/634-2277
1317 Inwood Rd.   Mon-Sat 10-5; Thu 10-7; Sun Noon-5
Inwood Trade Center   www.crateandbarrel.com
Dallas, TX 75247

Started in 1962 in an old elevator factory, Crate and Barrel is on a mission and they have a passion for what they refer to as the three P's: People, Product and Presentation. One visit to their stores, including their outlet stores, and you can see all three in action. The merchandise is part of that plan too, as they seek out the most wonderful and unusual items that represent the highest standards in housewares. From artisans to designers, manufacturers to those little unknown factories, that's why you don't see the same products at C & B that you'd see in housewares departments or specialty stores any where in the country. Their presentation is fresh and crisp and shopping at the outlet is no exception. Displays are in visual vignettes and somehow, you want it all. (As an aside, this company gives considerable sums to Aids and breast cancer-related causes.) So, if you have a charitable organization, stop by your local store to inquire about the giving of gift certificates with a donation. But back to their outlet. Let you plate run-neth over. The dinnerware and tabletop accessories are the objects of my affection for any of one's dish fulfillment. Since 80 percent of their stock is discontinued, strike while the bargains are hot; otherwise you'll starve to death. At the outlet, you'll save 20 percent, though specials net even deeper cuts. You'll see only first quality (an occasional irregular) resting on their butcher blocks: terra-cotta dishes, glass-ware, vases, kids' stuff, table runners, rugs, herb wreaths, salt and pepper mills, neat desk accessories, clocks and more—all for less. A great starter set for brides-to-be and those looking for a shower gift. Cart off a crate-full of bargains and "Have a nice day!" Here's the final resting place for those who have reached the bottom of the barrel. Saturday's—its elbow to elbow, but worth it if you're looking for a con-tainer for that elbow macaroni. Who would have thought!

◆◆◆◆◆ Dal-Tex Rental   972/495-8555
910 Belt Line Rd.   Mon-Sat 7:30-6; Sun 10-4
Mesquite, TX 75149

When our favorite Rent-all Centers flew the coop and all calls were transferred to Dal-Tex, we thought we'd be out of luck when we wanted to rent tables ($5) or chairs (35-cents), let alone the Moonwalk ($95.) But not to worry, they still rent-it-all. If you're feeling a little under the gun for spring-cleaning, then grab a pressure washer for $56. Or pull out all the stops and let's have a party, a wedding, or any kind of celebration will do. Just make sure you have all the right equipment to do it up right. After, rent some exercise equipment. But all is not fun and games. Medical equipment, power and hand tools, floor and carpet-care equipment, painting and plumbing equipment, camping and sporting equipment, auto-motive tools, equipment for your yard and garden, moving and towing supplies, video cameras, office equipment, stage/dance floors, machines to make cotton candy, snow cones, hot dog, popcorn and mar-garitas, $75/day plus delivery charge based on where you live. What more could you ask? OK! They also rent ice cream carts and a dunking booth. I can see it now. The next board meeting where all the mem-bers get soaked rather than drained when the annual report is read. Second location at 4504 Lakeview Parkway, Rowlett, TX 75088; 972/ 475-7773.

★★★★★ Decorators Warehouse   972/985-1078
1535 S. Bower   Mon-Sat 10-6
15th and Independence   www.decoratorswarehouse.com
Plano, TX 75075

Having the decorator's touch is like the Midas Touch at this Decorators Warehouse. Kin to founder Dave Hanson, this 15,000 square foot warehouse is overflowing with fabulous foliage-for-less. The forest is flourishing with some of the lushest artificial trees, floor plants, silk flower arrangements and table toppers in the Southwest. But it's their custom-made trees, as tall as 12 feet, that brings us to our knees. Want a ficus? No fuss. No muss. How about a palm? Not a problem. The six-footer was tall, dark and handsome. Select your tree branch and go from there. Save 40-60 percent off retail on florals, plants, trees, framed art, mirrors and occasional tables, too. Enjoy elegant accents at egalitarian prices. Shop where the decorators shop and grace your high ceiling ballrooms or atriums, if need be. Choose your tree type and watch them grow. (No watering required.) With several floral design-ers on staff, expect DW to offer creative solutions to boring blooms. With triple the space this year, it's no wonder folks from far away find their way to Decorators Warehouse. Scott Lincoln's in charge here. (His brother-in-law, Dave Hanson, started the concept in Arlington and still maintains a location at 1535 S. Bowen, 817/460-4488. Dave's the one who proclaims from billboards on Stemmons closer to the holidays that he's liquidating over $3 million dollars worth of Christmas trees and decorations called the Christmas Warehouse. I'll be telling you about it, no doubt, on radio and TV as the time draws near. Pay attention and shop when the sign goes up. His Garden of Eden keeps growing and growing at the southeast corner of Park Row and Bowen.) If ever there was a greener pasture of silk flowers, it hasn't been planted. Sales cut the stems to the bare roots. Everything's always 20-50 percent below retail. Once you find them, it's no secret anymore. You're sure to tell others how their garden is sowed. Choose from a veritable variety of floral displays such as silk flowers and trees (from only $89). Now, too, they also carry gifts and furniture. There's no better source for quality silk plants, silk arrangements, artificial trees, plants, vases, flowers, cabinet toppers, and other arrangements are always 40-70 percent off. Plants run anywhere from $15 to $500 depending on the size. Though it's a pretty nondescript store from the outside, it's a gold mine inside. Hit pay dirt and shop the Mother Lode, next door to Dickey's Barbecue and behind Cathy's Wok. Dig in and enjoy.

★★★★★ Dr. Livingston Group   972/438-7272
1502 E Irving Blvd   Mon-Fri 8:30-4
Irving, TX 75060

Here's an outlet that really gets out there. Finding it can be a challenge but once inside these doors, falling for the trip is a worthwhile adventure. Dr. Livingston, I presume, enjoyed finding his way around the world and sending home gifts. Give one to yourself: jewelry, lamps, artifacts, antique reproductions, woodcarvings, baskets, home accessories, and collectibles line the shelves. They have it all from market samples to closeouts, all below wholesale prices. Pay wholesale at their outlet in Irving and forever hold your piece.

★★★ Kitchen Collection   254/582-2577
Hillsboro Outlet Center   Mon-Sat 10-8; Sun 11-6
104 NE I-35, Suite 127   www.kitcol.com
Hillsboro, TX 76645

Factory-direct prices on current first-quality products, selected special purchases, manufacturer's closeout specials and items made exclusively for the Kitchen Collection, all at factory-direct savings. Sounds almost too good to be threw, but let's season the write-up even more and see what you think. They also carry seasonings and accessories to help spice up your life. (Hey, I thought that was Ainsley Harriott's job!) Head to Hillsboro for gourmet gizmos and gadgets for baking, broiling, boiling, mixing and fixing anything that smacks of food. Now here's some more food for thought: They also sell blenders, can openers, coffee and espresso machines, food processors, indoor grills, irons, mixers, ovens and slow cookers, pans and woks, refurbished **KITCHEN AID**, rotisseries, toasters. Ever wished you had a pencil during the middle of the night when something that looks so good that you want to get out of bed and order it? You can, during the day because lots of those cooking infomercial products wind up here. "As-Seen-On-TV" products and more at prices good enough to bring home to Mother. I did...along with ceramic mixing bowls, storage containers, some **CIRCULON** commercial cookware, a pasta set and a small omelet pan. Another location at Tanger Outlet Center, 301 Tanger Dr. Suite #208, Terrell, TX 75160; 972/524-7510. *Call toll-free: 888/548-2651*

Kiva Pottery   214/821-1700
1916 N. Haskell Ave.   Tue-Sat 10-6
Dallas, TX 75204

Don't crack up. This pottery oasis has an answering machine as their receptionist because they're out in the playing field, or Reggie's off to Mexico on a buying trip. Not to worry. Though erratic hours may leave you nervous, once you've seen the yard full of indoor and outdoor decorative planters, table tops and chimeras, alongside south-of-the-border's rustic wrought iron and pine furniture, you will be in the "Garden of Bargains", Mexican-style. Of course, the best selection of chimeras anywhere is one good reason this Diva loves Kiva. A decorative urn, sold elsewhere for $155, was unearthed here for only $50. Their selection also includes 150 lines of clay pottery with an old-world Greek style. Pottery is a wonderful decorative accessory in any home, indoors or out. For out-of-this-world prices and selection, long live Kiva Pottery. Check before you head out the door—as their hours are a bit unstable.

★★★★★ Liquidators Outlet   972/660-3206
2125 S. Great Southwest Pkwy.   Mon-Sat 10-6; Sun 1-6
Grand Prairie, TX 75051

My, what changes are in store for decorator wannabes. You'll be in hog's heaven once you've found that X marks the spot for bargains. Two warehouses full of them, including their newest expansion in front with room vignettes displaying all one-of-a-kind market samples. From the safari motif to the English pub, choose your decor and away you go. Furniture, art and lamps, home decorative items, china, dolls, seasonal items, bath accessories, more lamps and now, furniture galore, mostly from the World Trade Center. If you're looking for a wedding gift, their collection of wedding frames and crystal pieces can't be beat. Choose china and china dolls, crystal, designer housewares, Egyptian cotton bedding and towels, high-end toiletries (including French), objects d'art, hand-painted birdhouses, accent tables, planters, area rugs. Move over HGTV!

★★★★ Our Children's Store of Dallas   214/691-9411
437 NorthPark Center   Mon-Sat 10-9; Sun Noon-6
Dallas, TX 75225

These are Our Children, too, a charitable cooperative effort with the Dallas business community, non-profit organizations, community volunteers and others who are dedicated to providing relief to children in crisis. How do they do it? They raise money via this retail store generating revenues for more than 50 local children's charities. Donations from major manufacturers, samples from wholesale showrooms and others that are given freely; then proceeds of sales are distributed to the children's charities. Located between Neiman's and Lord & Taylor on the second, this in itself is a valuable charitable gift. Expect lots of housewares, china and crystal, fun gifts to expensive gifts, whatever's donated is what you'll see and generally not found in your typical department store, which makes it even a place for the unusual and the unique. Thousands of gift items—from cheap to costing thousands, though most are $50 and under. Shopping for the holidays is a smash hit with holiday items, pet gifts, greeting cards, picture frames, leather goods, specialty baskets, aromatherapy items, pottery, home accessories, birdhouses and garden tools, children's gift items and more. Sponsors include Frito Lay, TGI Fridays, NorthPark, Southwest Airlines, AT&T Media Services, Lennox International, The Hall Agency, John Stolly Design, Eller Media, Bland, Garvey, Eads, Medlock and Deppe, PC. Around the world with generous donors provides a gift for you, at a discount. Personally I bought both cappuccino mugs: Cora Cappuccino and Mary Mocha and saved $3 per mug in the process.

Pier 1 Clearance Store
2350 N. Belt Line Rd.
Irving, TX 75062

972/255-9811
Mon-Sat 10-9; Sun 11-6
www.pier1.com

When you can snare a $150 iron barstool for $5 because its leg was bent, I'd say, "Right on!" However, don't expect too many to have splinters or cause for pause. Most are all first quality but have just remained on the retail store shelves too long. It's like being on a treasure hunt where the bounty is hitting the Mother Lode. Like gold, these values are rock solid. If you like their retail stores, imagine the thrill of victory when you see their outlet. Now settled into their new bigger location, you can either sink or swim through the bargains. Rarely, though, will you walk out empty handed. In fact, you may have to make several trips. Their Clearance Store is located in Irving across from the Irving Mall. It's not unusual to case the joint first, load up with an armful, and wait at the check out counters with shoppers who have come from surrounding states. Word has spread. This place is the place to be. Since 1962, this Fort Worth-based charmer has let the deals out of their myriad of baskets without ever having to call in the snakes. Though the manager has moved up to the corporate level, the store remains her legacy. My, oh my, from love beads to their store of many splendid things, even with their enormous success, they are still generous with the savings and to the community. Locally they give to United Way; nationally they give to Susan G Koman Breast Cancer and Internationally to UNICEF. No stone is left unturned. Good Folks. Great retailer. Clearance Store, Wow!

★★★★ Promenade Clocks
1325 Promenade Center, #132
Richardson, TX 75080

972/644-3979
Mon-Fri 10-5:30; Sat 10-5
www.promenadeclocks.com

There are bubbies and zaydies (parents of our parents) but there's nothing quite as regal as a Grandfather...clock, that is. Though sexist in its intent, it's universal in its appeal. Since 1962, Promenade Clocks has been keeping time with the best of them. In fact, one shopper considers her grandfather clock as a member of her family. When he's having a time out, she does, too. No matter, it's always standing in her hallway, keeping a watch on everybody as they come and go. Its grandeur and presence reminds one of days gone by and happy days are here again...especially if a $16,500 model is reduced by 50 percent. Other models were 60 percent off. Located off Coit Rd. between Arapaho and Belt Line, they will meet or beat any advertised price on most grand brands like **HOWARD MILLER**, **RIDGEWAY**, **SEIKO**, **SETH THOMAS**, **SLIGH** and others. Practically a 1,000 clocks to choose from including cuckoos, mantle, desk, novelty and wall clocks, even hour glasses. What a neat idea for keeping your teen's phone conversations to a minimum. Gift items and expert clock repair, in home or out, also available.

★★★ Protecto-Pak
PO Box 5096
Longview, TX 75604

903/297-3985

Don't worry. Even if you wind up a bag lady, at least you'll be protected from the elements. Besides, you'll be saving as much as 35 percent off retail. If storage is your goal, **PROTECTO-PAK** products are designed to protect, store and display your valuable collectibles at an affordable price. So, what does that mean? It means, they make a patented hinged-back bag that is made of the finest crystal- clear heavy-duty plastic. Now that may not be important to you, but if you're a bag lady, it's crucial. These bags can be hung by the hook or stand free, either way, they're tough as nails (without getting nailed.) They are also acid free to protect valuables for years to come. Maybe you'd like to print your company name on them and use them for your storage needs. However, plan on a minimum order for printing of 25,000. Other good uses for these bags—carry home the catch of the day right off the boat, carry your craft projects to and from class, maybe you were asked to bring the silverware to the party, or baby food to the day care. What about sharing those seedlings with a neighbor or a place to store dog food when you're traveling with Fido in the car. See, I told you. Leave a message on the machine if they don't answer. Send a SASE (self-addressed stamped envelop) for a price list, or request by phone with a minimum order of $10. All products are guaranteed. Delivery time approximately four to six weeks.

★★★★★ **Tic Toc Clocks**   **214/321-9331**
8928 Garland Rd.   Mon-Fri 10-5; Sat 10-3
Dallas, TX 75218

Don't expect their website to be tictock.com; that's already registered to a Dallas Marketing and Promotions company. But they are trying to get going online. Stay tuned to this space. But if you have no time to shop for clocks, carve out an hour of my favorite things. Save up to 50 percent off, even if you're not in the same time zone or even looking to replace your grandfather. Expect all grandfather, mantel, wall and cuckoo clocks to sell for half price until they are going, going, gong. Do you know what time it is? Well, it's probably time to get the tick for your tock. Time to consider buying an **AMERICAN HER-ITAGE**, **ANSONIA**, **BALDWIN**, **BLACK FOREST**, **DOLD**, **HOWARD MILLER**, **LORICON**, **LINDEN**, **NEW ENGLAND**, **RIDGEWAY**, **SETH THOMAS**, **SLIGH** and more. Whether you feel more secure with a bat-tery-operated model or key-wound, the point is you know where the big hand and the little hand costs you. Hands down, this store will save you money on both new and antique clocks. Hands down, the **ATMOS** clocks and 400-day clocks were all present and accounted for. Expert clock repair (experienced since 1963) and restoration, cleaning, and oiling of any old clocks is available. Located eight blocks past Buckner Avenue and Garland Road, this old-favorite keeps getting better over time. Repairs take two weeks or longer, depending on parts needed. Talk to Shelly or Billy (the owners) if you're trying to hunt down an antique or unusual clock. Their contacts will help them track down or locate just about any clock or part.

PS Travis Mitchell Auctions   **972/276-3500**
3821 Dividend Drive   Mon-Fri 8-5
Garland, TX 75247   www.travismitchellauctions.com

Debating whether to house this write-up in Antiques & Auctions or Housewares, we finally decided this is where they belonged. Selling good used kitchen/restaurant and bar equipment, it's one of the few spe-cialists that homeowners can really save on commercial products at residential prices. Consignments (those consigning inventory to the auction) get the proceeds in 10 business days. In order to bid, you have to ante up a $100 Cash Deposit if you want to bid. It's refundable if you don't buy or it's applied to your purchase price if you do. Thank goodness the auction now takes place in a new air-conditioned ware-house on Dividend Drive. They boast they're the pinnacle of the new and used restaurant and bar equipment via the auction block, and they're not far from the truth. Find everything you'd find in a restaurant or bar, including dishes, glassware, freezers, icemakers and more. Sales are held at the ware-house approximately every three weeks. Auctions start at 10 on select Saturday mornings, with previews from 1-6 the preceding Friday afternoon. You can view the inventory that is expected to arrive on the auc-tion block during normal hours on any business day, but they will not be tagged for auction until Friday. *Call toll-free: 877/4-AUCTIO*

◆◆◆◆◆ United Rental
3749 N. Josey Lane
Carrollton, TX

972/492-0550
Mon 7:30-5; Tue-Sat 8-5
www.unitedrent-all.com

Yes, take me to Margarita-ville. Take me home to United Rental, the home to Margaritas-R-Us. Drink up with different sizes of Margaritas, Bellinis (peach, raspberry, strawberry), Cha-Ladas, Piña-Coladas, Hurricanes, Mai-Tai's, Long Island Iced Tea—just make sure you have a designated driver. Party items are everywhere. Serious party items are their specialty. Need something to display your ice sculpture (an ice-carving display stand) for $25? Or, what if you weren't born with a silver spoon in your mouth and you've got to feed peach melba to 100? Well, now it's the time to yell, "Hi-ho, silver." The finest silver serving pieces, china, flatware, serving utensils, champagne fountains (up to $60), punchbowls and glassware, table cloths and other linens (nobody will know you haven't raided your private attic trunk!) Add chairs, wooden lattice screens, flower stands and call in the troops. For business meetings, rent office equipment that you only need occasionally like lecterns, easels, projectors, video cameras and players. For a garden wedding, what about a gazebo for $115? For your school's fund-raiser, what about party and carnival games that include at 15 x 15-foot spacewalk for $120, or a quarterback toss game for $60? Keep it all under the Big Top and rent a tent. It doesn't come cheap but it does protect your guests from a downpour. (And it's certainly cheaper than adding a room addition just for this one occasion.) Dance under the stars with outdoor lighting and dance floors, concession and cooking equipment. Unexpected company can stay the night with rentals of rollaway beds, cribs, playpens, highchairs and strollers. You need it? They've got it. Delivery extra according to your zip code. Chuck Patterson, the head rental honcho, is the best, but he's the only thing not for rent!

★★★★ Weatherly's Clock
5041 Granbury Rd.
Fort Worth, TX 76133

817/294-1281
Mon-Sat 10-6

You can weather any storm with battery alarm clocks starting at under $20 so load up, you know the weather in north Dallas can take a turn for the worse within a moment's notice. Paying attention to timepieces can mean everything from getting to the church to getting to work on time (better late than never doesn't cut it with the boss!) If you're looking for a particular style of clock, this is the place to dial. Dial C for clocks, even if they don't have it in stock, they will special order. Time lines at Weatherly includes grandfather clocks, mantle clocks, cuckoo clocks and more. A new clock would look good hanging in your hallway. But a used clock would look just as good. That's right! They carry both new and antique clocks and who would know the difference? (Unless of course, the antique clock is running a few hours behind the times.) Repairs are available and take about two weeks (pretty standard since most clock stores researched average about two weeks on repairs—or they use the same repair service?) And if your watch needs help, they can repair those, too. All clocks are mechanical or battery—don't expect an electric clock here.

★★★★ World Market (Cost Plus)
1201 N. Central Expressway
Plano, TX 75075

972/509-1843
Mon-Sat 9-9; Sun 10-7
www.costplusworldmarket.com

All the world's a stage, and the players participating like a good thing or two. Enter World Market, when fun and functional furnishings fit the bill. Create that worldly environment from the deals you dig up here. The buyers at World Market travel the globe uncovering the treasures from remote villages, centuries-old villages and foreign bazaars. Based in California, they now bring forth their delicacies like baskets from Bali, Belgium chocolates, pottery from Portugal, other gourmet foodstuff and wine. Do they have the wine! Over 450 varieties, all at great prices. From Chardonnay to Cabernet, Merlot to Zinfandel, the pickings are vast and veritable. Merchandise arrives daily. They even produce their own coffees and biscotti and bring it forth to settle comfortably between floor lamps, sleeper sofas, rugs, chairs, pottery, housewares, home accents, even blinds. One of the most notable blinds included the cinnamon bamboo varieties, the matchstick versions, rice paper and paper accordian...not your usual or customary garden varieties. Check directory for a location nearest you. ***Call toll-free: 800/Cost-Plus***

Jewelry

★★ Bermuda Gold Custom Jewelers

404 S. Main St.
Grapevine, TX 76051

817/481-5115
Mon-Fri 10-6; Sat 10-3
www.bermudagoldjewelry.com

Their website is definitely a faux pas. Nothing to write home about, no history on the company, no jewelry designs to highlight, no online sales to order, so if you want to strike gold, you'll have to go to the bank. Well, this former bank in particular. In business since 1984, the building that they are housed in was a former bank that was held up by Bonnie and Clyde. Though the bank never re-opened, many years later, Bermuda Gold Custom Jewelers moved in. Their specialty is creating custom-designed jewelry utilizing 14-Karat and 18-Karat gold and platinum. If you want a more contemporary look, don't overlook their large selection of colored stones. A gem in any color, even colorless, is perfect in my book. They are located in historic downtown Grapevine (that in and of itself is a buried treasure.) Strike it rich or strike it for less in diamonds (round, emerald-cut, pear-cut, princess-cut, a solitaire, whatever's your pleasure, is available in small to large enough for you to own a piece of the rock. In-house custom designs and watch repair including wedding sets, sterling silver, certified stones, estate jewelry and more. Now, I hate to point a finger at a jewelry store, but it depends on which finger you're talking about. If it's my pinkie, I'm not complaining!

★★★ Big Apple Diamonds & Fine Jewelry

1301 Custer Rd., Suite 482
Plano, TX 75075

972/422-0899
Tue-Wed, Fri 10-6; Thu 10-7; Sat 10:30-4
www.bigapplediamonds.com

I hate websites that tell you to "call the store for details." What's the purpose of a website if you can't get additional information that the store doesn't have time to share? Here are some suggestions should you choose to accept them: Prepare a shopper with a history of your company, how to shop for diamonds, how not to get ripped off, get the message? Looks like you can't expect the Big Apple to take a big bite forward. This is just another way to market diamonds direct from an importer who prices them at direct-factory prices. If you don't "mine," prices for your wedding bands or engagement rings may be cheaper in the Big Apple. Now, since your already in the wedding bell blues state-of-mind, think wedding invitations—here they're 30-50 percent off depending on which competitor you're comparing them to and delivery in 24-hours (if it's a quickie!) Look for them under the Salon Unique sign on the southwest corner of 15th and Custer between Tuesday Morning and Coomer's. There's a trio of designers and jewelers on site: Angela and Martin and David, the owner, who happens to be a graduate GIA (gemologist).

★★★★ Billie B's   972/669-0510
18 Spring Valley Village   Tue-Sat 11-6
Richardson, TX 75080

This isn't the little ole lady from Pasadena but she could pass. Billie is semi-retired meaning for this dynamo, she prefers no set hours and she only likes to stay open until 4 on Saturdays (even at her age, she likes a hot date now and then). "B" tolerant of her unregulated times open and always call before you head out the door. But when her doors swing open, you can try to "B" first in line. She sells necklaces, earrings, wedding sets, rings, bracelets and more, from costume to custom at up to 75 percent off. Billie owns it but she doesn't make it. Her designers do and they can make most pieces overnight. An 18-inch string of fresh water black pearls was $25; or go for broke and string her along for the 22-inch model for $28. Get this, she has a picture of a string of pearls that sells for $1,600 at Tiffany's; she sells the same string for only $40. The only difference? Tiffany's has an 18K gold clasp. These are the twistee pearls and seeing is believing. By utilizing a cheaper clasp, she can reduce the price by $1,560. Now that's some kind of savings. I declare. Billie B saves lots of ads from magazines and catalogs and she copies them for a lot less. Who's to say she's not your guardian angel? As far as repairs go, Billie prefers just fixing your broken stringed jewelry. Located just off Central Expressway, tucked away in a little corner strip center. Call before you lose out on her collection of lapis and patina jewelry. Boy, Billie B, I was boiling when I couldn't get in! Of course, it was hot that day and all I could do was peer through the window. How frustrating! Shoppers don't browse well.

★★ Castle Gap   214/361-1677
8300 Preston Rd., Suite 500   Mon-Sat 10-6
Dallas, TX 75225   www.castlegap.com

Head to their stores or check out their website and see what Charlotte Bennett has brought back from the reservations. Castle Cap the gap on paying exorbitant prices for Indian Jewelry. For more than a quarter of a century, Charlotte and her family have been collecting sterling silver of North American handcrafted wares from the Indian reservations. In fact, she has served on many prestigious Indian craft jewelry organizations such as American Indian Arts Council and as a judge for the North American Indian Art for the AIAC in Dallas. From the ordinary to extraordinary, Castle Gap will serve as your conduit to Indian jewelry and now they've expanded to showcase silver jewelry worldwide via their website. Shop in Plano at the northeast corner of Preston and Park, next to Boston Market. *Call toll-free: 800/880-7407*

★★★ Charles Cohen Manufacturing Jewelers   817/292-4367
4747 S. Hulen St., Suite 107   Tue-Sat 10-6
Fort Worth, TX 76132

With a name like Cohen, of course they know how to sell it to you wholesale. Since 1947, Charles Cohen Jewelers has been providing a personal touch to generations of shoppers. This family-owned jeweler offers jewelry repair to appraisals, custom designs to help in picking out the perfect stone or setting. It's like having a gemstone in the family tree. Value pricing on diamonds, colored gemstones and gold jewelry is how they've managed to stay around for more than 50 years. Want to trade up to a larger diamond? Fine, that's their secret trade-in policy where if you buy the diamond from them, you'll receive the full current price back. Bigger is better, you know that. In addition to their raw gemstones, such as inlaid malachite, lapis, precious opals, black onyx and a staff of graduate gemologists (GIA), they even offer a two-year, no-interest layaway plan. They sell gold wholesale by weight. (Not yours but carat weight, silly!) Specials are active throughout the year on gold and diamonds. Set your dial to a discounted **ROLEX** or the newest addition, the **ROVEN DINO** watch with a five-year warranty (comparable to **TAG HEUER**). Located between Pearle Vision and Bank of America in a small office complex at the back, but is worth the treasure hunt.

★ Claire's Boutique
I-20, Exit 501
Terrell, TX 75100

972/524-6442
Mon-Sat 10-9; Sun 11-6
www.claires.com

Dare your little girl not to drag you to Claire's! Catering to the young and restless, regardless of her age, Claire's wants her! Play dress up in everything from rhinestone earrings and tiaras, friendship bracelets to fuzzy-top pencils; it's glow and go for all the girls. You go, girl. To the prom, they've got you covered from glitter glow to sparkles for your hair. Perfect little purses to handle only those little things, or back packs to carry your change of clothes and makeup must-haves. Add in your key chains, cartoon character diary and buy one, get one whatever, this is a must stop on the 99-cent trail. Or buy a certain dollar amount and get something else for 99-cents. For example, buy $10 or more and get the new Naturals sample CD for only 99 cents. Prices range from cheap on jewelry to I-can-get-that-cheaper-somewhere-else—especially on accessories and other little goodies. But if you watch the shoppers in action, you'll notice how they grab and go regardless of the limits of their allowance. Fun, fun, and more fun, but watch those mini-mavens lest they go crazy with their babysitting money. With 2,200 locations nationwide, surely there's one near you.

Dallas Gold & Silver Exchange
2817 Forest Lane
Dallas, TX 75234

972/484-3662
Mon-Fri 10-6; Sat 10-4
www.dgse.com

Crack open this oyster and you'll find more than a grain of sand inside. Billy Oyster's in charge and boy oh boy, when mother nature wants to compress something from a li'l ole oyster pearl, to a lump of coal for a diamond, to lava for tanzanite, well, just step back and watch her at work. Then, when you want to drop a little around your neck without dropping a lot of money, Dallas Gold & Silver Exchange is the place to dig. They're one of the few public companies in our book with a single location that has its own stock exchange symbol (DGSE). Find the best prices on pre-owned **ROLEX** watches that all come with a two-year warranty and a price tag that's substantially less. Starting this year they've launched a new consolidating jewelry portal, www.eJewelryPortal.com as well as their website above. Considered a category killer, they're one of the power players in the Metroplex who can deliver great prices on diamonds (certified), estate jewelry, watches, pearls, gold jewelry (sold by carat weight), pearls and one of the largest selections of wedding bands. They buy your own gems and watches so they're also a conduit for cashing out on jewelry that you're not wearing (or can no longer afford the insurance rider.) Besides Rolex, they also sell other popular designer watches, brand new or estate models. Personally, the old watches are much more classic than the new, but when you're talking saving money, watch out...either will do. Want a **DAVID YURMAN** bracelet? Well, go price them at Neiman's then shop here. Or a **BREITLING** man's Chronograph watch that lists for $11,700 for $4,700. Seeing is believing. But bring your sunglasses. The diamonds are brilliant and can cause a sudden case of cut-glass blindness, a rare and often di-Bill-ating condition that can only be remedied by a diamond purchase. Also, as their name indicates, stock up on gold and silver. Call for the latest price quotes on bullion. From LBJ, go south on Josey to Forest and turn right. You can see it from the freeway, but you have to go around to Forest to enter the front door. You'll then be buzzed in. Security is tight, and you can be, too. But you'll have to spring for something because the prices are that good, you won't be able to refuse. *Call toll-free: 800/527-5307*

★★★★★ **Dallas Watch & Jewelry Co.**   **972/484-6700**
12801 Midway Rd., Suite 505   Mon-Fri 10-6; Sat 10-3
Dallas, TX 75244   www.dallaswatch.com

One of the largest retailers of reconditioned **ROLEX** watches, it should come as no surprise that they've been around for 30 years. From the days of my first book in 1972, twenty years later they merged with Promenade Gold and Silver. Member of NAWCC, they carry **BREITLING**, **OMEGA**, Rolex to name-drop a few star-watchers but nothing's as chic as adding a custom-diamond-emerald bezel around your Rolex. This custom bezel adds a very special touch with oyster or emerald colored faces. Shop online for it for $1,095 instead of $1,800. They will install any new bezel that you buy at no additional charge. A bezel is that gold and jeweled ring around the watch face. And watch it you will. A diamond and sapphire bezel that retails for $2,650 was $1,100. They specialize in reconditioned Swiss watches so any kind will do. If your taste turns to tennis and you want to ace a large tennis bracelet, then wrap this doozie around your arm. A 10.42kt diamond tennis bracelet that retails for $8,995 was $7,800. Now that's more than a tennis membership to Brookhaven Country Club, but then again, you can't wear a country club! And if you want to assert your manhood, shower her with a trillion engagement rings. This rock is a whopping 3.25 carats for only $3,500. Now she, too, can own a piece of the rock. *Call toll-free: 800/345-0428*

★★★★ **Diamond Broker, The**   **972/490-6060**
11930 Preston Rd.   Mon-Sat 10-6; Thu 10-9
Dallas, TX 75230

Go for the broke-r! When the stock market cries out in pain, call this broker and consider the gain. With an inventory of over $2,000,000, this broker can call the (hot) shots. Buy direct and if you think you'll like a one-carat, consider instead one piece. After all, larger stones are their specialty and you know, girls like 'em big! Rather than bore you with a list of how-to-stay-on-a-diet, stick to this sure weight loss plan (it's based on carats.) Over 500 styles of platinum engagement rings available. A one-carat rounder was $2,750; a 9.91 carat round G-H Si was $97,5000. Surely, you'll find something you'll like from their vault. Oy ge-vault! It has such a nice ring to it.

★★★★ **Diamond Cutters Jewelry Mfg. Wholesale Exchange**
972/386-9088
14811 Inwood Rd.   Mon-Thu 9-6; Fri 9-3:30; Sun By Appt.
Addison, TX 75001

Never on Saturdays, but they will make a concession on Sundays—after church. Well, pray and save, that does have a nice "ring" to it. Diamond Cutters have been around a long time. As a matter of fact, since 1921 they have been laying out the velvet carpet showing you loose diamonds, mounted jewelry with diamonds, watches with diamonds and estate jewelry with diamonds if diamonds are still your best friend. If you prefer a pre-owned **ROLEX**, a work of art, an elaborate silver tea service, they take in those for cash and resell them for cash (check or credit card.) Either way, whether you're buying or selling, or making a private loan on your jewelry, you will no doubt find something that sings out "you" and nobody else will do. Not particularly friendly on our visit but then we were just "looking" and lookers are not what keeps them in business. Located between Spring Valley and Belt Line on Inwood, look for the sign with jewelry and watches. Isn't that special? But their attitude this year cost them a star. *Call toll-free: 800/458-4044*

Dixie's Fashion Accessories Outlet
2500 E. Randol Mill Rd., #113
Arlington, TX 76011

817/649-1112
Mon-Fri 9-6; Sat 10-5
www.dixiesoutlet.com

You'll whistle Dixie when you cross over to this side of the Mason-Dixie line. Scoring a home run is easy. Play dress up in costume jewelry at wholesale prices or below. Sterling silver is also a specialty alongside soft side bags and designer look-alike bags like **BRIGHTON** and **COACH**. There was a **TIFFANY** look-alike necklace with accompanying toggle heart that was an absolute knockout. Why pay Tiffany's price? Dixie's version was still sterling silver and it sure could pass for one costing hundreds of dollars. Instead, pay a pittance of the retail and brag all the way to the bank. See if heads don't turn. Choose from hundreds, no thousands of accessories priced at 50-90 percent off retail. Who doesn't need another pair of earrings anyway? Create a priceless charm bracelet for grandma or a necklace of liquid silver. My D.I.V.A. bracelet is loaded: shopping bags, mules, heels, dogs, credit cards, computer, TV, Radio mic, golfer...My life is a "charm". Say thanks to this family who rings in the New Year by not only getting older, but better. Add lots of gift sets, bath products, leather accessories, sunglasses and more and it spells Dixie's, now bigger and better for a lot less! *Call toll-free: 800/535-6825*

★★★★★ Euless Gold & Silver
1201 W. Airport Frwy., Suite 305
Euless, TX 76040

817/540-5242
Mon-Sat 9:30-6

Oh how we danced on the night we were wed. Remember that song? Have you remembered your anniversary? Well, head to Euless if you have one coming up soon and buy that gift for a lot less. Or, maybe buy an anniversary band that has been worn to celebrate someone else's wedding. Who cares? If it's beautiful and you like it, that's all that counts. Look for **ARTCARVED** wedding and anniversary rings brand new at substantial discounts, too. This company is well known in the Mid-Cities, as it is owned by the Bear family. Papa Bear and his family of Bears sell gold by weight, which means it's easy to comparason shop. (No, not by your weight, silly.) Diamonds are sold at 20 percent over cost, giving both the buyer and the seller a fair deal. As a matter of fact, all of their jewelry is tagged at rock-bottom prices. Take advantage of their cases of pre-owned jewelry that sparkle and shine just as new without the blinding price tags. Both new and used jewelry available for purchase as well as they buy, sell or trade jewelry if you run into a bind. Love to put a spin on that ball during a friendly game of tennis? Then consider their huge assortment of one-carat diamond tennis bracelets from $225 and up. Yes, they also sell used **ROLEX-ES**, refurbished to respond just like new, but with a one-year warranty. They have it all except porridge. Enjoy everything else that they have to serve you at the intersection of Airport Freeway and F.M. 157 (near Burlington Coat Factory).

★★★★ Family Jewels
221 W. Parker Rd., Suite 431
Plano, TX 75023

972/424-8348
Mon-Sat 10-6

Take your family jewels that you're not wearing for whatever reason and have this family jeweler reset and redesign a piece that will be what everybody asks, "Where did you get it?" Resetting and custom pieces take about ten days as all work is done in-house and on the premises. For example, an old brooch that my mother left me. I had something else in mind, other than a pin. Well, what about using it as the centerpiece for a necklace? Hey, I never thought of that. What a perfect idea. Or remove all the little stones and start from scratch. Maybe a necklace and earring set or possibly eke out a bracelet depending on how many stones are salvageable. See, this is just like reclaiming the remains of the day. Only today, the treasures are gems. Still, the sales gal had even another idea. Have the stones set for display like in an elegant silver picture frame alongside a picture of who left you the brooch to begin with. Now, we're onto something. What a great idea and at Family Jewels, they had plenty. Whatever you're not wearing, at least salvage the gold or silver, and then redesign a piece utilizing the basics. Watch the craftsmen at work on the benches in the back. Most of the jewelry is custom-made here but you've got to start with something from you. Reclaim your heritage and breathe new life into something old. There are plenty of mountings to choose from if you want to put your own stone(s) into a readymade. **SEIKO** watches, too, can keep you on time for the next important date. Just don't forget the family jewels.

★★★★★ Fossil Outlet

104 NE I-35, Exit 368
Prime Outlets of Hillsboro
Hillsboro, TX 76645

254/582-7785
Mon-Sat 10-8; Sun 11-6
www.fossil.com

Dig up a good deal at the fossil outlet, one of our hometown favorites with customers and Wall Street. If you already own a **FOSSIL** and it's in need of repair, save yourself the postage and drop it off here where they in turn will send it out for you. Then it's their responsibility for any loss or extra damage. (Always thinking!) New this year is the **HARRY POTTER** limited-edition watches starting at $90. Or get Buffy The Vampire watches for the same price. Either way, it's a small price to pay for the latest, and greatest! You've got to have a few Fossils in your watch wardrobe; otherwise, you're considered backwards in time. All Fossil collectible watches come with special packaging, which adds to their long-term value. Gotta love those collectible tin cans. Fossil started in 1984 with just watches but has now expanded to carry all the items listed above as well as over 300 different styles of watches. So what if you have to dig deep into your pocket to pull out your money? You're going to be saving 30-40 percent. Got a problem with that? Fossil also licenses other items such as purses, leather belts and wallets for men and women, jewelry, alarm clocks, caps, T-shirts and sunglasses. We eyed sunglasses from $6.99-$20 and purses that cost $60-$80, were bagged to $39-$49. The new laser crystal watches were $65 but hadn't arrived at the outlet yet but "watch" for them soon. Online shopping for everything, all except the other locations of their outlet stores. Receive second day air shipping FREE. With these prehistoric prices, you can't go wrong. Don't you just dig it?

★★★★★ Friendze

654 Grapevine Hwy.
Hurst, TX 76054

817/514-7700
Mon-Sat 10-6
www.friendze.com

Experience the frenzy that is sure to be ignited when you start to tap into your creativity. Steer clear of any distractions and take time to go online for workshops and discussion groups if you want an entire wardrobe of jewelry for yourself and your home. Whether you go into their stores or shop online, you'll get what you bargained for. There are some advantages, though, to shopping online. For example, if you're an angel and like to surround yourself with them, they'll even send you a FREE angel greeting card. What started as a jewelry-finding store with components to make your own creations has evolved into a complete one stop shop with all the elements to make your own adaptations of such in-demand designers as **LAGOS** and **DAVID YURMAN**. That's right. Make your own and save a ton of money. In store or online, you see most any motif: hearts and flowers, western, angels and cherubs, filigrees, crosses, Victorian luggage tags, frame corners or bar pins, drops, animals, novelty letters, religious, musical, school days, sports, stones, beads, kits—if you've got the gift of more than gab, grab the opportunity when it presents itself. Make your own designs for yourself or as a gift. The prices are heavenly. Meticulously detailed, Friendze's components are nearly indistinguishable from the originals—all except the final price. Ready-made necklaces from $7.98 to $14.98 were just the tip of the iceberg. New this year, cool Italian faux tortoise jewelry from earrings and neck baubles to bracelets and children's barrettes and key chains. Learn how to add a touch of elegance to wine glasses, too. Yep, bar glasses can be enhanced with jewelry. Their motto, "Look like a million without spending a fortune." Well, meet your new Friends at Friendze. ***Call toll-free: 888/591-4394***

★★★ Fuller's Jewelry   **972/484-7581**
15164 Marsh Lane   Mon-Sat 10-6; Thu 10-8
Addison, TX 75244   www.fullersjewelrystore.com

Since 1949, three generations have worked hard to make customers feel like family. Really? I certainly would never deny owning up to an Uncle in the business. But, I must have been the black sheep of the family, as I've never been treated like there was a genetic relationship. In spite of their radio ads claiming to treat you like family, I have known these folks for 30 years and have never even been introduced. Prices online are cheaper but will be honored in-store if you call them on it. It doesn't hurt, therefore, to check it out online before you head out. A platinum and gold diamond heart pendant was $149 and a pair of 1/4-ctw diamond stud earrings were just $199. Tell her you love her with a full 1-ctw diamond anniversary band. It was a mere $1,199 or 1-cwt tennis bracelet was sharply priced at $499. On the day we visited, all **CITIZEN** watches were an additional 35 percent off, but there were also similar deals on **ACCUTRON** and **SEIKO** watches. But don't expect a very big selection; you'll have to shop in person to experience the full jewelry box. So, how do they keep prices low? Manufacturer-direct is one way. For example, a diamond-cluster pair of earrings (retail $1,000) was selling for $250, and diamond ear studs (retailing $400) were slashed to $150. Read my lips: expect to shell out $2,610 for a pear-shaped .72-Carat I-SI1, $15,600 for a brilliant round 3.01-Carat K-SI2 certified diamond, $6,400 for a brilliant round 1.01-Carat D-VS2, or $6,925 for a pear-shaped 1.24-Carat I-VS1. Consolidated into their one location on Marsh, gaze at their glaringly beautiful presentation underneath lots of chrome and glass. Necklaces, rings and pearls are presented per piece by a salesperson and then calculated to determine the price after the discount. Fuller's guarantees that they're the lowest price from any "authorized" Seiko dealer. Take advantage of their gold card financial plan—no payments or interest for 90 days and say, "Fuller up!" In a strip shopping center one block north of Belt Line on Marsh, they also buy diamonds and estate jewelry as well as sell estate jewelry, offer insurance appraisals and expert watch and jewelry repair.

★★ Greene's Gold & Diamonds   **972/233-1181**
5519 Arapaho Rd.   Mon-Fri 10-6; Sat 10-5
Dallas, TX 75248

When you talk about taking the walk—down the aisle, I'll probably see you at Greene's Gold & Diamonds just behind Prestonwood Mall. Bobby Greene, a long-time fancier of the finer things in life continues to go for the gold. At one time, he had the largest discount jewelry chain in the Metroplex. But those were the good old days when folks were throwing money at him. Today, it's not so free wheeling and yet he still remains one of the biggest wheeler-dealers. Carrying a very large bridal selection coupled with an equally substantive selection of pre-owned **ROLEXES**, this is where dreams are actualized. How about a diamond, any size, shape or clarity? Expect a savings plan of up to 50 percent. They also can place that rock in a platinum mounting, too. And if you're lacking cash but have a collection of cache that you wish to convert to cash, Bobby Greene may be just the buyer you've been waiting for. Greene also buys and sells estate sets. But no website. Hey Bobby, get with the program!

★★★★★ Grissom's Fine Jewelry   817/244-9754
9524 Spur 580   Tue-Sat 10:30-5
Fort Worth, TX 76116

Tarrant County's golden goose is Grissom's Fine Jewelry. They've stood the strands of time and have bedecked the arms and necks of many Metroplex matrons of arms. Try them on yourself. If the shoe fits, well, same with the ring. After more than 30 years in business at the same location with the same traditions that have been handed down to the next generation, they pride themselves on being the manufacturers. And by shopping at the manufacturers, you're eliminating the middleman (the wholesaler or distributor) and can therefore save a lot of moola. Now twice the size than their humble beginnings, once you've entered through their custom doors, take a seat and be waited on hand to neck. Their inventory runs the full spectrum: from loose diamonds (in fact, Grissom's certifies more diamonds than any single outlet operation in Tarrant County.) to custom designs. And the kinds they sell that are certified diamonds, they are sent elsewhere for that certification. Therefore all diamonds are independently graded which helps when you're comparing the prices to the prices of other jewelers. If their diamonds are certified, you can comparison shop meaningfully. Choose custom designs in platinum, gold and silver. And if you're a novice when it comes to buying diamonds, expect a short course in Diamonds 101. Have a Swiss watch that has gone bonkers? Worry not, there's a full repair center on the premises; run by a watchmaker with years of experience in Switzerland. Expect repairs on watches to be about 50 percent less than repairs elsewhere. Then, watch out. **BREITLING** watches, sport watches and one-of-a-kind timepieces are on the shopping block alongside platinum and gold matching wedding bands. In fact, we priced a set that was $300 less than we saw in the bridal magazines. Every stone larger than .5-Carat is sent to an independent lab for grading. According to owner Pat Grissom, "It's the cut that counts!" If you'r busy and you can't get in, they will gladly mail you catalogs of merchandise, providing pricing, quality and such details over the phone. That way, you know a lot before you take the next stop. Michelle was our guide this year and was both knowledgeable and accommodating. *Call toll-free: 800/362-6645*

★★★ Harold's Jewelers   972/221-8581
1288 W. Main St.   Tue-Wed, Fri 9-6; Thu, Sat 9-4
Lewisville, TX 75067

Not exactly Harrods of London, but this Harold of Lewisville is the jeweler of choice to many localities who like that folksy approach. Formerly of Bachendorf's, he's been on his own for years and I'm sure you'll like him! Known as the Supreme Quartz, he's put more batteries into my watches than I can count on one hand. But watch out if you're in the market for watches. He can fix any of them in about a week; ring sizing takes about two days and other repairs such as remount takes about one-two weeks, depending on what's needed. He could write a tome on the history of timepieces because he's even restored old pocket watches. On a more contemporary note, plan on pocketing 25-60 percent on **BULOVA** and **SEIKO** watches, gold chains, pendants and rings.

★★★★★ Jewelry By Floyd   214/821-9155
3300 Swiss Circle   Mon-Sat 9-6
Dallas, TX 75204

Meet Floyd Bickel by heading towards Baylor Hospital, on the corner of Hall and Swiss Circle, and near Floyd St. Look for the white building with black trim and tell him the Diva sent you. Floyd's the Lloyds of London when it comes to buying and selling diamonds, gold chains, coins, platinum, silver, **ROLEX'S**, estate jewelry, just about anything of value that sparkles and shines. Redesigning jewelry is a specialty at "rock" bottom prices so what are you waiting for? Offering complete jewelry and watch repairs, since 1981, his motto has been, "Why Pay Retail?" This secret hideaway may be in a location that is only familiar to those in the Lakewood area, but it's worth an excursion if you need a diversion from retail prices. They boast of their artistry as they are one of the few small-time custom jewelers with big-time deals. They buy, sell or trade—whatever's your jewelry pleasure. Savings can be substantial due to the fact that some of the merchandise comes from repossessions, some from estate sales, and some, quite frankly, out of desperation. Whether it's an engagement or wedding ring, loose diamonds or the remounting of your old ones, semi-precious stones, restringing of pearls or a jewelry appraisal, you can trust this Floyd. He also pays cash for diamonds and other jewelry items. You might even think, without asking a single question, " He is the missing link!"

★★ Jewelry Connection
11427 Harry Hines Blvd.
Dallas, TX 75229

972/247-1477
Mon-Fri 9:30-6; Sat 10-5

I'm just wild about Harry Hines. Connect to this jeweler's store front on this street of dreams. Then dream on. High-fashion designer jewelry and not so designer (but still looks great) plus handbags, totes and clutches. Forget those needless mark-ups and buy direct from this wholesaler/importer. See the Tower of Baubles in watches, earrings, necklaces, sterling silver rings, look-alike handbags, accessories and gift items that are priced to suit "Hour Gang!" **ANNE KLEIN** and **FOSSIL** look-alike watches, **YURMAN** look-alike bracelets and earrings; **LOUIS VUITTON**-like purses (unless you prefer to fork over $785-$980 for a real one.) Then move on to **CHANEL**, **PALOMA PICASSO** and others who can pass as the truth, the whole truth. Large rhinestone selection is perfect for the bridal parties. Add accents like matching rhinestone hair accessories and you've got your bridesmaids all decked out in a row. And for the summer, who can go out without their sterling silver toe rings? Not moi! Toe nail polish and now the toe rings. What else do I need to do to meet the fashion code in the Metroplex? Perfumed tootsies, next?

Jewelry Exchange, The
318 S. Central Expwy.
Richardson, TX 75080

972/671-6700
Mon-Sat 10-6; Thu 10-8; Sun Noon-5
www.jewelryexchange.com

With jewelry and prices this good, who'd want to exchange them? Soon to open their internet buying site, with their ten or eleven stores across the country racking up $100 million in sales, it is any wonder their advertising budget is probably the highest in the Metroplex for a jewelry store.? You can hear them or see them standing outside their non-descript showroom on Central Expressway most days and nights and a few mornings too. You can't ignore them. Being the highest volume jewelry outlet in the country allows them the luxury of a multi-million dollar ad campaign. How do they do it? Well, for one, they import the complete site holder's box of diamonds, which they claim is the cheapest and most direct way of acquiring diamonds. (Here I thought marrying the owner of a diamond mine was the best way to owning a piece of the rock!) Then add to your jewelry chest an armload of bracelets, fingers full of rings, necks full of pendants, and then, it's full steam ahead. The Jewelry Exchange guarantees their jewelry will appraise at twice the full purchase price. I don't know if anybody's held their nose to the fire but when you're importing your diamonds directly from Israel and India, it's no wonder they can price them at such discounts. They also operate five other factories nationwide and can therefore price ready-made jewelry at rock-bottom prices. Boy, talk about hitting the Mother Lode! Not the finest quality, but very acceptable. Independent custom jewelers can't compete, it's true, so they claim the Jewelry Exchange's diamonds are not as fine as theirs. Whoever knows the truth hasn't come forward to spill the beans to date. One-carat tennis bracelets as low as $199 is not chopped liver, you know. JE is a great source for wedding bands, anniversary bands, diamond solitaires, hundreds of sizes, styles, shapes and settings. Thousands of center diamonds are sold loose (and that's the smartest way to buy them.) Don't let them show you a center diamond in a setting because the stone's flaws can be hidden. Then once you've picked the stone and you want to "Sharon the Stone", have them mounted while you wait. Then, you'll be able to get to the church on time.

★★★ Jewelry Factory, The   817/633-3333
2800 Forestwood Drive, Suite 114   Mon-Fri 10-6; Sat 10-5
Arlington, TX 76006

If your watch has lost its band width or your dial has died, you might rush your instrument to the Jewelry Factory for an emergency fix. Watches that are in need of repair can be made whole in no time. But the Jewelry Factory does more than watch repair. They are also home to custom-made jewelry and fine stainless steel watches at 25 percent off. Try on a **CITIZEN** watch or one called **BELAIRE** that they consider one of the finest. They stay on their toes by shopping the competition and pride themselves on keeping abreast of the latest jewelry trends. But their strength still lies on repairs. This husband and wife team can save you up to 66 percent on repairs. Located one block west of 360 off of NE Green Oaks Blvd. in northeast Arlington, take a peek at them in action. Manufacturing, importing, wholesaling and designing in ten, fourteen, eighteen and twenty-four carat gold. Watch them link you to chains, earrings, pendants, bracelets, rings, watches, silver and platinum jewelry. Pay the same price for quality stones that retail stores do and laugh all the way home. All services are performed on site—in most cases, while you wait! Layaway, available, for those who can wait.

★★★★ Jewelry Gallery, The   214/369-5361
5924 Royal Lane, Suite 170   Mon-Fri 10-5
Dallas, TX 75230

Did your dearly departed mother leave you her cache of crown jewels? Want to turn them into cash? Then consigning her jewelry here makes perfectly good sense. Whether you're buying or selling, if you've got an excess of success, not enough fingers or ears, or not just a sterling marriage, you might want to trade it all in and start anew. Consignment jewelry is priced at half of retail. Letting them sell them allows them to receive a 17 percent commission (two percent goes for insurance.) Dazzle them with estate rings, necklaces and bracelets but don't expect to get away cheap. A pair of dangling tanzanite and diamond earrings was $2,895 and an accompanying floral ring of tanzanite and diamond in 14 kt was $1,600. If it fits, fine; if not, they'll recommend someone who can resize it for you. Wait for the sales when prices are reduced. Margaret gathers her lode through estate sales, bank-ordered liquidations and closeouts from other retail stores and are priced at least half off or more. When their "countdown" sale's in progress, expect savings to descend to 60-75 percent off. Call at any given time for them to clue you in to what's in. Don't ask them what's out. They're not fashion consultants.

★★ Kazlow & Associates   214/373-3070
9400 N. Central Expwy., Suite 100   Mon-Fri 9-6 or By Appt
Dallas, TX 75231

The best, only the best, is how best to describe Kazlow's inventory. This first floor office tower showroom is a site worth seeking. Peek through their windows for the finest quality diamonds or gemstones. Ever wished for an S-link or bar/prong tennis bracelet that holds nothing under a full 1CTW but also nothing under $1,000? Well, I told you. They pride themselves on catering to the rich and famous who demand the very best. These downstairs jewelers sell their wares at wholesale prices because of lower overhead, no retail advertising, no mall security, and very little diversity of inventory. For example, no watches (though they'll order one through a catalog if you want.) Gold chains can be your unchained melody or you can link up with any other of their inventory of gold, bracelets, mounted rings and loose stones. The ambience is salon-chic all the way. Direct from the cutters helps chisel the ultimate cost to the bone. Loose diamonds are where they're at in all shapes and sizes. But don't look online for any info or inventory. They gave up with their website.

★★★★ King Arthur Clock and Jewelry

1201 N. Central Expwy., #3
Plano, TX 75075

972/423-2205
Mon-Sat 10-6
www.kingarthurclock.com

King Arthur Clock and Jewelry has been holding court for more than 16 years. As one of the premier retailers of grandfather clocks, curio cabinets, mantle clocks, wall clocks and jewelry for over 16 years, their incredible selection and low prices have held firm in spite of the rise and fall in the economy. Grandfather clocks start at $999 and up. **HOWARD MILLER** and **SLIGH** are two popular manufacturers who meet King Arthur's qualifications. But they rest easy next to all sorts of clocks including wall, table and novelty models, tick tock. Then we were curious about curio cabinets. It was time for my doll collection to relocate from the stairwell. A custom jeweler is on the premises for all your jewelry needs including jewelry appraisals, jewelry repair and restoration, custom jewelry and more. Between custom jewelry and curios and clocks, what's wrong with this picture? Well, I know one thing they carry that others don't and that's class rings and the popular two-tone gold jewelry. For the large clocks, delivery is available but for jewelry, they expect you to cash and carry. Their Lifetime Guarantee states that if your piece breaks, tarnishes, is defective or damaged in any way, simply return it for a new one...no charge. A wonderful pair of two-tone hoop earrings was only $28 and a two-tone 18" inch necklace was only $189. Gold crosses start at $38 and anklets as low as $20 (we're talking dainty, though.) Their philosophy is to ensure their customers will always get the best merchandise at the best price available. Shopping online makes it easier than ever. Sometimes it's hard staring at all those brilliant cuts, stone after stone. Then, it's off to preview their other fine jewelry, clocks, curios and more from the comfort of your home. Talk about the height of luxury as the dreams of carats and sugarplums dance in your head. *Call toll-free: 877/883-8300*

★★★★★ Medalias

4901 Cole Ave.
Dallas, TX 75205

214/526-1987
Tue-Fri 10-3 (Mon-Fri 8-5 online sales)
www.medalias.com

This Dallas-based custom jewelry designs by Foree Hunsicker are the rage. How lucky for Metroplex shoppers that this former interior decorator, oil painter and clothes designer decided to switch gears and start out in 1987 designing luggage tags. Today, sales includes a sterling-silver, Indian-head post set of earrings that retailed for $32 but were marked $12.50 in her retail outlet/showroom. Children's jewelry included bracelets and necklaces, semi-precious jewels, hematite, silver and crystal as well as a large selection of white, pink, lavender and black-purple pearls. A hand-mirror of blue and white porcelain and stone handle was originally $25 but on the day we visited, marked down to $12. Hundreds of items for under $50. Exit Monticello and head to the second floor. No signs. No address. Parking on the first level but believe me, it's worth the hunt. Save 50 percent and more off some of the most interesting silver items in anybody's fashion wardrobe. Vintage jewelry with silver and pearls, stone and ethnic beads, gifts and belts. You never know what's leftover in her outlet, but since she sells to more than 1,500 specialty and department stores, including Nordstrom and Dillard's, there's usually a little of this and a little of that. One day it could be a few pieces from her Ruff Hewn Silver Collection that features classic bead and link chains that are matched with reproductions of antique medallions and sports' medals. Another time, it could be faux ivory and buffalo horn combined with sterling silver accents that she called her Ivory Collection. Then it was the Ruff Hewn Milagro Collection—which were small silver, bronze and copper "miracle" charms. Tiny prayer-aids, minute charms, bleeding hearts, goats, donkeys and other animals inspired by designs seen at Santa Fe's Folk Art Museums are all here, too. Her designs are worn by Liz Taylor, Mary Ann Mobley, Candice Bergen and as the winner of the Dallas Fashion Award, you, too, can be proud to wear a Texan's creation—especially when it's marked at half off! Shop online and see the collection. Then when you discover the prices, you'll jump for joy. *Call toll-free: 800/772-1987*

★★ Nature's Gallery 972/446-1994
1106 South Elm St. Tue-Sat 10-5:30
Carrollton, TX 75006

You can't fool Mother Nature or anybody else that is made and nurtured from the stones, minerals and gems molded here. West of the gazebo in old town Carrollton, Nature's Gallery is where Donald molds nature's wonders into of art. See them glisten and glimmer as they are transformed into beautiful jewelry that bedecks the finest necks in town. Add a few ear pieces and encircle a matching bracelet and hands down, you've got a down-to-earth work of art. Quality, price and the variety of minerals, gems, custom lapidary items, gifts and carvings are unearthed by this guy who doesn't mind getting down and dirty. He happens to be a geologist and chemist turned artisan. So, mosey on down to the old town downtown and see his latest work in progress. There were some ready-mades available, but he prefers to be commissioned from the stash he has mined. I don't mind since they're so affordable. Do you mind?

★★★★ Oscar Utay Jewelry 214/363-6591
8300 Douglas Ave., Suite 725 Mon-Fri 9-4:30
Dallas, TX 75225 www.utay.com

Like father, like son. In the '30s, Oscar Utay began as a watchmaker in downtown Dallas. He moved to the Preston Center location in 1981 and continued to work every day until his death at the age of 85. Dedication was his middle name. Like the song in "Fiddler on the Roof," tradition! brought his son Eddie Utay into the business when his father passed away. He continues as his father before him with a jewelry business off the beaten path selling quality jewelry below retail prices. In fact, he works with each customer personally, with more than half of his sales custom made. Diamonds are handpicked, same with other gemstones, to ensure the best quality and pricing. Selling at a lower profit margin because of lower overhead makes for the perfect match. In fact, he's so sure of his pricing that if you show him a comparable deal that he can't beat, he tells you to buy it elsewhere. He'll gladly bring out all the jewelry left in the vault that his father hoarded from the early '30s and '40s. Talk about a pack rat. A two-tone 14 kt. **ROLEX** that retailed back then was $5,300 and Eddie sold it for $1,600. What a steal! Make a date because all of his prices are borne of the same ilk. Custom jewelry, diamonds, precious gems, gold and platinum, both in stock and custom made are part of his repertoire as well. After all, that's how daddy started and his son dutifully follows in his footsteps.

★★★ Palazzo Diamond Importer 972/239-3131
4532 Belt Line Rd. Mon-Sat 10-6; Thu 10-8
Addison, TX 75244

A short throw from the Tollway, shoppers at either end can exit for custom designs and imported diamonds at prices in cruise control. In Dallas for the past 17 years, they provide a resident GIA gemologist on site, custom jewelry designs and watch repairs on the premises, plus certified loose diamonds. Specializing in large diamonds, maybe Mark Cuban will find something special for one of the thousands of women clamoring for his attention. Prices from $2,820 to $37,000 are advertised specials including the three-carat marquise that my hands eyed. For a mere $20,000, wouldn't it be grand if my wallet were as big as my wants?

★★★★ Parkhill's   817/921-4891
2751 Park Hill Drive   Mon-Sat 10-5
Fort Worth, TX 76109

It may not be Park Ave. but **PARKHILL** has all the rudiments of success. Just like the high-price boutiques in New York City, but without the high price tags. Look for this little white house near TCU without all the presidential trappings. Lower prices on silver jewelry because they are the manufacturers. They own a factory in Bangkok and though you may not be as familiar with their line called **BARSE**, it is very similar in nature to the **BRIGHTON, MARY LOUISE, MEDALIAS** (see write-up under Jewelry) and **ROBERT CHIARELL**, which they also sell. But expect 30 percent off their own line. Silver chains, bracelets, rings, toe rings, anklets, earrings, keychains...if it dangles in silver, no doubt they've got it! Where else can you expect to buy a money clip? Not every store has them in their inventory. But at Parkhill, just park your car (not on a hill), and shop for all on your gift list. Then, call it a wrap and away it goes.

Sam Moon Trading   972/484-3083
11433 Harry Hines Blvd.   Mon-Sat 9-6:30
Dallas, TX 75229   www.sammoon.com (under construction)

Uncle Sam wants you! Enlist his help if you want the premier source for gifts, handbags and luggage and jewelry on the street of dreams, Harry Hines. In fact, when he opens his grand slam at the corner of Harry Hines and (Royal, Walnut Hill, I've forgotten which) in January, you will see 50,000 square feet of heavenly bliss and bargains. He will be your celestial super-duper source for Moon drops and other worldly possession. The entire Moon family is involved and if you want a pair of earrings, a handbag, a set of luggage, a brief case or attaché, a small electronic gift, frames, toys, backpacks to earrings, rings, bracelets, necklaces, costume watches...that's one small step for womankind... watch out, they are the one-stop mega-store for it all. After all, this is Texas and Sam Moon has landed!

★★ Silver Vault   214/357-7115
5655 W. Lovers Lane   Mon-Sat 10-5:30
Dallas, TX 75209

Take a flying leap over to this vault and see silver, "Hi, Low Silver." Expect savings of 25-50 percent yet they deny being a discounter. Looks like they were born with a silver spoon in their mouths and locating on Lovers Lane has put them into serious denial. Merchandise changes but not the categories. Expect to find the largest selection of unique silver gifts, collectibles, silver jewelry, silver photo frames, baby gifts, cigar smoker accessories, barware, decanters and other wine items, as well as antique and estate silver at this shop just west of the Tollway. Custom engraving services and gift-wrapping are also available. Look for extra savings (an additional 25 percent off prices) each January during the annual storewide clearance sale. And while you're there, ask them what they've got against discounting since that is the reason you're there shopping. They're really a five star in merchandising but we had to lower the boom since their attitude is so condescending.

Solitaires   **972/517-1969**
2070 W. Spring Creek Pkwy., Suite 306   Mon-Fri 10:45-5:30; Sat 10:45-4
Plano, TX 75023

Winston is good like a jeweler should. And one visit to his shop will confirm his lone star proof. Though he's a five star winner in our book, he's the jeweler that took an onyx and pearl Buddha pin that was a treasure my mom brought back to me from Hong Kong, but I never wore it. Instead, Winston transformed it into a ring. It's THAT ring—the one that wherever I am, in the elevator, the ladies' restroom, at a restaurant, in the courthouse, someone asks, "Where did you get that ring?" It's THAT ring that has made Winston Davis a star in my jewelry box. After 30 years in the business, he does have a few connections to get it to you wholesale. That means, up to 50 percent at this little neighborhood hideaway next door to Brookshire's at the corner of Spring Creek and Custer. It's where grooms-to-be line up for engagement rings; it's where brides and grooms circle around the corner to pick out their matching wedding bands. It's where husbands flock when they need to shop for an anniversary band. And it's where I dump all of my jewelry I'm not wearing into Winston's lap so he can make them it something new that I WILL wear. And proudly. Diamonds arrive directly from the cutting houses in Israel; hence the savings are stupendous!

★★★★ Travel Jewelry   **214/369-4722**
6123 Berkshire Lane   Mon-Sat 10-5
Dallas, TX 75230

From costume and CZs, to custom and estate jewelry, this place is a virtual trip in itself. Wander through cases of 14K, 18K and platinum—all glimmering like the sun setting on a beach horizon. Ask for Larry Albeita and he will create anything your imagination can conjure into charm bracelets, which, by the way, are all the rage. Then, you must shop here for a vast selection to charm you. Have jewelry you wish to sell? Then, consign it here and let them do all the work!

★★★★★ Two Divas   **214/696-6719**
4412 Lovers Lane   Mon-Sat 10-6; Thu 10-7; Sun 11-5
Dallas, TX 75225

You can ask a diva where she buys her jewelry, you can ask a jeweler where they shop for a diva, but you can't get this diva to multiply overnight. Lo and behold, that's just what happened. Last year, it was Diva; this year, there's Two Divas. One year and holding their own. Costume jewelry for the jet set is just what the doctor ordered. Looking for Azurite, one of the highest quality diamond simulations on the market today? Then get a peek at their fabulous collections. Rings that will knock your socks off. Imagine if they made toe rings like this! (You really would knock your socks off!)

★★★★ Ultra   **972/724-2559**
3000 Grapevine Mills Pkwy,   Mon-Sat 10-9:30; Sun 11-8:30
Grapevine Mills Mall   www.ultrastores.com
Grapevine, TX 76051

Can you imagine? Fixing what's broken right before your eyes? Well, it's true (but broken hearts do not count!) It's just one of the extras that this value jewelry retailer, who was named among the top 10 national jewelry chains by National Jeweler Magazine as one of the largest and fastest growing in the country provides. Whether you're buying gold or diamonds, having something repaired, buying a name brand watch. (**MOVADO**, **TAG HEUER** and others) at the lowest prices guaranteed, everything's 20-75 percent off period. End of discussion. Of course, they offer a six-month lay-a-way plan, 12 months with no interest charged with an Ultra card (card holders are also notified of special events and sales), fine jewelry cleaning inspections and more. Shop online for bigger discounts like signing up for e-mail notifications and getting an additional five percent off your purchase. Also available are three-year protection plans against loss or damage. Living the good life at half the price just got a little nicer. The ultra jewelry shopping experience also has locations in other outlet malls such as Gainesville Prime Outlets (940/668-2566), Hillsboro Prime Outlets (254/582-7070) and San Marcos Prime Outlets (512/392-2570).

★★ Village Jewelers & Diamond Cutters   **972/239-0323**
13534 Preston Rd.   Mon-Sat 10-6; Thu 10-9
Dallas, TX 75240   www.villagejewelers.com

You don't have to be the village idiot to know where the diamonds are! If you're a woman, you can spot them a mile away. Since 1980, this South African has established himself as the primo in loose diamonds priced at near wholesale. Of course, he imports them from South Africa and probably has a few connections. Regardless of how you cut it, be it a marquis to baguette, eternity bands to pavé rings with rope edging, the possibilities are forged in 14 ct, 18ct or platinum. Not a bad place to wind up. Want an invisible setting or a channel setting? Don't care? Don't know the difference? Well, these folks will show you the way. They provide custom designs and appraisal services along with watch repair and pearl restringing. So, don't let the competition string you along, all repair work is done in-house so nothing leaves their premises. They will remind you of the four C's when shopping for a diamond: Cut, Color, Clarity, Carat Weight. They all affect the bottom line. Keep in mind, the cut is just as important as the other criteria since the cut is what allows the diamond to let the sun shine in and display its brilliance. And if you want to keep time, they also discount **CITIZEN**, **MOVADO**, **OMEGA**, **PHILLIPE CHARRIOL**, **TAG HEUER** and other watches to encircle your wrists. Other locations that will dazzle you include Dallas, Plano, Fort Worth, Arlington, Southlake and Mesquite.

Zales (The Diamond Store) Outlet   **214/689-0492**
8701 John W. Carpenter Frwy., Suite 200   Mon-Sat 10-6
Dallas, TX 75247

Zales did not get to be the largest jewelry retailer for sitting around on the sidelines. No, sir. They know their business. And their business is diamonds. Let me introduce you to a pendant, earrings or a ring they've introduced called "The Diva." Now, who do you think they modeled this gorgeous set and charged so little for if it weren't for this Diva? Well, maybe not. Looks like any woman with an affinity toward diamonds would consider this line especially for their eyes only. Let's face it. We're all Divas, though some, I must admit, are DITS (Divas-In-Training.) Shopping at the outlet means, you're shopping with prices of 20-70 percent off traditional retail prices. Keep an active lookout at the outlet for other items for your consideration. Gift lists always seem long around Christmas time, so shop often and don't wait until D-Day. Win the war on high prices, from diamond solitaire earrings to a pair of gold hoops that will run circles around the competition. Brand-name watches, too, sit adjacent to some of the trendy jewelry sets in platinum and sparkling with tanzanite! Most jewelry is specially-purchased for their outlet division, and it is very fashion-forward, catering to a woman who wants a lot of bang for her buck! Know anybody like that? All "certified diamonds" will appraise at 20 percent more. Check directory for other outlet locations at Hillsboro Prime Outlets, Grapevine Mills, Gainesville Prime Outlets, and the new Allen Premium Outlets in Allen, opening in November. One particular ring in the "Diva" line is made up of two dozen princess cut diamonds invisibly set in white 14K gold on a yellow 14K gold band. Wow! The two-tone combination means it's so-o-o cool and versatile. And it comes in two sizes: one and two carat total weights. The one carat version retails at $1,480, at Zales Outlet/$799; the two carat version at the outlet is $1,499/retail $2,780. Now, can we talk?

Zozza Gallery
2260 Promenade Center
Richardson, Texas 75080
Dallas, TX

972/889-0440
Mon-Fri 10-6; Sat 10-5
www.zozza.com

When the passion of its owners meets art where the heart is, that's when you separate the ordinary from the extraordinary. Joe Raphael and Carole Altman have carved out an unusual niche in the Metroplex. Their gallery glistens with dazzling art glass and their jewelry displays a comparable reflection. From buying exquisite engagement and wedding bands to buying a wedding gift that's perfect for the couple in question, it might be your gift from God's ears. If it's a Jewish couple, their selection of Judaica gifts, for example, is the best in the Metroplex. For a mezuzahs, for instance, the miniature 10 Commandments that Jewish couples hang in the door jamb to welcome each and every entrant, can be a signed work of art with history accompanying your purchase, or just plain and simple, but a welcomed gift nonetheless. Choose from appropriate Jewish gifts from $30-$300 in glass or in metal. Why honor the couple with the ordinary? Surprise them with the extraordinary. Their motto is, "Where the Unusual is Usual!" And they mean it. Raphael and Altman travel the globe ferreting out the artisans who have not yet entered the marketplace with their work at untenable prices. Instead, you can buy the newest collectibles at the start of the curve and watch them appreciate. Special lighting accents the glass sculptures and vases, many of them signed by artists from across the globe. Then look in the jewelry showcases to see many handcrafted works of art for your fingers, wrists, neck or ears. Are you listening, God? Don't expect anything but the experience from four generations of jewelers. How else did they achieve such buying power to be able to sell diamonds at below wholesale prices? See one-of-a-kind pieces that are not only dramatic but conversation pieces. Once you've shopped Zozza's, you'll never shop anywhere else. As the exclusive distributor for the **HUBLOT** watch, how can you describe the most beautiful and technologically-enhanced watch piece in the country? Of course, you pay for it, but then, who could ever show you up (unless they also bought a Hublot from Zozza's)? Nobody else sells them in town and that's exactly what Zozza is all about. Each of their locations offers different merchandise, so you have to do double duty to experience the whole megillah (stuff!). Taste Zozza's across from NorthPark, next to the Cheesecake Factory. Forget dieting—then again, the carats at Zozza's are non-fattening. *Call toll-free: 800/992-2728*

36

Legal & Financial

◆◆◆◆ AA USA Insurance Agency   **972/644-7010**
9241 LBJ Fwy., Suite 108   Mon-Fri 8-6; Sat 9-4
Dallas, TX 75243

Start out revving their motors for your car insurance. You'll be tickled pink if they save you some green, then you can pursue their other insurance offerings. If you're longing for a company that represents more than 30 different companies and seeks out the best price and value for your money, you might find this agency a refreshing change of pace. Family-owned and operated, each member participates in the company's goings-on. No customer is denied coverage, regardless of past driving records. Seniors, young drivers under 25, first-time drivers, ticketed drivers, drivers with accidents, drivers with no prior insurance—no problem! So be it. Coverage is available for all 50 states and Canada. They even offer short-term policies (like one or two months) but they are no Rodney D. Young. If you prefer, they'll even split your down payment (not with them sill, but into two payments.) Now, where else have you ever heard of such generosity?

◆◆◆◆◆ Bud Hibbs, Credit & Financial Counseling   **817/589-4284**
PO Box 101672   By Appt. Only
Fort Worth, TX 76185-1672   www.budhibbs.com

This Bud's for you! Once he becomes your om-buds-man, move over credit bureaus. Bud Hibbs will tell you all the alternatives to filing bankruptcy or resigning yourself to a so-called non-profit credit-counseling agency. His book *Guilty! Until Proven Innocent* is FREE, you can't beat that! Get it all on his website and learn what to do if you're drowning in debt, get a FREE cease communication letter, know what you need to know before dealing with debt collectors and collection agencies, even learn who are America's worst Collection Agencies. (Hey, I know a few, too—one day late on Federal Express, even when THEY sent the bill to the wrong address, it was turned over to a collection agency. What gives?) Well, sure enough, there it was...in red on Bud's list of WORST! Right on!! If you should need the assistance of a consumer attorney regarding illegal collection efforts, credit bureau misreporting or other consumer abuses and don't know where to look, just send Bud an email outlining your problem and where you live and he'll give you the advice you need. He's smart. Cuts to the quick. And has done his homework. Meet him online and introduce yourself. He's the best friend a consumer can turn to.

◆◆◆ Consolidated Funding   972/644-4663
2301 Travis   By Appt. Only
Plano, TX 75093

Well, lo and behold. Getting advice from this slugger who's on your side is a breath of fresh air. Know how to do your own mortgage and save a few hundred, maybe a few thousand on that mortgage loan? Well, Larry Dugger has a better idea. His one page loan application is simple. You can't go wrong if you follow his instructions. Whether you're purchasing or refinancing, it pays to save with advice from this expert. At the time of our research, we could get a seven percent interest rate on a 30-year mortgage or a 6.5 percent rate on 15 years with no points. See for yourself and save the old-fashioned way.

◆◆◆◆ Consumer Credit Counseling Service (CCCS)   214/638-2227
8737 King George Drive, Suite 200   Mon-Fri 8:30-2:50
Dallas, TX 75235   www.cccs.net

Since 1973, this Dallas-based credit counseling service (CCCS) has helped the full spectrum of maxxed-out consumers. From financial counseling to debt management, their funding comes from contributions made by creditors and are usually given as a percentage of your payment to that company. For example, let's say you agree to pay a company $100 a month, $10 of it is returned to CCCS. But now the creditors are off your back. (A small price to pay for relief from all those calls.) You can even get advice online. However, credit counseling is noted on your credit report and from what I hear, most creditors see it similarly to bankruptcy; so don't think you're off the hook. And for sure, erasing your debts by filing bankruptcy is not at all like wiping the slate clean. Bankruptcy does not give you that "easy start" that is promoted on TV. After a bankruptcy, it is not easy getting credit for anything—a car, a home, a credit card, an education, sometimes even a job. Getting a handle on your finances is one of CCCS's best contributions to your out-of-control indebtedness. There are 14 offices throughout the Metroplex, with some having ATMs to take your payments. They do, indeed, take the pressure off. The percentage they charge is based on income, for no more than five years. To get to their main location, take I-35 to Regal Row, then east to King George and turn right. They're on the second floor of the second building on the right. *Call toll-free: 800/783-5018*

◆◆◆◆◆ Fathers for Equal Rights/Dallas   214/741-4800
PO Box 50052   Mon-Thu 8-4; Fri 8-3
Dallas, TX 75239   www.fathers4kids.org

Know a guy who's been shafted by his ex? This organization is like manna from heaven. Fathers have rights too, even though the courts don't often see it that way. This organization provides fathers, children, grandparents and families with current and relevant information about critical fathers' issues. Some of these include divorce, child custody, child support, parenting, father's rights, grandparents' rights, family court, kidnapping, parental alienation, fighting false and malicious child abuse accusations, false family violence accusations and step-parent issues. What a handful, but they're one of the most effective support and lobbying groups in the country. Weekly meetings, seminars, legal research training available to its members; with membership, you'll have access to a dozen or so simpatico attorneys and paralegals who will help you prepare court documents. You will, though, have to pay court costs, but it helps. Join in the war stories—there is comfort in numbers. Meetings are Thursdays at 7 where they do ask for a $100 membership fee. Fathers For Equal Rights, Inc. of Dallas is a nonprofit 501 (c) (3) organization, and is one of the oldest and largest civil rights, educational and advocacy organizations in the country with Steve Finstein, Director. Find chat and discussion groups in Dallas and online for support.

◆◆◆ Hayman & Company   214/953-1900

Dallas, TX   PS

Here's a new twist on an old subject—bankruptcy. A licensed attorney offers a $99 package seminar on avoiding judgments. Hey, I know a few folks who could or should be first in line! If you want to learn how the law permits you to restructure your assets and protect your income, you might want to find out when the next seminar is. Such hot topics as learning which assets a creditor can't touch, how to protect your spouse's assets, how to settle your judgments cheaply (hey, I didn't think a lawyer even knew that word!), how to set up checking accounts your creditors can't find or garnish, how to hide your money in untraceable credit and debit cards, even what to do when the constable knocks on your door. I'm not suggesting you sit in the front row, but you never know when this information could come in handy.

◆◆◆◆◆ Nick Mayrath, CPA   972/661-9055

13612 Midway, Suite 603   Mon-Fri 9-5 By Appt. Only
Dallas, TX 75244

Here's the scenario. My *former* CPA does my tax return and says I owe $600. Nick Mayrath does the same return, and says, I'm entitled to $6,000. Now which CPA do you think I use now? You'd be wise to seek his expertise and counsel. He won't steer you wrong.

◆◆◆ Simple Law   940/575-2731

PO Box 8   www.simplelaw.com
Bridgeport, TX 76426

Save money by preparing your own legal documents. Online, you can choose from the following: Name changes, wills and trusts, divorce and general documents which include affidavits, assumption deeds, medical treatment of a minor (that one is important to have on hand), bill of sale, land contracts, organ donation, power of attorney and more. All four come in CDs, downloadable versions and books. Also online updates available for FREE. CD Rom and downloadable versions with worksheets were just $24.95, books $19.95. Also individual forms can be downloaded for $4.95 such as Texas agent and artist contracts, Texas Affidavit for business records, Texas assumption of a mortgage note, Texas land and cattle leases, Texas non-marital cohabital agreement and more. Just maybe, just maybe, you can do-it-yourself and keep the legal bills under wraps. ***Call toll-free: 800/585-8481***

val-u-corp.com   800/555-9141

     24-7
     www.val-u-corp.com

Starting a new business? Want the protection of a corporation? Well, you can incorporate a small business the easy way, the cheapest way, and have all the benefits the big boys have—a Nevada corporation. In fact, if you find a price lower for incorporating than at val-u-corp, they'll beat it. You can form your own Nevada corporation, find an existing corporate shell and make it your own. Enjoy the benefits of a resident agent in Nevada, so if somebody is going to sue you, they have to serve those papers to your agent in Nevada. Get all the legal corporate kits, get custom mail forwarding service, have all the state and local business licenses, have them keep all your records, learn all the tax saving and asset protection strategies, FREE referrals to corporate and tax attorneys and accountants, what else do you want? Research corporate names for availability at the Nevada Secretary of State's site as well as download various forms. Go, man, go. Pick out your corporate name, pay with a credit card (secured site, of course) and you're in business! If you're leery about paying with a credit card online, call their toll free number. Forget incorporating in Delaware. Find out why Delaware USED to be the best state but why Nevada is now. It works. They're good. And they're the cheapest. Enjoy the best of all worlds.

37

Lighting & Lamps

★★★★ A Shade Better
4757 W. Park Blvd., #104
Plano, TX 75093

972/758-0926
Mon-Sat 10-6; Sun 1-5

Nothing shady about this lady. It's perfectly clear, this store was made for shopping. Topping off a beautiful base, choose from hundreds of shades, from pleated to plain, and make that lamp stand its ground. Turn on to more than 300 lamps, 200 finials and 2,000 lampshades. That's right. Thousands. Between the two locations, they can keep you out of the dark. Wrought iron, ceramic, crystal or brass, it's lights on at 20-25 percent off. They also breathe life into old lamps, rewiring that great garage-sale find, or they'll add oomph to plain and boring shades with the addition of rick-rack, tassels, or other interesting trim. Their buy one and get the second one at half price has become a ritual, so pay attention to sale dates and buy a shade better...for less. Turn to A Shade Better in Lewisville, too, at 500 E. FM 3040, #124 @ MacArthur, 972/315-6325.

★★ A to T Lamps
255A Huffines Plaza
Lewisville, TX 75057

972/219-9660
Mon-Fri 7-6:30; Sat 9-3

It took a while for the light to go on here. First, how did they get their name? A stands for arbitrary (basic light bulbs) and the T stands for tubular lights. Go figure. Located two doors down from Bob's Tires, they are the experts when it comes to bulbs or ballasts. So, it's not lamps but lights they sell. And we all need to switch. They carry fluorescents, floods, ballasts and specialty light bulbs including the full spectrum and daylight fluorescents. Call for a lightning quick quote on any of your lighting needs and get out of the dark ages.

★★★★ ARC Fan & Lighting
120 W. Bedford-Euless Rd.
Hurst, TX 76053-4098

817/268-2218
Mon-Fri 8:30-5:30; Sat 10-5

No need for a curve ball, ARC Fan & Lighting is on the straight and narrow when it comes to good deals. Cool your heels with ceiling fans from **CASABLANCA**, **CRAFTMADE**, **ELLINGTON**, **HUNTER** and more. Let them show you the light with over 50 different manufacturers of home lighting including landscape, decorative, or utilitarian lighting. Still can't see your way clear? Then, put on your reading glasses and flip through pages of catalogs 'til you find just watt your looking for. But since most fixtures are on display, deciding between **CALCO**, **CLASSIC**, **DOLAN**, **KICHLER**, **MINKA** and **WILSHIRE** may just be the hardest part. Ordering is easy and prices are still competitive and in some cases make a clean sweep of the competition. Life's all a glow with heavenly fixtures and fans from ARC.

★★★★ Benson Lighting   817/590-2266
2325 E. North Loop 820   Mon-Fri 8-5; Sat 9-1
Fort Worth, TX 76118   www.bensonlighting.com

Looking to shed some light on the subject of high-end lighting with some lower prices? Well, are you living in the Dark Ages? Or under a rock? This family-owned mother and son business has been lighting the homes of Tarrant County for years. In fact, you're welcome to shop their lighting showroom even if you're not a card-carrying resident of Tarrant County. They only request you remain orderly and not grab the sconces from the walls, see if the crystal chandeliers "ping," or play with the dimmers on all the light switches in their showroom. You see, they're used to a more sophisticated audience and prefer that when you see the prices and the selection of old world, Mediterranean and rustic styles that have joined the others on display, you will remain calm and collected. From contemporary to traditional, eclectic to elegant, economical to extravagant, it's all under one roof here. Expect to brighten more than just your space—by adding some dramatic finishing touches such as mirrors, paintings and furniture.

★★★★★ Classic Clearance Center   214/630-4074
7101 Carpenter Frwy.   Tue-Sat 10-6
Dallas, TX 75247

Classic Clearance Center (CCC) is to lamps and shades what the BBB is to bargains (bigger, better ones, that is.) Exit Mockingbird off the Carpenter Freeway, and enter what appears to be a run-down brick warehouse...hardly worth stopping by. But buy you will! Hundreds of lighting possibilities with lampshades starting at $5. Top it off with any one of their choice finials, hang out around the framed pictures, decorative accessories and pillows, and appreciate that life is good. At least 50 to 90 percent off those that have seen better days. Market samples, items that have been discontinued or slightly shopworn but worth every hour of display use. At the time of publishing, they were moving but could not tell me where. Call ahead to avoid disappointment.

✒ Cover Ups Light Switch Plates   972/496-3663
Garland, TX 75044   By Appt. Only

You never know what Tolanda McKinney is up until you see her latest light switch covers in leathers, granites and animal prints. That's right. What is hot in home furnishings is translated onto those plain vanilla light switches that when completed, add a dash of color and an air of the dramatic. Don't give up if the line is busy. She's a talker. But once she sets an appointment and comes out to your home or office, expect pound-for-pound, a perfect light switch matched to you fabric, colors, wallpaper, child's favorite sports or team logo, your hobby, your logo, or what I selected ultimately, the faux marble to match my kitchen walls and the leopard spots to match my guest bath. At $7 and up per switch plate, c'est la vie. But at least you won't be in the dark!

★★★★★ **Dealers Lighting (Lighting Showcase)**   **972/509-0116**
1400 Summit, Suite 3C   Mon-Fri 7:30-5; Sat 8-12
Plano, TX 75074

Let there be light resonating around the Metroplex and Dealers Lighting came forth to the Summit. What a suite deal to C. Seeing the light at wholesale prices is nothing to turn your nose up at. This east Plano showroom is the retail division of Dealers Electrical Supply, a lighting wholesaler. And what you see when you arrive (off-the-beaten-path) is worth taking that extra mile. The elegance of the findings belies the spiral of downward prices. Turn on to some of the best: **GEORGIAN**, **LIGHTOLIER**, **KICHLER**, **QUOIZEL** and **SCHONBECK** crystal and fine art lamps. Their 3,700 square foot showroom also features framed prints, mirrors, decorative accessories and occasional furniture. But it's lighting that still sets them apart from the maddening crowd. From specialty light bulbs to lighting packages for the entire home, lighten your load and save on energy; your budget will be grateful. And if you start to feel faint, fan yourself with a **CRAFTMADE** or **HUNTER** ceiling fan. Focus on your artwork with track lighting and if you're still in the dark, why not consider fluorescent lighting and light bulbs. Shop with the Dealers and enjoy dealer pricing.

★★★ **Elect-A-Van/dba EVS Supply**   **972/231-5351**
1350 E. Arapaho, Suite 126   Mon-Fri 8:30-5; Sat 10-3
Richardson, TX 75081   www.evssupply.com

If it's portable and you need it to go, than go to EVS supply. Battery packs are the specialty of the house—for laptops, camcorders and cellular phones. But remember, they haven't gotten so big that they've forgotten the little guys. They still sell watch batteries even if the big boys call on them for down-well drilling operations. Get powered up with batteries from **DURACELL**, **ENERGIZER**, **HAWKER**, **LENMAR**, **PANASONIC**, **POWER-SONIC**, **RENATA**, **SAFT**, **SANYO**, **TADIRON**, **VARTA** and others. If you're looking for all the right lights in all the wrong places, you might want to change to EVS Supply. So watt's up except all the filaments to light the way? Start with **ELKO**, **PHILIPS**, **OSRAM** and **SYLVANIA** light bulbs. Add in some good-looking light fixtures, chargers, ballasts, recordable media, even large specialty lamps. Business began in the back of a 1962 Plymouth and, like the Energizer Bunny, they keep growing and going. If you need to assault the high cost of batteries, just say charge it (though they accept checks, too.) If you're restoring a vintage lamp, for example, no doubt it'll require a vintage bulb as the standard grocery variety just won't do. The battery selection will drive you batty–there are so many, I lost count an hour ago. Batteries for every conceivable model, from custom to antique, incandescent to metal halogens. As an afterthought, they also sell audio and videotapes at 20 percent off. ***Call toll-free: 800/776-5267***

★★★★ **Fan Factory Outlet**   **817/244-5888**
7948 Hwy. 80 West   Mon-Sat 9-6
Fort Worth, TX 76116   www.fansales.com

Getting a good deal here is a breeze. Getting their website up and running is not. Somewhere in between, this ten-year-old-plus business has put up with a lot. A lot of fans, that is. From inexpensive to 52" **HUNTER** original fans for $245, you will become a fan of the Walter's family who will keep your cool forever more. There are fans everywhere hanging out with others of the same ilk: **AIRWIND**, Hunter, **LIGHTOLIER**, **ROYAL PACIFIC** and others. Whether you're blowing hot or cold, you can choose from lots of inexpensive fans priced lower than the home centers in a variety of styles and in a multitude of colors for under $39.95. Just don't expect them to last a lifetime or to be as effective as others with sturdier motors and the higher price tags. Mostly made in Taiwan or by low-end USA manufacturers, some were even as low as $25. Again, for a small utility room or a bathroom, it should do the job. Special orders are welcome.

★★★ Lakewood Lighting   214/826-5980
341 Hillside Village   Mon-Fri 9:30-5; Sat 10-4
Dallas, TX 75214

Forget the lake, there's a sea of value floating around this store in the Lakewood area. An area bordering east Dallas that still maintains the feeling of a neighborhood. And like this shop that caters to those newcomers who covet the houses of the '30s and '40s looking for restoration lighting, you can light up the night with some of the custom transformations here. Yes, they carry the traditional lighting fare: lamps, fixtures, ceiling fans, chandeliers, but their forté is topping them off with a shade (as low as $10) and taking your favorite or unusual container and turning it into a lamp. Take your favorite cowboy boot, your pewter coffee urn, your marble vase, your daughter's first ballet slippers and let them wire them for lights, action, and a dramatic addition to the end table. Too, Lakewood Lighting also carries market samples in table and floor lamps, which translates into dimming the prices. If your lamp needs some R & R (repair and restoration), these folks are experienced craftsmen and can repair them with ease, and are an authorized **STIFFEL** repair service. Turnaround time for the average fix-er-upper is about four-six weeks. After all, they've got to find the parts, don't they?

★★★★★ Lamp House   214/946-2372
923 Wynnewood Village   Mon-Sat 10-5:30
Dallas, TX 75224

Try leaving the porch light on just in case you've gone shopping. After 30 plus years, they don't even flicker. The flame burns brightly in the same location with the same hours and the same mission...to not leave a light unturned. No need to leave the home fires burning. The Lamp House will light the way with all kinds of lamps in every shape, size and intent. From decorative table lamps to floor lamps to sit behind a couch, a grand **SCHONBEK** chandelier for the dining room table or a smaller version for the entry way. **TIFFANY**-styles mean a stained-glass look and wall sconces mean you can throw some light off the wall. The market samples were not a filament of our imagination. They were half price and a Lamp House fixture. Expect to also see Country-French furniture and more contemporary brands such as **CELLINI**, **KIMBALL** and **UNION CITY**, all at excellent prices, and their standard of excellence hasn't dimmed over the years.

★★★★★ Lamps Plus   214/520-2995
3319 Knox Street   Mon-Fri 10-9; Sat 10-6; Sun 11-6
Dallas, TX 75205   www.lampsplus.com

Say hello to the new guy in town. Since 1974, Lamps Plus, is the largest specialty lighting company in the U.S. Their brightly lit, state-of-the-art showrooms carry a huge selection of functional and decorative lighting, with a complement of furniture and accessories. Save 10-50 percent on hundreds of items, and a smaller selection online. Expect prices to be lower than those at the typical lighting or department store. Opening day specials lured us in ignited by half-price savings on **CASABLANCA** fans, traditional stick lamps for $19.95, an Egyptian gold chandelier for $199.95 and a 3-for-1 torchiere for $59.95. Of course, if you're looking for a chandelier, there are over 660 to choose from. Register online for a free light bulb redeemable at the store. Second location opening soon in Plano which will join their 44 other stores across the country. Lights out! Prices Guaranteed! Isn't it time you turned on to saving money and energy (check out those seven-year bulbs——imagine, not changing bulbs every few months but years' worth of light!). *Call toll-free: 800/782-1967*

★★ Lighting Connection, Inc.   972/964-1946

2001 Coit Rd., #164   Mon-Fri 9-6; Sat 9-4
Plano, TX 75075   www.lightingconnection.com

In 1989, Lighting Connection, Inc. came upon the midnight clear and showed us another way to buy lighting fixtures in the Dallas/Fort Worth area. Since their inception, they've opened two other showrooms, Irving and Austin/San Antonio. Each location displays an A to Z inventory of possible lighting options. From chandeliers to ceiling fans, outdoor and landscape lighting, hall and bath lights, and table and floor lamps. In August of 1989, Lighting Connection Inc. opened as a new lighting fixture supplier in the Dallas-Fort Worth area. Since the early days, when there was a one-man, one truck crew, Lighting Connection, Inc. has become a conduit to keeping the cities of Dallas, Irving, Austin and San Antonio seeing more clearly. By focusing on more than 2,000 fixtures in stock, if you want to connect to saving at least 20 percent, let them be your connection. Online, there's a small closeout section and an online catalog with a few pictures (no shopping online yet.) Hang around with brands like **ART**, **FORECAST**, **GEORGIAN**, **MAXIM**, **THOMAS**, **SAVANT** and **WILSHIRE**—both classic and contemporary at prices several watts below retail. Connect to some of the best, but priced not at the very least. Turn on to their Irving store at 3301 Royalty Row. If it's good enough for David Weekly homes, it's good enough for the BBB (bigger better bargains, of course!)—the consumer's best friend.

Lights Fantastic   214/369-1101

4645 Greenville Ave.   Mon-Fri 9-6; Sat 9-5:30; Sun Noon-5
Dallas, TX 75206

Somehow Lights Fantastic was able to acquire the last remaining "original" **STIFFEL** lamps before the Salton Company acquired Stiffel. If you're a fanatic about history, there's still a few Stiffel's available at 25-75 percent off at this lighting outpost. The La Belle Rose table lamp, French gold finish with ivory antique highlights and an oyster brocade shade retailed for $359 but was marked $89. That's 75 percent off, dahling. Though there will be no more Stiffel lamps made from the original molds, there will be more branded Stiffels but they will never be the same. Then again, Salton makes a pretty good egg poacher and you know you can't tell a good yoke without putting some light on the subject. So, with that in mind, let's lighten up. Lights Fantastic is the granddaddy of the lighting specialists. They are also a manufacturer of fluorescent lighting. That's why you'll find a terrific selection of lights, lamps, lighting fixtures and bulbs. Love those bulbs that last for years. What a relief from not having to change those high-ceiling lights on a monthly basis. I finally found the **MOGUL BASE** bulbs here alongside **CASABLANCA** ceiling fans and the best in high-end designer lighting. Turn on to the **GEORGE KOVACS** collection of Halogen lamps and make tracks to **LIGHTOLIER** track lighting. They are the source for high-tech and contemporary lights that are often ignored in other lighting stores. Look for one of the most extensive collections of **QUOIZEL**, the only **TIFFANY**-endorsed replica. And for chandeliers, they've got them glistening in the sunlight. Then move on to specialty room lighting for the bath, the kitchen, under-the-counter lighting, outdoor lighting, and my personal favorite, the wire that is strung across the room with lights attached, dancers dancing, children riding bicycles; it's a way to keep you always looking up. Then, for the most extensive selection of bulbs, pick out plant lights, long-lasting bulbs and anything to do with fluorescent lighting. If you can't find it here, see how the view is with a flashlight!

★★ Nathan Frankel Electric
1109 Lamar
Fort Worth, TX 76102

817/336-5656
Mon-Fri 8-5; Sat 8-Noon

Let's be frank, Nate. I don't like to pay retail. That's why I like Nathan Frankel Electric because they fit the bill for service and low prices. Ceiling fans start at $50 but before you can buy it, they make sure you're getting what you need. How big is the room where the fan is going? What is the primary reason for the fan...to cool, circulate warm air, or just for good looks? What is the motif of the room? Is it already wired? Who would think there are so many questions that need answers? But when you finally select a fan, you'll be sure it'll get the job done. Then don't forget the light for the fan, too. This small mom and pop neighborhood shop keeps the overhead low, hence lower prices. But, there's plenty to choose from with quality and familiarity. Some, though, were unfamiliar but appeared to be a good value. For doorbells, you can ring the **NUTONE** chimes, then breeze through the collection of **QUOREM** (formerly called **DAVENPORT**) brands of ceiling fans. Other notable brands include **ADVANCE**, **PHILLIPS** and **PROGRESS** for a nice range of options. If you are looking for specialty items, ever consider a built-in vacuum system? A heat light for keeping foods warm? All lighting and electrical supplies are available for installation, all except the installer. A nice change of pace without the hustle put on the sale or "Can I help you, honey!" Now, that's a switch!

★★★★ Reese Interiors
3861 SW Loop 820
Fort Worth, TX 76133

817/292-9191
Mon-Wed, Fri 8-6; Thu 8-8; Sat 9-5

Here's the inside scoop on Reese Interiors and make it a double. There's no wrong way to eat (or beat) the Reeses. Neither can you go wrong by shopping at this interior design studio. Exit Granbury Road, loop around to the south side of the service road, and you have arrived. This one-stop showroom provides everything you may need for your home decorating plan of action. Lighting, flooring, area rugs, drapery and wallpaper. Their low-price guarantee on carpeting includes installation over premium padding, moving of furniture and vacuuming. No hidden costs. We saw pecan flooring (the most durable in the woods) and knew we were nuts to ever pay retail again. Next, on to lighting. They have one of the largest collections of **DALE TIFFANY** lamps in Fort Worth (that means lamps, pendants, chandeliers and fixtures). Another winner is their **FRANK LLOYD WRIGHT** lighting interpretations—close to museum-quality, but not museum-priced. You don't even need to add a rider to your insurance policy. If you need professional lighting design and planning, turn to their professional staff, including recommendations for energy-efficient fixtures for the politically correct. In fact, you can call for a **FREE** energy audit for your home and let them shed some interesting light on the subject. For window treatments, they can accommodate you in that department, too, since they own their own workroom. Custom draperies are a snap to coordinate with the thousands of rolls of wallpaper and borders. Custom lamps and window coverings, though, take about six-eight weeks. Seams like they're pretty busy! Six months same as cash with no interest or payments with approved credit. And that's the end of the story. ***Call toll-free: 800/479-0328***

★★★★★ Texas Lamp Manufacturers
505 E. Hwy. 80
Forney, TX 75126

070/661 6267
Mon-Sat 10-6

This is no blarney. Forney is where the lamps are made for Texas homes. If you live in Texas and you haven't shopped here, you might as well move back to Detroit. Y'all visit them one time and you'll be hooked. Custom lamps take two-four weeks, not bad. And new this year, a large selection of furniture. Make the trip and think destination shopping as if you were going on a grand excursion. Forney is home to lots of interesting and sought-after shopping sites for sore budgets. Exit Talty Road and enjoy one of the largest lamp manufacturing showrooms in the Southwest. If you can't find a lamp here, they'll custom make one for you. You have no excuse not to buy something—especially when I tell you you'll be saving 30-50 percent on hundreds, if not thousands of pretty typical lamps—brass, crystal and statues predominantly. And if yours is broken, they can fix it, sell you a shade, recover your old shade or make a custom shade. If you're looking for brass planters for your plants or other decorative accessories, their 7,000 square feet of options surely will satiate your appetite. Finally, your dim-witted days are over with all the lights here. Layaway is available with 20 percent down and monthly payments for up to a year. ***Call toll-free: 800/537-2675***

38

Lingerie

★★★★★ **L'eggs Hanes Bali Playtex Factory Outlet**   **972/881-1006**
1717 E. Spring Creek Pkwy.   Mon-Sat 9-9; Sun Noon-6
Plano, TX 75074   www.myfavoriteoutlet.com

Let comfort be your guide and savings be your reward. Find **BALI**, **BARELY THERE**, **BEYOND BARE**, **L'EGGS**, **LOVEABLE**, **PLAYTEX** and **WONDERBRA** in everything you need underneath it all. Whether it's bras, panties, intimates, socks, hosiery, legwear, sleepwear, slippers or apparel, you'll weather the storm of high prices here. Don't forget their FREE frequent buyers club where you get a stamp for every $10 you spend. Then after 15 stamps, you get 20 percent off your next purchase. Join the club and get advanced notice on special "members only" sales and events. Save 20-50 percent from the feet up, including fuller-figure queensize pantyhose and knee highs along with the accompanying undergarments to keep it up or covered. Find first-quality **HANES HER WAY** panties that were $1 less than what Wal-Mart was selling them for. Get the scoop online for everything that's going on in the outlets. Find the closest one to you, order their catalogs, or shop online. Love those **LOVEABLES**, **SHAPEWEAR**, **HANES HER WAY**, Socks and Trouser Socks. Are you a plus size? If so, what a selection! Plus size intimates, legwear, apparel, sleepwear and slippers, casual wear, **CHAMPION JOGBRA**. Men and kids are not ignored either. Indulge in bath and body products and you'll never look for odor-eaters again.

★★★★★ **Maidenform**   **972/355-4056**
3000 Grapevine Mills Mall   Mon-Sat 10-9; Sun 11-8
Hwy. 121 @ 2499   www.maidenform.com
Grapevine, TX 76051

From fair maidens to old hags, **MAIDENFORM** will shape, hold, firm and tuck you back into place. It's what to wear under what you're wearing. From full figures to petites and all sizes in between, save big on crop tops, minimizers, push-ups, soft cups, strapless, underwires and water bras, which is the rave these days, thanks to Julia Roberts. Achieve the appearance of a more natural curve, just don't allow any man to break your heart. Panties were as low as 99 cents a pair and shapewear (no longer called a girdle) was priced well under $20. (But why bother?) Here's an interesting piece of information that you may not have known. Maidenform invented the bra as we know it today. Before hand, it was more like a solid wrap but a husband and wife team of dressmakers in New York thought that dresses fit better over a natural bust line so they started making two separate cups to fit in their dresses. It became so popular so fast, women started asking for the cups separately. They designed the bra and offered it as a bonus undergarment with each dress sold. So much for history. Maidenform also makes the **FLEXEES** and **LILYETTE** brands. Expect savings to be around 40 percent off, but during sales, wow, it's a boon, not a bust!

★★★★★ VF Factory Outlet   903/874-1503
Factory Stores of America   www.VFFO.com
316 Factory Outlet Drive
Corsicana, TX 75110-9045

VANITY FAIR is far from being fair. It's one of the most powerful names and outlets in the country. If you want to shop direct from the manufacturers they represent, and achieve the ultimate...half off the lowest ticketed price, how's that for a company's mission statement? Visit online to find the VF Factory Outlet nearest you. Print out a FREE money-saving coupon and go forth into the world of savings. Born in The Outlet Capital of the World, in Reading, Pennsylvania, they have spread their wings and brought forth their brand names into the hinterlands. The line-up is mind-boggling: **BRITTANIA**, **HEALTH-TEX**, **JANSPORT**, **JANTZEN**, **LEE**, **RED KAP**, **RIDERS**, **VANITY FAIR**, **VASARETTE** and **WRANGLER**. So whether it's lacy or denim, it's materially coming from one of the big boys. Go online and print out a $10 coupon off a $100 or more purchase. Such a deal! Closest to the Metroplex, you can shop in Corsicana by taking I-45 S to Exit 229 to Hwy 287 S. to the Factory Stores of America; or 4500 Highway 180 East in Mineral Wells, TX 76067-8385, 940/325-3318 from either Fort Worth / Dallas, take I-20 / Hwy 180 to Mineral Wells; Wichita Falls: Hwy 281 S to Hwy 180 E.

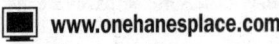 **www.onehanesplace.com**   800/671-1674
                                                   24/7
                                      www.onehanesplace.com

Settle down at One Hanes Place and dress comfortably all the rest of your life. This one-stop-shopping Nirvana brings you your favorite brands one "peace" at a time. Know their names? **HANES**? **L'EGGS**? **BALI BRAS**? **PLAYTEX**? all have their own registered trademarks and are part of the fabric of most shoppers' wardrobes. "Sheer Energy" and "Sheer Elegance" are almost household names. Since the early 1970s, when I first wrote about them as the "Family Showcase of Savings," it didn't take long for them to revolutionize the business. Was there even life before pantyhose in those egg shape cartons? Today, even **WONDERBRA** push-up bras are old hat. **CHAMPION** workout wear is typical to find in most gym bags and now you can experience the convenience and ease of shopping through their website. (Catalogs are still available, too, via their toll-free number above.) All those famous-name brands you love and can't live without: silky-soft Hanes "Silk Reflections" hosiery, including sheers, opaque tights and more; value-priced L'eggs pantyhose, including best-selling "Sheer Energy" and "Sheer Elegance"; beautiful Bali bras and lingerie, Playtex bras, Hanes underwear and **HANES HER WAY** bras should confirm their commitment to support your desire to save money. One click and you can start being picky. Once you've gotten the hang of it, you'll probably want to hang out online more often. Clearance items it where to start; otherwise, you'll be paying retail.

39

Medical

◆◆◆◆◆ AmeriPlan USA
14180 Dallas Pkwy., Suite 504
Dallas, TX 75240

972/671-9445
Mon-Fri 8-5:30
www.ameriplanusa.com

As a member of AmeriPlan, I can now smile and laugh all the way to the bank. Expect to pay $11.95 for individuals and $19.95 for the family plan (monthly) and have supplemental insurance for your health's sake. Your membership will get you discounts on dental, vision, pharmacy and chiropractic services in the Metroplex. Add a few bucks to your monthly plan, and Fido can enjoy trips to the vet, too. One price for a house full of dogs made sense to me. Everybody these days could use supplemental health care and AmeriPlan is the biggest and most well known. Since 1992, there's been no special claims forms, no restrictions on age, no worrying about pre-existing conditions; rather your monthly fees are guaranteed for two years and they offer a 100 percent satisfaction guarantee. Save over 50 percent on braces; if you need a filing, without this insurance, it might cost as much as $120 to walk through the doors of some dentists. But bite you tongue when I tell you this. On AmeriPlan, you simply pay $40. AmeriPlan is the only national discount eyewear plan endorsed by the Opticians Association of America. You'll also save 30-50 percent on diagnostic exams and treatment at chiropractic offices across the country. No restrictions. If you move, the plan moves with you. Also save up to 50 percent on generic drugs and up to 25 percent on name brand prescriptions. The card is accepted at many pharmacies including Eckerd, Walgreens, K-Mart, and Wal-Mart. Then for the animals, veterinary plans cost $6 per month for a single pet and $10 per month for multiple pets. In the Metroplex, there were over 200 dentists and specialists and pharmacies, over 100 eyecare and chiropractic centers and veterinarians. This is one sure way to beat the high cost of health care for yourself, your family, and man's best friends.

 discount-prescription-drugs.com

www.discount-prescription-drugs.com

First, I am not endorsing any of these "information only" prescription drug sites because there is still controversy over their legality. The selling of discounted FDA-approved prescriptions across the border is still a bone of contention with governmental agencies. Buying them is supposedly a customs violation. Customs stops prescriptions from coming into this country because supposedly, the manufactures of overseas drugs are not regulated. In their effort to protect consumers, the government intervened. But interestingly enough, it doesn't apply to orders purchased over the Internet. Loopholes in the bill submitted by the Clinton administration left it impossible to regulate Internet sales of prescription drugs from overseas; this resource gives you the names of where to buy these drugs wholesale for a membership fee of $19.99. Names to over 400 domestic and international pharmacies are listed for the expressed purpose of buying prescription drugs, non-prescription drugs, vitamins, minerals, herbs, supplements, anabolic steroids and veterinarian medications. In addition, they offer online consultants (I am assuming they are doctors who are available for prescriptions if needed). Just be sure to read all disclaimers. The site does keep up with current events in Washington over the purchasing of overseas prescription drugs. It does hold promising possibilities as far as money-saving is concerned. Also check out www.noprescriptionneeded.com, a similar site for the same $19.99 a year membership. Ver-r-ry interesting!

◆◆◆◆◆ **Hearing Aid Express**   **972/241-4620**
11888 Marsh Lane, Suite 111   Mon-Fri 9-5
Dallas, TX 75234

Now hear this. Hearing Aid Express has three locations, Dallas, Mesquite (3330 N. Galloway, #322, 972/270-4441) and Plano, (926 E. 15th St., #102, 972/881-4327.) Congratulations! If you have trouble hearing the fine print, you need Hearing Aid Express. At last, someone is meeting the needs of the aging population by providing discounts on private label hearing aids (Hearing Express brand.) Both in the ear (custom, $495) and (canal, $595) can get you hearing right off the bat. They also offer lower prices on programmable and digital hearing devices from $1,195-$2,500. With all the new and improved technology for the hard-of-hearing, nobody has an excuse these days to be reading lips. Hearing Express has been in the Metroplex for over 10 years so forget shouting, unless you're so excited, you can't help it. But really, they can save your money. They offer a 30-day trial period, so what do you have to lose? (except maybe that all important sales meeting, a marriage proposal, a symphony...get the message?) They also offer a one-year warranty, full FDA compliance, qualified repairs ($89-$119 any brand), batteries (50-cents) and fast service (in some cases, same-day) because they have their own on-site lab and full-time technicians on staff. Appointments are not required, but they are appreciated. *Call toll-free: 800/628-8250*

◆◆◆◆ **Hearing Professional Center**   **214/987-4114**
5462 Glen Lakes Drive   Mon-Fri 8:30-5
Dallas, TX 75231

Did you know that men and women hear pitches differently and that has proven to be the cause of a lot of marital strife? Did you hear that, Bob? I wish he would understand that not hearing is a serious ailment and so easily rectified. Why compound the issue by ignoring a hearing loss? Men often have trouble hearing the female voice (boy that better be true or some guy's come up with a great cop-out.) General screening is $130 and comes with a full report and audiogram results. This will also tell you what type of hearing loss you have and once that's determined, you can be fitted with the world's first and smallest 100 percent digital, completely in-the-canal, hearing aid called "Senso." New from **WIDEX**, it's practically invisible. You have to try it, to believe it. Its CD-quality sound processing within a discreet apparatus has no visible outward signs that you're wearing a hearing aid. Read my lips—is could be just what the doctor ordered. The same technology that is used in CD players, with as much computing power as a desktop computer, there are no buttons, no knobs, no manual adjustments because there's a built-in chip that makes 40 million calculations per second and pre-processes sounds up to 1 million times per second. It's so small, it can fit into the eye of a needle. Since 1983, this hearing center has been located near Presbyterian Hospital, and its "hearing aid with a brain" should revolutionize sound. Bob, are you listening? Appointments are scheduled usually the next day.

◆◆◆◆◆ Homecare Medical 214/696-2525
11130 Petal St., Suite 600
Dallas, TX 75238
Mon-Fri 9-5; Sat By Appt.

It doesn't get better than having the service you need without having to leave the comforts of your own home. In most cases, insurance and Medicare pay for in-home medical equipment. Therefore, Homecare Medical will come out to your home, do a complete evaluation for you, fill out all necessary paperwork and complete all the filings. And it won't cost you a dime. Get lift chairs, recliners, electric scooters, other mobility devices and health aides delivered right to your doorstep. Prices are below retail too. Need we say more? Ok, they've been doing business in the Metroplex for over 20 years. Now that ought to cure a few aches and pains. But don't confuse them with Home Care Medical in Fort Worth who offers a more general array of home health care items. *Call toll-free: 888/643-2525*

★★★★★ Medical Arts Pharmacy 817/558-2971
604 N. Nolan River Rd.
Cleburne, TX 76031
Mon-Fri 9-6

Medical Arts is a masterpiece of value and quality wear for men and women in the medical profession. From scrubs to medical duds all offered at discount prices. Staying on your feet all day can be taxing. **CALZUROS** shoes are just the right remedy. The fact that they will match competitor's prices and sever another 10% off the price can be almost therapeutic. Get an extra jolt by bringing in the whole gang. They'll give an extra 2% off the purchase price. But with all that, we still haven't gotten to their best feature. Discount prosthetics for women with mastectomies. Who would have thought swimwear, bras and lingerie for women with special needs would ever be discounted? Well, they are, with the same low price guarantee. Rest assured Medical Arts DME is just what the doctor ordered.

▣ Medicine Program 573/996-7300
PO Box 520
Doniphan, MO 63935
www.themedicineprogram.com

Looking for a way out of paying for prescription drugs if you really can't afford them? Well, download this book published by the *Cost Containment Research Institute* and find out which drug companies will fill your prescription for FREE. This publication offers an A to Z listing of manufacturers who have patient assistance programs. Most manufacturers do provide FREE medications but rarely publicize it. Since 46 million Americans lack health care insurance, if you're sick and need a prescription, you can't proceed without your doctor's assistance. You can't just call in your **PAXIL** yourself. Make sure you check the manufacturer's shipping policy. Try to anticipate your needs in advance since shipping times vary. (Another cost saver, if you're currently seeing a doctor, ask for samples.)

★ Mixables 214/341-5434
10201 Plano Rd., #112
Dallas, TX 75238
Mon-Fri 10-6; Sat 10-5

Get down to Mixables—Stat! Hurry in for one of the biggest and best selections of health care apparel in the Metroplex. Believe me, it's not just a stroke of luck that these prices are more than fair. Pump up the savings on scrub tops in hundreds of styles and prints, pants, jackets and lab coats all starting at just $10. Now don't have a heart attack over the news that you have to buy at least six pieces to receive these wholesale prices. Cast off the old and in with these new factory-direct uniforms sizes-small to 3XL for both men and women. Pace yourself without fracturing your wallet. You never know whose heart you'll get racing. Doctor up any uniform with pen necklaces and comfortable shoes. Mix and match to your heart's content.

■ **Patience Assistance Network**   **202/595-1038**
Dept. PPA-0109   24/7
PO Box 60382, Washington, DC 22039   www.patientassistance-network.org

Prescription SOS. A new service offered by the Patient Assistance Network in Washington, DC, is for folks unable to pay for their prescription medicine. The network helps people apply for assistance programs. Most provide free rX medications to individuals in need if they meet the sponsor's requirement. Being broke counts. Being out of work counts. Having a company stiff you on your paychecks counts. Consumers receive a personalize prescription application instruction package by mail. Send $5 to the Patient Assistance Network above and include the patient's name, your name if assisting the patient, name and address of the prescribing physician and the name of the drug is required. Call 202/595-1038 or visit www.patientassistance-network.org for more information. Talk about life or death. This could be your lifeline to maintaining good health or recovery. Don't wait another day.

★★★★★ **Radiant Research (formerly Hill Top Research)**   **214/265-1624**
7515 Greenville, Suite 801   Call For Appt. Mon-Fri
Dallas, TX 75231   www.radiantresearch.com

Chances are, whatever ails you will eventually end up on a list of investigative pharmaceutical medicines. If you want to be on the cutting edge of medical research, then volunteer yourself and your ailments to Radiant Research. Programs change frequently but this week's problems for research included Athlete's Feet, Contraceptives, Gastrointestinal Ulcers, Hot Flashes, Obesity, Osteoporosis and Overactive Bladder. The list didn't actually stop there, an additional 10 other medical conditions were also being researched. This may be an alternative to high cost doctor's office visits and prescriptions. Each study has certain requirements such as age, gender, etc., but most conditions offer free study-related medications and examination as well as travel compensation. Keep in mind you might get a placebo or you might get the real juice. After all, this is a study. But for some, it could be a welcomed relief to the pain of high prices. Visit this location or their other facility on Harry Hines Blvd. A quick phone call or trip online will show the current studies and qualifications.

★★★★★ **Reach Across America**   **972/4-DOCTOR**
RHD Medical Center   www.clinicaltrial.com
9 Medical Pkwy., Suite 202
Dallas, TX 75234-7851

Be a modern day hero and volunteer for medical research. Reach out and help someone, even if it's you. Reach Across America is where they conduct clinical trials for the pharmaceutical and nutraceutical industries. Volunteers receive up-to-date medical care including doctor visits, physical exams, regular follow-up evaluations, and laboratory and diagnostic testing at no charge as part of each study. There's also compensation for travel expenses. Readers Digest states that experts credit research volunteers with helping to develop treatments that have cut the male death rate from coronary heart disease by 50 percent and that now save the lives of 70 to 80 percent of the victims of childhood leukemia. Save yourself the medical bills and become a hero in eyes of those in need, too. Thanks to ongoing clinical drug trials, the American Lung Association anticipates important asthma treatment breakthroughs in the next five years. That should make you breath a little easier.

 **RxUSA.com**   **800/798-7248**
28-28 13th St.   www.RxUSA.com
Long Island City, NY 11101

Some discount mail order pharmacies are worth the extra effort and this one in particular is worth noting. They offer below average wholesale pricing on over 25,000 prescription drug and over-the-counter health and beauty aids. They also personally call your physician to be sure the order is correct and will help out in any way they can with all those insurance forms. They carry everything for every condition. Another discount pharmacy to consider is www.RxUniverse.com, located at 5090 North Dixie Hwy., Ft. Lauderdale, FL 33334, 800/794-6490. By purchasing a prescription drug card through this company for only $19.95 a year, you can save 5-40% off prescription retail prices at over 50,000 retail drug stores across the United States. But the real savings is in their mail order division where savings can soar to a whopping 80% and more off retail prices. Talk about relief! No matter how you look at it, discount mail order pharmacies are just what your accountant ordered. Another good choice to consider, check out www.USmedication.com, 524 Clarkson Ave., Brooklyn, NY 11203, 877/624-5879. Do your homework and save a ton on your fiscal fitness.

◆◆◆◆◆ **Senior Friends**   **972/420-1000**
Lewisville HCA Hospital
Lewisville, TX 75057

Are you a senior? Do you love a bargain? Is your name Goldstein or Blair? Well, CODE GREEN, CODE GREEN, all bargain hunters report to the hospital with their Senior Friends membership card and upgrade to first class. For $15 a year/$25 for couples, enjoy the benefits only this club can grant. Oh, mighty one. Want a private room for the price of a double? Want your spouse (or other family member) to enjoy a meal on the house while they're visiting you? These and other benefits await you just by knowing who to call. Her name's Mary Sue and she's the coordinator of this program that grants you these wonderful upgrades.

★★★ **Texas Dental Plans-D/FW**   **972/458-2020**
12850 Hillcrest Rd., #200   Mon-Fri 8-5
Dallas, TX 75230   www.texasdentalplans.com

Grin and bear it with savings on individual and family dental care. Texas Dental Plans is part of the Comp Benefits Family Plan and it has been offering Texas residents something to smile about since 1996. Save big with individual rates just $9.95 to family rates of $17-$34 per month. Don't forget, the one time enrollment fee of $19 and you're ready to turn over a new leaf on dental care. Count on these plans saving you and your family 30-80 percent on most dental fees from preventative, restorative and cosmetic dentistry that includes oral surgery, prosthetics, orthodontics and periodontics. Be sure to get your application in by the 15th of each month for policies to become effective the following month. If not, you might have to bite a bit softer on those aching molars for a while. Taking care of those pearly whites is not something to sneer about.

40

Music & Books

75% Off Books

972/243-3144

3844 Belt Line @ Marsh
Dallas, TX 75001

Mon-Sat 10-8; Sun Noon-6
www.75offbooks.com

Nothing suits me better than curling up in a comfortable chair, cross-legged with a good book, sipping on a tall glass of iced-tea with a twig of mint....and thou bestest bookstore. This is it. Consider reading this small chain of bookstores from cover to cover. Bookmark savings of 75-90 percent off. Did you read me loud and clear? I'm talking books for under $5. Books that retail for $15-$25-$50-$100 for under $5. Talk about reading the riot act! This is where the action is. It's criminal to pay more when you can amass a library full of art books, cookbooks, computer books, health and fitness books, maps, fiction, kids' books, coffee table editions, fiction, if it's in print, expect it here. All are new and all are less than $5. No need to read the fine print. Turn the pages to two other locations, Spring Creek Pkwy/Hwy. 75 in the Plano Market Square and 5152 Rufe Snow Drive, Suite 2872 (Rufe Snow and Loop 820).

★★★★ Bill's Records

972/234-1496

8136 Spring Valley   Mon-Thu 10:30-10; Fri-Sat 10:30-Midnight;Sun 12-10
Dallas, TX 75240

www.billsrecords.com

Hear it. See it. Buy it at Bill's. There's no other record store like it in the Metroplex. Is it a hangout? Yep! Is it a worldly source for rock and roll history? Yep! Is it the place to strike gold, platinum or any other record that has made it to the top? Yep! Will you feel old if you shop here? You might? But that's life. If you want the current rage on the Top 10 Billboard Chart or you want one that was a hit way back when, Bill's Records has it. Bill himself may have had it, too. A throwback to the 60s when flower children wanted peace and cigarettes were a- smokin'! Expect a puffin' and a blowin' when you go in but don't expect a fully functioning website. It was still under construction when we hit enter. "Somewhere over the Rainbow" you'll strike gold by purchasing CDs for just $6.99. Bill's is the place where you can "Boogie Woogie with the bugle boy from Company B" and every sound in between. Don't expect a long, drawn-out conversation unless it's about music. Bill's a "Yes" kind of man and man, oh man, he's a legend in his own time. Nostalgia plays a bigger role than sometimes rock and roll, but Bill's one of the music-aficionados in Texasville.

★★ Book Rack

214/221-0064
Mon-Sat 11-7

10233 E. Northwest Hwy., Suite 432
Dallas, TX 75238

Here's the epitome of *Trading Places*. Even Eddie Murphy would find the Book Rack a laughing matter (if he were looking for funny books.) Their trading policy, though, is somewhat limited. They only take back their books (previously sold) or new releases. No other trade-ins are allowed at this time. That tells me their shelves are overflowing. Thumb through thousands of paperback books that have been read before ending up at their final resting place. Take half off the cover price or trade two-for-one. Its' all the same to them. They also take magazines for in-store credit—but comic books, forget it. Leave the funny stuff to Eddie Murphy. Well-organized alphabetically by author and category, so if you're looking for the "Life of Reilly", you'll find it under Biographies or if Danielle Steele's your must-read, find her under Romance. But if you're looking for love, you're looking in all the wrong places. Try the *Dallas Observer* instead.

★ Booked Up

940/574-2511
Mon-Sat 10-5

216 S. Center St.
Archer City, TX 76351

If you're looking for some *Terms of Endearment*, this is the place that is all booked up. Larry McMurtry, author of *Terms of Endearment*, Lonesome Dove and The Last Picture Show has carved out his place both on the page and in the bookstore. History is in the making. Small towns and bookstores that are unique, different and a place where people meet is what McMurtry had in mind when he opened Booked Up a decade or so ago. Still four stores are scattered throughout the square with each having their own unique categories. Go to the main store (referred to as Store #1) and get the lay of the land throughout their other bookstores each organized by categories. Since none of their inventory is computerized, you'll only get a list of books by authors. Well, this is one chain store that does not want to be linked to the 21st century. I guess visiting where Cybil Shepherd slept is as close to contemporary as you're going to get. Often you'll run into Larry hauling off books and other famous folks thumbing through signed first editions of rare books. You never know who'll you're going to bump heads with but do not expect to find any new books. This bookstore is in a class by itself, a rare find indeed.

★★★★★ Budget CDs & Records

972/278-4333
Tue-Fri 11-7; Sat-Sun 10-7
www.budgetcd.com

2918 S. Jupiter
Garland, TX 75041

Owner Don Baker spent 33 years in the music business and wanted to do something else. So, what did he do? Open Budget CDs & Records. (I thought he wanted out?) Then in 1999, another milestone. Budget CDs went online. Talk about hearing the sites and sounds of music until you're IP pulls the plug. You'll never run out of options. Their extensive inventory contains thousands and thousands of new and used CDs, LPs, vinyl's and cassettes. You'll also find hard-to-find and favorite posters, concert T-shirts, photo albums, 45s, VHS movies, DVDs, accessories, music videos, stickers, buttons...I mean it's music-buyology 101. Musical tastes run the gamut, from country to comedy, gospel to New Age (how's that for a Leap of Faith?), rap to reggae, rock to R & B, sound tracks to sound effects, hold on to your batteries, there's still more. If you're in the store and note that there's a scratch in the CD, the manager will buff it out for a buck. Neato, eh? Whether you want the "best of" Sam Cook, Roy Orbison or KISS, here's the place to make a match. From Jimmy Buffet to the Cure, Pink Floyd to Lisa Loeb, you can connect in person or online. And their 30-day, money-back, if you're not satisfied policy, ensures your complete confidence whether you're buying from their west side location at Vikon Village, just north of Kingsley; or instead of walking for miles at the flea market, you stay home and shop online, you can buy in record numbers, save money, and have the world at your feet.

★★★★★ CD Source   214/890-7614

5500 Greenville Ave.   Mon-Thu 10-10; Fri-Sat 10-10:30; Sun Noon -10
Dallas, TX 75206

This Old Town source is for new town, uptown, downtown, all-around town CD music lovers. CD Source is the place to add to your **CHOPIN LISZT**, just don't expect Chopin, though, to be high on the list of frequent buys here. Stop doodling around and turn up the volume at the intersection of Greenville and Lovers Lane. The Rap Trap is just part of the scene here. Find old and new music on old and new CDs. In fact, they have more than 70,000 in stock at the best prices in this town. And what's nice, they are all co-mingled quite harmoniously with new and old, imports and rare products rather than be isolated in a world of their own. Expect thousands of new titles at $7.99 or less. Can't beat it (even if your name's Michael Jackson!) A 30-day guarantee assures your complete satisfaction; returns are accepted only with receipt. CD Sources pays more for your old CDs ($4.50 and up.)

★★★★ CD Warehouse   817/469-1048

1114 N. Collins St.   Mon-Sat 10-10; Sun Noon-8
Arlington, TX 76011   www.cdwarehouse.com

Another success story out of D/FW. Can you **HANDEL** it? Okay, let's get down to business. CD Warehouse started in a flea market by Mark Kane in 1992, an attorney, who obviously didn't want to practice law. He soon sold the concept in 1997 and an IPO was instituted giving the investment group who bought it plenty of cash. Today, there are almost 400 franchises not only in the U.S. but Canada, England, France South and Central America. Another of their companies they acquired under the CD Warehouse banner is the Disc Go Round stores. In 1998, they really expanded their reach when their website went live. Inventory from stores all around the company up-loaded their inventory onto the website and today, they're probably the largest supplier of pre-owned CDs on the Internet with over 1,000,000 items. I can't even fathom 1,000,000 anything, let alone CDs including rare, difficult and hard-to-find titles. But wait—where are these one million CDs? Anybody who can find them on their website, please let me hear from you on our website, www.biggerbetterbargains.com. I couldn't find a one. But it sure sounds good, doesn't it? In any event, pre-owned CDs are the way to go. Everybody comes out a winner, whether you're buying, selling or trading. As I say, when you build a better mousetrap, flaunt it. There are over 20 CD Warehouses in the Metroplex. Not bad. Expect savings of 30-50 percent off used and discounts on brand name titles, too.

★★★ CD World   214/826-1885

5706 E. Mockingbird, Suite 170   Mon-Sat 10-10; Sun Noon-8
Dallas, TX 75206

The world may take 24 hours to navigate but it'll only take you two-four minutes to find what you need and be on your way here. Why so short? Well, it's so well-organized and well-stocked without the long lines, you can get in and out in minutes. You'll even stay grounded as the inventory won't make your head spin, like some superstores. Being overwhelmed is not necessarily a good thing if you're a serious shopper. Furthermore, if there are lines forming at the checkout counter, it will sometimes deter you to turn around the leave. Though smaller than the superstores, their prices were as good, if not, occasionally better. But it's the used CDs that could really spin you out of control.

Half Price Books
5915 E. Northwest Hwy.
Dallas, TX 75231

214/363-8374
Mon-Sun 9:30-11
www.halfpricebooks.com

Got writer's block? Go to any location of Half Price Books, there's inspiration a block-long—and all at half price. See the millions of words that have been created in thousands and thousands of books from writers who have probably had at sometime in their career, a few writers' moments! At their flagship store, thumb through 53,000 square feet of books; surely you will find something to spark your interest. And think of the passion that was the foundation of this now 60-store chain when they first started. How many enterprises do you know that started in a converted laundromat? Today, there's even a "Half Pint Books" children's area (which includes a walk-in playhouse built by Habitat for Humanity and a dinosaur display from the Museum of Natural History, a community room for events, a coffee shop/bistro and even a post office substation. In spite of these amenities and their fabulous shop-online website, Half Price Books continues to be one of the leaders of the previously-read pack. Even though they're a formidable resource for the reading public, they are also a vast reservoir for half price software, videos, LPs, cassettes, CDs and even reading glasses. Whether it's new or used, they've probably got it. Half price PC software games like "Tome Raider Gold" for $7.98 and "Tomb Raider lll" or "Myst" for $14.95 may jumpstart your interest in electronic games; or the old-fashioned games like "Clue" may bring about a return to the days of playing games around the kitchen table. Half Price Books has many philanthropic endeavors, from literacy to donating their overstock inventory to nonprofit agencies around the world. Isn't it time you took those never-read-anymore books, or never-listen-to-anymore tapes, records, CDs, DVDs, movie videos and more off your bookshelves and traipse on over to the nearest location for an in-store credit. Look for 22 stores in the Metroplex including Irving, Lewisville, Mesquite, North Dallas, Plano and Richardson, as well as Arlington, Bedford and Fort Worth.

★★★★★ Movie Trading Co., The
6109 Greenville Ave. @ Caruth Haven
Dallas, TX 75206

214/361-8287
Sun-Thu 10 -11; Fri-Sat 11-Midnight

I knew Mark Cane of CD Warehouse was up to something. Since he sold CD Warehouse, he's shifted gears to concentrate on the next major trade in, trade out, trade up concept. (Note, trade is the operative word here.) Is there any reason not to cast your ballot for The Movie Trading Company? They are the best and most extensive movie/video/DVD store in town (and the next concept to wind up selling for beaucoup bucks.) Buy, Sell, Rent—any which way you can. The more than 20,000 copies of 15,000 titles should keep you entertained for a lifetime. Whether it's "Sesame Street" or "Barney," or "Die Hard" (With or Without Vengeance,) check 'em out. Six area stores besides the one above. Oak Lawn, Belt Line, Central Exp. in Plano, Arlington and Irving. Mark Kane has set the benchmark ahead of the trend and now he's laughing all the way to the bank. Pop your own popcorn, put your feet up on the chair in front of you, whistle, stop the action when you take a bathroom break, and enjoy the flick for years to come.

★ Paperback Trader
1112 W. Main
Lewisville, TX 75067

972/219-8400
Mon-Wed, Fri 10-6; Thu 10-8; Sat 10-5; Sun Noon-4

What a novel idea! After all, who reads a book more than once? Unless it's the Bible or a dictionary, perhaps, the only thing good about having all those books around is to fill your library's shelves. Maybe a few you've read twice, but the others are either decorative objects or space-wasters! Who cares if the book's been read or the pages dog-eared? It only makes the book easier to digest, and easier to open. You know, it's the groove and if you want to know how Stella got her groove back, there are thousands of options here. After eight years in the same place, turn to this neighborhood shop where used paperback, hardbacks and audiotapes are available at least half the cover price (and even cheaper for most hardbacks). For bigger better savings, bring in books to trade. For each trade-in title, you'll receive a credit of 25 percent of the publisher's price. Use that credit to buy another title and you'll end up saving at least 75 percent off the cover price. Isn't love lovelier the second time around? Well, so are books.

★★★★★ Recycled Books, Records & CDs   940/566-5688

200 N. Locust   Mon-Sun 9-9
Denton, TX 76201   www.recycledbooks.com

Since 1983, this Denton tower of babble has been the source of reading material for miles around. I really didn't want to Title Tattle, but it's really one of the best in the county. From required reading and esoteric titles, to books for under the hammock or around the fireplace, there are over 200,000 of them, 7,000 records and 16,000 CDs. A lifetime of collecting, and a lifetime of pages to turn before you sleep. If you're on your way to court, you can't miss it. Just look for the color purple (that's their building color) and then go inside and get a copy of *The Color Purple*. Both are quality words between the pages. Three floors of books, records, CDs and more for 50 percent off and less. No sales. No fooling. No overpriced anything.

41

Musical Instruments

★★★ Brook Mays Music Co.
2521 W. Airport Frwy.
Irving, TX 75062

972/570-1600
Mon-Fri 10-8; Sat 10-6; Sun 1-5
www.brookmays.com

No relation to babbling brooks but they do run deep—on sales, that is. But ordinarily, their low price guarantee means if you find it cheaper within 30 days, they'll refund the difference. In business over 100 years, they opened in 1891 and are still playing my song. Everything you need for guitars, amplifiers, the orchestra or band, keyboards, drums, recording, lighting, DJ equipment and musical education, what more could **LUDWIG** want? With 14 locations throughout the Metroplex, on one visit, we couldn't resist the **YAMAHA** vocal plug-in board for $113. Others in our party ogled the **FRANCISCAN** classic guitar for $117 and the **WINSTON** Black/Nichols sax for $1,200. This store means business, serious music business, though others will find it harmonious to making music, even if they're amateurs. Slide on in for a trombone or any other instrument to beat the band. Additional brands include **AMERICAN, HORST, KORG, KURZWEIL, IBANEZ, MARTIN, PEAVEY, ROGERS, ROLAND, SCHMIDT** and **SQUIER**. Join the Performer's Club for special prices all year 'round.

★★ Clearance Keyboard Outlet
14235 Inwood
Dallas, TX 75244

972/490-5397
Thu-Sat 10-6

Looks like they're replaying my song but reducing it to three days a week. Is business that good that the doors can be closed more than half the week? Well, they are available for appointments for other times if you're serious about buying, selling or trading any new or used keyboards. All of theirs on the showroom floor are ready to be played and are in tune with the times. The player grand pianos are too cool. There's a variety of keyboards to choose from that have come their way via consignment, bank or store repossession. But if the price is right, you and the outlet come out a winner. Play the field on multiple bands of instrumentation: **BALDWIN** (should become a collector's item since company is in bankruptcy at time of publication), **FENDER, GIBSON, KAWAI, KORG, MARTIN, ROLAND, SAMICK, SUZUKI** and **YAMAHA**—pianos, keyboards, electric guitars. But **SONIC**, that's a new one. I thought they were a drive-in? Get on the bandwagon and experience the sound of the times. Nationwide financing and layaway available for 90 days with 20 percent down.

★★★★ Dallas Piano Warehouse & Showroom   972/231-4607

9292 LBJ Frwy.   Mon-Thu 10-8; Fri-Sat 9-6; Sun 1-6
Dallas, TX 75243

Billy Joel may have been the piano man but it's Walt Birchfield, owner of Dallas Piano Warehouse & Showroom, who's stealing the show these days. Just pass his showroom on LBJ (exit Abrams Road) and look inside. Even if you're driving by, you're sure to remember that red (or whatever color) piano that is showing in the window! Tickle the ivories of **BOSENDORFER**, **KAWAI**, **ROLAND**, **SCHIMMEL**, **STEINWAY**, **TECHNICS**, **YOUNG CHANG** and more in pianos and keyboards. In fact, they are supposedly the largest Young Chang dealer in the country. But what if you wanted to "Play It Again, Sam"? Used pianos start at $1,195 but our attention was diverted when we heard the player pianos. What fun! Lay-a-way is available for up to six months with 25 percent down and 90-days financing is same as cash; or 10 percent simple interest for three years or 11.5 percent for five years. A "sound" investment for budding Beethovens or aspiring Elton Johns.

◆◆◆◆ Dallas School of Music, The   972/380-8050

2650 Midway Rd., Suite 204   Mon-Thu 10-9; Sat 9-4
Carrollton, TX 75006   www.dsminfo.com

You've heard of "Tickle me, Elmo," haven't you? Well, what instrument tickles you most? If it's the piano, you're really sharp because this school can teach you the difference between the sharps and the flats, the rests and the clefs. In fact, they can teach you how to play most any instrument. Lessons are available at their location or via the Internet at www.MusickEd.com. Can you believe they are playing your song? They also offer vocal education: soprano, alto, tenor, bass and speech therapy beside all the instrumental instruction you need to join the orchestra or band. From flute, clarinet, sax, oboe, bassoon, trumpet, trombone, horn, euphonium, tuba or percussion, why not drum on the drums and make those trombones ooze? If you're tired of being strung along, why not try your hands on the violin, viola, cello, double bass, guitar, electric guitar or electric bass? And to really drown out your sorrows, try a synthesizer or MIDI. Pianos, to the younger set, may be considered passé. Whatever tickles their fancy, let there be music, music, music.

★★★★★ Guitar Center   972/960-0011

14080 Dallas Pkwy.   Mon-Fri 10-9; Sat 10-7; Sun Noon-6
Dallas, TX 75240   www.guitarcenter.com

The story begins the night the Beatles appeared on "The Ed Sullivan Show" in 1964. Rock 'n Roll arrived and the electric guitar was born. Soon, Guitar Center began filling the need for aspiring artists to buy them. Now, 36 years later, Guitar Center has evolved into a multi-faceted music store, where musicians connect both locally and nationwide. It's the hubba-bubba of quality musical equipment. It's also the country's largest retailer of musical instruments at the guaranteed lowest price. Don't fret! Whether it's a keyboard or headphone, amps to drums, today it's far more than just an electric guitar store. Every music specialty is represented: Keyboards, MIDI peripherals, music software, pro audio recording equipment, dance music gear, percussions, amplifiers, basses, acoustic guitars, accessories to vintage instruments, nary a sound is ignored. The display of products is awesome with private acoustic rooms, innovative product demonstration facilities—a real exciting "hands on" environment. (They were first, MARS came after.) For home-recording professional tips, tune into their workshops at all locations (721 Ryan Plaza Drive, Arlington, 817/277-3510, 7814 N. Central Expwy, Dallas, 214/692-9999, far north Dallas, 14080 Dallas Parkway, 972/960-0011 or in Plano at 2333 N. Central Expressway, Suite 101, 972/422-7171). For their unrivaled Buyers Guide where you can find all the deals, expect to see a new one every 30 days. If you live within 50 miles of a Guitar Center, they're happy to put you on their mailing list. Walk-ins are welcomed, especially musicians for hi-fi talk and jammin'.

Jack Whitby Piano

8326 Scyene Rd.
Dallas, TX 75227

214/381-9571
Mon-Thu 10:30-7; Fri-Sat 10:30-5; Sun 3-6
www.jackwhitbypiano.com

The piano scene starts on Scyene, however you pronounce it. This 30-year veteran of the black and white piano business has the corner on refurbished pianos wrapped up with a great big yellow ribbon. Texan pianists like it big and Jack Whitby can supply them in a grand way. Since the early '70s, they have maintained an inventory of over 30 pre-owned grand and upright **KAWAI** and **YAMAHA** pianos. They also have **BALDWIN**, **MASON & HAMLIN**, **PEARL RIVER**, **STEINWAY** and then, occasionally they find a jewel like the **SAMICK** that I bought for $6,500 that would retail for over $15,000. By the way, the Samick piano is the only other brand sold through Steinway. And it's the best piano I've ever played a Bach fugue or a Chopin waltz on. Today, prices start around $7,500 for the Kawai and Yamaha baby grands and around $3,200 and up for Professional Uprights and $1,800 for Consoles. Believe me, you won't be able to tell the difference once they get their hands underneath the hood, tickle the ivories and strip off the old finish. The pianos all look brand new and at half the price, sound the same to me. All pianos are thoroughly serviced and checked string by string. You can even request one of those new player piano systems to be installed. Financing available. Now find them and you will have finished the symphony, at last! *Call toll-free: 888/381-7333*

◆◆◆◆ Karl's Piano Tuning

Dallas, TX

214/381-7390
By Appt. Only

If your C is flat and your F is sharp, then it's time to call in the tune-up medic. Karl maintains his home business by coming to your home for your piano's checkup. Don't wait until it's an emergency and Van Cliburn's coming to dinner and you've got to tune up! No, if you think dogs have great ears, you should see Karl in action. He can hear a flat a mile away. He'll come to the rescue with his perfect pitch and tuning fork anywhere in the Metroplex. Expect to pay a minimum of $75 for a house call. Make an appointment a few days ahead, but sometimes, he will make a special appearance for a calamity. Don't let your diminuendos sound like crescendos or your pedals hit the metals. He can work magic but not miracles. In that case, you may need an Orthopedic Surgeon.

★★★★★ Lone Star Percussion

10611 Control Place Drive
Dallas, TX 75238

214/340-0835
Mon-Fri 9:30-5:30
www.lonestarpercussion.com

Without inducing a concussion, these percussion instruments should strike a chord with anyone itching to launch a rock band, join in the marching band, contribute to an orchestra or make a living as a DJ. With over 6,000 items in stock, instruments that will ensure you strike up the band, and beat the competition by a mile. Over 40 percent off, sometimes more, sometime less, but overall an average of 40 off is music to our ears. Get a great deal on **PRO MARK** drumsticks for $4.70 (retail $13.25) or get an **IMPACT SIGNATURE BAG** starting at $29 (retail $42). See what I mean? Drums, brushes, books, mallets, sticks, sound effects and books are the beginning elements of the total sound. More than 20 years of pounding out a living, you'd think they'd stop beating around the brushes. Oh no. All you have to do is take a peek at their "Discount Price List" (online or by mail) and you'll see an extensive list of more items than you can shake a stick at. It's easy to get around the massive inventory with their index categories. And don't turn a deaf ear to their online specials. One was a five-piece **LUDWIG** junior drum set that listed for $350, but was $209.95; a 15-inch Ludwig snare bottom was $21 but was captured for $10.45. But it was the set of five dry **AGOGO** bells that were $127 that rang our chimes for $76.15 and that turned a Latin ensemble into a hotsy-totsy salsa band. Lastly, don't forget, if you need some specialty calls, consider an auk, quail, crow, nightingale or other jungle sounds without buying from a quack-quack. Be a sport...from $5.55 to $24.10. Professional wire **ZILDJIAN** brushes were found for $15.55 (retail $25.95) and **AMERICAN** snare drum sticks were $6.95 ($9 retail). Now, maestro, please, strike up the band!

★★★★ Mars Superstore   214/361-8155
8081 Walnut Hill Lane @ North Central Expwy.   Mon-Fri 11-9; Sat 10-7;
Sun Noon-6
Dallas, TX 75231   www.marsmusic.com

This is the big-band box of discount stores—this time, the category's musical instruments. With their out-of-this-world selection of more than 100,000 products and 500 brand names, many in stock, is there a sound that can not be heard from here? It's doubtful. They even offer a Mars Music credit card with no annual fee and special sales events and offers for "members only". Since 1996, this chain has played out their strengths within 38,000 square feet of traditional musical inventory and some within unique niches that are often ignored by others. For example, their demo room is a Top 10 hit! It's where musicians jam in a state-of-the-art recording studio and perform on the stage for in-store concerts and clinics. Then, there's the "Babies Make Music and Toddlers Make Music" for little ones. A nine-week class runs $149 and includes books and materials. Lessons are also offered seven days a week in all areas of music. Schedules change often so call and ask for the Learning Center. Now, let's get down to brass tacks. They also sell musical equipment for recording, lighting, microphones, sheet music and DJs can save up to 40 percent on cartridges, slip mats, single-sided headphones, gooseneck lights, LP and CD cases. Add turntables, mixers and CD players and you start to get a glimpse of the program in progress. While all this might come with a premium price, Mars guarantees it will beat any advertised price, plus refund double the difference, up to $50, if you see a lower price advertised within 30 days of purchase. Now, are you ready to hop aboard and take a trip to Mars? You might even find gossamer's wings to fly home on. Look for additional locations in Arlington, 817/465-1444, and Plano, 972/633-1250.

★★★★★ Piano Restoration by Bill Powell   972/285-9755
1320 Hwy. 80 E.   Mon-Sat 8-6
Mesquite, TX 75149

Nothing quite compares to a piano that has been restored by Bill Powell. Make an appointment for an estimate (he's busy, so be prepared to wait a few days, maybe a week) for his appraisal. A charge of $50 is assessed but will be taken off the final bill if you have him perform the necessary plastic and/or internal surgery. He can transform that pale and pathetic 88-keyed instrument to one of mint condition both inside and out! But really, it's the innards that make him a Master of Pianontology—a new and neglected discipline soon to be added to Southwestern Medical School's roster. An old, neglected **BALDWIN** was rescued in an estate sale for $2,000; restored completely inside and out including a new keyboard, sounding board and other intricate workings and when it was returned two months later, for approximately $5,500, it brought tears to my eyes. That investment brought an appraised value of over $15,000 and I'd say well worth the money spent. Dr. Powell, as he should be addressed, is the Miracle Man who has worked magic on many other pianos, grand or otherwise, in the Metroplex. Even dealers use him and then charge you twice the price. Shop direct and save. Sounds good to me, eh?

★★ Rhythm Band, The

1212 E. Lancaster
Fort Worth, TX 76101-0126

817/335-2561
Mon-Fri 8-5
www.rhythmband.com

If your kids are clamoring to start their own marching band, join in a neighborhood jam band, or just want to strut their stuff around the block, they will love that you've hopped aboard the Rhythm Band's bandwagon. Tom-toms start at $9.95, xylopipes were $8.95 and marching drums, a mere $11.95. A small price to pay for pounding out their aggressions and making some sounds of music? Well, maybe not music. Remember **CHARLIE HORSE** from TV? Well, your kids probably do and his 10-piece rhythm band set was only $24.95. Remember, he may be the next Gene Krupa! Ukuleles cost $32.50 but I doubt if Arthur Godfrey's on your five-year old's want list? Then what about the full scale of broomwackers for $22? First, you've got to find out what a broomwacker is. If it's a kitchen helper, you ought to consider. All infants love the rhythm of the band with a baby drum set with mallet, baby bell stick, maraca, red scarf, baby book and video for $40. You may remember some of these instruments from way back when. This company has been helping music educators since 1961. Come on...sing along. Expect to save about 15 percent with no minimum order. Same rates as those for schools. Order online or through their catalog such must-haves as: rhythm instruments like bells, bongos, castanets, cymbals, drums, glockenspiels, kazoos, maracas, rhythm sticks, ukuleles and xylophones. Can't live without some sand blocks? Triangles? That was my favorite when I was in the band! Remember? ***Call toll-free: 800/424-4724***

★★★★ Richard's Band Instrument Repair

1311-B E. Belt Line Rd.
Carrollton, TX 75006

972/446-4081
Tues-Sat 10-6

Richard's Band Instrument Repair is a great place to strike up the band if your children are looking to blow their own horn. But before you shell out a lot of cash for some brass, think again. Remember, often times, they change their minds a week or so into the lessons or the commitment to join the band and here you're stuck with an $800 trumpet. Save on these expensive instruments and buy them used instead. Let junior try the trumpet, trombone or tuba for less than you might pay for one instrument new. Aspiring musicians or their parents have turned to this Music Man for keeping their instruments in finely tuned shape. Just swing by if indeed your brass is sounding crass and you're ready to donate it to the dump. But don't think he's a Johnny one-note. He offers much more than just new pads for the saxophone or un-jamming a valve on the trumpet. Having taught band for years, he never ventured out to include the guitar or the drums. Actually, he's a sax virtuoso and plays professionally around town, but for the average Joe, he sells band instruments at really low prices. Swing low, sweet instruments. They now carry a tune, thanks to this Richard's almanac of tune-up virtuosity. Buying used instead of new makes a harmonic contribution to your budget's scale of diminishing returns. ***Call toll-free: 800/381-2263***

★★★★ Speir's Music/Roomscapes

510 S. Garland Rd.
Garland, TX 75040

972/272-1700
Mon-Fri 10-8; Sat 10-7; Sun 1-6
www.speirmusic.net

Music started blaring out of Speir's Music Store in 1962 and has been sounding loud and clear ever since. Speir's cuts to the heart of the music industry by offering band instrumentation, guitars, keyboards, percussion and amplifiers at very competitive prices. Heard around the world with amplifiers by **AMPEG**, **BUDDA**, **CARR**, **CRATE**, **DR Z**, **GIBSON**, **GOLDTONE**, **SWR** and **TOP HAT**. Then be sure to record every note with components by **AKG**, **ALESIS**, **AUDIO TECHNICA**, **CAD**, **EV**, **ROLAND**, **SENNHEISER**, **SHURE** and others. All under one roof, you'll find the instruments, repairs, and a policy of 90-days-same-as-cash. Now, where else can you find more than 1,000 guitars and this helpful financing incentive? All sales personnel are especially trained by the factory. The four S's make them a logical choice to escape to: service, sales, selection and then add Speir's to your shopping musical list. Oh, by the way, the **TOCA** conga drums for $299.95 came with a FREE stand so we couldn't stand it and bought them. *Call toll-free: 800/497-1703*

Sword's Music Co.
4300 E. Lancaster Ave.
Fort Worth, TX 76103

817/536-8742
Mon-Sat 10:30-7

Let's cut to the quick. First, ask for Anthony or Dave (they're always there) and let them lead the way. Since 1969, Sword's has been helping you slash the high prices on all band and orchestral instruments. Start out with **FENDER**, **GIBSON**, **IBANEZ** or **MARTIN** guitars; add in **CRATE**, **FENDER**, **MARSHALL** or **ROLAND** amps; strum on a CB-700, **LUDWIG**, **PEARL**, **TAMA** drum; tickle on a **KORG** or **ROLAND** keyboard; then swing on a P.A. system, trumpet, saxophone, clarinet, oboe, French horn, or viola——all priced at up to 40 percent off. Jump on the band wagon and show them a price that was advertised elsewhere, and they'll match it. Plain and simple. Occasionally, they have older/vintage instruments, too, if you're a collector. Check it out. Play it every which way—sales, rentals, repairs and lessons, too. They'll never string you along. You'll always be able to strike up the band. Why? Because their layaway plan is almost too good to be true. Here goes: You put down whatever you can afford and you pay monthly as much as you can, for as long as you need to, until it's paid in full. (Sounds like a Tommy Snodgrass layaway policy to me!) Ah, music to my ears. If you have to have it now, financing is available through Wells Fargo and approvals only take 30-45 minutes. This is the Speedy Gonzales approach to financing so you can cut out the mumbo-jumbo and be playing the high notes ASAP! *Call toll-free: 800/522-3028*

42

Office

★★★ **A-Box Connection**   214/357-2088
2671 Manana   Mon-Fri 8:30-5; Sat 9-1
Dallas, TX 75220

Help yourself, folks, when you're ready to pack it all in. This small store is housed in their offices but is set up to accommodate you whenever you're ready to move. Buy new and recycled boxes when packing time draws near. A perfect stop to shop before you call in the movers. Get packed and keep organized. You'll be so much happier when you finally reach your destination. Mark it—Living Room. Bedroom. Kitchen. Then when you get there, the movers can deliver it to the right room. Save time and money. Buy your boxes here. Overruns and misprints in boxes, just like in other merchandise categories, and save yourself a bundle. From small recycled packing boxes to the heavy-duty varieties that can handle the big stuff, to the delicate stuff such as glasses and dishware. From a low of 50 cents for a 16 x 12 x 12 box to one that can house your entire closet for $8, complete with metal bar rack so you can keep it all on hangers, you can be sure that your wardrobe can go from house to house with nary a wrinkle. Plus, after you've unpacked, you'll have an extra closet for the garage. Buy also all the packing materials to ensure a perfect move like bubble wrap, markers, foam and sealing tape. It's you're connection to boxes. So let's get moving!

★★★★ **Aaron Rents & Sells Office Furniture/BackRoom**   972/385-9472
14105 Inwood   Mon-Fri 9-6; Sat 9-5
Dallas, TX 75243   www.aaronrentsfurniture.com

If you haven't seen panel dividers for $19, folding tables for $19, computer desks for $39, desks for $99 or file cabinets for $39, you haven't been to *Aaron's BackRoom*. Remember, these are the guys who rent furniture, for both home and office, and these are their rental returns. So what? Unless you believe what goes around, comes around, you can make your business a success regardless if it came from a dot.com business who didn't. Your bottom line will know the difference. Office suites, desks, files and other storage units, seating, tables, panel systems, business equipment and more at a great savings. Aaron Rents is one of America's leading names in furniture rental, sales and leasing, so give A to their leadership and another A for effort. AAaron Rents and you can be the benefactor.

★★ Acquisition Specialists Inc. (ASI)   972/888-1500
15160 Marsh Lane   Mon-Fri 8-5
Dallas, TX 75001

Acquisition and mergers. Acquisition and office equipment. Of course, now I get it? Housed in CompUSA's old location and next to Fuller's Jewelers, this jewel may be the pearl in the oyster of office equipment. Got an old copier that doesn't work like it should? Well trade it in, trade it up, or go for the gold and get one that works from scratch. They sell refurbished copiers with three-year warranties on used models and five-year warranties on new. Now, you can start making copies by the copier. They carry other new and used electronic office equipment besides copiers. After all, man does not just live by copiers alone. They also carry printers and fax machines and sometimes very specific machinery such as a plotting machine or industry-specific equipment. Just don't ask me to explain. Get one of their sales reps to lead you by the hand. They're the specialists, remember?

★★★★★ Advantage Copier Equipment (ACE)   214/350-4532
2636 Walnut Hill Lane, #325   Mon-Fri 9-5
Dallas, TX 75229   www.acelaser.com

When you're the ace in the hole, you ought to take advantage of their cost-cutting copiers. Now, copy this. Nobody's better than Greg Budde (sounds like Booty). Since 1992, he's been specializing in selling and servicing remanufactured copiers, faxes and laser printers. Today, he has now branched out into selling remanufactured cartridges for laser printers, copiers, and fax toners and inkjet cartridges. Look to them for **BROTHER**, **CANON**, **HEWLETT-PACKARD**, **IBM**, **PANASONIC**, **RICOH**, **SHARP** and **XEROX**, they leave not a copier unturned. Same with the recycling and selling of toner cartridges. For example, remanufactured laser cartridges start at $39.95 and come with a full guarantee. Save at least 50 percent and more over new. Don't you dare throw those cartridges out. Every cartridge that is recycled saves pints of oil, as one advantage. Do your part to help reduce landfills and not pollute the environment. If for some reason you think that the quality is not the same as a new product, they will issue a 100 percent refund. Now, that's an ACE you'll have up your sleeve! Rated tops by both BBB's.

★★ Benefit Store, The   972/470-0700
235-B N. Central Expwy.   Mon-Fri 9-5:30; Sat 10-2
Richardson, TX 75080

One good deed deserves another. Donate used (and even slightly abused) office furniture of all types to this worthy charity. The move to Richardson has its benefits, too. Between Belt Line and Arapaho, some of the deals are actually finger-lickin' good. Just ask the Colonel (Col. James P. Caston, that is), who has been attached to this cause forever. Area offices can either be a beneficiary or a benefactor—either way, buying or donating, you'll be doing double duty. This colonel has office furniture that runs the gamut from extra crispy to regular fare. All items have been donated with proceeds benefiting the Children's Medical Center. Desks start as low as $80 and escalate to several thousands. Chairs go from $25-$400. Not only are you (the purchaser) the recipient of good deals at the office, but the children are the benefactors of the colonel and his caring platoon. For more than 10 years, this group has raised millions of dollars for Children's Medical Center, so when you buy that desk or file cabinet, there should be less pain all the way around. Donations arrive daily—so shop often. Pick-up and delivery available but prices vary by destination.

★★★ Bob Carney Office Furniture   214/827-2537
3901 Main   Mon-Fri 1-4; Sat 8:30-4:30
Dallas, TX 75226

This Carney isn't as funny; but when he's open for business, he means business with the furniture spilling out the front door. At the corner of Main and Washington (he recommends parking on Washington and coming in the middle entrance). because that's where all the furniture is parked. I suspect he's hanging on for something to do in his post-retirement. Rmember it's not over 'til it's over. The discounts are what make shoppers flock to the more than 350 items in stock. You can buy good-quality used office furniture cheap, whether it's a dented or scratched reject or a manufacturer's return; it's your bottom line that takes front row center. We carted off a four-drawer legal file for $75 and a teacher's desk for old-time's sake, that brought back nightmares from my teaching days for $100. Of course, I should have thought twice and considered the one for $45 and then refinished it myself. Just look for the two-story, red brick building and follow the stone walkway to the side door. Truly a remarkable shopping experience where office furniture, traditional and contemporary, sells to savvy purchasing agents like you and me. If no one answers the phone, it only means they're out delivering. Call ahead. And if you develop labor pains while you're waiting, Baylor Hospital is five blocks away. Delivery is available though Bob doesn't. He will recommend some area movers for you to hire.

◆◆◆◆ Business Furniture Services   214/637-2371
2777 Irving Blvd., Suite 208   Mon-Fri 8-5; By Appt.
Dallas, TX 75207

Got a few nicks and scratches that make your office look tired and worn? Or are you ready to move out, move away, move up? Then spruce up with the folks at BFS. What a suite deal. Have your office furniture refinished, the millwork touched up on wooden items, reupholstered, painted, repaired, sanded, whatever it takes to bring the furnishings up to snuff without having to throw it all out and start from scratch. Start with the desks, the chairs and the files. Then, move on to re-keying the locks, make the move to new quarters, or rearrange what you've got where you are. Reconfigure, or completely redo. If you need to reinstall or install totally new furniture in your new office environment, they can take it from there. If you need your old furniture warehoused until you're ready for the move, they can accommodate it. If you want to make some changes around your office and want to keep your people doing what they do best without the needless interruptions, here they come again. Their construction/remodeling services include all the necessary "fix-ups" like sheetrock repair, tape and bedding, painting and minor millwork. With their cleaning services, they offer construction site cleanup, post-move cleanup, weekly contracts and even carpet cleaning. They are fully insured with branches in Dallas (their home base) and Houston, Austin, San Antonio, Oklahoma City and Tulsa. Hourly rates are based on normal business hours and vary from $20 up to $40. If you need them on the weekend or at night, expect a night-owl premium of an additional 50 percent. Isn't that a hoot?

Cort Office Furniture Rental Clearance Center   972/445-2678
250 W. Airport Freeway   Mon-Fri 9-6; Sat 10-5
Irving, TX 75062   www.cortfurniture.com

Who would have ever thought that over 80 percent of Fortune 500 companies rent furniture from Cort? Why, oh why, pray tell. Well, for one, it preserves capital and remains flexible enough to change at the drop of a hat. When you just want to introduce a new color scheme or a new attitude, it's easy. Move it out and move some new in. There are over 100 showrooms nationwide offering 48 hour delivery, space planning and design assistance...all backed by the industry's only written "Personal Service Guarantee®." Then, when you decide it's time to buy, that's where the Furniture Rental Clearance Centers come in offering new and previously-leased brand name retail products at substantial savings of 30 to 70 percent savings. If you want to order in furniture nationwide for temporary housing coast-to-coast, no problem. One call and you can be set up. Online, click for coupons that will entitle you to additional discounts. The Clearance Centers marry the best of both worlds: quality office furniture at terrific prices. Other Cort Clearance Centers located at 14215 Inwood Rd., Dallas TX, 75244, 972-386-2981 and 2208 N. Collins, Arlington 817/274-2717. Live the good life in and out of your office, from one executive office to 100 **HERMAN MILLER** workstations, the brand names are more than meets the eye. **CHROMCRAFT**, **HON** and **UNITED**, too, meet all the requirements for an official inspection and at these prices, what are you waiting for? Another announcement from Alan Greenspan? Start with the reception area, and proceed full steam ahead to bookcases, chairs, conference rooms, desks, files, panels, tables and fill in the blanks with all the little extra accessories. *Call toll-free: 888/669-CORT (2678)*

★★★★★ Dallas Midwest

4100 Alpha Rd., Suite 111
Dallas, TX 75244

972/866-0101
Mon-Fri 7:30-7; Sat 9-1
www.dallasmidwest.com

Any company that is in business over a half a century must be one step from heaven. And that's exactly what is the chosen ministry at this industry treasure. Specialists in institutional furniture for schools, churches, day-care centers and libraries, you can finally get a new pew, a mobile desktop lectern ($79), a coat and hat rack ($59), a park bench, a picnic table, a bike rack, a storage unit, bulletin or magnetic boards with markers or magnets, indoor and outdoor signage and still save 30-60 percent off list. Order online or via their catalog which is now more than 120 pages of pews for churches, pulpits, choir risers, office furniture and more. They provide FREE color samples on some items and some come with a 50-year guarantee (instead of the usual 15- year.) Some assembly required but usually only the basic tools are needed. Prices are quoted with and without assembly. Additional savings are available for volume purchases over $1,000. If you'd prefer utilizing your own fabric for chairs, for example, they are likely to oblige. If you're a church, school or government agency, sometimes there's special credit extended. You can even lease furniture if your order exceeds $2,000. Holly rollers! *Call toll-free: 800/933-2731*

Desk & Chair Outlet, The

15301 Midway (retail store)
15307 Midway (outlet store)
Addison, TX 75001

972/661-2508
Mon-Fri 9-6; Sat 10-5
www.thedeskandchair.com

Only a few doors separate the retail from the outlet store, but many a dollar has been saved is reason enough to make the walk. Off Belt Line, this outlet can get your office machinery in gear as they deal in factory overruns, closeouts and showroom samples by some of the best names in the business. Add in the likes of **BODYBUILT**, **CHROMCRAFT**, **GLOBAL**, **GUNLOCKE**, **HARDEN**, **HON**, **KAUFMAN** at 55-70 percent off retail and you'll see why we got a promotion to a corner office. Choose from a variety of wood finishes, from cherry, mahogany, medium oak, natural maple, walnut, charcoal and light gray. Why not consider eliminating those steely-looking generic desks and classing up the joint? Here's the place to begin that transformation with computer desks, U-shaped desks, secretarial desks, pedestal desks, bookcases, chairs, credenzas, lateral files, storage systems and tables. They'll even throw in FREE space planning and design. Why pay full price when you can get all of this? You got something against utilizing these savings for a company cruise?

★★★★★ Executive Privilege   214/352-1588

2615 W. Mockingbird   Mon-Fri 9-4
Dallas, TX 75235

If you expect to be served during the 12-1 lunch hour, forget it. These folks are out to lunch and refuse to be rushed. But during their working hours, you can load up the truck and make a killing. How about saving 70-90 percent on pre-owned office furniture that has seen the boon of the dot.com business come and go? Or the conference room table and ten leather swivel chairs that was extricated from that bankruptcy auction to wind up here for $1,000 instead of $12,000? The names are stellar and the prices superb. It makes perfect sense to accept their benevolence with open arms. **D'USO**, **HERMAN MILLER**, **KEILHAUER**, **KNOLL**, **MAITLAND**, **NOVIKOFF**, **SMITH** and **STEELCASE**—names that you don't see often in the usual line-up of used office furniture. Whatever you need to open your doors and start the business ball rolling can be found at this executive hideout: desks, chairs, conference tables, computer desks and all the office accessories necessary to conduct business until the merger or acquisition is completed. Interior design services also available. Located one-half block west of Love Field, I'm sure you've past it a million times and never thought to stop. Now that you know its net worth, make it your business to enjoy all the privileges of smart shopping.

Express Furniture   214/637-1600

909 N. Industrial Blvd.   Mon-Fri 9-6
Dallas, TX 75247

If you're buying office furniture (and having it delivered by their sister store, Business Environments), you will find that deep in the heart of the industrial district, your wholesale connection to the actual furniture awaits. Make a date and express your frugality royally. Save at the corner of Industrial and Continental, with more office furniture down the street. Expect the same operator to answer the phones for both businesses; she'll transfer you to Business Environments if you want installation or keep you on the line for Express Furniture. New office furniture at wholesale prices, showroom samples, and used furniture for even additional savings is the ticket here. **PAOLI** is one of the big names in the business that will transform your business into a first-class act. Others are likely to do the same: **COUNCIL CRAFTSMAN**, **EFI**, **HAHN**, **HERMAN MILLER**, **LA-Z-BOY** and others, again at 50 percent off. OK, bossman, with savings like that, don't you think you can spring for the tab at lunch? If you prefer taking a front row seat, consider **SUPERIOR** and **UNITED CHAIRS** for executive offices, of course. If one of the desks has been returned, you can slash another 20 percent off. Paoli comes with a 10-year warranty and a promise that nothing will mar its surface, including nail polish. Just be sure you put in for a corner office with a view from the top; otherwise, who will you be able to impress? Express does offer financing but you have to come in for more information. *Call toll-free: 888/637-6337*

★★★★★ Front Desk Office Furniture Outlet   214/904-9045

10401 Harry Hines Blvd.   Mon-Fri 9-5
Dallas, TX 75229   www.frontdeskdallas.com

Jay and John Crisford take front and center at their showroom's door and lead you through the vignettes of new and used furniture officially designated for your office. Whether you pick from those in the front or not is immaterial as long as the price is right. Clean up your act and get ready for the laundry list of options: new and used office furniture, including executive chairs, **AERON** chairs, ergonomic computer task chairs, modular open plans, cubicles, executive desk sets, computer furniture, conference tables, reception stations, storage cabinets, credenzas, bookcases, vertical and lateral file cabinets, metal desks

and accessories. The brands have all passed an official inspection: **HERMAN MILLER**, **KNOLL**, **LA-Z-BOY**, **STEELCASE**, **THOMASVILLE** and more. Nary an item goes unnoticed if it means getting down to business. The Crisfords are also notorious for liquidating your excess office furniture when you want to trade in, trade up, even trade out. They will take a look, make an offer, pick up the furniture and give you a check, trade or donation receipt. The transaction's painless and then when you want to replace it, they're also available to handle the process from start to finish. Installers and delivery personnel are all bonded and professional. Buy it now. Enjoy it tomorrow. Plan for the future. It's all under one roof here.
Call toll-free: 800/299-8095

◆◆◆◆◆ Inhouse Couriers   214/351-5929
6115 Denton Drive
Dallas, TX 75235
When you want a document couriered over to wherever, these are the folks that deliver the best service at the lowest price. Of course, rush jobs cost a tad more; any calls after 5 PM, an additional $15 per run. Make sure your weight (on the package, silly) doesn't exceed 25 pounds, as the first 25 pounds are FREE; then it's two cents a pound thereafter. See, even fat packages are penalized.

★★★★★ OFCO Office Furniture   817/429-3553
200 W. Rosedale   Mon-Fri 8:30-5:30; Sat 8:30-5
Fort Worth, TX 76104   www.ofco.com
The domain's name registered and it's official, but there's no reason to hit the website yet. As soon as someone comes into the office, they'll get working on it. Check back later. But in the meantime, if you are looking to buy office furniture, don't ignore this Tarrant County favorite. OFCO stands for Office Company and if it's your company's office furniture you're needing to buy, why not buy it as direct as it gets. Bypass the middlemen and shop direct at the manufacturer or distributor, then pass those savings on to you as the final official user. Everywhere you look, you'll see that price tags are prominently displayed with the retail price and the OFCO price. If the executive chair you're looking at is used, depending on condition, it will be marked 60-90 percent off; or if new, prices are marked 40-60 percent off. Now who's complaining? Upon closer examination, some of those new items are part of the "scratch and dent" department so make sure whatever's the problem, it does not matter in its overall function. From the top drawers to the wastebasket, you'll see bargains at every turn. A four-drawer filing cabinet with a small dent in the side was $39 and another four-drawer one that was scratched and missing a lock was the same. One that was nearly new (or at least looked the part) was $69. Secretary chairs for $29 (if new, $249), or $49 for break room tables (new $245). If only new will do, what about a two-drawer mahogany lateral file cabinet for $149 (up to $935/new) or an executive walnut desk for $399 instead of $699? Officially speaking, you can find desks, credenzas, file cabinets, hutches, computer desks and more displayed throughout the 30,000-square-foot-showroom. Don't expect a hard sales approach either. The salesmen are not on commission. Other locations they office at include 740 W. Pipeline in Hurst, 817/268-0981 and at 4433 River Oaks Blvd. in Fort Worth, 817/625-1880.

★★★★ Office Depot   972/438-9177
1000 W. Airport Frwy.   Mon-Fri 7 AM-9 PM; Sat 9-9; Sun 10-6
Irving, TX 75061   www.officedepot.com
"Taking care of business, everyday" is their official message in song but they also mean it when the singing stops. Officially, they are the superstore of choice, the "big box" player in the world that other office stores model themselves after. Being one of the first does have its obvious benefits. One is, of

course, name recognition. Selection is next: office supplies, office furniture and all the latest and greatest when it comes to high-tech and novelty products. In-store, you can practically conduct your entire official duties: copy, fax, bindery and graphic design services for professional presentations. Looking for resources? Then look online where they list companies to assist with money management, marketing, communications, managing people and the office. They list companies that have worked with Fortune 500 companies as well as recommend companies that offer FREE services...yes, free! Pick the way you want to do business—online, in store, with their catalog or by phone just by calling 888-GO-DEPOT. Since 1986, Office Depot has grown to almost 900 stores and 30 of them are in the Metroplex. Talk about a growth spurt! *Call toll-free: 800/685-8800*

★★★ Office Liquidation Center   972/438-4499
3215 E. Carpenter Frwy.   Mon-Fri 8:30-5
Irving, TX 75062   www.officeliquidationcenter.com

This 35,000-square-foot showroom is bland next to the colorful Lone Star Boot building, but looks can be deceiving. These folks liquidate furniture fast but are slowly working on their website. Though not much there, yet, there is lots of new and used closeout furniture to choose from. Look no further than behind the hundreds of desks, credenzas, conference tables, bookcases, filing cabinets, artwork, partitions, cubicles and more. Put more than your mind at ease with lots of chairs including side chairs, task chairs, executive chairs, manager chairs, secretary chairs, guest chairs, conference chairs, banquet chairs, and at last, you can table the issue. They also offer minor refinishing services in case there's a nick or a scratch. As they say, "itch it!" and come out with a smooth finish.

★★ Office Max   972/613-4099
1515 Town East Blvd.   Mon-Fri 8-9; Sat 9-9; Sun Noon-6
Mesquite, TX 75182   www.officemax.com

In spite of their emphasis on buying for practically FREE after rebate, I have yet to snare a one. In fact, I find that approach of saving $10 or $20 a bit cumbersome. If I'm concentrating on business, I hate to have to save money with additional steps. Oh well, the luck may only be with the Irish. And McGoldstein, I'm not! Save up to 50 percent on more than 7,000 name-brand office products all with "pen-ache!" Take shopping for office supplies and equipment to the max and enjoy the power selection of a superstore. Then if you want to copy (and more), head to a CopyMax where they offer self-serve and full-service copying as well as graphic design, faxing, binding and even self-serve computers in most locations. Could I sense a Kinko's copycat? Order business cards for as little as $9.99 or send documents electronically (straight from your computer to theirs) and place your orders directly from the office...how convenient. FREE delivery on all orders over $50. Check directory for other locations before you max out.

★★★★★ PS Business Interiors   214/688-1925
3131 Commonwealth   Mon-Fri 8:30-5
Dallas, TX 75247   www.psbusinessinteriors.com

PS-don't forget to save some money when shopping for your favorite office furniture and modular workstations. With offices in Dallas, Atlanta, Baltimore, Philadelphia and San Diego, you can expect that whichever location you shop at, you'll be getting the best money can buy. For the fastest and bestest prices, pre-owned is what's recommended for the common cause. The website directs you to a front page highlighting the Philadelphia location, but just enter what you're looking for and you'll be taken care of. Since 1984, Dallas-based Robert Paul (the P) and Jack Shure (the S) have collaborated and developed the concept of buying and selling office furniture that is three to seven years old and in acceptable, if not superb condition. If not, you can bet your bottom dollar that it will be refurbished to a like-new status. Some of the brands to note included **GLOBAL**, **HAWORTH**, **HERMAN MILLER** and **STEELCASE**. Expect to save between 70-80 percent off retail on desks, credenzas, secretarial chairs, lateral and vertical filing cabinets, conference tables, chairs, storage cabinets—whatever it takes to run your office. Popular cubicle systems are always available, in new, used and refurbished varieties. No wonder their phones ring off the wall. Buy it when you see it and buy it fast. Tomorrow's another day, another dollar, and it may not be available if you're one of those doubting Thomas's. Check out their other location at the northeast corner of Miller and LBJ, 214/343-1925. Ask for Manuel—the guy with a hands-on approach to helping you solve your business interiors.

★★★ Sav-on Office Supplies   817/926-7071
2508 W. Berry St.   Mon-Fri 8-7; Sat 10-5
Fort Worth, TX 76109   www.sav-onofficesupplies.com

First there was Snap-on, now it's Sav-on and specifically, Sav-On Office Supplies. Save on a little of this and a little of that. With their full compendium of name brand office, computer and school supplies from 20 to 70 percent off, you can get off to the right start with the right stuff. Everything you may need to pass the grade in school and in business—from paper clips to copy paper, furniture to fax machines, computer printers to cartridges. Then, pay attention to the other services such as making of those rubber stamps, printing of business cards, faxing, special orders and the area they designated "Copies and More" a full copy center located in each of their stores. Headquartered in Fort Worth, there are locations in Dallas at 11333 Northwest Hwy., 310 Hillside Village and in Arlington at 2407 S. Cooper.

★★★★★ Signs Manufacturing & Maintenance Corp. 214/339-2227
4550 Mint Way   Mon-Fri 8-5
Dallas, TX 75236   www.signsmanufacturing.com

What sign are you? If you don't know, you might want to give this sign company a call. After all, their signs have been seen in national magazines, as well as newspapers, movies and commercials. So, why not yours, too? If you want to compete with the big boys, get you name out there. Choose channel letters, neon, illuminated or non-illuminated sign cabinets, pole signs, plastic lettering, trim-cap lettering, monuments, pylon signs and more! Their philosophy is, "If a sign is costing you money, it's not doing its job." In fact, on the contrary. They use only the highest quality technology available while presenting a bottom line that's competitive. They refuse to substitute a lesser quality sign just to cut costs; rather they throw in all the details that you'd expect with a top-notch signer. As far as the permits go, they deal with the appropriate municipality, so you don't have to, whew! A long and prestigious lists of clients include 20th Century Fox, Albertson's, Chili's Restaurant, Circuit City, Dairy Queen, Dallas Mavericks, Men's Warehouse, Sears, Victoria Secrets, Whataburger and just too many more to list. Want to know who makes the signs for Dallas? Addison, DeSoto and Duncanville, too? Guess?. Lighted or not, large or small, prices are wholesale to the public and customers are treated with fine, kid gloves. FREE estimates from this radio-dispatched company who'll get your name up there in lights. You can visit their south Dallas manufacturing plant or have them come to you, either way it's a snap.

★★★★ Staples   972/353-3877
997 Valley Ridge Blvd.   Mon-Fri 7 AM-9 PM; Sat 9-9; Sun 11-6
Lewisville, TX 75067   www.staples.com

This Massachusetts $9 billion retailer of office supplies, furniture and technology to consumers and businesses is a top dog in the office supplies industry. From home-based businesses to Fortune 500 companies,

Staples is credited with inventing the office superstore concept and today is the world's largest operator of office superstores. With more than 46,000 employees at more than 1,100 locations plus business via their mail order catalog, e-commerce and contract business, expect if it has anything to do with cut and paste, you can find it here, for less. Similar to Office Max, Office Depot, this completes the triangle of superstores where you run around in circles. In my humble opinion, I preferred the good old days of small, neighborhood office supply stores, all except the power buys that the big boys seem to finagle. Too, online, there are easier websites to navigate and better prices elsewhere. There, I said it! *Call toll-free: 800/STA-PLES(333-3330* 🇺🇸

★★★★★ TCS Corporate Services   972/238-9123
1571 N. Glenville Drive   M-F 7:30-5
Richardson, TX 75081   www.tcstoner.com

In business since 1986, TCS is the largest direct-selling toner cartridge remanufacturer in the country. Save up to 40 percent and keep that printer going and going and going. Who would have thought I'd be running to Office Max twice a month just to keep my printer going. Here I thought once I met my Prints Charming, I wouldn't have to keep replacing my cartridges, but no, not in this lifetime. TCS is authorized to sell and service all major brands of printers. Again, another office nightmare solved. Who do you call when your printer crashes? Let them help you uncover cost savings on your printing needs without sacrificing quality. Start with laser printers, faxes, scanners, remanufactured toner cartridges, inkjet supplies, printer accessories and more. Stock your office with envelopes, markers, labels, shelves, pens, hole punchers, clips, cords, binders, even coffee supplies. Brands include: **AVERY**, **BUSH**, **CANNON**, **GENICOM**, **HEWLETT-PACKARD**, **TEXMARK**, **PITNEY BOWES**, **TEKTRONIX** and **XEROX** for starters. Get with it and start saving the corporate way. *Call toll-free: 800/633-4935*

★★★ Xerox Service   214/503-5600
10490 Vista Park Rd.   Mon-Fri 8-5
Dallas, TX 75238   www.xerox.com

XEROX's a name that is as familiar as **KLEENEX**...the only difference, of course, is we don't blow our nose with a copier. (Though each is a staple in our everyday life at home and at the office.) Though this company has been around almost 100 years (founded in 1906), they officially became Xerox in 1961. If you're looking to duplicate your efforts and save more than 70 percent on refurbished copiers, here's your chance to do so. All come with a 90-day parts and labor warranty. Stop running all over town and run those efforts through a Xerox. You'll save on gas and you'll always have a back up paper trail.

★★ XPEDX Paper and Graphics   214/651-0331
501 N. Stemmons, Suite 300   Mon-Fri 7:30-5:30; Sat 8-Noon
Dallas, TX 75207   www.xpedx.com

By the time you read this, their website will be up and taking orders. Formerly Avery Paper, looks like they sat around and voted on a name like **XEROX** or **EXXON**—a made-up name that nobody would want or use. Stop chasing around for the perfect paper. Here's wher to land for paper, paper, and more paper, laser paper products, printer's supplies, stationery and more. Too, they're also a source for office supplies. Look for training offered throughout the country like Paper 101 that teaches consumers how to make informative choices when making paper purchases. I never knew there was so much to consider when buying paper! These people take the cut out of more than trees; they cut out the guesswork and also cut down the price. And that's a paper cut I can live with. Anything else not in stock, can be ordered and delivered in 24 hours. Visit also at 15408 Midway Rd. in Addison and 2158 Jupiter Rd. in Garland.

43

Outlet Centers

★★★★★ **Allen Premium Outlet Center**   972/678-7000
820 W. Stacy Rd.   Mon-Sat 10-9; Sun 11-6
US 75 N/Exit 37 (Stacy Rd.)   www.premiumoutlets.com
Allen, TX 75013

Fifty outlet stores are waiting for your beady bargain-shopping eyes. Give a look at the newest Chelsea Property Group and see what insiders are craving as they're raving. If discounted designer clothing, shoes, handbags, luggage, housewares, home furnishings, gifts, books, music, vitamins, jewelry and accessories get your attention, I won't even mention the food. Remember, I only said to put your BUDGET on a diet. The lineup here includes: Banana Republic Factory Store, Barney's/New York, Big Dog, Casual Corner (regular, petites and plus sizes), DKNY, Dress Barn, Eddie Bauer, Escada, Fubu, Geoffrey Beene, Greg Norman, Guess?, Izod, Jones New York, L'eggs/Hanes/Bali/Playtex, Liz Claiborne, Maidenform, Nautica, Perry Ellis, Polo Ralph Lauren, Reebok, Tommy Hilfiger, Van Heusen, Wilson Leather Outlet...got room for more? Then, slip into a pair of Bass, Cole Haan, Kenneth Cole, Liz Claiborne Shoes, Samsonite and Timberland. Decorate from The Bombay Outlet or The Crate & Barrel Outlet; cook up a storm with Le Creuset and dress your table with a sterling setting from Oneida. Lastly, sleep tight after a long day's night with a bevy of bargains from Westpoint Stevens. Accessorize with Claire's, Sunglass Outlet, Ultra Diamond and Gold and Zales, The Diamond Store, Outlet. And lastly, pray you've got some strength left to visit the Bible Outlet, Book Warehouse, Country Clutter, Earthbound Trading, Music for a Song and Vitamin World...with more signing up as we speak. Not as high-ended as their Woodbury Commons site outside New York City, but high enough to impress the Dallas palate. Oh, look who just moved in? Movado and K-B Toy Outlet...just in time for the holidays. Now, how convenient.

★★★★ **Denton Factory Stores**   940/565-5040
5800 N. I-35, Exit 470   Mon-Sat 10-8; Sun 11-6
Denton, TX 76207   www.dentonfactorystores.com

You don't have to drive a million miles for one of those sought-after styles because now, just north of the Dallas county line is a line-up of outlets under the umbrella of Denton Factory Stores. No doubt, Denton residents know a good thing when they see it. You can, too, just by heading north on I-35 past the Denton exits to Exit 470. Though what they lack in quantity, they make up in quality. One of the best reasons to cross the county line is the Bridal Company Outlet (See Bridal Chapter). Bridal gowns for as low as $99 is a good bet in anybody's book. Just ask my niece who bought her gown there. Dress Barn and Dress Barn Woman's another good companion piece. Need comfortable shoes? Try Famous Footwear. Need a wedding gift? You'll love the Lenox Factory Outlet, Suite 501, 940/891-6011. Not too shabby, eh? Stay out of the glare of the crowd by pairing with Sunglass Hut, Suite 309, 940/891-1380. And guys are not forsaken 'cause there's a Van Heusen Outlet, Suite 305, 940/382-3970. They might even give you the shirt off their backs. Then one of the best bed and bath resources in the country is Westpoint Stevens. Who can resist spending the night with them at these outlet prices? Shop US Factory Outlets, Suite 201, 940/384-0124 for everything else. Start early to avoid the gold rush, but when it comes time for a lunch break, enjoy Good Eats. But the real surprise this year is the opening of a Denton location of Antiqueland, a real plus in the asset department. There are over 200 dealers under one roof utilizing every inch of the 30,000 square foot display area and 78 showcases highlighting unique antiques, collectibles, decorative items, gifts and crafts. And for history buffs, don't forget to stop in at the Denton County Historical Museum. My only complaint? When Antiqueland took over one whole building, it included the public lounge which gave shoppers one place to rest their weary feet. To compensate, they now offer vending machines in the mall office. Big deal! Fortunately, they kept the restrooms.

★★★★ Factory Stores of America   903/439-0118
I-30, Exit 124   Mon-Sat 9-7; Sun Noon-6
Sulphur Springs, TX 75482

One new addition since last year and that's the World Beauty and Gifts outlet. However, this alone would not make you do a wheelie and head to Sulphur Springs, Exit 124. Nevertheless, if you want to salute the savings in total, you will find it patriotic to enlist the help of a few friends and make the drive. Some of the bargains are worth it. Bass Shoes, Bonworth, Dress Barn, Easy Spirit, Fieldcrest/Cannon, Factory Brand Shoes, Factory Connection, Kitchen Collection, L'eggs/Hanes/Bali/Playtex , Morgan Ashley, Paper Factory, Rue 21, Van Heusen and Vanity Fair. You'll notice that they have my support (Hanes and Vanity Fair, for sure!) Whether it's a comfortable pair of shoes that you buy after a few hours of walking, or a dress shirt for dad, your kid's birthday party invitations, a queen-size sheet set, believe me, you'll have enough choices to come home bearing gifts.

★★★★★ Grapevine Mills Mall   972/724-4900
3000 Grapevine Mills Pkwy.   Mon-Sat 10-9:30; Sun 11-8
Highway 12, Exit Bass Pro Drive   www.millscorp.com/grapevine
Grapevine, TX 76051

If you've heard it through the grapevine, it's probably true. This mega-marvel at the cornerstone of D/FW means over 1.5 million-square feet of pure shopping pleasure. Not all stores offer the biggest discounts but spend the day and you'll always come home a winner. From the big attractions like the AMC 30-screen theater to Bass Pro Shops Outdoor World, Bed Bath & Beyond, Books-A-Million, Burlington Coat Factory, GameWorks, Group USA, JC Penney Outlet, Last Call from Neiman Marcus (opening soon), Marshalls, Off 5th, Off Rodeo Dr, Old Navy, Polar Ice, The Sports Authority, Virgin Megastore and Western Warehouse. But don't stop——there's specialty attractions including Ann Taylor Loft, Carter's for Kids, Donna Karan Company Store, Gap Outlet, Guess? Outlet and more, this is tourist stop numero uno when visitors arrive in town. Be sure to stop by the Information Booth and pick up a Discover Card coupon book which offers even more savings when shopping with your Discover Card. Hey, we'll take the savings anyway we can get them. And since it takes at least a meal or two to make it through this place, be sure to stop by and enjoy dining at the Stockyards Food Court, the Rainforest Cafe or Dick Clark's American Bandstand Grill.

Don't get caught up in the outlet frenzy but bargains are definitely blooming for those willing to put up with a few weeds. Either way, your visit to this mega center will be more than just "run of the mill." This is where Mike Bryant and I filmed a segment of "Extra! with Leeza Gibbons". We did uncover a few examples where the savings were miniscule or non-existent but overall, a worthwhile shopping experience.

★★★★★ Inwood Trade Center   214/521-4777
1311 Inwood Rd.   Hours Vary with Merchants
Dallas, TX 75247

For an in-town shopping experience that's an outlet shopper's easy-in and out dream, here's where it's happening. Regardless of which side of the street you're bargains are buttered on, you can shop at a stellar line-up of merchants: Special Occasion Dresses has just opened its outlet and it's an outstanding ought-to-shop for the After 5, Bridal and Dressy set who are down right cheap; Circa Consignment Interiors (formerly Oak Lawn Antiques) is now home to another Peacock Alley Outlet department; Seventh Ave Plus Sizes is still heaven; Royal Optical Factory Outlet, Suzannes, Crate & Barrel Outlet, Far East Apparel, Shoe Fair, Everything Uniform, Interior Alternative, Simmons Mattress Outlet World of Sleep) and Lily's Children's Outlet make up the Inwood Trade Center family. Off I-35, two blocks west, pull up to their front doors and you're in business. If you consider yourself part of the "in" crowd, don't miss the "out-lets."

★★★★ Plano Market Square   972/578-1591
1717 E. Spring Creek Pkwy.   Mon-Sat 10-9; Sun 10-6 (Garden Ridge 9-9)
Plano, TX 75074

Do you realize that should this mall ever get monogrammed towels, it would read PMS (Plano Market Square—well, they could run monthly sales, couldn't they?) Conveniently located in the affluent suburb of Plano, there's nothing plain about it. Some good merchants and some great merchants co-exist. Read all about the great ones: 75 Percent Off Books is one and Factory Outlet Rugs is another. Load up on both. There's nothing quite like either of them in the Metroplex. Nostalgia Crafts and Antiques is one of the reasons the mall has steadily risen above the common ground. From crafts to antiques, you can wander the aisles until you think you cannot shop another store. But as the force be with you, you manage a few more steps. There are off-price powerhouses like TJ Maxx and Garden Ridge Pottery, the L'eggs/Hanes/Bali/Playtex Outlet, lest I fall down on my job. Too, you can order from Creative Gift Baskets & Balloons for last-minute gift ideas or try out a new computer at Daltex Computers. There's more—some good and some better than good. Enjoy a nosh at Reza's Café and your day is complete. Located on Spring Creek Parkway, just east of Central Expressway.

★★★★★ Prime Outlets at Hillsboro   254/582-9205
I-35 South, Exit 368A   Mon-Sat 10-8; Sun 11-6
Hillsboro, TX 76240   www.primeoutlets.com

Ninety stores and holding at their Prime, these outlets are worth the one hour drive south from Dallas/Fort Worth. Sign up online and get email notifications of special sales and events or if not online, call their toll-free number. Some of the big names are represented: Big Dog, Black & Decker, Bombay Company, Bugle Boy, Carter's, Casual Corner, Corning Revere, Dress Barn, Duck Head, Eddie Bauer, Elizabeth, Farberware, Florsheim, Fossil, G & A Furniture, Gap, Guess?, Haggar, J. Crew, Jones New York, Kasper, L'eggs/Hanes/Bali/Playtex, Liz Claiborne, Maidenform, Mikasa, Motherhood, Nike, Oshkosh B'Gosh, Polo by Ralph Lauren, Reebok, Rue 21, S & K Menswear, Samsonite, Sunglass Outlet, Ultra, Vitamin World, Zales, The Diamond Store Outlet and more. If your tummy starts a grumblin', then get your motor rumblin' over to the food court for everything from Subway Sandwiches,Pepperidge Farm, Rocky Mountain Chocolate Factory and well, give me strength to carry on! Groups of 10 or more get special coupons for additional savings. *Call toll-free: 800/866-5900*

★★★★★ Prime Outlets of Gainesville   940/668-1888

I-35, Exit 501   Mon-Sat 10-9; Sun 11-6
Gainesville, TX 76240   www.primeoutlets.com

Another Prime example of what you can deliver when you put 80 named outlets and specialty stores under one roof. Just three miles south of the Red River en route to Oklahoma, stop—in the name of the love of bargains. As always, shop with a critical eye. More than 80 stores line up to tempt each and every dollar. But oh, what fun: Baby B'Gosh, Big Dog, Bon Worth, Brooks Brothers, Bugle Boy, Carter's, Casual Corner, Chicago Cutlery, Claire's, Corning Clearance Center, Corning Revere, Greg Norman, Izod, Jones New york, K-B Toy Outlet, L'eggs/Hanes/Bali/Playtex, Mikasa, Motherhood Maternity, Naturalizer, Nike, Nine West, Nocona Boot Co, Olga/Warner (Calvin Klein), Oshkosh B'Gosh, Parkhill's Jewelry, Perfumania, Petite Sophisticates, Reebok, Rocky Mountain Chocolate, Rue 21, S & K Menswear, Samsonite, SAS, Savane/Farah, Springmaid/Wamsutta, Ultra, Van Heusen, Zale Outlet and more. No doubt you'll work up a sweat. Energize with a trip to GNC. And if you've worked up an appetite, there are seven stops in the food court to grab a bite; however fast, you're at least sitting down. Wheelchairs, strollers and gift certificates available through the mall office. *Call toll-free: 888/545-7220*

★★★★ Tanger Factory Outlet Center   972/524-6034

I-20, Exit 501   Mon-Sat 10-9; Sun 11-6
Terrell, TX 75160   www.tangeroutlet.com

Being one of the pioneers in the outlet center business, Tanger can be proud of its contribution to bargain shoppers everywhere. Since 1981, Tanger is no Sanger-Harris, but if you're a department store devotée, make a detour down I-20 and shop in Terrell. With over 35 stores including Bass, Bible Factory Outlet, Big Dog, Bon Worth, Casual Corner, Claire's, Corning Revere, Dress Barn, Factory Brand Shoes, Factory Shoe Warehouse, Gap, Jockey, K-B Toy Outlet, Kitchen Collection, Koret, L'eggs/Hanes/Bali/Playtex, Levi's, Liz Claiborne, Mikasa, Oshkosh B'Gosh, Paper Factory, Perfumania, Publishers Warehouse, Rocky Mountain Fudge Factory, Reebok, Rockport, Rue 21, Samsonite, SAS Shoe, Seiko, Sunglass World, Totes, Vitamin World and Welcome Home. If you're a member of AAA, show your card at the mall office and get a coupon book for additional savings. (You can also try your BBB book and see what it gets you!) By the end of the day, show receipts of $40 or more and get a $5 gift certificate; show receipts of $100 or more, get a $10 gift certificate. Too, if you like freebies, they also offer a FREE National Geographic Atlas and Travel Planner. Famous for their 4th of July and Labor Day Sidewalk Sales plus extra sales on Tax Free Shopping Days, even a special in August included FREE pocket calculators with any $100 purchase for back-to-school shoppers. A plus, an ATM machine. You'll need it. *Call toll-free: 800/4TANGER*

44

Party & Paper

★★★★ 1/2 Price Cards
2151 S. State Hwy. 121 @ Corporate
Lewisville, TX 75067

972/315-2591
Mon-Sat 9:30-7; Sun Noon-5

When you raise the rent substantially and your bread and butter sales are half price cards, no wonder you had to move! Plus, in their previous location, the parking was atrocious. Now, in a new shopping center with Albertson's, make this store a regular stop on your shopping list. If you're no longer getting "carded," you might as well double up your card buying and buy twice as much, or pocket the difference. Great selection of other party goods, decorative plates, party favors, balloon bouquets and anything else to complete the fête accompli. Gala events don't have to cost a fortune. But if you want to personalize that event, or send an invitation, expect to save about 20 percent. This neighborhood gathering hole is a place to bump into old friends around the greeting card aisles.

★★★★ Brass Register, The
610 James Drive
Richardson, TX 75080

972/231-1386
Mon-Sat 9-5:30
www.brassregister.com

Hop online to see a few of the highlights of the store but don't expect to shop on their website, yet. Just see the photos where they'll pique your interest, but I bet you'll want to make a pit stop ASAP. In fact, I guarantee it. Whether it's the mini-diner counter and stools or a jukebox, you will want to turn back the clocks and rock around The Brass Register. Well, if it's that mini-diner that turns you on your heels, grab it 'cause I have my eye on it. Whether you're looking to buy something out of your memory bank or rent a jukebox for that next sock hop, this is the place to register. And now they've expanded their inventory to include **GO-PED** motorized scooters where you can really "go-go." Start the engines and go, man, go. Kids love them and they are fun. Same with the jukeboxes. But consider renting one for a change of pace—for youngsters of any age. Let them do the Macarena while you do the mambo Italiano, ah, I remember it well. The Brass Register can ring it up on many nostalgic items ignited by a visit here—from soda fountains to antique cash registers, juke boxes, of course, to taxi stands, it's a trip, a real kick in the pants. But for a fun ride, consider their motorized products including the fun quad riders. The Go-Peds start at $495 and are a handy-dandy transport for getting around the back roads or the shopping center parking lots. It is not recommended for Central Expressway commutes, but to see them, you will need to travel on Central Expressway, between Belt Line and Spring Valley where The Brass Register is ready to ring you up.

★★★★★ Card & Party Factory
2215 S. Cooper
Arlington, TX 76013

817/274-8044
Mon-Sat 9-8

I huff, and I puff to blow those candles out! Party, party, burning bright, what's a girl to do if planning a party? Head to Card & Party Factory for a hula good time. Having a luau? Bring on the grass skirts and pineapple honeycombs. No poi, but chances are they have everything else. Then, add a little red, white and— break all the best party favors out for the 4th of July or any other holiday fare. Lots of children's themed-party goods for each and every occasion. Lei down the law and expect to pay a lot less for a whole lot of fun. Gracias, señorita, for the colorful piñatas hanging about but you might not want to hang around until Mardi Gras to enjoy its contents. For any holiday, wait until after the date, and then stock up. Be prepared and you'll never be victimized by a surprise party. You'll be ready from the Factory. Plan your next soirée by checking out any one of their 23 Texas locations.

★★★★★ Card$mart
6850-F N. Shiloh Rd.
Garland, TX 75044

972/496-5222
www.cardsmartofnorthtexas.com

Yards and yards of cards at 50 percent off is just the beginning of mowing you down with selection, service and savings. Gift-wrap, too, is half price. Boy, oh boy, **BOYD BEARS**, **CAMILLE BECKMAN**, **CHERISHED TEDDIES**, **DEPARTMENT 56**, **DREAMSICLES**, **FENTON**, **FONTANINI**, **HARBOR LIGHTS**, **LEE MIDDLETON DOLLS**, **MATCHBOX**, **PRECIOUS MOMENTS**, **SERARPHIM CLASSICS**, **SWAROVSKI**, **TY**, **UNITED DESIGN**, **VANMARK** and more are beckoning to be added to your collection. But for sure, you can add an in-store and online gift registry. What a smart way to shop for cards and collectibles. Just ask any of their customers who return to their stores an average of 3.5 times per month. (How does one return for 1/2 an experience?) Another location includes Cards For Less at 2000 West Parker Rd, in Plano (@ Custer), 972/964-8778.

Discount Paper Warehouse (Blue Sky)
207 E. Hwy. 80
Forney, TX 75216

972/552-5295
Mon-Sat 10-5:30
www.paperandparty.com

Never in a blue moon would you see prices this good for paper and party supplies. Expanded hours mean only one thing, the public demanded it. Across from Clements Antiques, this wholesaler has down-to-earth prices on pie-in-the-sky products. Everything you would ever want or need to tie one on, or package it up, including gift card enclosures are all under one warehouse roof. Save up to 70 percent on all the makings for gift baskets such as ribbons and bows. Need a bow to go? They've got them at wholesale prices, too. Got a sweet tooth? How about dandy candy at 60 percent off the mall prices? And gift wrap—enough to blanket the Metroplex! Get in the swing of things with their new "school spirit" selections including megaphones (rah! rah!) for $1.29, pom poms or point the finger with a big foam hand for $2.99. The inventory is so expansive, you'll be exhausted at the end of your shopping spree so what's left to say is, "It's a wrap!" Lots of gift boxes, gourmet baskets, totes and bags from super-sizes to micros, frosteds to metallics, glossies to naturals. Gift-wrap in all styles, colors, themes and you won't be foiled, they've got foils, too. Add special touches of colored and designer tissue paper, shrink-wrap and shreds. Not only do the kids love those party favors starting at under a buck (like the four-pack of play money for 80 cents and the four-pack of sheriff's badges for 96 cents,) but let them start arresting anyone's who paying full price! Banners were $2.99, pull bows, 34 cents and metallics were glistening for just 49 cents. Open the throttle and it's Blue Skies ahead! *Call toll-free: 800/258-3759*

◆◆◆◆◆ Entertainment Alliance   **972/495-3768**
2001 Lancecrest Drive   Mon-Fri 9-6
Garland, TX 75044   hometown.aol.com/mwmagic/page/index.htm

You can't help but smile when you place a call to Entertainment Alliance. They're the folks to call to arrange the perfect party all the way down to the entertainment. So, start the ball rolling. With 25 years of experience, Marty the Magician (a.k.a. as Marty Westerman) has more than magic up his sleeve. They also are "cape-able" of providing the catering, arranging for the decorations and supplying other entertainers like sketch artists, musicians and more. Why worry about who's going to tend to all these details? It's hats off to this group of dedicated master planners! *Call toll-free: 800/395-3768*

★★ Palmer Sales   **972/288-1026**
3510 E. Hwy. 80   Mon-Fri 9-6; Sat 10-4
Mesquite, TX 75149

Saving one-third on all your party favors, fund-raising and carnival supplies is how they've staked their claim at Palmer Sales. Since 1948, they have been selling balloons, toys, holiday and other religious items by shopping through their "wholesale" catalog. Have a ball. Celebrate your next happy occasion with thousands of little doodads that every teacher or parent would love. Items like plush animals, holiday decorations, confetti, party supplies, trinkets and charms, paperware, party favors, piñatas, all the accoutrements of a fun time in the old town tonight. You're nuts if you pay full price when you can save on all the **LOONEY TUNES** plush animals. One thing you won't find is popularly-themed children's party decorations. But if you want to be a **POWER PUFF GIRL**, you better go **POKEMON** someplace else. On all returns (30-day return policy), there is a 10 percent restocking charge, so be sure it's what you want. Most orders are shipped the same day they are received. Order in their FREE catalog and see what kind of party's just around the corner. *Call toll-free: 800/888-3087*

◆◆◆◆◆ Parties Portable   **817/467-3087**
PO Box 150001   By Appt. Only, 24-Hour service
Arlington, TX 76015   www.parties-portable.com

Taking talent on the road is what these portable entertainers do best. Add some life to the party and put the details in their hands. It doesn't matter where or when, or even what's the occasion, Lico Reyes will provide it all. Weddings, bar mitzvahs, showers, birthdays, it's your party and you'll cry if you want to. But do you know what Lico's favorite job is? Spending his most-profitable season (Christmas) throwing parties for the poor and homeless. Other times, he draws from his extensive repertoire and brings along professional DJs, sound systems, spectacular light shows, music from the '40s to the '90s, karaoke, magicians, dancers, comedians, clowns, bands and emcees, celebrity look-alikes or a carnival dunk tank. They may even have been the first mobile DJ in the country, having started in 1970. Packages start at $90 per hour with a three-hour minimum. This is such a deal, especially considering that Lico has not raised his prices since 1980. Services can be conducted in English, Spanish or Vietnamese. They will go anywhere you need them; previous parties have even taken them to the Bahamas and Mexico. Add video taping to their list of services this year. One of the most fun things to do is invite one of their celebrity look-alikes to join you. Imagine your guests' faces when they think Elvis, Marilyn Monroe, Selena, Michael Jackson, Liz Taylor, Cher, Bill Clinton, Al Gore or Ricky Martin shows up and throws their arms around you? They even go along and sign autographs.

◆◆◆◆◆ **Trax City USA**   **972/252-7827**
321 W. Airport Frwy.   Mon-Fri 10-7; Sat 10-6
Irving, TX 75062   www.traxcityusa.com

Looking for a karaoke clambake? Then dig in your heels and start the music with a song and a dance. From jive to hip hop, rap to mambo, cha-cha to the lindy, golden oldies to country-western, big band to the blues, rent a karaoke machine, roll up the carpet, and start filling up your dance card. Pick your sounds from over 80,000 sound tracks and if you really want them to trax down something out-of-the-ordinary, they're up for the challenge. For the past 15 years, they have been whoopin' it up for churches, schools, auditoriums, clubs, your next big party can really be the talk of the neighborhood (depending on how loud you go!)

★★★★★ **Treasure Chest (Holiday Market)**   **972/285-4113**
2414 Hwy. 80 E.   Tue-Sat 10-6 (Jan.-Sept.); 7 days 10-6 (Oct.-Dec.)
Mesquite, TX 75149

Making a move into Suite 130 brings them closer to the highway and a new name. It's business model is now bigger and better, with higher ceilings and brighter lights. Rather than hopping from little room to little room, everything's in one big room. If you're in the market for a wrap, this is the place to paper the town——from one end to the other. Furniture is placed outside, which is one big difference over last year's. Home accents include those with a western and Spanish motif. New, too, children's things for the holidays. Thousands of new items all over the showroom and hanging on the walls still at discounted prices. And the gift-wrap, well, they have the largest selection in the Metroplex, over 4,000 rolls. Seasonal items will be brought in at the appropriate hour, but until then, expect to see lots of primitive iron and wood furniture, things like baker's racks and etágéres. It's a catchers' catch can. Selection changes constantly and ebbs and tides according to seasonal demands. Ronnie Nalin's in charge here but he's also the chief cheese with another of his outlets at the CBI Laboratories Outlet Store, 2055-C Luna Rd., Carrollton.

★★ **Trophy Arts**   **817/336-4532**
519 Pennsylvania   Mon-Fri 9-5:30
Fort Worth, TX 76104

Shelve the idea of going anywhere else. Trophy Arts displays custom trophies and engravings along with plaques, medals and awards that give you some additional inspiration to go that extra mile. If men can have trophy wives, you can collect trophies for just about everything else—from sports to academic achievement, be proud and show them off! Turn around time is generally only three to five days for just about any order. Employers may want to reward sales if a certain goal was reached with a unique or functional pronouncement such as a trophy clock or plaque that doubles as a penholder. Whether it's carved in wood, engraved on a trophy or medal, printed on a ribbon, everybody wants recognition. Getting that pat on the back is always appreciated, even if they spell your name wrong.

★★★★★ **Under Wraps**   **972/669-9120**
13590 Floyd Circle, Suite 100   Mon-Sat 10-5
Dallas, TX 75243   -

Like the Energizer Bunny, these brothers are still going strong. Sure enough, they learned early on to roll with the punches. And it's their rolls that have fed the Metroplex with savings of up to 80 percent. Designer gift-wrap, tie-ons, ribbons and bows including several bins of 99-cent rolls on clearance are the tip of the paper chase. Their warehouse location is where it's all at, but expect them to multiply like rabbits during the holiday season (usually at area malls.) Accent those packages with punch and expect during the rest of the year, these guys are closed for lunch, from 12-1. (Man's gotta eat though wraps are not on their list of favorites.) Depending on their mood, they may leave before the closing bell at night so don't shop too close to the 5 o'clock bewitching hour. You can never anticipate their staying power. Now, let's call it a wrap!

45

Pets & Vets

ABT Tropical Aquarium   972/644-3474
1002 N. Central Expwy., Suite 699   Mon-Fri 10-8; Sat 10-7; Sun Noon-6
Richardson, TX 75080   www.abttropical.com

Fish gotta swim and if you want the best in fresh and saltwater tanks and water gardens, here's where to dive. No need to wear a wet suit, though. ABT is a water wonderland specializing in Central, South American and African Cichlids, saltwater fish, invertebrates, and live rock from around the world, plus a large variety of community fish. With more than 500 tanks on display stocked with fish, snakes and turtles, your lesson in aquatics begins here. Learn everything you need to know about aeration, nitrogen and maintaining the water quality and clarity. Then find out which fish are compatible? You don't want to incarcerate two enemies into one environment only to see one get tanked, do you? Expert advice comes FREE of charge; maintaining a tank can be a costly investment and you don't want to lose any one of your fine finned friends unnecessarily. Whether you choose a standard or custom aquarium, is up to you. From **ALL GLASS**, **D.A.S.**, **NATURE'S VIEW**, **OCEANIC** and **OCEANVIEW**, they not only house those moving creatures, but feed them, too. Accessories help separate the tanks from plain and boring to knockouts. Add live plants to create a one-of-a-kind wet and wild. Learn how to fish for the finest in **FLUVIAL**, **HAGEN**, **OCEANIC** and **TETRA'S**. Go online to find specials and coupons like buy one fish ($9.99 or less) and get one FREE. How's that? Improve the water in the tank by considering some of these enhancers: **AMQUEL**, **BACTER PLUS**, **CYCLE**, **FRITZYME**, **STRESSCOAT** and others. Nothing fishy about them—just don't think of them as suitable for a Friday night fish fry!

★★★★★ Backtalk Bird Center   972/960-BIRD
6959 Arapaho Rd., Suite 513   Mon-Tue, Sat 10-6; Wed-Fri 10-7; Sun 12-6
Dallas, TX 75248

If Polly takes flight, take her in for a wing clip and nail trim, only $10. Birds need their regular salon appointments, too, even if they continue to give you back talk. Sassy little things can also be boarded when you go out of town. Bird sitting now joins the ranks of other pet-sitting services around town. But if you're particular, you won't leave your bird with just anybody. Bird-watching costs begin at $5 a day. But you must bring your own cage (and their own bottle if they have their special preferences.) Leave any special meds, vitamins, instructions and if Polly likes her special crackers, bring them along, too. They probably do draw the line over bringing Polly's special blankie. (Even birds have to grow up sometime.) Now onto the other birds (and no squawking about the prices as they're the best in town.) Many were below dealer's cost and that means, "cheep, cheep!" Cockatoos to cockatiels, macaws to Amazon parrots, this is aviary heaven here on earth. Bring these flying friends home and get acquainted (though these friends don't fly free.) Start with some of the lower-priced birds selling for around $12/pair to some that cost thousands. The more exotic, the more expensive. One rare species was the **MAJOR MITCHELL LEDBETTER** priced at $3,499— to the **AFRICAN GRAYS** for $799 (the most popular.) They mentioned briefly if I would be interested in the **HYACINTH MACAW** for $7,000 but flying that high is not my idea of à la cage de faux.

★★ Boutique Pet Shop & Aquarium   214/321-1219
9035 Garland Rd.   Mon-Fri 8-7; Sat 8:30-6, Sun Noon-5
Dallas, TX 75218

We fell for this store hook, line and sinker until we had to give them a call. Though they've been a favorite since 1968, it's hard to believe this is a combination grooming salon and fish store. What an unlikely duo. Just hold the mustard? Don't reel in more than you bargained for, but if it has a fin or a big sloppy grin, pampered pooches and floppy fins win our vote until...well, I'm getting ahead of the story. Though they were voted the Best Fish Store in 1997 by *The Dallas Observer*, by the time we waded through being on hold for five minutes, and calling back three more times only to find the line busy, we almost had it up to the gills. Yes, they're a popular hang out but surely there's not a line-up of fishes waiting to finagle a salon appointment? They sell aquariums and all the accoutrements: plants and tropical and marine fish on one hand and dog supplies for your dogs and grooming for same with charges from $20-$50 depending on size and condition of your dog. On the other hand, same day grooming is possible unless Max has to be de-toxed and de-tangled. I'm still waiting on the line to make an appointment. What gives?

★★★ Canine Commissary   214/324-3900
11504 Garland Rd.   Mon-Wed, Fri 9-7:30; Thu 9-9; Sat 9-6; Sun Noon-6
Garland, TX 75218   www.caninecommissary.com

This is the ultimate in fancy feasts for your four-legged friends. Gourmet treats, peanut butter pops, biscuits and bones are just the beginning to whet their growing appetites. Bring Fido along when you shop and let him beg for his supper. Toy boxes for your pooch are coming soon (now if they could only learn to clean up after themselves) but pooper scoopers are available for your personal use just by asking. Both cat and dogs are treated as equal opportunity pets with discounts across the kennels, dogs runs, show supplies, grooming supplies, doggie fashions, car seats and carriers, bowls, bones, toys, "how-to" manuals and books, even cards that are dog-eared. Arf. Arf. Don't be catty. Spread the good word. Premium to economy-brand foods are available but if you're smart, you might want to serve it on "bone" china. To satisfy all of your animal instincts, the pet patrol is also maintained at 3614 Greenville Ave., Dallas, 214/821-7700 and 1301 Custer Rd., Plano, 972/985-3900. Watch for their website, which was under construction at the time of publication.

★★★ Diamond Pet Center   972/442-7500
4412 Dillehay Rd. (FM 2551)   Mon-Fri 10-7; Sat 8-6; Sun 1-5
Parker, TX 75002

When a bird flies the coop, all hell breaks loose in the store. Imagine our chagrin when this exotic birdhouse had such a "beakout." Close the escape hatch. All hands on deck. You can imagine the chaos that ensued when all we wanted was to bring Tweetie in for clip job. Anyway, all's well that ends well, especially since he got his nails done FREE with a wing clip. Parrots, cockatoos, cockatielsand several varieties of macaws, including **GREEN WINGS**, **HARLEQUINS** and **CAMELOTS** are swinging from their perches. Flutter at the thought of buying elsewhere but at this diamond in the rough. They have one of the most extensive and best-priced lines of bird products and accessories in the Metroplex. Is it a bird? Is it a plane? Is it a plain bird? Not here, oh eagle eyes.

◆◆◆ Find-A-Pet 214/827-4357

6301 Gaston Ave., Suite 600
Dallas, TX 75244

Mon-Fri 8:30-5:30
www.petdata.com

When Fifi or Fufu loses their way, where to go for help? Try this FREE Find-A-Pet service if your pet has been registered. Registration costs $7 for spayed or neutered pets and $20 for those that aren't. Senior citizens have up to three FREE registrations as do the pets that assist the disabled. Statistics show that you are 90 percent more likely to find your lost pet if they are registered with the city. Register every year and when the tag expires, it will be the same date as the expiration of your animal's rabies' shots. Help solve animal control problems and the heartache that goes with losing your best friend. ***Call toll-free: 888/738.3463***

◆◆◆◆ North Texas Emergency Pet Clinic 972/323-1310

1712 W. Frankford
Carrollton, TX 75007

Mon-Thu 6 PM-8 AM; Fri-Sun 24 Hours
www.ntepc.com

Moving into new digs this year from their original MacArthur location, bark when you have an emergency and they'll come running. This brand-new medical facility caters primarily to dogs and cats but they also have been known to take care of an occasional ferret and rabbit. Birds and exotic animal owners should call in advance to see if there's a specialist on duty; otherwise, they will recommend you to another clinic. As always, bring your dog on a leash and your cat in a carrier or box. Otherwise, they will provide one so as to not add insult to injury. ***Call toll-free: 800/362-8600***

◆◆◆◆◆ Operation Kindness 972/418-7297

3201 Earhart Drive
Carrollton, TX 75006

Mon-Wed, Fri-Sat 11-4:30; Thu 11-8; Sun 1-4:30
www.operationkindness.org

I double dog dare you to find a better place for finding a new home for your dog or cat whether you're giving or getting. Their new and improved expanded facility is one mile north of Belt Line and one street south of Keller Springs, west of Midway in Carrollton. Adoption rates have increased this year to $115 for dogs and $100 for cats but don't expect just any rummy off the street to be an acceptable parent for the animals here. Homes must meet the highest of standards and be willing to make the necessary commitment to ensure a lifelong relationship. Keeping a 100-pound sheepdog in an efficiency apartment, isn't an ideal match for either. If you're ever hungry, stop in at CiCi's Pizza on Trinity Mills in Carrollton the second Thursday of each month. Bring in your receipt and drop it in the box at Operation Kindness. CiCi's will donate 10 percent of all receipts collected. (CiCi's doesn't make it easy but at least they're trying.) Since pizza is one of Jazz's (my own OK adoptee) favorite snacks, save a little of the crust for her, won't you please? You can probably guess, I consider Operation Kindness to be A-OK and the greatest little pick-up joint in town. This no-kill animal shelter is where to find love and give love for the rest of your life. Besides, you know pet owners live longer? Too, if you're ever looking for a perfect pet present, what about a state-of-the-art litter box or crate, bandannas, sweaters, pet books, T-shirts, umbrellas, jewelry, photo frames, whatever's got a pet connection can be found in the gift shop. Johnny's on the spot as their fearless leader and welcomes donations any time. All proceeds benefit the 2,500 homeless animals they care for each year. And since Jazz is the best behaved of all of my dogs, I have to give Operation Kindness credit for good foster caring after she was dumped on LBJ Freeway and rescued.

◆◆◆◆ Paul's Pet Food Delivery Express   214/222-PETS
Lewisville, TX   By Appt. Only

Celebrating two years is a milestone in business these days and if having 1,000 customers is any indication, Paul is on the right road to success. Though their names are Greg and Michelle Gillogy, they brought Paul's Pet Food Delivery Express from California to the Metroplex and pet-lovers have embraced them with open arms. Not only do they deliver **NATURE'S SELECT** super premium pet food, they offer four different formulas covering the entire lifespan of your dog: Chicken, Rice and Lamb, Lamb and Rice, Puppy Formula and the Senior/Reduced Fat formula. Along with the food, they also deliver natural dog biscuits and liver treats. Why not call for a FREE sample to see if your four-legged friend(s) are ready to make the switch? Make your life easier. Why run out in the middle of the night when Fifi finds herself craving for a late-night snack?

★★★★★ Petco   972/221-8816
201 N. Summit Drive   Mon-Sat 9-9; Sun 9-7
Lewisville, TX 75067   www.petco.com

Go, pet, go. This pet company means business and if you don't know it, you haven't been to one of their stores where pets sometimes out-number the people and the personnel. Petopia.com is now part of Petco, so shopping online makes even more sense. In fact, their website is dog-gone great! Have your dog or cat at your computer's edge and forget the leash. However, if you want to adopt a pet, check with your nearest Petco location for times and dates. Grooming facilities are open seven days a week, dog-training classes are offered in-store and even veterinary services are available (though the location above is one of the few that doesn't offer grooming.) Veterinarians are mobile and have varying schedules; call in advance for times and dates. If you use their vet, expect to take advantage of their low-cost vaccinations, feline fecal exams, deworming and all of the other routine services that a stationary clinic would provide. The difference, though, the price. Check directory for locations near you. It's a dog's life after all. Order premium pet foods, toys, treats and supplies online with the support of their over 530 stores and eight product distribution centers around the country. They are substantial partners with animal welfare organizations besides their adoption events, contributing millions of dollars annually to a wide variety of animal rescue and spay/neuter programs. Their expanded "Yellow Page" directory of additional pet services is invaluable and their features on pets, from A to Z, makes good background reading. Remember, dogs and cats are not their only pet attraction. They also cater to birds, fish, reptiles and other creepy crawly creatures, too. ***Call toll-free: 877/738-6742***

◆◆◆◆◆ Petland   972/669-2728
Dal-Rich Shopping Center   Mon-Sat 10-9; Sun 11-6
101 S. Coit @ Belt Line   www.petland.com
Dallas, TX 75240

How much is that doggie in the window, arf, arf? The one with the waggity tail. But it's not just how much, it's also which one's right. Are you the perfect master to a Miniature Schnauzer or are you an Alpha-kind of guy? If so, you'll find the Akita to be your soul mate. From Beagles to Terriers, Bassets to Bloodhounds, Boxers to Black Labs, even a few mixed breeds thrown in for humility, now you can buy your pet from the largest Petland in the country. This franchise is owned and operated locally, but it also provides other pets for our land aplenty: Kittens, tropical and marine fish, reptiles, birds plus all the accoutrements to keep your pet alive and well and living in the laps of luxury. Since 1967, this company has morphed into a different kind of store than when it was first created. In the 70s and 80s, they became franchisers of retail pet stores. Soon they expanded internationally and currently operate 123 stores in the United States and 57 overseas. Since over 50 percent of the U.S. households have one or more pets, expect to find a pet here, if not through the shelters. American Kennel Club registerable puppies and Cat Fancier Association kittens are available, too. Trained sales counselors are really knowledgeable about each pet and their modus operandi. Though they haven't brought Fido into therapy and offered the couch to get him to talk, they do know more about each animal and its breed than the average clerk in a discount pet store. Petland also employs trained animal care technicians and retains the services of a licensed veterinarian to continue in-service training for all of the store's personnel. Visit also at 420 E. FM 3040, Suite 680 in Lewisville, 972/874-0770; in Southlake Marketplace, 2125 W. Southlake Blvd., Suite 345, 817/488-2488 and in Arlington, 642 Lincoln Square Shopping Center, 817/861-0131.

★ ★ ★ ★ ★ PETsMART   972/407-0101
6204 W. Park Blvd.   Mon-Sat 9-9; Sun 9-7
Plano, TX 75093   www.petsmart.com

If you're sMart, you'll shop PetsMart. If you're not, you'll pay retail. That's just how the raw hide goes. Similar websites makes fairly equal competitors, but PetsMart comes out ahead in the pricing department. Pennies from heaven are shaved from their site compared to Petco's, though I found Petco's site easier to navigate. How catty of me. From dogs, cats, birds, hamsters, fish, reptiles and wild animal supplies, you can literally shop from A to Z. They also have a VetsMart inside with it's own separate phone line (972/250-6428—yet no clinic hours, yet.) The VetsMart in East Plano, though, has clinic hours already, so call 972/423-6032 (which most locations do) where they can get vaccinations for just the cost of the shots. The office visit is FREE but it's only during special clinic hours, which vary by location. Watch for special LUV-A-PET promotions where shelters and humane societies bring in their prospects for adoption. Save money and save a pet at the same time. Though they are one of the big box superstores for pet supplies, don't think warehouse only means cheap treats. They are also the source for Three Dog Bakery, the gourmet chuck wagon full of rawhide treats, beef ears, pig ears, tail chips and ham bones. Yum-m-m. Then, for cats, expect to indulge them with **GYM PETS**, **TOPINI** (white cheese or trout-flavored) or mouse-shaped treats. Meow! Expect to find prescription pet food and all of the pet's necessary accoutrements from doghouses, leashes, toys, fashions—all at discounted prices. Check directory for location nearest you. ◀

★ ★ ★ Plano Pet & Do It Yourself Pest Control   972/423-1610
1120 E. Parker, Suite 112   Mon-Sat 8-9; Sun Noon-6
Plano, TX 75094

From premium foods to made-in-Texas varieties, it's food for thought for all your pets, including ferrets and birds, grooming supplies and more. The lineup is all over the map from **ALL GLASS**, **HIKARI**, **KENT**, **KT**, **LM PRODUCTS**, **OSI**, **PRETTY BIRD** and **WARDLEY** with the main pest control line being **PHOENIX**. Doing-it- yourself can be a blessing or a pain in the patootie. Call back in a few months when their website should be up and purring for online ordering. Red Rover, Red Rover, get Rover combed all over with fine toothcombs, slicker brushes, nail clippers and more. Then, when all is said and the do is done, add the final spritz of cologne and dog-gone-it, let's be on our way. Oh, don't forget the breath spray so the liver and bacon treats' odor will be-gone. At least at Plano Pet, they maintain their sense of humor while Jazz went wee-wee all the way home. But like my Mother always said, just in case, Jazz was all Jazzed up and smelling like a rose.

Puppy Love Mobile Dog Grooming
Dallas, TX

972/243-8331
Mon-Sat By Appt.

And they call it, Puppy Love. But at least having a crush on this puppy won't flatten your wallet. Book your appointments about two weeks in advance for Saturdays and one week for weekdays. (Hey, when you're haute, you're hot!) Grooming rates vary by breed but $3 is the only additional charge for the convenience of pulling up in your driveway. You won't get away cheap but then again, having a Bichon means detailed and meticulous grooming. Now, a Shepherd-mix doesn't require the same deft hands. Anyway, we can't sing their praises enough. The convenience alone is worth the price of admission. In the olden days, I trucked them to get their nails done; today, they have monthly standing appointments. And there are days when they actually jump with glee rather than flee when they know Puppy Love's pulling up. Their service extends to the mid-cities, Arlington and all of Dallas and their multiple vans are manned by professional groomers who know all the cuts, from French Poodles to Yorkies, Maltese's to Akita's. And yes, certain groomers also do "lion cuts" on our Himalayan, Persian and others who think they are.

◆◆◆◆◆ Riding Unlimited
9168 T. N. Skiles Rd.
Ponder, TX 76259

940/479-2016
Tues-Sat: Call for times
www.ridingunlimited.org

Three cheers for their sponsors: Lone Star Park, Texas Instruments and Wal-Mart as these folks provide horseback riding as therapy for both children and grown-ups. Ride 'em cowboy. Saddle up for their 10-week sessions in the spring and fall and six-week sessions in the summer. Want to help butthey can't squeeze a penny out of a turnip? Then listen up. Albertson's, Kroger and Tom Thumb donate a percentage of your purchases to Riding Unlimited. To acquire an Albertson's Community Partners Card or Kroger Cares card, simply call the Ranch above or the next time you are at Tom Thumb, ask the cashier to program your Reward Card with Riding Unlimited's number— 4842. How's that for a galloping gourmet. They are always looking for volunteers, so if you're a horse person who loves people, too, this program needs you. Now that makes horse sense, neigh?

★★★★★ Southland Farm Store
5855 Maple Ave.
Dallas, TX 75235

214/350-7881
Mon-Fri 8-6; Sat 8-5

Who would have thought that an out-of-the-way feed store would be the primo pet place for saving money? Make this a ritual as you make your monthly rite of passage for pet food. After all, these guys are the distributors of premium pet food, so why not shop where the retailers shop and guaranteed a low, low price? Shop and compare and you'll see why man's best friends' lap it up here. Variety is the spice of your pet's life so slice off some of the fat and save some money on all the staples within this 5,000 square foot of air-conditioned warehouse/showroom. Finish the rest of your shopping in the remaining 30,000 square feet of warehouse, (un-air-conditioned), then pull your car or truck up to the loading dock and pile it in. Retailers who are buying wholesale need to shop at their new warehouse in Irving (400 Cascade Drive), while the rest of us pet parents can fill up our canine pantry at the Maple Ave. location now with more elbow room. All of the popular and vet-recommended brands are available: **IAMS, KAL-KAN, KEN-L-RATION, NUTRO, PRO PLAN, SCIENCE DIET, SENSIBLE CHOICE, WAYNE** and more. But it doesn't stop there. Southland also is your source for saving green on all your lawn and garden supplies. But that's not all; they also offer a complete do-it-yourself pest control department and probably the largest selection of wild birdhouses, feeders and supplies in the Metroplex. Cheep! Cheep! ***Call toll-free: Metro 972/44***

◆◆◆◆◆ Spay-Neuter Assistance Program (SNAP)   214/372-9999

4830 Village Fair Drive   Wed-Sat 7:30-6 (Appt. for surgeries)
Dallas, TX 75224   www.snaptx.org

In by 7:30, off by 6! For less than it costs to tune-up your car, you "auto" fix your dog or cat. The Human Society of the United States operates this Spay-Neuter Clinic as well as the Animal Wellness Center (Open Wed, Fri & Sat from 10-6, with walk-ins welcome). Thought the prices are reduced, the state-of-the-art equipment or veterinarian's services are not. Top notch all the way, from spaying and neutering to rabies' shots (required by Texas law), nail trims, physicals, heartworm testing, flea and tick control and prevention, the works....for less. Located six miles south of downtown Dallas near I-35E and Ledbetter Drive (Loop 12), please help control the animal population. Do your part so there's no unwanted strays without a loving home.

▪ State Line Tack   800/228-9208

PO Box 935   24/7
Brockport, NY 114420   www.statelinetack.com

How tacky of me to look for a discount on tack! But it's time to stop horsing around and get down to brass tacks. Whether you order via their slick 236-page catalog or shop online, you can find discounts from 15-50 percent. Mount and then count the savings on breeches, chaps, jodhpurs, tights, jackets and coats, shirts and boots for the entire family (men, women and children.) If you're part of the jet set and ride the fox hunt, you'll find both formal and less formal footwear, outdoor gear, helmets and such. But now that we've dismounted, let's look to outfitting the horse next. Equipment and supplies for horses are available including saddles, bridles, horse-related jewelry, trailer equipment, blankets, medical aids; then be sure to check out the selection of "how-to" books and more. The catalog provides the more extensive selection of products for riding the range but online is on its way up. 🇺🇸

46

Plants & Gardens

Bright Flowers
11363 Denton Drive, #104
Dallas, TX 75229

972/247-8818
Mon-Sat 9:30-5:30

Flower, flower burning bright, want to bring a little sunshine into your life? Even if you can not speak the proprietor's first language, the language of flowers is first and foremost, universal. Carry on a conversation with the plants and flowers here as they will last forever, or until the last dust mite eats it away. These flowers never die—though they may just fade away. The benefits of silk flowers, of course, is the absence of the need to water. Thirst not. And at these dirt cheap prices, what do you have to lose—except maybe the ability to smell the roses? Save 50-80 percent on thousands of flowers and greenery that can be bought individually or in an arrangement. Located in the International Plaza complex with lots of other imported worldly finds, shop year 'round or during the holidays for Christmas trees and it's guaranteed that you won't be cut out of the loop. There are two sides to the story here; one side's for the flowers and greenery and the other is for imported dolls, doll furniture and collectibles. It's important, though, for you to remember that neither silk flowers or money grows on trees. And look at it this way. With the money you save on one half, you can spend on the other.

★★★ Bruce Miller Nursery
1000 E. Belt Line Rd.
Richardson, TX 75081

972/238-0204
Mon-Sat 8-6; Sun 10-5
www.brucemillernursery.com

If all your plants go from green to brown, then take a look around. Bruce Miller's the place for anyone looking for high-quality trees, shrubs, flowers, fertilizer, seeds, bulbs, soil, pots, tools and more—especially if you're beyond the nursery stage. Now that organic is becoming the "in" thing, you can expect plenty of the pure stuff here. Since they're located in a former Dairy Queen, what did you expect, a blizzard? Yuletide brings a mad rush for Christmas trees, and Bruce Miller is right up there front and center. Save some green from their seedlings that are all grown up and ready to be carted off. Looking for a great gift? What about a potted Rosemary plant shaped like Christmas tree, or a Christmas cactus, an ivy candelabra, wind chimes or the all-time favorite, poinsettias? See, you don't have to just bed down with the plants out front. There's plenty of the green stuff inside, too. You can't order anything online, but it's still a handy-dandy source for knee-deep gardening information. Isn't that right, Widetrack?

★★★★★ Cristina's Garden Center   972/599-2033
6250 Mapleshade Lane   Mon-Sun 8 AM-7 PM
Plano, TX 75093

This store's got flower power as well as buying power. With 18-count flats at $10.80 each, they were one of the lowest-priced nurseries in town. That's elementary, my dear. Figure it out. That's 60-cents each, folks. At the southeast corner of Preston and the George Bush Turnpike, across from Lowe's, Cristina's is raring to grow. Bedding plants were all over the place, side by side with shrubs and hanging baskets. They've got it all—from Alyssum, Begonias, Celosia, Shade Coleus, Dianthus, Dusty Miller, Impatiens, Marigolds, Moss Rose, Petunias, Snap Dragons, well the list is exhaustive enough to tire even Tiny Tim as he tiptoed through the tulips. Visit also at 4617 Lovers Lane, just West of Inwood.

◆◆◆◆ Do-It-Yourself Pest & Weed Control   972/867-7649
2109 W. Parker Rd., Suite 108   Mon-Sat 9-7
Plano, TX 75023

Bragging about having the biggest roach in Texas is nothing to be proud of. Get rid of those nasty critters (or sell them to the "Fear Factor", the latest survivor show to make your stomach turn!) Everything here is environmentally-safe for pets when used correctly, so pay attention. Since silver fish are often a problem in garages and closets, there's even bait to catch them, too. But no bait and switch. If there are fleas, they make them flee. If there are mites, they make them take flight. Just about any bug or pest (including rodents) can make an exit with this money-saving, take charge and do-it-yourself weed and pest control. Of if you're not convinced, let them do it for you.

★★★★★ Doan's Nursery   972/790-3500
622 S. Belt Line Rd.   Mon-Fri 8-5; Sat-Sun 9-4
Irving, TX 75060   www.doansnursery.com

Since 1991, they've been boasting the "lowest prices in town." So if you've got a pain over the high prices of plants and shrubs, go back to nursery school and start over from there. What a selection! Over 50,000 square feet to aid and abet the greening of America: shrubs, annuals, perennials, fertilizers, bird feeders, pots, statues, the works. Sure gets my attention. Add these to your studies: Butterfly Vines, Mandavilla , Purple Passion, Angel Wings, Blue Daze, Boston Ferns, Fuschsia, Geraniums, Ivy and New Wonder hanging around or in pots watching over the flats of Dianthus, Dusty Miller, Marigold, Moss Rose, Pursiane, Salvia and Zinias. Color, color everywhere but not a square inch left to plant. What a dilemma! Well, what about starting over? Okay, that sounds like a good idea. This time, should I choose Asian Jasmine or English Ivy? I declare. Is it any wonder my neighbors are green with envy? So what did they do to compete? Head to Doan's and load up with Azaleas, Boxwoods, Dwarf Buford Holly, Red Tip Photinia and Waxleaf Ligustrum. Why don't they just leaf me alone, already?

★★ Fannin Tree Farm   972/747-9233
Hwy. 121 @ Custer Rd.   Mon-Sat 8-5; Sun 1-5
Plano, TX 75024

Down by the ole mill stream is where Fannin Tree Farm now resides. At the northwest corner of Hwy. 121 and Custer, the forest now has some breathing room. There's nothing more idyllic than sitting under the shade of that ole apple tree and here is where you can buy them. Of course, the staple crops are the Red

Oaks, Live Oaks, Cedar Elms and Chinese Pistachios. Hundreds and hundreds are waiting to be uprooted and reestablished at your home and garden. This farm is a legacy in its own time. Expect prices, depending on the season, to be about $100 per caliper inch. A three-inch tree (round), for example, would cost around $330 delivered, planted and guaranteed, while a four-inch beauty could be yours for around $490. "I think that I shall never see, a tree as beautiful as these!"

★★★★★ Flower Ranch
901 Pearson Lane
Keller, TX 76248

817/431-3830
Mon-Fri 8-5; Sat 8-2

The hours can fluctuate with the high-demand season, but for right now, you can expect to be singing, "Don't Fence Me In" with flowers bought at this Flower Ranch. Giddy-up and get going. If you're looking for a flat of anything, ask before you pack up the kids and pack up the car. When you round the bend, there's usually upwards of 20,000 flats waiting to be lassoed. Expect most flats to cost $13.75, a 75-cents increase over last year (compared to Christina's for $10.80). This commercial grower has finally made the plunge and has decided to open to the public full time. The economy here is certainly "flat" but you'll be in the pink with the varieties: Alyssum, Begonias, Bougainvillea, Celosia, Coleus, Ferns, Hibiscus, Impatiens, Joseph's Coat, Marigolds, Moss Rose, Petunias, Salvia, what did you expect? A colorless canvas of nudes!

★★★★★ Hartwell's Landscaping Nursery
1570 N. Stemmons Frwy.
Lewisville, TX 75067

972/436-3612
Mon-Fri 8:30-5:30; Sat 8:30-5; Sun 10-4

What's a tree growing in Lewisville? I thought it was supposed to grow in Brooklyn? Even though she didn't have a New York accent, we understood Tammy very well. She's the decorator for your garden. For $250, she'll completely map out a recommended and functional design but if you then proceed with buying the plants, shrubs, trees, ground cover, it comes off the final bill. Or bring in your own plans, designs and ideas, and let them bid on it, no charge. Imagine this great oasis of greenery sitting between all the boat dealerships, barbecue joints, funeral homes and RV outlets on Stemmons. Nevertheless, just take a look at the Crepe Myrtle's like one-gallon pots for $1.89 or five gallon (five-six feet tall) for $9.95. Lots of trees line the freeway of opportunities; Bradford Pear, Chinese Pistachio, Fruit, Pecan—have them planted by their crew or plant them yourself and have a backache on Monday. Prices were also slashed on one-gallon shrubs and Hibiscus, two-gallon Wax Myrtles, Cedar Elms, Silver Maples, Live Oaks, Loblolly Pines, Globes and Weeping Willows—with a guaranteed lifespan of one year. Also, a good source for organic supplies approved by the naturalpaths such as green and lava sand, pine mulch, humate and plenty of "Garrett Juice" to keep those good intentions pure as the native sun.

★★★★ Joy Silk Flower Outlet
11252 Harry Hines Blvd., #201
Dallas, TX 75229

972/241-1466
Mon-Sat 9-6:30

Reading the *Joy Luck Club* may have been my inspiration to check them out, but seeing them was my lucky day. Putting the language barrier aside, these are the folks for fabulous silk flowers, custom made or ready-made for your own custom arrangement. Stems started at $1 and are perfect for any special occasion. Do buy them—'cause they never die. The more exotic the stem, the more expensive, but the time comes when you just have to spring for it. Occasionally, that's a thorn in my side, but it only hurts for a minute. For sprucing up those you've already planted on your dining room table, nightstand, bathroom counter or elsewhere, they stock all the silk flower cleaning supplies you could ever need.

362   **biggerbetterbargains**.com

★★★★ **Lake June Garden Center**   **214/391-4005**
8634 Lake June Rd.   Mon-Sat 9-5:30; Sun 10-3
Dallas, TX 75217

Don't get hosed by paying through the nose. Instead, plant your garden from the terra firma here. Plants, plants and more plants can be found at Lake June, minus the lake and during more months than just June. They've even busted out with a sister store called Pickerings, 8950 Kingsley Rd., in Dallas, 214/349-1077 if more convenient. As one of the sponsors of the Xeriscape Contest each year through the Dallas Water Utilities Department, you can expect participants to really do up some pretty snazzy displays of native and naturalized plants specific to our Texas climate. Expect discounts to be at least 20 percent off competing nurseries and more during special sales. Stop and smell the **STAR** brand roses, it's one of their mainstays. With the additional fencing, they've been able to increase their forest of shade and fruit trees giving yards the full spectrum of shrubs, ground cover, plants, trees and all things green and beautiful. There are plantiful opportunities for Robert to execute his landscaping designs. Make an appointment (a week to 10 days in advance) and he'll come back with a computer generated landscape plan for $25. If you use their products and services, you can deduct that $25.

★★★★★ **Little House on Pearl, The**   **214/748-1443**
514 S. Pearl   Wed-Sun 9-5
Dallas, TX 76201

What a gem! This pearl is a girl's best friend when it comes time to add some greenery to your life. In a mountain greenery, God is the only one that paints the scenery. But here is another good reason to head to the sheds at Farmer's Market. Millions of shoppers descend on downtown Dallas to shop Farmers Market and the Little House on Pearl is no exception. Mix and match, pick and play with a bunch of dried flowers, the more the merrier, all at a fraction of the cost if purchased pre-arranged. Gather ye rose buds while thee may, add a touch of sunshine with sunflowers, throw in some pepper or tallow berries, poke around the artichokes and, for spice, add some cinnamon sticks. For local color, assemble a gaggle of okra pods and a cayenne of chile peppers, gaze upon some pine or star cones, rough up some raffia, and tuck in the birch twigs—what a great little housewarming for a newcomer moving to Big D. Nobody west of the Mississippi can rival the selection at this Little House on Pearl. Curl your fingers around a bevy of dried flowers and plants that sit gingerly alongside candles and other tabletop accessories and enjoy your trip from bountiful.

★★ **Mary's Flowers**   **972/243-4333**
Farmers Branch Shopping Center   Mon-Fri 8-6; Sat 9-5
12895 Josey Lane
Farmers Branch, TX 75234

Mary had a little flower shop and decided to sell her cut flowers at cut prices. Whatever's the occasion, she'll try to sell both the traditional requests as well as the unusual. She's specializes in utilizing a plethora of pots, containers, usual baskets, urns, tea pots, whatever she can find to display the flowers and still save you 25-30 percent. April showers bring more than May flowers. Mary sells a dozen roses at $54.99, which includes the vase, greenery and baby's breath. Delivery is available with a minimum purchase of $25 ($5-8 delivery charge.) Looking to add some balloons? No problem, they have both Mylar and Latex for any occasions. Sending an "over the hill" balloon bouquet on a friend's 30th birthday was my just rewards. Exotic arrangements with such unusual varieties as Birds of Paradise, Spider Mums, Halliconia, Pineapple Plants, Honey Combs, little orchids on the side, well, you get the picture. Add ribbons and stuffed animals, maybe a green plant on a pedestal, there's bargains blooming everywhere. Flower arrangements that are imaginative, economical and fun rolled into one continues to make Mary not contrary. ***Call toll-free: 800/222-6507***

◆◆◆◆◆ Metro Irrigation   817/877-5052
1622 Rogers Rd.   Mon-Fri 8-5
Fort Worth, TX 76107

If your lawn's begging for a drink and the occasional downpour in the hot Texas sun doesn't quite cut it, keep it raining with an irrigation system from Metro Irrigation. With three locations (North Richland Hills and Arlington, too) it's the company that will make your garden grow. They are also highly mow-tivated to install a custom system, from one-inch heads (they'd never sell anything smaller to keep you from having to deal with the headaches of a broken system.) If you want smaller ones, do-it-yourself from Home Depot. But remember, those smaller ones can't take the big jobs and break down from having too much water pressure and not big enough valves. Do not call them for repairs but they will try to talk you through any job for FREE. Choose from stationary heads, pop-ups and gear-driven for just the right combination of coverage. If you want the Doctors of Sprinklers, these folks are the hands-on experts.

★★★ Oncor Factory Outlet   214/689-8833
Inwood Trade Center   Mon-Fri 9-5
1325 Inwood Rd.
Dallas, TX 75247

What is an answering machine doing taking the place of a live person? Well, the store is 7,000 square feet with a warehouse in back, so we'll give them the benefit of the doubt. We know you're there. We know you're open. We tried to talk to you, but, each time we called, we got the same two seconds, a beep and hang up. There wasn't even time to tell you to chop down the cherry tree. Anyway, this is an Oklahoma-based manufacturer (well, they're actually made in China) of faux flowers and plants. See bushes and blossoms and berries, oh my. When the season looms front and center, expect Christmas trees at prices reminiscent of the good old days. The prices here garner rave reviews like seven heads of flowering bush-es for 50-cents; or $2 for 14 heads. Now compare a six-foot ficus tree, including basket for $20 (to the eight-foot beauty for $699 at Luckman Silks.) Granted, the quality may be reduced, but a tree is a tree. Unless you want museum-quality (à la Luckman), these trunks are well-rooted in dirt cheap prices. For-get that fear of dying. These are destined from here to eternity. Why close on the weekends, though, when most people can shop?

★★★★★ P & E Plants   214/741-9209
1204 S. Central   Mon-Sun 6 AM-6 PM
Dallas, TX 75201

If you love flowers, you'll want to buy them out at P & E, lock, stock and barrel. I hate to accuse them of being bloomin' idiots, but a three-gallon Azalea pot was $15 and the price of flats were $12 (same as last year's.) Though Pansies were out-of-season at the time, we were particularly pleased with the Peri-winkles. Is it any wonder why millions of shoppers make the trek to Farmer's Market just to get in the thick-of-et? P & E Plants and Mr. Eddie Comer are a big draw to plant yourself downtown and add col-or to them thar front and backyards. Bring a truck or your trunk will runneth over. Three-gallon shrubs were gathered up as thee may. The Azalea, Boxwoods, Buford Holly, Red Tip Photiniaand Yaupon Holly were all jolly-good prices, $5.50. With over 20,000 scrubs to choose and over 10,000 hanging baskets, is it any wonder folks from miles around come to cozy up to the greenery? Don't expect a lot of personal service. They are so busy, they can hardly come up for air.

★★★★ Plant Market, The

972/867-1105
Mon-Sun 9-5:30

500 Spring Creek Village
Belt Line and Coit
Dallas, TX 75248

To market, to market, have yourself a field day. Just how green is your valley anyway? If it's not, The Plant Market is the place to sow. It's all a matter of how your garden grows. From custom landscaping to flower beds, this company has it all. Planted on solid ground, turn your barren backyard into a blooming arena. From Alyssum to Passion vines, don't overlook the myriad of possibilities of planting it all. And for eager beavers, there's nothing better than your own vegetable or herb garden. Adding wonderful color, aromatic aromas, and hearty accents for cooking, the time is ripe to consider all the growing options. All plants are grown in their greenhouses in McKinney, hence "Direct from Grower." Expect prices to reflect this. Have it all, from landscaping plants, seasonal flowers, some trees, Christmas trees, clay pots and other seasonal items to a complete line of organic products for the yard including Howard Garrett's in case he has you under his thumb. Spring and summer, expect hours to extend to accommodate the rush for Begonias and the petulance for Petunias. Plant yourself at their Plano location, 3200 Thunderbird if you're in that far north corridor. You can't miss it. It's next door to Thunderbird Skating Rink. Spring into action. Don't fall!

★★★★ Plants and Planters

972/699-1281
Mon-Sat 9-6; Sun 10-6

1050 N. Greenville Ave.
Richardson, TX 75248

Just north of Arapaho, plant this twosome on your list of "To Shop" and get thee to their greeneries. Herbs for $1.19, geraniums for $4.95, fruit trees for $19.95, azaleas from $4.95-$12.95, well, what you get here is basically twice as many plants for the money. From organics to perennials, vegetables to pots, get that landscape and flower bed in tip-top shape with the custom green thumbs here. Whether it's landscaping, or your own weekend project, these folks can keep you bedded down for life. From ground cover to houseplants, floor-size tropicals to baby versions for $1.25, life is good. Life is green. Life is saving you money. Now, how much green was your valley? Second location at Northwest Highway and Plano Rd., 214/340-1020.

 proflowers.com

888/FRESHEST(373/743
24/7
www.proflowers.com

The service, the prices, the convenience, they are the pros in the know. In fact, they probably wrote the book on online shopping for flowers. Based in San Diego, and holder of many prestigious awards in the business arena, they remind you of special occasions, keep your credit card on file for when you place your next order, give enough space to create a personal card enclosure, send an update when the flowers leave the grower, and so far have never missed a date. This site is coming up roses each and every time you click or call. Personally, they are the freshest I have ever received and last longer than any others. Of course, you're limited to their choices, but there's enough variety, you won't feel like they've cut you short. Twenty blue irises were $29.95 plus delivery, one dozen long-stemmed summer roses (usually arriving in their bud stage), the same. And always via Federal Express. Returning time and time again should tell you something. I never send flowers without them. Even the president of the company emails me when I place an order. Now, isn't that's something! Since 1998, Proflowers has grown to be the largest domestic direct-from-the-grower Internet flower company with an unparalleled seven-day "Freshness Guarantee." Read their roster of talent and you'll understand why. Unlike most retail floral companies, they bypass the wholesalers and distributors (making flowers, by that point, already five-10 days old.)

Since they ship direct from the grower, you're getting fresher, more beautiful flowers, plain and simple. In fact, after I read about all of their proprietary software, and how a human is never even involved in the shipping process, I am not so sure the president, Bill Strauss, really does email me after all. Oh shucks! Foiled again.

Rose Petal, The   972/262-5253
515 E. Main   Mon-Sat 10-5
Grand Prairie, TX 75050

He loves me, he loves me not, let me count the ways. The only way I know to profess your love is to find something to love from The Rose Petal. Now, put your petal to their metal yard furniture—a summer glider for the front porch is too good to be threw. Add a few original birdcages as decorative elements, and a few to hang up to actually feed the birds. Surround yourself with the lushest hanging ferns at the lowest prices on earth; mix in a veritable variety of unusual geraniums...like chocolate (no, I'm not kidding) or more traditional scents like mint. Save a mint, too, on the kinds of flowers your grandmother planted and return to the days when you held her hand and walked to your "secret garden." Located next to Tommy Snodgrass Discount Furniture, it's worth the drive to Grand Prairie. Forget shopping online. There's too much in their back yard showroom and it changes too often. Gaze at more than just crystal balls. They have those wonderful gazing balls for the garden that mirror nature like nothing else can do. Choose bric-a-brac to hang over the garden wall, planters to hang on the fence, all one-of-a-kind and not right off the assembly line. Then turn to the barn-board potting benches, wicker chairs that serve as plants, wind chimes, concrete benches, fountains, statues, birdbaths and now even jewelry, all priced rosier than elsewhere. Bet if you added a few items from the Rose Petal, your house will increase in value; add a few items to your back yard, and your time gazing out the window will increase tenfold.

Ruibal's Plants of Texas   214/744-9100
601 S. Pearl Expwy.   Mon-Sun 8-6
Dallas, TX 75201   www.ruibals.com

Now we're talking a blanket of carpet bushes, climbing roses, rose bushes and more than what meets the eye of any Ivy Leaguer. Seven days a week, the Ruibal boys are at it, knee deep with bedding plants, tropicals, landscaping, topiaries and making deliveries to area offices and household gardens. Pat those Petunias, sweet pea, for $12/flat. Lilies, well, they're the hottest flowers growing. Create stunning vertical color online, too, with their topiary basket system. A 12" basket that fits a 14-16-inch pot for $24.99. Their world-famous topiaries bring folks from around the world to check them out. Going online, though, brought a skeletal template of what their website will look like when it gets filled in. Trust me, you'll wind up a basket case after you've taken a look at the over 5,000 baskets hanging overhead. Keeping their own overhead low is one of the reasons they can sell their plants-to-go so low. From their shed to your yard, patio, pool, front or back yard, ground cover, bedding plants, perennials, tropicals, herbs, what is it that you want? Two sheds full of all the garden varieties from simple to elaborate, dainty to dramatic, if it's green, has flowers, can grow, Ruibal's the place to stake out.

★★★★★ Season Flower International   972/488-3073
11398 Harry Hines Blvd., Suite 101   Mon-Sat 9:30-6
Dallas, TX 75229

You can't smell the roses, but what the heck, spray them with air freshener or cologne instead. There's nothing seasonal about the flowers here. In fact, they cover all the seasons, never die, and live on in infamy. From silk to Latex blooms, these folks are blooming with them all. From delicate roses to magnificent magnolias, you can join the Bush administration and blow your tax rebate all in one place. Prices start as low as 50-cents for a single stem to $7 for potted bushes. Flowers and fruits are their specialty, all arranged for easy picking. Have yourself a field day with the artificial fruit—from apples to grapes, bring on the reds and the purples and set them in bowls on tables throughout your house. No watering required. An occasional dusting should do the trick.

★★★ Sunshine Miniature Trees

7118 Greenville
Dallas, TX 75231

214/691-0127
Mon-Sun 9-6
www.sunshinebonsai.com

Add a little sunshine to your life and you'll be better off in every direction. It's true, Sunshine Miniature Trees has the largest bonsai nursery in North Texas and has been refining their delicate art for the past 35 years. The Sunshines (that's their name) have been serving the needs of discriminating plant enthusiasts based on the proposition that "Excellence at the most reasonable price," makes for good bedfellows. Expect to save 20-40 percent throughout the many rooms that meander back until you think you're going to exit the back door. Though they do import some of their plants from Asia, most are started from seed, tissue cultures and cuttings and grown right in the heart of Texas. Looking for a good deal? Then ask about their monthly specials like a Bonsai Juniper. This hearty two-year old plant comes completely landscaped with moss and rocks and planted in a brown plastic bonsai pot. It also includes a free humidity tray and a comprehensive care sheet for only $26.95. What a unique gift that transcends just an ordinary gesture, but one that lasts. If you are not happy with your purchase, you may return it with a receipt within 10 working days for a full refund. For orders outside the area, there's FREE UPS shipping available. *Call toll-free: 800/520-2401*

★★★★ Willhite Seed

PO Box 23
Poolville, TX 76487

817/599-8656
Mon-Fri 8-Noon, 1-5
www.willhiteseed.com

Call for their FREE catalog and soon you'll be able to shop online from this 75-year old source for top-quality seeds. Though they started out with watermelon, today's a whole other ballgame. From peanuts to beans, peas, tomatoes, onions, spinach, potatoes, corn, cucumbers, squash and peppers, too, plant your garden in July and come fall, you'll be wallowing in the fruits of your labor. Willhite Seed is one of the largest mail-order seed companies in the country. Texas-born and bred, Willhite's actually located between Weatherford and Bridgeport; so if you're in the area, why not "see'd it" for yourself? Family-owned and operated, dig around and see what materializes. Sow the seed directly into the ground or seed ahead for planting after the last frost, you will be able to turn your garden into a green, eating machine. It's fun. It's cheap. And it's satisfying. *Call toll-free: 800/828-1840*

47

Pools & Yards

Aquatic Landscapes
9132 Sweetwater Drive
Dallas, TX 75228

214/327-POND
By Appt. Only
www.aquaticlandscapes.com

Oh how I wish I could go with the flow. Though no Henry David Thoreau, there's nothing quite as inviting as dreaming by golden pond created by these specialists. Ten years and growing, they maintain a 16-acre research and development facility with a one-ton backhoe and offer some of the most imaginative backyards in the business. Their philosophy is simple...build it right the first time and make it low maintenance. Believe it or not, almost 70 percent of their business is fixing or rebuilding other's designs that are less than 24 months old because they are too complicated for the average consumer to maintain. Their staff continues to create award- winning user-friendly water gardens and koi ponds, as well as movie and television set designs and exquisite low light designs, just to name a few. Also, they create living eco-systems that not only increase the value of your home, but help to rejuvenate the soul. Creative touches such as low-voltage lighting, cedar arbors and hardscape construction, as well as ecologically safe organic planting methods, set them apart from the crowd. Give me an Aquatic Landscape or give me nada! *Call toll-free: 972/562-8119*

★★★ Aries Spa Manufacturer
4176 I-30
Rockwall, TX 75087

972/771-6286
Mon-Fri 8-5; Sat 9-3; Sun 10-4
www.ariesspas.com

So, what is your sign? If you're an Aries, you might have found a place to cool off. Since they're the manufacturer, customization for you spa is no problem. Start by simply choosing your color and finish. Then go a little deeper, under water that is, and feel the placement of each jet as it personally suits your needs, aches and pains. And every spa is available as a portable model, a spa shell with or without plumbing or a deck model. A few noticeable differences between Aries and other spas include the extra depth, a user-friendly, top-loading filtration system and topside controls, an extra-heavy shell and easy-care finish. Over 15 years in business should tell you something. Here you can try and keep your head above water. They also sell all the hot tub/spa supplies. Located on the eastern edge of Rockwall near I-30 and FM 549 (Exit 70), these are some of the best-price spas in town. Why spend a fortune? You'll end up all wet anyway?

★★★★★ Artforms Fountain Outlet — 972/494-6787
3828 Cavalier Drive
Garland, TX 75042

Mon-Fri 8-4; Sat 10-5; Sun 1-5

Well, how art thou form? If you want your fountain to appear a work of art, try shopping in Garland of all places as opposed to Venice or Paris. What's there? Copper fountains, whimsical garden sculptures, garden and gift accessories all priced at wholesale or there about. Don't let your cup runneth over. Try a fountain instead. If not, you may have to have your head examined. They don't always answer their phones, but assuming they're still creating forms that follows function, you'll score at this garden bonanza.

◆◆◆◆ B & B Lawn and Tree Care Co. — 972/475-9813
Rowlett, TX

Mon-Fri 9-5

Here's someone who's cutting costs in the Garland and Rowlett area. Looking for regular maintenance on your lawn and garden? Then they limit their territory to a manageable area. But if you want the works, they will goto the ends of the earth to get the job done. From regular mowing, wedding, trimming of hedges to cutting back large trees to full-scope landscaping, Bill Blundell, the owner, is the chief with the golden eye. Seniors, take advantage of additional discounts. FREE estimates gladly given. Weekly yard service for an average yard (exclusive of acreage, hills, and extra services) runs $25-$30. They also offer fertilizing, planting, sod installation, pruning and shaping of trees.

★★ Blue Haven Pools and Spas — 972/644-0494
13349 N. Central Expressway
Dallas, TX 75243

Mon-Sat 9-5; Sat 10-5
www.bluehaven.com

Though I haven't fallen off the deep end of the pool yet, I still can say I have never seen a pool as lovely as thee. Blue Have Pools and Spas, according to their press materials, is trusted by more schools, hotels, resorts, country clubs, and athletic centers from coast to coast than any other "pool company". Suppose they can handle a little hole in your backyard? They have been building custom gunite pools (concrete) since 1954. Choose from hundreds of models that are their standard and usual configurations. Go one step further, and let them design a custom pool with added features of tranquility, versatility and fun. From Grecian calming spas, lap lanes to lagoons, the latest trends and styles are sure to add value and comfort to your home (but dollars to your final bill.) Consider it your vacation for a lifetime. They private-label every one of their parts and accessories. They offer their own line of smart...everything: SmartVacs, SmartControls, SmartSavers, SmartLight, SmartPure, SmartBright, Smart-Filter and SmartFlow that allow for additional features, savings and easy maintenance. How cool! Now dive into your new Blue Haven Pool. We understand that each Blue Haven Pool location is a franchise, so differences do exist. Whichever one you select, always get references from Blue Haven Pool owners in your area. *Call toll-free: 800/543-3883*

★★★★★ Brandon Industries — 972/542-3000
1601 Wilmeth Rd.
McKinney, TX 75069

Mon-Fri 8:30-5
www.brandonmail.com

For 20 years, Brandon Industries has been the leading the way out of the Dark Ages. As a manufacturer of aluminum outdoor lighting, signage and mailboxes, they have made antique reproduction lamp posts, period street lights, deck lights, wall sconces, stop signs, cast aluminum mailboxes and mailbox posts for both commercial and residential use. Look to them for many charming styles and sizes that are made to complement any landscape or architecture. Expect only quality exterior fixtures in their FREE catalog or shop online. Everything they craft is similar to the originals after which they were modeled. Combining turn-of-the-century casting methods with today's technology, Brandon Industries offers the best of both worlds. Orders delivered to your home or office via UPS usually within two weeks. They only use name brand UL-approved parts from **ADVANCE TRANS-FORMER**, **GENERAL ELECTRIC** and **LEVITON** to electrify the way. Whether you're a builder, a developer, or a property owner (for your home or office), you might consider adding something more attractive to light the way. All prices are wholesale or below. Find them on exit north of U.S. Hwy. 380 on U.S. Hwy 75.

★★   Breez-Lite Awning Co.   214/321-2626
8940 Garland Rd.   Mon-Fri 9-4; Sat 9-1
Dallas, TX 75223

About 30 percent less than the competition, this company's a breeze to consider for the long hot Texas summers. One way to reduce your electric bills is to shade your windows or cover your patio with an awning. Canvas awnings may need to be replaced but the ones that are baked-enamel aluminum don't. They come in a myriad of colors and a lifetime FREE of maintenance. That means, they don't have to be replaced. Stay warmer in the winter, cooler in the summer, your initial investment may be higher than you'd like (about $1,000 or more) but remember, you're never going to replace it. Breeze-Lite also builds patio covers and carports. If you like that look, you'll like their price.

★   Care Free Plastic Fence & Design   214/339-1396
4307 Shilling Way   Mon-Fri 8-5
Dallas, TX 75237

Save a tree and erect a fence with polyethylene instead. Whether it's for commercial or residential use, the 20-year warranty you get means you can throw away the paint brushes and forget having to replace that fence again. One new modification has been introduced into their fence plans this year. Instead of using all plastic fencing that didn't quite cut it through our storms, they now use metal posts and edges to secure them. It would now take a tank to knock them down and yet they're still maintenance free. Give your nosey neighbors the brush-off and consider recycled, high-density polyethylene the way to fence yourself in.

◆◆◆◆   Chair Care   214/638-6416
8804 Sovereign Row   Mon-Fri 8-4
Dallas, TX 75247

Why buy a whole new chair when repair will do? The remedy is Chair Care, where there are two businesses rolled into one. Chair Care and Custom Powder Coating operates out of this Sovereign Row location and reigns supreme in the category of restrapping or restoring your better brands of patio furniture. Here, every strap is replaced and, if need be, your frames are restored to like-new condition. Don't bother to bring in a cheapo chair, it's not worth it. But for chairs that cost $200-$300 or more, that's another story. Brands such as **BROWN JORDAN**, **TROPITONE** and **WOODARD** (in either wrought iron or aluminum,) are examples that meet the criteria for cost-saving repairs. If, for example, you had a Brown Jordan set that you wanted re-strapped and repainted, the arm chairs would cost you $130 per chair. A standard 36-inch table would cost $120. So, for less than $900 (table and six chairs), you could be living in the lap of luxury with what looks like a brand new set that would new cost two to three times that if bought new. But don't expect next day service. Restrapping just four chairs would take approximately two weeks.

Comfort Cushion   214/748-2242
1717 Levee St.   Mon-Fri 7-3; Sat (summer only)
Dallas, TX 75207

This manufacturer and wholesaler is a cut above the others, especially if you want to cushion the blow of paying retail. Whether you want new ones, replacements, or repairs on your own, make sure you know your sizes since all cushions are not created equal. Both ready-mades and custom cushions are available. Standard sizes can be anywhere from 18 x 18-inches up to 23 x 72-inches. From PVC furniture slings to umbrellas, you can pick from hundreds of fabric swatches and coordinate your entire patio ensemble with matching fabric. Open on Saturdays during the summer months only.

◆◆◆◆◆ Crack Doctor, The   972/420-6442
1702 S. Hwy. 121, Suite 303   Mon-Fri 8-5 (By Appt. Only)
Lewisville, TX 75067

Here is the scoop. If you've got a crack in your pool, don't crack up. You're a fool to think you have to replace the entire pool. For $125, they come out and do a structural damage analysis. Then it's $4 a foot for the crack repair. Other cracks around skimmers, drains, pumps, etc. are priced $75/an hour and are billed at actual time. The Crack Doctors are underwater repair specialists who can repair any crack in your pool regardless of its origin. Cracks, grout, tile, mastic repair, stain removal and leak detection are just part of their everyday repair duties. They perform underwater inspections, acid washes, and year-round underwater service. But no more free estimates. Only a warranty comes FREE with every repair job. Don't ignore it. Your water bills will soar and ultimately, you'll have serious pool damage that may be irreparable. Expect a three-week wait for an appointment. *Call toll-free: 800/404-8234*

★★ Dallas Custom Swings   214/341-3727
11660 Plano Rd.   Mon-Sat 10-5
Dallas, TX 75243

Since its founding in 1984, Deborah Muse has been musing over Custom Swings. If she's any relation to the founder of Muse Air, she's a high flying entrepreneur in her own right. Her "Explorer Series" is as all of the kits, a challenge to assemble, but surely you have a honey-that-can-do-it for you. Have the kids, regardless of age, ready to go in no time. Then, for other backyard swing-dings, don't forget all of the other accessories that Dallas Custom Swings is notorious for like: swings, swing hangers, tent tops, porch swings, picnic tables, swing frames and slides. Have yourself a field day on the "Amazing Imagination Machine Play Systems, their large systems that are designed to spark a child's imagination and improve playtime on the equipment. For a price, equipment can be installed and sealed for you. Swing by their second location at 17435 Preston Rd. in Dallas (972/818-3727) and have a real good time.

★★★★★ Decksource   972/539-6948
1000 Spinks Drive   Mon-Fri 8-5
Flower Mound, TX 75028

This subsidiary of Superior Forest Products provides homeowners an opportunity to deck out their back-yards at the price of what the contractor's pay. If you want to build your own deck, they will help you design it and install it at their store or over the phone, and sell you all the ingredients at 10 percent less than the competition. Woodn't that be lovely? And why not. What you get delivered to your back yard is pressure-treated cedar, **CHOICE DEK**, pine, redwood or **TREX**, at no charge (unless you are building a lanai in Costa Rica.) If you'd rather just save on the materials and have someone else build it for you, they have several reliable deck hands they will recommend. Remember, unless you're not handy with a hammer and nails, you're just ordering the supplies here. These guys are not one to lend a helping hand.

◆◆◆ Dickson Brothers   972/288-7537

204 N. Galloway Ave.   Mon-Fri 8-5:30; Sat 8-5
Mesquite, TX 75149

The Wright Brothers knew the blue sky and what makes planes fly and Dickson Brothers know the ropes about blue waters and the pumps that make it flow. Bring in your broken parts to your spa, pool or pump and someone in their service department will point you in the right direction. Better yet, have them service the part or system on location. It's a bit much to haul in your pool to their shop. They are the fixer-uppers to do the job. Though they used to build water gardens and ponds, today they just sell the equipment and hook you up with those that do. Broken pool filters, no-bubble **JACUZZIS**, clogged-up pipes on your pond, that's what they're all about. They also sell water garden and pool supplies, too, but I promise, you won't drown.

★★★★ Elliott's Spas, Pools & Service   972/562-7902

1505-B W. University Drive   Mon-Fri 10-7
McKinney, TX 75070

Call before you dive it as the Elliotts may be out on a call for a spa who's got a leak or a pool with a problem. After more than 15 years in the business, **SUNBELT SPA MANUFACTURING COMPANY** has designated them as the authorized dealer for Sunbelt's 15 models and five jet system spas. You can choose from 14 different colors in gemstone, marble and granite-like and each comes with a three-year lifetime structural warranty. They know their stuff and if you want a value-priced spa, these are at least 20 percent less that Morgan Spas. Besides selling them, you know they can service them if something goes on the blink.

Executive Jungle   817/251-6606

567-B Commerce St.   Mon-Fri 9-4; Sat 9-Noon
Southlake, TX 76092

In business over 18 years, when it comes to either interior or exterior landscaping, this must be the place. It's still a jungle out there and you don't want to be swinging from one vine to the next. These folks are rock solid. They also offer landscape maintenance services and design consultation. If you want to transform your home into a showplace, in and out, consider the options here. Everything is priced at wholesale prices. See iron tables, accessories and pottery with some of the same items that have decorated restaurants such as El Chico and others. Since 1979, they've been one of the best-kept secrets. (Well, so much for hidden treasures.) When you think pottery, think chimeras, talavera, sconces, iron, gazing balls, baskets and more, turn to the one and only, Executive Jungle. You don't need to be a CEO to figure how this company will help you climb the corporate grapevine

Fireplace & Grill Factory Outlet

4301 Westgrove
Addison, TX 75001

972/250-2006
Mon-Sat 10-6

Having a symbiotic relationship with the national fireplace manufacturer **GOLD-EN BLOUNT**, when it gets too hot to cozy up around the fireplace, then these folks turn up the heat with their gas grills. Golden Blount is the source for high-quality gas logs, gas fireplaces, gas grills, glass doors, folding screens and other fireplace accessories. They are home to the "Texas Bonfire" gas log and the revolutionary new "Texas Stack." Sounds like we're listening to KYNG, doesn't it? In fact, they were voted best designed gas log in the fireplace industry. Bet you can't even tell if it's real or not! And if you're looking for grills, girls, the "Texas Sizzler" is one hot tamale. Manufactured also by Golden Blount, the Sizzler is one particular grill that is the thrill of the hunt-er. Grill those birds over the ceramic infra-red heat just like they do in the finest steakhouses in town at 1,650 degrees. Infra red sears the meat fast...hence, it seals in the flavor. Cook chicken, steaks and more in half the time. Shop direct at the manufacturer and save your ashes. See why Fireplace & Grill Factory Outlet is the #1 Retailer for the **DUCANE** Gas Grills. Fire away year 'round and see what the largest inventory in the Metroplex looks like. Of course, discounts day in and day out. Now we're cookin'!

◆◆◆◆ Green Thumb Lawn, Tree Care, Inc.

Dallas, TX

972/727-9595
By Appt. Only
www.getgreenthumb.com

Since 1976, this company has been digging around the Metroplex providing professional lawn care with a "We'll match any competitor's price on the same size lawn....and won't ask you for their coupons!" They don't do your basic cut; rather they're the ones who come dressed to kill...weeds, that is. All kinds of insect control, fire ant mounds, nutrients for a healthier greener lawn, fertilize your shrubs and of course, your lawn for year-round protection. And moving into the information age, check out their website for helpful hints, a specific list of what they do, check your account, or even get a job. If you don't have a green thumb, get one from here. First-timers get their first application up to 6,000-square-feet for $19.95 instead of $45.

◆◆◆◆◆ Hobert Pools

300 S. Central Expwy.
Richardson, TX 75080

972/690-8118
Mon-Fri 8-5; Sat 8-4; Sun 1-5
www.hobertpools.com

Ho-Ho-Hobert. For the past 25 years (he started in 1975 when Central Expressway was just two lanes,) today there are five locations throughout the Metroplex. With 100 percent financing (with approved credit), you, too, can jump in over your head with manageable payments. A free consultation is available to have someone give your yard a once over. They will build a pool within a 70-mile radius of Dallas. They take pride in building one pool at a time and built it to last. Secondly, along the way, they try to save time and money. A timely competition date, quality construction and at a competitive price sums it all up at Hobert Pools. If you want to take a peek, they have pools on display at select locations. Check directory for the location nearest you. The one above is one block south of Belt Line.

Inside Out Patio and Fireplace
17390 Preston Rd., #120
Dallas, TX 75252

972/931-0626
Mon-Fri 10-8; Sat-Sun 10-6
www.insideoutshop.com

One of the most aggressive and sharp retailers in the patio and fireplace business continues to help us live the best casual lifestyle without the rigors of formal lifestyle prices. Relax, shoppers, in casual and cast aluminum, wicker and wood furniture for the patio (and fireplaces when the season arrives) in only the best names in the business: **BROWN JORDAN**, **HOME CREST**, **JENSON JARRAH**, **KINGSLEY BATE**, **MALLIN**, **O.W.**, **LEE**, **SAMSONITE**, **WINSTON**, **WOODARD** and **WROUGHT IRON**. And for the fireplace: **BECKWOOD**, **GOLDEN BLOUNT**, **HARGROVE**, **HEATALOR**, **MAJESTIC**, **PETERSEN**, **PILGRIM**, **RASMUSSEN**, **SUMMER CLASSICS** and **UNIFLAME**. Go north of Campbell and save money on each and every purchase. Load up on umbrellas and cushions and then when you think it doesn't get any better, go next door to their 3,000-square-foot outlet for even further discounts. And last, visit online for additional money-saving coupons that you can print out to be used for web purchases or in-store. Their newest location is 439 I-30, Rockwall Village, Rockwall, TX 75087. *Call toll-free: 800/329-0626*

Kiva Pottery
1916 N. Haskell Ave.
Dallas, TX 75204

214/821-1700
Tues-Sat 10-6

Vive la company! Except, this one's name is Kiva, a popular name in Southwestern, primitive and Santa Fe pottery. If you've ever lived in Arizona, New Mexico, Southern California, trust me, Kiva is like a middle name to designer products. Now shop like you mean it—especially when I tell you the prices are wholesale. Located between City Place and Ross Avenue, there are yards and yards of decorative planters (usable inside or out) for you to choose. The shapes, sizes and styles are plentiful including the popular chimineas. What patio can be without? For indoor accoutrements, the pottery, the rustic wrought iron and patio furniture and accessories make for warm and inviting conversation pieces, containers for plants, or just lay them down on their sides and use them to cover that stain in the carpet or that blank space in your floor plan. They do wonders for your decorating scheme.

★★★ Leslie's Swimming Pool Supply
1260 W. Spring Valley Rd.
Richardson, TX 75080

972/231-3793
Mon-Sat 10-6; Sun Noon-5
www.lesliespoolsupplies.com

They're everywhere, they're everywhere which tells you there's a pool practically on every residential street corner. With more than 38 years in the business, they are the largest and most well-know swimming pool supplier who'll keep you in the swim of things. Dependable and well-priced, Leslie's is an **AQUA QUEEN**, **ARNELSON**, **KREEPY KRAULY** and **POLARIS** pool-sweep dealer but they also carry solar covers, pumps, heaters, motors and lights. They also offer repair service and leak detection so you won't have to float a note to keep from drowning in debt. Look to Leslie's private-labeled goods for their best buys as well as specials. For example, with any inflatable purchase over $49.99, you would get a FREE electric pump. You don't have to be a blow-heart to appreciate the wind-power that you will conserve. One of my favorite features is their FREE water tests. That's just one of the FREE in-store perks. They also offer FREE labor on in-store repairs, FREE seminars, their X-press parts program, their 100 percent satisfaction guarantee which is right up there with their 120 percent best price guarantee. Float to the center of the pool with a fort and slide; or hydra-lounge around complete with water guns for a real duel, $49.99. Check the directory for the location nearest you.

Little Red's Antiques   972/564-2200
10274 W. Hwy. 80   Mon-Tue, Thu-Sat 9-5; Sun 1-5
Forney, TX 75126

What do you get when you open your doors to 40,000 square feet of European antiques and reproductions? Little Red's, that's what. Richard Whaley is behind Little Red's (dad was the original Red) and has located his treasure-trove in the groves of Forney's Antique Row. Whatever your pleasure, whether an antique or a reproduction, they've got it. Even if you don't have a cast-iron stomach for wandering down the many miles of aisles, if you're looking for cast-iron, it's one of their specialties. Looking for something to flank your entryway? This is where I bought my two stately Great Dane guard dogs...ceramic, of course. From majestic ironworks to Majorca pottery, patio sets to old-fashioned street signs, urns to yard ornaments, it's their outdoor lamps for $250 (wired and ready to glow) that light my fire. One of the highlights in the Forney strip.

◆◆◆◆ Marjorie's Lawn & Garden/Fence Repair   214/350-4238
3044 Webb Chapel Extension   Mon-Sat 8-5; or By Appt.
Dallas, TX 75220

It may take a village to —well, it may take a woman to deliver good, old-fashioned service at affordable prices. Marjorie's a one-stop landscape service business. If it has something to do with your yard, she's the one to call. Overcoming poverty by working is her motto, she offers ten-year guarantees on new fences and five-year guarantees on fence repairs. For your yard, she also does weekly maintenance, one-time yard sprucing up, sprinkler systems and tree trimming. Don't be a prune, your trees need attention, too. They're not the cheapest, but they're one of the most reliable. They actually show up, do the job and leaf without leafing a mess. And if in a pinch, they offer plumbing, aid-conditioning and handyman services, too. What they don't do? Well, haven't found one yet!

★★★★ Mobile Mini   214/333-2222
3550 Duncanville Rd.   Mon-Fri 8-5; Sat 8-Noon
Dallas, TX 75236   www.mobilemini.com

This is so cool. Containers delivered to your home or office to act as mini-storage units. Low-cost, ground-level and portable, they pick up and deliver these mini- storage vaults and you're practically home free. They are custom-built from five to forty-square-feet and delivered to your site direct from the manufacturer. Hate keeping those lawn mowers or pool equipment strewn about the lawn? Are your golf clubs, tennis rackets, racing bike and mini-gym cluttering your garage? Then, pack it up and store it if you're not using it. Same with all your Christmas paraphernalia. Pack up the tree, trimmings, ornaments and such until next year. With one call, they'll be returned coming down the chimney. (Okay, so it's really the driveway.) Moving boxes and supplies also available. Click online for special coupons like a $50 off rental. Have a business? Become a Preferred Customer. It's FREE and you'll get reduced rates, rebates, FREE clean up on returns, priority pick up and delivery and your satisfaction guaranteed or your next local delivery is FREE. ***Call toll-free: 800/950-6464***

★★ Mower World
435 E. Danieldale Rd.
Duncanville, TX 75137

972/298-7554
Mon-Fri 9-6; Sat 8-5

Mow'er down and keep that lawn cut to the quick with a new **HONDA**, **LAWN BOY**, **STIHL** or **TORO** lawn mower, trimmer, blower, if it was meant to do hard labor on your lawn or garden, this is your world of options. From a Lawn Boy single-speed, self-propelled mower for a low of $324 to a **MASSEY FERGU-SON** tractor for several thousand, cut up at the largest lawn, garden and outdoor equipment place on the planet. Orbit around and while you're at it, save some green. If it's mowers you want, they have every brand, every size, and every price range. Bet you didn't know there are special lawn mowers just for women? (I can just see it now. Full makeup. Darling sling mules and a mower! Wow!) The same holds true for garden and lawn tools. This is the place for all those great gadgets you see in gardening magazines but never can find—like that bulb planter that looks like a hole digger, or barbecue grills, wood swings and more. Sales are where you'll get the best prices, as much as 60 percent off. Too, at Christmas time, they have some of the best prices on Christmas trees (starting in October)? In fact, there's over 20,000 square feet of trees, ornaments and trimmings ready to blow and go. But they're missing the boat not having a website. They'd probably make a killing. Repairs available but during the busy season (spring and summer), expect about a two week wait, unless it's minor and then it'll take only a few days. During slow times, though, repairs take about a week. *Call toll-free: 888/80-MOWER*

Patio One/Fullrich Industries
1501 Summit Ave., Suite 4
Plano, TX 75074

972/633-5522
Mon-Fri 9-5; Sat 10-6

Patio One is no second best. In fact, they're probably the only designer teak garden furniture manufacturer's outlet in the Metroplex and they're at your service. How does a serving cart sound for $39 instead of $100? Or a round end table for $18 instead of $60? Well, if you are in the market to outfit your outdoor environment, here's the outlet for imported teak and **NYATOH** furniture from Indonesia. Displayed in their 3,000 square feet warehouse/showroom, you'll be showered in tables, chairs, benches, sun umbrellas, lounges and more. As an afterthought, we saw a $400 five-piece aluminum patio set for $199.95/ retail $400, a teak armchair retailing for $300/their price, $187.50; a four-foot teak bench that retailed for $400 was $225. See first hand what saving 50 percent and more is like. If it's in the cards for your al fresco dining, head to Plano Parkway, off Central Expressway and say aloha to high prices. Oh lei! Call for directions. Once you get the hang of it, it's a cinch.

Pool & Patio Landscaping
2026 SE 14th St.
Grand Prairie, TX 75051

972/263-6606
Mon-Fri 8-6; Sat 8-4; Sun Noon-5 (Summer only)
www.pool-and-patio.com

Talk about living, selling and displaying your entire life's activities in one place, Pool & Patio Landscaping is living testimony to keeping your overhead down. When you arrive at Pool & Patio's showroom, you can't help but notice that this is Nancy and Bill Sexton's homesite, their warehouse and their Landscaping Visitor Center all sharing the same roots. Their homestead is their business and vice versa. Twenty years ago, Nancy Sexton decided to get into the pool business and use the **VISION** filtration system for the lowest levels of chlorine. Building a pool business based on integrity, quality and workmanship is what has kept this company crystal clear. Noticing shoddy work of other pool builders, she decided to keep her fine reputation intact. From the basic package (where the homeowner can do some of the work himself) to the elite "Champagne Edition", you can have your pool and drool, too. Jump into a Sexton pool for less than a one-time luxury vacation and keep enjoying it year after year. During the winter months, they do not stay open on Sundays; but the rest of the year, weather permitting, you'll have a pool in two weeks. What faces the visitor's center is Bill and Nancy Sexton's backyard pool. Their pool contains a majority of the most popular features customers request when considering a new pool including a **CHAMPAGNE SPA**, waterfall, fountains, slide, **OKLAHOMA FLAGSTONE** coping and deck, and all controlled by a wall-mounted computer control inside the Sexton's home. If you're looking for advice, Nancy is likely to show you her own pool. Do ask her what she can do with old pantyhose, it may surprise you. A lifetime warranty is offered on all of their pools. So, don't worry, you won't take a bath on your investment.

★★★ Recreational Factory Warehouse   972/509-9707

700 Alma Rd., Suite 116   Mon-Fri 10-8; Sat 10-6; Sun Noon-5
Plano, TX 75075   www.LeisureBay.com (under construction)

Head north to Plano for a plain old source for recreational products like tanning beds, spas, and above ground pools. At the northeast corner of Plano Parkway and Alma, you can fill up your after-hours with recreational activities that are sure to relax, refresh or reduce the stress of everyday living. They guarantee the lowest prices on all Leisure Bay products. No big deal since they are the only source for them and we couldn't compare the prices if we wanted to. For $99, you can just add water to an above ground, family size **SEARAY** pool. But, read the fine print. That is only for the installation. The cheapest way to take a dip is around $699 up to $999 (compared to $2,000.) Another good buy, however was their **HOUSTON VII** slate pool table. For $1,399, as the maker, they've got you cued to low prices. Then, for grins, they'll throw in a $350 bonus package with deluxe playing accessories and professional delivery. Too good to be true? Accordingly, several shoppers again this year, find the prices reasonable, but the sales approach radical. Worse than the slimiest used-car salesman, probably commissioned-only and determined sales personnel make their desire to close a sale anxiety-provoking. Besides, prices are not firm. Make them an offer and see what you wind up paying. Same with tanning beds. As the maker, they control the prices which should bring about lower prices. No doubt, compared to like products, prices are lower. In fact, a lot lower on most. But a $3,500 swing set left us dumb-founded! Swing to their other locations and see what you think: 6801 NE Loop in 820 North Richland Hills (817/498-4811) and Garland at I-30 and Belt Line Road (972/203-2220).

The Rose Petal   972/262-5253

515 E. Main   Mon-Sat 10-5
Grand Prairie, TX 75050

He loves me, he loves me not, let me count the ways. The only way I know to profess your love is to find something to love from The Rose Petal. Now, put your petal to their metal yard furniture—a summer glider for the front porch is too good to be threw. Add a few original birdcages as decorative elements, and a few to hang up to actually feed the birds. Surround yourself with the lushest hanging ferns at the lowest prices on earth; mix in a veritable variety of unusual geraniums...like chocolate (no, I'm not kidding) or more traditional scents like mint. Save a mint, too, on the kinds of flowers your grandmother planted and return to the days when you held her hand and walked to your "secret garden." Located next to Tommy Snodgrass Discount Furniture, it's worth the drive to Grand Prairie. Forget shopping online. There's too much in their backyard showroom and it changes too often. Gaze into more than just crystal balls. They have those wonderful gazing balls for the garden that mirror nature like nothing else can do. Bric-a-brac to hang over the garden wall, planters to hang on the fence, all one-of-a-kind and not right off the assembly line. Then turn to the barn-board potting benches, wicker chairs that serve as planters, wind chimes, concrete benches, fountains, statues, birdbaths and now even jewelry all priced rosier than elsewhere. Bet if you added a few items from Rose Petal, your house would increase in value; add a few items to your back yard, and your time gazing out the window will increase tenfold.

★★★★ Splash Pools & Spas   817/590-0333

827 Airport Frwy.   Mon-Fri 10-6; Sat 9:30-5:30; Sun 1-5
Hurst, TX 76053

Splash round in one of their pools or spas, but cash reigns supreme here. The lowest-priced model started at $4,000 and did a double gainer up to $9,000. Though financing is available, that's almost a price of a car. Now, would you rather drive to the lake, or bring the water to your own backyard? But let's talk drying off on any one of the more than 500 patio sets in stock. What a selection: wrought iron, aluminum, resin—pick your pleasure. They promise a low price guarantee, but not the lowest. Nevertheless, you certainly can count on them to deliver on their promise. In business since 1951, they carry only top-of-the-line products, like **HOMECREST**, **RANDAL** and **WINSTON**. Because they deal directly with the manufacturer, they can cut you a great deal—especially during clearance sales. So, this is where I'd concentrate my money. Take a shower, stay wet, and dry off outside on one of their patio sets. Too, they are also the exclusive **DOUGHBOY** dealer with 30-year warranties on their above-ground pools. Now, we're talking. Seasonal sales on patio furniture begin with Labor Day and that's when they really unload the truck loads. For spas, they carry the **MAJESTIC** line of **ARTESIAN**. The best time to shop for pools, spas and patio furniture, believe it or not, is Christmas even though the seasonal sales start as early as September; by Christmas, they're desperate. Can you wait? Try it. Then you'll get at least 50 percent off all patio furniture in stock and rebates on all their pools in stock. All in all, Splash lives up to its reputation for quality, service and reliability as well as maintaining a sales staff who are knowledgeable, courteous and attentive. How refreshing!

★★★★★ Sun Time Pool, Spa & Patio   817/548-8100

1001 NE Green Oaks Blvd., Suite 131 Mon-Fri 10-7; Sat 10-6; Sun Noon-5
Arlington, TX 76006

When the sun shines Nellie, it's time to call in the pros at Sun Time Pool, Spa & Patio. If it's a big job, call and ask for Chris Perry or Lance Jones; otherwise, anyone can help you with an impressive selection of pool and spa supplies, patio furniture and accessories. Though located in Arlington, their service area extends to the entire Metroplex when it comes to servicing and remodeling pools as well as decorative resurfacing of decks. Have your pool decks, coping or pool surface face-lifted or completely redone, be it a commercial or residential pool. To keep you swimming not in the thick of things, they are the distributors for **SUN CHEMICALS**—the ideal concentrate for keeping clear, cool water. Use less, save money. To continue a clean sweep of things, save at least 20 percent on patio equipment and furniture—and only the better brands: **AQUA-RITE**, **HAMAMINT**, **HAYWARD**, **JACUZZI**, **LETRO**, **PAC FAB**, **POLARIS**, **SARATOGA SPAS**, **SUN COAST**, **TELEDYNE** and more. Expect the best for less, none of those rinky-dinky types. All patio furniture is made of heavy-gauge aluminum or slings and last from season to season. Stay in the shade with an impressive array of umbrellas, and don't forget they also offer pool and spa supplies, equipment, water toys, as well as servicing and remodeling of all pools. They do complete and full pool renovations but limit their new pool construction to about 15 pools a year. Financing available in-house through Wells Fargo or Compass Bank. So, point yourself in the right direction and get into the swim of things. ***Call toll-free: 817/265-9800***

378   **biggerbetterbargains**.com

★★★★ Texas Greenhouse Co.
2524 White Settlement Rd.
Fort Worth, TX 76107

817/335-5447
Mon-Fri 8-5; Sat 10-2
www.texasgreenhouse.com

Growing since 1948, you can stay in the pink with the greenhouses here. Manufacturing their own greenhouses and accessories, expect prices to be factory-direct. Don't be a hot-head, either. If you really build your own with a **TEXAS GREENHOUSE** kit, you will save lots of green, then your plants can get steamed. Carrying a full line of accessories including heating, cooling, ventilation, misting and watering systems, shaders, timers, controls, benches, shelves and hundreds of other items ensuring your green thumb will not turn black and blue. Styles include free-standing, lean-to, bay window and outdoor fog systems. They'll even help the novices find the right style to suit their space and needs. But don't expect them to make house calls. They also carry other brands besides their own including **MODINE** heaters and **CHAMPION** coolers. Prices are extremely competitive and most orders are delivered in six to eight weeks with a one-year guarantee. Also, take note. If you return it because of indecision on your part, you'll be paying a 15 percent restocking charge. A 50 percent deposit is required upon ordering and balance is due upon delivery. Call, write or order online for their catalog. *Call toll-free: 800/227-5447*

★★★★★ Texas Patio
5742 Airport Frwy.
Haltom City, TX 76117

817/831-2266
Mon-Fri 10-7; Sat 9-6; Sun Noon-5
www.texaspatios.com

It may be hush hush and not nice to name drop, but once we found it, we had to call it as we saw it. We ran into **DAYVA, HATTERAS HAMMOCKS, HOMECREST, KETTLE, LANE VENTURE, TELESCOPE CASUAL** and **WOODSTOCK CHIMES** while winding through the myriad of patio sets and patio accessories on display at this two-story showroom. It's size is formidable and it's probably safe to call them a category killer in selection as well as price. In between the fountains and bird baths, you'll find every kind of patio set—from aluminum, iron, steel and whatever's the latest material. Boo on their website, it's zilch! It's basically a request form for information. But you should be tempted to seek your semi-fortune of savings by shopping in person. Once there, they'll even give you a blow-by-blow description of how-to-build you own fish pond. They've got all the elements to do so and we dug it! We sought out the water fountains, waterfalls, even the black fiberglass lines to add to a kidney-shaped fish or lily pond, but it took us forever to decide —koi or joy? We finally opted for the koi and once we decided on at least one bird bath and the pumps, we were on our way. Located near the Carson Street exit on the south side of Airport Freeway, you can reach them easily. Second floor views of the skyline of downtown Fort Worth is a breath-holding experience. Frankly, this 30,000-square-foot showplace is a landmark for many Tarrant County old-timers. If you care enough to sit on the very best, you might as well buy it here, for less. Exclusive lines such as **BROWN JORDAN, TROPITONE** and others made us ready for some R & R. But instead, we started digging our koi pond. You, too, can reel in similar opportunites at their second location, 6080 S. Hulen St. in Fort Worth, one mile south of Hulen Mall, 817/292-7599.

Venture Pools
2550 Trinity Mills Rd.
Carrollton, TX 75006

972/416-1324
Mon-Sat 8-5; Sun 11-4

The referrals are long and vocal but these guys left **CHALLENGER POOLS** and started their own company. Though only three years old, John Carney ensures a start to finished pool with nary a leak in the process. They offer a three-year, bumper-to-bumper, so to speak, guarantee on equipment and labor at no additional cost. What a relief! They are also members in good standing of the National Spa and Pool Institute and the Dallas Better Business Bureau. All the popular brands are carried: **LAARS**, **POLARIS**, **TANDY**, **TELEDYNE** and their **HAYWARD** equipment comes with a 10-year warranty. They have plenty of referrals and happy letters on file, so be sure to ask. If they've made all of their pool owners happy in their three-year history, they are on solid footing in my book. Only in-ground swimming pools and spas are offered. Please don't ask for an above-ground model. Add a heater and though your electric bills may soar, but you can get your workouts in all year long. With 400 pool builders in the Metroplex, in such a short time, they went from a start-up to number 11 in just two years and that's pretty impressive.

★★★★★ Vita Spa Factory Outlet   817/226-7727
2542-C E. Abram St.   Mon-Sat 10-6; Sun Noon-5
Arlington, TX 76010

We softened our appraisal of being a smacked mackerel last year to one of a catfish this year. A few whiskers still tickled our thoughts of their hard-sales approach but somehow, this 27-year old company this year greeted us with warmth and no sales pressure. Hurray, Hurray. They must have been read their writeup and took note. So, let's proceed full steam ahead. All of their spas come with a 25-year warranty and a lifetime structural warranty. That's good. All spas were user-friendly with top-loading filters and since they use silver and zinc, there's no need for chlorine. That's very good. Then to make you even more relaxed, they offered aromatherepy scents to add a lot more steam to your spa experience. And that's very, very good. And their pricing just can't be beat since it's one-price period—including spa, delivery, cover, chemicals and redwood steps. Now get this. They also include beverage holders, Euro-tech handles and a filter cover that converts to an ice bucket. Spas start at just over $1,000 ($1,400 but on sale often for $1,200 and sometimes a $999 offer appeared but that's not a usual event. Your best bets are on discontinued floor models but who can tell last year's models from this years? I can understand having gazebos for sale, but pool tables, too? That's right, I guess they are trying to model the inventory mix of Recreational Factory Warehouse, but the prices can not compare. You do the shopping. An eight-foot slate pool table by **AMERICAN HERITAGE** and **KASSON** were priced from $1,000-$2,700 but since they're not one of the top three manufacturers, I can't determin their credibility. Don't put them behind the eight ball just yet. You need to shop around. Vita is one of the largest spa showrooms in the Metroplex with susbstantial savings, don't you agree? One hundred percent financing available with approved credit. Congratulations, Vita Spa, you're back in our good graces!

★★★ Wooden Swing Co./Children's Furniture   972/386-6280
13617 Inwood Rd.   Mon-Sat 10-6
Dallas, TX 75244   www.woodenswing.com

For the active tykes, get them a tree house in the August moon. Imagine keeping them up a tree, without costing a fortune. Just think what a pool costs? Sleep-a-way camp? A trip to Grandma's? For a fraction of the price, build them a vacation in the backyard and keep them looking up. Or keep them occupied indoors with lots of space-saving bedroom suites such as modular bedrooms that grow with them through their teen years and beyond. What kid wouldn't dream of bunk beds complete with a slide or canopy beds, trundle beds, captains beds, and lots of imaginative twin beds. Then, add in all the matching furniture and accessories to complete their sweet dreams. Lots of styles from big to bigger to keep them out of your hair and having fun in the sun. **BRIO** toy railroads are always 10 percent off suggested retail. Since 1978, this company has been building their business while building their market share selling market samples of children's furniture taking over about half the store. Children's furniture was definitely a void in the marketplace and often at the lowest prices in town. Novelty beds will bring a smile, from racecars to bunk beds. And of course, outdoors, they can be swingers in wooden swing sets, or on the lookout inside the fort. Imagination and safety always tantamount in their strategy.

Yard Ideas
136 N. Main St.
Keller, TX 76248

817/379-5644
Mon-Sat 10:30-5:30

This husband and wife team had a better idea. In fact, they had plenty of ideas so they decided to make their own yard art and go from there. Located on the Main Street drag in Keller (the old Hwy. U. S. 377), you'll find a home for small statues starting at around $25 all the way to giant garden varieties for $225. Yard Ideas offers mostly rounded models; very few square ones to go into backyard corners. But not to side-step the issue of stepping stones or wall hangings, they offer lots of the most popular models, from angels to sun signs. You can ogle their massive yard display as you drive down Main Street and marvel at their ingenuity. Since they make their own, they've eliminated the middlemen and can chisel off the excess clay and go from there. Prices are so low, a shopper said even when she was in the nursery business herself, she couldn't find wholesale containers or fountains priced as low as here. Now how's that for a savvy former New York retailer endorsement? Furnish you're entire backyard with concrete bird baths, benches, tables, decorative animals, bird-houses, children's tables and both white and terra-cotta pottery. Save at least 20-40 percent on statuary, fountains and concrete patio sets and you will never have to tiptoe through the garden again. Most are displayed outside so what you see is what you can buy. A small three-tier fountain with a pump and a three-foot tall pedestal was watered down to $175 and not even carved in stone. We left with it for $150. Sorry, the early bird gathers the best-priced moss-less fountains.

48

Shoes

★★★ Converse Factory Store

3844 Belt Line Rd.
Addison, TX 75234

972/488-9252
Mon-Fri Noon-8; Sat 10-6; Sun Noon-6
www.converse.com

This oldie but goodie is making a strong return if you're ready to dunk and discount. Okay, so let's **CONVERSE** over the possibilities. Save 20-50 percent and more off the retail on these popular sports shoes starting as early as infants through size 4-10 for girls. After infants, though, girls are out of luck, until they're big enough to slip into a women's size 4-12. Some cheerleaders would fit the bill perfectly. For guys, you have it made in and out of the court, for they can outfit you up to a size 17. Basketball players need to go that extra mile. Most men's shoe sizes stop at 13, and this is where this factory store shines. Nothing's over $40—with the clearance corner scoring the extra points in a sudden death showdown. Since 1908, Converse has been in the ball park selling athletic shoes for casual or serious play. In the 1920s, they introduced the "Chuck Taylor" shoe and it remains the most popular shoe today. In April, 2001, Converse was acquired by Footwear Acquisition, Inc., so they should be on solid footing from here on out. Their online store is limited to just the Chuck Taylor All Star shoe with sizing tips reflecting how they fit if you're not familiar with this model. For men, it is recommended to choose 1/2 size down from the labeled size and women should choose two sizes down from the labeled size. ***Call toll-free: 800/547-2667***

★★★★★ Crown Shoe Warehouse

900 W. Parker Rd.
Plano, TX 75075

972/424-0158
Mon-Sat 10-9; Sun Noon-6

When it doesn't sell at Designer Shoe Warehouse (DSW), it winds its way down the hierarchy to those that peons would find palatable. Less pricey and perhaps more appropriate for the common man (woman or child). Or so the tale is told. So why not kick up your heels and enter the kingdom of shoes where before no man dared to tread—to the bottom of the heap. Who would know the difference? When you get your invitation to the ball, or are taking a leisurely stroll over the moat, gloat that you are wearing a pair of shoes from here. You don't have to be well-heeled to take the walk. However, don't expect to be served royally. This is a buy-all-you-can-wear and serve yourself kind of store. Aisle after aisle, you'll be left to your own defenses. Armed with checkbook in hand, you will be surprised how little your final total will be. Several pairs later, you'll be strutting your stuff. Keeping a low profile, they don't make a big deal out of the brand names they keep but you've certainly heard of them: **ADIDAS, JONESWEAR, NATURALIZER, NEW BALANCE, NUNN BUSH, STACY ADAMS** from $16 and up. Didn't see any higher than $49 for men or women or on average, $9 for children. Slip into women's sizes 5-12 in narrow and wides (commendable) and men's sizes 6-14. Athletic shoes were performing well in the $29-$49. One location and one location only.

★★★★★ DSW (Designer Shoe Warehouse)   972/233-9931
13548 Preston Rd.   Mon-Sat 10-9; Sun Noon-6
Dallas, TX 75240   www.dswshoe.com

Joining the movement north, DSW (Discount Shoe Warehouse) has entered the fray in Frisco and now boasts two stores on Preston Road, the newest being the one at 3333 Preston Rd., north of Stonebriar Centre at Hwy. 121 and Preston, 972/668-4510, Mon-Sat 10-9; Sun 11-7. Ladies and gents can slip into either one of the other Metroplex locations and be shod to the nines (though their sizes go from 5-12 for women and 7-15 in men's). If you're shoesy, then only the best will do. Guys line up in **BALLY, FLORSHEIM, NUNN BUSH** and **STANLEY BLACKER** for starters and gals slip out in **AIGNER, AMERICAN EAGLE, ANNE KLEIN, BASS, COLE HAAN, DEXTER, ENZO, EVAN PICONE, HUSH PUPPIES, LIZ CLAIBORNE, NINE WEST, SELBY, VIA SPIGA, ZODIAC** and more including the coveted **DOC MARTENS** for either. Over 36,000 pairs to choose from in 900 different styles. Their "Reward Your Style" frequent shoppers program gives you $25 off for every $250 spent and that's another good reason to shop. This division of billion-dollar off-price Value City Department store (both headquartered in Columbus, OH) has 80 stores nationwide and four DSW's in the Metroplex where everything's 20-50 percent off department store prices. Also you can bag discounts on handbags, totes and hosiery. Check out their other locations in Fort Worth at Bellaire and Hulen, Lewisville, southwest corner of Round Grove and MacArthur, and the newest location in Frisco.

★★★ Famous Footwear   817/732-8491
Overton Park Shopping Center   Mon-Sat 10-9; Sun Noon-6
4656 W. I-20   www.famousfootwear.com
Fort Worth, TX 76109

Want to be one of the shoe-sen few who have met their sole mate? Then slip into a pair of Famous Footwear and see if you're a match. This power chain is famous for brand name shoes for the entire family. Save 20-40 percent across the platform, be it athletic, dress, casual, boots or slippers. From hiking to slippers, sandals to accessories, name your favorite: **ADIDAS, ASICS, AVIA, BASS, BUSTER BROWN, CARLOS FALCHI, CATERPILLAR, CLARKS, CONNIES, CONVERSE, DEXTER, DOCKERS, DUCKHEAD, EASY SPIRIT, ESPRIT, ETONIC, FILA, KEDS, FLORSHEIM, FOOTJOY, FREEMAN, GOODY TWO SHOES, HUSH PUPPIES, KEDS, LIFESTRIDE, MAINE, NATURALIZER, NEW BALANCE, NIKE, NUNN BUSH, PUMA, REEBOK, ROCKPORT, SAUCONY, SEBAGO, SKECHERS, SPERRY, STACY ADAMS, TIMBERLAND, VANELI, WEEBOK, WESTIES, WOLVERINE** and more. Full size ranges in both mediums and wides; narrows, well, pretty slim. Watch newspapers for additional savings when coupons appear. Online shopping, a breeze, even if it's just for a new pair of slippers. *Call toll-free: 800/40FAMOUS*

★★★★★ Fossee's   214/368-1534
5925 Forest Lane, Suite 600   Mon-Wed, Fri-Sat 10-6; Thu 10-8; Sun 1-5
Dallas, TX 75225   www.fossees.com

No relation to Bob Fosse, but if you want to head to Broadway without leaving home, these are the shoes to take you there. Fossee's is home to sizes 4 through 12 and a particularly stellar selection in the long and the narrows. Don't even bother side-stepping the issue of paying full price. These are all stars in the savings department, too, from 30-60 percent off in most cases. Don't expect to walk out with a pair or two. It's hard to "Stop" in the name of love when so many of the better brands are beckoning. Right off the fashion runways of New York's Seventh Ave., coordinate all of your designer clothes with the appropriate bottom half; otherwise, they'll think of you as a clod rather than a clog. Here are some of the stars that take a bow: **AEROSOLES, AMALFI, ANDRÉ ASSOUS, ANNE KLEIN, ARCHE, BANDOLINO, CALVIN KLEIN, CHARLES JOURDAN, COLE HAAN, DONALD PLINER, EVAN PICONE, FERRAGAMO, J. MILLER, J. RENEE, LIZ CLAIBORNE, MR. SEYMOUR, PREVATA, SESTO MEUCCI, RANGONI, STUART WEITZMAN, UNISA, VANELI, VIA SPIGA, YSL**—you will be the hit of the "Chorus Line". Hundreds and hundreds of shoes from the fanciest shoe salons around priced elsewhere at $250 can be shod for generally one-third or more off. Slip into their second location at 19009 Preston Rd. in North Dallas (972/380-0992).

◆◆◆◆◆ Mehl's Shoeland   817/924-9681

2900 S. Hulen St.   Mon-Sat 10-5:30
Fort Worth, TX 76109   www.mehlsshoeland.com

Myer Mehl opened this shoeland in 1950 and solved many a foot problem from day one. In his particular land of plenty, you'll find names like **CLARKS, EASTLAND, HUSH PUPPIES, KEDS, MUNRO, NATURALIZER, NEW BALANCE, REIKER, SPERRY, STRIDE RITE** and **TROTTERS**. Well, that's just the start of it. Woman can finally find a full size range, from Cinderella's size 4's to big and tall size 12's. At last, gals with a lot of leg room don't have to get blisters squeezing in to too tight shoes. Widths are offered in S, N, M, W and WW. And, too, footwear here can accommodate inserts and orthotics. Mehl's offers a FREE shoe clinic with a certified orthotist on the last Monday of each month. Rest assured, even kids can be sized up. Each customer's name is kept on file with date of purchase, style numbers and sizes so that they can follow little Joey and Jill right up the hill. Choose **FOOTMATES, HUSH PUPPIES, JUMPING JACKS, KEDS, MARKELL, MOLLIE MUNRO, NINE WEST, SPERRY, STRIDE RITE** and more. Take advantage of their children's program of buy 12 get the 13th FREE. They also offer a supply of children's corrective footwear. So, shake those booties and bring in your doctor's prescription if you're new to the store. Shopping here will allow your child to walk through life taking one comfortable step at a time. Do not expect any high heels hanging around here. These shoes are all in the comfort zone: loafers, pumps and sandals are the usual and customary choices. Sales offer the best price but the service here is superb. And at least, you can slip in and out with a pair to wear that won't hurt.

★★★★★ National Shoes   972/387-8329

102 Preston Valley Shopping Center   Mon-Fri 10-8; Sat-Sun 10-6
Dallas, TX 75230   www.national-shoes.com

Three generations of shoe sellers should tell you these guys are sole survivors in the shoe biz. Since the depression of '29, the line-up of brand name shoes for men have rocketed the industry. Walking all over the competition, you don't have to be a clod to be shod. Just slip into a pair of **BOSTONIANS, BRASS BOOTS, COLE HAAN, DEXTER, EKTELON, EVANS SLIPPERS, FLORSHEIM, FOOTJOY, NEW BALANCE, ROCKPORT, TIMBERLAND** and more. You may not think 20 percent off MSRP is anything to rave about, but this is the only full-service men's shoe discounter in the Metroplex. Just staying alive is enough to write home about. National Shoes has a financial interest in trying to save your assets. For example, a pair of Timberland "Ridge Riders" retailing for $90/retail price, $72. That's $18 to spend on dinner. Or a Bostonian pair that retailed for $140 was $112. Hey, you can even have dessert with the savings on these. How can you not take her to dinner, pal, I've just saved you all this money and National's located next to Chili's at the southwest corner of 635 and Preston Road? *Call toll-free: 800/564-3878*

★★ Off Price Shoes   214/327-1150
410 Big Town Mall   Mon-Sat 10-7; Sun Noon-5:30
Mesquite, TX 75149

Conversation here is still a hit and a miss. Mostly a miss. Nary a word was spoken, but we were able to manage a few sporadic sentences such as..."No more children's shoes." Still, you can be off price and running in women's shoes for $9.99. Occasionally, they were even lower...like $6.99. Men, too, have plenty to choose in sizes 6 1/2 to 13 (and a few 14's) with prices tagged $14.99. Now, how can you lose, unless you snooze. Choose sandals, canvas slip-ons, boots, dressy and casual, lace-ups, tasteful, professional and perfect for that lost sole you've been searching for. Locations include Wynnewood Village Shopping Center in Dallas and also Preston Rd. in Dallas, Big Town Shopping Court in Mesquite and East Division Street in Arlington.

★★ Payless ShoeSource   817/460-4714
1071 N. Collins St.   Mon-Fri 10-9; Sat 9-9; Sun 11-6
Arlington, TX 76011-6133   www.payless.com

You may not consider Payless Shoes as some little secret that you haven't heard about before, but maybe their baby program is one that will catch you by surprise. It's baby's first shoes. Bring in your little one when you think it's time to move their feet from under their jammies to their first pair of shoes, fill out a registration card and choose from a little pair of white, pink or blue canvas sneakers for FREE. Okay, so they don't stay on, but they're so cute. This nice gesture surely will endear you to Payless, where you do pay less for lots of shoes for the entire family. Being one of the biggest (over 220 stores around the country) offering some of the best values for your money means you can slip into a pair and not have to take out a second mortgage. Go to their website if you need to find larger sizes 13+ or wider widths. They don't have printable coupons online anymore, just current sales and specials but they will keep you up to date. Payless ShoeSource is your source for inexpensive shoes that are indeed fashionable. They're not museum quality; expect prices to be affordable. Check directory for the location nearest you.

★★★★ Rack Room Shoes   214/327-3663
Casa Linda Plaza, Suite 294   Mon-Sat 10-9; Sun Noon-6
Dallas, TX 75218   www.rackroomshoes.com

Join in the celebration of the opening of the seventh Rack Room Shoes at Gateway Plaza, 2900 E. Southlake Blvd. in Southlake. In 1920, they had 12 stores; since 1984, when they were acquired by a European family, they have grown to over 330 stores and are now the largest privately-owned shoe retailer in the world. So, what are you waiting for? This powerhouse is walking all over the competitors with number of stores and making their mark known on the Metroplex pavement. Why not rack up savings every step of the way? Choose from more than 17,000 pairs in each store's inventory with brands such as **ADIDAS**, **AIRWALK**, **BONGO**, **CANDIES**, **CAPEZIO**, **CHILIS**, **DEXTER**, **EASTLAND**, **ESPRIT**, **FLORSHEIM**, **GAROLINA**, **IMP**, **MIA**, **MOOTSIES TOOTSIES**, **MUSHROOMS**, **NEW BALANCE**, **NICOLE**, **9 & CO.**, **OSHKOSH B'GOSH**, **ROCKPORT**, **SKECHERS**, **TIMBERLAND**, **WEEBOK**, **WHITE MOUNTAIN** and more. Rack after rack, don't get your back up against the wall, redneck Mother. They also sell shoes for men, women and children with their slogan screaming, "Big brands at big savings!" Save up to 30% off suggested manufacturer's retail prices with private labels offering additional savings without sacrificing quality or fashion sense. Online, download coupons and see what specials are in-store at the moment. Additional locations include Grapevine Mills (972/539-2818); Cameron Crossing in McKinney (972/542-7155); 2823 Market Center Blvd. in Rockwall (972/722-3747); LBJ at MacArthur in Irving; and also in Hurst.

★★★★★ Shoe Cents   972/964-5900
Preston Town Crossings, Suite 310   Mon-Sat 9:30-9; Sun Noon-6
2432 Preston Rd.   www.shoecents.com
Plano, TX 75093

Not all Shoe Cents makes sense. Some locations sell both men's and women's, one sells men, women and children's shoes and some don't. Here's the deal: Hillside Village (Mockingbird & Abrams), Market East, 1515 Town East Blvd, Mesquite sells men's and women's; Stonebriar Center, 3333 Preston Rd. in Frisco sells men's, women's and kid's shoes. The Dallas stores have different hours, too, so check before you head out. The Plano location above, though, sells only women's. Phew! That's a mouthful. You need a Ph.D. in shoe memory so I thought it best to finally spell it out (Shoe Cents has more than 30 stores nationwide). If you're choosy about your shoes, take the walk test and step into a pair from here. At the northeast corner of Preston and Park (next to Ulta), load up on lipsticks and loafers, you never have enough, right? Department store brands at discounted prices include: **AIGNER, BASS, CALICO, CLARKS, ESPRIT, HUSH PUPPIES, IMPO, KEDS, LIFESTRIDE, MUSHROOMS, NATURALIZERS, NICOLE, NINE WEST, RED CROSS, REEBOKS, SAM & LIBBY, SRO, WESTIES** and more—your basic standard fare, but solidly built to last. Regardless of the occasion, pick your pair—from dressy to casual, career to play—if it's shoes, they've got you covered from 20-40 percent off. In fact, if you're counting, you may hit as many as 14,000 pairs on any one given day, most priced under $25. They even have extra small and extra large sizes to size 11 in pumps, loafers and casual leather shoes. Is it any wonder The Container Store has to sell a ton of shoe closet accessories to accomodate a Shoe Cent's customer? How else would you be able to find all those shoes anyway? Locations throughout Texas, but in the Metroplex, try making Shoe Cents at 3907 West Airport Freeway, #104 in Irving for women's shoes, 1515 Towne East Blvd., Suite 156, Mesquite, men's and women's shoes, 344 Hillside Village, Dallas, for men's and women's shoes, and the Plano store above, for just women's. Isn't it time you put your best foot forward?

Vantage Shoe Warehouse   214/678-9967
2222 Vantage St.   Mon-Sat 9:45-6; Sun Noon-6
Dallas, TX 75207

Vantage Shoe Warehouse returns to the days of yesteryear, where every woman within a 500 mile radius slipped into a pair or two from here. Vantage is one of the places to shop and " shoes" the best shoes in the business. Why not dance, walk, skip, boogie, kick your heels up, step out in a pair by **NINE WEST, ANNE KLEIN, ENRO, ENZO, DONALD PLINER, FERRAGAMO, J. RENEE, MARGARET JERROLD, NATURALIZER, STUART WEITZMAN, VANELI, ZALO**——for starters? Then, make sure your man can keep up with appearances. Men can shop for **BASS, BOSTONIAN, FLORSHEIM, ROCKPORT, SEBAGO, ROCKPORT** and more. So, what does it take? An engraved invitation? Let me give you an inside report: **MARTINEZ VALLERO ORIGINALS**, retail $150/ VS $69. Or, look at a knock-off of the same shoe by **NINE WEST** and buy them retail at $85/VS $9.99. Pay retail or pay Vantage Shoe's (VS) price and you be the judge. Pay $49.99 for a Donald Pliner Pony mule instead of $190; pay $169.99 for a pair of Ferragamos retail or VS $49.99. Don't be a heel. Save tons of money on the whole shoe, and nothing but. Even if you're big foot, you can get covered. Sizes 4-12 in women's and 8-13 in men's. In-season, upscale specialty and department store shoes at 40-90 percent off. Now do you see why I say they run circles around the competition? Shop, too, at 11255 Garland Rd., Dallas, 214/328-3603 and their new location in North Dallas at the old Arnold Square, just north of LBJ, 13410 Preston Rd., 214/231-0027.

WeLoveShoes.com

When we want to kick back and enjoy a walk through thousands and thousands of pairs of designer shoes for men, women and children, here's where to land. Just imagine every designer name brand, priced at 50-90 percent off, organized by sizes and widths and tell me you're not in heaven. It may even be better than winning the $50,000 on the "Fear Factor" just by eating worms. Be the "Sole Survivor" and walk a million malls in a pair of these shoes and I guarantee, this is the easiest shopping experience you'll ever have. You'll never exclaim, "The prices to cover my feet are killing me!" Let's see. **BANDOLINO**, **BRUNO MAGLI**, **COLE HAAN**, **DOC MARTENS**, **FERRAGAMO**, **KENNETH COLE**, **NATURALIZERS**, **NINE WEST**, **SKECHERS**, **STEVE MADDEN**, **TIMBERLAND**, **VANELI**, and **VIA SPIGA** to name a few. Whew! I'm exhausted. And my feet still don't hurt. Kids can get shod, too. But back to women's shoes. I saw a pair of **STUART WEITZMAN** shoes at a store who shall remain nameless. It had my name on it. But it was $200. Thank goodness I waited a week and found them at www.weloveshoes.com for $24.99—that's a savings of 87.5 percent. So, put this website on your favorite list and I don't want to hear another word. Narrows and wides, smalls to large, and lots in between. If you'd rather be seen and not heard, don't tell another living sole!

49

Sporting Goods

★★★★ **Academy Sports & Outdoors**   **817/346-6622**
6101 W. I-20   Mon-Sat 9-9; Sun 10-7
Fort Worth, TX 76109   www.academy.com

This super duper sports chain offers an academic lesson in saving money. Since 1938, when Max Gochman opened the first Academy Tire Shop in San Antonio, he started by selling military surplus and then ultimately called the business Academy Super Surplus in Austin where he expanded to four stores. In 1973, his son Arthur began opening similar stores in Houston and the rest is history. Now selling sporting goods and outdoor items, Academy is one of the biggest sporting goods discounters in the Southwest and now exploding on to the Southeast scene with over 50 stores in seven states. The selection is broad enough to satiate most sports enthusiasts—in equipment, apparel and footwear at everyday low prices. Combining low prices with a large selection, Academy Sports & Outdoors has the highest sales per store and highest sales per square foot of any sporting goods retailer in the country with a consistent 25 percent sales growth for the past ten years. Grandson David Gochman is now Chairman, President, and CEO overseeing over 4,500 employees. Wow! And they're all in pretty good shape, too. Whether you're into golfing, camping, fishing, biking, swimming, basketball, football or soccer, let them sock-it-to ya with how they buy 'em low and sell 'em even lower. Though no online sales yet, you can find the store nearest you by clicking to their site. Their jingle sticks in my mind—it's the place to find the right stuff at the right price! Whether you're looking for hunting gear or fitness machines, you'll find it all with name brands like **ADIDAS, BROWNING, COLEMAN, COLUMBIA, CONVERSE, DIAMOND BACK, EVERLAST, IGLOO, NIKE, REEBOK, ROADMASTER, SHAKESPEARE, SPALDING, TIMBERCREEK** and so many more, it would tire even Lance Armstrong. To find the store nearest you, be a sport and check directory assistance or click online.

★★★ **American T-Shirts**   **972/289-8262**
1228 Scyene Rd.   Mon-Fri 9-5; Sat 10-3
Mesquite, TX 75149

This is the all-American way of keeping the family in T-shirts. Order their FREE catalog and buy in bulk to save any money. Though single T's are not full price, expect to pay $4.53 per shirt; buy them by the dozen or more of the same size and the price drops to $4.09. These are adult sizes. Children's were priced $3.61 for under a dozen and $3.01 for a dozen or more of the same size. Now we're talking. Especially notably for school or sport teams where the logo and the kid's name are the most important elements, you can almost forget the shirt, but not the name. A variety of shirts available such as baseball shirts, coach's shirts, even a fan club can order here. We're thinking about silk-screening our own T-shirts, "We are your cheapest link" where proceeds would go to my favorite charity; keep tuned to our website for that announcement soon. Any T-shirt agents or manufacturers up interested in giving us a bid? Send all inquiries to our website, askthediva@biggerbetterbargains.com, remember?

★★★★ Athletic Wearhouse

972/219-0073

1780 N. Stemmons Frwy.

Mon-Fri 10-7; Sat 9-6

Lewisville, TX 75067

www.athleticwearhouse.com

The Athletic Wearhouse finally has established itself as a home run. Shop in person or from their catalog, you can strike while the game's still hot: bats, balls and gloves by **ATEC**, **DIAMOND**, **EASTON**, **LOUISVILLE SLUGGER**, **MARKWORT**, **MIZUNO**, **RAWLINGS**, **SSK** and **WILSON**. Catch a good deal on an **ALL-STAR** catcher's helmet for only $150; or hold on to a fast ball with a pair of **LOUISVILLE TPX** batting gloves for $11 or throw a fast ball with a Rawlings Radar Ball for $20. And when all else fails, they even can call it a wrap with ice wraps for those injuries that are inevitable. Play the game with all its parts. Shop here for shoes and accessories for any major sporting event. Be a baseball fashion plate and slide into home base with T-Shirts. Or don any of the related baseball fashion jackets and jerseys by all of the above plus **NIKE**. Whether it's padding, bats, balls or any other accoutrement to play the game, you can find children's and youth sizes available. Older kids and their dads are not in their game plan. However, if your little one is needing a uniform that they don't stock, they are happy to order it. A two-week turnaround on uniform orders is promised but not guaranteed. Unless their site's up and running, you might strike out like we did. *Call toll-free: 800/435-6485*

★★★★★ Ball Billiards Ltd.

972/424-4533

1305 Summit Ave, Suite 10

Mon-Fri 6-4:30; Sat 9-3:30

Plano, TX 75074

You might as well rise to the "Summit" and get from behind the 8-ball. Arthur Ball is the owner of this custom-billiards business. In business for eight years, looks like eight is his lucky number. Don't expect him to ever pressure you into buying a table. He probably won't even ask you to buy one. Simply stop by, he'll give you a tour and explain how all his custom tables are made and then, have a nice day. But if you're in the market for a billiard table, you probably will place your order here if you want to cue up with a custom pool table starting at $2,395. Now we're talking custom made complete with delivery and set up. Choose your choice of felt and pocket colors as well as four cue sticks and cue rack, a slate top, oak or mahogany wood, **BELGIUM ARIMUS** balls and chalk, too. No assembly-line here. Each table is hand-made and carefully crafted. Even an exotic African mahogany table with six legs is within the realm of possibility. Have you priced ready-mades lately? This is their only business and unless your name's Minnesota Fats, there's none better in the Metroplex. Exit Plano Parkway off Central, go east to Avenue K, turn left and take the first right, which is Summit. They shoot straight but don't expect a big sign on their door. They like to keep a low profile. Except during Christmas, they can produce a custom table in about two weeks. Order before Thanksgiving to be guaranteed delivery in time for the holidays. All tables come with a lifetime guarantee and are totally handmade. Do you think their name had anything to do with their ultimate life's work?

Bicycle Exchange
11716 Ferguson Rd.
Dallas, TX 75228

972/270-9269
Mon-Fri 9-7; Sat 9-5

If I could have but one bike in my life, let it be an electric one complete with a recharge and let me race up to 18 MPH without having to do much of anything except to look cute with my helmet and short shorts. (Okay, so I can dream, can't I?) Bicycle Exchange is one of the few guy shops where you get personal attention and women are welcome, regardless of proficiency. They carry mostly new but do carry a few used bikes to accommodate their customer base. Bikes for every skill level—from beginners who need training wheels to those aspiring to ride in the Tour de France. Lance Armstrong wannabes have to start somewhere, even if it's on a three-wheeler. Whatever your starting point, it's important to wheel and deal and have a mode of transportation that will keep you blowin' and goin' in the wind. Get a grip on all-terrain, freestyle and **BMX** bikes, especially if you're looking for an "easy rider." Bikes in all sizes—from children's models to adult mountain bikes; even custom-made wheelchairs and special-needs cycles (as well as repair or modification) can be handled, bar none. Brands are the best: **CANNONDALE, DIAMOND BACK, GT, LOWRIDER, MONGOOSE, ROLAND, SHIMANO, TREK, YAKIMA** and more. They maintain an in-store technical staff who can fix any kind of bike, but they won't guarantee their turnaround time on repairs. They do guarantee their service. Expect them to probably sell more bikes than anyone else in the Metroplex. For the past 25 years, they have not boasted being a discounter, but they are proud of being a wheeler-dealer. Pedal over to their second location in Carrollton in Old Town at 1305 S. Broadway (972/245-5510) if it's more convenient. ***Call toll-free: 800/583-7269***

★★★★★ Billiards & Barstools
1803 W. Airport Frwy.
Euless, TX 76040

817/467-7665
Mon-Fri 10-7; Sat 10-5

This power player has cued up and placed several locations in the Metroplex for your gaming pleasure. Pool tables start at $1,395 and include delivery and set up. Choose from over 31 cloth covers and not pay extra for the option of choice. Six months with no interest financing through American General is another plus. They are considering changing their hours to be from 10-9 during the week, so call ahead and see if they've followed through with their intentions. The selection here is probably the best around with at least 50 pool tables and over 200 bar stools. If you've got an interest in the game, or a game room that needs some interest, here is where to start. In-home service a plus with custom two-piece cues, cue racks and cases an interesting and unique service. Add in the other entertaining options of foosball tables, shuffleboard, ping-pong tops, poker tables, juke boxes and billiard lights and it spells hours of leisure-time pleasure. Names are some of the best: **AMF, BRUNSWICK, GANDY, PETER VITALIE, PLAYMASTER, POLHAUSEN, RENAISSANCE** and **STERLING**. Check out their other locations in Richardson at 2080 N. Collins Blvd., 972/445-5485, in Dallas at 4004 Ross Ave., 214/821-5744, in Carrollton at 1702 Vantage Dr., 972/478-8451 and Lewisville at 2061 S. Stemmons Frwy., 972/434-4434. You might as well rack up the savings before the game begins.

★★★★★ BSN Sports
PO Box 7726
Dallas, TX 75209

800/292-7772
Mon-Fri 7:30-6
www.bsnsports.com

A quarter of a century and still going strong. If you want a place to soccer-to-me, call for your FREE BSN Sports catalog or shop online, it's a breeze. This is your one-stop sports headquarters for any sport available at the high school or college level. Shop where the coaches and athletic directors shop. All sports. All brands. That should get your heart rate pumping and the cash registers humming. Brands include

ATEC, **BULLDOG**, **EASTON**, **GAMECRAFT**, **HUFFY**, **IGLOO**, **MITRE**, **MIZUNO**, **PORT-A-PIT**, **PRO DOWN**, **REEBOK**, **ROL DRI**, **SPALDING**, **VOIT**, **WILSON** and **WORTH**. There's always a deal, a great deal. Just one example, a **MACGREGOR** soccer ball for $7.97 that retails for $15.95. Score Points is a program where you earn points for FREE gear. Hey, what a novel idea! Every dollar you spend equals one point (Promotion ends September 27, 2002). Redeem those points for specific merchandise that they will make available. The minimum cash out on points is 1,000 points (in other words after spending $1,000); although, if you order online, you can earn double points. Yea! Rah, Rah, Sis-Boom-Bah! What a great incentive for a team so they can end up with some freebies. **AQUA**-sports, archery, badminton, baseball (softball), basketball (benches and bleachers), boxing, camping, fitness, football, golf, gymnastics, hockey, La Crosse, physical medicine (P.E.), playground equipment, racquet ball (scoreboards), soccer, sports medicine, handball, tennis, track & field, volleyball, weight-lifting and wrestling. Got a choke-hold on paying full price? Here's the place to avoid the obvious, sport, and catch some MVPs (most value-oriented pricing.)

★★★★ Buddy's Sporting Goods Athletics   214/941-5506
123 W. Jefferson Blvd.   Mon-Fri 9:30-6; Sat 9-5
Dallas, TX 75208   www.buddyssportinggoods.com

Look great, no matter your passion. Is it football, basketball, baseball, soccer, track, boxing, volleyball, hockey...even the best-looking officials around can make the call in these uniforms. This is the place for team uniforms and equipment customized with screen-printing and embroidery. We found some blow-out prices on gear like chest protectors for only $5, socks for $3 and helmets as low as $10. How low can they go? Well if limbo were a sport, it would be priced be rock bottom, too. Sales mean taking an extra 20 percent off their already discounted priced gloves and finding baseballs, softballs and 12" softy balls starting at just $1.99. Name brands include **ADIDAS**, **CONVERSE**, **HIGH FIVE**, **NIKE**, **RAWLINGS**, **REEBOK**, **WILSON** and others. This Oak Cliff sporting goods source is an institution in Oak Cliff. Teams have been courting them for years and years. See what's online and get in the mood with the "Rocky" theme song. You'll be ready to climb the stairs of the Philadelphia library when you're finished outfitting the kids and the refs. Play ball at their second store in Duncanville at 749 W. Wheatland Rd. (972/780-8177) and then call it a day.

★★★★★ Cheaper Than Dirt   817/625-7171
2522 NE Loop 820   Mon-Fri 7-8; Sat 9-3
Fort Worth, TX 76105   www.cheaperthandirt.com

Now that the millennium scare is over, Cheaper than Dirt can get back to normal. Within their 4,500 square feet of possibilities, there are over 1,800 items lurking in every inch of display space. Don't expect the website and store to carry the same merchandise, however, though the store can order anything if you find it on their website. Come and admire their trophy room with game animal mounts and full-body mounted Black Bear, African Lion, Jaguar, Trophy Deer, Elk, Cape Buffalo, Alligators and dozens more game to get up close and personal. If you're looking for a macho vicarious experience, get ready for the hunt. This is the place to find the fruits of that expedition. When you find it, you will have landed on one of the most popular hideout for hunters, shooters, law enforcement and collectors who intend to be armed with the best: **BERETTA**, **COLT**, **DAKOTA RIFLE**, **GLOCK**, **H & K**, **KEL-TEC**, **KIMBER**, **MARLIN**, **REMINGTON**, **RUGER**, **SAVAGE**, **SIG**, **S & W**, **TAURUS**, **WINCHESTER** and more. Plus tons of camping equipment, military surplus and closeout items—just in case you need to head to the woods. Located next to the large dark gray TTI building, just north of the Sheriff's office, it must have been fate to have wound up so close to the local armed forces. Ammo, holsters, scopes, air-guns, clothing, cooking gear, mags & clips, archery, electronics, military surplus, black powder, optics, police gear, books & videos, camping gear, knives—all cheaper than dirt! *Call toll-free: 888/625-3848*

★★★★★ Consignment Sports & Fitness   972/437-1222
300 N. Coit Rd.   Mon-Fri 10-7; Sat 10-6; Sun Noon-5
Richardson, TX 75080

Two locations to work up a sweat, their original one on Coit Road and their warehouse location in Farmers Branch, 3340 Garden Brook, 972/488-3222. Either place, whether you're consigning or buying, they are a solid source to reduce the fat. The choice of sports equipment is as varied as the myriad of sporting activities and it's forever changing with the times. If skate boarding is hot, they'll have plenty of them; same if skate boarding is not. It depends on when the enthusiast loses interest or wants to trade in or trade up. Whether you are buying, selling, trading or renting, you'll be saving money. Try out that treadmill at half the price before buying a new one for twice the money only to discover you really prefer it as a planter or a clothes rack. We've seen all kinds of fitness gear, from **STAIRMASTERS** to **PRECOR BICYCLES**, weight benches to circuit weight training apparatus, hockey skates to in-line skates, racquetball and tennis rackets, golf clubs to an occasional recumbent bike or **WEE JOGGER**, you just have to be a sport and shop a lot. Equipment comes and goes just like the craze.

★★★★★ Cycle Spectrum   972/480-9588
1310 W. Campbell Rd.   Mon-Sat 10-6; Sun Noon-5
Richardson, TX 75080   www.cyclespectrum.com

Take advantage of their FREE service policy for life on all bikes sold. That's right. This solid performer has been riding the high road since 1970 and they have all of their shops nationwide humming. Round and round they go as they ride the competition. When was the last time you were told to bring in your bike and receive FREE tune-ups, check ups, regular maintenance and repairs? Try asking your doctor or your hair-dresser for a similar plan and they'll want to lock you up. Better yet, ask your local car dealer if they'd replace parts when and if you needed them and all you would have to pay for is the part? Well, aren't they all looking for customers for life? The spectrum of cycles here is monumental: from road bikes to mountain bikes, from a cruiser to a **BMX**; even kiddy bikes complete with training wheels for that very first ride will start your relationship with them early. Then you'll grow as you go. For the serious biker, we eyed the **MOTOBECANE LE CHAMPION** bike that retails for $1,600 but was here for $1,095 (that's a savings of over 35 percent). Expect other top dogs to complete their discounting cycle such as: **BELL, BLACKBURN, DYNO, FREE AGENT, FUJI, GT, KRYPTONITE, LOOK, MOTOBECANE, PEUGEOT, PRIMAL, PURE SHIMANO, POWERLITE, RALEIGH, RHODE GEAR, ROCK SHOK, SRAM, TEKTRO, UNIVEGA** and **VISTALITE** — at some of the best prices in town. All you need is the helmet. Don't forget. They carry the Bell helmets. Since you can't buckle up, the least we can do is give you a heads up! Check directory for one of their eight locations.

★★ Dallas Golf   972/270-0989
2100 Eastgate Drive   Mon-Fri 9-7; Sat 9-6; Sun Noon-5
Garland, TX 75043   www.dallasgolf.com

Dallas may be known to have the quickest draw in the Southwest but Dallas Golf has the quickest repair service in the world. And believe me, that should count for something when those 18 holes are beckoning. After seventeen years in the business, they know a panic attack when they see one. Since they specialize in custom fitting clubs, it doesn't matter if you're a Sunday golfer or tournament pro, they treat you the same. Four locations and swinging, you can also see them in action at 3963 Belt Line Road, Addison, 972/866-0007; 429 N. Central Expressway, Richardson, 972/231-9399 and in Irving at 2326 W. Airport

Freeway, 972/255-3639. Want to demo the equipment on your home course? No problem. Have at it! Their knowledgeable staff shouldn't tee you off with any of the popular brand names on the floor: **MCHENRY METALS**, **PING**, **PRO-LINE**, **TITLEIST**, **WILSON** and others. Just don't expect sizeable slices in the prices. Look online for the best deals on auctioned and used equipment. Now we're getting closer to that hole-in-one.

Doug & Lynda's Ski Shop   **972/542-0214**
227 E. Louisiana St.   Mon-Sat 10-6; Sun 1-5
McKinney, TX 75069

When the first snow flakes start to fall, spring to this shop and make your skiing more affordable. Schuss down by shopping for your entire ski/snow/winter wardrobe here where savings of 20-70 percent off are possible. Championship names include: **AIRWALK**, **ATOMIC**, **BLACK BEAR**, **CB SPORTS**, **COLUMBIA**, **DESCENTE**, **DYNASTAR**, **FILA**, **HEAD**, **K2**, **MORROW**, **NORDICA**, **OAKLEY**, **OBERMEYER**, **RAICHLE**, **ROFFE**, **ROSSIGNOL**, **SALOMON**, **SIMS**, **SNUGGLER**, **SPYDER**, **TECHNICA**, **VOLANT**, **VOLKYL**, **WHITE STAG** and more. Before you make your move, though, be sure you've also loaded up with all the other ski-time accoutrements. Don't take that downward spiral without goggles, gloves, headbands or fanny packs. But if you really want a cheap ride, wait until the end-of-the-season sales where markdowns can descend to 75 percent off snowboards and skis with bindings. This shop is no lightweight in the service department either. Keep those skis and snowboards in tip-top shape at their full-service repair facility. The drive to McKinney is worth the savings, unless of course, you prefer to spend all your money on lift tickets. And now that the Ladylike Shop in Wylie has taken a powder, this is the reigning far North Dallas ski king. *Call toll-free: 972/562-5743*

★★★★★ Edwin Watts Golf Outlet   **817/861-6677**
901 W. Lamar   Mon-Fri 9:30-7; Sat 9:30-6; Sun 12-5
Arlington, TX 76012   www.edwinwattsgolf.com

From one small pro shop in Fort Walton Beach to 48 superstores today, Edwin Watts and his brother Ronnie are still going strong. Adding a third partner thirty years ago, they're all still together and their lives have been good ever since. Today, they offer some of the latest high-tech golf equipment in the country with a large selection of pro-line equipment——from clubs and bags to shoes, balls, apparel and more. Their Dallas stores feature indoor hitting rooms, putting greens (one's even outdoors), and fitting rooms. To make their stores even more visual, they intersperse displays of antique clubs and memorabilia. There are three locations in the Metroplex, but the one above is the only half and half store which we consider the cream of the crop. Half retail but the other half is their outlet. The 5-star rating, of course, applies to the outlet half. You'll still see all the big names in golf: **ADAMS**, **APEX**, **ASHWORTH**, **BAG BOY**, **BEN HOGAN**, **BUSHNELL**, **CALLAWAY**, **COBRA**, **DEXTER**, **FOOT-JOY**, **MAXFLI**, **MIZUNO**, **NIKE**, **ODYSSEY**, **OAKLEY**, **PING**, **PINNACLE**, **PURE SPIN**, **REEBOK**, **SKB**, **SPALDING**, **TITLEIST**, **TOP FLITE**, **US KIDS GOLF**, **WILSON**——frankly, there are just too many to list. Whatever you're looking for, you'll find it here. From balls, bags, belts and books to clubs, cleats and carts. And if you think that's it, forget it. Now it's time to dress the part. Look good in men's and ladies' apparel, gloves, hats, sunglasses, even magnetic bracelets if that wrist is bothering you. Be prepared for the heat or the rain with large umbrellas, training aids, software and travel covers. Even gifts for the real golf enthusiast like "Golf Monopoly" for $30 and "Golf Scrabble" for $20 make for the perfect stocking stuffer or last-minute gift for the golfer. Their outlet side is where the buys are. Sales are not final because they willingly accept exchanges and provide refunds. Swing to their other Dallas locations at 2320 Stemmons

Trail in Dallas, 214/352-9431 and 5955 Alpha Road, 972/404-4424. Online closeouts provide almost instant gratification, which is par for the course at Edwin Watts.

★★★ Finish Line   972/881-1213

Plano Outlet Mall
1717 E. Spring Creek Pkwy.
Plano, TX 75074

Mon-Sat 10-9; Sun Noon-6
www.finishline.com

If you'd like a good deal on logo T-Shirts, tank tops, sunglasses, socks, duffel bags, ball caps, even watches by **FOSSIL** and **OAKLEY**, here's the place to finish off your last-minute shopping. To entice you further, print coupons online and take them into the store for additional savings. Wow! How's another $10 off a purchase of $50 or more sound? Shoes, too, for men sizes 5-18, women 5-11, kids 1-6 and yes, even preschoolers size 3-13. Unless you wear the box, they can get you covered. Plus, there's always a sale and always a reason to finish off your shopping, sport, with an athletic shoe, regardless of the model number, or the color, as long as they're a matching pair. The Finish Line could be the perfect line of defense against allowing your budget to run rampant. We ran with a New York Yankee's jersey for $19 (instead of $45) and a pair of **CONVERSE** basketball shoes for $9.98 instead of $24. Ten area locations, check online for the one nearest you as well as their online outlet offerings.

★★★★ Golfsmith Pro Shop   972/991-9255

4141 LBJ Frwy.
Dallas, TX 75052

Mon-Sat 10-7; Sun Noon-6
www.golfsmith.com

I remember them well. Ah, Carl and Frank Paul, brothers from Plainfield, NJ, who started out in one little basement location and moved to Austin in 1969. Today, they're one of the big boys in the industry who have struck it rich with first selling their own line of golf equipment via mail order, then to their bricks and mortar stores and now their online supercenter (including a partnership with www.golfonline.com for all the latest tournament and golfer scores in real time along the way). Today, they are head and shoulders above par. Should a little birdie find a lower price on the same item online, they will match it plus 15 percent. Inside their stores, you'll find Golf Simulators (featuring virtual golf), **SWINGTEK** swing analyzers, expansive putting greens, and large screen TV(s) showcasing the current tournament or latest in golf and sports programming. Shop the major manufacturers including: **ADAMS**, **ALIEN SPORT**, **ASHWORTH**, **BEN HOGAN**, **TOP FLITE**, **CALLAWAY**, **CLEVELAND**, **COBRA**, **DATREK**, **ETONIC**, **FOOTJOY**, **FORRESTERS**, **GOLFSMITH**, **IZZO KILLER BEE**, **LA JOLLA**, **LYNX**, **MAXFLI**, **MIZUNO**, **NIKE**, **ORLIMAR**, **PING**, **PRECEPT**, **REEBOK**, **SNAKE EYES**, **STX**, **SUN MOUNTAIN SPORTS**, **TAYLOR MADE**, **TITLEIST**, **WILSON**—there's enough to link you up to every golf course in the country. Between the metals, woods, irons, putters, wedges, drivers, add in their collections of Junior Sets, Women's Clubs, Starter Clubs, a golfer could go crazy. Then dress 'em up, practice them up, and send them out. Oh shame, I almost overlooked the four-leaf clovers in closeouts, the "Hot Buys," the "Pro Pointers"—all the extras you didn't know who to ask but couldn't resist when you saw them online. All that's left is to either ask for their catalog, sign up for their newsletter, and tell them whether you want to communicate in English, Español, Français, Italiano or Deutsch. Ihr seid a bargain shopper! Ya? Their 20,000-square-foot stores provide a haven for every golfer (or golfer's widow if they tag along—male or female). They also own the **HARVEY PENICK** line which you will find putting around the showroom. If you're ever in Austin, visit and play their corporate golf course at 11000 N I-35 (512/837-3878). Or shop closer to home in Arlington at 1001 W. I-20 (between Matlock and Cooper; 817/557-5077) or in Plano at 900 Central Expwy. (972/424-4823). *Call toll-free: 800/815-3873*

★★ Las Vegas Golf & Tennis
8612 Preston Rd.
Plano, TX 75024

972/668-5090
Mon-Sat 9-6; Sun Noon-5
www.lvgolf.com

How often during a golf match do you wish you could try the shot first, and then try again? Well, LV Golf & Tennis franchises have such a program. "Try Before You Buy" your next set of clubs by taking a demo set onto the course to see if it's the perfect match. Everything else, you buy, you keep: Clubs, balls, gloves, racquets, bags, shoes, apparel and accessories with an unbelievable line-up of great names including **ADAMS, ADIDAS, ARMOUR, ASHWORTH, BOBBY JONES, CALLAWAY, CLEVELAND, COBRA, CUTTER & BUCK, DUNLOP, ETONIC, FOOT-JOY, GOLF PRIDE, HEAD, GREG NORMAN, LBH, MAXFLI, MIZUNO, NIKE, OGIO, PING, PRINCE, PURE SPIN, SPALDING, TAYLOR MADE, TITLEIST, VISION, WILSON** and more. They even have their own line of clubs called **VISION GOLF**. All clubs are backed by a lifetime warranty on both defects and quality. Take a 30-day trial run; receive a full refund if not completely satisfied. They also have a guaranteed trade-up program. What a winning combination! You can hit the jackpot, too, in Hillsboro, at Hillsboro Prime Outlets, 104 N.E. I-35, Ste. 162, 254/582-1022.

★★★ North Texas Golf World
1100 E. I-820 S.
Fort Worth, TX 76112

817/457-9345
Mon-Fri 8-5; Sat 9-2

Golfers, take a back seat and relax. Here's your source for new and used golf clubs and carts. But I bet if you could have but one piece of equipment, you would die for a cart before a **BIG BERTHA**. Eh? Golf carts with names like **BOMBARDIER, E-Z-GO** and **YAMAHA** at prices from $750 for a fabulous three-wheeler to more expensive models three to five years old. Like-new, rebuilt carts range from $2,850-$3,400 but new ones can set you back $4,000 or more. They also have a store in Granbury (817/578-8720). Fly like an eagle and take a swing at their new and used club selection like **CALLAWAY, COBRA, PING, TAYLOR MADE, TITLEIST** and more. There's always something new (well new to you even if it's used) coming and going. Word of finding a Tiger in the Woods was a hoax!

★★★★★ Oshman's SuperSports USA
4620 Cooper & I-20
Arlington, TX 76017

817/467-0090
Mon-Fri 10-9; Sat 9-9; Sun 11-6
www.oshmans.com

When you're big, there's nowhere to go but to get bigger. And that's what Oshman's has done. They have experienced monumental store growth since Jake Oshman first opened Oshman's Dry Goods in Richmond, Texas in 1919. After moving to Houston and opening another store by buying up bankrupt stock of another dry goods store while liquidating the inventory of his store in Richmond, he was on to something. Strike while the iron was hot and the birth of the superstore was in its infancy. In 1990, the Oshman's SuperSports USA megastore concept began to take hold into 80,000-square-foot monsters with so much going for them, you'd get dizzy just walking the perimeters. There are product demo areas where you can try out the equipment right there and they've integrated entertainment into each of the merchandised areas. As a result of all this activity, it has become an entirely energized family shopping experience. Named one of the most innovative store concepts today and "Best Store" in the Mall of America by *USA Today*, no wonder we can now all be a super sport. They sell equipment and accessories in xtreme sports including **CWB SLAYER WAKEBOARDS** (1999-2000 editions) for $189 (retail $279) and **FILA FF 70** In-Line Skate for women just $99 (retail $134) and the **HOT WHEELS** Folding Kick Scooter With Front Suspension (only the blue model) for $79 (retail $109). But who's picky at these prices? Ride out on a mountain bike with names like **HUFFY, JEEP, MONGOOSE** or **ROYCE UNION**. What about backboards—the Huffy Power Force for $199 (retails $249) or an **IMAGE** 800Q treadmill for $499 (retail $899)? Get customized **MLB** (Major League Baseball) jerseys as low as $59. Oshman's supports many different charities but one in particular is noteworthy——their grants for girls' athletic sports called "Grants for Girls." Check directory for the closest of their 13 stores in the Metroplex. With a female Oshman at the helm, they're being steered in the right direction for explosive growth and this Texas-bred bargain empire will soon be turning heads everywhere. ***Call toll-free: 800/PLAY-OSH***

★★★★★ Play It Again Sports   **972/720-9666**
14902 Preston Rd., Suite 506   Mon-Fri 10-8; Sat 10-6; Sun Noon-5
Dallas, TX 75240   www.playitagainsports.com

No, this is not a Humphrey Bogart licensed store. Instead, this Sam plays sports and doesn't pay attention to Lauren Becall. Play It Again Sports is in the game of selling sports equipment as long as it's been played before. This franchised nationwide-network of sporting goods stores sell it again and again. Too, they service what they sell and with 11 area stores (Arlington, Carrollton, Dallas, Flower Mound, Fort Worth, Irving, Mesquite, Plano, Rockwall, Southlake, Wichita Falls), surely each sport is an equal opportunity location. However, since each site is individually-owned and operated, not every location is equipped equally. But each store does have loads of equipment. Why? Because every year, your kid (grown-ups included) likes to trade up into something more advanced, or retreat into something more elementary. That's for starters. Or, they've lost interest in the barbells and want a stationary bike. Or, instead of baseball, they want to try hockey this year. It never fails. But this is the place where you can trade or sell your gently-used sports equipment on consignment. When it sells, get the money and run; or apply it to something new in the store. To fill in the empty spaces, each store also buys new closeouts and overstocks from major manufacturers though some locations do better with new. Nevertheless, these guys have been around for 18 years and nothing is stopping them from gaining an international foothold as the world's leader where sporting goods are their currency and buying them for less is the consumer's mantra.

★★★★★ Ray's Sporting Goods   **214/747-7916**
730 Singleton   Tue-Sat 9-6
Dallas, TX 75212   www.rayssportinggoods.com

Forty-six years of aiming to please combined with their killer instincts is why big game hunters and other gun enthusiasts consider Ray's a sanctuary from high prices. Called "the firearms specialist," Ray's has been the target of pot shots with my puns for years, but if you're a serious shooter, when it comes to custom rifles, shotguns and pistols, there is none better in the Metroplex. Their arsenal of weapons are not the only items for sale in their game plan. Dress the part in camouflage clothing, sign up for a deal on their frequent hunting trips, and buy all of your supplies, optical equipment and accessories to hit the mark, too. Major brands to brandish include **BENELLI, BERETTA, BIANCHI, BLASER, BROWNING, COLT, DESERT EAGLE, GLOCK, GRIZZLY, HAHR, H&K, KRIEGHOFF, MOSSBERG, REMINGTON, SKB, SMITH & WESSON, UBERTI, WALTER, WEATHERBY, WINCHESTER** and more. Whether it's a pistol, a rifle, a shotgun, ammo, knives, even targets, you can be sure the conversation turns to ease, reliability and price (and this shop's a straighter-shooter in all three departments). Ready, aim, and fire away. Make sure your licenses are all in order and head to near the corner of Sylvan Ave and Singleton in Oak Cliff. ***Call toll-free: 800/440-3323***

★★★ REI Recreational Equipment   **972/490-5989**
4515 LBJ Frwy.   Mon-Sat 10-9; Sun 11-6
Dallas, TX 75244   www.rei.com

One block west of the Galleria, and actually within the boundaries of Farmers Branch, you only have to have a zest for the great outdoors to escape city life and head for the hills. Maintaining one of the finest catalogs for the well-endowed sporting class, if you'd like to climb to greater heights, REI is the place to camp. They offer the most extensive clothing and equipment inventory for the serious mountaineer in the world. And if it anything breaks, be it a zipper on a jacket, pair of pants, sleeping bag, or you need to patch a parka, tent or backpack, they'll fix you up. If you are a member (see below) prices on zipper pulls for members is $8 while non-members pay $10. Those prices are also good for packs and sleeping bags. Not significant by itself, but they add up. Most repairs are under $20 anyway, with very few exceptions. Are you looking to explore a new sport? Then take advantage of their rental gear program and try before you buy. If it's Adventure Travel, get your discounts here. Sign up for your own REI Bankcard with cash back and other benefits alongside their $15 yearly REI membership where you get cash back at the end of the year on your total purchases. Add to those special sales and discounts on merchandise and repairs as well as reduced Avis car rental rates, you'll be raring to go. Skiers have a field day with everything they need to deliver that sermon on the mount and serious bike riders love the selection of high-tech gear. Too, they wouldn't be caught dead not dressing the part. After all, the former president of REI has climbed Mount Everest and was one of the first Americans to do so, you wouldn't expect anything less, would you? Prices, though, are a slight melt-down from retail. But remember that 10 percent rebate at the end of the year? A few well-known brands are visible like **JANSPORT**, **KELTY**, **SIERRA DESIGNS** and **WALRUS** but 90 percent of the stock is private labeled with their name (another way to keep costs under control without sacrificing quality.) Join their cooperative club like millions of others have done and share in the profits at the end of the year. And be happy there's a store in the Metroplex that has "The Attic"— their name for a clearance department. Online, load up on the best prices yet from their outlet.

★★★★ Richardson Bike Mart

1451 W. Campbell Rd.
Richardson, TX 75080

972/231-3993
Mon-Fri 10-8; Sat 9-6: Sun Noon-5
www.bikemart.com

Stop spinning your wheels riding the wave of new retailers who take you out for a spin and then drop you like a hot potato. No, ma'am, this is a long-time name in the area though their name implies only a Richardson location. They're also at 9040 Garland Rd. near White Rock Lake, 214/321-0705, hours are Mon-Fri 10-7; Sat 9-6; Sun 12-5. There you'll see plenty of riders getting in gear for a ride around the lake. If you, too, want a leisurely bike ride, get in shape for a triathlon, or if you're a first-timer, here's where to go. Expect to see brands like **BIANCHI**, **CALFEE**, **CERVELO**, **CIOCC**, **COLNAGO**, **COPI**, **DE BERNSRDI**, **GRIFFEN**, **IBIS**, **INDEPANDANT FABS**, **KLEIN**, **LEMOND**, **MERLIN**, **QUINTANA ROO**, **SCHWINN**, **SEROTTA**, **SEVEN**, **SPECIALIZED**, **TREK**—well, all I was looking for was a Schwinn since that was a name I remembered from my childhood. See how progress has ridden right by and I haven't even noticed. But never mind, I'm up for learning. Same with kids—to grandparents, bicycling is great fun and great exercise. Every bike sold here gets a FREE six-month check up, FREE brake and derailleur adjustments for one year, and one FREE clinic in cycling techniques or basic maintenance. Price guaranteed that if you find it at another dealer priced less within 30 days of purchase, they will refund the difference. So it pays to shop around. If you visit their website, you'll be able to retrieve a list of bike trails both locally and nationally.

★★★★★ St. Bernard Sports Outlet

2707 W. Mockingbird
Dallas, TX 75235

214/352-1200
Tue-Sat 10-6
www.stbernardsports.com

Bark when you see this St. Bernard coming to the rescue. Great prices (Arf! Arf!) like on a pair of **SALOMON** X-SCREAM skis for $550, (MSRP: $675) or a pair of the new 2002 **VOLANT** Gravity Chubbs (available here before any other retailers were even opening up the cartons) for $300. Some hard-to-find brands that you might find only in the more exclusive ski boutiques like **BURMA & BIBAS**,

CHACO, DIESEL, FRESH PRODUCE, HELEN KAMINSKI, LUCKY, MAUI JIM, OAKLEY, PAUL FRANK, QUICKSILVER, REEF, SOLITUDE and TOMMY BAHAMA plus all the popular brands you'd expect in the typical ski shops like BURTON, K2, NORDICA, SALOMON, TYROLIA, VOLANT and others. From bindings, boots, poles to skis, snowboards and accessories, you'll find in all under one roof. Head to their warehouse where savings ascend to 50 percent. Start at the top of their 3,500-square-foot warehouse and don't look back. Slalom all the way down to the bottom and enjoy the ride back up knowing you saved all that money. Near Love Field, before you take that charter flight to Vail, make sure you've back-packed all the terrific deals here before you get your boarding pass. If they're giving out lift tickets, you're too late.

★★★★★ T-Shirt Outlet

14015 N. Stemmons
Farmers Branch, TX 75234

972/241-7030
Mon-Sat 10-8

Prices on shirts start at $3 each for S-M-L-XL and $4 each for 2XL-4XL but for the whole team, that's a different story. Win the game on high prices and shop at this bold yet beautiful bargain T-Shirt Factory. For silk-screening t-shirts, expect to pay a $35 set up charge per color to be imprinted. Then it'll cost $1 per side of printing on a white shirt and $1.50 per side of printing on colored shirts. The minimum order for printed T-Shirts is three dozen but smaller orders for just T-Shirts can be had at a price slightly higher. They can be either be 100 percent cotton or 50-50 (cotton/polyester combination). Why not get with the program and get your team's name up there front and center, or back and center, either side will generate results. The T-Shirts are so inexpensive, and these folks have all the equipment to churn out the quantities fast, in time for the first batter to go to bat. The children's T-Shirts cost five for $10 (that's $2 a shirt) and are the lowest we've found in the Metroplex. Too, adults can get the same quantity at the same price. No kidding. But oversized T's (2XL and 3XL) are a tad higher, three for $10. Still the lowest in town. Looks like this is where we'll be getting our "cheapest link" shirts. Stay tuned.

Tour Line Golf

7616 Spur 580
Fort Worth, TX 76116

817/560-4700
Mon-Fri 10-6; Sat 9-5
www.tourlinegolf.com

The game doesn't get better than this. Play with the pros...their equipment that is. The pro shops from country clubs nationwide send their clearance items and used clubs that they take in trade to these two shops in Dallas and Fort Worth. They are, in fact, the largest clearinghouse in America for such pro lines. In turn, they sell the clubs at a fraction of the cost of new. Major players include CALLAWAY, CLEVELAND, KING COBRA, HOGAN, PING, TAYLOR MADE, TITLEIST, TOP FLITE—typically always on hand but they do keep their "eagle" eye out for others like. DEXTER, DUNLOP, FOOTJOY, LIQUID METAL, MAXFLI, MIZUNO, ODYSSEY, PRECEPT, PROLINE, US KIDS, WILSON, YAMAHA, ZEVO and others who make an occasional appearance. You can return within 48 hours (even if you used the equipment) for a full refund. After that you have 30 days but there will be a 20 percent restocking fee. Since clubs are used, they must pass two inspections before being placed on the floor for sale. If they've never been used, they will be labeled "new;" if they were only slightly used or used as a demo, they will be labeled "demo" and if they've seen more than two rounds of golf, they'll be labeled "used." We found a used Bobby Jones' putter from CALLAWAY for $49, that is if you're right handed. Or a woman's right handed BIG BERTHA 5 wood graphite for only $79. A NICKLAUS "Air Bear" right 3-PW were $329. Of course, for that price, those had seen the course more than a few times but still looked great and performed as well according to one happy golfer. And if it's just got to be new, how about NIKE hats for $10 and COBRA putters for $65? No clones or copies, just the originals to get you out of that sand-trap. A stellar selection at great prices, so who's going to set the tee time? Great prices on golf balls, too, and if you want to talk golf, this shop walks the talk all the way to the cash register. Shop online for some of the "Hot Buys" and lots of information for the golf enthusiast or fanatic. How about Callaway Hawk Eye Woods for $219.99 , Titleist 975 D Drivers, $229.99, Cleveland Quad Pro Woods, $99.99 or a Callaway Great Big Bertha Woods, $169.99? Grab while the irons are hot. See what's available for women, locate a golf pro, find a coach, or other informative links. Also swing into their Old Town location in Dallas at 5500 Greenville, Suite 502 at Lovers Lane (NE corner), 214/692-9411. ***Call toll-free: 800/530-5767***

★★★★★ Wally's Discount Golf Shop

817/261-9301

900 E. Copeland Rd.
Arlington, TX 76011

Mon-Fri 9:30-6:30; Sat 9-6

What a sport! Wally wonders why you haven't taken up his favorite game yet after all these years? He even takes Sunday off to hook up with his customers on the course where all life begins, teeing off at 6 AM, even in the dark. So, when you are ready to get with the program, whether you're looking for one club or a set, stay focused on Wally's because with his multiple stores, he has what you're looking for. In fact, he can get most anything withint two days since he stocks the most popular sizes and brands in his Garland warehouse. Otherwise, the wait may be up to two weeks. (Then again, have you ever ordered furniture from North Carolina? You could probably walk there faster.) So be grateful for their speedy recovery. All the top names from **CALLAWAY** to **TITLEIST**, **MIZUNO** to **PING**, well he carries them all. Hey anything's worth a try if it'll lower your score, right? Tee off at their other locations at 126 Town East Shopping Center in Mesquite, 1332 S. Plano Rd # 400 in Richardson, 915 Main St. in Garland and at 1820 Coit Rd., # 140 in Plano. But start at their outlet location first at 9090 N. Stemmons Fwy. in Dallas, 214/637-2944 before you lay down the green. Some golfers I know stop by a Wally's location at least once a week, just to talk golf! ***Call toll-free: 800/249-2559***

50

Surplus, Pawn & Thrift

★★ **American Pawn Superstore**   **972/203-2020**
1785 E. I-30   Mon-Sun 9-9
Garland, TX 75043-4456

An all American activity that has been ignored in good times comes back into favor when times go south. The pawn shop is sometimes the only place that can provide cash for products. Try taking your computer or **ROLEX** watch to the bank. Other than admiring it, they give you squat! When shopping, try to avoid Frank. He's so fast-talking, you may pawn the clothes on your back without wanting to do so. But the good news is that almost anything that can bought, sold or loaned-on can be found here. Within 32,000 square feet, it's probably the largest pawn shop in the Metroplex. Pawn shops in general are great places to learn to shop with the sharks. You won't be over your head in debt shopping here for sporting goods, electronics, musical instruments, electronics, luggage, lawn mowers, vacuum cleaners, TVs and stereos, TVs and more stereos, VCRs, clocks, guns, jet skis, bikes, power tools, clocks, lamps, jewelry (costume and fine), diamonds, watches and more. Or, if you're drowning in debt, this is a good place to relieve some of it by selling some of those things that are taking up space in your life. Either way, it's the American way. Visit their smaller satellite locations at LBJ and Midway and another in Arlington.

★★ **Cash America Pawn**   **214/948-1522**
626 W. Jefferson Blvd.   Mon-Fri 9-7; Sat 9-5; Sun 11-4
Dallas, TX 75208-4724   www.cashamericapawn.com

Remember not so long ago when pawn shops were scattered all over the country and the industry was fragmented mom and pop concerns with no universal voice? Well, welcome to the world of high finance and smart marketing. Headquartered in Fort Worth with other companies under their corporate umbrella (they also own Mr. Payroll and Rent-A-Tire), Cash America Pawn not only has the largest number of locations in the United States, but is the most recognizable brand in the pawn shop industry. Just for your edification, pawn loans were made as far back as 3,000 years ago, so the concept is nothing new. When Cash America Pawn was born in 1984, the image changed dramatically. Now it's known as the "non-bank" with over 470 locations in 18 states. It's where people go to get cash as well as a great place to buy something at a great price. In fact, CAP is a little shopping mecca of previously-owned stuff. From TVs and VCRs to guns, cameras, sporting goods, guitars, bicycles, drums, saxophones, a treadmill and some household items like blenders, microwaves and silver, conceivably, it's even a goldmine. And speaking of gold, if you want jewelry, you can buy jewelry. Lots of it. Examine all merchandise before making that final decision. Get cash quick; loan documents only take minutes to print and you're outta there. Visit the 42 other Metroplex locations.

★★★ Freight Outlet, The   972/240-6678
6545 Duck Creek Drive   Mon-Sat 9-8; Sun 1-6
Garland, TX 75043

New address and phone number does not a difference make. But they have made a move in the right direction by getting closer to the greater good. (Garland is closer than Balch Springs.) That means, the freight stops here where "it's been shipped by truck. We have it, had it, or will have it." And everything's on the up and up. All killer-priced. New merchandise is sold on an old premise. Buy it right, sell it low and the customers will come. The adventure of it all is one big surprise. You never know what lies ahead in the search. Standard surplus items included food items (canned and boxed), sundries, beauty supplies, your typical grocery and drug store items. Occasionally, they offered some perishables, too, like corny dogs and bacon. But man does not live by the fat of the land only. Save lots by buying lots. Load up and make every dollar count. Personnel are helpful and typical of small-town America. Located near the corner of Duck Creek and Broadway, across the street from K-Mart. trek over to their second location called Freight Outlet Plus in St. Joseph, Texas. If you need directions, call 940/995-2776.

★★★ Goodwill Industries   214/638-2800
2800 N. Hampton Rd.   Mon-Sat 9:30-6; Sun Noon-6
Dallas, TX 75212   www.goodwilldallas.org

How about "*Good Will, Hunting?*" Well, you won't have to look very far. Goodwill Industries means not only are you buying right, you could be giving for all the right reasons. Benefit this worthy cause and strike a deal in any of the area Goodwill stores around town. You never know how good it can get until you try. Besides knick-knacks and odds and ends, you'll see small appliances, dishware, glassware, family clothing and toys. Just exactly what does Goodwill do? Well, how does providing jobs for those who may not otherwise be able to work? On one visit, we unearthed some great uses for some old-looking painted metal decorator tubs (with stands) in three different styles for just $9.99 each. Then, we crowed when we discovered a **MURANO** glass rooster for $14.99. These were the real genuine Venetian glass sculptures and at these prices, we bought two. If you're looking to make a donation, they have 26 attended drop-off locations throughout the Metroplex that are open seven days a week. Just about anything can be found. Clothing, household items, electronics, small sporting equipment, small accent pieces of furniture, small office equipment and small appliances. Don't expect large furniture or appliances. Goodwill does not accept them. Basically if you need a dolly to lift it or it won't fit in your car, they're probably not interested. This is a fairly new rule since large furniture was seen several months ago. Well, that was yesterday and today's a new day. You can also give by using your reward cards at Tom Thumb and Kroger and by designating Goodwill as your charity of choice. (You can also give by shopping through www.igive.com and designating Goodwill Dallas as your charity.) Although Goodwill is about to reach their 100th birthday (founded in 1902 in Boston), they've been in Dallas for 77 years. Check directory for the closest location and lend a helping hand. Every little bit helps. Remember, generosity begins at home.

Habitat for Humanity (ReStore)   214/827-9083
3020 Bryan   Mon-Fri 10-6; Sat 8-6
Dallas, TX 75204   www.dallas-habitat.org

Ready to sweat the good stuff? Then ReStore is the place for in-store savings on all your home improvement projects benefiting Habitat for Humanity. No spoils in this victory when savings abound on new and used appliances, doors, windows, tile, tubs, sinks, plumbing supplies, flooring, hardware, fixtures, wiring and more for any home improvement project. Illuminate the possibilities with 50 percent off wholesale prices on premium manufacturers' lighting. Lock down a good deal on door locks from names like **MASTER** and **SHLAGE** that start at just $2.99. Turn your house inside out with interior and exterior white paint for just $2.99/gallon. Open the door to savings with doors starting at just $2 and then the windows will open up a whole new world at just $8 and up. Pucker up to new 8- and 9-ft. garage doors for just 50 smackers. New **WHIRLPOOL** tubs were $400 and **CORIAN** sinks were $30. And remember, all purchases are tax deductible and donations are always welcome. In Dallas, look for their one-story warehouse three blocks east of Central Expressway or call for directions. Don't be shy. Now that you've helped yourself to some good deals, be sure to remember that shopping here helps others find a place to call home. The Dallas Habitat for Humanity started in 1995 and with their new goal of Vision 100, they plan to build 100 new houses per year for area families. Wanna help? Join Jimmy Carter and the rest of the helpful weekend warriors to build a better America. Call for information on how you can hammer away at providing low-income housing for the needy. Visit also their location at 3420 S. Grove St, Fort Worth, TX 76110-4307, call 817/926-3585 or visit online at www.habitat.org/restore.

★★★★★ Hope Chest   214/520-1087
4209 McKinney   Tues-Sat 10-5
Dallas, TX 75204

If there's hope, there's charity. And this thrift store could be your guiding light. New and gently used resale with all proceeds benefiting Hope Cottage (where parents are made through adoptions). Lots of babies, children's and maternity wear as you might expect. Donations are welcome. Now their parking lot sits on the property of my old office building on Fitzhugh. How the world turns. And as an adoptive mother myself, I feel even closer than most. Besides, where else would I suggest you fill up a hope chest than with the finds from here? It's worth a lifetime of happiness to lucky parents everywhere—with a little help from our community.

★★ Pennies From Heaven   214/823-5851
1605 N. Haskell   Tue-Sat 10-5
Dallas, TX 75204

Penny Pinchers might just find that their prayers have been answered. When you're feeling under the weather and want to bring a little sunshine back into your life, donate what you're not using to this charitable cause. Whether it's an item of value or your valuable time, you will be giving Pennies From Heaven without experiencing a thunder shower. Discounts on thrift goods such as clothing,dishes, small housewares, books, belts, shoes, furniture, bric-a-brac, books, lamps and whatnots arrive Tuesdays through Saturdays via the gracious generosity of others and recycled to those in search of a good deal. It's a win-win situation. And the pennies add up to dollars which goes to help Reconciliation Outreach, an organization that helps homeless women and children in the Metroplex. A worthwhile trip to this thrift shop for a worthwhile cause just might have you sitting on "Cloud Nine".

★★ Salvation Army
5554 Harry Hines
Dallas, TX 75235

214/630-5611
Mon-Sat 10-6
www.salvationarmy.org

We want you—to be a price-conscious shopper, that is. Even if it means stopping by the local Salvation Army to rummage around the boxes, shelves, racks and displays. You just never know what you'll find. The hunt is on for perfectly-priced clothing in sizes for men, women and children that are big, small, short and tall. Fall in love with the housewares, baskets, lamps, toys, bikes, furniture, small office equipment, yard tools and appliances and come out a winner. Win the war on high prices. One man's trash is another man's treasure, so just about anything goes here. And don't forget to give your unused items along with your spare change to the ringing bells during the Holiday Season. All those pennies you save at the store can be turned around and put to good use. Spare a dime? How about a hundred? A thousand? These days, anything goes. The Salvation Army is now accepting boats, cars, motorcycles and trailer donations. Don't forget it all goes to a worthy cause and every penny is tax deductible. This generosity could be your salvation come April 15th. Watch for their online store soon and if interested, you can donate online as well. Their website is internationally full of feature material and information on their charitable activities.

★★★★★ Trading Post
818 W. Main St.
Grand Prairie, TX 75050

972/263-7117
Mon-Sat 9:30-6; Sun 9:30-5

Mosey on over and put a stake at this station of value. Hear thee, pardner, the Trading Post exchanges quality merchandise for cash or trade. From TVs to VCRs, appliances, furniture, tools, whatever, it's all fair game. Dust if off, polish it up and bring it on in. New and used as long as it hasn't been abused. Merchandise changes frequently. Last month, washers and dryers tumbled in and cleared out. This month it was refrigerators and stoves changing the temperature in these here parts. Next month, it might be a stampede of CD players. (Now that would be music to my ears.) Ride 'em off into the sunset but before howling at the moon, be sure to pull on those heartstrings. Dress the part and round up your posse. Head out to the Trading Post where they'll wheel and deal their way into your heart. Don't dress in your finery; they might think you don't need to save money. From appliances to tools, electronics to housewares, **BEANIE BABIES** to animal bean bags, you'll roar with the best of them—both new and used. What fun, even if you're not Emily Post. Shop if for no other reason than to see a dying breed of bargain haunts.

51

Toys

★★★★★ **Constructive Playthings/U.S. Toy**   **972/418-1860**
1927 E. Belt Line   Mon-Fri 9-7; Sat 9-5; Sun 12-5
Carrollton, TX 75006   www.ustoyco.com

Party, party, let's have a party, smarty. And if you're one of us, you already know where to get your party, carnival, educational, seasonal, novelty decorations plus stuffed animals, balloons and more with one quick click of the mouse. No, not THAT mouse, your computer's mouse. When you enter their store, in person, via their catalogue, or online, you're a Mickey if you don't buy here. Most things are priced so low. How low? How does one cent low sound? So, if I could give you a penny for your thoughts, what would you say? "Happy Days" are here again and it's time for a celebration. Browse through three different divisions until you find the perfect ...whatever. The U.S. Toy Magic division is dedicated to promoting the wonders of the mysterious and fascinating world of magic. There's an an immense selection and a full line of challenging stage magic supplies, tricks, videos and magic books. Abracadabra! Move on, funny face and choose from a clowning section with videos, costumes, professional make-up and more. A lot more. Constructive Playthings is made up of the School Division and the Parent/Family Division, award-winning suppliers of the finest early childhood educational toys, equipment, books, records, tapes, videos, art supplies and teaching aids. They search the world and pick only those products that promote, enhance and enrich the growth of children. Want to stay home, no problem. Shop online. Or request a catalogue. It's as easy as 1-2-3, A-B-C, OK? *Call toll-free: 800/841-6478*

★★★★ **Discount Model Trains**   **972/931-8135**
4641 Ratliff Lane   Mon-Sat 10-6
Addison, TX 75248

I think I can, I think I can...well here, you definitely can!!! For an extensive website about toy trains, read all about it at www.trains.com. Then shop at this bricks and mortar store in Addison. Discount Model Trains, since 1989, has provided in-stock-year-round, over 60,000 G to Z scale items, with most products discounted 20 percent off manufacturers' suggested retail price. Only a small sampling of their inventory is available at www.trains.com where they have a presence. Most things in the current *Walther's Catalog* plus hard-to-find and unique items are either in-stock or readily available from here. Nothing gets run over without notice from this couple who decided to retire over 10 years ago, yet still are going strong. Model trains in sizes H (the most popular size requested), N and G, too, hit the tracks with brand names like **ARISTOCRAFT**, **ATLAS** and **CATO**. Located just around the corner from the Wilson Building on the right, pull into the parking lot and follow the signs. Track your savings while you shoot the breeze with the Peterson's. Not only do they offer the largest selection of model railroad equipment in town, they also have the scenery and glue to put your railroad depot on the map. Expect to hop aboard with a starter set starting around $80, all the way up to $8,000. To keep on track, be sure to get on their newsletter list. *Call toll-free: 800/387-2460*

★★★★ Doll Village

817/329-1333
Fri & Sat 10-5 or By Appt.

1110 E. Northwest Hwy.
Grapevine, TX 76001

Reduced from seven rooms to four with the addition of a sale room with specials like "buy one, get one free" and 40 percent off selected items, how can you not make out like the Frito Bandito. Two days for browsers, or by appointments for serious shoppers, now, that makes sense. Owner Nancy Csolk has been a collector herself for well over a quarter of a century. So, she knows her stuff. You're not buying from some rummy out to sell you a doll, dummy. She is considered a doll connoisseur and maintains an inventory of hundreds of doll babies waiting for a new home. Doll furniture is used but not in abused condition. New furniture is extremely pricey and few folks can afford it. So, why not buy used? The kids won't know the difference. All the same coveted dolls line the shelves like: **ANNETTE HIMSTEDT**, **DADDY'S LONG LEGS**, **EFFANBEE**, **MADAME ALEXANDER**, **MATTEL**, **MIDDLETON**, **RAIKES BEARS**, **ROLANDA HEIMER**, **XAVIER ROBERTS** plus certified one-of-a-kinds, porcelains, antique, artist dolls, doll clothing, furniture, collector doll and bear books and of course, there's **BARBIE**. When summer comes, she never forgets to have a Barbie Q! If it does take a village to sell dolls, Doll Village contains a mixture of collectibles and wooden dolls, porcelains and hand-crafted dolls and high-class dolls like **GOETZ**, **LUNA BABIES** and **ZWERGNASE** (Zwergnase are German dolls by artist Nicole Marshcholland that look like real children ranging in price from $500-$1,500.) Only 250 are made per series. Doll Village is located on the corner of Dallas Road and Hwy. 114 business exit. Oh, you beautiful doll.

★★★★★ Dolls of Yesterday & Today

972/242-8281
Wed-Sat 10:30-4:30
www.dollsoldandnew.com

1014 S. Broadway, # 108
Carrollton, TX 75006

Hello Dolly. Say hello to hundreds of current and discontinued **MADAME ALEXANDER'S** in stock Great prices on clearance **BARBIES**, **GENES** and **TONNER'S**, too. They are such experts, they can provide an Alexander appraisal as well. Looking for dolls, well, how can you keep them in boxes forever? Put them in an upright position on a doll stand and show them off! They have a large library of collectors' books and catalogs available for sale. All of the books are in new condition. You'll find **ALEXANDER BABIES**, **ANN & ANDY**, **RAGGEDY ANN & ANDY**, and other vintage dolls that only get better with age. Yeah! Want a play doll or a bear to hug? They've got them, too. Did you miss the Jackie White House fashions' exhibit? No problem. You can still buy fabulou **JACKIE** dolls online and at their overstock clearance price. Wow! Since 1981, Marilyn and A. Scott Dundon have made shopping for dolls a state-of-the-heart. Shopping online is a cinch. FREE shipping on U.S. orders of $100 Layaway available.

■ econotrain.com

24/7
www.econotrain.com

I've seen it all. A knock-off of **THOMAS THE TANK**®. Since 1951, Sandy Walkes has been in and around the toy business in some capacity. In fact, he's got lots of family members involved in helping fans of pre-school toys save money. Wood trains are his passion. All of his toys are based on "play value" which are considered the highest quality yet fairly priced. Since they are both the manufacturer and the importer, they sell the toys at the same price they sell to retailers. They offer 46 train and train accessory products on their website but are growing by leaps and bounds. Besides that, in 1997, they entered into an agreement with Brio® Corporation, which allows them to say that their components are compatible to Brio® components. Truer words were never spoken. They are not, in any way, affiliated with Brio® Corporation. Same goes with the sought-after **THOMAS THE TANK**® wooden trains distributed by Learning Curve International. But their components are compatible. Children love **THOMAS THE TANK**® trains for their names and beautiful faces. When you want to add to a **THOMAS THE TANK**® layout, compare their prices for track, switches, track-side accessories, bridges, tunnels, etc, to theirs. Their tracks don't go "Clickity-Clack." You'll love them. If you don't agree that their quality is superior to Thomas, then send the toys back. So, what are you saving? How about 50 percent off or more off Brio's® selling prices. How do they do it? You'll eliminate the middleman, multi-million dollar advertising campaigns and no royalties (sometimes up to 25 percent) to designers or inventors. Plus, remember, you pay for those elaborate four-color boxes you see on retail shelves. Eliminate the box, you eliminate that expense, too. Your toys come in a poly bag, or in a plain undecorated box. And listen to this assurance! If you buy a toy and are disappointed, return it within 30 days for a full refund, either to your credit card or a check if you've paid cash. No hassle. No questions! Hurray! FREE shipping to all 50 states. A $50 minimum purchase is required. All toys have been kid-tested and mother-approved.

★★ Game Exchange   972/420-4263
1118 W. Main   Mon-Fri 11-8; Sat 11-6; Sun Noon-5
Lewisville, TX 75067

If you love me, you'll stop playing games. If you love to play games and would rather shop for them at a discount, here's an opportunity to have it your way.

★★★★★ K-B Toys Outlet Store   254/582-1052
Prime Outlet Center at Hillsboro   Mon-Sat 10-8; Sun 11-6
104 I-35 NE   www.kbtoys.com
Hillsboro, TX 76645

It's A-OK at K-B Toys if you're looking for the ABCs of gift-giving. Thousands of toys, collectible toys, video games and software titles at great prices. You'll have no problem finding what you want. Browse the main departments: Toys, Software, Video Games, Collectibles or just land at the Outlet. Or if you prefer, simply shop by Age, Price or Brand. It's so simple a child could do it! If you're looking for a birthday or holiday gift, visit the Gift Center. Find expert gift advice and specially-created Gift Guides. Can't resist a bargain? Check out the "Surprise of the Day"–and don't miss their "Great Values". Thousands of items in every brand: **BARBIE**, **CRAYOLA**, **FISHER-PRICE**, **LITTLE TIKES**, **POKÉMON**, **RADIO FLYER**, **STAR WARS**, trading cards, it's like being in a candy store without it being fattening. If you need to return or exchange a product, you can take it to one of the 1,300 KB Toys stores nationwide. Since they recently purchased the eToys name, features and merchandise, there is nary a toy that can't be found. Watch for new features like "Wish List" and "Gift Wrap" coming soon. *Call toll-free: 877/522-8697*

★★★ Merrill Discount Trampolines   972/424-2285
1909 Hillcrest   Mon-Sat 9-5
Plano, TX 75074   www.discounttrampolines.com

Jump around, turn around and do a pirouette. Jump upon the only discount trampoline source in town, be it round or rectangle. Since they represent a company who manufactures them locally, you'll be a jumping bean in no time. Both new and used models available, from $300-$500. They're the only dealer in the U.S.A to carry the **JUMP KING** European model, a rectangular 9 x 15-foot model with heavy-duty pads, brand new for $550. *Call toll-free: 800/449-3598*

★★★★ Not Just Dolls

2447 Gus Thomasson
Dallas, TX 75228

214/321-0412
Tue-Sat 10-5
www.notjustdollsdallas.com

Oh, you beautiful doll, you great big beautiful doll. But if you think there's just dolls, think again. Since 1988, they have been the doll-babies of choice with one of the largest selections in Texas. Consider any one of them part of the family and add generations to your collection. From **ANNETTE HIMSTEDT'S** to **DADDY'S LONG LEGS**, **MADAME ALEXANDER** to **MARIE OSMOND**, take your pick and adopt them all. Line up the beauties. **BARBIE 2000** and **2001** were waiting to be picked up while **ANNETTE FUNICELLO BEARS** and **BEANIE BABIES** were waiting to be hugged. Please don't leave without some doll furniture. A doll house is not a home without it. After all, girls do not live on clothes alone. Their dolls also need an appropriate living environment including a single wicker stroller for taking your doll out for a walk ($58) to a cloth double stroller for twins, starting at $59. Not Just Dolls provides a home for both antique and new dolls, porcelains to ones with just pretty faces. Other collectibles included **EFFANBEE**, **GINNY**, **GOTZ**, **JERRI**, **LEE MIDDLETON** and **MUFFY** dolls, too. Prices are excellent but beware as they are co-mingled with retail prices on lots of accessories like doll cases, trunks and stands.

★★★★★ Toys From the Attic

2159 Buckingham Rd.
Richardson, TX 75081

972/671-0770
Mon-Fri 10-6; Sat 10-8; Sun Noon-5

If you want to buy a toy, lots of luck getting through the busy signal. Maybe it was trouble on their line, or maybe **THOMAS THE TANK**® was off line. However, when all's clear, these folks are on the right track. Somewhere throughout their 2,000-square-feet of collectibles, hard-to-find, unusual, current and popular toys, surely something will delight every little girl and boy. Dive into this treasure trove and reel in the steals. Who cares if they were enjoyed before. And not just toys, either, but baby equipment like car seats, cribs, baby swings, toddler beds, high chairs, strollers—pretty much anything a baby cries for. Then, for the backyard, there's the sandboxes and cozy coupe cars. Or what about dining al fresco on a **FISHER PRICE** picnic table? Located at the northwest corner of Buckingham and Jupiter, if you play your cards right, you'll find a veritable variety that will delight any child, from infants to when toys become a thing of the past and are then packed away for posterity.

52

Travel

★★★★★ **Best Fares Discount Travel Magazine**   **817/261-6114**
PO Box 170129   www.bestfares.com
Arlington, TX 76003

Tom, Tom, the Travelin' Man. If you've seen him once, you've seen him a million times. He's every media's travel guru spewing out the latest hidden fares or best buys from Point A to Point B. If you want to be in the know, go to his website, sign up for his magazine, and be the travel shopper in the driver's seat. Membership is still $59.90 which will give you the maximum in travel benefits: 12 issues of *Best Fares Magazines*, the lowest prices on airfare, hotel, car rental and cruise discounts and more. Plus, you'll receive a valuable coupon entitling you to a $99 companion fare certificate, four FREE one-class upgrade certificates and all the information you can digest in one seating. Find discounts of up to 70 percent off rack rates at more than 6,000 hotels around the world. Receive your FREE copy of Tom's 446-page *Insider Travel Secrets* book and beat the travel industry at their own game. Even if you forgo membership in the club, there are plenty of non-member deals for the general public. Check out "Snooze you Lose," "Seniors Special" and "Internet Only" specials for over 200 deals to whet your wandering appetite. But remember, time is of the essence. *Call toll-free: 800/880-1234*

 Cheap Tickets   **800/877-1265**
                                                                    24/7
                                                      www.cheaptickets.com

No beating around the bush, this is one of the best airfare discounters around. For the past 15 years or so, I have been trying to get through their 800-lines and have often been close to thinking it would be faster driving than waiting for an operator to answer. But, now, things are different. Their website has relieved a lot of the extra frustration and if you can travel to New York City for $172, Sacramento for $234 or Cancun for $343—I'd say you've got a hum-dinger. Yes, that's round-trip. They're not just dropping you off and leaving you stranded. Affordable travel made easy has generated countless of satisfied customers. All major airlines are represented. If they're flying, there's a cheap ticket out there, somewhere, somehow. All transactions are secure and include additional options at equally appealing prices for rental cars, hotels and cruises. "Spend your money there—not getting there!" There are more than 1 million non-published discount airfares that are offered on 40 airlines through Cheap Tickets. You'll leave on a regularly-scheduled flight from major airports in the United States, Europe, Asia and South America. No, you're not leaving from an airstrip out in no man's land. Hundreds of thousands of repeat customers and more than nine million registered website users are committed to flying via a Cheap Ticket. Specials and customer service also ensures a perfect take-off and landing each and every time. Create a customer profile, and get all your personal requests—like I always request a bulkhead seat, a special meal and a strong he-man sitting next to me.

D-FW Tours	**972/980-4540**
7616 LBJ Frwy., Suite 524	24 Hours
Dallas, TX 75241	www.dfwtours.com

Established in 1978 as a wholesale tour operator, today they are one of the largest volume airline consolidators. Don't be fooled by the localized name. These guys can fly you anywhere, except the moon. Buckle your seat belt, put your chair in an upright position, and it's up, up and away. Having contracts with over 35 major air carriers, D-FW Tours offers the almighty discounted consolidator fares (those are the fares that the airlines sell off to third parties for seats that have gone unsold). Anywhere you want to go, except the moon for the time being, there's a flight for it. Destinations are worldwide from more than 200 U.S. departure cities. Online, you'll find a scheduled airline service (no charter airlines count) at wholesale rates. It doesn't get better than this. Most international fares are sold as air only, and most require no advance purchase. Some routes allow one-way travel, and first and business class fares are available in some markets. D-FW Tours also offers senior, student, military, missionary and child fare discounts. (Shopping missions were unacceptable. I tried!) International published sale fare-matching is permitted for select carriers and destinations. Visit them online to request a fare quote, to book a reservation and for information on domestic tours and reservation policies. To show you how significant online travel has grown, in 1999, D-FW Tours issued over 68,000 tickets, with gross sales of over $51 million. In the first quarter of 2000, sales were up 52 percent over the same period last year. D-FW is one of the five founding companies of Travel Services International, Inc. TSI was established to create the leading single source distributor of specialized leisure travel services and in April, 2000, TSI, Inc. became part of the UK-based Airtours PLC and hence became the largest vacation packager in the world. Still, with all the dollars involved, I still did not see an indication of secured shopping. Be sure to ask before giving them your credit card number. You can also shop by phone. ***Call toll-free: 800/527-2589***

◆◆◆◆◆ **Hartmann Travel**	**972/392-9797**
7616 LBJ Frwy., Suite 421	Mon-Fri 8:30-6
Dallas, TX 75251	www.hartmanntravel.com

Since opening their doors in 1993, Hartmann has taken off. Focusing on the needs of the traveler through a personalized approach to service, this could be the difference between flying high and landing without a hitch. Their goal at this agency is to help you select and prepare for your vacation or business trip by creating an experience that equals or exceeds your expectations. From white water rafting, deep sea diving, hiking and African safaris, to mountain climbing and dude ranches, your adventure awaits you. Looking for a trip on short notice? You'll find their weekly specials are always a great bye-bye! Be sure to check out their up-to-date specials online which you may take notice, with or without packing. They find it a challenge to match up dreams and budget to give you the best value for your dollar. They will even schedule after-hour and weekend appointments, if that's the only way for you to go. With all the click-and-shop-only operations, this is the pause that refreshes. I mean, one traveler had to leave within the hour and her tickets were hand-delivered to her as her car was pulling out the driveway. That's service where both parties ended smiling. (LOL) ***Call toll-free: 800/577-1960***

▪ Help-U-Move,Inc.
131 Bishopwood Dr.
Jupiter, FL 33458

561/625-6683
Mon-Fri 9-5 EST
www.helpumove.com

This is a way to go from point A to point B without hiring a moving company. In fact, they are the rental truck alternative. Listen up. If you want to save money on moving, you load and unload, and they'll do the driving. It's the low cost, hassle-free alternative to a rental truck or an expensive full service mover. Save time and money—'course you do the bulk of the work. But really, the most expensive part of the move is the driver and the truck. Cost it out and see how much money you can save over a traditional moving company. They utilize some of the best trucks in the industry and can be particularly cost-effective if you're moving a long distance. Compare the prices and leave the driving to them. How do they do it? First, they deliver a 28-ft. trailer to your home, storage facility or other loading point, giving you enough time to load it. From one hour, several hours, overnight or over the weekend, you decide. You load and secure your furniture and other belongings and you only pay for the space you actu-ally use. When you're finished, they pick up the loaded trailer and move it back to the terminal where they load commercial goods such as computers, TV's or VCR's into the empty space that remains. And then, they're off. Your shipment is driven to your new hometown where it will be held at their nearby terminal until you are ready to move your belongings into your new home. If the trailer arrivers before you do, don't worry; they will hold your goods at the terminal for two days, worry and cost FREE. Lastly, you unload the trailer and call them to pick it up. That's it in a nutshell. Look, I'm only the messenger. You can save money, my friends. FREE estimates online or via phone.

▪ Hotel Reservations Network
8140 Walnut Hill Lane, Suite 203
Dallas, TX 75231

214/361-7311
Mon-Fri 8-6
www.hoteldiscount.com

After they were acquired by a big online travel site, Hotel Reservations Network instantly became the Internet's primary source for discount accommodations worldwide, with savings up to 65 percent off regular hotel rates in some of the world's most popular and expensive cities. Of course, now talking to Bob Diener, one of the founders, is beyond the realm of possibilities. He's prob-ably curled up with a good book in a suite at the Plaza. But if you want to travel in style and stay in all the right places, this Internet booking service is for you. What a way to go. Now, you, too can stay over where "leaving the light on" isn't so important. Yes, some of best rooms can be booked, from medium to the best, both quickly and efficiently. Compare price, quality, location, amenities and availability of hotel rooms, then make your reservation which is confirmed in just seconds. Through its affiliate program, they are partnered with over 4,000 travel-related Internet sites, which offer dis-count hotel rooms through HRN's booking engine. Check out discount accommodations in more than 2,500 premier properties in over 90 major destinations in the U.S., Europe, the Caribbean, Canada and Hong Kong including New York, Boston, San Francisco, Orlando, Miami, London, Frankfurt, Toron-to and Vancouver BC. The only way they could improve is to offer travelers Frequent Flyer miles. Well, your wish is their command. Now you can qualify to earn 500 Frequent Flyer Miles when booking accommodations with this site on **DELTA**, **NORTHWEST**, **TWA**, **CONTINENTAL** or **USAIR**. *Forbes Magazine* named them one of the best on the web, and Sue Goldstein already named them a 5-star contender years before. One night at San Francisco's upscale Mark Hopkins InterContinental for $260, as opposed to the going rate of $349 made me a believer. If you ever get lost on the site, Hotel Discounts' toll-free reservations service helps you out of the maze. But that rarely happens; the online reserva-tion's process is relatively straightforward and hassle-free. Hotel Discounts also features a host of other useful applications, such as a currency converter and links to informative city guides. Hey, what about our Top 10 bargain shops in those cities? Log on to our website and shop our favorites in cities across the world. Their newest acclaim is a separate website for four- and five-star luxury hotels, www.all-luxuryhotels.com. It's the ultimate way-to-go! *Call toll-free: 800/964-6835*

★★★★★ Snowballers Tours   817/335-SNOW
1500 W. 5th St., Suite 5A
Fort Worth, TX 76102

I don't have a snowball's chance in you know where to ever make it beyond the Bunny Slope. But whatever your skill, there's only one way to go—up. And there's only one way to get there and— that's down. Unless you're got a friend who pilots a helicopter, this is an inexpensive way to go. Snowballers Tour is a Metroplex tradition that makes that downhill slope less slippery. All you have to do is join the club. They make ski trips affordable by providing group rates without hefty membership fees. Just put down a deposit when you sign up for one of the multiple trips this group arranges each year. Ski outings and other options available, too, with prices usually always under $400, with many in the $250-$300 range per person. Getting there is half the fun. Travel varies from sleeper bus to a 727 charter jet. Destinations include Crested Butte, Squaw Valley, Mount Rose and Taos. Since 1972, this club has been satisfying many skiers regardless of proficiency. Even if you're a master of hot toddies, you're welcome. Since trips sell out even before the season gets underway, get on the list so you can make that downhill journey for less. *Call toll-free: 800/SNO-SKII*

53

Windows & Walls

★★★★ Artistic Design
1322 Levee St
Dallas, TX 75207

214/742-1996
Mon-Fri 9-5; Sat Appt. Only

Design Resource and Remodeling on Dragon Street is now Artistic Design and has relocated to a new address for all your decorating desires. Wishful thinking? Not any more. Casey still reigns supreme as the interior design guru. And this is how she works step by step. Simply bring her a magazine picture of a room that you admire. She will not only duplicate the window treatments but the upholstery, bedding and walls as well! Although they have stopped selling blinds, you can find an amazing array of fabrics for every room, and they can even do special designs on your walls! Just come in a browse through amples of samples. Wholesale to the public in the Dallas Design District is no big deal, you say? Well, try going into a retail showroom at the Design Center and see what the going rate is. Everything here is sold at practically 40 percent off MSRP plus shipping charges. Casey goes to bat for you with an hourly rate of $75 for an in-home consultation and installation depends on products and services. Dreaming of that perfect room where every piece complements each other right down to the walls and floors? Then wake up, little Susie, and meet your artistic alter ego!

★★★★★ Blind Alley
7211 Authon Drive
Dallas, TX 75248

972/404-1944
Mon-Sun 8 AM-9 PM
www.blindsonthenet.com

You won't have to worry if I recommend you travel down this Blind Alley. All you really have to do is keep your eyes wide open for the savings of 65-80 percent on window treatments like blinds and shutters. Since 1993, this company's been making house calls or you can visit their north Dallas showroom for an onsite birdseye view. Another option these days is to shop online at their website www.BlindsOn-TheNet.com. FREE installation with the purchase of 10 or more blinds within the Dallas, Plano, Richardson, Allen, Rowlett, or McKinney areas. They carry all major brands of blinds, shades and arches (except those that fall). Let them bid on any specific product and see how low they will go. How to measure doesn't take a Ph.D., so let them tell you how to do-it-yourself. This year, they're not only selling window treatments like two-inch wood blinds, pleated and double-cell shades, mini-blinds, verticals, arches and shutters, but carpet and upholstery, too. Name brands like **HUNTER-DOUGLAS** can be relied on for quality with the Blind Alley leading the way. The newest in wood blinds and wood shutters with premium woods are now also available. What do you have to lose? The finest brands, the finest materials, the finest fabrics and all at discounted prices. No more of the blind, leading the blind. *Call toll-free: 888/243-6974*

★★★★ Blind Connection, The   214/731-1599
Dallas, TX   By Appt.

Susan is waiting with baited bargain breath, ready to remedy all those interior aches and panes! While you won't find anything in-stock, you can custom order blinds and shades from **TIMBERLAND BLINDS**, **ROYAL**, **KIRSCH**, **SKANDIA** and others. A standard wood 32" x 72" blind in white wood will cost $99 and slightly more if you prefer a little color. No curtains or draperies can be found hanging around, but if you are in need of window hardware, there's hardly a better place to connect. With discounts ranging up to 75 percent off, color your budget...happy. *Call toll-free: 877/708-3361*

★★★★ Blind Place, The   972/881-0201
601 W. Parker, Suite 105   Mon-Fri 10-6; Sat 10-4
Plano, TX 75074

Owner Clarence Stark will gladly walk you through the wonders of window treatments. From blinds and shades to draperies and swags, this is your one stop shop for all your window needs. With savings of 80 percent off MSRP, a standard wood blind, measuring 32" x 72" was only $105 (higher than the Blind Connection!) Bring in your favorite magazine picture and see what materializes. There's nothing like custom-made to make a house a home. Find names like **HUNTER-DOUGLAS** and **SKANDIA**. The Blind Place is solely a place for custom work, so don't expect instant gratification. Everything must be ordered; home estimates are FREE and no installation charges on orders over 10 windows. With 90 days same as cash, every little extension helps.

★★ Blind Spot   972/669-1383
2067 N. Central Expwy.   Mon-Fri 9-5:30
Richardson, TX 75080

Are you seeing spots? If so, correct it immediately with designer names like **DEL MAR**, **KIRSCH**, **LEVOLOR**, **SKANDIA** and **TIMBERLAND BLINDS**. Any room in your house that has a window is a candidate for custom window treatments. Bring in a magazine picture and Dorothy will work her magic. Find a variety of savings depending upon the manufacturer. For example: get 75 percent off Skandia MSRP. A standard wood-stained, wood blind measuring 32" x 72" will cost you $108.75. While there is no cost for an in-home estimate, there is a cost for installation. First the trip charge of $22 plus $6 per blind and $4/foot for draperies, then buy a swag...and brag! *Call toll-free: 800/527-4585*

★★★ Casa Linda Draperies   214/388-4721
4111 Elva Ave.   Mon-Fri 8-5
Dallas, TX 75227   www.altavista.com

The saying here is "Mi Casa su Casa." Elaine, a highly qualified interior designer, will ring your doorbell with over 300 books of manufacturers and fabrics like **GRABER**, **HUNTER-DOUGLAS**, **KIRSCH**, **SCHUMACHER/WAVERLY** and others for you to browse through FREE of charge. She will gladly design a room for you or simply help you place your own designs into action. From window treatments and hardware to bedding, pillows and slip covers, get everything for a dazzling new room all under one roof. They can also contract for help with floors and wallpaper. You'll find 30-40 percent off fabrics with various other discounts depending upon manufacturer. Installation fees are incorporated so you won't be left hanging out alone on the shelf.

Christy's Resale Drapes   **972/403-1543**
Antiqueland   Mon-Wed 10-6; Thurs-Sat 10-8; Sun 10-6
1300 Custer @ 15th
Plano, TX 75075

Christy's is located inside Antiqueland at 258 Broadway.(the front left corner) If you think you've heard it all, you haven't. This is the newest category to enter the resale marketplace, and long overdue. But first a note to those wanting to sell; you must make an appointment with Christy, although the store may be open, she may not be there, and if she's not, you won't have the opportunity to sell your goods until she returns. Though we might have to rewrite the "Planet of the Drapes," this is the origin of smart shopping. You'll be surprised how often a home buyer will discard the previous owner's drapes so they can replace them with ones that better suit their color scheme. Or, replace them with hard treatments like blinds or shutters. It's often the first thing to go. Too formal. Too informal. Too fussy. Too classy. Change to blinds. Add shutters. Want balloon shades. Okay, but what to do with those drapes? Turn them over to Christy. Her store inside Antiqueland's in Plano, where naturally, the housing boom is busting at the seams. Ninety-five percent of her inventory has been custom-made. Of course, this is Plano, remember? All sizes, toppers, panels, tassels, rods, shower curtains, Roman shades, you never know what "Window of Opportunity" is waiting for a transfer of ownership. Prices are particularly pleasing. A topper or cornice board may start as low as $50 to $300 for a floor to ceiling beauty. Hang out with the best. Stylish and affordable drapery treatments that look like new including dust ruffles, cornice boards, valances--just less expensive ways to dress up your windows, protect your privacy, and ensure you keep out the riff-raff. Let's talk savings! A king-size duvet, matching sheets, pillow shams and five pillows was priced at $75 for the whole she-bang, part of an estate sale in Arkansas. This is typical of the possibilities. Among the brands hanging around were **KRAVETS**, **SCALAMONDRE**, **RALPH LAUREN**, **SCHUMACHER**, and more. Then for the baby's room, you should see the adorable draperies and matching wall hangings I got for Hannah Rose's room. Too cute! So cheap!

Claire & Co.   **214/752-7474**
1400 Turtle Creek Blvd., Suite 137   Mon-Fri 9-5 Preferably By Appt.
Dallas, TX 75207   www.claireandco.com

Willowy, billowy, and pillowy are just a trio of words to describe this custom shoppe's repertoire. Voted best in draperies locally and now named to the TOP 10 "To Die For" by the BBB's (biggerbetterbargains's) staff, rest assured, these women are top drawer in the "Harlequin" Romance department. Pillows, tableskirts, lampshades——like I've said, decorative accessories including a custom cover-up for a water cooler. Unusual trims you haven't seen before, fabrics from the sublime to the extravagant, custom bedding, swags and valances over a headboard or to make a dramatic statement in the grand room. Creating luxury looks by giving your home the royal treatments, that's what they're all about.

★★★★ Creative Shutters   **972/423-3967**
2700 Avenue K, Suite 500   Mon-Fri 8-4; Sat- By Appt.
Plano, TX 75074   www.gtesupersite.com/cshutters/

Creatively speaking, you might shutter at the thought of putting anything but Creative Shutters on your windows. Their quality is their hallmark along with great prices. These window covering experts use only northern bass wood for their window coverings to ensure a superb finish. They offer custom designed window fittings, French and patio doors along with bay windows as well as their own brand of beautifully-crafted Plantation shutters. This family-operated business offers a range of services to enhance your windows, including wood blinds, pleated shades, Roman shades, single-cell and double-cell shades. In addition, they offer FREE in-home consultations and estimates as well as a lifetime manufacturers' warranty. Shutters here are not only top-quality, custom interior shutters, they are also energy-efficient and economical—the ultimate in privacy and security. Their Plantation shutters are hand-crafted exclusively at their Plano, Texas plant. Renowned for meticulous color matching, you'll get a custom decorator look in every room. With professional installation, lifetime manufacturers' warranty, and very competitive pricing, it's a cinch to see why Creative Shutters is the complete window-covering specialist. Feel free to contact them for a tour of their facility and see for yourself the craftsmanship that goes into each of their window treatment in progress. It's like being at the car wash, only the final product is a Creative Shutter.

★★★★★ Curtain Exchange, The   214/350-3045

Inwood Village   www.thecurtainexchange.com
5470 West Lovers Lane
Dallas, TX 75209

It's curtains on custom draperies here. A concept whose time has come, this new money-saver lets you hang it all out...from previously draped curtains. Seen in *Southern Accents* and *Metropolitan Home*, The Curtain Exchange is expanding across America with franchisees who offer shoppers a cost-effective, high-quality, and immediate solution to their window covering needs. Why wait? You can even take them home for their famous 48-hours hanging test. All have been custom-made and rather than taking a small fabric swatch home to see if the color works, take the entire drapery treatment with you and see what materializes. They also sell new draperies in fabulous silk colors: toffee, mocha, cinnamon, vanilla, raspberry, cherry, Merlot and plum if you've got your color scheme picked out. This is The Curtain Exchange...beautiful, ready-made draperies in all kinds of colors and designs, from solid silk taffetas, to sophisticated stripes and plaids, to delicate printed cotton florals. They also have both consigned and gently-hung to brand-new original designs. Bring in your measurements and save time and money. They're cool. They're eclectic. They're artsy. They're sophisticated. They're elegant. They're funky. It's curtains. And they're ready and willing to make the move and hang out at your house. Based in New Orleans, it all started with an advertisement in the 1996 New Orleans Junior League Showhouse by interior designer, Georgina Callan, advertising custom-made curtains for sale. When the phone began ringing off the wall, people not only wanted new draperies, they wanted to get rid of the old. The first franchise was opened in Baton Rouge, Louisiana, in August 1998; the rest is history.

★★ Custom Coordinates   817/498-7353

4709 Colleyville Blvd., #500   Mon-Fri 10-6, Sat 10-5
Colleyville, TX 76034

Traveling the road to Colleyville is getting bigger and better. Custom Coordinates in that local conduit to coordinating all of your home interiors. Super friendly and ready to assist with every question, they offer **WAVERLY** fabrics and more. You can also find **GRABER**, **HUNTER-DOUGLAS**, **KIRSCH** and **LEVOLOR** window blinds and hardware. Choose your coordinates: wallpaper, fabrics, draperies, bedspreads, furniture, blinds or shades. In-home estimates and consultations require a $75 fee and installation charges depend on your purchases. The discounts are par for the course (nobody pays retail these days.) Based on the manufacturer, you can save, for example, 40 per cent off Hunter-Douglas wood blinds...expect to pay $242 for a standard 32" x 72" window. Definitely more than others in this chapter. But coordinating patterns for different accents and accessories are what make this company somebody to C. Waverly's the main name here with 50 percent off all in-stock patterns (and there were over 100 to choose from) but the rest of the fabric and wallpaper offerings were a mere 20 percent off. Mini-blinds were blind-sidingly discounted up to 70 percent off. If you want to borrow their sample books, it'll cost you a $25 deposit (just in case you never return it and they've got to pay to replace it). However, don't expect overdue notices to be sent. Books are due back the next day, promise.

★★★★★ Dallas Draperies
214/654-0177; 214/65
2970 Blystone
Mon-Fri 9-5; Sat 9-2
Dallas, TX 75220

Talk about good karma! What goes around, comes around. And around the corner from this factory, a magic genie surfaces. Shop this outlet showroom if you want to save up to 70 percent on custom-made window treatments and bedding. During special sales, expect to pick up fabric slashed to 90 percent off. This decorating dynasty has been custom-making draperies, top treatments, swags, cornices, valances, bedspreads, pillows and more for as long as I've been writing books. Having their own in-house workroom keeps costs to a bare minimum and for a custom fit, it's the only way to go. Ever try to keep those sheets on a pillowtop mattress? They also sell **GRABER** mini-blinds, verticals, duettes, roman and balloon shades, shutters and more. In stock bedspreads, blow out the door for $29.95 (an occasional windfall.) They also do headboards, fabric walls and upholstery with your choice of over 25,000 square yards of fabric as low as $4.99 square yard. Visit their Plano showroom on Central Expressway @ 15th., 972/881-0233, if more convenient.

★★ Designer Draperies Floors & Furniture
817/451-6890
5324 Brentwood Stair Rd.
Mon-Fri 9-5:30; Sat By Appt. Only
Fort Worth, TX 76112
www.flexsteel.com

Max and Beverly are reigning supreme as the "designing duo" of Fort Worth. Their motto, "You want it, we have it!" Find quality furniture with names like **ESTATE HOUSE** and **FLEXSTEEL**. You can see what's here ahead of the curve if you simply check the possibilities at www.flexsteel.com. Adorn your eyelids of the great indoors with window hardware from **GRABER**, **HUNTER-DOUGLAS** and **KIRSCH** and add the touch and whisper of luxurious fabrics from **ROBERT ALLEN**, **WESTGATE** and **WAVERLY**—all favorites of designing women. Lengthy in-home estimates do require a minimum of a $50 charge while installation fees depend on the individual products and services chosen. You will find that everyday prices are lower than "below MSRP" promised elsewhere! With up to six months same as cash and all major credit cards accepted, what are you waiting for? So if your eyes are sore, soothe them with fresh designs, bright colors and a new landscape, indoors of course!

Draperies & More
972/353-2672
1565 W. Main St., Suite 220
Mon-Fri 10-6; Sat 10-4:30
Lewisville, TX 75067

When you wish upon a star, don't forget to include Draperies and More into your dreams. After thumbing through enough decorator magazines to earn a place in the *Guinness Book of Records*, pick your favorites and dream on. Then take those dreams and have Karen Moore (though she does *more* than others in her field of dreams) whip up a drapery treatment or a bedding ensemble that looks just like the ones that retail for thousands for a fraction of the price. 'tis true, 'tis true, there is a fabric fairy that can make dreams come true. Whether you shop her Lewisville shop that will WOW you when you walk in, or her Carrollton location at 3733 Josey Lane, Carrollton, Texas, 972/394-4893, you can expect the most extensive and some of the most creative window treatments and matching or coordinating ensembles in the Metroplex. This is it. Don't even look elsewhere. Head to the corner of Garden Ridge and Main, you'll see horizontal and vertical blinds, shutters, carpet, custom furniture, reupholstery, custom draperies and shades. Hang out with brand names from **CAROLE**, **GRABER**, **HUNTER-DOUGLAS**, **KASHMIR**, **RALPH LAUREN**, **ROBERT ALLEN** and **WESCO**. Deck the walls with grand names in wall coverings such as **IMPERIAL** and **YORK**. Discounts soar to 70-80 percent off list price on wood blinds, PVC blinds, mini-blinds, vertical blinds, pleated shades; up to 30 percent off fabric/lining on valances and window treatments; 10 percent off comforter sets; 30 percent off carpet and wallpaper. Shop 'til you drop off to sleep in either custom or ready-made spreads (even her ready-mades are to die for!) Here, you've got it made in the shade!

★★★★★ Dungan's Floors/Blinds & More   972/562-9444

1434 N. Central Expwy., Suite 109   Tue-Fri 8:30-5:30; Sat 10-4
McKinney, TX 75070   www.ccvm.com/dungan's_floors/index.html

Explain the phenomenon where a husband and wife can stay happily married for more than 20 (or is it 30?) years, raise a family, and corner the McKinney market on window and floor coverings, too. What is their secret? They should package them and make a fortune, too. They certainly have the bull by the horn and can put a wrench into any merchant trying to horn in on their territory. They're one of the originators of custom tile on both floors and counter-tops, laying imaginative patterns that you'd only see in million-dollar mansions. Let them install **ARMSTRONG**, **BRUCE**, **MANNINGTON**, **PHILADELPHIA** and **SALEM** carpet and hardwoods. Choose adobe, brick, ceramic tile, hardwoods or laminates. It's a never-ending tribute to overwhelming you with options. There's the newest stain-resistant fibers, custom ceramic tiles to match your wallcoverings, to match your back splash, to match your...whatever. Then, if you're not satisfied showing your flooring to your neighbors peeking through the front windows, cover them up with a myriad of window coverings. They're noted for being a one-stop three-S store: Style, Selection and Service = Savings. Another plus, they maintain their own installation crews and Lou Jenkins is a master craftsman himself. Lennie's the decorator and together, they make quite a team. FREE estimates and doing it right the first time out of the box will ultimately save you time, money and aggravation. Bruce hardwood flooring started at $6 a square foot but that included installation. Allow for waste, so an 11 x 11-foot room would run just under $800. Not a bad investment to transform a room into a showplace (and add resale value to your final selling price, too.)

★★★★ Elegant Shutters Plus   972/437-9081

13566 Floyd Circle, Suite G   By Appt. Only
Dallas, TX 75243   www.elegantshutters.com

Why not enjoy a room with a view with Elegant Shutters. Open sesame and let the sun shine in; or close out the world and cocoon, the choice is yours with custom shutters from this company. One of the most sought-after window treatments, Plantation shutters, wood blinds and mini-blinds cover a multitude of options for your window panes. The double-pleated cellular shades not only filter light and soften the glare but also provide additional insulation for any room in your house. Don't shutter. These folks have been shuttering the world for the past 25 years. In home consultation, professional installation, FREE estimates and lower overhead equals lower prices, plain and elegant. Eliminating the middleman, and let them display their craftsmanship is all you need to call it a day. Check out their special of eight windows or more, $19 a square foot, including rectangular shutters, trim, paint finish and installation. For special windows such as doors or arches, call for pricing and expect a trip charge for traveling outside of the Metroplex.

◆◆◆◆◆ Fine Art Finishes   817/992-9230
Fort Worth, TX   By Appt. Only
http://web2.airmail.net/all2real

Fie, Fie, FAUX, fun. That's what you'll see by enrolling in the classes at this finishing school. So, if you're looking for that "Trompe Card," this is where they teach you how the palette meets the painter. You'll learn a myriad of painting techniques for your walls and ceilings. One which is particularly mesmerizing is multi-color glazing over hand-troweled plaster. You'll fall in love with this kind of wall. Or perhaps you're more a meet and beat-it kind of gal. Then, you'll probably pick the textured and realistic faux brick placed throughout a room. Faux concrete walls can be antiqued to resemble those of ancient Italy which have begun to crumble and are discoloring with age. Who are we kidding? It's not the real wailing wall but it's so realistic, it will transfix you to another time and place. Head online to learn of their courses which are the talk of the decorative painting message boards. Expect one of (if not *the*) most comprehensive course on the subject of faux painting. They will introduce you a myriad of imported materials and layering techniques, and explain why certain materials are used the way they are. All aspects of this business-including installs, pricing and design are included in your coursework. So, if you're considering a side business, you will get a gallon's full here. It's all a "working studio", the artists that are teaching you are actually working on jobs during their off times. They will teach you to create new and exciting finishes rather than just rehashing the same old stuff you've seen a million times. ***Call toll-free: 888/508-FAUX (3289)***

★★★★★ Leland Interiors   817/226-7890
2021 S. Copper   Mon-Fri 9-6; Sat 10-5; Sun Noon-5
Arlington, TX 76010   www.lelandswallpaper.com

Celebrating their 20th year, Leland Interiors offers everything from antique reproductions, window coverings like blinds and draperies, plus stencils, murals, wallpaper and more! Find manufacturers like **ASHFORD HOUSE, GRAMERCY, PARKVIEW DESIGNS, SCHUMACHER/WAVERLY** and **YORK**. They offer a discount book list of wallpapers for online customers only as well as FREE shipping on orders over $100. Shop here for the newest look in windows: "Wallpaper" for windows. Recreate the timeless look and feel of etched glass with this adhesive-free, easy to install, vinyl film. Or let the experts at Leland's do it for you. As part of their line-up, expect 45 percent off in-store wallpapers and on all special-order books. There are literally hundreds of books to choose thousands of wallpaper choices. If Gary Leland's on a roll, he'll buy out another store's inventory and add it to his Bargain Corner where the rolls are really rock-bottom priced. Also Leland sells window treatments like mini-blinds, Duette shades, wood blinds, custom shutters, verticals, floor coverings, matching bedspreads and more. Names that are discounted include **DAVID & DASH, FABRICUT, GRABER, GRAMERY, HUNTER-DOUGLAS, IMPERIAL, KAS-MIR, M&B, ROBERT ALLEN, WARNER, WAVERLY/SCHUMACHER, WESTGATE** and others are either in stock or can be ordered in a matter of days. ***Call toll-free: 800/560-9725***

★★★★ Lone Star Blinds   214/766-0330
Dallas, TX   By Appt. Only

This is strictly a Shop-At-Home business that can provide a remedy for any window treatment. Ram will knock on your door armed with samples and ready-to-please pricing. Low overhead equals lower costs to you. Forget the time-consuming effort it takes to get in your car, find a parking place, sweat all the way into the shop and have to stand on your feet while looking at all the window options possible. Stay home. Stay cool. Have a tall glass of iced tea by your side and shop for hours in the comfort of your home. Hassle-free, relaxing and effortless, that's what shopping at Lone Star Blinds is all about. Take your time and take care of all your window needs from blinds to solar screens without leaving home. The discounts vary between manufacturers and installation difficulty. All the national brands like **GRABER**, **HUNTER-DOUGLAS**, **LEVOLOR** and **KIRSCH** are represented and more. Say hello to Ram, yes that's his name, and expect to be in good hands. After 17 years of selling window treatments with low prices and high-quality name recognition, you can expect to eliminate any kinks in the ordering or installation process. His repertoire is extensive and varied. Choose: shades (Pleated, Cellulars, Silhouettes, Duettes, Luminettes), roller and roman shades, louvers, one- and two-inch blinds, aluminum, vinyl, polywood and verticals, woven woods and shutters. Isn't it time you took your blinders off and recognized by that nobody in the Lone Star State pays retail?

★★ Mini Blind Warehouse   817/277-1014
2707 S. Cooper, #105   Mon 10-5; Tue-Sat 10-6
Arlington, TX 76015

Forget name brands here. Mini Blind Warehouse manufactures their own and after 15 years of doing so, you can expect quality at a price that can't be beat. In business for 14 years, they do shop their competitors to ensure they are keeping the quality as high. To them, quality is the most important ingredient in duplicating the other, well-known brands. Everything from blinds and shades are custom-made to size except shutters. A standard 32" x 72" two-inch wood blind will cost $119. They will gladly come out to measure or if you already know what you need, then just call for an estimate.

★★★★★ Smart Looks Window & Wall Decor   972/699-1151
101 S. Greenville Ave.   Mon-Fri 9-5; Sat 9:30-5
Richardson, TX 75080

Forget running around all over town to coordinate your entire house, or just a room, if that's your plan. Instead, be smart. Shop smart. Smart shoppers are the "norm" here at this old-time favorite. What was once a shop for exterior shutters has now evolved into a worldly wall and window emporium. The best, for less. More than 30 individual vignettes showcase ideas are there for you to embrace. In-stock wallpaper plus the hundreds of books to browse through will keep your nose buried in the books for hours. Norm and Lucy Morrow have been in the business at the same corner location for more than 20 years. Without compromising service one iota, they continued their expansion beyond the usual custom blinds, verticals, Plantation shutters, exterior shutters, balloon shades, pleated shades, Silhouettes, rolling shutters, woven woods and of course, custom draperies. Want them motorized so you don't have to get up to close the drapes? No problem. Want matching bedspreads, pillows, boudoir chairs, benches, ottomans? No problem. See why they've been your best friend in this business for years now saving you 30-75 percent on the finest fabrics by **FABRICUT**, **KASMIR** and more. And expect the lowest prices on **SHUTTERCRAFT SHUTTERS** because they own the factory. Always free estimates and all custom prices include installation. From commercial to residential, bay-bow or arched, they can get you covered.

★★★★★ Sunburst Shutters   214/343-2601
10990 Petal St., Suite 100   Mon-Fri 8:30-5
Dallas, TX 75239   www.sunburst-shutters.com

With a burst of energy and a Sunburst Shutter, life on the fast slat is good. Keeping the rays at bay, Sunburst Shutters has been crafting wood shutters for almost 25 years. They offer a unique louver tension system, premium finish and the highest structural integrity in the industry today. In fact, their reputation has followed them all along the way. Being "The Best Built Shutter in America" today does have its burdens. It takes a real commitment to continue on the path that has been carved out from preceding products. But don't expect them to rush the process. Turnaround time is between five and seven weeks. PolyWood Shutters are made of an engineered wood substitute that won't chip, crack, warp or split. They are moisture- and fire-resistant and impervious to termites. Made of natural gas with 50 percent more insulation than traditional wood shutters, you really do get more bang for your buck. In-home measurements are taken to ensure the perfect fit. Pay $22.50/square foot which includes tax and installation. Located just off 635 and Jupiter, they are easy to find and easy to fall in love with. Ask for their FREE video and see first-hand why over 300,000 shutters have graced the windows of fine homes in Phoenix, Houston, Tampa, Orlando, Las Vegas and Dallas. Note, warmer climates seem to really warm up to these window treatments. Shutter at the thought of buying them elsewhere. Sunburst Shutters are all custom made: measured, manufactured and finished by the craftsmen themselves. Hands-on does makes a difference.

★★★★★ Texas Galleries
206 N. Greenville, Suite 300
Allen, TX 75002

972/396-1001
Mon-Sat 10-6
www.texasgalleries.com

Formerly Wall & Window Gallery, if you want to spend a lifetime browsing through wallpaper books, start now and don't miss a lick. Over 1,000 books from all the national suppliers will be at your beckon call at a fraction of the price. Save up to 80 percent off retail prices on wallpapers. All these specially-priced wallpapers are double rolls, and prices include ground freight and taxes. All other wallpapers and borders not in their gallery are priced at 30 percent below retail. Not bad, not bad at all. Then to complete the picture, try their custom window treatments in wood and PVC blinds, Plantation shutters and draperies. You'll pay a $25 in-house estimate charge but if you buy, it's credited to your purchase price. Visit a wallpaper retailer in the area, pick your wall covering, manufacturer's name and number, then record that information on their online form for a price quote. Manufacturers include all the popular ones: **BAYSIDE, BEACON HOUSE, BEACON STUDIO, BIRGE, EISENHART, FOREMOST, HORIZON, IMPERIAL, MAXWELL, PATTON, PELICAN, REGALLIA, SCHUMACHER, SEABROOK, SHELBOURNE, SUNWALL, SUNWORTHY, TALMADGE, WALL TRENDS, WESTCHESTER, YORK** and others. See how much they'll save you in the long run. Voilá! You're in the money. ***Call toll-free: 877/347-1001***

★★ Wallpaper For Less
1288 W. Main, Suite 109
Lewisville, TX 75067

972/219-9985
Mon-Sat 10-6

If accessorizing your home for less sounds appealing, then consider the expanding inventory at Wallpaper For Less. This neighborhood wallpapering hole serves up some savings on your liquid assets. Unique home accents now permeate the rolling inventory including plate racks, plates, lamps, orbs, framed prints, crosses, candles, plant stands and more. Too, custom bar stools, mantel pieces and wall shelves complete the picture. Want to paint over old wallpaper? No problem. They carry the product "Readywall" which does the trick. No paint, though, but enough paste and buckets to wallpaper the town from the ground floor up. Then, if you remembered what you came for, don't forget they do have wallpaper and fabric, for less. Locations in Arlington, Rowlett, and Mesquite, 2110 N. Galloway Ave., Suite #104, 972/329-3414.

Wallpaper Source & More
612 Preston Forest Shopping Center
Dallas, TX 75230

214/987-2369
Mon-Thu 10-7; Fri-Sat 10-6
www.wallpapersource.com

Paper! Paper! Read all about it. Business has been so good for Wallpaper Source & More, they've expanded big time. Wallcoverings, of course, with over 1,200 in-stock patterns and over 1,500 special order books are still their stock in trade. But now, they also offer rugs, art, custom draperies, bedding and floral arrangements to their ever expanding list of options. They're the Rolls Royce choice when it comes to wallcoverings at savings from 30-75 percent. At the southwest corner of Preston and Forest, at any time of the day, there's a store full of eager beavers at their wallpaper book corner flipping pages until they land "the one!" Laura Marlowe is the driving force behind the scene with her hands-on approach to serving her loyal following and overseeing all of the decorator personnel who are experienced Certified and Registered Design and Decorating Consultants. With their expansion, they don't intend to "roll" over and play dead. They're one of the movers and pasters in the Metroplex. ***Call toll-free: 800/987-2369***

★★ Wallpapers Galore for Less   972/381-7664
17194 Preston Rd.   Mon-Fri 10-6; Sat 10-5; Thu 10-7
Dallas, TX 75230

With over 300 wallpaper patterns in stock, Wallpapers Galore for Less will keep you glued to your money! But that's not all. You'll also find window treatments, blinds, shades, wood shutters, fabric and more all rolled into one neighborhood outpost. They don't do free estimates and installation themselves but can recommend someone who can. You'll find discounts off MSRP ranging from 30 to 80 percent. While they carry most name brands, you won't find any **HUNTER-DOUGLAS** products here. Don't know why, but who cares? With so many wallpaper books to wade through, who has time to look behind company policies. Some of the brands of wallpaper included: **ANTONIA VELLA**, **GRAMMERCY**, **LAURA ASHLEY**, **KATZENBACH & WARREN**, **MOTIF**, **RALPH LAUREN**, **RONALD REDDING**, **SEABROOK**, **STERLING PRINTS**, **VILLAGE**, **WAVERLY**, **WESTMONT** and **YORK**. And that's just a few to impress you. Though wallcoverings are their forté, they also showcase **KASMIR**, **LADY ANNE** and **NORBAL** fabrics and custom blinds at similar discounts. Remember, windows to your soul start with the appropriate window treatments; otherwise, they'll catch you, butt naked!

★★★ Wallpapers To Go   972/503-8616
14560 Midway Rd.   Mon-Fri 9-7; Sat 10-6; Sun Noon-5
Dallas, TX 75244   www.wallpaperstogo.com

Go online and receive an additional 20 percent off an in-store purchase to make these rolls even more delicious. This almost national chain (they have locations in 17 states) offers over 1,400 patterns in stock (wallpaper and borders) in brands like **SUNWALL**, **WARNER** and **WAVERLY** plus the hundreds of special order books to browse through. Their website offers do-it-yourselfers the tricks of the trade including how to measure (an all-important step in successful wall covering). Or wait for their "how-to" clinics in store. Area designers and decorators line up at the bins to pick and choose. One of the easiest wallpaper stores to shop.

★★★★★ Window Fashion Center   817/261-5009
2590 Pioneer Pkwy.   Call for Appt.
Arlington, TX 76013

You don't have to be a pioneer to celebrate your independence from high prices. This high-fashion window store exudes all your window needs right down to the bedding and upholstery, so that everything can mix and match. Nary a whim is left unattended. Want some good-looking furniture that you can sit on as well as count on? Consider names such as **BASSETT**, **BECKMAN**, **HOOKER** and more. But it doesn't stop there. Add up the discounts of up to 75 percent off name brand blinds such as **HUNTER-DOUGLAS** and 30 percent off wallpaper on any name in the book. While an in-home estimate for windows is FREE, expect to incur a $75 retainer for interior design work which is then deducted from your total bill. Debbie does decorating! Seek them out and ye shall prosper. Custom draperies, shutters, upholstery, mini-blinds, verticals, pleated shades, wood blinds, area rugs, carpet, plus the bedding ensembles and furniture make window treatments just the beginning to a *House Beautiful*.

Brand Name Index